THE

# BOOK OF PROVERBS.

PART FIRST.

THE HEBREW TEXT, KING JAMES' VERSION, AND A REVISED VERSION,

WITH AN INTRODUCTION AND CRITICAL AND PHILOLOGICAL NOTES.

---

PART SECOND.

THE REVISED VERSION,

WITH AN INTRODUCTION AND EXPLANATORY NOTES.

---

FOR THE AMERICAN BIBLE UNION.

BY THOMAS J. CONANT.

---

*NEW YORK:*
SHELDON & COMPANY, NO. 677 BROADWAY.
LONDON: TRÜBNER & CO., 60 PATERNOSTER ROW.
1872.

T. Holman, Printer and Stereotyper, New York.

The reader will please make the following corrections.

IN PART FIRST.

Ch. 26:26 (rev. vers.,) for "congregation," read assembly.

Ch. 27:22 (rev. vers.,) for "a pestle," read, the pestle.

P. 7, 2d col. of notes, 5th line, read, *aculeate.*

P. 56, 1st col. of notes, 13th line, read, § 5.

P. 127, 2d col. of notes, 14th line, read, § 5.

P. 135, 2d col., note (*) read, *gefasst.*

P. 137, 1st col. of notes, 8th line, read, 1–9. *Ibid.*, read § 5.

IN PART SECOND.

P. 40, 2d col., end of 1st line, read, all, *to.*

P. 66, 2d col., 16th line, for "3 : 27," read, 20 : 9, 10.

# TO THE READER.

In the plan of the following work, the critical and exegetical notes designed for the learned, and the strictly expository notes for English readers, are printed separately, the former in connection with the Hebrew text and the revised version, the latter in connection with the revised version alone. In the former division, for convenient comparison the entire Hebrew text,* the common English version, and the revised version, are printed side by side in parallel columns; and in the subjoined notes are stated the grounds, critical, philological, and exegetical, for the renderings in the revised version. In determining the proper rendering of the text into English, the principal questions in exegesis, as well as in criticism and philology, are necessarily considered.

The plan here adopted combines in one work the advantages both of a learned and of a popular commentary, while neither interferes with the other. The course of critical and philological discussion, in which the different views of scholars on questions of translation and exegesis have to be fully discussed, can not without inconvenience be interrupted by purely expository commentary for practical use. On the other hand, the union of expository and practical with learned commentary, on the same page, embarrasses the mere English reader, by the occurrence of foreign words and extended critical discussions, unintelligible to him, and on subjects of no interest to him.

For the use of scholars, and of ministers of the gospel and others to whom the Hebrew text is familiar, the two parts are bound together in one volume. For the convenience of the common English reader, the Revised Version, with Introduction and Explanatory Notes, is bound in a volume by itself, and is complete in itself for the use of the common reader, having no connection with the other division of the work, and no dependence on it.

---

* As edited by Theile; with the correction of typographical errors, of which a remarkable instance occurs in ch. 27 : 3, where by an oversight of the printer the word אבן is omitted after כבד.

In the critical and philological notes every available help has been consulted. In the part containing the revised version with explanatory notes, the writer has not drawn from commentaries already before the public; preferring that his work should be a contribution to the subject, rather than repeat what others have written. His own observation of life, and reflection upon it, have been his guide in unfolding and applying the teachings of this wonderful book. With its religious principles his own mind and heart are in full accord. But he has not sought for religious instruction where the sacred writer has not furnished it, nor to find everywhere material for a religious homily. His aim has been, to bring out the original thought, and to make the obvious and direct application of it; leaving the reader, in most instances, to trace out for himself its more remote and indirect bearings.

The translation and notes, in both parts of this work, were in type as far as ch. xxvi., when the further preparation of it was interrupted, early in 1862, by circumstances beyond the writer's control, and was not resumed till near the close of the last year. In the mean time valuable contributions were made to the literature of the book. Among these is the elaborate commentary of Zöckler in Lange's Bibelwerk (1867), with important additions and corrections by Dr. Aiken in the American edition (1870); Kamphausen, Die Sprüche, in Bunsen's Bibelwerk (1865); Böttcher, Ausführliches Lehrbuch der Hebräischen Sprache (1866–68), and his Neue exeget.-krit. Aehrenlese, 3te Abth. (1865); Delitzsch, art. Sprüche Salomo's, in Herzog's Realencyclop. (1861); Muehlau, De Proverbiorum quae dicuntur Aguri et Lemuelis Origine atque Indole (1869). These writers are accordingly first referred to in the portion commencing with ch. 26 : 19, and the earlier part has been carefully compared with the views expressed in these later works.

The references to Gesenius' Hebrew lexicon are to Dr. Robinson's latest American edition of it, enlarged by additions from the Thesaurus, and by new matter (as far as the letter *Cheth*) communicated to him by Gesenius in manuscript, giving the results of his more mature investigations. It is necessary to remark this, to prevent occasional misapprehension, as his authority is sometimes still quoted in support of views corrected by himself in the later American edition of his work.

T. J. CONANT.

*December*, 1871.

# INTRODUCTION.

## § 1.

### GNOMIC LITERATURE.

The earliest ethical and practical wisdom of most ancient nations found expression in short, pithy, and pointed sayings. These embodied, in few words, the suggestions of common experience, or of individual reflection and observation. Acute observers and thinkers, accustomed to generalize the facts of experience, and to reason from first principles, were fond of clothing their results in striking apothegms ; conveying some instructive or witty reflection, some moral or religious truth, a maxim of worldly prudence or policy, or a practical rule of life. These were expressed in terms aptly chosen to awaken attention, or inquiry and reflection, and in a form that fixed them indelibly in the memory. They thus became elements of the national and popular thought, as inseparable from the mental habits of the people as the power of perception itself.

Such germs of philosophic thought, the ground-ideas of ethics and œconomics, become the proverbial philosophy of a nation, and develope themselves in the popular life. Their value consists in condensing the most comprehensive wisdom into the briefest possible expression, furnishing for ready use on every occasion a wise and safe rule of conduct.*

The classic student is familiar with a rich and varied literature of this class in the remains of what was once the popular philosophy of the Greeks. Such were the sayings of the (so called) Seven Wise Men of Greece ;† the Aurea Carmina attributed to Pythagoras ;‡ the remains of the Poetae Gnomici ;§ maxims and rules contained in Hesiod's Works and Days. Scattered through the Greek classic writers are remains of gnomic wisdom ; polished and sparkling gems, such as an inspired Apostle thought not unworthy to point his own earnest admonitions (1 Cor. 15 : 33).|| But though adorned with all the elegancies of

---

* As said by Cicero : Gravissimae sunt ad beate vivendum breviter enuntiatae sententiae.

† Orelli, Opuscula Graecorum vet. sententiosa et moralia, 1819.

‡ Ed. Knauth 1720, Schier 1750, Günther 1816.

§ In the several collections of them ; by Glandorf and Fortlage 1776, Brunck 1784, 1817, Schäfer 1817, Boissonade 1832.

|| Jerome, on Galat. 4 : 24, Necnon et illud, *corrumpunt bonos mores confabulationes pessimae*, trimeter iambicus de comoedia sumptus est Menandri ; and on Tit. 1 : 12–14, Ad Corinthios quoque, qui et ipsi Attica facundia expoliti . . . sunt, de Menandri comoedia versum sumsit iambicum, *corrumpunt mores bonos colloquia mala*. Compare Menandri Frag. *Thais*, ed. Meineke, Vol. IV. p. 132.

Grecian genius and art, they will not bear comparison, in native wit, profound wisdom, and comprehensive application, with the remains of the same class of literature in the Hebrew Scriptures.*

Roman literature also is rich in the treasures of gnomic wisdom. The admirable sayings of Publius Syrus would alone justify this statement. Among the few quoted by Aulus Gellius (Noct. Att. Lib. xvii. c. 14, 1), as examples of his sayings then in current use,† are the following favorable specimens of his manner, and of the spirit of his moral and practical precepts:

Malum est consilium, quod mutari non potest.
Beneficium dando accepit, qui digno dedit.
Feras, non culpes, quod vitari non potest.
Cui plus licet quam par est, plus vult quam licet.
Comes facundus in via pro vehiculo est.
Ita amicum habeas, posse ut fieri hunc inimicum putes.
Veterem ferendo injuriam invitas novam.
Pars beneficii est, quod petitur si belle neges.

The four books on morals by the Pseudo-Cato (Dionysii Catonis disticha de moribus ad filium) are also favorable specimens of gnomic wisdom, and contain many truthful observations on life and its proper direction. These, and the sentiments of Publius Syrus, have often been published, either separately, or in collections of Roman authors, and in connection with similar gems of wit and wisdom gathered from others.‡

Roman writers, no less than the Greek, abound in pointed moral sayings, containing some ethical truth, some practical rule of life, or pungent rebuke of vice. The collections already made from them are far from exhausting the treasures of gnomic wisdom scattered through their writings. Within their range, they are among the best moral precepts on record; regarding human life in many of its varied aspects, and in these giving the wisest rules for its direction. They are interesting and instructive, as showing that God has not left himself without a witness in man's intellectual and moral nature. But they lack the profound religious teaching of the Hebrew writings, which takes hold on the deepest springs of moral action, and controls the whole inner and outer life.

With the Arab sages the construction of moral and prudential maxims was a favorite pastime. It was an exercise well suited to their peculiar genius and habits of thought, and to the popular taste. Hence Arabic literature is prolific in these brief and pointed

* Rhode (De veterum poetarum sapientia gnomica, Hebraeorum in primis et Graecorum, 1800) is singularly unjust in his estimate of their comparative merits, and seems to have been misled by his classic tastes, and by his want of sympathy with the spirit of the Hebrew writings and their simple graces of expression.

† Hujus Publii sententiae feruntur pleraeque lepidae, et ad communem sermonum usum commodatissimae.

‡ Most fully by Orelli, Syri Publii et aliorum sententiae, cet., 1822–24, and supplement 1832. Also in Auctores Lat. Minores, ed. Tzschucke, Vol. I. 1790, containing among others Syri Publii sententiae, Dionysii Catonis disticha de moribus; and in Bibliotheca Lat. classica, ed. Titze, Vol. I. 1804, containing with others Catonis Disticha, and Syri Sententiae.

sayings, bearing the strongly marked characteristics of the national mind. Gravity and humor, wit and wisdom, jest and earnest, seriousness and levity, shrewd observation, practical good sense, furnish alternate matter for reflection and merriment, along with sagacious counsels, and genial correctives of the lighter and graver foibles of human nature. But they are superficial and showy, lacking in the profound moral earnestness essential to true worth in character.*

The Chinese have also their gnomic literature. Of its spirit and manner the following are favorable examples. Morrison's Chinese Dictionary, Part III. p. 191 :

"On him who does good all blessings will be conferred;
On him who does evil all curses will descend."

Page 342 :

"Although a snake enter a straight bamboo tube, it is impossible to alter its nature."

Ibidem :

"The virtuous are not prosperous, perhaps contrariwise meet with calamities; the wicked receive not calamities, but perhaps contrariwise obtain prosperity; and therefore continually raise men's sceptical doubts."

Ibidem :

"Repress your momentary anger, and your whole life will be without vexation or sorrow."

Marshman's Chinese Grammar, Append. p. 7 :

"On the bathing laver of Thang was engraved, 'Would you thus daily cleanse your mind, correct some evil habit every day, yea continually renovate yourself.'"

Page 21 :

"The peach tree how pleasant!
Its leaves how blooming and luxuriant!
Such is a bride, when she enters the house of her spouse,
And duly regulates his family."

More interesting in this connection, on account of their resemblance in form to the Hebrew gnomic poetry, are the following examples from the work of J. F. Davis on the poetry of the Chinese,† repeated in Vol. II. of the Transactions of the Royal Asiatic Society.

Vol. II. page 405 (of the Transactions) :

"The fine flower unblown exhales no sweets,
The fair gem unpolished exhibits no radiance.
Were it not that once the cold penetrated its stem,
How could the plum-blossom emit such fragrance?"

Page 411 :

"The white stone, unfractured, ranks as most precious;
The blue lily, unblemished, emits the finest fragrance."

Ibidem :

"The heart, when it is harrassed, finds no place of rest;
The mind, in the midst of bitterness, thinks only of grief."

* Anthologia Sententiarum Arabicarum, cet., H. A. Schultens, 1772. Specimen Proverbiorum Meidani ex versione Pocockiana, H. A. Schultens, 1775; also in Fundgraben des Orients (durch eine Gesellschaft von Liebhabern, Wien, 1809 ff). Arabum Proverbia Sententiaeque Proverbiales, G. W. Freytag, 1838–43.

† Poeseos Sinensis Commentarii. On the Poetry of the Chinese.

Ibidem :

"Be not discontented, though your land be narrow, your garden small;
Be not disturbed, though your family be poor, and your means contracted."

Page 413 :

"With few cravings of the heart, the health is flourishing;
With many anxious thoughts, the constitution decays."

Ibidem :

"Unsullied poverty is always happy;
Impure wealth brings many sorrows."

Due allowance must be made for defects of expression in translation. But apart from this it will be admitted, that in beauty and delicacy of the conception, as well as in depth of meaning, the palm must be given, without hesitation, to the products of the Hebrew mind in the same field of thought.

## § 2.

## GNOMIC POETRY OF THE HEBREWS.

When we pass to the gnomic wisdom of the Hebrew Scriptures, as exhibited in the Book of Proverbs, we find ourselves on a higher plane. There is a certainty in its ground principles, a positiveness in their assertion, a sharpness of outline between the right and the wrong in thought and action, an authority which allows no question or appeal, and a power to enforce from which there is no escape.

Its starting point, the spring of all true moral action, is the distinct and positive recognition of a spiritual Personality as the Creator and universal Sovereign, and of his will as the supreme law.* "The fear of JEHOVAH is the beginning of knowledge," (ch. 1 : 7), is its opening assertion; the developement of this ground thought, in its application to the life, is the substance of its teachings.

Accordingly, true knowledge has its beginning, its initial step, in that harmony of the human spirit with the DIVINE, without which the soul is a chaos of conflicting impulses, without order and without direction. This principle once received into the mind, and made its central law, all its impulses move in harmony therewith and with each other. Man's spiritual nature and his relations to the spiritual world thus recognized, his lower faculties and instincts, his appetites and passions, become subservient to his higher intellectual and spiritual developement. In this distinct conception of his relation to the spiritual and eternal, and of his duties in that relation both to himself and others, there is a profound significance, and a moral grandeur, unapproached in any other writings of antiquity. The

* Compare with this the faltering and hypothetical statement (Dionysii Catonis disticha moralia, lib. i. 1) :

Si deus est animus, nobis ut carmina dicunt,
Hic tibi praecipue sit pura mente colendus.

moral teacher has then a hold on the central springs of action. His precepts cease to be merely an outward restraint, and become an inward law.

The application of this primary law is first made in a series of continuous discourses, of singular power and beauty, pointing out the duties and the special dangers and safeguards of the young.* They lay the foundations for true moral developement, and of intellectual and moral greatness, in reverence for the Supreme, in respect for law, in truthfulness, kindness, and fidelity to every relation in life.

In these discourses, much stress is laid on the value and the claims of WISDOM, as an emanation from Jehovah the source of intelligence and moral influence,† as clothed with his authority, as claiming the regard and obedience of man, his sure and only safe guide. The striking and beautiful personification of Wisdom,‡ her counsels and warnings, her faithful admonitions, tender expostulations, and fearful threatenings, are among the finest strains of sacred poetry, and are matchless in their simple grandeur and pathetic earnestness.

True wisdom is higher, purer, nobler, than anything of human birth. "Her seat is the bosom of God; her voice the harmony of the world." By her the creative power of God was inspired and directed. In a paragraph of unequaled beauty and sublimity, she is described as the associate and guide of the Divine Architect in the work of creation.§ She therefore personates a principle which is the law of his universe, and to which all created things are subject. In another passage, allusion is made to the knowledge and skill shown by the Divine Architect in his work. (Ch. 3 : 19, 20):

Jehovah by wisdom founded the earth;
established the heavens by understanding.
By his knowledge the deeps were broken open,
and vapors distill the dew.

God therefore accomplishes his own wise ends in the exercise of those attributes, of which human reason and understanding are the feeble reflection. Man, formed in the image of God, was allied to the Supreme Intelligence; was capable of intelligent moral action, and of directing his powers to the wisest, noblest ends. The first step in his moral recovery is the fear of Jehovah, that moral element which brings him again into harmony with the Divine.

Thus is shown the dignity and worth of that principle which alone ennobles the life and destiny of man. As a practical principle in the conduct of life, wisdom appears in seeking the best ends by the best means. The truly wise is one who chooses for himself the best

---

* The general topic of each discourse is stated in the Explanatory Notes. A more minute analysis of each was furnished by the writer for the American edition of Smith's Bible Dictionary, in an addition to the article Proverbs.

† For Jehovah gives wisdom;
from his mouth are knowledge and understanding. (Ch. 2 : 6.)

‡ Ch. 1 : 20–33; ch. 2 : 10 (comp. expl. note); ch. 8 : 1–36; ch. 9 : 1–6.

§ Ch. 8 : 22–31. The reader is referred to the writer's closing remarks on the passage.

and noblest aims, and has discernment and knowledge to select and use the best means for their attainment. Practical wisdom, therefore, includes both a moral and an intellectual element; namely, a right moral direction of the will, and intelligence for its guidance. Both are properly required in the instructions of this book; both being, in great part, the result of individual culture. Hence the frequent commendation of *shrewdness*,* which is only natural sagacity, cultivated by that habit of observation and reflection which every one owes to himself and others. Hence too the sharp dealing with the *simple*;† whose indolent neglect of faculties given for his guidance and protection, and sluggish inattention to what passes around him, make him the easy prey of the designing. Such are justly censured in this book; for no one, possessing the powers of an accountable being, has a right to be a simpleton, with all the opportunities this world affords for learning better.

The obligation of the law of chastity, so necessary to the well-being of society, and to the healthy developement and the physical and moral perfection of the race, is enforced in terms so direct and explicit as not to be misunderstood, and yet so delicate that maiden modesty may read them without a blush; and its observance is commended by appeals to the purest and noblest sentiments of the human heart.

The chaste relations of husband and wife, as represented in this book, are pure, elevating, and refining, in their influence on both. But illicit connexions, under whatever name, are corrupting and debasing, and leave the noblest nature sullied with stains that neither time nor remorse can efface. One such has left a voice of fearful warning, in the lament:

> "Worlds could never,
> Restore me those pure feelings—gone forever!"

In the brief proverbial maxims which follow, we find the same religious elements. The will of the Supreme Creator is the law of his creature; his favor is the reward of obedience; his displeasure follows surely on every violation of his law, and there is no escape from its penalty. Right and wrong, obligation and duty, are no abstractions here. They are not matters of human speculation, about which men are permitted to differ. The supreme Lawgiver is no ideal conception, the offspring of human thought. His requirements, though adjusted to the nature of man and his wants as a social being, are not speculative deductions from them. Man is here brought face to face with his Maker and Judge, and lives and acts as in his presence and under his eye. He is taught to regard him as the infinite Father; of boundless pity for the weak and erring, ready with his help to second every striving after the right and good, to reclaim the wandering, to succor the tempted. But he is also taught to know him as the stern avenger of wrong, the vindicator of the violated and oppressed; that the victims of fraud, and treachery, and

* Ch. 1 : 4 (comp. phil. note); ch. 8 : 5 (comp. expl. note).
† Ch. 8 : 5 (comp. expl. note); ch. 14 : 15 (and expl. note).

violence, have in him an almighty friend, who will not suffer the wrong-doer to go unpunished. As the helper of the helpless, that truly divine prerogative, he rebukes the insolence of the strong, and confounds their arrogant self-confidence. To all such it is said (ch. 22 : 22) :

Rob not the weak because he is weak;
and oppress not the poor in the gate.
For Jehovah will plead their cause.

And again they are told (ch. 23 : 10, 11) :

Remove not an old landmark ;
and enter not into the orphans' fields.
For their deliverer is strong ;
he will plead their cause with thee

Thus are the proud taught, that the weak are not so helpless and defenseless as they might seem ; that they have a "strong deliverer," who "will plead their cause." The preacher of righteousness, who has the courage to rebuke wrong-doing, and to wage war with all forms of wickedness, will find effective weapons for every conflict, in this divine armory.

Nothing is more noteworthy than the number and variety of human relations, and of representative characters, exhibited in this book. Every domestic, social, civil and political relation, that can exist under any form of society, is here recognized in its essential features. Every form of virtue, every phase of vice and crime, is here typified, with its appropriate reward and punishment. There is no type of human character that is not found here, in sharply-defined and unmistakable outlines ; and few strokes are needed to fill in the personal lineaments of an individual representative of the type to which the sitter belongs.

In comparison with the gnomic wisdom of the Hebrews, that of pagan literature is shallow in its ground principles, weak in its penal sanctions,* meagre in its details, and narrow in its scope.

## § 3.

## STRUCTURE OF THE BOOK.

The Book is single in its design, the object of the whole being practical instruction. It is not so, however, in its structure or form. It is constructed on no regular plan, and has much variety of form. Of the parts which compose it, eight in number,† each has a

* The writer does not forget the admirable treatise of Plutarch, De sera Numinis Vindicta, edited by Profs. Hackett and Tyler ; a beautiful and instructive exhibition of what man can attain by reason, observation, and reflection, as one groping in the dark. But how weak, indefinite, and uncertain, compared with the force, and precision, and positiveness, of the instructions in the Book of Proverbs !

† It is common to reckon three main divisions, with supplements and appendixes (Delitzsch, Sprüche Salomo's, in Herzog's Realencyclop. ; Smith's Bib. Dict. art. Proverbs) ; but all may properly be reckoned as constituent parts of the book.

certain consistency and uniformity in itself, and all have a common relation in their object.

The book commences, after the inscription, "Proverbs of Solomon son of David king of Israel," and a brief introduction setting forth its design and uses, with a series of admonitions and warnings in the form of continuous and somewhat extended discourse. These constitute the first part (chs. 1–9); and are distinguished from the other parts, both in form, and in their general spirit and tone, especially in poetic fervor occasionally rising to sublimity.

At the tenth chapter a second division, extending to ch. 22 : 16, commences with its own separate heading, "Proverbs of Solomon;" clearly indicating that it is a distinct collection, having no organic connection with the preceding discourses. This is confirmed by its contents; being short isolated sayings, having no connection with each other, rarely exceeding two lines, and each making a complete sense by itself; wholly unlike the form of continuous and connected discourse in the preceding division. They are constructed in couplets* on the model of the Hebrew parallelism; the antithetic, more or less perfect in structure, being predominant, but alternating quite frequently with the other forms.

This collection of single isolated maxims is followed, in chs. 22 : 17—24 : 22, by short admonitory discourses, less extended and in a lower tone of poetic conception and expression than in the first division, and alternating with brief moral and prudential precepts of from two to four lines. Prefixed are a few lines of introduction, in which allusion is made to previous written instructions.

These are succeeded by a shorter collection (ch. 24 : 23–34) under the separate heading, "These also are of the Wise."

Then follows another collection of Solomon's proverbs (chs. 25–29) under the heading, "These also are Proverbs of Solomon, which the men of Hezekiah king of Judah copied out;" the inscription implying that it is added to a collection already given. In form and spirit they do not differ essentially from the former one; except that in a very few instances they are slightly more extended, some making from three to six lines.† Included in it is the lovely picture of rural economy, in ch. 27 : 23–27.

Another division (ch. 30) bears the heading, "Words of Agur son of Jakeh," consisting partly of enigmatical sayings of a moral import; followed by another (ch. 31 : 1–9) with the heading, "The words of king Lemuel; an oracle with which his mother instructed him." In the spirit of their instructions these two divisions correspond with the other

* Except the triplet in ch. 19 : 7; a fact which stands in the way of Ewald's theory of the composition of the book, and which he arbitrarily seeks to get rid of by critical emendation. In ch. 11 : 18, 19, two couplets are united in one statement by the particle of comparison; an example of the so-called introverted parallelism. In ch. 16 : 29, 30, the two couplets are probably connected, the subject in both referring to the same person; but the case is not so clear.

† The allusions to royalty and to other distinctions of rank, and to litigation, are not, as has been thought, specially characteristic of this collection in distinction from the former one. They are found in both.

portions of the book ; but with very marked peculiarities of language of which there will be occasion to speak in the section on the writers of the book (§ 5).

The book closes (ch. 31 : 10–31) with an acrostic poem of twenty-two couplets, corresponding to the number of letters in the Hebrew alphabet; a beautiful portraiture of the ideal Hebrew matron.

It thus appears, that the book has not a proper unity, except in its general design and object, being the product of different writers, and having no regularity of structure, and much variety in form. Some critical ingenuity has been expended to little purpose (as may be seen in § 5) in attempting to account for its present arrangement, and to show from what nucleus, how, and at what period of time, it has grown up into its present shape. As usual in such cases, the simplest supposition is most likely to be the true one ; namely, that materials having the same general purpose have been here combined, under some competent and recognized authority, in one collection as a book of practical wisdom. That it could not have assumed its present form earlier than the age of king Hezekiah, is evident from ch. 25 : 1 ; and this is all that can be certainly known, or even conjectured on any satisfactory grounds. The canonicity of the book, in the form in which it has come down to us, is beyond question.*

## § 4.

## POETIC FORM.

The Hebrew word rendered *proverb*, (*mâshâl*,) meaning *likeness, similitude*, or *comparison*, answers to the characteristic form of the Hebrew poetic diction ; namely the couplet, of which the two members have more or less correspondence in sense or structure, or in both. In this book it is applied to a short, pointed saying, so constructed, in which the two members have some obvious relation of resemblance or contrast in thought, or a similarity of verbal structure ; and also to continuous discourse consisting of sentences so constructed.†

The poetic couplet here takes the three typical forms of parallelism ; but with more than ordinary variations from them, in adapting it to its peculiar uses in this book. A few of these will be referred to, as illustrations of the freedom with which these general forms are here varied. Other variations will be observed by the attentive reader.

I.—*The synonymous.* For example :

Ch. 11 : 25. The liberal soul shall be enriched ;
and he that waters shall himself be watered.

---

* The proofs of this statement, which in part are applicable to all portions of the Old Testament, are reserved for a general Introduction. For the recognition of the teachings of this book in the New Testament, see § 1 of the introduction to the revised version with explanatory notes.

† But not necessarily so named for this reason alone. Compare the remarks on ch. 1 : 1.

The reader, who may wish to compare the statements in this section with the contents of the book, is desired to use the version as printed by itself or in connection with the explanatory notes, where it is arranged in accordance with its poetic form.

The correspondence, both in sense and structure, is here perfect; "the liberal soul" in the first member answering to "he that waters" in the second, and "shall be enriched" in the first, to "shall be watered" in the second.

Ch. 17 : 27. He that has knowledge is sparing of his words;
and a man of understanding is cool in spirit.

Ch. 19 : 8. He that gets wisdom loves his own soul;
he that lays up understanding finds good.

The order of the terms may be inverted. For example:

Ch. 18 : 15. The heart of the discerning will get knowledge;
and for knowledge the ear of the wise will seek.

In the following example, one term in the first member is only implied in the second:

Ch. 16 : 32. The slow to anger is better than the mighty,
and he that rules his spirit than he that takes a city.

In the following example, two terms of the first member are only implied in the second:

Ch. 17 : 28. Even a fool when he is silent may pass for wise,
while he shuts his lips, for a man of discernment.

Less exact forms of this class are very frequent. For example:

Ch. 16 : 11. A just scale and balances are of Jehovah;
all the weights of the bag are his work.

In this class, two things may be grouped together, whose only correspondence is in their accidental relations and effects. For example:

Ch. 19 : 13. A foolish son is a calamity to his father;
and the bickerings of a wife are a continual dripping.

A "foolish son" and the "bickerings of a wife," though very different things, are closely related in their influence on domestic happiness. Hence their connection here.*

Other instances are synonymous in sense without parallel terms. For example:

Ch. 15 : 12. The scoffer loves not one that reproves him;
he will not go to the wise.

There may be a consonance in the grouping of opposites and their proper predicates. For example:

Ch. 27 : 6. Faithful are the wounds of a friend;
and plentiful are the kisses of an enemy.

The precept may take the form of an illustrative case. For example:

Ch. 18 : 22. He found a wife—he found good,
and obtained favor from Jehovah.

II.—*The antithetic.* For example:

Ch. 13 : 9. The light of the righteous shall be joyous;
but the lamp of the wicked shall go out.

Corresponding terms: "light of the righteous" in the first member, "lamp of the wicked" in the second; "shall be joyous" in the first, "shall go out" in the second.

* It is but just to the party of the second member, who is not allowed a hearing, to ask the reader's attention to the second paragraph of the explanatory note.

Ch. 12 : 22. Lying lips are an abomination to Jehovah;
but they that deal truly are his delight.

Ch. 12 : 24. The hand of the diligent shall bear rule;
but the slothful shall be under tribute.

Ch. 14 : 1. Every wise woman builds her house;
but the foolish plucks it down with her own hands.

Ch. 14 : 2. He that walks in his uprightness is one that fears Jehovah;
but he that is perverse in his ways despises him.

Antithetic in sense and terms, without formal antithesis of members:

Ch. 13 : 7. There is that makes himself rich, and has nothing at all,
that makes himself poor, and has great substance.

Antithetic in sense without regular antithesis of terms:

Ch. 12 : 3. A man shall not be established by wickedness;
but the root of the righteous shall not be moved.

Ch. 13 : 22. The good will leave a heritage to children's children;
but the sinner's wealth is laid up for the righteous.

Ch. 20 : 17. Sweet to a man is the bread of deceit;
but afterward his mouth shall be filled with gravel.

Contrast, without direct antithesis:

Ch. 12 : 12. The wicked delights in the net of the evil;
but the root of the righteous will bring forth.

Ch. 12 : 15. The way of a fool is right in his own eyes;
but he that hearkens to counsel is wise.

Often the second member is merely adversative, expressing contrariety, correction, limitation, and other relations. For example:

Ch. 16 : 14. The king's wrath is as messengers of death;
but a wise man will appease it.

Ch. 16 : 2. All a man's ways are pure in his own eyes;
but he that trieth spirits is Jehovah.

Ch. 16 : 33. The lot is cast into the lap;
but its decision is all of Jehovah.

As in the synonymous couplet, the precept may take the form of an illustrative case. For example:

Ch. 27 : 12. The shrewd saw evil, he hid himself;
the simple passed on—they were punished.

III.—*The synthetic;* here, only a rhythmical parallelism, in lines of about equal length, without direct correspondence in the sense or construction. In couplets of this class, the second member may merely complete the sense, making with the first a single sentence; or it may add a kindred and parallel sentiment; or may amplify or limit, or otherwise qualify, the sentiment commenced in the first; or may be an inference from it; or may add a condition, or an illustration or confirmation of it, or its cause, ground, reason, intent, effect, or result. The following examples will serve as illustrations; and still other relations may occur to the attentive reader:

Ch. 20 : 10. Divers weights, divers measures,
are both an abomination to Jehovah.

Ch. 21 : 3. To do righteousness and justice,
is more acceptable to Jehovah than sacrifice.

Ch. 21 : 23. He that keeps his mouth and his tongue,
keeps his soul from troubles.

---

Ch. 18 : 16. A man's gift makes room for him,
and leads him before the great.

Ch. 17 : 6. Children's children are the crown of old men;
and the glory of children are their fathers.

---

Ch. 12 : 28. In the path of righteousness is life,
even a beaten way, where is no death.

Ch. 18 : 17. The first in his suit is right;
his fellow comes and searches him out.

Ch. 10 : 22. The blessing of Jehovah, that makes rich;
and he adds no sorrow therewith.

---

Ch. 15 : 11. The underworld and destruction are before Jehovah;
how much more the hearts of the sons of men.

---

Ch. 16 : 31. The hoary head is a crown of glory,
if it is found in the way of righteousness.

---

Ch. 16 : 24. Words of kindness are as the honey-comb,
sweetness to the soul, and a healing to the bones.

Ch. 16 : 12. It is the abomination of kings to do wickedness;
for by righteousness is the throne established.

---

Ch. 21 : 25. The sluggard's longing slays him;
because his hands refuse to work.

---

Ch. 25 : 8. Go not forth hastily to contend at law;
lest thou do aught in the end of it,
when thy neighbor has put thee to shame.

---

Ch. 16 : 26. The laborer's appetite labors for him;
for his mouth has laid a burden on him.

---

Ch. 13 : 14. The law of the wise is a well of life,
to turn from the snares of death.

Ch. 15 : 24. The path of life is upward for the wise,
that he may turn from the underworld beneath.

---

Ch. 19 : 3. A man's folly subverts his way;
and his heart is angry against Jehovah.

---

Ch. 16 : 3. Commit thy works to Jehovah,
and thy purposes shall be established.

Ch. 20 : 4. Because of cold the sluggard will not plough;
he shall beg in the harvest, and have nothing.

Couplets of this class often express comparison; especially in the illustration of a spiritual or moral truth, by some analogy in physical nature. For example:

Ch. 27 : 19. As face to face in water,
so is the heart of man to man.

Ch. 26 : 8. As binding a stone in a sling,
so is he that gives honor to a fool.

Ch. 27 : 8. As a bird wandering from her nest,
so is a man that wanders from his place.

With the omission of the particles of comparison :*

Ch. 26 : 21. A coal to burning coals, and wood to fire,
and a contentious man to the kindling of strife.

Ch. 27 : 21. A refining pot for silver, and a furnace for gold,
and a man to the mouth that praises him.

Many other peculiarities might be pointed out, in each of the above classes. But these will serve to indicate the great variety in the forms of the couplet, and in the relations of its members.

Two couplets, connected in a stanza of four lines, may be related to each other like the two members of a couplet; as in ch. 3 : 9 and 10, 11 and 12; ch. 11 : 18 and 19; ch. 25 : 4 and 5.

By certain writers much account is made of more numerous groups, forming a stanza of an even number of lines (from six to eight), or with an isolated member prefixed interposed or appended making an odd number (from five to seven), as though such a stanza was a studied and artistic form. The stanza of five lines in two couplets with an intervening isolated member, and of seven lines in three couplets with an intervening member, certainly has this appearance. For an example of the former, see chs. 23 : 4, 5, 24 : 13, 14, and of the latter, ch. 23 : 6–8. With these two exceptions it is not certain, and hardly probable, that there was any significance or studied purpose in the particular number of lines in a stanza. The writer completed the expression of his thought, under its several aspects and relations, in any number of lines required, and whether in even or odd numbers. Compare a stanza of six lines (ch. 9 : 7–9, and 10–12); and one of eight lines, in six conditional couplets followed by one expressing the result of compliance (ch. 2 : 1–5), and one of nine lines with a similar close (ch. 3 : 1–4).

The triplet has various forms and uses; as when an isolated member is followed by an antithetic couplet, of which the second member is adversative to the first (ch. 22 : 29); or when a synonymous or synthetic couplet is followed by an isolated member (chs. 27 : 22, 24 : 27, 28 : 10, 19 : 7); or when the thought in the isolated member is followed by a couplet expressing the ground of it (ch. 25 : 8); or when the isolated member expresses the ground of the thought in the preceding couplet (ch. 27 : 10); or when two things are compared in a couplet followed by the point of comparison in the isolated member (ch. 25 : 13); or when the comparison is with two objects forming a couplet (ch. 25 : 20), or with a single object expressed in a couplet (ch. 26 : 18, 19).

* In the version for common use, the obviously intended comparison is expressed.

A peculiar stanza, the numerical, is formed by groups of couplets, in which objects having a certain relation are enumerated under a common characteristic. Chs. 6 : 16–19 ; 30 : 15 and 16, 18 and 19, 21–23, 24–28, 29–31. The acrostic (alphabetic) poem which closes the book (ch. 31 : 10–31) betrays its artistic design by its form.

## § 5.

## WRITERS OF THE BOOK. THEORIES OF ITS COMPOSITION.

The name of Solomon is prefixed to the whole book as the reputed author, and also to two of its large divisions. But certain portions, small and inconsiderable indeed, are expressly ascribed to others.* Moreover, its want of uniformity in structure, and the variety of form in its contents, as shown in §§ 3 and 4, preclude the supposition that it was written as a continuous composition, on a definite and regular plan. It was a compilation from already existing materials and collections, as sufficiently shown, and in part expressly stated, in the book itself. Hence it could not, in its present form, have proceeded directly from the hand of Solomon; and his name is prefixed to the whole as the reputed author of most of its contents.

With the exception of the slight reservations named in the book itself, indicating the care with which the different portions were ascribed to their proper authors, it has come down to us accredited to Solomon from the date of its existence as a book. It is not customary, nor is it safe, to reject such evidence of authorship, against which there is no counteracting external testimony, except on clear and decisive internal grounds.

The question to be considered is this: Do the contents of the book, except the small portions expressly reserved, belong to Solomon as their author? The critical question is not such as would be raised by characteristic peculiarities in its different portions, were nothing said in it respecting the author ; but whether its contents contradict its own statements in regard to authorship, and can not be reconciled with them on any reasonable supposition.

That Solomon was not the author of much that here passes under his name, is asserted on the following grounds :

1. Very marked diversities in general form and manner, and in single words and phrases.

2. Repetitions, of the same thoughts and imagery, and of proverbial sayings in the same or nearly the same words or sense.

3. Sentiments that could not have been uttered by Solomon ; as being inconsistent, (1) with his domestic relations, (2) with his official (regal) position, (3) with the state of society in his time.

* Ch. 24 : 23–24 ; chs. 30—31 : 9. Some include chs. 22 : 17—24 : 22, on account of the expression, "hear the words of the wise" (22 : 17).

In estimating the force of these objections it must be borne in mind, that the portions ascribed to Solomon are not represented as having been written, or uttered, continuously at any one time. From the nature of the case, they must have been composed, or uttered, at different times and at long intervals, as they were suggested by passing occurrences, or as inferred from protracted observation and reflection on the course of human life. It is not to be supposed that a man sits down to the composition of a book of isolated sayings, having no coherency or connection with each other, and no law of association by which one should suggest another.

Under the first head, it is alleged that the portions ascribed to Solomon are quite various in their contents, both as to form, and in words and phrases; so much so as to preclude the supposition that all proceeded from the same writer. The first nine chapters are in the form of continuous discourse, in which the same train of thought is continued at some length, in a series of connected sentences. But chs. 10–29 consist of short independent sayings, in isolated couplets, or at most in isolated stanzas of a few lines, having no connection with each other, and no mutual relation. Moreover, these disconnected sayings in chs. 25–29 occasionally differ in form from those in chs. 10–22 : 16; the former having sixteen variations from the couplet form, namely, five of four lines each,* nine of three lines each,† and one of five lines,‡ while the latter has only three such variations, namely, one of three lines (ch. 19 : 7) and two of four lines (ch. 11 : 18 and 19; ch. 12 : 29 and 30). In chs. 22: 17–24 : 22 the contents are still more varied in form; containing, besides the couplet, triplet, and four-lined stanza of the two divisions just mentioned, stanzas of from five to thirteen lines, in short connected discourse.

The objection to the general form in chs. 1–9 is valid only on the assumption, that one who may have spoken or written in short and unconnected proverbial sayings, can not be supposed to have ever used continuous discourse; an objection not likely to be pressed. It is further objected, that here the parallelism is almost uniformly synonymous; while in chs. 10–22 : 16 (with partial exceptions admitted to be Solomon's by common assent of critics) it is said to be as uniformly antithetic.§ But for this there is an obvious reason. The antithetic couplet is not adapted to continuous and connected discourse, but is often the happiest, as being the most pointed, form of a proverbial maxim.

It is further alleged, that we do not find in the first nine chapters examples of the peculiarly artistic structure occurring in some other portions. The objector has overlooked the passage in ch. 2 : 1–5, consisting of five synthetic couplets, the first four conditional, and the fifth expressing the result of compliance with the conditions. Another stanza

* Ch. 25 : 4 and 5, 9 and 10, 21 and 22; ch. 26 : 24 and 25; ch. 27 : 15 and 16.

† Ch. 25 : 8, 13, 20; ch. 26 : 10, 18 and 19; ch. 27 : 10, 22; ch. 28: 10, 24. ‡ Ch. 25 : 6 and 7.

§ This is true of chs. 10–15, in which there are very few couplets (not more than sixteen out of a hundred and eighty-three) that are not antithetic in form or in substance. But chs. 16–22 : 16 have comparatively few such couplets, not more than forty-eight out of a hundred and ninety-two, the remainder (a hundred and forty-four) being loosely synonymous or synthetic.

consisting of a group of three synonymous couplets occurs in ch. 1 : 27–31; and another of two synonymous couplets in the two following verses.

Against the unity of authorship in the first nine chapters is further alleged the dissimilarity of style in certain portions; as in ch. 2 : 6–20, where one sentence is said to drag heavily through eleven verses, compared with ch. 7 : 4–27, where the same subject (as alleged) is treated in a very different manner. But the two passages are unlike in subject as well as manner. In the latter there is only a single point of view; in the former many are combined, and are presented at once for combined effect.* The latter, moreover, is descriptive and dramatic, with its peculiar advantage of picturesque delineation of incident and character. The former is simply reflective and parenetic; and its purpose requires a manner adapted to it. Yet there is some striking similarity in construction; namely, in the continuance of the same sentence through four verses in ch. 7 : 6–9, and of another through six lines, rather loosely connected, in vv. 22, 23.

Another argument against this unity, and for an authorship of ch. 2 distinct from that of other portions of the book, is found in the use of the divine name God; occurring (as alleged) only in ch. 2 : 5, 17, and in the Words of Agur ch. 30 : 5, 9, the name Jehovah being elsewhere used. But the former occurs also in chs. 3 : 4, and 25 : 2. In chs. 2 and 3 it alternates with the name Jehovah; and in every passage there is a just reason for its use. In ch. 2 : 5 the parallelism makes it necessary to use one of these divine names in the first member, and the other in the second. In ch. 2 : 17 the writer puts the criminality in strong relief, by its disregard of the twofold relation to "the partner of her youth," and to "the covenant of her God." He could not say, her Jehovah; and yet her twofold relation, recklessly violated, must be recognized. Her God, in his covenant relation,† has claims as strong as the partner of her youth. The name itself, moreover, seems the more appropriate one here, the aggravation of the crime being failure of duty to HER God.‡ In ch. 3 : 4 the proper contrast is between "God" and "man;" as in ch. 25 : 2 the proper contrast is between "God" and "kings." There is no ground, therefore, for an argument founded on the distinction between *Elohists* and *Jehovists*.

Ewald regards the construction of שפתים with a *masc.* and a *fem.* in two successive verses (ch. 5 : 2, 3) as indicating a late date in the degeneracy of the language. But it may be construed either way, according as its own subject is *masc.* or *fem.* Compare ch. 5 : 3 with chs. 15 : 17 and 18 : 6. The *plur.* אישים (found only in Prov. 8 : 4, Is. 53 : 3, Ps. 141 : 4), which Ewald thinks can hardly be older than the seventh century, is the shorter and more poetic form of the plural, and in sense is the appropriate one here.§

* See the analysis of its structure in the explanatory note.

† Compare the explanatory note on the passage.

‡ Compare the emphatic claim to this relation, "Jehovah YOUR GOD," so often reiterated in the Old Testament.

§ *Alltagsmenschen* (Böttcher, Lehrb. der Hebr. Sprache, § 554, 6).—Dichterisch selten (Ewald, Lehrb. der Hebr. Sprache, § 186, 2, *c*) is true; but whether, relatively to the point at issue, mehr spät, and neugebildet (*ibid.*), is not so evident. It occurs in Ps. 141, regarded by very able critics as one of the oldest psalms. So De Wette: Mit Psalm 10 halte ich ihn für einen der ältesten (introductory remarks on Ps. 141).

Delitzsch* admits that the contents of chs. 1–9 are in every respect worthy of Solomon ; but finds in the new heading, "Proverbs of Solomon" (ch. 10 : 1), an insuperable objection to his claim of authorship. It seems not to have occurred to him, that a distinct collection properly bears a distinct and separate heading. His theory is, that chs. 1–9 were written by the compiler, whoever he might be, of the first collection of Solomon's proverbs (chs. 10–22 : 16) as a suitable introduction to it. But the occurrence of such *un*-suitable matter as ch. 3 : 27–35, ch. 6 : 1–19, is inexplicable on this supposition. Moreover, this portion far exceeds, in æsthetic merit, all other parts of the book. In the graphic distinctness, and now delicate now gorgeous coloring, of its descriptions, in the tender earnestness of its appeals and the startling sternness of its threatenings, in its poetic fervor rising sometimes to sublimity, in the depth and compass of its teachings, in its mastery of poetic imagery and expression, it compares favorably with any portion of the Old Testament. If these chapters were written by the collector, as an introduction to his gleanings from older writings, then the humble and nameless compiler far outstripped his masters, and has reared before their work a structure of surpassing architectural beauty, throwing it quite into the shade.

It is further said that Solomon, with his multitude of wives, could not so forcibly have conceived and described the blessing of a single one (ch. 5 : 15–19). The contrary might be inferred. Certainly the sentiment, *video meliora proboque*, had never a fairer opportunity for illustration. It can hardly be supposed that Solomon, wise as he was, and observant of life in all its aspects, could not estimate the worth, the felicities, the supreme delights, of a true marriage with a wise and virtuous woman. He could not have seen all of life, if he had not seen this. Hebrew annals show that opportunities were not wanting for such observation. It is no unnatural or improbable supposition, that he may have looked back from his crowded harem, with fond remembrance, to an earlier and happier relation.

The recurrence of the same topics, and of the same images and figures, alleged against unity of authorship in the first nine chapters, is rather in favor of it ; for it is more probable that a writer would repeat himself,† than "that fragments of a number of writers should be found, distinguished by the same way of thinking, and by the use of the same striking figures and personifications."

Delitzsch has shown,‡ in opposition to Ewald, a very remarkable linguistic unity in all the portions ascribed to Solomon § The conclusion, which he admits to be a near one, of a unity of authorship‖ is not set aside by the occurrence of eight or nine words peculiar to

* Herzog's Realencyclop. art. Sprüche Salomo's pp. 691, 705, 712.

† As suggested by the writer of the article Proverbs, in Smith's Dictionary of the Bible, p. 2613, Am. edition.

‡ Herzog's Realencyclop. art. Sprüche Salomo's, pp. 709–10.

§ Terms and phrases do indeed occur in some parts that are not found in others. But a writer's range of phraseology is not exhausted in every minute portion of his writings, and may vary much in the course of a long life.

‖ Die Schluss—[dass die Einleitung nicht minder altsalomonisch sey als 10 : 1—22 : 16]—liegt nahe (Herzog's Realencyclop., as above, p. 710).

the first nine chapters,* nor by the greater variety and fullness of expression suited to continuous discourse, and the recurrence in it of favorite thoughts and images, fondly dwelt on, and importunately pressed on the reader's attention.

It has already been shown (p. xvii.) that the two divisions expressly ascribed to Solomon (chs. 10–22 : 16, and chs. 25–29) are distinguished by considerable varieties of form. The objection to a common authorship, based on these variations, is valid only on the assumption that a man can not write, or utter, proverbial sayings except after a single model.† But one who speaks "three thousand proverbs" (1 K. 4 : 32) will be likely to use some variety of form, in adapting the expression to the thought he wishes to utter. In making from these a small and select collection, it would be natural to choose, for the most part, such as are closely related by some striking peculiarity of construction. Another selection, afterwards made, may contain a still greater number of those that slightly vary from this peculiar form.

In making these different selections, some proverbs have been repeated, as might easily occur. But the repetitions are fewer than has been supposed. It should be observed, that the use of similar, or nearly the same, phraseology and imagery in different proverbs is not repetition, in the sense required in this argument ;‡ and that the first or the second member may be used more than once in constructing different proverbial sayings. For the former case, compare ch. 21 : 9 and 19 ; 14 : 31 with 17 : 5 ; 19 : 12 with 20 : 2. For the latter case, compare ch. 10 : 1 with 15 : 20 ; 10 : 2 with 11 : 4 ; 10 : 15 with 18 : 11 ; 15 : 33 with 18 : 12 ; 11 : 21 with 16.: 5. In these and similar cases, there is no such repetition as might not reasonably be expected in the construction of a great number and variety of these proverbial sayings.

In the second collection, made by the men of king Hezekiah, some repetitions and occasional variations might reasonably be expected. But only two are identical with proverbs found in the former collection ; namely, 25 : 24 with 21 : 9, and 26 : 22 with 18 : 8. Slightly different are 26 : 13 and 22 : 13, 26 : 15 and 19 : 24, 27 : 13 and 20 : 16 ; materially different, 28 : 6 and 19 : 1, 28 : 19 and 12 : 11 (the former far more pointed) ; wholly different in sentiment, 29 : 22 and 15 : 18. It is quite as probable that such variations, in the expression of nearly related thoughts, were found among the numerous utterances of Solomon, as that his sayings were partially adopted by others for models of their own.

There is no ground for questioning the extent and accuracy of Solomon's observation of man and of nature, as set forth in 1 K. 4 : 29–34. He was doubtless competent to give just and instructive precepts on all the subjects of this book. It has been thought, however, that

* Especially as they are not characteristic of a writer, in the sense that he must use them in whatever he writes, however brief.

† It has been shown (p. xvii.) that in the portion conceded to be Solomon's (chs. 10–22 : 16), there are marked differences of construction in chs. 10–15 compared with chs. 16–22 : 16. See the foot-note (§).

‡ Of the alleged instances of repetition in the first selection (chs. 10–22 : 16) only one, 16 : 25 compared with 14 : 12, is strictly a repetition of the same proverb. In ch. 19, vv. 5 and 9 differ only in the last word, the former having "shall not escape," the latter, "shall perish."

many of its sentiments and precepts can not be ascribed to him, as being inconsistent with his personal or official (regal) position and relations. Such, for example, as relate to husband and wife (12 : 4 ; 25 : 24) implying a state of monogamy, as though that were not a matter of observation as well as of experience ; and such as relate to husbandry and the duties and interests of the husbandman (chs. 10 : 5, 12 : 11 and 28 : 19, 14 : 4, 27 : 23–27). But may not a man of discernment and observation give wise general directions on such subjects ? What shall we say of Socrates' practical precepts on various industrial interests, in Xenophon's Œconomics ? Such sentiments, moreover, as chs. 16 : 10, and 12–15, 20 : 26, 28, 25 : 2–7, are thought to indicate a writer who was not himself a monarch. They seem rather to be the sentiments proper to be uttered by a wise monarch, giving just precepts for the guidance of a prince. Ch. 28 : 16 could not be Solomon's, being at variance with the spirit of his own reign (1 K. 12 : 4). He doubtless viewed the matter differently ; and certainly did not regard himself as "a prince lacking in understanding," and as one loving "plunder." Equally futile are other similar objections ; assuming that every allusion to any particular condition in life implies that the author of it was of that condition.

A state of society, supposed to be implied in certain portions, is made an argument for a later date of composition.* Proofs of such a state are supposed to be found in chs. 1 : 11–19, 2 : 12–15, 4 : 14–17, 24 : 15, showing that many robbers and other lawless men were roaming through the land, and by their seeming good fortune tempting the young to similar lawlessness ; in ch. 24 : 21, warning against sedition ; in ch. 24 : 11, showing a decay of justice pervading the whole state. But there is nothing in these passages that may not be seen wherever there is a lax and insufficient police, as there has always been in eastern lands. A moderate and just interpretation of ch. 1 : 11–19 shows that the inference drawn from these verses is overstrained. Nothing is there said of numerous robber bands roaming the country, and nothing of their success except their own boast, coupled with the certain fate of such lawless men (v. 18) :

For their own blood they lie in wait,
and lurk for their own lives.

General reflections on public affairs, on the relations of rulers and subjects, on the evils of misgovernment and anarchy, are not of necessity drawn from a local and temporary condition of things in the existing state of society. They are settled and permanent truths. The records of history, of what has been and will be again, are the fruitful source of such lessons of human experience for all time. It certainly did not exceed the wisdom and knowledge of Solomon, and his opportunities for observation on the past and present in his own and other lands, to make such general reflections as are found in chs. 28 : 2, 15, 29 : 2, 4, which Ewald thinks could have been suggested only by experience of the later fortunes of the state. He sometimes finds what seems not easy to discover ; petty and greedy tyrants,

* Ewald, Sprüche Salomo's, pp. 43, 44, and 48, 49.

for example, in ch. 28 : 3. Instead of a guarded and mournful tone in speaking of rulers, which he finds in what he regards as the later portions, I can find only frank and outspoken criticisms,* the utterances of one who was raised above any fear of man. It is admitted that these portions deal with certain subjects not within the prescribed range of chs. 10–22 : 16; and this is accounted for by the more limited design of that earlier and select collection.

When it is considered, that these proverbial sayings are successive gleanings from a far greater number (three thousand are mentioned in 1 K. 4 : 32); that the Hebrew word *mâshâl* means a short instructive discourse, as well as a single sententious maxim; that, from the nature of the case, these discourses and maxims were the product of many years of observation and reflection; that a writer's style necessarily differs much, in the free flow of continuous discourse, from its abrupt and condensed form in sententious sayings, of which the alternate members and single terms are studiously chosen, and adjusted to each other, for verbal correspondence and effect; that a writer's manner varies at different periods of his life, and new terms and favorite forms of expression are adopted from time to time; it will not be thought strange, that successive selections from a much larger amount of material should exhibit some few diversities in general form, and in the use of certain words and phrases, and some repetitions and slight variations of the same sentiment.

Of others to whom portions of the book are attributed, only two, Agur and Lemuel (ch. 30 : 1; ch. 31 : 1) are mentioned by name; and of these nothing is historically known. Ewald† regards the whole of chs. 30–31 : 9 as the production of a single poet, who calls himself *Agur son of Jakeh;* of whom we know nothing more, though we can not doubt that in his own time he was regarded as a very skillful poet.‡ By others, however, something further has been attempted. Setting out with the assumption, that למואל מלך (ch. 31 : 1) is not good Hebrew for "King Lemuel" (or, "Lemuel, king"), the following theories have been proposed in regard to the nationality of Lemuel and Agur.§

1. Hitzig,‖ holding that the word king, if in apposition with Lemuel, must in Hebrew have the article, claims that it is here construed with the following word (*Massa*) as a genitive, and hence this must be the proper name of the country or kingdom over which Lemuel reigned. This kingdom must have been foreign, since elements of decidedly foreign and un-Semitic origin (ch. 30 : 15, 16) are found here, and at the same time Israelitish, the sentiments being unquestionably such. But was there a "kingdom of Massa," as Delitzsch pertinently asks. Massa occurs (Gen. 25 : 14) among Ishmael's descendants (heads of tribes), in connection with *Duma*, and the territory so named must therefore be sought in northern

* Chs. 28 : 15; 29 : 4, 12, 14.

† Sprüche Salomo's, p. 59.

‡ Muehlau says justly of his manner: Memoratu digna nobis videtur orationis et elegantia et suavitas nec non eloquendi varietas (De Proverb. quae dicuntur Aguri et Lemuelis origine atque indole, p. 34).

§ See the closing paragraphs (1, 2, 3) of the remarks on ch. 30 : 1, p. 129.

‖ Zeller's theolog Jahrbb., 1844, pp. 269–305; Die Sprüche Salomo's, introductory remarks and annotations on chs. 30–31 : 9, pp. 310–315, and on ch. 31 : 1, p. 330.

Arabia, and in the neighborhood of Duma.* The next problem is, to people this originally Ishmaelitish territory with Israelites, and to found there an Israelitish kingdom for Lemuel to reign over. The solution is discovered in the migration of Israelites into that region in the days of Hezekiah (1 Chron. 4 : 38–43), and in the conquest of Mount Seir by five hundred Simeonites, and their permanent occupation of the country (vv. 42, 43). Having thus obtained a kingdom for Lemuel, Hitzig next provides for Agur; and by a change of the punctuation and division of consonants in ch. 30 : 1, finds him to have been the son of Lemuel's mother.†

Delitzsch‡ adopts Hitzig's suggestion of a "kingdom of Massa," as the true solution of the grammatical difficulty in ch. 31 : 1, and explanation of the foreign elements in this section. Accordingly he translates, "Lemuel, king of Massa;" but while accepting this the main point in Hitzig's theory, he rejects its details as untenable. That the territory of Massa should lie in the highland of Arabia, and yet this should bear the name of Mount Seir, he regards as a very doubtful supposition; and the use made of Is. 21 : 11 he condemns as wholly unauthorized. He denies the assumed necessity of an Israelitish origin of chs. 30 and 31; referring to the similar cases of Job and Balaam. Job was not an Israelite, nor of a country peopled by Israelites; and yet his discourses were thought worthy to be transplanted to the soil of the sacred literature of the nation.§ The Old Testament was not so narrow-hearted (*engherzig*), that it did not recognize workings of the spirit and utterances of human piety, resembling the patriarchal, though outside of the sphere of Israel and of the Mosaic Thora. The last writer of the book, who affixed to these chapters the seal of truth, was of course an Israelite; but not so Lemuel and Agur. Lemuel was an Ishmaelitish king of Massa, or rather (with a more suitable punctuation) of Mesha, Gen. 10 : 30. The sayings of Agur, in his opinion, have an Arabic origin. They bear numerous proofs of an extra-Hebraic though Semitic source. Among these are the divine name *Eloah*, the spectral *'aluqa* and her two daughters (reminding one of the *Ghoul* in the Arabian Nights, and belonging perhaps to an Indian legend that had wandered into Arabia),‖ and certain Arabic words and forms. He admits, however, that the latter do not, in our want of acquaintance with the Arabic of that period, justify more than a conjecture as to the author's nationality. Hitzig's construction of ch. 30 : 1 he declares to be quite as adventurous (*ein ebenso abenteuerliches*

* He thinks that Isaiah (ch. 21 : 11) may have said *Massa*, instead of *Duma;* and that a copyist substituted *Duma*, because the appellative *massa* (burden) preceded. The text, when it happens to stand in the way of some critics, is easily brushed aside. Hitzig said long ago, that one can no longer be accounted a Hebraist who does not take the text in hand. He has taken it in hand, and has certainly magnified his office.

† See No. 2 of the different constructions, on p. 129.—Muehlau, while accepting Hitzig's suggestion of a "kingdom of Massa," refutes his arguments in regard to its location (as above, pp. 22–26).—Zöckler, who had not seen Muehlau's more full examination of the case, approves Hitzig's view against Delitzsch (Lange's Bibelwerk, on ch. 30 : 1).

‡ Herzog's Realencyclop., art. Sprüche Salomo's, pp. 693-4, 711–12

§ With singular inconsistency confounding Job, the chief character of the book, with its author.

‖ See the note on ch. 30 : 15.

*Hebräisch*) as that which it would set aside. But he finds himself obliged by his theory, not merely to alter punctuation, and the division of the consonant text, but to re-write the text itself.*

Muehlau (as above, pp. 26–32) holds that the site of the Ishmaelitish city or land of Massa is determined by that of another *Duma*, situated at the eastern base of Mount Hauran; and that it was taken possession of by Israelites in the days of Saul (1 Chron. 5 : 10), or in a subsequent invasion (vv. 18–22). Among these are to be sought the inhabitants of Massa, over whom Lemuel reigned, and among whom Agur was distinguished as one of the wise men of the East (1 K. 4 : 30). They were not, therefore, pagans or proselytes from paganism, but Israelites by birth. He deals very freely with the text in ch. 30 : 1, changing the consonants and re-arranging the order of words.†

On the whole it seems pretty clear, that nothing of value has been gained by the violent conjectural emendation of the Hebrew text, and the assumption of a kingdom unknown to history, whose locality and population are so indefinite and uncertain. In the opinion of so competent a judge as Ewald,‡ there is no grammatical necessity for this in ch. 31 : 1.§ Still less is there occasion to found a kingdom and a permanent monarchy for Lemuel, who may very probably have been the sole representative of a locally quite restricted and merely temporary reign. Within the bounds of certain portions of Palestine, provincialisms, and among them Arabisms,‖ have either arisen, or have been locally perpetuated. Such may have been אלוה (Prov. 30 : 5; poet. Deut. 32 : 15, Pss. 50 : 22, 139 : 19); יקהת (Prov. 30 : 17; Gen. 49 : 10); and more certainly, אלקום (Prov. 30 : 31; comp. analogous cases in Ges. Thes. I. 92 ff.) This sufficiently accounts for all the admitted, as being fully proved, linguistic and historical peculiarities of these chapters, without assuming for them a foreign origin.

Of the writer of the beautiful portraiture of the model Hebrew matron¶ nothing certain can be known. It has not the distinctive peculiarities of the two short sections immediately preceding it. The alphabetic arrangement, and the *scriptio plena* (עוז) in vv. 17 and 25, are thought to indicate a late date. Not decisively, however, both being found in early psalms, the former in Pss. 25 (imperfectly alphabetic), 34, 37, the latter in Ps. 84 : 6.

Many attempts have been made to account for the structure of the book and the peculiarities of its various contents, and to show how, at what times, and under what influences, its several portions originated, and were brought into their present relation. The following are the most worthy of notice.

---

* See No. 3 of the different constructions, on p. 129. Muehlau (as above, p. 16) thinks Hitzig's construction grammatically admissible (referring to Böttcher's Lehrb. § 734); but properly objects to it as wanting in simplicity, and not justified by similar combinations, that of Is. 11 : 14, for example, as rendered by Hitzig himself.

† See No. 3 of the different constructions, p. 129.

‡ See No. 10 of answers to objections, and foot-note, p. 129.

§ A similar case of apposition is found in the connection, Jehovah God.

‖ Böttcher, Lehrb. § 36. Muehlau shows (as above, p. 55), that ליש 30 : 30, and תלשין 30 : 10, reckoned by Böttcher (§ 36, *d*), and חלוף 31 : 8, reckoned by Delitzsch (as above, p. 712) as Arabisms, are not to be accounted such.

¶ See Explanatory Notes, introductory remarks to ch. 31 : 10–31.

Ewald* finds in it the following four sections: (1) the oldest collection, chs. 10–22 : 16; (2) the later collection, chs. 25–29; (3) the still later addition of chs. 1–9, and ch. 22 : 17—ch. 24; (4) later and final additions, chs. 30–31 : 9, and ch. 31 : 10–31. The first and oldest of these, in chs. 10–22 : 16, was the original ground-work of the book. It was a collection, made about two centuries after Solomon's reign, of the proverbial wisdom of Solomon and of others before and after him, of the period commencing in the tenth century and continuing into the ninth. The stream here flows clear and limpid, near to its source, and in its original vigor and freshness. In the second collection, of a later period, in the ninth century and extending into the beginning of the eighth, it begins to be disturbed by new influxes, though not with strongly marked change. Later still, at a period of deeper and wider develpement in the first half of the seventh century, a gifted didactic poet reproduced the oldest collection (chs. 10–22 : 16), prefixing his own introduction in praise of wisdom (chs. 1–9). In this he shows himself independent and original, though reflecting the finest thoughts and images of the book now reproduced by him. In prefixing the general title, "Proverbs of Solomon, son of David, king of Israel," he clearly intended what followed from his own hand to be merely an introduction to the earlier work, with its distinctive title, "Proverbs of Solomon" (ch. 10 : 1).

To the oldest collection, thus enriched with the introduction by this gifted poet, a mere compiler, towards the middle of the seventh century, appended the portions embraced in ch. 22 : 17—ch. 29. But in the mean time new books of proverbs had appeared under the title, Sayings of the Wise. From two of these he selected the portions contained in chs. 22 : 17–24 : 22, and ch. 24 : 23–34, and attached them, abridged indeed in various ways, to the earlier collections; but not as Solomon's, as is shown by the heading in ch. 24 : 23. This collector's work proceeded no further, and chs. 30 and 31 were afterwards added.

This view is characterized by the genius, learning, and exhaustive research of its distinguished author. On very many points his more detailed statements in support of his theory are exceedingly instructive. But it is obvious how much it assumes hypothetically, and against historical probability, while it signally fails to account for the statements of the book itself in respect to its authorship.

According to Hitzig's theory,† the first part, ch. 1 : 6—ch. 9, is the oldest portion of the book,‡ composed as early as the ninth century, and holding the first place in its construction. Next came, probably after the year 750, the second part, chs. 10–22 : 16, and ch. 28 : 17—ch. 29. But in the last quarter of that century the anthology, ch. 25–27, was formed; and this, falling into the hands of a possessor of the previous collection, early after the exile, inspired him to compose ch. 22 : 17—ch. 24. Placing his own work first, he inserted both in the previous collection before the last sheet, which may be assumed to have begun with ch. 28 : 17.

* Die Sprüche Salomo's, pp. 4–63.

† Zeller's Jahrbb. (as above); Die Sprüche Salomo's, pp. xvii. foll.

‡ Rejecting as interpolated what Ewald regards as proofs of a later date.

But he was aware that he had thus severed sixteen verses from a new section, the twenty-second chapter, and supplied them by ch. 28 : 1–16 on his last blank-leaf. As to the "Words of Agur, and to Lemuel," they might very early have come next to chs. 25–27 as a natural continuation ; but not in all copies, and not in those of the author of chs. 22 : 17 and foll. Being of foreign origin, they the more easily remained longer a separate composition ; and though written perhaps in the eighth or beginning of the seventh century, they were first annexed after the section ch. 22 : 17—ch. 24, and not by the author of that section. The last portion, ch. 31 : 10–31, is to be regarded, on linguistic and orthographic grounds, as the latest of all. As an appropriate place, it could be appended to the instructions given to Lemuel by his mother. But more probably, in view of the relation of v. 20 to v. 9, and of v. 26 to v. 9 and the whole connection in vv. 2 and foll., and of the matron's purple attire (v. 22), the section 31 : 1–9 was itself the occasion of the concluding poem. According to this view, the several portions of the book originated, substantially, in the order in which they now stand.

Bertheau* remarks the uncertainty of the criteria for determining the relative age of these several collections, when they lead to opinions so diverse as those of Ewald and Hitzig. He holds in opposition to Ewald, after a careful examination of his arguments, that there is nothing in the contents of the first and second collections (chs. 1–9, and chs. 10–22 : 16) which requires us to assume for them different dates. As to the third collection (ch. 22 : 17—ch. 24), which Ewald regards as synchronous with the first, we can infer nothing more, from examination of all that bears on the case, than the probable conjecture, that the earlier writings referred to in ch. 22 : 20 were those contained in the first two collections. After a minute and careful consideration of all Ewald's grounds for the relatively later date of the fourth collection (chs. 25–29), he comes to the just conclusion, that nothing appears in the historical background indicating a later date than that of the second collection ; that, moreover, in the first and third we find references to the same historical relations as in the second. These conclusions are highly significant ; as, if well founded, they effectually set aside the most formidable objections to Solomon's authorship of all that is ascribed to him in the contents of the book.

He holds that the statement in ch. 25 : 1 is the only clue to the age of these proverbial sayings. From this we learn, that those of the fourth collection were in the time of Hezekiah regarded as Solomon's. But many of the second are found also in the fourth ; showing that they too were not only extant in the age of Hezekiah, but were also regarded as Solomon's. As nothing in the form or contents of these indicates that they are older than the rest, we are at liberty to conclude, that all of the second collection were then extant under the name of Solomon's proverbs. Since many, at least, of the second collection, and all of the fourth, were held to be his so early as the age of Hezekiah, when clear and positive

* Die Sprüche Salomo's, pp. xxi. and foll.

remembrances of his literary activity (1 K. 4 : 32 foll.) must still have been extant, we are not authorized to assert that he can not have composed them. Not that they all proceeded from his hand as they now lie before us. A comparison of those in the second and fourth collections shows that in the course of centuries they underwent manifold changes. Nor is it meant, that he composed all the proverbs ascribed to him in this book.* But a large part of the second and fourth collections must certainly be attributed to him.

The book, in its present form, he regards as the work of a single collector, who must have lived after the age of Hezekiah, namely, towards the end of the seventh century, or even later; who wrote the superscription (ch. 1 : 1–6), and made the first two collections (ch. 1 : 7—ch. 9, and chs. 10–22 : 16), adding the two smaller collections already made (chs. 22 : 17–24 : 22, and ch. 24), and also chs. 30, 31, all of which are included in the superscription, ch. 1 : 1–6.

Delitzsch† has made a very critical and exhaustive examination of this subject, under the four following heads: (1) Structure of the book, and its own testimony to its origin. (2) Its several parts, viewed with reference to the manifold form of its contents. (3) Its repetitions. (4) Its manifold characteristics in style and teaching.

The investigation under the first head shows the structure of the book to be as follows: (1) The title of the book, ch. 1 : 1–6, leaving it to be determined, how much of the present book was originally included in this general title. (2) The admonitory discourses in ch. 1 : 7—ch. 9, leaving it undetermined whether the work of Solomon begins with them, or they are only an introduction to it by another, perhaps by the writer of the general title in the first six verses. (3) The first great series of the Solomonic proverbs, chs. 10–22 : 16. (4) First appendix to this first series, namely, "Words of the Wise," chs. 22 : 17–24 : 22. (5) Second appendix, a supplement of some words "Of the Wise," ch. 24 : 23–34. (6) The second great series of the Solomonic proverbs, by the men of Hezekiah, chs. 25–29. (7) First appendix to this second series, "Words of Agur son of Jakeh," perhaps an Arabian, of Massa (or Mesha), ch. 30. (8) Second appendix, "Words of king Lemuel," perhaps king of Massa (or Mesha), ch. 31 : 1–9. (9) Third appendix, the acrostic poem, ch. 31 : 10–31. These nine parts form three groups; namely, the introductory discourses with the collective title prefixed, and the two great series of the Solomonic proverbs with their respective appendixes.

As the result of the investigations under the other heads, he holds that the book consists of two principal divisions; the first extending to ch. 24 : 22, the second embracing the remainder of the book. These two divisions are from different hands. The former was the work of a single compiler. Its nucleus and principal part is contained in chs. 10–22 : 16,

* His grounds for this reservation are (p. xxiv.): (1) Differences in structure, and in the relation of the two members. (2) The same thought occurring more than once. (3) The same member repeated in two proverbs in other respects different; as if only part of a saying was remembered, and was then used by another poet in forming a new one. (4) Repetition of smaller portions of some proverbs in others—Compare, on this point, what has been said above, p. xx., in the first, second, and third paragraphs.

† Herzog's Realencyclop., art. Sprüche Salomo's, pp. 690–718.

derived mainly from the three thousand proverbs spoken by Solomon (1 K. 4 : 32). But a considerable time having intervened before its preparation, the old Solomonic *mashal* had meanwhile, in the mouth of the people and of poets, put forth a multitude of side-shoots. These, only mediately Solomonic, the collector incorporated with the genuine sayings of Solomon. But if this first collection had its origin at a time when the old Solomonic sayings were already multiplied to some extent, by new groupings, variations, and imitations, no more suitable time will be found for it than the age of Jehoshaphat; whose reign (commencing sixty-four years after Solomon's death) was an era of popular instruction, and of many noble productions in psalmic poetry. The compiler prefixed his own introduction (ch. 1 : 7—ch. 9), in which he shows himself a highly gifted didactic poet and an instrument of the Spirit of Revelation, and closed the whole with the "Words of the Wise" (chs. 22 : 17–24 : 22). Of this appendix the author does not indeed give an intimation (as some think) in ch. 1 : 6; but it may be expected of him after these words in the title of the book, and the introduction to it (ch. 22 : 17–21) is like a supplement to the greater introduction, its brevity corresponding to the smaller compass of this appendix.

The book of proverbial wisdom, thus originated, was enlarged by a later compiler after the age of Hezekiah. He added the collection made by Hezekiah's men, and also a small supplement of words "Of the Wise" (ch. 24 : 23–34), placing the latter, according to the law of analogy, immediately after chs. 22 : 17–24 : 22. There is no ground for denying to this second compiler the supplements in chs. 30, 31. He may have intended, in adding them, to make the conclusion of the enlarged work uniform with that of the older one. As the older collection of Solomonic proverbs, so now that made by Hezekiah's men, has Words of the Wise on the right and on the left, and the king of proverbial poetry stands in the midst of a worthy retinue.

In this theory of the origin and structure of the book, he lays much stress on diversities of outward form (see above, p. xx), and a supposed gradual developement, in successive stages, of its doctrinal teachings. His analysis of its instructions is discriminating, and mainly just. But in what he regards as distinctive forms of teaching (*Lehrtypus*), there is no such expression of individuality as necessarily implies variety of authorship, much less a gradual developement, from time to time, in doctrinal views.

Notwithstanding some fanciful conceits and occasional exaggeration, the theory of Delitzsch is in many points worthy of special attention. Zöckler (Lange's Bibelwerk, § 12) approves and adopts it; excepting among other minor points to the view, that chs. 10–22 : 16 contain much that is Solomon's only in a secondary sense, and holding that we find here only "fruits of Solomon's gnomic wisdom in the narrowest and strictest sense."

The writer of the article Proverbs, in Smith's Bible Dictionary, reviews the subject in a spirit of moderate and judicious criticism, and with results differing considerably from the position taken in this section. As the canonicity and divine authority of the book, and the worth of its instructions, do not depend on the question of authorship, the inquiry is one rather of literary interest than of practical significance.

TEXT AND REVISED VERSION,

WITH CRITICAL AND PHILOLOGICAL NOTES.

TO THE MEMORY

OF MY BELOVED WIFE

HANNAH C. CONANT

THE FOLLOWING PAGES

READ BY HER IN PROOF

ARE SORROWFULLY

DEDICATED

THIS work is appropriately dedicated to the memory of the late MRS. H. C. CONANT, the translation and notes in both parts having passed under her revision in the proofs, as far as the twenty-sixth chapter. The preparation of the work was interrupted at that point, and was not resumed till after her decease.

Six and thirty years we had prosecuted our studies and literary tasks at the same table. She was a proficient in several of the modern languages, and the German, with its world of literary wealth, was as her mother tongue. Of the ancient languages, the Latin was familiar to her, and of Greek and Hebrew she had sufficient knowledge to be helpful in tracing and verifying references. From childhood, the best English authors were her familiar companions, and her judgment of English expression was almost infallible.

She was a ready and versatile writer; and though burdened with the care of a large family she was a regular and frequent contributor to the literary and religious periodicals, and was equally at home in the discussion of the gravest themes, and in the lighter essays of fancy and humor. Her mental organization was of peculiar feminine delicacy. But she had disciplined her mind to severe study, and found her chief pleasure in difficult and laborious investigation, seeking only recreation in her lighter studies and the more playful productions of her pen. Her correspondence, which was extensive and fills several volumes, was distinguished by the same traits; and her most familiar letters exhibit the rich and cultured thought with which her mind was stored.

She first became known to the public as editor of the *Mother's Journal*. Of the volumes published by her the most important are: *History of the Translation of the Bible into the English Tongue; The Earnest Man, a Sketch of the Life and Labors of Adoniram Judson; The*

*New England Theocracy*, a translation of Uhden's *History of Congregationalism in New England; Translations of Neander's Commentaries, on the Epistle of Paul to the Philippians, on the Epistle of James, and on the First Epistle of John.* For other publications, showing the same love of earnest work, she had made collections and partial preparation; namely, *The Mythic Age of the Nibelungenlied*, illustrated from the poem and from contemporaneous legends; *The Influences and Agencies in the Revival of Literature; Erasmus and his Times.*

# THE BOOK OF PROVERBS.

| KING JAMES' VERSION. | | HEBREW TEXT. | REVISED VERSION. | |
|---|---|---|---|---|
| CHAP. I. | | CHAP. I. | CHAP. I. | |
| THE proverbs of Solomon the son of David, king of Israel; | א | מִשְׁלֵי שְׁלֹמֹה בֶן־דָּוִד מֶלֶךְ יִשְׂרָאֵל׃ | PROVERBS of Solomon, son of David, king of Israel: | 1 |
| 2 To know wisdom and instruction; to perceive the words of understanding; | 2 | לָדַעַת חָכְמָה וּמוּסָר<br>לְהָבִין אִמְרֵי בִינָה׃ | for knowing wisdom and instruction,<br>for understanding sagacious words; | 2 |
| 3 To receive the instruction of wisdom, justice, and judgment, and equity; | 3 | לָקַחַת מוּסַר הַשְׂכֵּל<br>צֶדֶק וּמִשְׁפָּט וּמֵשָׁרִים׃ | for receiving instruction in prudence,<br>in righteousness, and justice, and rectitude; | 3 |

V. 1. *Proverbs* corresponds more nearly with מָשָׁל, in its leading use in this book, than any other English word. The Heb. word properly means a *likeness, similitude,* or *comparison.* It may be used of a short discourse or narrative, in which a comparison is traced, by imaginary scenes and occurrences, for the illustration of events in real life. Of this use a good example is found in Ezek. 17 : 2–10 (where, in v. 2, it is properly translated *parable*), and in Judges 9 : 8–20 (Jotham's parable). It is also applied to any short saying, in which two things are aptly compared, from some similitude traced between them, especially for the illustration of some moral truth; as in ch. 26 : 20. As these readily passed into proverbial sayings (compare 1 Sam. 24 : 13, *as says the 'mashal' of the ancients,* where it is properly rendered *proverb*), the word came to mean simply a common or proverbial saying, without reference to its *form;* as in 1 Sam. 10 : 12; Ezek. 12 : 22, 23; 18 : 2, 3; in all of which it is properly rendered *proverb.* So *παραβολή* is used in Luke 4 : 23.

Accordingly, in the predominant usage of this book, the word means a short, pithy saying, embodying some maxim of experience, some lesson of sagacious wisdom or acute observation of life, such as constitute the proverbial treasures of a people. In form, it consists of two parts or parallel members, related to each other by resemblance or contrast in the thought, or simply by similarity of verbal structure, in order to give greater point to the expression and fix the truth in the memory; as below, in vv. 7, 8, 9. Sometimes, especially in the first division of the book (chs. 1–9), they follow one another in a series, making a connected body of instructive and pointed admonitions on some one topic, as below, in vv. 10–19. But here the use of מָשָׁל has reference to the form of the single couplets, and not to their connection in a series. The principle, *a potiori nomen fit,* requires that the Heb. word should be expressed in English by the term which most nearly corresponds with its prevailing usage in the book.

V. 2. *For knowing* = in order to know, i. e., that one may know, expressing the object of the writer. The simple infinitive, *to know,* does not give the proper effect of this *gerundial form* (§45, 3).*

Second member:—*Sagacious words:* properly *words of insight,*† genitive of quality; words showing deep insight, viz., into moral truths and their relations.

The first paragraph embraces vv. 1–6, showing the design and uses of this collection of proverbs (see Expl. Notes). Bertheau supposes that two classes of persons are distinguished in v. 2, the first member referring to the young and inexperienced, the second to those more advanced in age and knowledge; and that the first member is resumed and amplified in vv. 3, 4, and the second in vv. 5, 6,—the voluntatives (יִשְׁמַע, יוֹסֶף, יִקְנֶה) in v. 5 taking the place of the infinitive with לְ in vv. 3, 4. But this ingenious and rather intricate arrangement has nothing decisive in its favor; and the more simple conception, given in the Explanatory Notes, is preferable.

V. 3. *In prudence,* the objective genitive, expressing the object

* Maurer: *ad cognoscendam* (discendam) *sapientiam.*

† Bertheau: *die Worte der Einsicht.*

| KING JAMES' VERSION. | HEBREW TEXT. | | REVISED VERSION. | |
|---|---|---|---|---|
| 4 To give subtilty to the simple, to the young man knowledge and discretion. | לָתֵת לִפְתָאיִם עָרְמָה<br>לְנַעַר דַּעַת וּמְזִמָּה׃ | 4 | for giving shrewdness to the simple,<br>to youth knowledge and reflection. | 4 |
| 5 A wise *man* will hear, and will increase learning; and a man of understanding shall attain unto wise counsels: | יִשְׁמַע חָכָם וְיוֹסֶף לֶקַח<br>וְנָבוֹן תַּחְבֻּלוֹת יִקְנֶה׃ | ח | The wise will hear, and shall increase knowledge,<br>and guidance the discerning will obtain; | 5 |

of instruction, viz., *in prudence, in righteousness*, etc.*—השׂכל, from שׂכל to view attentively, to consider well, expresses the habit of reflection and consideration, and then, as a practical virtue, *prudence*. Second member:—*In righteousness*, etc., the nouns in this member standing in the same relation to מוסר as the one immediately following it.† Bertheau's objection, that the parallelism is incomplete,‡ is not valid; for there are many instances of this and the like freedom in the relation of the two members. Nor is this construction, as he alleges,§ in itself the most direct one. This is true only of the external relation; in sense, the connection is more immediate with מוסר than with לקחת.‖

V. 4. *The simple* (Expl. Notes; comp. ch. 14 : 15).—ערמה, Gesenius, *craftiness, guile* (Ex. 21 : 14, Josh. 9 : 4); and in a good sense, *prudence* (Prov. 1 : 4; 8 : 5, 12).¶ So Lee, Heb. Lex., (a) *craftiness, cunning;* (b) *prudence*.

This word, belonging to a stock in which the idea of *craft, cunning, shrewdness*, predominates in the usage of the language, is to be carefully distinguished from those expressing the more generic idea of *wisdom, prudence*. Of this stock, the earliest application is to the serpent (Gen. 3 : 1) as *subtile, crafty*. It is used also of the cunning craft of the murderer, in effecting the destruction of his victim (Ex. 21 : 14); of the wily stratagem of the Gibeonites, for obtaining an advantageous peace on false pretenses (Josh. 9 : 4); of the adroit shifts, by which a fugitive evades his pursuers (1 Sam. 23 : 22); of the crafty counsel of embittered enemies (Ps. 83 : 4 [3]); of those who contrive evil devices (Job 5 : 12), and of the craft of the worldly-wise (Job 5 : 13); of one whose words are skillfully chosen to deceive (Job 15 : 5).

* So Bertheau: *damit man annehme Unterweisung der Besonnenheit;* das kann nur sein zur Besonnenheit. So Ewald: *Zucht zu Besonnenheit.*

† So Ewald: die Zucht zu Besonnenheit, zu Recht, Billigkeit und Redlichkeit . . . . (so hängen die Worte des 2ten Gliedes v. 3 noch von מוסר ab). Maurer: *disciplinam prudentiæ, Justi et legitimi et recti.*

‡ Erst durch Ergänzung des Verbs קחת bei dem zweiten Gliede tritt der Parallelismus der zwei Glieder hier ganz so wie v. 4 und 6 deutlich hervor.

§ Diese Auffassung liegt an und für sich am nächsten.

‖ So these words are construed by Maurer: צדק וגו׳ v. 3 pariter atque השׂכל pendent ex מוסר non ex לקחת. Sunt vero השׂכל et rel. Genitivi non Subjecti sed Objecti.

¶ Hebr. u. chald. Hdwbch. (5te Aufl. 1857) עָרַם, 2) listig, auch nur klug sein, . . . eig. abgerieben, abgefeint sein, wie *περιτριβής, τριβακός, τρίβων*, im guten und übeln Sinne.

These are all the examples of this stock, out of the book of Proverbs. In all of them, with the exception of 1 Sam. 23 : 22, it expresses a moral perversion of natural acuteness to an evil end, in the sense of *cunning, craft*. In Proverbs, it occurs in thirteen passages; in all of them denoting sagacity, shrewdness, directed to just and worthy ends; and in some, that habitual exercise of it which becomes a practical virtue, in the sense of *prudence, discretion*. I have expressed it in some instances by *shrewd, shrewdness*, in the sense recognized in the Dictionaries of Worcester and Webster, and authorized by good English usage. It rarely happens, however, that words expressing complex ideas have exact synonyms, in all their comprehension, in another language.

Second member:—מזמה, *meditation, thought, reflection, consideration* (comp. the verb in 31 : 16); here, the habit of reflection.*

V. 5. *The wise will hear, and shall increase knowledge;* the *Jussive* (ויוסף) indicating the subjective view of the writer. The first clause expresses what the truly wise will do; the second the writer's assurance, that in so doing they shall not fail of the object sought. Or, the general sense may be: the wise, by hearing, shall increase knowledge; but more probably, the first clause is an independent proposition, declaring what may be expected of the truly wise.

Some suppose a transition here, from the *Infin.* construction to that of the finite verb (§ 132, Rem. 2), *that the wise may hear*, etc.;† others, that the first verb also (ישׁמע) has the sense of the *Jussive, let the wise hear*, etc.‡ But neither supposition is necessary; for the ordinary use of the form, as expressed above, gives a more pertinent and effective sense. The writer, moreover, by changing his construction after four successive clauses, would seem to intend a change of relation in this clause.—It is not necessary to understand by *the wise, the discerning*, those who are already far advanced in wisdom and intelligence; rather

* Ewald: *Ueberlegung;* De Wette: *Besonnenheit.*

† Ewald (*in loc.*): die *imperf.* ישׁמע u. s. w. v. 5 hängen von ל v. 4 ab, nach § 621 [6te Ausg. § 350, *b*]. De Wette: *dass der Weise höre.* Maurer: *ut audiat qui sapit.* Latet ea conjunctio in ל particula præmissa לתת v. 4. . . . cf. חמה 2 : 2.

‡ Bertheau: Das Imperf. als Voluntativ, wie aus dem folgenden ויוסף wo Voluntativ-Bedeutung auch durch die Form ausgedrückt werden konnte, hervorgeht (?), *hören möge;* in der unmittelbaren Fortsetzung des Vorhergehenden würden wir den Infinit. לשׁמע erwarten, *damit höre;* statt dessen der Voluntativ, weil nach vorläufigem Abschluss die Rede von neuem anhebt.

| KING JAMES' VERSION. | HEBREW TEXT. | | REVISED VERSION. | |
|---|---|---|---|---|
| 6 To understand a proverb, and the interpretation; the words of the wise, and their dark sayings. | לְהָבִין מָשָׁל וּמְלִיצָה<br>דִּבְרֵי חֲכָמִים וְחִידֹתָם׃ | 6 | for understanding a proverb and a byword,<br>the words of the wise and their dark sayings. | 6 |
| 7 The fear of the LORD *is* the beginning of knowledge: *but* fools despise wisdom and instruction. | יִרְאַת יְהוָה רֵאשִׁית דָּעַת<br>חָכְמָה וּמוּסָר אֱוִילִים בָּזוּ׃ | 7 | The fear of Jehovah is the beginning of knowledge;<br>wisdom and instruction fools despise. | 7 |

those in whom is the spirit of wisdom and discernment, who have a natural aptitude and disposition for learning.*

Second member:—*Guidance*, viz., for himself, for his own direction, so as to conduct him aright. So the word is used in Job 37 : 12, *and it turns with his guidance every way*. In this sense, of *guidance, direction, administration, management*, it is used also in the only other passages where it occurs, viz., Prov. 11 : 14, 12 : 5, 20 : 18, 24 : 6. The guidance of others, as understood by Bertheau, is quite foreign to the connection.

V. 6. להבין is subordinate to the finite verb which it follows, as maintained by Bertheau;† not, as understood by some,‡ coordinate with the infinitives in vv. 2, 3, 4.

The word מליצה occurs in only one other passage, viz., Hab. 2 : 6, where also it is connected, as here, with משל and חידות. That it denotes a common saying, one that has passed into general use, is evident from this passage; that it is of the nature of sarcasm, exposing folly and wickedness by just mockery or raillery, is also evident from its etymology and its use in Hab. 2 : 6.§ To this we have nothing so nearly corresponding as *by-word*, a current saying among men, very commonly (though not exclusively) reproachful and taunting in its character.‖ Compare, e. g., Deut. 28 : 37; 1 K. 9 : 7; 2 Chr. 7 : 20; Job 17 : 6, 30 : 9; Ps. 44 : 14. So Shakesp. 3 K. Henry VI. i. 1; *hath made us by-words to our enemies*.

According to Gesenius it means in Hab. 1 : 6, *a song of derision, a taunt* (*carmen irrisorium, dicterium*); but here (prop. *interpretation*) by metonymy, something requiring interpretation, an *obscure maxim, enigmatic aphorism*.* To the latter Maurer justly objected, that it is far-fetched; and that the signification *irony*, or in general a *sarcastic saying*, better accords with its use in Hab. 2 : 6.† His own version (*aculeata dicta*) expresses rather the force of שְׁנִינָה Deut. 28 : 37; 1 K. 9 : 7.

The word has been understood in various, and even opposite senses.‡ Sept. σκοτεινὸν λόγον is not specific (in Hab. πρόβλημα); Aquila and Theodotion ἑρμηνεία, Vulgate *interpretationem*; Symmachus πρόβλημα; Syriac and Chaldee § *parable*. The Vulg. rendering (retained by Pagnino), was followed in all the English versions, but is now rejected by scholars.

Second member:—חידות, prop. something *knotted, entangled*, and hence difficult of solution (see Expl. Notes); applied in Judg. 14 : 12, etc., to Samson's *riddle*; in 1 K. 10 : 1, to the tests by which Solomon's wisdom was proved; in Ezek. 17 : 2, to a parable or apologue with a latent sense (vv. 11 foll.); in Num. 12 : 8, to the indirect and obscure intimations given to prophets (e. g., in visions, dreams, etc., v. 6) in contrast with the more direct and plainer communications made to Moses; in Ps. 49 : 4, and 78 : 2, to what is of deep and mysterious purport in doctrine and in providence, not apprehended by the superficial observer.‖

V. 7. *The fear of Jehovah*, etc. This thought has no connection with the topic of vv. 1–6 (the design and uses of the book),

* לקח propr. λῆψις, *acceptio*, hinc pass. *id quod accipitur* (discitur), *doctrina, scientia*; cf. קַבָּלָה al. (Maurer).

† Weil nach den Voluntativen in V. 5, und somit diesen untergeordnet stehend, muss der Infin. mit ל zu ihrer weiteren Bestimmung dienen.

‡ So C. B. Michaelis (Annot. Uberior.): constructio ex v. 2, 3, 4, continuata, adeoque pendens a v. 1. So also Maurer: להבין, v. 6, non pendet ex v. 5, sed referendum est ad v. 1, ut לדעת, לקחת, להבין, vs. 4, 3, 2.

§ Where the Genevan, and after it the Bishops' and com. version, render מליצה and חידות together *a taunting proverb*; the earlier English versions (Tyndale, Coverdale, Cranmer) more freely, *mock him with a by-word*.

‖ Nearly to the same effect (though omitting the proverbial element clearly belonging to this word) Ewald renders it, *ernsten Scherz*; and remarks very justly: Dergleichen ironische Form gar nicht so selten diesen Sprüchen gegeben wird, um die Beschränktheit, die Trägheit, die Laster überhaupt desto schärfer obwohl im besten Wohlwollen und im ernstesten Scherze zu geisseln.

* Heb. u. chald. Hdwbch., (1) *Spottlied* Hab. 2 : 6; (2) Dolmetschung, dah. was einer Dolmetschung bedarf, Räthsel, räthselhafter Lehrspruch; Spr. 1 : 6.

† Quod longius petitum videtur. Malo voci convenienter ad Hab. 2 : 6 significationem tribuere *ironiæ* vel gener. *aculeate dicti*.

‡ Rarior vocula מליצה . . . distrahit (says Schultens); aliis enim est *oratio obscurior, interpretatione egens*, aliis *clara et diserta*, quæ sit ipsa *interpretatio*. Of the latter class Cocceius (Lex.) defines it: *ἑρμηνεία, clara oratio*, . . . oppositum חידה *αἴνιγμα*. Cevallerius (Pagnini Thes. Ling. Sanct., 1575): *interpretationem*; vel, *orationem artificiosam*. Idem Chab. 2 : 6.

§ In the Polyglotts, improperly, *interpretationem*.

‖ Its relation to the two synonyms, and particularly to the more generic מָשָׁל, is well stated by Hitzig (Kl. Propheten, Hab. 2 : 6): Am nächsten dem משל steht חידה *das Räthsel*; . . . ein solches wird der מָשָׁל, wenn der Vergleichungspunct dunkel, oder das Verglichene, das Subject der Prädicate, nicht genannt ist. The general sense is given by Cocceius: חידות *ænigmata*, id est, sermones reconditioris sensus, ad quorum intelligentiam requiritur exercitatio prævia, et præcognitiones.

| KING JAMES' VERSION. | HEBREW TEXT. | | REVISED VERSION. | |
|---|---|---|---|---|
| 8 My son, hear the instruction of thy father, and forsake not the law of thy mother: | שְׁמַע בְּנִי מוּסַר אָבִיךָ<br>וְאַל־תִּטֹּשׁ תּוֹרַת אִמֶּךָ׃ | 8 | Hear, my son, the instruction of thy father,<br>and reject not the law of thy mother. | 8 |
| 9 For they *shall be* an ornament of grace unto thy head, and chains about thy neck. | כִּי ׀ לִוְיַת חֵן הֵם לְרֹאשֶׁךָ<br>וַעֲנָקִים לְגַרְגְּרֹתֶךָ׃ | 9 | For a garland of grace are they to thy head,<br>and chains for thy neck. | 9 |
| 10 My son, if sinners entice thee, consent thou not. | בְּנִי אִם־יְפַתּוּךָ חַטָּאִים<br>אַל־תֹּבֵא׃ | י | My son, if sinners entice thee,<br>do not thou consent. | 10 |
| 11 If they say, Come with us, let us lay wait for blood, let us lurk privily for the innocent without cause: | אִם־יֹאמְרוּ לְכָה אִתָּנוּ<br>נֶאֶרְבָה לְדָם<br>נִצְפְּנָה לְנָקִי חִנָּם׃ | 11 | If they say: Go with us;<br>let us lie in wait for blood;<br>let us lurk for the innocent, without cause; | 11 |
| 12 Let us swallow them up alive as the grave; and whole, as those that go down into the pit: | נִבְלָעֵם כִּשְׁאוֹל חַיִּים<br>וּתְמִימִים כְּיוֹרְדֵי בוֹר׃ | 12 | Let us swallow them up alive, as the underworld,<br>and whole, as those who go down to the pit. | 12 |

V. 11. for the innocent in vain

and should not be united with them in the same paragraph. On the contrary, in connection with vv. 8, 9, it sets forth the grounds for giving earnest heed to the admonitions which follow; and these verses should, therefore, stand in a paragraph by themselves.

V. 9. *Garland of grace;* expressing both its beauty, and the favor it secures from the beholder.* Second member:—ענק, *chain* (i. e. *neck-chain*) as properly translated in the com. version, Judg. 8 : 26; Cant. 4 : 9.

V. 11, third member. Many take חנם in connection with the preceding adj. *the innocent in vain* = *him who is innocent in vain*, i. e., whose innocence avails him nothing. But it seems rather intended to repeat the aggravation of their guilt, implied in the innocence of the victim, viz., that no just cause is given them. The position of חנם proves nothing in favor of the former view; comp. below, 3 : 30; Job 2 : 3; 9 : 17; 22 : 6.

V. 12. *Let us swallow them up alive,* another aggravation of their crime; *living men* are their prey (not merely goods, inanimate substance), whom they destroy as the underworld devours its victims. In Maurer's construction, *let us devour them, as the underworld* (devours) *the living,* the emphasis is lost.† *Whole:* entire, leaving nothing of them; as utterly consumed, as those who go down to the pit. Some take תמימים in its moral sense, *the upright;*‡ but that is less pertinent here, where the theme is the unsparing rapacity of the plunderer, whom nothing satisfies but the entire destruction of his victim. According to others, it means *whole in health,*§ of sound body, unharmed. Of course they understand the comparison thus (as explained by Ewald):* let us swallow them as suddenly and unexpectedly, as if the abyss should yawn beneath, and instantly engulph them alive and in full health (as in the case of Korah and his associates, Numb. 16 : 31–33). But, with every allowance for the compressed brevity of the language, I am unable to make out such a comparison from the author's words, as translated by Ewald himself.† The idea is: their destruction is sudden and complete; they are as utterly consumed, as are those who go down to the pit; the plunderer is as unsparing in his voracity as the grave.

Happily, the translation itself is not affected by this difference of opinion. *Whole* is the literal meaning of תמימים; and, like that, means also *whole in body* in distinction from the *sick;* e. g., *The whole need not a physician, but they that are sick.* Ewald interprets, instead of translating, when he says *of sound body* (*gesunden Leibs*).

The force of the comparison, in the second member, is greatly weakened in Bertheau's conception of it. *Those who go down to the pit* (he says) are the dead, who have no strength for defense; and the sense is:—we will make way with them as easily, and with as little resistance on their part, as if they, the living and sound in health, were without strength and life like the dead.‡ The strong and bold comparison of the original is belittled and frittered away, in this minute induction.

* Bertheau: *eine Krone der Gunst* ist die, welche schön steht und überall gefällt.

† *Devoremus eos* (insontes) *ut orcus* devorat *viventes.* Ewald, correctly: *Verschlingen wir sie, wie die Hölle, lebend.*

‡ Rödiger (Thes. fasc. poster., p. 1509): (b) *integer moribus, innocens, probus,* . . . Prov. 1 : 12.

§ Gesenius (Lex.): *incolumis, salvus* (Hebr. u. chald. Hdwbch.: *unversehrt, wohlbehalten*); Ewald: *gesunden Leibes;* Bertheau: *Gesunde.*

* (S. 52): als thäte der Abgrund seinen Schlund auf im Nu die zu verschlingen, welche ohne Krankheit und gewöhnlichen langsamen Tod in ihn fahren, die in demselben Augenblick gesund lebend und todt sind.

† Verschlingen wir sie, wie die Hölle, lebend,
gesunden Leibs, wie die zur Grube fahren.

‡ *In die Gruft hinabsteigende* sind die Todten (Ezek. 26 : 20, 31 : 14, und häufig in den Psalmen) denen die Kraft sich zu vertheidigen fehlt, Ps. 88 : 5; der Sinn ist, wir wollen sie so leicht und ohne allen Widerstand von ihrer Seite hinmorden, als wären sie, die ganz Gesunden, ohne Kraft und Leben den Todten gleich.

| KING JAMES' VERSION. | HEBREW TEXT. | | REVISED VERSION. | |
|---|---|---|---|---|
| 13 We shall find all precious substance, we shall fill our houses with spoil: | כָּל־הוֹן יָקָר נִמְצָא<br>נְמַלֵּא בָתֵּינוּ שָׁלָל׃ | 13 | All precious substance shall we find;<br>we will fill our houses with spoil. | 13 |
| 14 Cast in thy lot among us; let us all have one purse: | גּוֹרָלְךָ תַּפִּיל בְּתוֹכֵנוּ<br>כִּיס אֶחָד יִהְיֶה לְכֻלָּנוּ׃ | 14 | Cast in thy lot among us;<br>let there be one purse for us all. | 14 |
| 15 My son, walk not thou in the way with them; refrain thy foot from their path: | בְּנִי אַל־תֵּלֵךְ בְּדֶרֶךְ אִתָּם<br>מְנַע רַגְלְךָ מִנְּתִיבָתָם׃ | טו | My son, go not in the way with them;<br>withhold thy foot from their path. | 15 |
| 16 For their feet run to evil, and make haste to shed blood: | כִּי רַגְלֵיהֶם לָרַע יָרוּצוּ<br>וִימַהֲרוּ לִשְׁפָּךְ־דָּם׃ | 16 | For their feet run to evil,<br>and haste to shed blood. | 16 |
| 17 Surely in vain the net is spread in the sight of any bird. | כִּי־חִנָּם מְזֹרָה הָרָשֶׁת<br>בְּעֵינֵי כָּל־בַּעַל כָּנָף׃ | 17 | For surely, in vain is the net spread<br>in the sight of any bird. | 17 |

V. 17. *For surely, in vain is the net spread*, etc.* (See Expl. Notes.)—כִּי = *for surely* (Gesenius' Lex. 2, a, end of 3rd ¶), in an appeal to what is well understood and is of common notoriety. The implication is: For surely one already forewarned, and with eyes open to the danger, will shun it as the bird does the snare spread in its sight. *Of any bird* (lit. *of any thing that has wings, any winged thing*). A bird of any kind = any bird, is meant. (Gr., § 111, 1, N. B.)

The true sense of the words was given by C. B. Michaelis;† viz., that they practice fowling in vain, when the nets are spread openly in sight of the birds, and will take nothing.

To his application of this sentiment, some of the objections are given in the Expl. Notes. He supposes the writer to mean, that these open plots against the innocent will certainly be detected, and will fail of their object; and this view is more fully developed by Bertheau. But none who adopt it explain the bearing of the words, *spread in the sight of any bird*. Their proper import is well expressed by Bertheau: "for if the birds see the net, they all fly away; not one is taken, and the fowler loses his pains. It is (he adds) a proverbial saying, to denote plots which fail of their expected results, and are suddenly turned to shame."‡ But to what purpose, in such a proverb, is the expressed condition, that the net is spread *in sight of the expected prey?* This is not the practice of the fowler, nor of those who seek to circumvent and destroy their fellow-men.

The very obvious sense of the words above given from Michaelis is rejected by Maurer.* He understands by them, not a net spread openly and in sight of the intended prey; but a net so spread, that *its bait* is in sight of all birds. From this forced construction of the words, he assumes as the sentiment of the passage: in vain they lay snares for as many as possible of the good, no one is taken; but they themselves are taken, and rush into the destruction which they prepared for others. That the net is spread in vain, *with its bait in the sight of all birds*, is something novel in human experience. The sentiment of the text is at least as old as Ovid, and we may very well believe is as old as this book.

Still another and more singular view is taken of the import of this verse; viz., that the net is in vain spread in sight of the prey, because they nevertheless rush into it and are taken.† But as the net is spread for that very purpose, it is not easy to see that it is done in vain.‡ The application of the verse they thus explain: These plunderers rush on to certain ruin, even as the bird descends into the snare though spread for it in its sight.§

* *Spread*, מְזוֹרָה *Pu. Part.* of זָרָה *to scatter*, and gen. *to spread out* (Ges., Lex. 3). Gesenius, Thes. I., p. 430: *nam frustra conspergitur rete* sc. granis. "Sed malim, coll. Kal no. 3, *frustra expansum est rete.* Ewald: *wird ausgespannt das Netz.* De Wette and Umbreit: *ist ausgespannt das Netz.* Maurer: *expansum est rete,* . . . a *spargendo* enim proficiscitur *expandendi* notio, cf. זרע et alia. Bertheau: *ist ausgebreitet das Netz.* Septuagint: *ἐκτείνεται δίκτυα.* Chald. פְּרִיסָא מְצוּדְתָא. Syr. ܡܬܦܪܣ ܡܨܝܕܬܐ. Vulg. *jacitur rete.*

† (Annott. uberior.) Sensus autem est: frustra aucupes esse, cum retia palam et spectantibus avibus volvunt revolvuntque; nec eos quidquam facile capturos. Insidias enim tectas et occultas esse oportet, quia (ut Ovidius ait) *Quæ nimis apparent retia, vitat avis.* So Schultens: Nulla ales tam stupida, quæ se in rete ante oculos ventilatum, ejectumque, induat.

‡ Nämlich sehen die Vögel das Netz so fliegen sie alle davon, auch nicht einer wird gefangen und die Mühe des Netzstellers ist umsonst gewesen. Sprüchwörtl. Rede zur Bezeichnung von Anschlägen die den sicher erwarteten Erfolg nicht haben und ganz plötzlich zu Schanden werden.

* *Rete expansum in oculis omnium avium* . . . est rete expansum ita, . . . ut in oculos cadat ejus esca omnium avium. . . . Sensus: frustra isti scelerati insidias ponunt piis (v. 11) quam possunt plurimis (v. 17), nemo illorum capitur; sed capiuntur ipsi, ruunt ipsi in exitium quod pararunt aliis (v. 18).

† *Aves in retia, ante oculos ipsarum jacta, involare,* non consciscant magistri aucupiorum (Schultens).

‡ It is well said by Schultens: Constructio quoque חנם מזורה *frustra spargitur* aliud spirat, atque *jactum frustratum* suggerit; and by Schnurrer (Diss. III., § 1, p. 99): haud facile quisquam dixerit retia esse frustra posita, hoc sensu, ut innuat, noluisse se aves a reti absterreri; ad capiendas enim non vero ad abstinendas aves retia ut plurimum usurpantur.

§ So Rosenmüller (after Jarchi and Aben-Ezra): Latrones

| KING JAMES' VERSION. | HEBREW TEXT. | | REVISED VERSION. |
|---|---|---|---|
| 18 And they lay wait for their *own* blood; they lurk privily for their *own* lives. | וְהֵם לְדָמָם יֶאֱרֹבוּ<br>יִצְפְּנוּ לְנַפְשֹׁתָם׃ | 18 | And they, for their own blood 18<br>they lie in wait,<br>and lurk for their own lives. |
| 19 So *are* the ways of every one that is greedy of gain; *which* taketh away the life of the owners thereof. | כֵּן אָרְחוֹת כָּל־בֹּצֵעַ בָּצַע<br>אֶת־נֶפֶשׁ בְּעָלָיו יִקָּח׃ | 19 | So are the ways of every one 19<br>greedy of gain;<br>it takes its possessor's life. |
| 20 Wisdom crieth without; she uttereth her voice in the streets: | חָכְמוֹת בַּחוּץ תָּרֹנָּה<br>בָּרְחֹבוֹת תִּתֵּן קוֹלָהּ׃ | כ | Wisdom cries abroad; 20<br>in the streets she utters her voice. |

V. 19. greedy of spoil

It is very evident, from comparison with the above views, that the interpretation given in the Expl. Notes is the true and the only consistent one.*

V. 18. והם emphatic (§137, 3, Rem. 2), *and as for them.*

V. 19. *Greedy of gain;* בֹּצֵעַ בָּצַע a strong tropical expression, applied to those who are greedy after gain,† consequently reckless of the means of obtaining it. It occurs again in ch. 15 : 27; and in Jer. 6 : 13, 8 : 10 (com. vers., *given to covetousness*), Ezek. 22 : 27 (com. vers., *to get dishonest gain*); in Hab. 2 : 9, it is strengthened by the addition of רע, *greedy of evil gain* (com. vers., *that coveteth an evil covetousness*).

Second member:—*It* (viz., this spirit of unlawful gain) *takes its possessor's life,* proves fatal to himself in the end. But the version, as well as the sentiment, will be the same, if we refer '*it*' to '*gain,*' as some prefer.

Umbreit is correct in saying that the old versions have erred in the construction of the second member; e. g. the Vulgate, *animas possidentium rapiunt;* Luther, *that one takes the life of the other;* Tyndale, Coverdale, Cranmer, *one would ravish another's life.* Equally inappropriate (though grammatically admissible) is the Genevan: *he would take away the life of the owners thereof;* and the Bishops': *who taketh away the life of the owner thereof.*‡ The guilty course of the plunderer has already been exhibited; his *fate* is the topic here. The proper construction is given in the text; and in this all modern scholars agree.*

V. 20. חכמות *fem. sing.* (Gesenius, Lex.; comp. ch. 9 : 1); according to Ewald, a later poet. formation for the simpler חכמה.† But according to others, a prop. *plur.* (of חכמה), the abstract idea of *Wisdom* as personified in this book; hence construed not only with the *plur.* in ch. 24 : 7, but also with the *sing.* in ch. 9 : 1, and here with both.‡ תָּרֹנָּה, according to Ewald, the *3rd sing. fem.*, energic form.§ Gesenius regards it as *plur.*,‖ though followed by another verb in the *sing.;* the first standing in close connection with the *plur. form* of the subject, while the more remote is construed *ad sensum* with the implied pronom. subj.

---

illi incauti nimis et præcipites in suum exitium ruunt; . . . ita avibus frustra est rete expansum, quod eas a descendendo ad grana devoranda deterrere debuit. Umbreit: gleichwie u m s o n s t das Netz vor den Augen der Vögel ausgespannt ist, d. i. sie fliegen dennoch hinein; also stürzen sich die hinterlistigen Bösewichte . . . in das von ihnen unbemerkte Verderben. To the same effect, it is explained by Ewald.

* So Schnurrer (Diss. III., §1, p. 99): cum ne aves quidem sint tam stupidæ, ut in rete irruant, quod est palam ipsisque spectantibus positum, scito eosdem, dum aliis insidiantur, in præsentissimo suæ ipsorum vitæ discrimine versari; quodsi itaque, monitus de certitudine periculi, irretiri tamen te passus deinde fueris, sane oporteat te avicula esse multo stupidiorem. So also Dathe: Deest applicatio similitudinis, uti sæpe, sic fere instituenda: Rete tibi tenditur; sed jam admonitus de isto periculo volucres imitare, quæ cum viderunt rete sibi tendi, aucupum spem frustrantur atque avolant.

† Ewald: *jeder der sucht Raub;* De Wette, *die nach Gewinn geizen.*

‡ The Belgic, on the contrary, has the correct construction: *sy sal de ziele harer meesters vangen;* (Note) der gener, die de gierigheyt plegen.

* Rosenmüller: *animam dominorum illius capiet* scil. lucrum. . . . . Vocis בעליו pronomen suffixum spectat ad בצע, quod præcedit; et ad hoc ipsum nomen, ut ad suum Nominitivum, referendum est verbum יקח. De Wette: *er* [Gewinn] *raubt das Leben seines Besitzers.* Umbreit: *das Leben raubt er* [Gewinn] *dem, der ihn besitzt.* Maurer: *vitam domini ejus* (rapinæ), i. e. vitam ejus qui rapinam facit, *aufert* (ea rapina). Ewald: *die Seele seines Herrn nimmt er.* . . . Also nimmt ungerechter Gewinn (Raub), wie zur Vergeltung, das Leben dessen der ihn besitzt. Bertheau: *das Leben seiner Herrn,* d. i. derer die ihn gemacht haben, *rafft er fort,* nach Massgabe der Beschreibung v. 18. Stuart: *it taketh away the life of its master.*

† Sehr selten ist die Abartung dieses *ût* in *ôt*, nach §19, *c*, welche sich besonders findet (*a*) in חכמות *Weisheit,* eine neue dichterische Bildung für das einfachere חכמה Ps. 49 : 4, Spr. 1 : 20 (Lehrb., §165, *c*).

‡ Dietrich (in Gesenius' hebr. u. chald. Hdwbch., 5[te] Aufl.): Der *Plur.* חָכְמוֹת Inbegriff der Weisheit, eine dicht. Steigerung, wird in den Spr. personificirt, und daher nicht nur mit Plur. Spr. 24 : 7, sondern auch mit dem Sing. 9 : 1, mit beiden 1 : 20 construirt.

§ Lehrb., §191, *c*: mit . . dem tonlosen ־ַa des Willens . . . תָּרֹנָּה Spr. 1 : 20, 8 : 3.

‖ Thes. I., p. 473: חרנה rectius pro plur. habetur, quam pro sing. parag.; sequitur tamen sing. תִּתֵּן קוֹלָהּ.

KING JAMES' VERSION.

21 She crieth in the chief place of concourse, in the openings of the gates: in the city she uttereth her words, *saying*,

22 How long, ye simple ones, will ye love simplicity? and the scorners delight in their scorning, and fools hate knowledge?

23 Turn you at my reproof: behold, I will pour out my spirit unto you, I will make known my words unto you.

24 Because I have called and ye refused; I have stretched out my hand, and no man regarded;

25 But ye have set at nought all my counsel, and would none of my reproof:

26 I also will laugh at your calamity; I will mock when your fear cometh;

27 When your fear cometh as desolation, and your destruction cometh as a whirlwind; when distress and anguish cometh upon you.

HEBREW TEXT.

21 בְּרֹאשׁ הֹמִיּוֹת תִּקְרָא
בְּפִתְחֵי שְׁעָרִים
בָּעִיר אֲמָרֶיהָ תֹאמֵר׃
22 עַד־מָתַי ׀ פְּתָיִם תְּאֵהֲבוּ פֶתִי
וְלֵצִים לָצוֹן חָמְדוּ לָהֶם
וּכְסִילִים יִשְׂנְאוּ־דָעַת׃
23 תָּשׁוּבוּ לְתוֹכַחְתִּי
הִנֵּה אַבִּיעָה לָכֶם רוּחִי
אוֹדִיעָה דְבָרַי אֶתְכֶם׃
24 יַעַן קָרָאתִי וַתְּמָאֵנוּ
נָטִיתִי יָדִי וְאֵין מַקְשִׁיב׃
כה וַתִּפְרְעוּ כָל־עֲצָתִי
וְתוֹכַחְתִּי לֹא אֲבִיתֶם׃
26 גַּם־אֲנִי בְּאֵידְכֶם אֶשְׂחָק
אֶלְעַג בְּבֹא פַחְדְּכֶם׃
27 בְּבֹא כְשׁאָוה ׀ פַּחְדְּכֶם
וְאֵידְכֶם כְּסוּפָה יֶאֱתֶה
בְּבֹא עֲלֵיכֶם צָרָה וְצוּקָה׃

V. 27. כשואה ק׳

REVISED VERSION.

At the head of the thronged 21
ways she calls,
at the openings of the gates;
in the city she utters her words:
How long, ye simple, will ye 22
love simplicity!
and scoffers delight themselves
in scoffing.
and fools hate knowledge!
Turn ye at my reproof; 23
lo, I will pour out to you my
spirit,
I will make known to you my
words.
Because I have called, and 24
ye refused;
I have stretched out my hand,
and no one regarded;
and ye have refused all my 25
counsel,
nor would receive my reproof:
I also will laugh in your ca- 26
lamity,
I will mock when your fear
comes;
when your fear comes as a 27
tempest,
and your calamity shall come
as a whirlwind;
when distress and anguish come
upon you.

V. 23. to my reproof

V. 26. at your calamity

V. 21. הֹמִיּוֹת, prop. *noisy*, from the multitudes passing to and fro;* hence put for the *thronged ways*, or principal avenues of a city.†

V. 22. *How long!* An exclamation of surprise and pity, seems to pass in the second member into the affirmative form, *and scoffers they delight*, etc.; which accounts, I think, for the *perf.* between the two *imperf.* forms in the first and third members. Bertheau, less satisfactorily, explains it by the idea of *duration, permanence*, in the signification of חמד, which must ordinarily be expressed by the *imperf.*‡

V. 23. Bertheau: *Turn ye to* (i. e. towards, unto) *my reproof;* in the sense of giving heed to it instead of turning away from it.* Rather, *at* (at the voice of) *my reproof*, turn from the ways of folly; לְ *at*, denoting cause or occasion, Lex. 3, e; comp. Ps. 18 : 45. *I will pour out*, etc. (see Expl. Notes.)

V. 26. *In your calamity* (in the time of it) is evidently the meaning, both from the order of the Heb. words (*I also, in your calamity, will laugh*), and from the parallel member, *when your fear comes.*†

V. 27. *As a tempest* (Gesenius, Lex.), as the word is evidently used in Ezek. 38 : 9.‡

* Part (הָמָה) vim habens nominis substantivi: *loca strepentia*, turbis discursitantibus (Maurer).

† Bertheau: *An der Ecke der Heerstrassen.* Der Plur. des fem. Part. Qal המיות *die lärmenden*, Jes. 22 : 2, kann in diesem Zusammenhange nur besuchte Heerstrassen bedeuten. Ewald: *Vorn an den lärmendsten Wegorten rufend.*

‡ Der Wechsel der Zeitf. kann nicht aus ihrer Folge und ihrem Verhältnisse zu einander erklärt werden, da nach עד מתי ein *Imperf.* nach dem andern folgen kann, z. B. Ps. 94 : 3 ff.; sondern nur aus dem Begriffe des Verbi חמד, welches schon im *Perf.* die beharrliche Stimmung, den dauernden Zustand ausdrückt, zu deren Bezeichnung gewöhnlich das *Imperf.* dienen muss.

* *Wendet euch um, hin zu meiner Zurechtweisung;* der ihr jetzt, weil sie verschmähend, gleichsam den Rücken zugekehrt habt. Ewald: *Umkehren müsset ihr zu meiner Rüge.*

† So Maurer (and Rosenmüller): *in exitio vestro ridebo;* Bertheau: *Bei eurem Schrecken;* Umbreit: *bei eurem Unglück;* Dathe: *in calamitate vestra ridebo.* Ewald, on the contrary: *So will auch ich verlachen eure Noth.*

‡ So Maurer: *ut tempestas;* Ewald (and Bertheau): *wie Ungewitter;* Umbreit: *wie ein Donnerwetter.*

| KING JAMES' VERSION. | HEBREW TEXT. | | REVISED VERSION. |
|---|---|---|---|
| 28 Then shall they call upon me, but I will not answer; they shall seek me early, but they shall not find me: | אָז יִקְרָאֻנְנִי וְלֹא אֶעֱנֶה<br>יְשַׁחֲרֻנְנִי וְלֹא יִמְצָאֻנְנִי׃ | 28 | Then shall they call on me, but 28<br>I will not answer;<br>they shall seek me early, but<br>shall not find me. |
| 29 For that they hated knowledge, and did not choose the fear of the LORD: | תַּחַת כִּי־שָׂנְאוּ דָעַת<br>וְיִרְאַת יְהוָה לֹא בָחָרוּ׃ | 29 | For that they hated knowledge, 29<br>and chose not the fear of Jehovah; |
| 30 They would none of my counsel: they despised all my reproof. | לֹא־אָבוּ לַעֲצָתִי<br>נָאֲצוּ כָּל־תּוֹכַחְתִּי׃ | ל | they consented not to my coun- 30<br>sel,<br>they despised all my reproof; |
| 31 Therefore shall they eat of the fruit of their own way, and be filled with their own devices. | וְיֹאכְלוּ מִפְּרִי דַרְכָּם<br>וּמִמֹּעֲצֹתֵיהֶם יִשְׂבָּעוּ׃ | 31 | therefore shall they eat of the 31<br>fruit of their way,<br>and be filled with their own<br>devices. |
| 32 For the turning away of the simple shall slay them, and the prosperity of fools shall destroy them. | כִּי מְשׁוּבַת פְּתָיִם תַּהַרְגֵם<br>וְשַׁלְוַת כְּסִילִים תְּאַבְּדֵם׃ | 32 | For the turning away of the 32<br>simple shall slay them,<br>and the security of fools shall<br>destroy them. |
| 33 But whoso hearkeneth unto me shall dwell safely, and shall be quiet from fear of evil. | וְשֹׁמֵעַ לִי יִשְׁכָּן־בֶּטַח<br>וְשַׁאֲנַן מִפַּחַד רָעָה׃ | 33 | But he that hearkens to me 33<br>shall dwell in safety,<br>and be at rest, without fear of<br>evil. |
| CHAP. II. | CHAP. II. | | CHAP. II. |
| MY son, if thou wilt receive my words, and hide my commandments with thee; | בְּנִי אִם־תִּקַּח אֲמָרָי<br>וּמִצְוֺתַי תִּצְפֹּן אִתָּךְ׃ | א | MY son, if thou wilt receive 1<br>my words,<br>and treasure up with thee my<br>commands; |
| 2 So that thou incline thine ear unto wisdom, *and* apply thine heart to understanding; | לְהַקְשִׁיב לַחָכְמָה אָזְנֶךָ<br>תַּטֶּה לִבְּךָ לַתְּבוּנָה׃ | 2 | so as to direct thine ear to wis- 2<br>dom,<br>incline thy heart to understand-<br>ing; |
| 3 Yea, if thou criest after knowledge, *and* liftest up thy voice for understanding; | כִּי אִם לַבִּינָה תִקְרָא<br>לַתְּבוּנָה תִּתֵּן קוֹלֶךָ׃ | 3 | yea, if thou criest out for in- 3<br>telligence,<br>for understanding utterest thy<br>voice; |

V. 30. *Consented not to,* as the Heb. phrase is used in Deut. 13 : 9 (8).*

V. 32. *The turning away,* viz., from the paths of wisdom; comp. v. 23. Second member :—*Security of fools;* the false trust of those who depart from God. Comp. Jer. 22 : 21, and the use of the verb in 2 Chron. 29 : 11, to express the careless security and remissness of men unmindful of their duty to God, and the use of the derivative שָׁלֵו in Ezek. 23 : 42.†

V. 33. Second member :—מִן, Lex. 3, f.‡

Ch. II.—The structure of this discourse is as follows :—The conditional protasis ends with v. 4. The apodosis is twofold, marked in both instances by אָז; viz., one in v. 5, and another in v. 9, each followed by reflections confirming and illustrating the statement. Moreover, vv. 12, 16, 20 are coördinate, and all stand in the same relation to vv. 10, 11, showing what *wisdom, reflection,* and *understanding* shall do for their possessor. The last (v. 20) is a more comprehensive summary of the whole, and hence is expressed in a more definite form, *to the end that.*

V. 1. אִם *conditional* (Ewald, Umbreit, Bertheau); not *would that,* as understood by some, e. g., by Maurer (though doubtful himself of its correctness),* and by De Wette.

V. 3. כי אם; *yea if,* as now understood by most philologists.† בינה *intelligence,* the power of discerning, of which

* Ewald, happily: *nicht willigte in meinen Rath.*

† Ewald: *der Thoren Sicherheit.* Bertheau: שלוה hier die träge bequeme Ruhe, welche der lauten Mahnungen der Weisheit nicht achtet; vgl. Jer. 22 : 21.

‡ Ewald: *und Ruhe haben ohne Schreck vor Uebel.*

* Dubitabundus equidem hæreo inter utramque interpretationem, nec quidquam audeo definire.

† Ewald (Lehrb., § 356, *b*): Anders wo כי אם fortsetzend ist, *ja wenn,* Spr. 2 : 3; and in his version of the book: *ja wenn du rufst.* Umbreit: *ja der Erkenntniss rufst.* Bertheau: v. 3

| KING JAMES' VERSION. | HEBREW TEXT. | REVISED VERSION. |
|---|---|---|
| 4 If thou seekest her as silver, and searchest for her as *for* hid treasures; | 4 אִם־תְּבַקְשֶׁנָּה כַכָּסֶף<br>וְכַמַּטְמוֹנִים תַּחְפְּשֶׂנָּה׃ | if thou search for her as silver, 4<br>and as hidden treasures dig for her; |
| 5 Then shalt thou understand the fear of the LORD, and find the knowledge of God. | ה אָז תָּבִין יִרְאַת יְהוָה<br>וְדַעַת אֱלֹהִים תִּמְצָא׃ | then shalt thou understand the 5<br>fear of Jehovah,<br>and find the knowledge of God. |
| 6 For the LORD giveth wisdom; out of his mouth *cometh* knowledge and understanding. | 6 כִּי־יְהוָה יִתֵּן חָכְמָה<br>מִפִּיו דַּעַת וּתְבוּנָה׃ | For Jehovah gives wisdom; 6<br>from his mouth are knowledge and understanding; |
| 7 He layeth up sound wisdom for the righteous: *he is* a buckler to them that walk uprightly. | 7 וצפן לַיְשָׁרִים תּוּשִׁיָּה<br>מָגֵן לְהֹלְכֵי תֹם׃ | and has help in store for the 7<br>upright,<br>a shield for those who walk in integrity; |
| 8 He keepeth the paths of judgment, and preserveth the way of his saints. | 8 לִנְצֹר אָרְחוֹת מִשְׁפָּט<br>וְדֶרֶךְ חֲסִידָו יִשְׁמֹר׃ | to keep the paths of rectitude, 8<br>and the way of his pious ones he guards. |
| 9 Then shalt thou understand righteousness, and judgment, and equity; *yea*, every good path. | 9 אָז תָּבִין צֶדֶק וּמִשְׁפָּט<br>וּמֵישָׁרִים כָּל־מַעְגַּל־טוֹב׃ | Then shalt thou understand 9<br>righteousness and justice,<br>and equity, every good way. |

V. 7. יצפין ק׳   V. 8. חסידיו ק׳

V. 9. every way of the good

תבונה *understanding*, is the result. They are so nearly related, therefore, as to be interchangeable.

V. 7. תושיה, here in the sense of *help, deliverance* from danger or difficulties.* Maurer is mistaken in saying that this sense is not apposite here, and that *correct counsel, sound wisdom*, better suits the connection; † for the proof in vv. 6, 7, of the assertion in v. 8, consists of these two things:—1. That wisdom proceeds from God alone. 2. That he is ever ready to bestow needed help, whatever it may be. It better accords, also, with *shield* in the next member. *Kethibh*, correctly: וְצָפַן.

Second member:—מגן is most naturally a second object of צָפַן,‡ not in apposition with its subject, as construed by some. The translation, like the original, admits either construction.

V. 8. חסידו; in the *Qeri*, and in many MSS., חסידיו. In either case the effect is plural, and the word should be so translated.§—I take ישמר affirmatively, as is done by many; the more natural construction, and most effective expression of the thought.* The inf. לנצר is subordinate to צָפַן and its complement in the preceding verse, or to the thought in the two verses preceding (not a "continuation of the imperf. *he will protect*"—Stuart); expressing the object for which Jehovah imparts his help to the upright,† and which is declared affirmatively (as I construe the words) in the second member.

V. 9 commences the second part of the twofold apodosis, as remarked above. *Every good way* accords best with the abstract form in the parallel member; ‡ and I therefore put the version, *every way of the good*, which is admissible and preferred by many, in the margin.§ There is no solid objection to the division of the members made by the accentuation, which is followed by Ewald, Umbreit, and others. The copula is omitted with the last of the four objects of the verb, because it sums up all in one. ||

u. 4 wird das אם aus v. 1 und zwar v. 3 durch כי verstärkt wieder aufgenommen: *ja wenn.* Maurer: fortasse, *imo si.* Stuart: *Yea, if thou wilt call.* So Dathe: *Quin si intelligentiam desiderabis.* De Wette, on the contrary: *Denn wenn du der Erkenntniss rufest.*

* Gesenius: *auxilium, salus* (Sept. σωτηρία, Vulg. *salus*). De Wette, Umbreit, and Bertheau: *Heil.* Ewald: *wahres Heil.* Stuart: *help.*

† תושיה non, quæ est interpretatio Umbreiti, de Wettii, Ewaldi, aliorum, *salus* est, qui significatus a nexu alienus, sed, quæ est primaria notio, *ratio recta, consilium rectum.*

‡ Bertheau: מגן abhängig von יצפן, *Jahve bewahrt einen Schild* = er hält ihn immer bereit um mit ihm, wenn es Noth thut, die unsträflich-wandelnden zu beschirmen. Maurer: *clypeum integre viventibus.* On the contrary, Ewald (and Umbreit): *ein Schild.*

§ Maurer: *et viam* (agendi rationem) *piorum suorum* (ut) *custodiat.* Umbreit: *und seiner Frommen Weg behütet er.* Ewald: *und seiner Frommen Weg bewahre.* De Wette: *und dass er den Weg seiner Frommen bewahre.* Bertheau: Qri חסידיו im Plural; ob das Ktib den Sing. bezeichnen soll bleibt ungewiss, da es als Plur. חֲסִידָו gelesen werden kann.

* Rosenmüller: *et viam piorum ejus custodit.* Maurer: Alii tamen . . . non dubitant posterius hemistichium absolute capere hoc modo: *et viam piorum s. custodit;* quod et ipsum ferri potest.

† So Maurer: *ut servet.* De Wette (in immediate dependence on v. 7): *zu beschützen die Pfade des Rechts.* Bertheau: *Dass er hüte* (= hütend) *die Pfade des Rechts*, und somit die auf diesen Pfaden wandelnden. Ewald: *dass er behüte die gerechten Pfade.*

‡ Maurer: *omnem orbitam* (viam) *bonam.* מעגל טוב possit esse *orbita* (viri) *boni.* Sed suadet parallelismus, ut טוב habeatur pro abstracto. Umbreit: *jeden guten Weg.* De Wette: *jeglichen guten Pfad.*

§ Ewald: *jede Bahn des Guten.* Bertheau: *jeden Pfad des Guten.*

|| Bertheau: Das letzte von den vier Objecten schliesst die

| KING JAMES' VERSION. | | HEBREW TEXT. | REVISED VERSION. | |
|---|---|---|---|---|
| 10 When wisdom entereth into thine heart, and knowledge is pleasant unto thy soul; | י | כִּֽי־תָבוֹא חָכְמָה בְלִבֶּךָ<br>וְדַעַת לְנַפְשְׁךָ יִנְעָם׃ | For wisdom shall come into thy heart,<br>and knowledge shall be sweet to thy soul: | 10 |
| 11 Discretion shall preserve thee, understanding shall keep thee: | 11 | מְזִמָּה תִּשְׁמֹר עָלֶיךָ<br>תְּבוּנָה תִנְצְרֶכָּה׃ | reflection shall watch over thee,<br>understanding shall keep thee: | 11 |
| 12 To deliver thee from the way of the evil *man*, from the man that speaketh froward things; | 12 | לְהַצִּילְךָ מִדֶּרֶךְ רָע<br>מֵאִישׁ מְדַבֵּר תַּהְפֻּכוֹת׃ | to preserve thee from the evil way,<br>from the man that speaks perverseness; | 12 |
| 13 Who leave the paths of uprightness, to walk in the ways of darkness; | 13 | הַעֹזְבִים אָרְחוֹת יֹשֶׁר<br>לָלֶכֶת בְּדַרְכֵי־חֹשֶׁךְ׃ | who forsake the paths of rectitude,<br>to walk in ways of darkness; | 13 |
| 14 Who rejoice to do evil, *and* delight in the frowardness of the wicked; | 14 | הַשְּׂמֵחִים לַעֲשׂוֹת רָע<br>יָגִילוּ בְּתַהְפֻּכוֹת רָע׃ | who rejoice to do evil,<br>exult in the perverseness of the wicked; | 14 |
| 15 Whose ways *are* crooked, and *they* froward in their paths: | טו | אֲשֶׁר אָרְחֹתֵיהֶם עִקְּשִׁים<br>וּנְלוֹזִים בְּמַעְגְּלוֹתָם׃ | whose paths are crooked,<br>and they are perverse in their ways: | 15 |
| 16 To deliver thee from the strange woman, *even* from the stranger *which* flattereth with her words; | 16 | לְהַצִּילְךָ מֵאִשָּׁה זָרָה<br>מִנָּכְרִיָּה אֲמָרֶיהָ הֶחֱלִיקָה׃ | to preserve thee from the strange woman,<br>from the stranger that flatters with her words; | 16 |
| 17 Which forsaketh the guide of her youth, and forgetteth the covenant of her God. | 17 | הַעֹזֶבֶת אַלּוּף נְעוּרֶיהָ<br>וְאֶת־בְּרִית אֱלֹהֶיהָ שָׁכֵחָה׃ | who forsakes the partner of her youth,<br>and forgets the covenant of her God: | 17 |

V. 10. ינעם impersonally (§ 147, Rem. 2); *and knowledge, it shall be sweet*, etc.*

V. 11. מזמה, *reflection;* compare the use of the verb in ch. 31 : 16.†

V. 12. *To preserve;* see introductory remarks to this chapter. *From the way of evil = from the evil way.*‡

V. 14. *Perverseness of the wicked;* רָע, simply, for a wicked man (as in ch. 11 : 21; Job 21 : 30; Ps. 5 : 5), as understood by the Jewish scholars Aben Ezra and Levi Ben Gersom. The sentiment of the verse is similar to that in Rom. 1 : 32, *not only do the same, but have pleasure in them that do them.*

Many regard רע as a substantive expressing a quality of the preceding noun, *wicked perverseness*, an intensive form.|| But this is feeble; the other construction, equally correct, gives a spirited and appropriate sentiment. The earlier Eng. versions (Tyndale, Coverdale, Cranmer) follow the Vulgate: *and delight in wicked things.* Genevan, as I think, correctly: *and delight in the frowardness of the wicked.* Bishops: *and delight in the wickedness of the evil.*

V. 16. *To preserve*, etc.; another end which wisdom and reflection (vv. 10, 11) will effect for their possessor. *Strange woman* (see Expl. Notes). In the use of נכריה also, there is no reference originally to foreign birth;* foreign to one's self and one's own is meant, as the masc. is used in Eccl. 6 : 2.

V. 17. *Partner;* אַלּוּף (from אָלַף prop. *to join together, to associate.*†) Gesenius' Lex.: *familiaris, socius, amicus.*

drei ersten zusammenfassend das Ganze ab, daher wohl ohne Copula beigeordnet.

* *Und Erkenntniss* (was die betrifft), *deiner Seele wird es lieblich sein* (Bertheau).

† Maurer: *considerantia.* Ewald: *die Ueberlegung.* De Wette: *Besonnenheit.* Umbreit: מזמה ist hier die vorsichtige Ueberlegung. Stuart: *Reflection.*

‡ Bertheau: רע Subst. *das Böse*, dem stat. constr. דרך untergeordnet. Ewald: *um dich vor bösem Weg zu retten.*

|| Sept. ἐπὶ διαστροφῇ κακῇ (Gr. Venet. on the contrary: ἐν διαστροφαῖς κακῶν). Chald. בְּהוּפְכָא דְבִישְׁתָא.

* Maurer: אשה זרה *mulier aliena*, quæ est alius, alieni tori socia. Eadem est נכריה, minime barbara, cf. v. 17. Bertheau: אשה זרה *das fremde Weib* 5 : 3, 20, 22 : 14, wie hier neben נכריה 5 : 20, 7 : 5, während letzteres neben אשת רע und זונה 6 : 24, 23 : 27 vorkommt, bezeichnet demnach das ehebrecherische Weib; dies wird ausdrücklich bestätigt durch die weitere Beschreibung in v. 17. Gleiche Bedeutung kommt dem Worte נכריה zu, die nicht zum Hause gehörige und somit nicht rechtmässige Frau, vgl. איש נכרי Qoh. 6 : 2, Ps. 69 : 9. Nicht die *Ausländerin*, die *Nicht-Israelitin*, woran viele denken, meinend dass die öffentlichen Buhlerinnen vorzugsweise ausländische Frauen gewesen seien. Comp. *strangers*, Ezek. 16 : 32.

† Robinson (in Gesenius' Lex. sub voc.) Fürst, heb. u. chald. Hdwbch.: eig. *sich verbinden, vereinigen* mit Jem.

| KING JAMES' VERSION. | HEBREW TEXT. | | REVISED VERSION. |
|---|---|---|---|
| 18 For her house inclineth unto death, and her paths unto the dead. | כִּי שָׁחָה אֶל־מָוֶת בֵּיתָהּ<br>וְאֶל־רְפָאִים מַעְגְּלֹתֶיהָ׃ | 18 | for her house inclines to death, 18<br>and her ways to the shades : |
| 19 None that go unto her return again, neither take they hold of the paths of life. | כָּל־בָּאֶיהָ לֹא יְשׁוּבוּן<br>וְלֹא יַשִּׂיגוּ אָרְחוֹת חַיִּים׃ | 19 | none that go unto her return 19<br>again,<br>nor attain to the paths of life : |
| 20 That thou mayest walk in the way of good *men*, and keep the paths of the righteous. | לְמַעַן תֵּלֵךְ בְּדֶרֶךְ טוֹבִים<br>וְאָרְחוֹת צַדִּיקִים תִּשְׁמֹר׃ | כ | to the end that thou mayest 20<br>walk in the way of the good.<br>and keep the paths of the righteous. |
| 21 For the upright shall dwell in the land, and the perfect shall remain in it. | כִּי־יְשָׁרִים יִשְׁכְּנוּ־אָרֶץ<br>וּתְמִימִים יִוָּתְרוּ בָהּ׃ | 21 | For the upright shall inhabit 21<br>the land,<br>and the perfect shall remain in it. |
| 22 But the wicked shall be cut off from the earth, and the transgressors shall be rooted out of it. | וּרְשָׁעִים מֵאֶרֶץ יִכָּרֵתוּ<br>וּבוֹגְדִים יִסְּחוּ מִמֶּנָּה׃ | 22 | But the wicked shall be cut off 22<br>from the land,<br>and transgressors shall be rooted out of it. |

V. 18. There can be no reasonable doubt that ביתה is the subject of the verb;* any other construction being very unnatural (for the second member particularly) and feeble in effect. But as בית is everywhere else *masc.*,† either the true construction was misapprehended by the Masorites (as Umbreit supposes),‡ or they had in mind the neutral construction (§146, 3), with reference to both the subjects which follow.§ Bertheau's suggestion, that the principal subject, the adulterous woman, is before the writer's mind, and accounts for the *fem.* construction with בית in this single instance, seems not very natural.*

Second member :—רפאים, *shades,* see note on Job 26 : 5.

V. 19. כל—לא = *none* (§152, 1, 2nd ¶).

V. 20. *To the end that,* coördinate with vv. 12 and 16, and summing up the whole.

V. 21. *Perfect* = *integer*, complete in all that constitutes the righteous man.

V. 22. בגד, prop. *to act treacherously, perfidiously;* and hence the *part.* is often used in general for *transgressors,* as being faithless to their covenant obligations to God, recognized in the national economy of the Hebrews. Comp. Ps. 25 : 3; 59 : 5. Sept. *παράνομοι.*

*Shall be rooted out,* as a plant plucked up by the roots. The form יסחו *Kal Imperf.*, is the *indeterminate 3rd pers.* for the *pass.* (§137, 3, *b.*)†

---

* As understood by Jerome: *inclinata est enim ad mortem domus ejus;* and by Pagnino: *quia inclinata est ad mortem domus ejus.* So it is construed by nearly all modern scholars; e. g. Dathe: *nam deorsum ad mortem declinat domus ejus;* Ewald: *denn hin zum Tode sinket schon ihr Haus;* Umbreit: *denn zu dem Tode sinkt ihr Haus hinab;* Bertheau: *denn zum Tode senkt sich hinab ihr Haus;* Hitzig: *denn hinab senkt zum Tode sich ihr Haus;* Stuart: *for her house sinketh down to the dead.*

Others: *she sinks down to death* (the realm of death) *her house;* Geier: tanquam ad *domum suam.* Others, as De Wette: *denn sie sinkt zum Tode mit ihrem Hause, und zu den Schatten mit ihren Pfaden;* so, nearly, C. B. Michaelis: quod ad *domum suam;* sicut e. g. *ablatus* quoad *prævaricationem,* et *contectus* quoad *peccatum,* dicitur cujus prævaricatio ablata, et peccatum contectum est (Ps. 32 : 1). To all these may be objected, that the fate of the adulteress is not the writer's point, but that of her victims,—of all who suffer themselves to be enticed to her house. *It inclines* (tends down) *to death;* and all who enter it take that downward way to death and hell.

† And probably here. Ewald, indeed, includes it in his list of *fem.* nouns (§174, *d. γ*), but with no other proof than this passage: sehr selten בַּיִת *Haus,* אֹהֶל *Zelt,* מָקוֹם *Ort,* Spr. 2 : 18, Ijob 18 : 14, 20 : 9.

‡ שחה ist als 3te pers. sing., masc. gend. zu nehmen, insofern בית ein masc. ist, nicht das fem. von שוח, welches freilich die gewöhnlichere Form in Kal ist.

§ Maurer: Aut de ipsa muliere cogitavit scriptor initio hemistichii prioris, tum vero in fine ad complendam sententiam loco mulieris subjectum fecit ביתה, aut neutraliter positum est שחה quum præter ביתה sequantur מעגלתיה.

* בית ausnahmsweise hier als Feminin, eine leicht zu erklärende Unregelmässigkeit, da dem Verf. im Anfange noch das Hauptsubject, die Frau, vorschwebt.

† Bertheau: יסחו von נסח Deut. 28 : 63; Ps. 52 : 7; Prov. 15 : 25, also Imperf. Qal, nach dem passiven יכרתו so aufzufassen: *und Treulose werden sie herausreissen aus dem Lande,* welches, da das Subject unbestimmt gelassen wird, gleich ist dem passiven Ausdrucke, *werden herausgerissen werden.*

| KING JAMES' VERSION. | HEBREW TEXT. | | REVISED VERSION. | |
|---|---|---|---|---|
| CHAP. III. | CHAP. III. | | CHAP. III. | |
| MY son, forget not my law; but let thine heart keep my commandments: | בְּנִי תּוֹרָתִי אַל־תִּשְׁכָּח<br>וּמִצְוֺתַי יִצֹּר לִבֶּךָ׃ | א | MY son, forget not my law,<br>and let thy heart keep my commands. | 1 |
| 2 For length of days, and long life, and peace, shall they add to thee. | כִּי אֹרֶךְ יָמִים וּשְׁנוֹת חַיִּים<br>וְשָׁלוֹם יוֹסִיפוּ לָךְ׃ | 2 | For length of days, and years of life,<br>and peace, shall they add to thee. | 2 |
| 3 Let not mercy and truth forsake thee: bind them about thy neck; write them upon the table of thine heart: | חֶסֶד וֶאֱמֶת אַל־יַעַזְבֻךָ<br>קָשְׁרֵם עַל־גַּרְגְּרוֹתֶיךָ<br>כָּתְבֵם עַל־לוּחַ לִבֶּךָ׃ | 3 | Kindness and truth, let them not leave thee:<br>bind them on thy neck;<br>write them on the tablet of thy heart. | 3 |
| 4 So shalt thou find favour and good understanding in the sight of God and man. | וּמְצָא־חֵן וְשֵׂכֶל־טוֹב<br>בְּעֵינֵי אֱלֹהִים וְאָדָם׃ | 4 | So shalt thou find favor, and good understanding,<br>in the eyes of God and man. | 4 |
| 5 Trust in the LORD with all thine heart; and lean not unto thine own understanding. | בְּטַח אֶל־יְהוָה בְּכָל־לִבֶּךָ<br>וְאֶל־בִּינָתְךָ אַל־תִּשָּׁעֵן׃ | ה | Trust in Jehovah, with all thy heart,<br>and lean not on thine own understanding. | 5 |
| 6 In all thy ways acknowledge him, and he shall direct thy paths. | בְּכָל־דְּרָכֶיךָ דָעֵהוּ<br>וְהוּא יְיַשֵּׁר אֹרְחֹתֶיךָ׃ | 6 | In all thy ways acknowledge him,<br>and he will make plain thy paths. | 6 |
| 7 Be not wise in thine own eyes: fear the LORD, and depart from evil. | אַל־תְּהִי חָכָם בְּעֵינֶיךָ<br>יְרָא אֶת־יְהוָה וְסוּר מֵרָע׃ | 7 | Be not wise in thine own eyes;<br>fear Jehovah, and turn from evil. | 7 |
| 8 It shall be health to thy navel, and marrow to thy bones. | רִפְאוּת תְּהִי לְשָׁרֶּךָ<br>וְשִׁקּוּי לְעַצְמוֹתֶיךָ׃ | 8 | It shall be health to thy sinews,<br>and moisture to thy bones. | 8 |

V. 4. good repute

V. 8. Let it be

Ch. III.—V. 2. *And years of life.* Some, as Maurer e. g., make שנות a second *gen.* after ארך (*length of days, and of years of life*),* without necessity, while it weakens the expression.

V. 3. (See Expl. Notes.)

V. 4. *And find thou = so shalt thou find* (§ 130, 2, *a*). *Good understanding* (see Expl. Notes). So it is understood by Ewald,† and Bertheau.‡ Maurer: *shalt find favor and kind regard;* from the use of the verb, *to consider*, i. e., *to have regard for, to care for*, Ps. 41 : 2 (1).§ From the primary sense of the verb, *to view attentively, to regard*, שכל טוב might mean *favorable regard*, and hence objectively *good repute;** which is better suited to the second member. But such a usage is without support in the traditional exegesis.

V. 5. In the two members, אל expresses the direction of the mind toward the object of trust, and of reliance, where we use *in* and *on*.

V. 6. *Know him;* according to a common Heb. idiom, act as knowing him, recognize or acknowledge him.

Second member:—הוא is not specially emphatic—*he himself* and not another,† which would have no force here. What he, on his part, will do in return for the acknowledgment of him on thy part, is the point intended by the separate expression of the *pronom. subject* in Hebrew; and this is obvious in the English form, where the subject must be separately expressed.

V. 8. *It shall be health* (in distinction from *it will be*), the

* Maurer: *Nam longitudinem dierum annorumque vitæ.* So Umbreit: *denn Verlängerung der Tage und der Lebensjahre.* Ewald: *denn langes Alter, Lebensjahre.* De Wette: *denn Länge der Tage und Lebens-Jahre.* On the contrary, Rosenmüller: *Annis vitæ* . . . non simpliciter longævitas denotari videtur, sed simul etiam vita jucunda et felix, ut et alias.

† Als schön verständig betrachtet werden (S. 55).

‡ Es sollen grade Gunst und Einsicht bezeichnet werden, die nicht nur vor dem oft einseitigen und falschen, sondern auch vor dem scharfen untrüglichen Urtheile Gottes bestehen.

§ *Gratiam et curam benignam.* . . . שכל prop. attentio, hinc h. l. *studium* erga aliquem, *cura*, a שָׂכַל *Hi.* attendere ad, hinc curare aliquem; cf. imprimis Ps. 41 : 2.

* So Hitzig (die Sprüche Salomo's, 1858): שכל seinerseits ist eig. und so im Aram. *ansehen, betrachten* (vgl. שכל 1 Sam. 25 : 3 = شَكْل *species* [?]) . . . Demnach erklären wir: *eine* dir *günstige Ansicht, gütiges*, dir gewogenes *Urtheil.*

† והוא nachdrücklich *und er*, kein anderer (Bertheau).

| KING JAMES' VERSION. | HEBREW TEXT. | | REVISED VERSION. | |
|---|---|---|---|---|
| 9 Honour the LORD with thy substance, and with the firstfruits of all thine increase: | כַּבֵּד אֶת־יְהוָה מֵהוֹנֶךָ<br>וּמֵרֵאשִׁית כָּל־תְּבוּאָתֶךָ׃ | 9 | Honor Jehovah from thy substance,<br>and from the first fruits of all thine increase. | 9 |
| 10 So shall thy barns be filled with plenty, and thy presses shall burst out with new wine. | וְיִמָּלְאוּ אֲסָמֶיךָ שָׂבָע<br>וְתִירוֹשׁ יְקָבֶיךָ יִפְרֹצוּ׃ | י | So shall thy barns be filled with plenty,<br>and thy presses shall burst out with new wine. | 10 |
| 11 My son, despise not the chastening of the LORD; neither be weary of his correction: | מוּסַר יְהוָה בְּנִי אַל־תִּמְאָס<br>וְאַל־תָּקֹץ בְּתוֹכַחְתּוֹ׃ | 11 | Spurn not, my son, the chastening of Jehovah,<br>and loathe not his rebuke. | 11 |
| 12 For whom the LORD loveth he correcteth; even as a father the son *in whom* he delighteth. | כִּי אֶת אֲשֶׁר־יֶאֱהַב יְהוָה יוֹכִיחַ<br>וּכְאָב אֶת־בֵּן יִרְצֶה׃ | 12 | For whom Jehovah loves he rebukes,<br>even as a father the son he delights in. | 12 |
| 13 Happy *is* the man *that* findeth wisdom, and the man *that* getteth understanding. | אַשְׁרֵי אָדָם מָצָא חָכְמָה<br>וְאָדָם יָפִיק תְּבוּנָה׃ | 13 | Happy the man who finds wisdom,<br>and the man who obtains understanding. | 13 |
| 14 For the merchandise of it *is* better than the merchandise of silver, and the gain thereof than fine gold. | כִּי טוֹב סַחְרָהּ מִסְּחַר־כָּסֶף<br>וּמֵחָרוּץ תְּבוּאָתָהּ׃ | 14 | For her gain is better than the gain of silver,<br>and her increase than gold. | 14 |

effect of the *Jussive* here; the verb conforming to the prædicate preceding it (*health shall it be*) as the prominent thought. Others: *let it be health,** with the same effect. Bertheau prefers, *so shall there be health;*† but in that case, the connecting ו could hardly be omitted (comp. v. 10). שרך *thy sinews*, as shown by Rödiger, Thes. fasc. poster., p. 1483.

V. 9. מן, properly *from*, the expression of honor being made *from* the products of the earth, etc.‡

*With a part of thy substance* (Bertheau,§ and others) is not the thought; for he is to be honored *from all* of it, as giver and rightful proprietor of it all, and so recognized by the offering made from it.

V. 10. תירוש, the fresh juice of the grape, as it issues from the wine-press, properly called *must.*‖ יקב, the *wine-press*, as in Job 24 : 11.* *Shall burst out.* Gesenius' objection to this is not valid; viz., that "neither the wine-press nor wine-vat can be said to burst from the quantity of wine made, the figure applying only to a cask or wine-skin." (Lex., פרץ, 2.) By a common figure, the press is said to burst out (not burst) with the juice of the trodden grapes; which *breaks forth*, or *bursts out*, with a violence proportioned to its abundance. So the Sept., *thy presses gush out with wine.*

V. 13. *Who obtains*, viz., from the kindness and concession of another; the proper sense of the Heb. verb,† as in chs. 8 : 35; 12 : 2; 18 : 22.

V. 14. *Her gain*, viz., the gain she brings; not (as Ges. Lex.) *the gain of her* = to gain her.‡ חרוץ, Gesenius (Thes. and Lex.), "poet. for *gold*, prop. something dug out, fossils." This etym. (proposed by Cocceius§) is doubtless the correct one; but

* Rödiger (Thes. fasc. poster., p. 1483): *sanatio* s. medela hoc sit nervis tuis (in his enim sedes est roboris) *et recreatio ossibus tuis.*

† *So wird sein Heilung deinem Leibe*, indem der Voluntativ תהי hier ohne anknüpfendes ו den die Verheissung enthaltenden Nachsatz bezeichnet; vgl. יהי 5 : 18 (?), Ex. 7 : 9, und viele andere Beispiele der Art in späteren Psalmen. For the true relation of 5 : 18, see remarks on it.

‡ Maurer correctly: *Honora Jovam de tuis opibus*, etc.

§ *Ehre Jahve mit einem Theil deines Vermögens*, z. B. mit dem Zehnten wie Jaqob, Gen. 28 : 22, und die dem Mosaischen Gesetze gemäss lebenden Israeliten.

‖ Hence it is the usual term for the yearly product of the vine.—Fürst, Heb. Hdwbch., תירוש; *Most, . . . ungegohrenes Wein*, Mich. 6 : 15, von יין unterschieden, Hos. 4 : 11.

* So Bertheau: *und von Most überfliessen deine Keltern.* Sept. *αἱ ληνοί σου ἐκβλύζωσιν.* Vulg. *torcularia tua.*

† Gesenius (Thes. and Lex., 2) fecit, ut prodiret ab aliquo i. e. ab eo erogaretur, præberetur, inde *impetravit ab* aliquo. Bertheau: פוק *hervorgehen*, Hif. *hervorgehen lassen* = spenden Jes. 58 : 10, Ps. 144 : 13; sodann = sorgen dass etwas hervorgeht, herauslocken um in Besitz zu nehmen, das ist erlangen nämlich von Jahve Prov. 8 : 35, 18 : 22, denn aus seinem Munde kommt die תבונה 2 : 6.

‡ Maurer: *Nam melius* est *lucrum ejus* . . . (i. e. lucrum quod ex ea redundat), *lucro argenti*, quod redundat ex argento. Bertheau: *Ihr Gewinn* = was sie als Gewinn bringt 31 : 18, wofür 8 : 19 פרי. . . . *Besser als Gold ihr Ertrag* = was sie hervorbringt 8 : 19.

§ Lex.: חָרוּץ *χρυσός, aurum*, forte fossile.

| KING JAMES' VERSION. | | HEBREW TEXT. | REVISED VERSION. | |
|---|---|---|---|---|
| 15 She *is* more precious than rubies: and all the things thou canst desire are not to be compared unto her. | טו | יְקָרָה הִיא מִפְּנִיִּים<br>וְכָל־חֲפָצֶיךָ לֹא יִשְׁווּ־בָהּ׃ | More precious is she than pearls;<br>and all thy delights can not compare with her. | 15 |
| 16 Length of days *is* in her right hand; *and* in her left hand riches and honour. | 16 | אֹרֶךְ יָמִים בִּימִינָהּ<br>בִּשְׂמֹאולָהּ עֹשֶׁר וְכָבוֹד׃ | Length of days is in her right hand;<br>in her left hand riches and honor. | 16 |
| 17 Her ways *are* ways of pleasantness, and all her paths *are* peace. | 17 | דְּרָכֶיהָ דַרְכֵי־נֹעַם<br>וְכָל־נְתִיבוֹתֶיהָ שָׁלוֹם׃ | Her ways are ways of pleasantness,<br>and all her paths are peace. | 17 |
| 18 She *is* a tree of life to them that lay hold upon her: and happy *is every one* that retaineth her. | 18 | עֵץ־חַיִּים הִיא לַמַּחֲזִיקִים בָּהּ<br>וְתֹמְכֶיהָ מְאֻשָּׁר׃ | A tree of life is she to them that lay hold on her,<br>and blest is every one that retains her. | 18 |
| 19 The LORD by wisdom hath founded the earth; by understanding hath he established the heavens. | 19 | יְהוָה בְּחָכְמָה יָסַד אָרֶץ<br>כּוֹנֵן שָׁמַיִם בִּתְבוּנָה׃ | Jehovah by wisdom founded the earth;<br>established the heavens by understanding. | 19 |
| 20 By his knowledge the depths are broken up, and the clouds drop down the dew. | כ | בְּדַעְתּוֹ תְּהוֹמוֹת נִבְקָעוּ<br>וּשְׁחָקִים יִרְעֲפוּ־טָל׃ | By his knowledge the deeps were broken open,<br>and vapors distil the dew. | 20 |
| | | V. 15. מפנינים ק׳ | | |

V. 15. than corals

V. 19. in wisdom

V. 20. the deeps broke forth

there is no ground to assume any thing more than a poetic usage for gold.

V. 15. פניים, (Keri פנינים, as in many MSS.; comp. also ch. 8 : 11) *pearls*, as in the Targum, Jarchi on Prov. 8 : 11, Pagnino, and others. So Ewald (*more precious is she than pearls*), Bertheau,* Umbreit, De Wette, Rosenmüller, Lee (Heb. Lex. and Job), and others. Margin: *corals*, as understood by Gesenius, Maurer, Winer (Simonis' Lex.), and others. The grounds for the former opinion are given by Bochart, Hieroz., P. II., l. V., cc. vi., vii., and by Rosenmüller, Alterth., 4ter B., V. 5; for the latter by J. D. Michaelis Suppl., Gesenius, Thes., and Maurer, Comm. crit., I., p. 705 (Threni 4 : 7). The chief argument against the former is founded on Lam. 4 : 7, *were more ruddy* (*than peninim*); but its force is lessened by allusions in ancient writers to pearls of a ruddy hue, and by the rare occurrence still of those of a crimson tinge.† The milky *white water* is less prized among Orientals than in the West, the gayer and rarer colored varieties (especially the delicate *yellow water*, and the *black*) being preferred to it. I agree, therefore, with Rosenmüller (though on different grounds), that the passage in Lam. furnishes no argument against the opinion, that the פנינים were pearls.‡

* *Kostbarer ist sie als Perlen;* פניים nur hier im Ktib, sonst immer פנינים; vgl. Job 28 : 18, Prov. 8 : 11, wo unser Vers fast ganz wie hier wiederkehrt.

† Bruce describes a shell called Pinna, found in the Arabian Gulf, the inside lining "white, tinged with an elegant blush of red. Of this delicate complexion is the pearl found in this fish." Travels, Appendix, vol. VI., p. 277, art. Pearls.

‡ Alterthumskunde, 4ter B., 2te Abth., S. 459. Die erwähnte Stelle der Klagelieder steht folglich der Meinung, dass *Peninim* Perlen seyen, keineswegs entgegen.

V. 18. מאשר *sing.* construed with the *plur.*, attention being fixed on each individual of the number (§146, 4).

V. 19. Bertheau infers, from v. 16 compared with ch. 8, Job 28 : 12 fol., that *wisdom, understanding, knowledge*, are here personified, being only different expressions for the same thing.* But the form of expression in the first member of v. 20 (*by his knowledge*) does not favor this view. The personification in v. 16 is not necessarily continued in the new paragraph (on the same general topic), which evidently begins with v. 19. Moreover, these words are not to be so confounded. Each has its distinctive and appropriate import. *Wisdom* is the most comprehensive of them all; combining the highest moral purpose with the intelligence and foresight requisite for carrying it into effect; *understanding*, which comprehends relations, and adapts means to ends; *knowledge*, viz., of the natures and powers of all things, so as to be able to use them for his purpose. Such *wisdom, understanding*, and *knowledge*, has the divine Architect shown in the structure of the world.

V. 20. *The deeps;* the abysses of water. *Were broken open,*—

* "בחכמה, not *with* wisdom, as though only the divine attribute of wisdom employed in creation were meant, but *by wisdom*, according to the passages just quoted [ch. 8; Job 28 : 12, foll.; Sir. 24 : 3 foll.], and because here also in v. 16 (comp. 1 : 20 ff.) wisdom is clearly personified, appearing not as a divine attribute but as an independent personality. Accordingly, the words תבונה (comp. on 5 : 13 foll.) and דעת, only other expressions for חכמה, are also to be taken personally."

| KING JAMES' VERSION. | HEBREW TEXT. | | REVISED VERSION. | |
|---|---|---|---|---|
| 21 My son, let not them depart from thine eyes: keep sound wisdom and discretion: | בְּנִי אַל־יָלֻזוּ מֵעֵינֶיךָ<br>נְצֹר תֻּשִׁיָּה וּמְזִמָּה׃ | 21 | My son, let them not depart<br>from thine eyes;<br>keep true wisdom and reflection; | 21 |
| 22 So shall they be life unto thy soul, and grace to thy neck. | וְיִהְיוּ חַיִּים לְנַפְשֶׁךָ<br>וְחֵן לְגַרְגְּרֹתֶיךָ׃ | 22 | and they will be life to thy<br>soul,<br>and grace to thy neck. | 22 |
| 23 Then shalt thou walk in thy way safely, and thy foot shall not stumble. | אָז תֵּלֵךְ לָבֶטַח דַּרְכֶּךָ<br>וְרַגְלְךָ לֹא תִגּוֹף׃ | 23 | Then shalt thou go thy way<br>securely,<br>and thy foot shall not stumble. | 23 |
| 24 When thou liest down, thou shalt not be afraid: yea, thou shalt lie down, and thy sleep shall be sweet. | אִם־תִּשְׁכַּב לֹא־תִפְחָד<br>וְשָׁכַבְתָּ וְעָרְבָה שְׁנָתֶךָ׃ | 24 | When thou liest down thou<br>shalt not fear;<br>yea, thou shalt lie down, and<br>sweet shall be thy sleep. | 24 |
| 25 Be not afraid of sudden fear, neither of the desolation of the wicked, when it cometh. | אַל־תִּירָא מִפַּחַד פִּתְאֹם<br>וּמִשֹּׁאַת רְשָׁעִים כִּי תָבֹא׃ | כח | Be not dismayed at sudden<br>fear,<br>nor at the destruction of the<br>wicked when it comes; | 25 |
| 26 For the LORD shall be thy confidence, and shall keep thy foot from being taken. | כִּי־יְהוָה יִהְיֶה בְכִסְלֶךָ<br>וְשָׁמַר רַגְלְךָ מִלָּכֶד׃ | 26 | for Jehovah shall be thy confidence;<br>and he will keep thy foot from<br>being taken. | 26 |
| 27 Withhold not good from them to whom it is due, when it is in the power of thine hand to do *it*. | אַל־תִּמְנַע־טוֹב מִבְּעָלָיו<br>בִּהְיוֹת לְאֵל יָדֶיךָ לַעֲשׂוֹת׃ | 27 | Withhold not good from them<br>to whom it is due,<br>when it is in the power of thy<br>hands to do it. | 27 |

V. 27. ידך ק׳

by cleaving passages for them through the earth, to form fountains on its surface. To the same effect, Gesenius (Lex. בקע, Niph. 2): "Spoken also of waters which *break forth*, Is. 35 : 6; Prov. 3 : 20."* This language is not to be referred, as some suppose (C. B. Michaelis, Rosenmüller), to the origin of the ocean itself, bursting forth from the bowels of the earth (Job 38 : 8). This is contrary to the parallelism; for the next member shows, that the provision for the irrigation of the earth's surface is the subject of the verse. The act of *breaking open*, having been done once for all, is expressed by the perfect; while the formation of dew, continually recurring, is expressed in the next member by the imperfect. By these two provisions, the earth is abundantly supplied with moisture, from beneath and from above.†

Bertheau understands by the first member the division of the whole mass of waters, at the creation, into waters above and waters below the expanse (Gen. 1 : 7‡). But the verb נבקעו is not at all suited to the expression of this idea. It expresses the act of violently cleaving, sundering, parts which firmly cohere;

* Transfertur etiam ad aquam prorumpentem; Jes. 35 : 6, . . . *nam aperiuntur* s. *prorumpunt aquæ in deserto;* Prov. 3 : 20. (Thes.)

† Roris meminit ceu insignis Dei beneficii, in regionibus præsertim calidioribus, ubi raræ sunt pluviæ, adeoque rore nocturno summe opus est (Rosenmüller).

‡ So Ewald: *Es spalteten sich* bei der Schöpfung, nach Gen. 1 : 6–8, die Fluthen, so dass nun die obere Hälfte derselben, die wässrige Luft, stets den befruchtenden Thau träufelt. So also Umbreit: *Durch seine Weisheit theilten sich die Wassertiefen; . . .* ein malerischer Ausdruck.

not simply of keeping separate and apart, which is the idea in Gen. 1 7. The proper sense of the verb, with reference to the *abyss of waters*, is shown in Gen. 7 : 11.

Second member:—שחקים, fine watery vapors; commonly, for the region occupied by them, viz., the upper atmosphere, hence *the sky, the heavens.* Here, in its proper signification, for *vapors*, as in 8 : 28 for *clouds.*

V. 21. ילזו most naturally refers to the subjects already before the mind, not, as supposed by some, to those about to be mentioned in the second member.* For the *gend.* comp. v. 2.

Second member:—תושיה, *true wisdom;*† i. e. *real*, in distinction from imaginary and false notions of wisdom, current among men.

V. 24, second member:—*thou liest down*, etc., with the effect of the future (§126, 6, *a*). Bertheau, less happily: *and hast thou lain down* = after lying down.

V. 26. יהיה בכסלך = *shall be for thy confidence*, i. e., shall be as such to thee: Gesenius, Lex. בְּ, C. Comp. Ewald, Lehrb., §217, *f*, 1, *b*.‡

V. 27. בעל, Gesenius, Lex., 4, *extr.* לאל; לְ *of condition* or

* Quæ structura licet ferri potest, necessaria tamen non est, quum ex prægressis quænam illa sint, quæ non debeant recedere, satis superque perluceat (Maurer).

† Ewald: *wahren Rath und Ueberlegung.*

‡ Zur blossen Einführung des Prädicats *worin ein Subject bestehe,* aber sehr selten und nur dichterisch, הוּא בְּאֶחָד *er ist ein einziger*, Ijob 23 : 13, etc.

KING JAMES' VERSION.

28 Say not unto thy neighbour, Go, and come again, and to-morrow I will give; when thou hast it by thee.
29 Devise not evil against thy neighbour, seeing he dwelleth securely by thee.

30 Strive not with a man without cause, if he have done thee no harm.
31 Envy thou not the oppressor, and choose none of his ways.

32 For the froward *is* abomination to the LORD: but his secret *is* with the righteous.

33 The curse of the LORD *is* in the house of the wicked: but he blesseth the habitation of the just.
34 Surely he scorneth the scorners: but he giveth grace unto the lowly.
35 The wise shall inherit glory: but shame shall be the promotion of fools.

HEBREW TEXT.

28 אַל־תֹּאמַר לְרֵעֶיךָ ׀ לֵךְ וָשׁוּב
וּמָחָר אֶתֵּן וְיֵשׁ אִתָּךְ׃
29 אַל־תַּחֲרֹשׁ עַל־רֵעֲךָ רָעָה
וְהוּא־יוֹשֵׁב לָבֶטַח אִתָּךְ׃
ל אַל־תָּרוֹב עִם־אָדָם חִנָּם
אִם־לֹא גְמָלְךָ רָעָה׃
31 אַל־תְּקַנֵּא בְּאִישׁ חָמָס
וְאַל־תִּבְחַר בְּכָל־דְּרָכָיו׃
32 כִּי תוֹעֲבַת יְהוָה נָלוֹז
וְאֶת־יְשָׁרִים סוֹדוֹ׃
33 מְאֵרַת יְהוָה בְּבֵית רָשָׁע
וּנְוֵה צַדִּיקִים יְבָרֵךְ׃
34 אִם־לַלֵּצִים הוּא יָלִיץ
וְלַעֲנָיִים יִתֶּן־חֵן׃
לה כָּבוֹד חֲכָמִים יִנְחָלוּ
וּכְסִילִים מֵרִים קָלוֹן׃

V. 28. ק׳ לרעך V. 30. ק׳ תריב V. 34. ק׳ ולענוים

REVISED VERSION.

Say not to thy neighbor: Go, 28
and come again,
and to-morrow I will give,
when it is by thee.
Devise not evil against thy 29
neighbor,
when he dwells securely by
thee.
Strive not with a man with- 30
out cause,
when he has done thee no evil.
Envy not the man of vio- 31
lence,
and choose none of his ways;
for the perverse is the abomina- 32
tion of Jehovah,
but his favor is with the upright.
The curse of Jehovah is in 33
the house of the wicked;
but the habitation of the righteous he will bless.
Though he mocks at those 34
who mock,
yet gives he favor to the lowly.
The wise shall inherit honor; 35
but fools he exalts to shame.

V. 35. But fools bear away shame | *Others*, But shame lifts fools on high

*state* (Lex. B, 3); אֵל, Lex. 2 (comp. Thes. I., p. 48). *Thy hand* ידך, as in the Keri, and many MSS., and EDD.

V. 28. *Thy neighbor* רעך. For the *plur.* of the text, very many MSS. and some EDD. have the reading of the *Keri*, which is every way more pertinent.

V. 29. חָרַשׁ, *to fabricate, to work out,* and hence *to devise,* e. g. evil (Ges. Lex., 2).*

V. 32. סוד as in Job 29 : 4.

V. 34. *Though he mocks,* etc. So Ewald, Umbreit, Maurer, Rosenmüller,† and others. The construction proposed by Bertheau, viz., to make v. 34 the conditional protasis, of which v. 35 is the apodosis, gives a very feeble sense. Nor is such a construction necessary. The parallelism in v. 34 is by contrast: though so severe to the proud scoffer, he is gracious to the humble.

V. 35. *But fools he exalts to shame.* This seems to me preferable to any of the numerous constructions heretofore given of this member. The subject of מרים readily suggests itself, as in several other instances (e. g., 10 : 24, 13 : 22) where the nature of the act makes an obvious reference to the just Dispenser of reward and punishment. There is a happy irony in the expression of the antithesis, between honorable distinction on one side, and exaltation to shame on the other.

The following are examples of other constructions:—Ewald: *but shame lifts fools on high;** . . . as fearful examples of depravity and of divine punishment. Gesenius, Lex.: *but fools take up* (and bear) *shame.*† Maurer: *but whoever is a fool, he bears off shame.*‡ Umbreit: *but shame takes away fools.*§ Bertheau: *and shame snatches fools away.*‖ C. B. Michaelis: *but fools shall receive shame*¶ (after the Chald. and Syr.). Vulgate: *stulto-*

* Bertheau: *Nicht schmiede* = nicht ersinne, 6 : 14, 18; 12 : 20; 14 : 22; für welche Bedeutung des Verbi Ezech. 21 : 36 entscheidet. Nach dem Vorgange Anderer Ewald: *nicht säe*, auf welche Auffassung man von חרש *pflügen*, doch erst durch willkürliche Beziehung des Pflügens auf das Unterpflügen der Saat kommt.

† אם h. l. membrorum antithesis coæquationem significat, quasi hæc sint ἀντιστρέφοντα. Similiter Threni 3 : 32.

* *Doch Thoren hebet Schande hoch;* . . . als schreckliche Beispiele der Verkehrtheit und der göttlichen Strafen.

† Thes., *stulti auferunt* (tragen davon, reportant) *ignominiam.*

‡ *Et* (sed) *quicunque stultus est, aufert ignominiam.*

§ *Aber Thoren nimmt Schande hinweg.*

‖ *Und Thoren rafft fort Schande.*

¶ הרים *tollere* notare potest *accipere; tollere* tanquam *portionem* suam.

| KING JAMES' VERSION. | HEBREW TEXT. | | REVISED VERSION. | |
|---|---|---|---|---|
| CHAP. IV. | CHAP. IV. | | CHAP. IV. | |
| HEAR, ye children, the instruction of a father, and attend to know understanding. | שִׁמְעוּ בָנִים מוּסַר אָב<br>וְהַקְשִׁיבוּ לָדַעַת בִּינָה׃ | א | HEAR, children, the instruction of a father;<br>and attend, to know understanding. | 1 |
| 2 For I give you good doctrine, forsake ye not my law. | כִּי לֶקַח טוֹב נָתַתִּי לָכֶם<br>תּוֹרָתִי אַל־תַּעֲזֹבוּ׃ | 2 | For I give you good instruction;<br>forsake ye not my law. | 2 |
| 3 For I was my father's son, tender and only *beloved* in the sight of my mother. | כִּי־בֵן הָיִיתִי לְאָבִי<br>רַךְ וְיָחִיד לִפְנֵי אִמִּי׃ | 3 | For a son was I to my father;<br>tender, and an only child, in the sight of my mother. | 3 |
| 4 He taught me also, and said unto me, Let thine heart retain my words: keep my commandments, and live, | וַיֹּרֵנִי וַיֹּאמֶר לִי<br>יִתְמָךְ־דְּבָרַי לִבֶּךָ<br>שְׁמֹר מִצְוֺתַי וֶחְיֵה׃ | 4 | And he taught me, and said to me:<br>Let thy heart retain my words;<br>keep my commands, and live. | 4 |
| 5 Get wisdom, get understanding: forget *it* not; neither decline from the words of my mouth. | קְנֵה חָכְמָה קְנֵה בִינָה<br>אַל־תִּשְׁכַּח וְאַל־תֵּט מֵאִמְרֵי־פִי׃ | ה | Get wisdom; get understanding;<br>forget not, and turn not from the words of my mouth. | 5 |
| 6 Forsake her not, and she shall preserve thee: love her, and she shall keep thee. | אַל־תַּעַזְבֶהָ וְתִשְׁמְרֶךָּ<br>אֱהָבֶהָ וְתִצְּרֶךָּ׃ | 6 | Forsake her not, and she will keep thee;<br>love her, and she will preserve thee. | 6 |
| 7 Wisdom *is* the principal thing; *therefore* get wisdom: and with all thy getting get understanding. | רֵאשִׁית חָכְמָה קְנֵה חָכְמָה<br>וּבְכָל־קִנְיָנְךָ קְנֵה בִינָה׃ | 7 | The first thing is wisdom; get wisdom,<br>and with all thy getting, get understanding. | 7 |

V. 7. The chief thing | *Others*, The beginning of wisdom is to get wisdom

*rum exaltatio ignominia* (followed in the early Eng. versions, and in the com. ver.) Müntinghe: *but shame is the nobility of fools.* *

Ch. IV.—V. 1. *To know understanding* † may mean to acquire it, to obtain through instruction and reflection the power of understanding; or, not improbably, to know what it is, so as not to be imposed on by false pretensions to it. The literal form should, therefore, be retained.

V. 3. *For a son was I to my father;* ‡ the literal form and exact sense of the Hebrew. *Son*, in its obvious emphatic sense. *To my father* (Lex., לְ, A, 3, c), viz., in his regard; I was viewed and treated by him as a son.

Second member:—*An only child, in the sight of my mother*, means, I was so regarded by her, i. e. with the affection felt for an only child. If he was literally an only son, it would not be proper to add the limitation, *in the sight of my mother.* § *A tender and only child* (Umbreit,* Stuart) is contrary to the Hebrew construction.

V. 7. *The first thing*, either in rank or order of time, corresponds to the twofold use of ראשית. The construction: *The beginning of wisdom is, get wisdom* (i. e. wisdom's beginning is, to get wisdom), though favored by good authorities, † will not bear comparison with the one given in the text and margin. *With all thy getting*, i. e. in connection with it; among all thy acquisitions, neglect not to get understanding; let it have an

* Aber Schande ist der Adel der Thoren.

† Maurer: *Attendite, ut cognoscatis intelligentiam;* discatis recte intelligere. Bertheau: *um kennen zu lernen Einsicht.* Ewald: *und merket auf, Einsicht zu wissen.*

‡ Pagnino: *Quia filius fui patri meo.* Maurer: *Nam filius* (i. e. cum vi, veri nominis filius ideoque carissimus) *fui patri meo.* Ewald: *Ich war ein Sohn ja meinem Vater.* The erroneous construction of the Vulgate: *Nam et ego filius fui patris mei*, was followed in the Genevan, and adopted thence in the com. version.

§ Pfeiffer (Dubia Vexata, Cent. 3tia, Loc. lxxxv): Unicus fui non nativitate, sed ex æstimatione matris meæ, quæ me non aliter adamavit atque in oculis gestavit atque unicum filium.

* *Vor meiner Mutter Augen zartes, einz'ges Kind.*

† E. g. C. B. Michaelis: *Principium sapientiæ* est hoc: *Compara sapientiam;* i. e. is demum sapere incipit, qui de comparanda sapientia vere sollicitus est. Maurer: *Initium sapientiæ* est: *compara sapientiam* . . . pro, initium sapientiæ est comparare cet. De Wette and Ewald: *Der Weisheit Anfang ist: erwirb Weisheit.* Umbreit: Der Vorsatz, sich Weisheit zu erwerben, ist schon der Anfang derselben. Gesenius (Thes., ר, 1, *extr.*), *summa sapientia.*

On the contrary, Lud. de Dieu: *Præcipuum est sapientia, acquire sapientiam.* Schultens: *Princeps sapientia, vindicato sapientiam.* . . . Languidiuscule exit, quod multi dant: *principium sapientiæ* est, *acquire sapientiam.* Dœderlein: *Das erste* (das vornehmste und beste) *ist Weisheit; kaufe Weisheit.* Dathe: *Præstantissimum est sapientia, compara ergo sapientiam.* Stuart: *The principal thing is wisdom, get wisdom.*

| KING JAMES' VERSION. | HEBREW TEXT. | | REVISED VERSION. | |
|---|---|---|---|---|
| 8 Exalt her, and she shall promote thee: she shall bring thee to honour, when thou dost embrace her. | סַלְסְלֶהָ וּתְרוֹמְמֶךָּ<br>תְּכַבֵּדְךָ כִּי תְחַבְּקֶנָּה׃ | 8 | Exalt her, and she will promote thee;<br>will honor thee, when thou dost embrace her. | 8 |
| 9 She shall give to thine head an ornament of grace: a crown of glory shall she deliver to thee. | תִּתֵּן לְרֹאשְׁךָ לִוְיַת־חֵן<br>עֲטֶרֶת תִּפְאֶרֶת תְּמַגְּנֶךָּ׃ | 9 | She will give a garland of grace for thy head;<br>a crown of beauty will she deliver to thee. | 9 |
| 10 Hear, O my son, and receive my sayings; and the years of thy life shall be many. | שְׁמַע בְּנִי וְקַח אֲמָרָי<br>וְיִרְבּוּ לְךָ שְׁנוֹת חַיִּים׃ | י | Hear, my son, and receive my words;<br>and years of life shall be multiplied to thee. | 10 |
| 11 I have taught thee in the way of wisdom; I have led thee in right paths. | בְּדֶרֶךְ חָכְמָה הֹרֵתִיךָ<br>הִדְרַכְתִּיךָ בְּמַעְגְּלֵי־יֹשֶׁר׃ | 11 | I have taught thee in the way of wisdom;<br>have led thee in paths of rectitude. | 11 |
| 12 When thou goest, thy steps shall not be straitened; and when thou runnest, thou shalt not stumble. | בְּלֶכְתְּךָ לֹא־יֵצַר צַעֲדֶךָ׃<br>וְאִם־תָּרוּץ לֹא תִכָּשֵׁל׃ | 12 | When thou walkest, thy step shall not be straitened;<br>and when thou runnest, thou shalt not stumble. | 12 |
| 13 Take fast hold of instruction; let *her* not go: keep her; for she *is* thy life. | הַחֲזֵק בַּמּוּסָר אַל־תֶּרֶף<br>נִצְּרֶהָ כִּי־הִיא חַיֶּיךָ׃ | 13 | Lay hold on instruction, let not go;<br>keep her, for she is thy life. | 13 |
| 14 Enter not into the path of the wicked, and go not in the way of evil *men*. | בְּאֹרַח רְשָׁעִים אַל־תָּבֹא<br>וְאַל־תְּאַשֵּׁר בְּדֶרֶךְ רָעִים׃ | 14 | Enter not into the path of the wicked,<br>nor go onward in the way of the evil. | 14 |
| 15 Avoid it, pass not by it, turn from it, and pass away. | פְּרָעֵהוּ אַל־תַּעֲבָר־בּוֹ<br>שְׂטֵה מֵעָלָיו וַעֲבוֹר׃ | טו | Avoid it, pass not over it;<br>turn off from it, and pass on. | 15 |
| 16 For they sleep not, except they have done mischief; and their sleep is taken away, unless they cause *some* to fall. | כִּי לֹא יִשְׁנוּ אִם־לֹא יָרֵעוּ<br>וְנִגְזְלָה שְׁנָתָם אִם־לֹא יַכְשׁוֹלוּ׃ | 16 | For they sleep not unless they do evil;<br>and their sleep is taken away, if they cause none to fall. | 16 |
| | V. 16. יכשילו ק׳ | | | |

V. 13. Let her not go.

equal place with all of them. So Gesenius understands קִנְיָן here.* Others take it in the sense of *possessions, property, wealth* (ב *pretii*); *with all thy getting* (acquisition, wealth) *get understanding*,† i. e. at whatever price. The translation should be such, that the reader can judge of the meaning for himself.

V. 9. *Garland of grace;* 1 : 9. מִגֵּן *to deliver up*, viz., to another, to put into another's possession, Gen. 14 : 20, Hos. 11 : 8; here in a favorable sense.‡

V. 13. *Let not go*, prop. *relax not*, viz., the hand, as the verb is often used absolutely. Others, less forcibly, *let her not go.**

V. 15. Second member:—מֵעָלָיו, lit. *from upon it*, implying that it has already been entered on.†

V. 16. Second member:—יַכְשִׁילוּ,‡ the reading of the *Keri*,

* (Thes., קִנְיָן, 2) *acquisitio, emtio*, Lev. 22 : 11; Prov. 4 : 7.

† E. g. Bertheau: *Und für deinen ganzen Besitz erkaufe Einsicht*, denn alle deine Güter, und wären sie die kostbarsten, sind nicht so viel werth wie sie, 3 : 14 ff.

‡ Maurer: *Corona splendida dondbit te.* Dathe: *Coronam decoram tibi largietur.* Ewald: *Mit einer schmucken Krone dich beschenken.* De Wette: *Eine prächtige Krone verleihet sie dir.* Bertheau: *Mit einer schmückenden Krone wird sie dich beschenken*; מִגֵּן sehr selten, Gen. 14 : 20, Hos. 11 : 8, mit zwei Accusativen, Ewald. Lehrb., 283, b. Die Bedeutung ist gesichert. Sept. *ὑπερασπίσῃ σου*, als wäre מִגֵּן von מגן *Schild* abgeleitet, was etwa zu einer Mauer oder schon zu einem Panzer passen würde, nicht zu der schmückenden Krone des Hauptes.

* E. g. Maurer: *Ne missam facias. . . .* אל תרף etiam *ne remittas* manum significare possit, omisso יד, ut alias. Sed simplicior alia ratio. Rosenmüller: *Ne remittas* scil. manum (cf. Jos. 10 : 6, אַל תֶּרֶף יָדֶיךָ) ab ea tenenda, ne excidere aut extorqueri illam tibi sinas. So De Wette and Umbreit: *Lass nicht davon.* Second member:—נצרה injecto Dag. ut נצרה Ps. 141 : 3 (Maurer). Der Imperat. Qal נצרה in den meisten und besten Handschriften mit Dagesch dirimens in dem צ wie Ps. 141 : 3 (Bertheau).

† Bertheau: *Biege* wenn du dennoch auf ihn (עָלָיו) gekommen bist *von auf ihm ab*, und so ihn verlassen habend *ziehe einher.*

‡ This is expressed by the Vulg. *nisi supplantaverint*, and is

| KING JAMES' VERSION. | HEBREW TEXT. | | REVISED VERSION. | |
|---|---|---|---|---|
| 17 For they eat the bread of wickedness, and drink the wine of violence. | כִּי לָחֲמוּ לֶחֶם רֶשַׁע<br>וְיֵין חֲמָסִים יִשְׁתּוּ׃ | 17 | For they eat the bread of wickedness,<br>and wine of violence they drink. | 17 |
| 18 But the path of the just *is* as the shining light, that shineth more and more unto the perfect day. | וְאֹרַח צַדִּיקִים כְּאוֹר נֹגַהּ<br>הוֹלֵךְ וָאוֹר עַד־נְכוֹן הַיּוֹם׃ | 18 | But the way of the righteous is as the clear light,<br>shining more and more, to the noon-day. | 18 |
| 19 The way of the wicked *is* as darkness: they know not at what they stumble. | דֶּרֶךְ רְשָׁעִים כָּאֲפֵלָה<br>לֹא יָדְעוּ בַּמֶּה יִכָּשֵׁלוּ׃ | 19 | The way of the wicked is as thick darkness;<br>they know not at what they stumble. | 19 |
| 20 My son, attend to my words; incline thine ear unto my sayings. | בְּנִי לִדְבָרַי הַקְשִׁיבָה<br>לַאֲמָרַי הַט אָזְנֶךָ׃ | כ | My son, attend to my words;<br>incline thine ear to my sayings. | 20 |
| 21 Let them not depart from thine eyes; keep them in the midst of thine heart. | אַל־יַלִּיזוּ מֵעֵינֶיךָ<br>שָׁמְרֵם בְּתוֹךְ לְבָבֶךָ׃ | 21 | Let them not depart from thine eyes;<br>keep them within thy heart. | 21 |
| 22 For they *are* life unto those that find them, and health to all their flesh. | כִּי־חַיִּים הֵם לְמֹצְאֵיהֶם<br>וּלְכָל־בְּשָׂרוֹ מַרְפֵּא׃ | 22 | For life are they to every one that finds them,<br>and healing to all his flesh. | 22 |
| 23 Keep thy heart with all diligence; for out of it *are* the issues of life. | מִכָּל־מִשְׁמָר נְצֹר לִבֶּךָ<br>כִּי מִמֶּנּוּ תּוֹצְאוֹת חַיִּים׃ | 23 | Above every care, keep thy heart;<br>for out of it are the issues of life. | 23 |

V. 23. Above all that is kept

and of twenty-six MSS. of Ken., followed by C. B. Michaelis, Rosenmüller, De Wette, Umbreit, Bertheau, and others.

V. 18. *As the clear light,** bright, shining out without obstruction; here, from the visible sun. The expression itself does not necessarily refer to the sun's light (as some assume), but the next member makes this reference clear.

Second member:—נכון היום *fixed* or *stationary day,* when the sun seems to stand fixed in the heavens, neither ascending nor declining; a Heb. expression for noon-day,† like *σταθερὸν ἦμαρ, σταθερὰ μεσημβρία,* etc., quoted by Gesenius, כּוּן Niph. 1.‡

V. 19. They stumble, without knowing at what; and hence, can take no precautions against it, and find no remedy for it.

V. 22. Second member:—*His flesh* (בשרו) often used, as here, for the physical nature of man. It is better to retain it, therefore, than to represent it by *body,* as in many versions.

V. 23. *Above every care*§ gives the sense with better effect than is done by the solution of the thought, *above all that is kept* (margin), adopted by many.*

Second member:—*For out of it* (as from a fountain) *are the issues of life*† (תוצאה, prop. *a going forth, an issuing out*). The sentiment is the same as in Matt. 15 : 19, *out of the heart proceed evil thoughts, murders, adulteries,* etc. In other words, the outward life of man proceeds from the heart; and hence the keeping of the heart is his first and chief care.

The translation should be the same, if by *life* we understand *happiness* (according to Gesenius and others); and also if by תוצאה is meant the *exit* or *issue* of a thing, i. e. its end or termination, according to Ewald‡ and others.

---

paraphrased by the Chald. עַד מָה דְּעָבְדִין תַּקְּלָא, and the Gr. Ven. *ἣν μὴ συμποδίσουσι.*

* Ewald: *Wie das helle Licht.* Bertheau: Strahlendes Licht.

† Mercer (Pagnini Thes. Ling. Sanct.): Concretum pro abstracto, *perfectionem diei* (seu, *certitudinem et stabilitatem*) vernacule, *Plein jour.*

‡ Maurer: הולך ואור procedens, incrementa capiens, *crescens et lucens est,* nam אור hic participium est, i. e. *crescit et lucet,* i. e. *magis magisque lucet,* parataxi posita pro syntaxi [§ 131, 3, Rem. 3].

§ Rosenmüller: *Præ omni custodia,* i. e. majore solicitudine, quam ullam earum rerum, quæ a te custodiuntur. Ewald: *Vor jeder Hut behüte du dein Herz. . . . Vor aller Hut,* d. h. mehr als alles, was man sonst sorgsam zu hüten pflegt. Maurer: *Præ omni custodia,* i. e. præ omnibus rebus custodiendis *custodi cor,* animum, *tuum.* De Wette (well as to the sense): *Mehr denn alles bewahre dein Herz.* So Dathe: *Ante omnia mentem tuam observa.*

* Gesenius, Lex. Bertheau: *Mehr als jeglichen Gegenstand sorgsamer Bewahrung.* Umbreit: *Mehr als alles was zu behüten ist.* C. B. Michaelis: *Præ omni* alia *custodia,* Neh. 4 : 3; seu *re servanda.*

Mercer (Pagnini Thes. Ling. Sanct.): Alii, *præ omni . . . cautione,* i. e. eo quod cavendum sit.

† Maurer: *nam ex eo sunt exitus vitæ;* i. e. nam ex eo exit vita, nam cor, animus, sedes ac fons est omnis vitæ. Bertheau: *denn aus ihm sind Ausgänge des Lebens.*

‡ *Denn von ihm gehen aus des Lebens Enden.*

KING JAMES' VERSION.

24 Put away from thee a froward mouth, and perverse lips put far from thee.

25 Let thine eyes look right on, and let thine eyelids look straight before thee.

26 Ponder the path of thy feet, and let all thy ways be established.

27 Turn not to the right hand nor to the left: remove thy foot from evil.

CHAP. V.

My son, attend unto my wisdom, *and* bow thine ear to my understanding:

2 That thou mayest regard discretion, and *that* thy lips may keep knowledge.

3 For the lips of a strange woman drop *as* a honeycomb, and her mouth *is* smoother than oil:

4 But her end is bitter as wormwood, sharp as a twoedged sword.

5 Her feet go down to death; her steps take hold on hell.

HEBREW TEXT.

24 הָסֵר מִמְּךָ עִקְּשׁוּת פֶּה
וּלְזוּת שְׂפָתַיִם הַרְחֵק מִמֶּךָּ׃

כה עֵינֶיךָ לְנֹכַח יַבִּיטוּ
וְעַפְעַפֶּיךָ יַיְשִׁרוּ נֶגְדֶּךָ׃

26 פַּלֵּס מַעְגַּל רַגְלֶךָ
וְכָל־דְּרָכֶיךָ יִכֹּנוּ׃

27 אַל־תֵּט יָמִין וּשְׂמֹאול
הָסֵר רַגְלְךָ מֵרָע׃

CHAP. V.

א בְּנִי לְחָכְמָתִי הַקְשִׁיבָה
לִתְבוּנָתִי הַט־אָזְנֶךָ׃

2 לִשְׁמֹר מְזִמּוֹת
וְדַעַת שְׂפָתֶיךָ יִנְצֹרוּ׃

3 כִּי נֹפֶת תִּטֹּפְנָה שִׂפְתֵי זָרָה
וְחָלָק מִשֶּׁמֶן חִכָּהּ׃

4 וְאַחֲרִיתָהּ מָרָה כַלַּעֲנָה
חַדָּה כְּחֶרֶב פִּיּוֹת׃

ה רַגְלֶיהָ יֹרְדוֹת מָוֶת
שְׁאוֹל צְעָדֶיהָ יִתְמֹכוּ׃

V. 26. בנ״א יכונו

REVISED VERSION.

Put away from thee froward- 24
ness of the mouth;
and perverseness of the lips put far from thee.

Let thine eyes look right for- 25
ward,
and thine eye-lids be straight before thee.

Ponder the path of thy foot; 26
and let all thy ways be established.

Turn not to right or left; 27
remove thy foot from evil.

CHAP. V.

My son, give heed to my 1
wisdom;
to my understanding incline thine ear:

so as to regard counsels, 2
and that thy lips may keep knowledge.

For the lips of a strange woman 3
drop with honey,
and her mouth is smoother than oil.

But her end is bitter as worm- 4
wood,
sharp as a twoedged sword.

Her feet go down to death, 5
her steps take hold on the underworld;

V. 25. *Be straight before thee* (§ 53, 2, Rem.) *

V. 26. *Ponder the path*, etc. Gesenius: *Level the path of thy foot;* i. e. make a plain and even way for it.† But the other sense of the verb, recognized by Gesenius in ch. 5 : 21, seems more pertinent here; referring to the caution and circumspection necessary, in order that one's way (his course of action) may be stable, and not uncertain and fluctuating.

Second member:—*Be established* (see preceeding paragraph). De Wette: *And let all thy ways be right.* But the other sense of יכנו is more appropriate, as expressed in most of the critical versions. *

Ch. V.—V. 2. מזמות, prop. *meditations, reflections;* by meton. *counsels,* as maturely considered and thought out. †

V. 3. נפת is the *dripping honey* (not honeycomb), i. e. the purest, as it drips spontaneously from the comb; fully נֹפֶת צוּפִים *the dripping of the combs,* and then by itself in the same sense. זרה, 2 : 16. חך, prop. the *palate,* and then the *inside mouth* as the organ of speech.

V. 4. *Her end;* not her own fate, evidently, but the fate which she prepares for her victims; Gesenius (Lex., אחרית, 1, a):

* Maurer: *Et palpebræ tuæ in rectum tendant ante te.* Bertheau: *Deine Augen sollen gradaussehen, deine Augenlieder grade Richtung einhalten vor dir.*

† Dathe: *Expende tramitem pedis tui.* Maurer: *Expende* (accurate examina) *orbitam* (viam) *pedis tui.* . . . Alii, in his Gesenius, De Wette, פלס *complana, æqua* interpretantur, sensu minus commodo. Cf. præterea 5 : 6, 21. Rosenmüller: *Pondera semitam pedis tui.* . . . Sensus est: caute et sollicite instituas vivendi et agendi rationem. Ewald: *Wäg' wohl ab deines Fusses Bahn.* Umbreit: *Wäg' deines Fusses Steig wohl ab.* Bertheau: *Wäg wohl ab das Geleise deines Fusses,* damit du nicht in ein verkehrtes Geleise hineingeräthst.

* Maurer: *Et omnes viæ tuæ sint firmæ.* Dathe: *Et omnes viæ tuæ stabilientur.* Rosenmüller: *Et omnes viæ tuæ stabiles sint.* Umbreit: *Und fest mögen alle deine Wege sein.* Bertheau: *Und alle deine Wege mögen sicher sein,* nicht bald diese bald jene Richtung verfolgen. Ewald: *Und alle deine Wege seien aufrecht.* So the Vulgate: *Et omnes viæ tuæ stabilientur.*

† Bertheau: *Kluge Rathschläge.* Umbreit: *Dass Vorsichtsregeln du behaltest.*

| KING JAMES' VERSION. | HEBREW TEXT. | | REVISED VERSION. | |
|---|---|---|---|---|
| 6 Lest thou shouldest ponder the path of life, her ways are moveable, *that* thou canst not know *them*. | אֹרַח חַיִּים פֶּן־תְּפַלֵּס<br>נָעוּ מַעְגְּלֹתֶיהָ לֹא תֵדָע׃ | 6 | that thou mayest not ponder the way of life:<br>her paths waver, ere thou knowest. | 6 |

V. 6. { That she may not ponder the way of life,
her paths waver, ere she is aware.

"the final lot of those whom the adulteress seduces, compare 23 : 32."

V. 6. *That thou mayest not ponder*, etc., to prevent which is the tendency and effect of her ways; he who follows her steps is lead far from the way of life, and from all thought upon it.

By this connection (with the previous verse),* פֶּן has its proper and usual force, *lest, that not*, after an action that prevents or hinders another from taking place (as in v. 9).† The construction of תפלס as *2nd pers. masc.* (instead of *3rd pers. fem.*, as understood by many) is in harmony with the writer's purpose. It is not his object, certainly, to describe the fate of the adulteress; but to warn against the perils of yielding to her solicitations. To this construction Bertheau objects, that she alone is the subject of discourse in vv. 3—6. But she is not mentioned at all, except to warn against the dangers of being ensnared by her; and the direct, personal application of the warning is more natural than a merely implied and inferential one—the fate of her victim inferred from her own.‡ Maurer: *thou canst not ponder* (פן = לא).§

Many regard תפלס and תדע as *3rd pers. fem.;* but the interpretations founded on this construction, as was justly remarked by Maurer, are all embarrassed and artificial.‖ So Gesenius (Thes. and Lex.); who supposes that פן, in this one passage, "approaches to the power of a negative adverb, i. q. לֹא. . . . *The way of life she prepares not* for herself, i. e. walks not in it; fully, (she takes care) *lest she walk*," etc.* [i. e. she studiously avoids it.] But aside from the unauthorized use of פן, there is little force in the thought, after the much stronger tone of the preceding verse. Others, taking פן in its proper sense, suppose the dependent clause to stand first,† the hindrance being expressed in the second member. According to Ewald, the adulteress is here represented as already so fallen that she can no longer even reflect on the path of life, or ponder and choose it as the better way; and this is briefly expressed under the form: *that she may not ponder it* (for that purpose, so to speak), her paths waver before she is aware, and she sinks into hell.‡ Bertheau: "*That she may not ponder the way of life* (and so enter it, turning from the way to Sheol), *her paths have become wavering, while she observed it not.* And because her paths have, unlooked for, become wavering, i. e., turning aside from the firm ground of life have hurried on to Sheol the land of the shades, therefore she can not choose the way of life; which (putting the necessary consequence as the object) may be thus expressed: that she may not choose the way of life, her paths have become wavering."‖ Stuart: "*That she*

* Schultens makes the same connection, but takes תפלס as *3rd fem., lest she ponder*, etc. Habes quod cum præced. vs. intime cohæret. Audacissime se mediam in mortem vitiorum demittit ac demergit; . . . ne forte, morsu tacta conscientiæ, minus audacter minus secure peccet, atque iter vitæ incipiat librare.

† Gesenius, Lex., פן, 1. Ewald (Lehrb., § 337, *b*, 2nd ¶): Bestimmter ist jedoch פֶּן־ (W. פנה *abwenden*) mit dem *imperf.* kurzer Ausdruck für *damit nicht.*

‡ As conceded by Hitzig (in his just published work, Die Sprüche Salomo's): Wäre פן bloss = *quo minus*, so würde תפלס wahrscheinlicher 2. Pers. (Ibn E.), und dann würde in erwünschter Weise sein Schicksal ausdrücklich mit dem ihrigen verbunden sein. His objection to this construction, I trust it will appear, is not valid: Allein es geht sodann weiter in *b* die Erkl. nicht von statten. He is obliged to regard לא תדע as expressing the *accus. of direction*, under the relative form: *Her paths* (her mode of life) *wander* (whither), *she knows not* = *she knows not whither;* i. e. knows not that it is to destruction. *Ihre Geleise schweifen, sie weiss nicht wohin* . . . weiss nicht, dass zum Unglück, 4 : 19, zum Tode, v. 5. So ist לא תדע auch nicht Adv. (Zustandsatz), sondern Akkus. der Richtung, und hiemit als Relativsatz unterzuordnen.

§ (Comment.): פן vero, . . . eadem vi gaudere judico quam sæpe alias habet אל, ut פן תפלס sit *non poteris, tibi non licebit expendere.* (Later, in in his Hdwb., as in note †.)

‖ (Comment. gram. crit.): Ad mulierem תפלס et תדע referunt interpretes reliqui; quorum impeditæ et artificiosæ sunt interpretationes. Later, however (hebr. u. chald. Hdwbch., 1851, art. פלס): *abwägen*, Spr. 5 : 5 (wo die זרה Subject ist).

* Sed integra sententia est: (cavet) ne in via vitæ incedat So Umbreit: *Dass sie ja den Weg des Lebens nicht abwäge!*

† Maurer (Hdwbch.): פן, *dass nicht*, . . . in vorangestelltem Abhängigkeitssatze, Spr. 5 : 6.

‡ *Den Lebensweg, dass sie den nicht abwäge,*
*schwanken schon ihre Bahnen unversehens.*

Welche [das schmeichelnde Weib] schon so tief gesunken und der Hölle anheimgefallen ist, dass sie nicht einmal mehr den Weg des Lebens frei bedenken oder abwägen und als bessern Weg vorziehen kann; welche also, wie man kurz sagen kann, gleichsam damit sie jenen nicht abwäge, unversehens (לא תדע, *sie weiss nicht*, Zustandsatz, § 608) ihre Bahnen schwanken fühlt und in die Hölle sinkt.

‖ *Den Pfad des Lebens* (2 : 19, 10 : 17) *damit sie nicht abwäge* (und somit vom Wege zum Scheol umkehrend ihn einschlage), *sind schwankend geworden ihre Geleise, indem sie nicht bemerkte.* . . . Eben weil ihre Geleise unversehens schwankend geworden sind, d. i. vom festen Grunde des Lebens abweichend dem Scheol, dem Lande der Schatten, zugeeilt sind (2 : 18), kann sie den Weg des Lebens nicht erwählen; was auch, wenn die Rede die nothwendige Folge als das Ziel setzt, so ausgedrückt werden kann: damit sie den Pfad des Lebens nicht erwähle, sind ihre Geleise schwankend geworden.

| KING JAMES' VERSION. | HEBREW TEXT. | | REVISED VERSION. | |
|---|---|---|---|---|
| 7 Hear me now therefore, O ye children, and depart not from the words of my mouth. | וְעַתָּה בָנִים שִׁמְעוּ־לִי<br>וְאַל־תָּסוּרוּ מֵאִמְרֵי־פִי׃ | 7 | Now then, children, hearken to me;<br>and turn not away from the words of my mouth. | 7 |
| 8 Remove thy way far from her, and come not nigh the door of her house: | הַרְחֵק מֵעָלֶיהָ דַרְכֶּךָ<br>וְאַל־תִּקְרַב אֶל־פֶּתַח בֵּיתָהּ׃ | 8 | Remove thy way far from her,<br>and come not nigh the door of her house: | 8 |
| 9 Lest thou give thine honour unto others, and thy years unto the cruel: | פֶּן־תִּתֵּן לַאֲחֵרִים הוֹדֶךָ<br>וּשְׁנֹתֶיךָ לְאַכְזָרִי׃ | 9 | that thou give not thy strength to others,<br>and thy years to the cruel; | 9 |
| 10 Lest strangers be filled with thy wealth; and thy labours *be* in the house of a stranger; | פֶּן־יִשְׂבְּעוּ זָרִים כֹּחֶךָ<br>וַעֲצָבֶיךָ בְּבֵית נָכְרִי׃ | י | that strangers may not sate themselves on thy wealth,<br>and on thy labors, in the house of a stranger: | 10 |
| 11 And thou mourn at the last, when thy flesh and thy body are consumed, | וְנָהַמְתָּ בְאַחֲרִיתֶךָ<br>בִּכְלוֹת בְּשָׂרְךָ וּשְׁאֵרֶךָ׃ | 11 | and thou groan in thy latter end,<br>when thy flesh and thy fullness are consumed; | 11 |
| 12 And say, How have I hated instruction, and my heart despised reproof; | וְאָמַרְתָּ אֵיךְ שָׂנֵאתִי מוּסָר<br>וְתוֹכַחַת נָאַץ לִבִּי׃ | 12 | and say: How have I hated instruction,<br>and my heart despised reproof; | 12 |

V. 9. thy bloom

V. 10. and thy labors be in

*may not ponder the path of life, her ways are become unsteady while she regards it not.*"

Such is the best that be made out, if we regard these verbs as the *third pers. fem.* A comparison of the two, as it seems to me, is decisive in favor of the former construction; and I therefore place it in the text, and the other in the margin.

The error of the ancient versions (Sept., Chald., Syr., Vulg.), in all of which פֶּן was expressed by the absolute negative, was pointed out by C. B. Michaelis.* It is followed, however, by Dathe,† Dœderlein,‡ Müntinghe,§ and others.

Second member:—*Her paths*, viz., in which she leads her followers; comp. *her end*, v. 4. They are said to *waver*, as an insecure pathway over an abyss, that trembles under the footsteps of the adventurous traveler. (Comp. Expl. Notes.) The fine Heb. idiom לא ידע can be preserved in English; comp. Job 9 : 5.

V. 7. *Now then*, Lex., וְ, 4. *Children:* so pupils were addressed by the teacher. Whether this, or the parental relation, is intended in any given case, must be judged by the reader, and is generally clear from the connection.

V. 9. *That thou give not*, the idea of simple prevention (the primary force of פֶּן) is more appropriate here than the expression of apprehension (*lest*), for which this particle sometimes serves. *Strength*, viz., physical vigor,* accords best with the subject and with the parallel member. *Thy years*, equivalent to *thy life*, yielded up to the insatiable and remorseless consumer of thy youthful strength. *Cruel*, as being selfish and mercenary, and without pity for the victim of her fatal snares.

The use of the masculine in this and the following verses (אחרים ,אכזרי, etc.) is no objection to the natural reference to the adulteress. The writer uses a general form, *cruel* e. g., for one of whom this is characteristic, a *cruel one.*†

V. 10. That thy wealth may not go to satisfy strangers, and thy labors those not of thy own house, but in the house of another. The second member makes the emphatic contrast between his own house, for whose inmates it is his duty and happiness to provide, and that of a stranger where his earnings are consumed.‡ עצבים *labors*, by a natural and frequent metonomy, for *fruits of labor*, as in Deut. 28 : 33, and Ps. 78 : 46.

V. 11. *Vav. consec.* connecting with the *imperf.* dependent on פֶּן.

---

* (Annotat. uber.): Sed obstat huic explicationi, quod particula פֶּן alibi nusquam significet *non*, ad simpliciter negandum, sed constanter *ut ne*, *ne forte*, ad præcavendum.

† *Iter vitæ nequaquam ingreditur; Nutant ejus orbitæ, nec curat.*

‡ *Auf den Lebensweg lenkt ihre Strasse nicht ein: ihre Bahn bebt, und sie merkt es nicht.*

§ *Sie schlägt den ebnen Lebensweg nicht ein,*
*Ihre Tritte gleiten, eh' sie's bemerkt.*

* Gesenius, Thes. II., p. 856, pr. *turgor*, *vigor*, quo turget corpus humanum juvenile cet. The true signification of this word is there established.

† Maurer: Loquitur universe, sed nefandas intelligit mulieres exhaurientes vires (v. 9, cf. 11) et opes (v. 10) miseri juvenis.

‡ I find the same view taken by Hitzig, in his work just published on this book: Die Gunst des Weibes wird er durch Geschenke gewinnen wollen und sich bewahren müssen; er wird durch habsüchtige Forderungen der Hure (vgl. 6 : 26) ausgebeutet, möglicher Weise mit Wissen und Zulassung ihres Mannes, und sein Vermögen geht so nach und nach in fremde Hand über (Sir. 9 : 6).

| KING JAMES' VERSION. | HEBREW TEXT. | | REVISED VERSION. | |
|---|---|---|---|---|
| 13 And have not obeyed the voice of my teachers, nor inclined mine ear to them that instructed me! | וְֽלֹא־שָׁמַעְתִּי בְּקוֹל מוֹרָי<br>וְלִמְלַמְּדַי לֹא־הִטִּיתִי אָזְנִי׃ | 13 | and I hearkened not to the voice of my teachers,<br>nor inclined my ear to my instructors. | 13 |
| 14 I was almost in all evil in the midst of the congregation and assembly. | כִּמְעַט הָיִיתִי בְכָל־רָע<br>בְּתוֹךְ קָהָל וְעֵדָה׃ | 14 | Almost was I in all evil,<br>in the midst of the congregation and assembly. | 14 |
| 15 Drink waters out of thine own cistern, and running waters out of thine own well. | שְׁתֵה־מַיִם מִבּוֹרֶךָ<br>וְנוֹזְלִים מִתּוֹךְ בְּאֵרֶךָ׃ | טו | Drink waters from thine own cistern,<br>and streams out of thine own well. | 15 |
| 16 Let thy fountains be dispersed abroad, *and* rivers of waters in the streets. | יָפוּצוּ מַעְיְנֹתֶיךָ חוּצָה<br>בָּרְחֹבוֹת פַּלְגֵי־מָיִם׃ | 16 | Shall thy fountains spread abroad,<br>streams of water in the streets? | 16 |

V. 14. כמעט, *with a little* (i. e. a little more; wanting but little) = ὀλίγου δεῖν. *In all evil*, i. e. in all wickedness; aggravated by the fact, that this evil is done in the midst of God's people, in the congregation and assembly of his chosen. Compare the frequent expression, *wrought folly in Israel* (Gen. 34 : 7; Deut. 22 : 21; Judg. 20 : 6), and the implied guilt of desecrating a holy relation.

According to a suggestion of Schultens (on v. 9), more fully carried out by Ewald and Bertheau, and adopted from them by Stuart, the offender is here represented as sold into slavery by the injured husband. Thus (v. 9) his *strength* (or *youthful bloom*) is given to others (his purchaser), *cruel* meaning a cruel master, such as the injured party would be likely to select; his wealth and earnings (v. 10) belong to another, *labors in the house of another* meaning labors performed there; in which bondage (v. 11) *his flesh and fullness are consumed* away; and finally, (v. 14) he had barely escaped stoning by the whole congregation.

But to this representation there are serious objections. The law in Deut. 22 : 22 (and Lev. 20 : 10) is explicit, that both the guilty parties in such a crime shall be put to death (by stoning, according to Ezek. 16 : 40; comp. John 8 : 5). This punishment, on proof of the crime, the tribunals could legally inflict, but no other. To get over this difficulty, it is assumed that the husband could, if he chose, proceed more mildly, and sell the criminal into slavery. But, first, by what right or authority he could sell the offender into bondage, or by what title the purchaser could hold him, is not explained; nor, secondly, how the writer could represent an exceptional case, depending on the option of the husband, as the common fate of the offender.* This explanation more than borders on the ludicrous, when we are told that v. 14 means: *I had almost been in all evil* (i. e. the worst of all) *in the midst of the assembly*, for I was near being stoned by them;† the point of which (as Ewald seems to think*) is the solacing reflection, that his fate might have been worse than it is!

V. 15. *Streams* (נוזלים), as the same word is properly rendered in the com. version, Ps. 78 : 16. מתוך *from the midst of* = *out of*.

V. 16. *Thy fountains*, those at which thou drinkest. Shall they be such (i. e. wilt thou resort to such) as are common to all,—streams of water in the streets, where all that will may drink? The tone is that of indignant remonstrance; and the same sentiment is expressed affirmatively in the next verse.

That the verse is to be read as a question,† there can be no reasonable doubt. For, first, as affirmative, it is absurd in itself,‡ and is in direct contradiction with the next verse; and, secondly, if we make it negative by rewriting the author's text (for the insertion of the negative [not], on the misapprehension of the Lxx. and Aq.,§ is nothing less) still the case is no better; for who ever needed such a caution?¶ Schultens, in his objection to this

---

* This whole theory of selling the offender into bondage is justly characterized by Hitzig (in loc.) as a mere assumption, without any foundation in the text. Die Hypothese überhaupt, dass der ertappte Ehebrecher vom Manne zum Sklaven gemacht wurde, ist rein aus der Luft gegriffen.

† Bertheau: *Um ein weniges wäre ich gewesen im ganzen*, d. i. schlimmsten *Unglück mitten in der Versammlung und in der Gemeinde*, weil ich nahe daran war in der Volksversammlung gesteinigt zu werden.

* (S. 64): zufrieden, nicht noch schimpflicher gleich nach der That von der Gemeine als Ehebrecher gesteinigt zu sein.

† Ludov. de Dieu, Critica Sacra. Clericus: *An dispergentur fontes tui foras?*

‡ The notion that offspring are meant (Grotius: Ibi sere ubi prolem metas) will now hardly be taken into account.

§ And even of this slight support it is not sure; for the Alex. Codex (in Baber's *fac simile*) omits μή, as also the Complutensian and Aldine Edd., and it is wanting in twelve of the Codd. collated for Parsons' Ed., and in other authorities quoted by him. Aquilæ autem interpretationi, quæ ex *ed. Rom.* prolata, neque a Montefalconio in ullo Cod. Msc. reperta est, ne a librariis μή additum sit e Versione Alexandrina, jure vereor. (Vogel, Annot. ad Capelli Crit. Sacr., Lib. IV., cap. X., II.)

¶ Since sending the above to the printer, I have received the recent work of Hitzig on Proverbs, and find that he also reads the verse as a question. Unfortunately, he misses the delicate import of the verse; supposing it to mean, that one is to prevent these streams from spreading abroad, by drinking them himself (er soll das Ausströmen jener eben dadurch verhüten, dass er sie wegtrinkt); that the wise man asks: Shall the affection, which thy spouse cherishes for thee, be imparted to others on account of thy neglect? (Der Weise fragt: Soll der Minnesold, den dir

| KING JAMES' VERSION. | HEBREW TEXT. | | REVISED VERSION. | |
|---|---|---|---|---|
| 17 Let them be only thine own, and not strangers' with thee. | יִֽהְיוּ־לְךָ לְבַדֶּךָ<br>וְאֵין לְזָרִים אִתָּךְ׃ | 17 | Let them be for thee, by thyself,<br>and not for strangers with thee. | 17 |
| 18 Let thy fountain be blessed: and rejoice with the wife of thy youth. | יְהִֽי־מְקוֹרְךָ בָרוּךְ<br>וּשְׂמַח מֵאֵשֶׁת נְעוּרֶֽךָ׃ | 18 | Let thy fountain be blest;<br>and have joy of the wife of thy youth. | 18 |
| 19 *Let her be as* the loving hind and pleasant roe; let her breasts satisfy thee at all times; and be thou ravished always with her love. | אַיֶּלֶת אֲהָבִים וְיַֽעֲלַת־חֵן<br>דַּדֶּיהָ יְרַוֻּךָ בְכָל־עֵת<br>בְּאַהֲבָתָהּ תִּשְׁגֶּה תָמִיד׃ | 19 | The lovely hind, and graceful roe!<br>let her breasts satisfy thee at all times,<br>and be thou always ravished with her love. | 19 |
| 20 And why wilt thou, my son, be ravished with a strange woman, and embrace the bosom of a stranger? | וְלָמָּה תִשְׁגֶּה בְנִי בְזָרָה<br>וּתְחַבֵּק חֵק נָכְרִיָּה׃ | כ | And why wilt thou, my son, be ravished with a strange woman,<br>and embrace the bosom of a stranger? | 20 |
| 21 For the ways of man *are* before the eyes of the LORD, and he pondereth all his goings. | כִּי נֹכַח ׀ עֵינֵי יְהוָה דַּרְכֵי־אִישׁ<br>וְכָל־מַעְגְּלֹתָיו מְפַלֵּס׃ | 21 | For a man's ways are before the eyes of Jehovah,<br>and all his paths He ponders. | 21 |
| 22 His own iniquities shall take the wicked himself, and he shall be holden with the cords of his sins. | עֲוֺנוֹתָיו יִלְכְּדֻנוֹ אֶת־הָרָשָׁע<br>וּבְחַבְלֵי חַטָּאתוֹ יִתָּמֵךְ׃ | 22 | His own iniquities ensnare him, the offender,<br>and in the toils of his own sin shall he be holden. | 22 |

construction,* seems to have overlooked the language of the writer below, in v. 20.

The passage is a delicate commendation of connubial over illicit love; and the application of the figure in v. 16 is felicitous and beautiful. The thought, and the imagery it is clothed in, are equally delicate and refined (Expl. Notes, vv. 15, 16); nor is there the slightest ground for the offensive image attributed to the writer by Schultens, Rosenmüller, and others.

V. 18. *Let thy fountain* (as in v. 16, that at which thou drinkest) *be blest*, be one that is blest, as a relation divinely instituted, and blest of God;† all other is forbidden and unblessed. שמח with מן is a continuation of the figure of a fountain.‡

V. 19. It is very generally held§ (Bochart, Hieroz., Lib. III. cap. XXIII.; Gesenius, Thes. and Lex.; Winer, Rwbch., art. *Steinbock*) that by יעלה is here meant the female of the *Ibex*,* or of some species of the *Capra Ibex*. But, as usually represented, it does not correspond with the יַעֲלַת חֵן in this passage, which more probably refers to some similar and related species.† By some a class intermediate to the deer and goat is supposed to be meant here;‡ the less improbably, as these were not accurately distinguished in common Heb. usage (Gesenius, Lex., אַיָּל and אַיָּלָה).

As the word *roe* denotes the female, in good Eng. usage, and gives the general import of the original, I prefer not to change the rendering of the com. version (which is that of all the early Eng. versions) for any other that at present occurs to me.

Third member:—*Ravished* ("transported, delighted to rapture," Johnson§), the rendering of the Common Version, is the best expression of תשגה here, and in v. 20.‖ The verb is used again

deine Gattin bereit hält, deshalb, weil du sie vernachlässigst, Andern zutheilwerden?) No such matter! The caution is a very different one, and is rightly applied.

* Qui tam potenter detonaverat in amplexus adulterarum, non ad idem tam dilute rediret.

† Not (as Rosenm. and others): *Erit scaturigo tua benedicta*, i. e. large aquas emittens (sit uxor tua prole fecunda; Maurer); erroneously referring vv. 16, 17, to the offspring of connubial intercourse, without any appreciation of the depth and delicacy of tone in the whole passage.

‡ Bertheau: שמח hier mit מן, vielleicht des Bildes wegen, weil die Freude wie erquickendes Wasser *aus* der Quelle geschöpft werden soll.

§ With exceptions, however. Ipsum יעלה esse ibicem, verisimilibus argumentis, non certis, adstruxit Bochartus (Michaelis, Suppl. N. 1016, p. 1124).

* Haller described one, in his possession, as elegans et alacre animal, . . . ovi similius, come et animosum (Michaelis, Suppl., p. 1122). But this seems not to have been properly the Ibex, of which the usual descriptions and delineations give a very different impression.

† Winer (Rwbch., art. *Steinbock*): Bei aller Gewissheit dass وعل den Steinbock bezeichne, bleibt es indess immer zweifelhaft, ob dieses arab. Wort und das hebr. יָעֵל eben nur von diesem Thiere gebraucht worden sei, oder auch (etwa 1 Sam. 24 : 3) eine ähnliche und verwandte Species mit befasst habe.

‡ Lee (Heb. Lex.): *the graceful antelope.* Grævius: *the Gazelle.*

§ So in the best Eng. usage; e. g., *Ravish, like enchanting harmony* (Shakesp.). Richardson, Eng. Dict., "*Ravish*, to affect or move, with ecstacy, with excess of delight or pleasure."

‖ Ewald (with similar effect) *lose thyself: In ihrer Liebe magst*

| KING JAMES' VERSION. | HEBREW TEXT. | | REVISED VERSION. | |
|---|---|---|---|---|
| 23 He shall die without instruction; and in the greatness of his folly he shall go astray. | הוּא יָמוּת בְּאֵין מוּסָר<br>וּבְרֹב אִוַּלְתּוֹ יִשְׁגֶּה׃ | 23 | He shall die, without instruction;<br>and shall reel with the abundance of his folly. | 23 |
| CHAP. IV. | CHAP. VI. | | CHAP. VI. | |
| MY son, if thou be surety for thy friend, *if* thou hast stricken thy hand with a stranger, | בְּנִי אִם־עָרַבְתָּ לְרֵעֶךָ<br>תָּקַעְתָּ לַזָּר כַּפֶּיךָ׃ | א | MY son, if thou hast become surety for thy friend,<br>hast struck thy hands for a stranger; | 1 |

V. 23. and shall perish in the

V. 1. thy neighbor

in v. 23; and there it aptly expresses the giddy whirl of an overmastering passion. Stuart: *With her love do thou continually inebriate thyself.* But the idea of intoxication is not inherent in the verb.

V. 23. *Without instruction.* (See Expl. Notes.)

Second member:—ישגה (see note on v. 19, third member). Gesenius (Lex. 2): "*to perish*, Prov. 5 : 23. Comp. אָבַד, no. 2." So the Sept., καὶ ἀπώλετο δι' ἀφροσύνην. So also the Syr. ܢܐܒܕ may be understood here, as in Judges 21 : 3; in the Polyglott (erroneously, after the Vulgate), *decipietur.* But Rödiger (Thes. fasc. poster., p. 1362 *), more consistently with the ground idea and prevailing use of the verb as well as the connection here: "Of one *carried away* by his folly and *reeling* to destruction, Prov. 5 : 23" (as given in the fifth Am. ed. of Gesenius' Lex., 1854).

Ch. VI.—V. 1. ערבת ל, *hast become surety for.* So Gesenius (Thes. and Lex.), Ewald,† Rosenmüller, Maurer, and others.‡

By לרעך is meant, not the one *to* whom the surety is given, but the one for whom (in whose behalf) it is done; being the *dativus commodi*, as in Deut. 3 : 22, הַנִּלְחָם לָכֶם *that fights for you.*§ The use of the *dative* ל (instead of the usual construction with the *accus.*) has the effect to give prominence to the *motive* of kindness and goodwill which led into the error, and to justify the claim, implied in vv. 3–5, on the one thus befriended.

Second member:—* *Stranger* (*alienus*, one of another family; Gesenius' Lex., זוּר, Part. b, and the ref. to Deut. 25 : 5), is added as a further qualification of רעך, showing that there is no natural obligation in this case, as in that of a kinsman. So the word is used again in ch. 11 : 15. *A stranger*, in the sense of *one unknown*, would have no pertinence in either passage; for men are not accustomed to become surety for those personally unknown to them. The case supposed is that of a friend, though not of one's own kindred.

The sentiment of the passage is: One who becomes surety for a friend puts himself in the power of another, by whose act alone he can become free again. It is an admonition to beware of such improvidence;† or, if already ensnared, to lose no time in providing against the evil consequences.

But what is to be done in such a case? This is indicated in v. 3: *Go humble thyself, be urgent with thy friend,* Here, some understand by *friend* the creditor to whom the security is given;‡ who, if kindly disposed towards the bondsman, might be induced to be lenient to him. But this assumes an occasional and exceptional case; whereas, the writer evidently supposes the general and usual one, such as may be expected to occur, and therefore needs to be provided for. The one in whose behalf the surety is given, it might always be expected, would heed solicitations to make timely provision for payment, or to secure an

---

*dich stets verlieren.* So Cocceius, Lex.: Dicitur *inerrare alicui*, h. e, tanquam sui oblitum et mente motum rei alicui affixum esse. . . . Prov. 5 : 19, . . . *in amore ejus erres semper;* h. e. perpetuo te oblectes ejus amore, tanquam tui oblitus aut abalienatus mente.

* 1. *Erravit, oberravit* . . . 2. mente errabunda *titubavit* ex vino; . . . porro de homine, qui percitus amore est licito et conjugali non minus quam incesto (ausschweifen [?]), Prov. 5 : 19, 20; denique de eo qui se dementia et omni temeritate abripi patitur (in Thorheit dahintaumeln), ib. v. 23. Cf. שָׁגַע.

† *Sohn! hast du dich verbürgt für deinen Nächsten,*
*Handschlag gegeben für den Fremden.*

‡ Le Clerc: לרעך *amico tuo;* hoc est, in gratiam amici, pro amico spopondisti ejus creditori. Jun. & Tremell.: *si spopondisti pro amico tuo.*

§ C. B. Michaelis: לרעך *pro amico tuo.* Præfixum ל hic non eum significat cui, sed in cujus gratiam spondetur, coll. quod mox sequitur, *et alieno;* adeoque facit *dativum* non objecti sed *commodi*, ut Deut. 3 : 22, *pugnans vobis*, i. e. pro vobis.

* Rödiger (Thes. fasc. post., p. 1517): *spondes pro peregrino.*

† Melanchthon: In sexto capite prima sententia dissuadet sponsiones, narrans esse periculosas, quia plurimi fallunt sponsores. . . . In genere autem hoc dictum monet, ratam esse fidem pactorum, et raros esse sinceros et fideles.

‡ So Stuart (on v. 3): "ריעך here is not the same as in v. 1, but the friend *to* whom (not *for* whom) the pledge is given." But this assumes a case in which the surety is given, not only *for* a friend but *to* a friend; which so narrows the application of the rule, that few chances are left of its being of any service. On the contrary, as a man becomes surety only for a friend, the rule rightly interpreted is universal, and covers all cases that can be expected to occur.

Moreover, the writer's position in vv. 1 and 3 is this: *by becoming surety for thy friend thou hast come into the power of thy friend;* with manifest reference to the same person in both verses. On any other supposition, the second clause of v. 3 is a palpable *non sequitur.* Bertheau, with more logical consistency, refers *friend* in both verses to the creditor, *to* whom security is given.

| KING JAMES' VERSION. | | HEBREW TEXT. | | REVISED VERSION. | |
|---|---|---|---|---|---|
| 2 Thou art snared with the words of thy mouth, thou art taken with the words of thy mouth. | | נוֹקַשְׁתָּ בְאִמְרֵי־פִיךָ<br>נִלְכַּדְתָּ בְּאִמְרֵי־פִיךָ׃ | 2 | thou art snared with the words of thy mouth,<br>art taken with the words of thy mouth. | 2 |
| 3 Do this now, my son, and deliver thyself, when thou art come into the hand of thy friend: go, humble thyself, and make sure thy friend. | | עֲשֵׂה זֹאת אֵפוֹא ׀ בְּנִי וְהִנָּצֵל<br>כִּי בָאתָ בְכַף־רֵעֶךָ<br>לֵךְ הִתְרַפֵּס וּרְהַב רֵעֶיךָ׃ | 3 | Do this now, my son, and deliver thyself,<br>for thou art come into the power of thy friend;<br>go humble thyself, and be urgent with thy friend. | 3 |

accommodation with the creditor, even at personal loss, rather than jeopardize the interests of his bondsman.*

A new turn has been given to this whole passage by Bertheau, one of the latest and ablest of the commentators on this book. To the above construction of ערב ל and תקע ל he objects, that one is driven by it to a forced and unnatural explanation of the following verses, and especially of v. 3.† He has not shown, however, that such an explanation is necessary; though some of those given are certainly liable to his objection.‡ He understands the writer to mean: *If thou hast become surety to thy friend, hast struck hands to a stranger;* i. e. if thou hast become surety *to* another, be it friend or stranger. The *ensnaring* spoken of in v. 2 (*if thou hast ensnared thyself*, as he translates), he assumes can take place only at the time when one is *claimed* as a surety; viz., when the time of payment comes, and he finds himself already "in the grip."§ In this state of things, he is directed (v. 3) to seek humbly and earnestly for a *delay of payment.* The respite obtained, "then (v. 4) labor day and night, in order to earn the amount of thy debt;" ‖ and so (v. 5) *deliver thyself*, etc.

How much is here assumed, not only without ground, but against very plain facts as well as laws of language, is apparent on slight inspection. E. g. that one is not ensnared by his words

* So Le Clerc: Qui nempe fidejusserat, ne pecuniam reddere ipse cogeretur, necesse habebat eum pro quo fidem suam interposuerat (si timebat ne mala fide, aut negligentia, æs alienum dissolvere non curaret) humilibus precibus orare ut vellet creditori satisfacere, operamque daret ut præstituto tempore paratam pecuniam haberet; ne ipse fidejussor de suo satisfacere creditori cogeretur. C. B. Michaelis: Sensus est, non expectandum esse donec debitori, pro quo spopondisti, te a suscepto nexu liberare lubuerit; sed adeundum eum tibi ac urgendum esse ut solvat. To the same effect, Müntinghe, and Dœderlein.

† Fasst man mit vielen Erklärern, auch Ewald, ערב ל so auf: "Hast du dich verbürgt für deinen Nächsten," . . . so wird man, um die folgenden Verse, zumal V. 3 zu erklären, zu den gezwungensten Deutungen seine Zuflucht nehmen müssen.

‡ As Ewald's: So bleibt nichts über, als ohne Zeitverlust sich wieder davon loszumachen, indem man mit aller Anstrengung den Freund, in dessen Gewalt man durch die Bürgschaft für ihn gekommen ist (denn der Bürge wird der Schuldner des Schuldners [?]), zur Rücknahme des Versprechens drängt.

§ Was erst dann der Fall ist, wenn er als Bürge in Anspruch genommen wird; also v. 1. wenn du Bürge geworden bist, v. 2. und als Bürge dich in der Klemme befindest.

‖ Hast du Aufschub erlangt, nun so arbeite Tag und Nacht, um den Betrag deiner Schuld zu verdienen.

in the very act of pledging his own property and person, as surety to another; nor will be so, till the time of payment comes, and convinces him of it! Again, nothing can be plainer than the relation of v. 4, as a merely subordinate qualifying sentence in the connection, expressing the utmost haste; the same as to say: do this, giving no sleep to thine eyes, etc., i. e. with all diligence and dispatch.* Yet it is made the leading sentence in the connection, and is interpreted to mean hard labor, day and night, at something by which money can be earned. Other assumptions, equally groundless, need not be specified.

V. 2. *Thou art snared*, etc., the apodosis of v. 1.† He who becomes surety for another, thereby ensnares himself by his own words; hence the emphatic repetition, *with the words of thy mouth.*

It was suggested by C. B. Michaelis,‡ that this verse should be regarded as a part of the protasis (*art snared* = *if thou art snared*), and that the apodosis should commence with v. 3; it being the object of the writer to show what is to be done and how, when one has already become surety for another.

This construction is grammatically admissible, since the effect of אם may be carried on to v. 2, as it is to the second member of v. 1; and this is now generally regarded as the writer's construction. But, as it seems to me, the true force of the passage is thus lost. The emphatic assertion, *thou art snared,—thou art taken,*—exposes the rashness and folly of making one's self liable for another's debt, and is the most pointed and effective warning against it. It should be proved, that the writer's *only* object is to provide against the consequences of the error, before the direct warning against the error itself is blotted out, or merged in a hypothetical form.

V. 3, second member. *For* (כי) is the proper rendering,

* C. B. Michaelis: *Ne des* (permittas) *somnum*, sc. priusquam te liberaveris.

† So the Vulgate and Pagnino; so also the earlier Christian scholars generally, as Le Clerc, Schultens, Junius & Tremellius, Dœderlein, Dathe, etc. Teller (Auctar. ad Schultens. Comment. ed. Vogel): Omnia sponte fluunt, si vertas: *cura hoc quam primum mi fili et extrahe te* h. e. *ut extrahas* te (sc. ex isto nexu fidejussoris); *quando nimirum adjunxisti te sponsioni sodalis tui* (pro altero fidem tuam interposuisti), *age, accinge te, urge socium tuum* (ut scil. solvat).

‡ Ceterum protasis hujus orationis continuatur v. 2; apodosis vero sequitur demum v. 3 seqq. Ac adeo si iste nexus observetur liquebit, scopum Salomonis hunc esse, ut doceat quid et quomodo in casu susceptæ jam sponsionis agendum sit.

| KING JAMES' VERSION. | HEBREW TEXT. | | REVISED VERSION. | |
|---|---|---|---|---|
| 4 Give not sleep to thine eyes, nor slumber to thine eyelids. | אַל־תִּתֵּן שֵׁנָה לְעֵינֶיךָ<br>וּתְנוּמָה לְעַפְעַפֶּיךָ׃ | 4 | Give not sleep to thine eyes,<br>nor slumber to thine eyelids; | 4 |
| 5 Deliver thyself as a roe from the hand *of the hunter*, and as a bird from the hand of the fowler. | הִנָּצֵל כִּצְבִי מִיָּד<br>וּכְצִפּוֹר מִיַּד יָקוּשׁ׃ | ה | deliver thyself as the roe from the hand,<br>and as the bird from the hand of the fowler. | 5 |
| 6 Go to the ant, thou sluggard: consider her ways, and be wise: | לֵךְ אֶל־נְמָלָה עָצֵל<br>רְאֵה דְרָכֶיהָ וַחֲכָם׃ | 6 | Go to the ant, sluggard;<br>observe her ways, and be wise; | 6 |
| 7 Which having no guide, overseer, or ruler, | אֲשֶׁר אֵין־לָהּ קָצִין<br>שֹׁטֵר וּמֹשֵׁל׃ | 7 | who, having no prince,<br>overseer, or ruler, | 7 |
| 8 Provideth her meat in the summer, *and* gathereth her food in the harvest. | תָּכִין בַּקַּיִץ לַחְמָהּ<br>אָגְרָה בַקָּצִיר מַאֲכָלָהּ׃ | 8 | provides her meat in the summer,<br>gathers her food in the harvest. | 8 |

expressing the ground of the earnest warning in the preceding member. *Into the power of thy friend;* viz., the one for whom thou hast pledged property and person, the security of both being now dependent on him.*

*Humble thyself.* The suggestion of Cocceius† is sustained by the etymology and use of the word, and is now generally adopted.‡ *Be urgent with thy friend;*§ viz. to take whatever course may be necessary for the security of his bondsman. רעיך *sing.* (§ 93, 9, Rem. and Lex. רֵעֶה).

V. 5. *The roe.* Gesenius, Lex.: "See Bochart, Hieroz. I., p. 895 sq., 994 sq. (or II., p. 304 Lips.), where he shows that צבי is to be referred to the whole genus of the roe and antelope, and not to a particular species."

*From the hand* (first member), as the Hebrew text stands in all the MSS.; viz., from the hand of the capturer. Compare 1 Kings 20 : 42. There is no good reason for the conjectural reading (מִפַּח),|| founded on the free paraphrase of the Sept., Chald., and Syr.¶

VV. 6–11. There is no occasion to seek, as many have done, for a ground of connection between these and the preceding verses. A distinct and independent topic is treated in this paragraph, as also in those which follow.

V. 7. שֹׁטֵר (etym. *writer, scribe*) seems, from its connection with נֹגֵשׂ in Ex. 5 : 6, 14, to be there applied to an *inspector* or *overseer*, whose business it was to take account of the work done, and to see that it was the amount required by the taskmaster, to whom he was accountable (Ex. 5 : 14; com. version, "officers," as also in vv. 6, 10, 15, and 19). This is its most natural use in this connection. *Who, having no prince, . . . . provides,* etc., expresses the full effect of the relative on the following clause.*

V. 8.† Bertheau supposes that the *imperfect and perfect* refer, respectively, to a *continued* and to a fully *perfected* action. During summer, she continues collecting her food; and in harvest, when the grain is brought or is about to be brought from the field, she has already gathered her store‡ (reversing, by the bye,

---

* In cujus potestatem qui pro eo fidem suam interposuit, eatenus venit, ut si negligens iste vel dolosus sit, perdere potest cunctas sponsoris facultates, dum pro eo solvere tenetur (Rosenmüller).

† Lex.: *humilia te,* prosterne te et quasi conculcandum præbe. Wirf dich unter die Füsse, und lass dich treten.

‡ C. B. Michaelis: Hinc malumus cum Cocc. Lex. 628 exponere, *humilia* s. *prosterne te;* q. d. conculcandum te præbe. Cum nempe ad pedes alterius provoluti eum demisse ac instanter oramus, hoc ipsum est *se conculcandum* alteri *dare.* Conf. Ps. 68 : 31. Rosenmüller: *prosterne te,* i. e. humillimis precibus adi, demisse et instanter ora eum pro quo spopondisti, ut solvat quæ creditori debet, ne tu pro eo solvere tenearis. So Bertheau: התרפס (von רפס *treten,* Hitp. *sich treten lassen,* was das Hinwerfen zu den Füssen eines anderen und das Liegenbleiben in sich schliesst) steht Ps. 68 : 31 vom dringenden Bitten.

§ Bertheau, happily: *und bestürme deinen Freund.* Sept., παρόξυνε δὲ καὶ τὸν φίλον σου. Ewald: *und dränge deinen Nächsten.*

|| Ewald: *Von dem Netz.* Für מיד, welches wohl aus dem zweiten Gliede hier eingedrungen, lesen [?] LXX. מִפַּח oder

* Vulgate: *Quæ cum non habeat ducem, . . . parat in æstate cibum sibi.*

Latine duo hæc commata sic construe: *Quæ cum non habeat principem . . . Parat,* cet. (Maurer.)

† Ewald: *Welche ihr Brod im Sommer rüstet,*
*zur Erntezeit einsammelt ihre Speise.*

‡ Das Imperf. תכין von der dauernden Arbeit des Bereitens

מוֹקֵשׁ, welches wirklich sowohl an sich als auch wegen des entsprechenden Bildes V. 2 besser passt. Bertheau: *Aus der Schlinge* (statt מִיַּד, welches leicht durch Vertauschung des hier ursprünglich stehenden Wortes mit dem מִיַּד in *b* in den Text kommen konnte, lesen wir mit Sept., Pesch., Targ. etwa מִפַּח). On the contrary, the Vulgate: Quasi damula de manu, et quasi avis de manu aucupis.

¶ C. B. Michaelis: Chald. et Syr. *ex reti;* sed sensum illi potius quam significationis proprietatem expresserunt. Rosenmüller: *sicut caprea* se eripit *e manu* scil. venatoris qui rete ei tetenderat, uti יקש in hemistichii secundi fine est subaudiendum. . . . Absolute ut hic illud et 1 K. 20 : 42 ponitur: . . . *virum a me devotum dimisisti e manu* scil. tua.

KING JAMES' VERSION.

9 How long wilt thou sleep, O sluggard? when wilt thou arise out of thy sleep?

10 *Yet* a little sleep, a little slumber, a little folding of the hands to sleep:

11 So shall thy poverty come as one that travelleth, and thy want as an armed man.

12 A naughty person, a wicked man, walketh with a froward mouth.

13 He winketh with his eyes, he speaketh with his feet, he teacheth with his fingers;

14 Frowardness *is* in his heart, he deviseth mischief continually; he soweth discord.

HEBREW TEXT.

9 עַד־מָתַי עָצֵל ׀ תִּשְׁכָּב
מָתַי תָּקוּם מִשְּׁנָתֶךָ׃

י מְעַט שֵׁנוֹת מְעַט תְּנוּמוֹת
מְעַט ׀ חִבֻּק יָדַיִם לִשְׁכָּב׃

11 וּבָא־כִמְהַלֵּךְ רֵאשֶׁךָ
וּמַחְסֹרְךָ כְּאִישׁ מָגֵן׃

12 אָדָם בְּלִיַּעַל אִישׁ אָוֶן
הוֹלֵךְ עִקְּשׁוּת פֶּה׃

13 קוֹרֵץ בְּעֵינָו מוֹלֵל בְּרַגְלָו
מֹרֶה בְּאֶצְבְּעֹתָיו׃

14 תַּהְפֻּכוֹת ׀ בְּלִבּוֹ
חֹרֵשׁ רָע בְּכָל־עֵת
מִדְנָיִם יְשַׁלֵּחַ׃

V. 13. בעיניו ק׳ Ib. ברגליו ק׳
V. 14. מדינים ק׳

REVISED VERSION.

How long, sluggard, wilt thou lie; 9
when wilt thou arise from thy sleep?

A little sleep, a little slumber, 10
a little folding of the hands to rest;

and as a prowler comes thy poverty, 11
and thy want as an armed man.

A vile man, a base man, 12
is he who walks in falsehood;

winking with his eyes, talking with his feet, 13
pointing with his fingers;

in whose heart is perverseness; 14
devising evil at all times;
who scatters discords.

V. 11. like a robber

V. 14. who sends out

the order of the grain-harvest and summer in the East). But this is a false distinction. *In the harvest, she is gathering* (is occupied with gathering) is the idea, in the expression of which the *perf.* and *imperf.* may be interchanged (§126, 3, 2nd ¶).*

V. 10. Not the words of the sluggard in reply to the preceding expostulation,† but the writer's expression of his conduct, the consequences of which he declares in the following verse. *To rest* (Lex. שׁכב, a), as the verb is often used, e. g. Job 30 : 17.

V. 11. מהלך (*grassator*) one who roves about, specially for plunder; to which the English *prowler* corresponds, meaning both a *wanderer* and a *robber*.‡

oder Sammelns der Speise während des קַיִץ, d. i. während des früheren Theiles des Sommers; nachher das Perf. אגרה, weil die Ameise בקציר in der Erntezeit, wo das Getraide vom Felde weggeholt ist oder doch bald weggeholt wird, ihren Vorrath schon gesammelt hat.

* Especially for varying the expression in *Parallelism*, as admitted by Ewald: Und ähnlich wechseln die zwei Ausdrücke auch wohl bloss um des dichterischen Gliederwechsels willen. Lehrb. (6te Ausg.), §136, *b*, *a*.

† Maurer: Sunt verba pigri, qui excitatus ad surgendum (v. 9) surgere recusat, quod quietis paulum desit.

‡ Sept., κακὸς ὁδοιπόρος. Gesenius (Lex.): *a rover, ravager, robber*. Ewald: *Landstreicher*. In der That ist dies das wichtigste Wort im Satze, welches durch איש מגן im zweiten Gliede nur näher bestimmt wird, da doch der Sinn fordert, sich einen den einsamen Wandrer überfallenden Landstreicher zu denken. Bertheau: מהלך . . . wird durch איש מגן dahin bestimmt, dass wir an einen bewaffneten Umherstreicher (Sept., κακὸς ὁδοιπόρος) denken müssen; der, weil sein Angriff mit dem Nahen der Armuth verglichen wird, auf räuberische Weise die Wanderer um ihre Habe bringt.

V. 12.* אדם בליעל and איש און, it is manifest, do not stand in the relation of subject and predicate. This would be almost an identical proposition;† and in the most favorable expression of it, *a worthless* (useless) *man is a bad man*, is nothing to the purpose here. Both stand in the same relation, as predicates to the subject of the next member. The predicate here, as very often in this book, is placed first for the sake of emphasis (§145).

Second member:—(lit.) *perverseness of mouth* = *falsehood*. *Walks in falsehood*, an habitual course of action, a life of false dealing.

This character is particularly described in the two following verses (see Expl. Notes). The same subject is clearly intended by the following participial forms; and this relation is best expressed in English by rendering them in that form

V. 13. *To nip the eyes* (lit., *with the eyes*, ב *instr.* in place of the *accus.*, as explained §138, 1, 3, foot-note), the sudden compression of the eye in giving a significant wink. *Talking with his feet:* as well paraphrased by the Sept., *makes signs with his feet*. *Pointing*, etc., in the proper signification of the verb.‡

V. 14. *In whose heart* (§123, 3, *b*). The relative construction

* So Ewald construes the two members:

*Ein Taugenichts, ein Heilloser*
*ist wer in Mundes-Falschheit lebt.*

† Subject und Prädicat dann ziemlich ganz zusammenfallen würden (Bertheau).

‡ *Zeichen gibt mit den Fingern*, מרה Part. Hif. von ירה hier in seiner ursprünglichsten Bedeutung (Bertheau).

KING JAMES' VERSION.

15 Therefore shall his calamity come suddenly; suddenly shall he be broken without remedy.

16 These six *things* doth the the LORD hate: yea, seven *are* an abomination unto him:

17 A proud look, a lying tongue, and hands that shed innocent blood,

18 A heart that deviseth wicked imaginations, feet that be swift in running to mischief,

19 A false witness *that* speaketh lies, and him that soweth discord among brethren.

20 My son, keep thy father's commandment, and forsake not the law of thy mother:

21 Bind them continually upon thine heart, *and* tie them about thy neck.

22 When thou goest, it shall lead thee; when thou sleepest, it shall keep thee; and *when* thou awakest, it shall talk with thee.

HEBREW TEXT.

טו עַל־כֵּן פִּתְאֹם יָבוֹא אֵידוֹ
פֶּתַע יִשָּׁבֵר וְאֵין מַרְפֵּא׃

16 שֶׁשׁ־הֵנָּה שָׂנֵא יְהוָה
וְשֶׁבַע תּוֹעֲבוֹת נַפְשׁוֹ׃

17 עֵינַיִם רָמוֹת לְשׁוֹן שָׁקֶר
וְיָדַיִם שֹׁפְכוֹת דָּם־נָקִי׃

18 לֵב חֹרֵשׁ מַחְשְׁבוֹת אָוֶן
רַגְלַיִם מְמַהֲרוֹת לָרוּץ לָרָעָה׃

19 יָפִיחַ כְּזָבִים עֵד שָׁקֶר
וּמְשַׁלֵּחַ מְדָנִים בֵּין אַחִים׃

כ נְצֹר בְּנִי מִצְוַת אָבִיךָ
וְאַל־תִּטֹּשׁ תּוֹרַת אִמֶּךָ׃

21 קָשְׁרֵם עַל־לִבְּךָ תָמִיד
עָנְדֵם עַל־גַּרְגְּרֹתֶךָ׃

22 בְּהִתְהַלֶּכְךָ ׀ תַּנְחֶה אֹתָךְ
בְּשָׁכְבְּךָ תִּשְׁמֹר עָלֶיךָ
וַהֲקִיצוֹתָ הִיא תְשִׂיחֶךָ׃

V. 16. תועבת ק׳

REVISED VERSION.

Therefore shall his calamity 15
come suddenly;
in a moment shall he be destroyed without remedy.

Six things there are Jehovah 16
hates;
and seven are the abomination of his soul.

Lofty eyes, a lying tongue, 17
and hands that shed innocent blood;

a heart devising wicked coun- 18
sels,
feet running with haste to evil;

who breathes out falsehoods, 19
a lying witness,
and who scatters discords between brethren.

Keep, my son, the command 20
of thy father,
and reject not the law of thy mother.

Bind them on thy heart con- 21
tinually;
fasten them on thy neck.

When thou walkest, she will 22
guide thee;
when thou liest down, she will watch over thee;
and when thou wakest, she will talk with thee.

V. 16. the abominations (V. R.)

V. 22. it will

is required in English, for the proper expression of the more simple Hebrew conception.*

*Scatters discords* (properly, *sends out, sends abroad,* in the sense of originating and disseminating them); setting men at variance who would otherwise be at peace with one another. Here (third member), the participial construction passes over to that of the finite verb (§ 134, Rem. 2).

V. 16. *Six things there are;*† the best expression of this emphatic use of הנה (comp. § 121, 2; Ewald, Lehrb., § 297, *b*).

V. 18. *Running with haste* (§ 142, 4, Rem. 1).‡

V. 22. *She will guide thee,* etc.; a natural personification of the parental discipline spoken of in the two preceding verses. So this use of the *fem. sing.* is correctly explained by Rosenmüller,* and by Gesenius as quoted below (note §). Bertheau suggests, that *wisdom* may be the collective *sing.*, which, as the discourse proceeds, comes in place of the two ideas of *command* and *precept* in v. 20.† But for this substitution there is no just ground; and it would be better to regard the *fem. sing.* as a *neut.* (*it will guide*), as it is understood by C. B. Michaelis.‡

Third member:—*Will talk with thee* (תשיחך); Gesenius, Lex.: "c. acc. *to talk with,* to converse with, Prov. 6 : 22."§ Ewald:

* Bertheau; *In dessen Herzen Verkehrtheit ist.* So vv. 13, 14 are construed by Ewald:

Wer winkt mit Augen, spricht mit seinen Füssen,
wer weist mit seinen Fingern,
in dessen Herz Verkehrtheit ist,
wer säet Böses alle Zeit,
lässt lauter Hader los.

† Ewald: *Sechs Dinge sind's.*

‡ Ewald: *Füsse, die eilig hin zum Bösen laufen.*

* *Cumque* a somno *evigilaveris, ea* scil. parentum institutio, tuo animo obversata, *tecum colloquetur,* sicut familiaris cum familiari confabulatur.

† Der Singular . . . bezieht sich auf einen den zwei Wörtern *Gebot* und *Unterweisung* V. 20 im Verlauf der Rede substituirten Singular-Begriff, etwa auf Weisheit.

‡ *Id ipsum* (quod modo præceptum patris, doctrinamque matris nuncupavi v. 20) *loquetur tibi,* s. *tecum* suaviter *colloquetur.*

§ Thes. III., p. 1328: Ubi *evigilaveris, ea* (disciplina parentum) *te alloquetur;* tecum quasi colloquetur instar amici familiaris, i. e. largam tecum colloquendi et meditandi materiam tibi præbebit. Hebræi explicant תְּדַבֵּר עִמָּךְ .תָּשִׂיחַ עִמָּךְ, LXX. συλλαλῇ σοι. Gr. Venet. διαλέξεται σοι.

| KING JAMES' VERSION. | HEBREW TEXT. | | REVISED VERSION. | |
|---|---|---|---|---|
| 23 For the commandment *is* a lamp; and the law *is* light; and reproofs of instruction *are* the way of life: | כִּי נֵר מִצְוָה וְתוֹרָה אוֹר<br>וְדֶרֶךְ חַיִּים תּוֹכְחוֹת מוּסָר׃ | 23 | For the command is a lamp, and the law is a light;<br>and instructive reproofs are the way of life: | 23 |
| 24 To keep thee from the evil woman, from the flattery of the tongue of a strange woman. | לִשְׁמָרְךָ מֵאֵשֶׁת רָע<br>מֵחֶלְקַת לָשׁוֹן נָכְרִיָּה׃ | 24 | to keep thee from the evil woman,<br>from the flattery of the strange woman's tongue. | 24 |
| 25 Lust not after her beauty in thine heart; neither let her take thee with her eyelids. | אַל־תַּחְמֹד יָפְיָהּ בִּלְבָבֶךָ<br>וְאַל־תִּקָּחֲךָ בְּעַפְעַפֶּיהָ׃ | כה | Covet not her beauty in thy heart,<br>nor let her take thee with her eyelids. | 25 |
| 26 For by means of a whorish woman *a man is brought* to a piece of bread: and the adulteress will hunt for the precious life. | כִּי בְעַד־אִשָּׁה זוֹנָה עַד־כִּכַּר־לָחֶם<br>וְאֵשֶׁת אִישׁ נֶפֶשׁ יְקָרָה תָצוּד׃ | 26 | For, for a harlot is but a round of bread;<br>but the married woman hunts for the precious life. | 26 |

V. 23. corrective reproofs.

*she will muse with thee.** Bertheau: *will make thee thoughtful;*† in which the spirit of the figure is lost.

V. 23. *Instructive reproofs* (or *corrective reproofs,* marg.); מוסר being the qualifying genitive.‡

V. 24. *The evil woman;*§ the adulteress is meant (as the parallelism and connection show); one regardless of every obligation human and divine.

Second member:—(as the text is pointed) *From the flattery of the strange tongue.*‖ The meaning evidently is, *of the tongue of the strange woman;*¶ and so the text itself is expressed (as if read לְשׁוֹן נָכְרִיָּה) by the Chald., Syr., and Vulgate,** the Sept. also admitting this construction.

Ewald: *from the smoothtongued, the strange woman;* חלקת *fem.* of the adjective חָלָק* (lit. *smooth of tongue,* Ges. Gram., §112, 2). So also Bertheau.† To Ewald's objection (repeated by Bertheau‡) that חלקת can not be a subst., because an *abstract* here is not suited to אשת in the parallel member, Maurer replies that חלקת corresponds with רע and not with אשת; strictly, however, the correspondence is not between single words, but between the combinations אשת רע and ח״ ל׳ נכריה.

V. 26. עד ככר ל׳, *unto a round of bread* (usque ad); to that extent, and no more.§ So much suffices for her hire. So the Sept. and Vulg.‖ It is so understood by many of the leading modern scholars.¶ *A round* (ככר) *of bread = loaf of bread,* from its shape.

* *Wird sie mit dir sinnen.*

† *Sie wird dich sinnend machen,* gleichsam zum Morgengruss dir Ueberlegung, Nachdenken schenken.

‡ Ewald: *Die züchtigenden Rügen.* Umbreit: Statt תּוֹכְחוֹת will Ziegler mit den ältesten Codd. bei de Rossi, vielen Editionen und allen alten Uebersetzungen (welches letztere falsch ist, indem wenigstens *Vers. Veneta οἱ παιδείας ἔλεγχοι* hat) תּוֹכַחַת im Singular lesen. Aber diese Lesart des Singular gebietet weder strenge kritische Autorität, noch exegetische Nothwendigkeit. Vielmehr sagt der Plural mehr als der Singular.

§ Sept. *married woman, γυναικὸς ὑπάνδρου,* reading the Heb. רֵעַ. But the Masoretic text has evidently preserved the true sense. Schultens: *Mulier mali* est cujus pectori malitia incocta; atque adeo *τὸ πονηρὸν* ipsum malum medullis implicitum penitus, et infixum.

‖ Pagnino: *A blanditiis linguæ extraneæ.*

¶ Gesenius (Lex. נכרי): "*a strange tongue,* i. e, the tongue of a strange woman, Prov. 6 : 24." Rosenmüller: *Linguam peregrinam* esse linguam mulieris peregrinæ, vix est quod moneamus. Poetice linguæ tribuit, quod mulieri competit. Maurer: Quasi *lingua aliena* non commode et eleganter dicatur pro *lingua mulieris alienæ!*

** לִישָׁנָא דְנוּכְרֵיתָא; ܠܫܢܐ ܢܘܟܪܝܬܐ; *blanda lingua extraneæ.*

* *Vor der von glatter Zunge* = der Gleissnerinn, *der Fremden,* d. h. Frau eines andern Mannes, dem sie untreu wird; richtig Symm. Theod. *ἀπὸ λειογλώσσου ξένης*; anders aber die Accente, wonach der Sinn wäre: *vor Glätte einer fremden Zunge.*

† חלקת stat. constr. fem. vom Adject. חָלָק; *die Glätte der Zunge* ist eine welche glatt macht ihre Worte, 2 : 16, 7 : 5; נכריה ein in Apposition hinzugesetztes Adject.: *vor der fremden Zunge-Glatten.*

‡ Dem Weibe in *a* gegenüber erwartet man in *b* kein abstractum *Glätte,* welches c. 7 : 21 auch nicht חלקת, sondern חֵלֶק lautet.

§ Ewald (Lehrb., §217, *e*): Aus dem Begriffe der Steigerung folgt der *sogar* als Conjunction, 1 Sam. 2 : 5, oder auch *sogar nur* als Präposition, Spr. 6 : 26.

‖ *Τιμὴ γὰρ πόρνης ὅση καὶ ἑνὸς ἄρτου.* Vulgate: *Pretium enim scorti vix est unius panis.*

¶ E. g. Dathe: *Pretium mulieris meretricis est panis.* Opponuntur sibi h. l. scortum, s. prostibulum sui copiam faciens cuique pretio soluto, et adultera, cujus consuetudo vitæ est perniciosa propter zelotypiam maxime mariti, de qua vers. 34, 35.

Ewald: *Denn für 'ne Hure nur ein Stückchen Brod.* Für eine blosse Buhlerin gebe man *sogar* nur (עד) ein Bischen Brod . . . da sie nur elenden Lebensunterhalt erjage. So Bertheau: *Denn für eine Buhlerin sogar nur ein Brodkuchen;* d. h. die ist auch mit geringem Geschenke (Gen. 38 : 16, f.), ja, wenn es sein muss, mit einem Stücke Brod . . . zufrieden.

| KING JAMES' VERSION. | HEBREW TEXT. | | REVISED VERSION. | |
|---|---|---|---|---|
| 27 Can a man take fire in his bosom, and his clothes not be burned? | הֲיַחְתֶּה אִישׁ ׀ אֵשׁ בְּחֵיקוֹ<br>וּבְגָדָיו לֹא תִשָּׂרַפְנָה׃ | 27 | Can a man take up fire into his bosom,<br>and his clothes not be burned? | 27 |
| 28 Can one go upon hot coals, and his feet not be burned? | אִם־יְהַלֵּךְ אִישׁ עַל־הַגֶּחָלִים<br>וְרַגְלָיו לֹא תִכָּוֶינָה׃ | 28 | Or can a man walk on the hot coals,<br>and his feet not be scorched? | 28 |
| 29 So he that goeth in to his neighbour's wife; whosoever toucheth her shall not be innocent. | כֵּן הַבָּא אֶל־אֵשֶׁת רֵעֵהוּ<br>לֹא יִנָּקֶה כָּל־הַנֹּגֵעַ בָּהּ׃ | 29 | So he that goes in to his neighbor's wife;<br>no one shall be innocent that touches her. | 29 |
| 30 *Men* do not despise a thief, if he steal to satisfy his soul when he is hungry; | לֹא־יָבוּזוּ לַגַּנָּב כִּי יִגְנוֹב<br>לְמַלֵּא נַפְשׁוֹ כִּי יִרְעָב׃ | ל | They slight not the thief, when he steals,<br>to satisfy his spirit when he is hungry; | 30 |

Another construction, proposed by Gersonides, has been adopted by many; viz., *for, for the sake of a harlot, a man comes to a round of bread;** i. e. to a single loaf, as all that is left him.† So Gesenius (Lex. בַּעַד, 1, *a, γ*), "*for a harlot* (one comes) *to a piece of bread*; i. e. he who yields to her, lives for her and comes to want." So Le Clerc,‡ Rosenmüller, Umbreit, and others.§

It is obvious that the ellipsis, in this construction, is not the one most naturally and readily supplied.‖ The subst. verb, the natural and usual copula, is the only ellipsis that spontaneously suggests itself in such a case.

Prof. Stuart objects to the first construction and explanation, on the ground that it makes the writer say merely, "that harlot-hire is very cheap, and the price of adultery very high;" and "that the moral tone of the verse is much lowered in this way."¶ But this is a misconception of the writer's point of view. He is describing what the common harlot and the adulteress respectively seek; the one simply her infamous hire, the other the almost certain destruction of her victim.* As to the moral tone, nothing is gained by the second construction; according to which the writer would say merely, that harlotry is a very expensive pleasure, and adultery a very hazardous one.

Second member:—*Wife of a man* for *married woman.* Adultery was punished with death (Lev. 20 : 10, Deut. 22 : 22; compare John 8 : 5, with Ezek. 16 : 40). She is, therefore, properly said to *hunt for the precious life;* since, as remarked by Ewald (foot-note *), if not always the immediate object sought, it was one of its direct consequences.

VV. 27–29. The application (*So he*), in v. 29, follows naturally the cases supposed in the preceding questions, and with more effect than if a comparison were expressed, or were implied as unnecessarily assumed by Bertheau.†

VV. 30–31. *They slight not the thief*, etc., as though unworthy of notice and punishment. On the contrary, even such thefts as are committed under the pressure of urgent need, and only to the extent of nature's present wants, are visited with exemplary punishment; restoration being required to seven times the amount of the injury done (see Expl. Notes).‡ This (as well said by

---

The clause is so construed also by J. D. Michaelis, Dœderlein, and others. Müntinghe: Es ist gefährlicher, will der Verfasser sagen, mit einem verheiratheten Weibe, als mit einer Hure in Unzucht zu leben.

* כי בעבור אשה זונה יבא איש עד ככר לחם. Pagnino (Thes. Ling. Sanct., כִּכָּר): Nos vertimus, ut exponitur in commentariis Rab. Himmanuel, *Quia propter mulierem meretricem mendicabit homo usque ad buccellam panis.*

† Munster (Biblia Hebraica, 1546): *Quoniam propter mulierem meretricem* (pervenit fornicator) *usque ad massam panis.* Capitur hic בעד pro בעבור, et est sensus: qui scorto sese associat in tantam veniet egestatem, ut cogatur mendicare frustum panis.

‡ *Nam propter mulierem meretricem ad placentam panis* devenitur. Supplevi *devenitur;* possis et *devenies*, quasi fuisset תבוא, quia antecessit secunda persona.

§ Maurer: *Nam pro meretrice usque ad placentam* venitur, redigitur homo ad ultimam placentam, ad mendicitatem, ad incitas. Fürst (Heb. Hdwbch. בַּעַד, *extr.*): *denn für* (um) *eine Buhlerin* (giebst du alles) *bis zum Brodkuchen hin.*

‖ The cases referred to by Umbreit (Gesenius, Lehrgebäude, S. 850), do not justify it. In the first (Job 39 : 24, *that* it is *the trumpet's voice*), fourth (Ps. 3 : 9, *thy blessing* be *on thy people*), and fifth (Ps. 7 : 9, be it *unto me*), the subst. verb is spontaneously suggested; the second and third (Is. 66 : 6, Ps. 6 : 4) are simple exclamations.

¶ He translates and explains the clause thus: "For by reason of a woman who playeth the harlot, [one cometh] to a piece of bread." "Meaning: 'a man comes to abject poverty, by lavishing his money on harlots.'"

* As the case is well stated by Ewald, p. 74 (see remark, in the text, on the next member): Aber ein Eheweib jage eine theuere Seele, oder das kostbare, durch nichts einzulösende Leben des von ihr Getäuschten, wenn nicht immer ihrer nächsten Absicht, doch den nächsten Folgen nach.

† Da in den Fragen mit הֲ und אִם und ihren respectiven Nachsätzen liegt: wie dessen Kleider, der Feuer holt in seinem Schosse, verbrannt werden, wie dessen Füsse, der auf Kohlen geht, versengt werden, so kann, als gingen Sätze mit כְּ oder כַּאֲשֶׁר vorher, V. 29 als ein correlat. Satz durch כֵּן eingeführt werden: *So der, welcher hinkommt*, u. s. w.

‡ So these words were correctly explained by Le Clerc: *Non spernent furem;* hoc est, non habebunt homines furtum pro nihilo, nec negligent pœnas propterea a fure exigere, eo quod esuriens furatus fuerit, quo fami urgenti satisfaceret. Schultens:

| KING JAMES' VERSION. | HEBREW TEXT. | | REVISED VERSION. | |
|---|---|---|---|---|
| 31 But *if* he be found, he shall restore sevenfold; he shall give all the substance of his house. | וְנִמְצָא יְשַׁלֵּם שִׁבְעָתָיִם<br>אֶת־כָּל־הוֹן בֵּיתוֹ יִתֵּן׃ | 31 | and if found, he shall restore sevenfold,<br>all the substance of his house shall he give. | 31 |
| 32 *But* whoso committeth adultery with a woman, lacketh understanding: he *that* doeth it destroyeth his own soul. | נֹאֵף אִשָּׁה חֲסַר־לֵב<br>מַשְׁחִית נַפְשׁוֹ הוּא יַעֲשֶׂנָּה׃ | 32 | He that commits adultery with a woman is without understanding;<br>a destroyer of his own soul is he that does it. | 32 |
| 33 A wound and dishonour shall he get; and his reproach shall not be wiped away. | נֶגַע־וְקָלוֹן יִמְצָא<br>וְחֶרְפָּתוֹ לֹא תִמָּחֶה׃ | 33 | Blows and shame shall he get;<br>and his reproach shall not be wiped away. | 33 |

Schultens) confirms the preceding assertion, *shall not be innocent*, by an argument *a minimo ad maximum.** So Ewald translates and explains the passage.† Gesenius (Lex., בּוּז): "*Men do not despise a thief*, i. e. do not overlook his crime and let him go unpunished." So also Müntinghe, Dœderlein, Rosenmüller, Maurer (Comment. and Lex.), Bertheau,‡ De Wette,§ and others.

By some the words are understood to mean: "Men do not treat with ignominy the thief who steals only to satisfy the cravings of hunger;‖ on the contrary, they pity him, and are ready to overlook his offense."¶ They punish him as a thief, however (according to the next verse), and with the severest penalties provided for theft (see Expl. Notes). The palliations of the offense are, therefore, without practical effect; for the worst case of theft could not be punished more severely. There is, consequently, in this view of the words, no pertinency in the statement of these palliations.

As thus explained, moreover, the bearing of this clause (as well objected by Schultens) is against the writer's argument;* for he should rather have said: Do they not punish, with severity, even thefts committed under palliating circumstances? How much more adultery, etc. The objection can be obviated only by giving the clause another turn, to this effect: Men do not despise one who steals for such a purpose; but if detected, he is severely punished; how much more does the adulterer deserve, for whose offense there is no such mitigation? But there is an obvious want of coherency in the statement: They do not despise such a thief; but, if detected, they punish him with none the less severity.† It can not be said, moreover, that men do not despise the thief under such circumstances. The inherent meanness of theft can be covered by no palliations, whatever pity may be felt for the weakness of the offender. Starve rather than steal! is the dictate of just pride, where any self-respect is left.

V. 31. *All the substance of his house*, etc. There is no reference here to a special and more aggravated case. The meaning is, he shall make the required restitution, though it take all that he has.

V. 32. *Is he that does it*, gives the best English expression of the emphatic form of the original.

The same *neutral* use of the *fem. suff.* (יַעֲשֶׂנָּה) occurs in Mal. 2 : 12,‡ and with the same reference to an act, or course of action. There is, therefore, no occasion for referring the *Suff.* to אִשָּׁה.

---

Videri posset res *tolerabilis*, utcumque saltem *excusabilis;* nec tamen vel tale furtum pro vili ac nullius momenti delicto sperniitur, sed cum rigore vindicatur.

* Clausulæ prægressæ . . . *non immunis, non innoxius erit*, insistitur per comparationem a *furti specie levissima;* quod, vel sub stimulo famis commissum, neutiquam tamen impunitum dimittatur, sed gravi mulcta vindicetur.

† *Man übersieht's dem Dieb nicht, dass er stiehlt.* Auch der aus Hunger stehlende Dieb werde ja in viel geringerer Sache empfindlich gestraft (S. 74).

‡ *Nicht pflegt man zu übersehen dem Diebe, wenn er stiehlt,* thäte er es auch von Noth getrieben, *um anzufüllen seine Seele, wenn er hungert.*

§ *Man sieht dem Diebe nicht nach, wenn er stiehlt, um seine Begierde zu stillen, weil er hungert; und ertappt, muss er siebenfach erstatten*, u. s. w.

‖ Cocceius, Lex., בּוּז: *Non ignominia afficiunt furem;* Pisc.: *Man thut einem Dieb keine Schmach an; οὐκ ἀτιμοῦσιν, οὐ παραδειγματίζουσι.*

¶ Geier: Commiseratione hujus hominis tanguntur, ita ut æquanimiter maleficium ferant, atque delinquentem facile posthac in gratiam recipiant. Cocceius (Annott.): Nam furi impenditur commiseratio; et tantum cogitur vel tantundem, vel duplum, vel certe septuplum, et nihil amplius solvere. Parcitur enim ipsi, quod propter egestatem furatus fuerit.

* Nam relaxasset Paræmiastes, quod rigide voluit intendere, a furto omnium levissimo ad gravissimum illud, quod in adulterio patratur, argumentando. . . . Hoc exegisset potius: *An non contumelia afficiunt* vel *talem* etiam *furem*, qui saltem speciem potest prætexere necessitatis? nedum adulterum, etc.

† Stuart (v. 30): "*Men do not despise a thief, when he stealeth to satisfy his appetite, because he is hungry.* . . . [Note]: Men have regard to the temptation of such a man, and look on his fault with a feeling of pity. . . . (v. 31): *But when caught, he must render a recompense sevenfold; all the wealth of his house shall he give.*" The stress seems to lie on the Spartan distinction, "if detected."

‡ Femininum pro Neutro, ut Mal. 2 : 12 (C. B. Michaelis). Suffixum femininum pro neutro, ut Malach. II., 12 . . . *exscindet Jova virum qui hoc fecerit* (Rosenmüller). Das Suff. in יעשנה ganz unbestimmt, *es, solches* (Bertheau). *Zerstörer eigner Seele —der nur thut's* (Ewald). *Wer sich selbst verderbt, der thut es* (De Wette). Suffixum f. in יעשנה pro neutro est (Maurer).

| KING JAMES' VERSION. | | HEBREW TEXT. | REVISED VERSION. | |
|---|---|---|---|---|
| 34 For jealousy *is* the rage of a man: therefore he will not spare in the day of vengeance. | 34 | כִּי־קִנְאָה חֲמַת־גָּבֶר<br>וְלֹא יַחְמוֹל בְּיוֹם נָקָם׃ | For jealousy is the husband's rage;<br>and he will not spare in the day of vengeance. | 34 |
| 35 He will not regard any ransom; neither will he rest content, though thou givest many gifts. | לה | לֹא־יִשָּׂא פְּנֵי כָל־כֹּפֶר<br>וְלֹא־יֹאבֶה כִּי תַרְבֶּה־שֹׁחַד׃ | He will regard no ransom;<br>nor consent, though thou make many gifts. | 35 |
| CHAP. VII. | | CHAP. VII. | CHAP. VII. | |
| MY son, keep my words, and lay up my commandments with thee. | א | בְּנִי שְׁמֹר אֲמָרָי<br>וּמִצְוֺתַי תִּצְפֹּן אִתָּךְ׃ | MY son, keep my sayings;<br>and treasure up with thee my commands. | 1 |
| 2 Keep my commandments, and live; and my law as the apple of thine eye. | 2 | שְׁמֹר מִצְוֺתַי וֶחְיֵה<br>וְתוֹרָתִי כְּאִישׁוֹן עֵינֶיךָ׃ | Keep my commands and live,<br>and my law as the apple of thine eye. | 2 |
| 3 Bind them upon thy fingers, write them upon the table of thine heart. | 3 | קָשְׁרֵם עַל־אֶצְבְּעֹתֶיךָ<br>כָּתְבֵם עַל־לוּחַ לִבֶּךָ׃ | Bind them on thy fingers;<br>write them on the tablet of thy heart. | 3 |
| 4 Say unto wisdom, Thou *art* my sister; and call understanding *thy* kinswoman: | 4 | אֱמֹר לַחָכְמָה אֲחֹתִי אָתְּ<br>וּמֹדָע לַבִּינָה תִקְרָא׃ | Say to wisdom: My sister art thou!<br>and call understanding: Kinswoman! | 4 |
| | | V. 4. בנ״א ומודע | | |

V. 4. and call understanding: Friend!

V. 34. The connection shows that קנאה is the *subject*, and not the *predicate.** The object is to show the immediate risk incurred; for *jealousy* is no ordinary passion; it is the *rage of the husband,*† proverbial in all ages as the most violent and relentless. By גבר is here meant *husband*, in distinction from *wife* (Gesenius, Lex. 1, b).

*The day of vengeance;* including the private, personal chastisement referred to in v. 33, as well as the public penalty of the law, for which (as declared in v. 35) no ransom will be accepted.‡

V. 35. By כפר, in this connection, is meant *ransom* (as is evident from the next member), the price offered for exemption from public exposure, and from the legal punishment of the crime (Lev. 20 : 10; Deut. 22 : 22).

*Will regard,* etc., a tropical expression. A fallen, dejected countenance is the natural index of *anger* or *sorrow* (Gen. 4 : 5, 6). Consequently, *to raise the countenance* of one is to appease or avert his displeasure (comp. Expl. Notes, Job 29 : 24), or to make him happy and cheerful, by regarding him with favor; hence, simply, to have regard for, to accept, with reference either to persons or things.*

Second member:—*Consent* (יאבה), the abs. use of the Heb. verb, as in ch. 1 : 10. All thy gifts will not move him to compliance; he will insist on the extreme penalty of the law.

*Nor consent* (Bertheau, with too restricted an application), to forego the utmost rigor of the law;† (Maurer), to accept the proferred gifts, and overlook the offense.‡ *Though* (כי), Lex. 4, *extr.*§ *Gifts* (שחד, sing. collect.).

Ch. VII.—V. 3. *Bind them on thy fingers.* The language, of course, is figurative, meaning: Let them be ever at hand, ready for use, as if engrossed and bound on the fingers. Comp. Deut. 6 : 8; 11 : 18. Bertheau: "*Around thy fingers,* like a brilliant ring;" ‖ which is not the proper force of the image.

V. 4. *And call,* etc.; lit., *and thou shalt call,* imperative in

* Maurer: Subjectum esse quod nonnulli Prædicatum faciunt קנאה docet nexus. Bertheau (with a different use of גבר): *Denn Eifersucht* (27 : 4) *ist Mannesgrimm* (Jes. 22 : 17), d. i. ein nicht leicht vorübergehender Grimm. It is a trivial objection to this construction, "that women also are jealous" (weil auch Weiber eifersüchtig werden—Hitzig). This is not denied by affirming, that jealousy is the husband's most violent passion, and consequently dangerous to provoke. If the writer were speaking of the risk incurred from the jealousy of an injured wife, he could have said with equal propriety (so far as grammar and logic are concerned), *for jealousy is the rage of the wife.*

† C. B. Michaelis: חמת גבר non vulgaris est ira, sed *excandescentia viri* s. mariti, cui sustinendæ adulter haudquaquam par erit; c. 27 : 4.

‡ Rosenmüller: Occasionem sese vindicandi nactus non parcet vel in articulo temporis, quo deprehenderit, vel dum pœnam publicam apud judices persequitur.

* Bertheau: Das Gesicht des Bittenden erhebt man, wenn man seine Bitte freundlich gewährt; so würde der eifersüchtige Mann *das Gesicht irgend welcher Lösesumme erheben,* wenn er sie annehmen und damit zufrieden sein würde.

† *Und nicht wird er willig sein* auf sein strenges Recht zu verzichten.

‡ *Nec volet,* nec consentientem, i. e. ad accipienda dona, ad ignoscendum paratum habebis eum.

§ Rosenmüller: *Etiamsi multiplicaveris munus.* Maurer: *Si* (etiamsi) *multa facias dona,* et quamvis multa offeras dona. De Wette: *Wenn du auch Geschenke mehrest.* Hitzig: *Ob du auch bietest grosse Schenkung.*

‖ *Um deine Finger,* einem glänzenden Ringe gleich. Hitzig: Allein der Ring wird an den Finger gesteckt, nicht umgebunden.

| KING JAMES' VERSION. | HEBREW TEXT. | | REVISED VERSION. | |
|---|---|---|---|---|
| 5 That they may keep thee from the strange woman, from the stranger *which* flattereth with her words. | לִשְׁמָרְךָ מֵאִשָּׁה זָרָה<br>מִנָּכְרִיָּה אֲמָרֶיהָ הֶחֱלִיקָה׃ | 5 | to guard thee from the strange woman,<br>from the stranger who flatters with her words. | 5 |
| 6 For at the window of my house I looked through my casement, | כִּי בְּחַלּוֹן בֵּיתִי<br>בְּעַד אֶשְׁנַבִּי נִשְׁקָפְתִּי׃ | 6 | For at the window of my house,<br>through my lattice I looked forth ; | 6 |
| 7 And beheld among the simple ones, I discerned among the youths, a young man void of understanding, | וָאֵרֶא בַפְּתָאיִם<br>אָבִינָה בַבָּנִים<br>נַעַר חֲסַר־לֵב׃ | 7 | and saw among the simple,<br>I discerned among the youths,<br>a young man without understanding, | 7 |
| 8 Passing through the street near her corner ; and he went the way to her house, | עֹבֵר בַּשּׁוּק אֵצֶל פִּנָּהּ<br>וְדֶרֶךְ בֵּיתָהּ יִצְעָד׃ | 8 | passing along the street by her corner,<br>and he went the way to her house ; | 8 |
| 9 In the twilight, in the evening, in the black and dark night : | בְּנֶשֶׁף־בְּעֶרֶב יוֹם<br>בְּאִישׁוֹן לַיְלָה וַאֲפֵלָה׃ | 9 | at twilight, in the evening of the day<br>in the depth of night and gloom. | 9 |

V. 6. behind my lattice

V. 9. in the midst

effect (compare §130, 1).* The Heb. קרא ל is a common form for naming, or calling by a name or title ; Gen. 1 : 5, 8, 10, etc. מודע (and *fem.* מוֹדַעַת) *acquaintance* (notitia, familiaritas), spec. the intimacy of members of the same family or kindred ; † hence *relation*, and concr. a *relative*, ‡ of either sex.

V. 6. אשנב, *a lattice, a latticed window ;* Rödiger, Thes. fasc. poster. R. שׁנב. *Through*, etc. Ewald : *Behind the lattice*, i. e., standing behind it. § So Hitzig : *Behind my lattice I looked forth.* ‖

V. 7. *Youths ;* בנים being here a designation of age (Lex., 3), a use to which *sons* does not correspond. *And saw ;* not, *that I might see* (וארא and אבינה voluntatives—Bertheau). The latter verb has properly the ending ָה, in accordance with the verbal idea, in which effort and direction of the mind are implied.

V. 8. *Her corner ;* viz., of the street on which she lived, and which he entered (as the next member shows) and went the way to her house.* It is not necessary to understand by this, that he was seeking her house, as assumed by Bertheau and Hitzig ; the contrary seems to be implied in v. 21.

V. 9. נשף, *twilight ;* but used with some latitude, as extending far into the night (comp. Is. 21 : 4 ; Job 24 : 15).

Second member :—Prop. *in the eyeball of night*, etc. In the term *eyeball* (the dark centre of the eye), the tertium comparationis is twofold,† equivalent to *mid-darkness*. As the expression *eyeball of night* would not be intelligible in English, the thought must be expressed by a phrase of the same import. *And gloom :* אפלה being a second genitive after אישון, the construction "*in the black and dark night*" is inadmissible.

* Rosenmüller : *Et, nota* (cognata) *intelligentiæ acclama.* Dathe : *Et cognatam voca prudentiam.* De Wette : *Und nenne die Klugheit deine Verwandte.*

† Kimchi (Lib. Rad.) : ולפי שקרוב האדם ואשר הוא ממשפחתו יודעו ומכירו נקרא בן המשפחה מודע.

‡ As evidently used (both *masc.* and *fem.*) in Ruth 2 : 1, and 3 : 2 ; where the circumstances show that it must be understood (as by Bertheau in loc.) in the sense of *relative, kinsman.* So the early Christian Hebraists (after their Jewish teachers) ; e. g., Munster (Dictionarium Heb., 1523) : *Propinquus, consanguineus ;* (Proverbia Salomonis, 1524) : *Et propinquam ad intelligentiam clamabis ;* Mercier (Pagnini Thes.) : *Notus*, i. *cognatus*, vel *affinis.* So Schultens : *Et cognatam appelles prudentiam.* Bertheau : *Und Verwandtschaft* (= Verwandtin s. zu Rut 2 : 1, 3 : 2) *nenne die Einsicht.* Fürst, Hdwbch. : *Bekannt-, Verwandtschaft*, concr. *Verwandter*, Spr. 7 : 4.

Others : *A familiar, a friend* (as in the margin). Gesenius, Lex. : *Familiaritas, consuetudo*, et concr. *familiaris, amicus, amica.* Umbreit : *Und Vertraute ! ruf' der Klugheit zu.* Ewald : *Und als Bekanntin grüsse die Vernunft.* Hitzig : *Und Vertrauter nenne den Verstand.*

§ *Hinter dem Gitter blickt' ich aus.*

‖ *Hinter meinem Gitter blickte ich hervor.*

* It is without reason, therefore, that the Masoretic reading פִּנָּהּ is rejected by Ewald and questioned by Bertheau. Hitzig's explanation is insufficient ; viz., that "her corner" is put for *her house*, as marking the limit of her sight towards the neighboring houses (weil die Ecke das Ziel seiner Augen gegen die Nachbarhäuser markirt). C. B. Michaelis : Intelligitur autem angulus sive ipsius domus (Job 1 : 19), sive plateæ in qua domus adulteræ erat, nempe compitum, cujus altera via ad domum ejus ducebat. Maurer : Juxta angulum illius plateæ, in qua domus meretricis constituta erat ; cui interpretationi favent quæ subjiciuntur.

† Hitzig : Das Dritte der Vergleichung suche man nicht in der Mitte allein, noch in der Schwärze ; sondern daher, weil Beides in אישון zusammenfällt, rührt eben die Wahl des Bildes.

| KING JAMES' VERSION. | HEBREW TEXT. | | REVISED VERSION. | |
|---|---|---|---|---|
| 10 And, behold, there met him a woman *with* the attire of a harlot, and subtile of heart. | וְהִנֵּה אִשָּׁה לִקְרָאתוֹ<br>שִׁית זוֹנָה וּנְצֻרַת לֵב׃ | י | And, lo, a woman meeting him,<br>with harlot's attire, and deceitful in heart. | 10 |
| 11 She *is* loud and stubborn; her feet abide not in her house: | הֹמִיָּה הִיא וְסֹרָרֶת<br>בְּבֵיתָהּ לֹא־יִשְׁכְּנוּ רַגְלֶיהָ׃ | 11 | She is loud and stubborn;<br>her feet abide not in her house. | 11 |
| 12 Now *is she* without, now in the streets, and lieth in wait at every corner. | פַּעַם ׀ בַּחוּץ פַּעַם בָּרְחֹבוֹת<br>וְאֵצֶל כָּל־פִּנָּה תֶאֱרֹב׃ | 12 | Now before the house, now in the streets;<br>and by every corner she lies in wait. | 12 |
| 13 So she caught him, and kissed him, *and* with an impudent face said unto him, | וְהֶחֱזִיקָה בּוֹ וְנָשְׁקָה לּוֹ<br>הֵעֵזָה פָנֶיהָ וַתֹּאמַר לוֹ׃ | 13 | And she laid hold on him, and kissed him;<br>with impudent face she said to him: | 13 |
| 14 *I have* peace offerings with me; this day have I paid my vows. | זִבְחֵי שְׁלָמִים עָלָי<br>הַיּוֹם שִׁלַּמְתִּי נְדָרָי׃ | 14 | There are peace-offerings by me;<br>to-day I have paid my vows: | 14 |

V. 12. Now in the street, now in the broad ways

V. 10. *With the attire of a harlot** (comp. Gen. 38 : 14, 15); disguised as such, to avoid detection,† though she does not so represent herself in v. 19. *Deceitful in heart;*‡ both with reference to her husband, from whom she conceals her lewdness (v. 19), and to her victim whom she inveigles by her arts into crime and danger.

V. 11. *Loud*, etc. She is boisterous and wayward, submitting to no restraint. This and the following verse describe her general character and deportment.

V. 12. בחוץ, prop. on the outside of the house (in distinction from the inside), hence the same as in Eng. *before the house.*§

V. 13. *With impudent face*, etc. Literally: *She strengthened* (hardened) *her face, and said to him;* i. e., with a face of unyielding effrontery. This phrase, in effect, qualifies the following verb (§ 142, 3, *a*, and Rem. 1).‖

V. 14. *Peace-offerings*, as in the last American edition of Gesenius' Lex.;¶ in earlier editions, *thank-offerings* (margin), as still held by some, though at variance with Lev. 7 : 12, 13, 15, where the *thank-offering* (offering of praise, or acknowledgment, for mercies received) is distinguished from them by the addition of תּוֹדָה. The form of the expression, על תודה (Lev. 7 : 12, etc.) clearly designates the *occasion* and *ground* of the offering; not, as assumed by Ewald,* the outward pomp and ceremony (of music and song) attending its celebration.

*Are by me* (with me, at my house); עָלַי = *apud me* (as shown by Maurer on Jer. 8 : 18), Gesenius (Lex. 3, b), "*ad, apud* (Germ. *an, bei*), *at, by, near.*"†

The preference is now generally given to the version *upon me*, in the sense of *binding, obligatory, upon.* Gesenius (Lex. 1, a, δ): "*Thank-offerings* were *upon me;* i. e., were due from me."‡

* Rödiger (Thes. fasc. poster., p. 1401): *Habitus* (i. e. vestes, fucus et lenocinia) meretricis.

† Ewald: Im gewöhnlichen Hurenanzuge (שית *accus.* nach § 521 f), um unkenntlich zu sein.

‡ Gesenius, Thes.: [*M*ulier] *animi occulti*, i. e. astuta. Comp. Is. 48 : 6. Bertheau, less well: *Bewachte des Herzens* = eine, deren Herz verwahrt und unzugänglich (vgl. Jes. 65 : 4, נצורים) ist, . . . welche mit ihren Plänen zunächst zurückhält, um desto sicherer zu verlocken; C. B. Michaelis vergleicht schon das französ. *retenu.*

§ Ewald: *Bald vor der Thür, bald in den Strassen.*

‖ Ewald: *Und frecher Stirn sprach sie zu ihm.* Hitzig: *Mit frechem Antlitz sprach sie zu ihm.* Sept., ἀναιδεῖ δὲ προσώπῳ προσεῖπεν αὐτῷ. Vulg., *procaci vultu.*

¶ Rödiger (Thes. fasc. poster., p. 1422): *Sacrificium pacificum* (vulg.) θυσία εἰρηνική (ut LXX plerumque vertunt), hoc est, tale sacrificium quod ad pacem et amicitiam cum Deo colendam et testificandam offertur sive in usum publicum, sive privatarum rerum respectu. He concedes, however (p. 1423), that the signification *thank-offering* is not at variance with the laws of the language.

* Alterthümer des Volkes Israel, S. 55: Man wird dies daher nicht als ein nach der Veranlassung, sondern als ein nach der Feierlichkeit verschiedenes Opfer auffassen. Es scheint, dass dann der Opfernde zugleich von gelernten Sängern und Musikern herrliche Lob- und Preislieder aufführen, und dadurch der Feierlichkeit ein noch höheres öffentliches Ansehen verleihen liess.

† So the Septuagint: Θυσία εἰρηνική μοί ἐστι. Syriac: ܕܒ̈ܚܐ ܐܝܬ ܠܝ ܫܠܡ̈ܐ. Pagnino: *Victimæ pacificorum sunt mihi.* Le Clerc: *Victimæ salutaris sacri apud me sunt.* Junius & Tremellius: *Sacrificia eucharistica apud me sunt.* So Dathe (freely): *Epulas sacrificales paratas habeo.* Müntinghe: *Ich hab' ein Opfermahl bereitet.* Dœderlein: *Ich hab' eine Opfermahlzeit.* Ewald: *Dankopfer hab' ich zu verzehren.*

‡ C. B. Michaelis: עָלַי fuerunt huc usque *super me;* i. e. ad præstanda illa me voto quodam obstrinxeram. Rosenmüller: *Victimæ salutum* sunt *apud me;* vel, quod malim: *super me*, i. e. mihi incumbunt parare, . . . ad quæ me voto quodam obstrinxeram. Umbreit: *Dankopfer lasteten auf mir.* De Wette: *Dankopfer lagen mir ob.* Maurer (Comment.): *Sacrificia eucharistica super me* erant, incumbebant mihi; (Hdwbch.): *Dankopfer* עָלַי *lagen mir ob.* Bertheau: *Dankopfer lagen mir ob.* Hitzig: *Vorausopfer lagen mir ob.*

| KING JAMES' VERSION. | HEBREW TEXT. | | REVISED VERSION. | |
|---|---|---|---|---|
| 15 Therefore came I forth to meet thee, diligently to seek thy face, and I have found thee. | עַל־כֵּן יָצָאתִי לִקְרָאתֶךָ<br>לְשַׁחֵר פָּנֶיךָ וָאֶמְצָאֶךָּ׃ | טו | therefore came I forth to meet thee,<br>to seek thy face, and have found thee. | 15 |
| 16 I have decked my bed with coverings of tapestry, with carved *works*, with fine linen of Egypt. | מַרְבַדִּים רָבַדְתִּי עַרְשִׂי<br>חֲטֻבוֹת אֵטוּן מִצְרָיִם׃ | 16 | With coverings I have spread my couch,<br>with embroideries of Egyptian thread. | 16 |
| 17 I have perfumed my bed with myrrh, aloes, and cinnamon. | נַפְתִּי מִשְׁכָּבִי<br>מֹר אֲהָלִים וְקִנָּמוֹן׃ | 17 | I have sprinkled my bed,<br>with myrrh, aloe-wood, and cinnamon. | 17 |

V. 16. embroidered with

But there are the following objections:—1. This is an indirect way of saying, by inference, what the other version says directly and to the point. 2. In such connections, of subject and predicate by juxtaposition, the proper copula (proper, because the natural and spontaneously suggested one) is the *pres. subst. verb*, unless the mind is already directed to the past or future.* The form of the copula is not to be assumed *ad libitum*, but must naturally suggest itself from the connection. For example, 2 Sam. 18 : 11 is referred to by Gesenius in support of his view ("*on me* it lay *to give*, i. e., was my duty"); but the mind is there expressly directed to the past: *Why didst thou not smite him there to the ground? And on me* (had been, or, would now be) *to give thee*, etc. 3. The use of the past (*peace-offerings were due from me*) has a singularly unnatural and awkward effect in this clause, as an introduction to her solicitations. On the contrary, the direct statement that all is now ready (*I have peace-offerings by me* = a banquet is prepared), is natural and appropriate.

As both versions are grammatically correct, I think the preference is clearly due, on other grounds, to the older one first given.

V. 16. *With coverings*, etc., including all that was spread upon the couch, to make a place of luxurious repose.† *Spread* is the proper translation, and not *decked*, which is at least ambiguous. See Gesenius, Thes., art. רָבַד.

*With embroideries*,* etc., as translated by Ewald.† Gesenius (Lex., חָטַב), as in the margin. *Of Egyptian thread*:—"The Egyptians, from a remote era, were celebrated for their manufacture of linen and other cloths, and the produce of their looms was exported to, and eagerly purchased by, foreign nations. The fine linen, and embroidered work, the yarn, and woolen stuffs, of the upper and lower country are frequently mentioned, and were highly esteemed. Solomon purchased many of those commodities,‡ as well as chariots and horses, from Egypt." (Wilkinson, Manners and Customs of the Ancient Egyptians, Vol. III, Ch. IX, p. 113.)

V. 17. *I have sprinkled*, as in all the ancient versions.§ It is a trivial objection, that the bed could not be *sprinkled* with these solid substances (wood and gum), nor with water impregnated with them, which would render it unfit for use (Hitzig); as though there were no part of an ornamental couch, where fragrant substances, reduced to powder, might be sprinkled to

*Are due from me* (Stuart), is altogether inadmissible. The day was already past, and with it the time for making the offering, and the time for the feast was now come. It is well said, moreover, by Hitzig: Auch kann nicht gemeint sein: Gelübde lasten auf mir; heute entrichte ich sie = will ich sie entrichten. Auf den Grund der Thatsache V. 14 geht sie ja V. 15 erst ihn zu suchen.

The whole is well stated by Calovius (Biblia V. T. illustr.): In Ebr. *Victimæ pacificarum apud me.* Sub schemate pietatis allicit, quod *sacrificia eucharistica*, ex voto pridem facto, jam obtulerit, et *convivium sacrum* pro more inde apparârit, ad quod juvenem sibi occurrentem invitatum cupiat.

* This is felt by Hitzig, who seeks (ineffectually) to obviate it thus: Im eig. abhängigen Nebensatze 14 *a* bestimmt die Zeit sich durch שלמתי in *b* als Vergangenheit (vgl. dgg. z. B. Ps. 22 : 26).

† Rosenmüller: Aquila et Theodotion, *περιστρώμασι περιέστρωσα. Περίστρωμα* Lœsnerus, in Commentat. Theologg., P. III., p. 301, ejusdem significationis esse ostendit cum *στρῶμα*, *vestis stragula*, vel *ὑπόστρωμα*. Hitzig: 1 Sam. 9 : 25 ist וירבדו (LXX) *und sie betteten*, richteten ein Bett her. Also, werden hier nicht die Decken auf ערש hingebreitet, sondern dieses, das Bette, besteht aus denselben, wenn auch nicht aus ihnen allein.

* Rosenmüller (in loc.); Gesenius, Thes., art. חָטַב.

† *Mit bunten Decken von ägypt'schem Garn.* Vulgate: *Tapetibus pictis ex Ægypto.* Bertheau: *Mit Tapeten von ägyptischem Garn;* חטבות, von חטב = חצב *hauen* = Striemen machen, bedeutet den Uebers. gemäss *gestreifte Stoffe, Tapeten.*

‡ This statement is doubtless true; but it seems, from its connection here, to be founded on the questionable translation of מִקְוֵה 1 Kings 10 : 28, first introduced into the vernacular Eng. version by the Genevan (*fine linen*) after a suggestion of Gersonides (הנה הרצון במקוה בגדי שש כי כמו שהחוט יקרא תקוה כן יקרא הנארג מהחוטין מקוה), and thence into the Bishops' (*fine linen*) and the Common Version (*linen yarn*).

§ Sept.: *Διέῤῥαγκα τὴν κοίτην μου κρoκίνῳ.* Vulgate: *Aspersi cubile meum myrrha.* Chald.: רַסֵּית. Syriac: ܪܣܣܬ. Ewald; *Habe besprengt mein Lager.* Pagnino: *Suffivi.* Genevan (and the Common Version): *I have perfumed my bed.* So Hitzig: *Ich habe mein Bette durchduftet.* . . . Eig., ich habe angeschwungen mein Bette mit Myrrhe ff., welche im Rauchfass geschwungen wird. But his objections to the usual rendering are of little weight

| KING JAMES' VERSION. | HEBREW TEXT. | | REVISED VERSION. | |
|---|---|---|---|---|
| 18 Come, let us take our fill of love until the morning: let us solace ourselves with loves. | לְכָה נִרְוֶה דֹדִים עַד־הַבֹּקֶר<br>נִתְעַלְּסָה בָּאֳהָבִים׃ | 18 | Come, let us drink our fill of love till the morning,<br>let us delight ourselves with love. | 18 |
| 19 For the goodman *is* not at home, he is gone a long journey: | כִּי אֵין הָאִישׁ בְּבֵיתוֹ<br>הָלַךְ בְּדֶרֶךְ מֵרָחוֹק׃ | 19 | For the goodman is not at home;<br>he has gone on a journey far away. | 19 |
| 20 He hath taken a bag of money with him, *and* will come home at the day appointed. | צְרוֹר הַכֶּסֶף לָקַח בְּיָדוֹ<br>לְיוֹם הַכֶּסֶא יָבֹא בֵיתוֹ׃ | כ | The purse of silver he has taken in his hand;<br>at the day of the full moon he will come home. | 20 |
| | V. 20. בנ״א יבוא | | | |

perfume the air around, without coming in contact with the person.

*Aloe-wood.* See Gesenius, Thes. I., p. 33,* and Dioscorides as there quoted.

Fürst, heb. u. chald. Hdwbch. (art. אָהָל): "*Aloe-wood, ξυλαλόη,* the fragrant and precious wood, which the Hebrews used with מֹר *myrrh,* and קִנָּמוֹן *cinnamon,* for sprinkling and perfuming the couch."† "The proper *aloe-wood,*" says Sprengel,‡ "comes from a tree yet little known, of the family of the leguminosæ, *aloexylon agallochum* of Loureiro."

The researches of Celsius, Rumpf, Loureiro, and others, are believed to have established the identity of the Hebrew אהל with the *ἀγάλλοχον* of Dioscorides, and the *ξυλαλόη* of later writers.§ The tree is described as tall, with an erect trunk and lofty branches; compare Num. 24 : 6, prop. (as in the Genevan version): *As the aloe-trees, which the Lord hath planted.* The fragrant wood, referred to in the text, is an excrescence‖ (called *calambac*), and is so rare as to be worth its weight in gold. It is discovered by the fragrance with which it fills the air, or, as said by some, by a phosphorescent light perceptible in the dark.¶

The name *aloe-tree* (and, for the fragrant substance obtained from it, *aloe-wood*), is the proper designation of it,* in distinction from the plant called *aloe.*

V. 19. *The goodman;* meaning the master of the house, and also expressing his relation to herself, as in early English usage.† No other English word corresponds to the Heb. usage here.

*He has gone on a journey far away;* as the thought is expressed with marked emphasis in the original.‡

V. 20. *Of the full moon* (כסא), as shown by Gesenius, Thes. II., pp. 698–9.§

* Genus arboris indicæ odoriferæ, Græcis *ἀγάλλοχον,* sequioribus *ξυλαλόη* quoque dictæ, . . . recentioribus *lignum aloes.* . . . In ipsa India tantæ est raritatis, ut æquo auri pondere redimatur. Ligni frusta resinosa, subnigra, gravia, et velut a vermibus perforata *Calambac* dicuntur, arbor ipsa . . . Japanensibus *Kaworiki,* i. e., arbor odorata.

† Aloëholz, *ξυλαλόη,* das wohlriechende und kostbare Holz, welches die Hebräer neben מֹר (Myrrhe) und קִנָּמוֹן (Zimmtrohr) zum Besprengen und Beräuchern des Lagers gebrauchten.

‡ Ersch u. Gruber's Encyclopädie, 1te Sect., 39ter Th., S. 355. Das eigentliche Aloëholz von einem noch wenig bekannten Baume aus der Familie der Leguminosen, Aloexylon Agallochum *Loureiro,* kommt.

§ Græcum nomen *ἀγάλλοχον,* cui respondet arab. اغلاجون (*Agalladschun*), a priscis Ebræis אהלים aut אהלות vocatur (Sprengel, Comment. in Dioscor., Lib. I., cap. 21). So Winer, Rlwbch.. art. *Aloë, Aloëholz.*

‖ Est autem lignum gongrodes, i. e. morbo quodam natum, quo gemmæ propaginesque reprimuntur, idque oritur, quod nostrates *Maserkröpfe,* Galli *Madreure,* Itali *Marezzi* vocant (Sprengel, as above).

¶ Plurimi autem Sinenses dicunt . . . istius loci aut regionis dominum, circa hanc ambulantem arborem, aliquando percipere jucundissimum odorem, quem naso suo, tam diu et uno ex quinque sensibus prosequi et investigare debet, donec percipiat talem odorem prope hunc vel illum truncum aut ramum esse gratissimum, unde dijudicat *Calambac* in hoc contineri. Alii autem dicunt, per noctem observari lucentem et igneum quasi splendorem, ubi maturum reconditur *Calambac* (Rumphius, Herbar. Amboin., Lib. II., cap. XI., p. 30).

* Primitivum autem nomen in arabicis appellationibus الوة (*Allowat*) et اليه (*Allijath*) servatum esse videtur. . . . . Ex ultima arabica voce *Allowat* Græci *ἀλόην* et *ξυλαλόην* formarunt (Sprengel, as above). Cum ipsa autem merce nomen الوه *Alluwe* ad illos (Arabes) forte manavit; unde factum deinde a Græcis et Latinis hominibus *aloë.* Hebræis autem אהלים *Ahalim,* et אהלות *Ahalot,* sub duplici terminatione, hæc ligna dicebantur (Celsius, Hierobot., Vol. I., p. 136).

† E. g., Shakesp., *T. of the S.,* Induc. II.

‡ Bertheau: Der Gatte *ist gegangen auf einen Weg fern hin.* (מרחוק): was *von fern* ist, liegt fern hin. Hitzig: Wo wir sachlich *in die Ferne* sagen, setzt der Hebräer die Beziehung auf das Subject, wie ihm die Handlung erscheint, *von ferne her.*

§ Aquila: *Εἰς ἡμέραν πανσελήνου.* Vulgate: *In die plenæ lunæ.* Chald.: וּלְיוֹמָא דִיעְדָא; from a comparison of which with Ps. 81 : 4 it is higly probable, that חכסא was used *κατ' ἐξοχὴν* of the full moon of the seventh month, the time of the great convocation at the *feast of tents* (Lev. 23 : 34–36). So it is understood by Ewald here (um den *Vollmond* wahrscheinlich des Hüttenfestes; vgl. zu Ψ. 81); and this, it must be admitted, is more consistent with the statement in the first member, than the usual supposition of the next following full moon. Hitzig: *Auf den* (nächsten) *Vollmond;* also, da jetzt (vgl. v. 9) ungefähr Neumond sein wird, etwa in vierzehn Tagen. Bertheau: Bis *zum Tage des Vollmondes* . . . müssen demnach noch einige Tage sein.

| KING JAMES' VERSION. | HEBREW TEXT. | | REVISED VERSION. | |
|---|---|---|---|---|
| 21 With her much fair speech she caused him to yield, with the flattering of her lips she forced him. | הִטַּתּוּ בְּרֹב לִקְחָהּ<br>בְּחֵלֶק שְׂפָתֶיהָ תַּדִּיחֶנּוּ׃ | 21 | With her much ensnaring art she inclines him,<br>impels him with the flattery of her lips. | 21 |
| 22 He goeth after her straightway, as an ox goeth to the slaughter, or as a fool to the correction of the stocks; | הוֹלֵךְ אַחֲרֶיהָ פִּתְאֹם<br>כְּשׁוֹר אֶל־טָבַח יָבֹא<br>וּכְעֶכֶס אֶל־מוּסַר אֱוִיל׃ | 22 | He goes after her straightway;<br>as an ox comes to the slaughter,<br>and as a fool to the gyves for correction: | 22 |

V. 22. בנ״א פתאום

V. 21. with her smooth speech she impels him

V. 22. and as to the gyves, to the correction of a fool

V. 21. *Ensnaring art;* לקח (לֶקַח *to take, to captivate;* comp. ch. 6 : 25) Gesenius' Lex., *taking arts, artes* quibus animus alicujus *capitur.* *

Others take לקח in the sense of *talk, speech;* on no better ground, however, than that it means *instruction, teaching,* and hence (as this is done by words) *speech* or *discourse* in general. † But the ground idea is of something *taken* or *perceived* (by the senses), something learned; and hence what one learns, whether as received from another, or as imparted by him. There is, therefore (as rightly asserted by Arnold), ‡ no philological ground whatever for this meaning.

Umbreit takes the word in the sense of *teaching, instruction;* § acknowledging, however, that it must be used here *satirically,* since in its proper sense this beautiful term is ill adapted to her corrupting discourse. ‖ Precisely so; nor could such irony be more out of place, than in the grave simplicity and directness of the writer's language.

V. 22. *He goes after her,* * as the *part.* often stands for the finite verb; though it is more probably used (as suggested by Hitzig) † to express a closer connection with the preceding *pron. suff.*

The spirited description is thus fully carried out to its close, and the willing victim "goes as an ox to the slaughter, and as a fool to the gyves for correction." Nothing is wanting to the completeness of this lively picture of tempted folly, and of its sure and speedy reward. In place of this, Bertheau gives a tame and unseasonable generalization, under the moral reflection: *He who goes after her* (= *whoever goes after her*) *will suddenly come as an ox to the shambles.* ‡

Second member:—עכס, § accus. of direction (§ 118, Rem., *a*). ‖ Literal form: *And as to the gyves, for correction, a fool;* a frequent arrangement, by which the emphatic words are placed at the beginning and end.

The Masoretic pointing (מוּסַר) also gives a pertinent sense: *And as to the gyves* (goes *as to the gyves*) *to the correction of a fool* (the correction due to, or appointed for, a fool). So Bertheau: *And as to a foot-chain* (laid) *for correction of the fool.* ¶

The ancient versions are wholly at fault here. ** There is no

---

* As explained by Arnold (zur Exegetik u. Kritik des A. T.): Dem Sprachgebrauch des Zeitworts לקח, und dem חלק שפתיה in der folgenden Periode ist nichts gemässer, als durch לקח hier Künste zu verstehen, wodurch jemand gefangen wird. Dathe: *Pellexit eum multis suis artibus.* Winer (Simonis Lex.): *Ars,* qua quis *capitur,* corrumpitur, Prov. 7 : 21. Maurer (Hdwbch.): Das Einnehmen, die *Kunst* der Buhlerin einzunehmen, Spr. 7 : 21. Fürst, Hdwbch. (as an alternative): Entweder *Einnehmendes* (s. Spr. 6 : 25, 11 : 30), wie c a p e r e, Horat., sat. 2, 7, 46, Liv. 30, 12; oder, etc.

† Bertheau: לקח *Lehre,* sofern diese hingenommen wird aus dem Munde eines anderen, daher allgemeiner *Rede.* Stuart: *She turneth him aside by the abundance of her speech; she forceth him along by her smooth talk.*

‡ (Ubi supra): Die Alten übersetzen fast alle לקח durch Reden, Gespräche, nur um etwas zu sagen, welches sich in den Zusammenhang schickte; denn philologische Gründe für diese Bedeutung wüsste ich nirgends aufzutreiben.

§ So Ewald: *Sie beugte ihn durch ihrer Lehre Fülle.*

‖ *Durch die Fülle ihrer Lehre* ist satirisch zu nehmen; denn eigentlich ziemt sich das schöne Wort לקח nicht für die verführerischen Reden der Buhlerin. Rosenmüller: Hic vero per ironiam de libidinosæ mulieris sermonibus dicitur, quibus incauti juvenis animum demulcet et capit. So C. B. Michaelis (somewhat too naively): Volebat enim hæc mulier sapientiæ magistra videri, cum ad stultitiam et impietatem præiret.

* Rosenmüller: *Vadit post eam subito.* Umbreit: *Er folgte ihr mit einem Male.* Maurer: *Sequitur eam subito.*

† הולך knüpft eigentlich als Participium locker sich an das vorhergehende Suffixum, und beschreibt sein Verhalten als des מַדָּה.

Ewald: *Durch ihre Lippenglätte treibt sie ihn,*
*der da ihr folgt im Augenblick.*

‡ Der Schluss redet nicht mehr von dem einzelnen נער (v. 7), sondern davon, dass jeder solchen Lockungen nachgebende in sicheres Verderben rennt. *Wer ihr folgt, plötzlich gleich einem Stiere wird er zur Schlachtbank kommen.* Stuart: *He that goeth after her, will speedily go as an ox to the slaughter.*

§ *A fetter, shackles* (*compes*), *gyves;* Gesenius, Thes. R. עָכַס.

‖ Geier (with אל of the preceding member): *Et sicut ad compedes, quæ sunt ad castigationem stulti.* So Bertheau: *Und wie zu einer Fusskette,* etc. . . . . vor עכס das אל aus dem vorhergehenden ergänzt.

¶ *Und wie zu einer Fusskette, zur Züchtigung des Thoren gelegt.*

** Sept.: *Καὶ ὥσπερ κύων ἐπὶ δεσμοὺς* (Chald. and Syr. the same). Vulg.: *Et quasi agnus lasciviens, et ignorans quod ad vincula stultus trahatur.*

| KING JAMES' VERSION. | HEBREW TEXT. | | REVISED VERSION. | |
|---|---|---|---|---|
| 23 Till a dart strike through his liver; as a bird hasteth to the snare, and knoweth not that it *is* for his life. | עַד יְפַלַּח חֵץ כְּבֵדוֹ<br>כְּמַהֵר צִפּוֹר אֶל־פָּח<br>וְלֹא יָדַע כִּי־בְנַפְשׁוֹ הוּא׃ | 23 | till an arrow cleave his liver;<br>as a bird hastes to the snare,<br>and knows not that it is for his life. | 23 |

ground for doubt as to the literal meaning of single words, עכס e. g.; but the use of this word here, and the construction of the clause, have occasioned no little difficulty.* Gesenius (Thes. עֶכֶס) gives the preference† to the Rab. interpretation adopted by Buxtorf (עֶכֶס = אִישׁ עֶכֶס *vir compedis*‡), *a fetter* for *one that is fettered: and as one fettered to the punishment of a fool.*§ But the metonymy (a harsh one, at the best) is singularly infelicitous in such a connection as this: *And as a fetter* (the instrument of correction) goes *to* [receive] *the correction of a fool.* The resort to it, moreover, is unnecessary; for we have already the appropriate subject (אויל), and the proper term for his punishment (עכס). Preferable to this is the construction of Cocceius|| (commended by Schultens,¶ and followed by C. B. Michaelis,** and by De Wette††): *And as in fetters to the punishment of a fool* (for an example to all such). But to both these views it may be objected, that the image of one bound, and forced away to anticipated punishment, is at variance with the case here supposed; viz., of one who goes blindly and unconsciously to his fate, "as an ox to the slaughter, as a bird hastes to the snare, and knows not that it is for his life."

According to Umbreit, the meaning is: *He goes after her as the ox comes to the slaughter, and as a fetter for the chastisement of a fool.* But in what sense he goes after her *as a fetter*, etc., is not very clear. Its *passivity* he supposes to be the point of comparison; it being the involuntary instrument of another's will, as he is of the pleasure of the adulteress.‡‡ The amount of which is: He is as passive in following her, as is the fetter used for the punishment of folly!

V. 23. The retribution comes suddenly and unlooked for, as the arrow from an unseen bow. It can not be denied that the thought, as expressed in the received Hebrew text, is pertinent, and in the highest degree spirited and effective. The culprit goes thoughtlessly on, "till an arrow cleaves his liver; as a bird hastes to the snare, and knows not that it is for his life." Nothing is wanting to the completeness and symmetry of the thought; nor could it be expressed with more vivacity and point.

The objection made to the present form of the Heb. text,* particularly on the ground of defective parallelism, is certainly not without weight. But it should be considered that the writer, though studiously observant of the parallelism of thought, is not a slave to it. Moreover, the external evidence against the present form of the text is of trifling amount; while the aptness and coherency of thought, and the singular felicity of expression, are strongly in its favor. The force of this suggestion will be felt the more, on comparison with Hitzig's elaborate emendation of the text:†

V. 22. He followed after her at once,
as an ox, that goes to the slaughterhouse,
and as a bird hastes into the snare.

---

* Schultens: Torquet nodus, et torquetur, in vocabulo וכעכס. Gesenius (Thes.): Sic in loco multum vexato Prov. VII. 22, etc.

† Thes. (l. c.): Apparet etiam עכס in altero membro respondere *bovi* in priore, et מוסר אויל respondere *laniena*, locum igitur significare quorsum ducatur עכס. (*Ducatur* corresponds to *trahitur* in the quotation given in note (§), and shows that but one view is intended in the Thesaurus.) See, also (second col.): Flagitante parallelismo, עכס non potest non esse sive persona sive res, quæ in *perniciem trahitur.*

‡ *Compedem* concr. dici posse pro *compedito* vel *compeditis*, non dubium est.

§ *Sicut* maleficus *compeditus in castigationem stultorum*, i. e., in ergastulum trahitur.

|| Lex. עכס: *Et tanquam in compede ad pœnam* exemplarem pro וכבעכס. Gesenius formerly (as an alternative, Lex., 1833): *Et sicuti in compedibus ad supplicium* (it, s. trahitur) *improbus*, i. e., maleficus.

¶ Subtilius adhuc cl. Cocceius: *Et tanquam in compede.* Id dextre expositum palmam ferre poterit.

** *Et velut in compede ibat . . . ad castigationem* punitivam s. *pœnam stulti*; q. d. ut hoc modo justas pertinacis stultitiæ suæ pœnas luat.

†† *Und wie in Fesseln zur Züchtigung des Thoren.*

‡‡ Was ist *passiver* bei der Züchtigung eines Verbrechers, als die Fessel die seinen Fuss umschliesst? Ein blosses *todtes Werkzeug* ist sie; und ein solches auch der Jüngling, welcher der Buhlerin folgt, ihren Lüsten zu dienen.

* By Bertheau, e. g., "The sense . . . . is this: The one seduced is compared, 1. with the ox; 2. with a man taken in a foot-chain, . . . . and held fast till sudden death comes, one knows not whence, as the ensnared beast is slain by the arrow of the lurking huntsman; 3. with the bird. One can not but perceive, however, that the sense expressed by these words is unsatisfactory, for the reason, especially, that the parallelism of members is almost wholly wanting. . . . The original has been deranged, perhaps, by the omission of a whole line, to which the repetition of the words לא ידע (as may be inferred from the Vulg.) might have given occasion. We do not attempt its restoration." So, also, Maurer: Ceterum haud improbabilis est conjectura Rosenmülleri verba corrupta esse suspicantis, quum "quæ proxime sequantur v. 23, et quæ statim subjiciatur comparatio cum ave laqueo capta, fere flagitent, ut bovem inter et avem secundo loco fera aliqua alia commemoretur, quæ pedicæ irrita a venatore occidatur." Stuart: "The last two verses [22 and 23] are, as they strike us, somewhat involved and apparently defective. V. 23 has three clauses, the first of which seems to belong to something which should precede, i. e., either to the last clause of v. 22, or to something dropped from the text. . . . That the text has in some way been disturbed, seems quite probable from its present *abnormal* condition."

† V. 22. Er folgte ihr nach mit einem Mal,
wie ein Stier, der zur Schlachtbank geht,
und wie ein Vogel sich beeilt in das Garn.

| KING JAMES' VERSION. | HEBREW TEXT. | | REVISED VERSION. |
|---|---|---|---|
| 24 Hearken unto me now therefore, O ye children, and attend to the words of my mouth. | וְעַתָּה בָנִים שִׁמְעוּ־לִי<br>וְהַקְשִׁיבוּ לְאִמְרֵי פִי׃ | 24 | Now then, children, hearken to me, 24<br>and attend to the words of my mouth. |
| 25 Let not thine heart decline to her ways, go not astray in her paths. | אַל־יֵשְׂטְ אֶל־דְּרָכֶיהָ לִבֶּךָ<br>אַל־תֵּתַע בִּנְתִיבוֹתֶיהָ׃ | כה | Let not thy heart turn aside to 25 her ways;<br>go not astray in her paths. |
| 26 For she hath cast down many wounded: yea, many strong *men* have been slain by her. | כִּי־רַבִּים חֲלָלִים הִפִּילָה<br>וַעֲצֻמִים כָּל־הֲרֻגֶיהָ׃ | 26 | For many has she cast down 26 wounded,<br>and numerous are all her slain. |
| 27 Her house *is* the way to hell, going down to the chambers of death. | דַּרְכֵי שְׁאוֹל בֵּיתָהּ<br>יֹרְדוֹת אֶל־חַדְרֵי־מָוֶת׃ | 27 | Ways to the underworld—is 27 her house,<br>going down to the chambers of death! |

V. 25. wander not into her paths

V. 23. For the fool is offended at reproof,
and knows not that he is acting for his life,
till an arrow cleaves his liver.

The significant and spirited irregularity of the received text, it may be presumed, will hardly be exchanged for the tame propriety of the emendation.

*That it is for his life** (ב de pretio et permutatione, Lex., B, 3), at the price of life; that life is the forfeit. הוּא *it, id ipsum*, with emphatic reference to the *action* just described; † not (as Hitzig ‡) with a *personal* reference to אויל.

V. 24. *Now then* (ועתה, Lex. ו, 4), a form of summing up, in conclusion. §

V. 26. *For many has she cast down wounded.* The object of the verb (רבים) has the emphatic position at the beginning of the sentence, and is followed by חללים as an attributive. There is no necessity, therefore, for the far less spirited construction: *For many are the wounded, whom she has cast down.* ||

Second member:—*And numerous are all her slain;* the only admissible construction, as given in nearly all of the modern versions. ¶ The words רבים and עצמים are used here as in Am. 5 : 12. *All her slain* is an emphatic form, in itself implying a large company. Bertheau: "*And strong ones are all her slain* (= all has she slain), of course only when they have allowed themselves to be enticed by her; and if these, how much more the feeble stripling." * But the words can by no construction yield this sense (which would require כֻּלָּם); and with this use of עצמים they can only mean: *all her slain are strong ones,* which certainly is not intended. †

V. 27. *Ways*, etc. ‡ The plural is intensive, implying that her house is the home and representative of every evil way; and all lead down to perdition.

V. 23. Denn der Thor ärgert sich über Verweis,
und merkt nicht, dass er's um sein Leben thut,
bis ein Pfeil seine Leber spaltet.

He assumes (v. 23, *a*) that כעכס is an error for פִּי כֻלָּם, and construes the latter as *inf. constr.* followed by אויל in the *genitive.*

* Ewald (Lehrb., § 217, *f*, 3, *a*): בנפשו *um sein Leben*, mit Lebensgefahr, Spr. 7 : 23.

† Maurer: Cum vitæ periculo *id* esse, fieri, i. e., nesciens hic agi suam vitam.

‡ *Dass er's um sein Leben thut.*

§ Bertheau: ועתה führt die abschliessende, durch das vorhergehende begründete Ermahnung ein.

|| C. B. Michaelis: Vel potius *multi* sunt *confossi*, quos *cadere fecit.* Quia hic adjectivum præcedit, ideo verbum substantivum subintelligitur, ut Ps. 32 : 10, ac adeo relativum אשר supplendum est, ut supra c. 3 : 13.

¶ Rosenmüller: Græcus Alexandrinus bene sic expressit: *καὶ ἀναρίθμητοί εἰσιν οὓς πεφόνευκεν, et innumerabiles sunt quos occidit.* Nam עצמים hic parallelum est voci רבים in priori hemistichio, denotatque *numero validos*, copiosos, ut Joel 1 : 6, Ps. 35 : 18, et sæpius. Dathe: *Nam multos confossos dejecit, et complures sunt quos occidit.* Schelling: *Et magna copia eorum, quos omnes interfecit.* Müntinghe: *Die Zahl der von ihr Ermordeten ist gross.* Umbreit: *In starker Anzahl alle, die von ihr getödtet.* Ewald: *Denn viel Erschlagene hat sie gefällt; und zahlreich sind alle, die sie gemordet.* Maurer: *Et copiosi* (sunt) *omnes interfecti ejus;* ingens est omnium ab ea interfectorum copia. Hitzig: *und zahlreich all' ihre Gemordeten.*

* *Und Starke sind alle ihre Erwürgten* = hat sie alle erwürgt, natürlich nur wenn sie sich von ihr verlocken liessen; wenn aber diese, um wie viel eher den schwachen Jüngling. So Stuart: "*Even the mighty are all her slain*, i. e., she slays all of them who go in unto her, but not all the mighty among men. The appeal is on this wise: 'If even the *mighty* are destroyed by her, how can the mere *youngling* expect to come off with impunity?'"

† Bertheau's conception of the sense is pointedly condemned by Hitzig: Falsch deuten Vulg. und die Aramäer עצמים als *Starke,* und hiernach Bertheau auch רבים durch *Mächtige* (dgg. 4 Mos. 32 : 1, Jes. 31 : 1, Ps. 35 : 10 ff.); vollkommen richtig übersetzen den Vers Schelling und Umbreit.

‡ Sept.: *Ὁδοὶ ᾅδου ὁ οἶκος αὐτῆς.* Vulg.: *Viæ inferi domus ejus.*

Quidam sic exponunt: viæ, quibus ejus domum itur, at inferos ducunt, sunt ipsissimæ orci viæ. Sed hoc potius dicunt verba, domum adulteræ esse viam quæ in orcum ducit, quod qui illam frequentant in suum interitum ruunt (Rosenmüller). Maurer: *Viæ orci domus ejus;* . . . ad orcum ducit domus ejus, se præcipitant in perniciem qui illam frequentant. Ewald: *Wege zur Hölle ist ihr Haus.* Umbreit: *Wege zur Unterwelt—ihr Haus.*

| KING JAMES' VERSION. | HEBREW TEXT. | | REVISED VERSION. | |
|---|---|---|---|---|
| CHAP. VIII. | CHAP. VIII. | | CHAP. VIII. | |
| DOTH not wisdom cry? and understanding put forth her voice? | הֲלֹא־חָכְמָה תִקְרָא<br>וּתְבוּנָה תִּתֵּן קוֹלָהּ׃ | א | DOES not wisdom call,<br>and understanding utter her voice? | 1 |
| 2 She standeth in the top of high places, by the way in the places of the paths. | בְּרֹאשׁ־מְרֹמִים עֲלֵי־דָרֶךְ<br>בֵּית נְתִיבוֹת נִצָּבָה׃ | 2 | At the head of the high places, by the way,<br>in the cross-ways, she takes her stand. | 2 |
| 3 She crieth at the gates, at the entry of the city, at the coming in at the doors. | לְיַד־שְׁעָרִים לְפִי־קָרֶת<br>מְבוֹא פְתָחִים תָּרֹנָּה׃ | 3 | By the gates, at the mouth of the city,<br>at the entering of the gateways, she cries aloud: | 3 |
| 4 Unto you, O men, I call; and my voice *is* to the sons of man. | אֲלֵיכֶם אִישִׁים אֶקְרָא<br>וְקוֹלִי אֶל־בְּנֵי אָדָם׃ | 4 | Unto you, O men, I call;<br>and my voice is to the sons of men. | 4 |
| 5 O ye simple, understand wisdom: and ye fools, be ye of an understanding heart. | הָבִינוּ פְתָאיִם עָרְמָה<br>וּכְסִילִים הָבִינוּ לֵב׃ | ה | Learn shrewdness, ye simple,<br>and fools, be wise in heart. | 5 |
| 6 Hear; for I will speak of excellent things; and the opening of my lips *shall be* right things. | שִׁמְעוּ כִּי־נְגִידִים אֲדַבֵּר<br>וּמִפְתַּח שְׂפָתַי מֵישָׁרִים׃ | ג 6 | Hear, for of noble things I speak;<br>and the opening of my lips is with right things. | 6 |
| 7 For my mouth shall speak truth; and wickedness *is* an abomination to my lips. | כִּי־אֱמֶת יֶהְגֶּה חִכִּי<br>וְתוֹעֲבַת שְׂפָתַי רֶשַׁע׃ | 7 | For my mouth shall utter truth;<br>and wickedness is the abomination of my lips. | 7 |

V. 6. of princely things

We are not justified in restricting this expression (*ways to the underworld*) to the risks of the death-penalty incurred in the house of the adulteress.* It comprehends all the fatal influences, which there lead on from crime to crime, and to the inevitable reward.

*Chambers of death*† (see Expl. Notes).

Ch. VIII.—V. 2. *Crossways* (בית נתיבות), lit. *house*, i. e., place, *of ways*. viz., where several ways meet.‡

*Takes her stand* (נִצָּבָה),§ said (as well as the kindred יצב) of one who takes a stand, or position, at some favorable point for a specific object; e. g., of Moses (Ex. 7 : 15, prop. *station thyself*, or *take thy stand*) to meet Pharaoh; 17 : 9; of the sister of Moses (Ex. 2 : 4, prop. *stationed herself*) to watch the fate of the infant child; of Goliath (1 Sam. 17 : 16, prop. *stationed himself*) for challenging to single combat.

* Stuart: "By the Mosaic law, the adulterer could be put to death. . . . Hence the propriety of holding up the terrors of death before the person inclined to commit the offense in question."

† Rosenmüller: *ad penetralia mortis*, i. e., inferni; ad intimos orci recessus. Bertheau: *Zu den Kammern*, den geheimnissvollen Räumen, 18 : 8, *des Todes*, 9 : 18, 5 : 5.

‡ Propr. *domus semitarum* (viarum), i. e., locus qui plures vias in se continet, ubi plures viæ concurrunt, compitum, bivium triviumve (Maurer). *Wo viele Stege;* am Orte (בית) von Stegen, das ist, an einem Orte, wo viele Wege zusammentreffen in der Stadt (Ewald).

§ Ewald: *Hat sie ihren Stand.*

V. 3. *At the mouth*, etc. The metaphor is a natural one, founded on no peculiar idiom or use of words in Hebrew, and should therefore be retained.* תרנה; see note on ch. 1 : 20.

V. 4. בני אדם, *plur.* (§108, 3, *a*) of בן אדם *a son of man*, one of the human race; Eng. idiom requires *sons of men.*

V. 5. *Learn*, etc. The verb means both *to perceive, to come to know*, and, *to have understanding, to be wise;* and the expression of it must be varied, as in other cases where we have not a word of sufficient comprehension. *Shrewdness:* see note on ch. 1 : 4.

In the second member, Geier and others take לב in the sense of *understanding*,† as in ch. 15 : 32, 19 : 8; where, however, it is connected with the verbal idea *to get, to obtain.* The word does not mean absolutely *understanding*, as something that can be *learned*, but rather the organ to which it is ascribed.

V. 6. *Noble things.*‡ Tyndale, Cranmer, and Bishops: *For*

* Ewald: *Wo die Stadt sich mündet.* Umbreit: *Wo die Stadt sich aufthut.*

† So De Wette and Umbreit: *Und, ihr Thoren, lernet Verstand.* Bertheau: *Und, ihr Thoren, lernet kennen Einsicht.* On the contrary, Ewald: *Und Thoren, fasst verständ'ges Herz!*

‡ Gesenius (Lex., 3): Plur. neut. *nobilia*, honesta, Prov. 8 : 6. Maurer: *Nam generosa* (eximia, egregia) *loquor.* De Wette: *Denn Edles red' ich.* Ewald: *Denn ich rede Fürstliches.* Second

| KING JAMES' VERSION. | HEBREW TEXT. | | REVISED VERSION. | |
|---|---|---|---|---|
| 8 All the words of my mouth *are* in righteousness; *there is* nothing froward or perverse in them. | בְּצֶדֶק כָּל־אִמְרֵי־פִי<br>אֵין בָּהֶם נִפְתָּל וְעִקֵּשׁ׃ | 8 | In righteousness are all the words of my mouth;<br>there is nothing crooked and perverse in them. | 8 |
| 9 They *are* all plain to him that understandeth, and right to them that find knowledge. | כֻּלָּם נְכֹחִים לַמֵּבִין<br>וִישָׁרִים לְמֹצְאֵי דָעַת׃ | 9 | They are all plain to him that has understanding,<br>and straight to them that find knowledge. | 9 |
| 10 Receive my instruction, and not silver; and knowledge rather than choice gold. | קְחוּ־מוּסָרִי וְאַל־כָּסֶף<br>וְדַעַת מֵחָרוּץ נִבְחָר׃ | י | Take my instruction, and not silver;<br>and knowledge rather than choice gold. | 10 |
| 11 For wisdom *is* better than rubies; and all the things that may be desired are not to be compared to it. | כִּי־טוֹבָה חָכְמָה מִפְּנִינִים<br>וְכָל־חֲפָצִים לֹא יִשְׁווּ־בָהּ׃ | 11 | For wisdom is better than pearls;<br>and all objects of delight will not compare with it. | 11 |
| 12 I wisdom dwell with prudence, and find out knowledge of witty inventions. | אֲנִי חָכְמָה שָׁכַנְתִּי עָרְמָה<br>וְדַעַת מְזִמּוֹת אֶמְצָא׃ | 12 | I, wisdom, dwell in prudence,<br>and find out the knowledge of wise counsels. | 12 |

V. 9. are all right — Ib. and just — V. 11. all precious things

*I will speak of great matters.** The writer refers, evidently, to the dignity and nobleness of what is said. Genevan: *For I will speak of excellent things;* followed in the Common Version.

V. 9. *Plain* (נכחים); i. e., direct, straight forward, opposed to *crooked* in the previous verse. Gesenius (Lex.), "*right, just;*" but the literal image should be preserved in both members (second member:—*straight*), to correspond with the preceding verse.†

V. 11. *Pearls;* see note on ch. 3 : 15.

V. 12. *Prudence* (ערמה); see note on ch. 1 : 4. *Dwell in prudence* (inhabit prudence),‡ make her my abode. This is commonly understood to mean the most intimate familiarity and companionship.§ But, as ערמה is here the proper use of sagacity in the practical concerns of life (see note on ch. 1 : 4), the meaning is rather: I, wisdom, make my abode in this practical virtue, and am exhibited and represented in it. Accordingly, WISDOM here claims to be the animating spirit, from which "all good counsels and just works proceed;" and the parallel member favors this view.

The idea of *possession, control, use* (C. B. Michaelis,* Rosenmüller), as of one's own habitation, and hence of *property* ("*belongs to me, is mine,*" Bertheau†), is not the natural import of the expression;‡ nor is it a happy conception, to say the least, of the supposed relation between wisdom and prudence. The idea of *protection* (Umbreit§) is still less admissible.

Second member:—מזמות, in its favorable sense, wise or prudent counsels.‖ *Find out the knowledge of*, is not simply = *know* (Hitzig),¶ but implies effort of thought and reflection.

---

member:—מישרים, Gesenius (Thes. 1, a): *Quod rectum, jus fasque est;* Prov. 1 : 3, 8 : 6, cet. Here, adverbial accus.

* Vulgate: *De rebus magnis.*

† Ewald:

*Sie alle klar sind dem Verständigen,*
*und grade denen, welche Wissen fanden.*

‡ Rödiger (Thes. fasc. poster., p. 1408): *Ego sapientia . . . . habito in prudentia,* tota ego in ea versor, peculiaris mihi est.

§ So Ewald (followed by Hitzig) translates, or rather paraphrases: *Ich, die Weisheit, bin vertraut mit Klugheit.* To this, it is well objected (by Bertheau), that *to dwell in, to inhabit*, is not the same as *to dwell with, to dwell together* (aber bewohnen ist nicht zusammenwohnen); and that wisdom, which it is the object of the passage to exalt, is not to be thus put on a level with prudence (und nicht ist es passend, dass, dieser Auffassung gemäss, die so hoch gestellte Weisheit auf einer Linie mit der Klugheit erscheint).

---

* *Habitare* igitur hic valet *tenere et usurpare* aliquid tanquam suum; quomodo 1 Tim. 6 : 16, *lucem habitans* dicitur, ita ut *habitans* coordinetur præcedenti *qui solus habet.*

† Vielmehr setzt dieses, dass die Weisheit die Klugheit bewohnt, ihre freie Verfügung über die Klugheit wie über ein ihr zugehörendes Haus voraus, und der bildliche Ausdruck bedeutet: *sie gehört mir, ist mein Eigenthum.*

‡ The proof-passage referred to (1 Tim. 6 : 16) is not in point. The assumption, that *οἰκῶν* is simply parallel in meaning with *μόνος ἔχων*, can not be admitted.

§ Die Klugheit ist die schützende Wohnung der Weisheit im Leben; letztere braucht die erstere nur als Verwahrungsmittel gegen den Trug des Lebens.

‖ Cocceius, Lex.: *Et cognitionem dexterarum cogitationum invenio.* Fürst, Hdwbch.: Erkenntniss sinniger Rathschläge. Hitzig: *Verständige Ueberlegungen.* Bertheau: *Und die Erkenntniss sinniger Rathschläge erfasse ich.* Theodotion: *Καὶ γνῶσιν διαβουλιῶν εὑρήσω.*

¶ מצא דעת, v. 9 (vgl. Hiob 32 : 13), steht für ידע selbst, und so hier die Formel statt des einfachen וְאֵדַע מזמות = *und ich verstehe mich auf* מזמות (vgl. zu 1 : 4).

| KING JAMES' VERSION. | HEBREW TEXT. | REVISED VERSION. |
|---|---|---|
| 13 The fear of the LORD *is* to hate evil: pride, and arrogancy, and the evil way, and the froward mouth, do I hate. | 13 יִרְאַת יְהוָה שְׂנֹאת רָע<br>גֵּאָה וְגָאוֹן ׀ וְדֶרֶךְ רָע<br>וּפִי תַהְפֻּכוֹת שָׂנֵאתִי׃ | The fear of Jehovah is to hate evil; 13<br>pride, and haughtiness, and an evil way,<br>and a perverse mouth, do I hate. |
| 14 Counsel *is* mine, and sound wisdom: I *am* understanding; I have strength. | 14 לִי־עֵצָה וְתוּשִׁיָּה<br>אֲנִי בִינָה לִי גְבוּרָה׃ | Counsel is mine, and true wisdom; 14<br>I am understanding; strength is mine. |
| 15 By me kings reign, and princes decree justice. | טו בִּי מְלָכִים יִמְלֹכוּ<br>וְרֹזְנִים יְחֹקְקוּ צֶדֶק׃ | By me kings reign, 15<br>and princes decree justice. |
| 16 By me princes rule, and nobles, *even* all the judges of the earth. | 16 בִּי שָׂרִים יָשֹׂרוּ<br>וּנְדִיבִים כָּל־שֹׁפְטֵי אָרֶץ׃ | By me princes rule, 16<br>and nobles, all the judges of the earth. |
| 17 I love them that love me; and those that seek me early shall find me. | 17 אֲנִי אֹהֲבַיה אֵהָב<br>וּמְשַׁחֲרַי יִמְצָאֻנְנִי׃ | Them that love me I love; 17<br>and they that early seek me shall find me. |
| 18 Riches and honour *are* with me; *yea*, durable riches and righteousness. | 18 עֹשֶׁר־וְכָבוֹד אִתִּי<br>הוֹן עָתֵק וּצְדָקָה׃ | Wealth and honor are with me; 18<br>enduring riches and righteousness. |

V. 13. בנ״א תחפכת   V. 17. אהבי ק׳

V. 17. that love her (V. R.)

V. 13. *The fear of Jehovah*, etc., is the usual construction,* and the only natural one. It is fully justified, against such objections as Bertheau's, by the import of the verse as a whole, viz., that to wisdom belongs this fear of Jehovah.†

VV. 14–16 (see Expl. Notes). תושיה, *true wisdom*, what is really and truly such, in distinction from what often passes for it among men.

In the second member, the expression is varied with happy effect (*I am*, etc., alternating with *mine is*), giving emphasis as well as variety to the form.‡ There is, therefore, no occasion for construing אני as a *dat.* (with ל implied), suggested by Bertheau as a possible alternative.§

VV. 15, 16. The idea is: Without these qualities (which are mine, and imparted by me, v. 14), there can be no government, no administration of justice. Rightful authority, which alone is government in distinction from usurpation and oppression, is such as is claimed and exercised in obedience to her dictates.

The reading צדק (for ארץ, end of v. 16) in many MSS. and some Edd. (so Chald., Syr., Vulg.,* Gr. Ven.), adopted by Norzi as the reading of the text, has too much the appearance of a gloss, or of a repetition from the end of v. 15. The limitation, *all righteous judges*, is out of place here; on the contrary, *all the judges of the earth* is in harmony with the previous clauses, and the statement is to be understood in the same sense.

V. 17. *That love me* (the *Qeri*), as in many MSS. and Edd.,† the Sept.,‡ Chald., Syr., Vulg.§ The *Chethibh* (margin) is to be referred to wisdom herself (as an object already before the mind of the reader), not to יראת (v. 13), as supposed by Hitzig.

V. 18. Of the ἁπαξ. λεγ. עתק, the most reliable as well as appropriate sense is, *long continuing, enduring.*‖ *And righteousness* (see Expl. notes).

* C. B. Michaelis: *Timor Domini* . . . . est *odisse malum.* Ewald: *Jahve fürchten—das ist Böses hassen.* Maurer: *Timor Jovæ* est *odisse malum.* Hitzig: *Die Furcht Jahve's ist das Böse hassen.*

† Maurer: Quibus ostendit, timoris Jovæ se magistram esse.

‡ So Bertheau: Mit לִי *mir gehört*, wechselt אני *ich bin Einsicht.* Stuart's construction (*as for me, my might is understanding*) is altogether inadmissible, the use of לִי, in this clause, being determined by the other two clauses in immediate connection with it. Such a statement, moreover, is out of place here. The Jewish accentuation gives, without doubt, the true relation of the words.

§ Doch könnte man auch vor dem Pronom. אני das ל aus *a* ergänzen; in welchem Falle, eben weil ל nicht wiederholt ist, אני stehen muss in der Bedeutung von לִי.

* Sept., on the contrary, *κρατοῦσι γῆς.*

† De Rossi: In textu אהבי multi codices et editiones. Inter meos eminent 304, et 414 hispanici, et Hillelianus 413.

‡ *Ἐγὼ τοὺς ἐμὲ φιλοῦντας ἀγαπῶ.*

§ *Ego diligentes me diligo.*

‖ Sym. and Theod., *παλαιὸς*; so the Syriac. Bertheau: Das Wort bedeutet *alt*, das soll sein *gediegen* oder *dauernd.* Rosenmüller: הון עתק proprie sunt *opes vetustæ*, . . . a longo congestæ, hinc durabiles et solidæ, quæ non cito dispererunt. Aben-Ezra עתק exponit עובי וחוזק *densum et robustum*, quia quæ longius durant robusta sunt. Gesenius (Thes. II., p. 1085): Vulg. *opes*

| KING JAMES' VERSION. | HEBREW TEXT. | | REVISED VERSION. |
|---|---|---|---|
| 19 My fruit *is* better than gold, yea, than fine gold; and my revenue than choice silver. | טוֹב פִּרְיִי מֵחָרוּץ וּמִפָּז<br>וּתְבוּאָתִי מִכֶּסֶף נִבְחָר׃ | 19 | My fruit is better than gold, 19<br>yea than refined gold;<br>and my increase than choice<br>silver. |
| 20 I lead in the way of righteousness, in the midst of the paths of judgment: | בְּאֹרַח צְדָקָה אֲהַלֵּךְ<br>בְּתוֹךְ נְתִיבוֹת מִשְׁפָּט׃ | כ | I walk in the way of righteous- 20<br>ness,<br>within the paths of rectitude; |
| 21 That I may cause those that love me to inherit substance; and I will fill their treasures. | לְהַנְחִיל אֹהֲבַי יֵשׁ<br>וְאֹצְרֹתֵיהֶם אֲמַלֵּא׃ | 21 | to make those who love me 21<br>inherit substance,<br>and their storehouses I will fill. |
| 22 The LORD possessed me in the beginning of his way, before his works of old. | יְהוָֹה קָנָנִי רֵאשִׁית דַּרְכּוֹ<br>קֶדֶם מִפְעָלָיו מֵאָז׃ | 22 | Jehovah possessed me in the 22<br>beginning of his way,<br>before his works of old. |

V. 21. There is to bestow on those who love me

V. 22. possessed himself of me | *Or*, established me the beginning of his way (*or*, in the beginning of his way). *Others:* created me.

V. 19. חרוץ; see note on ch. 3 : 14. פז *refined gold*, gold in its purest state.

V. 20. "I lead" (Common Version) is not a recognized use of the Piël form in this verb.

V. 21. יש, *substance*,* as in the Sept. and Vulg.;† so many of the earlier and later Jewish and Christian hebraists.‡

The construction attributed to Jarchi (though his expression does not make this necessary),* has been adopted by many,† viz. *There is to bestow on those who love me;* = this is not wanting,‡ q. d., it is within my power. Michaelis' objection to this construction (footnote ‡, first col.) is not obviated by reference to 1 Sam. 21 : 5 (Gesenius, Thes. II., p. 637). Moreover, the connection of the passage (vv. 18–21) is destroyed; for the connecting thought§ between vv. 20, 21 and the previous context (giving unity to the whole) is lost, and these two verses stand isolated, as well from each other, as from those which precede.

*Inherit* (not simply *possess*), as something transmitted and conveyed by the good will of another.

V. 22. *Possessed*, etc., a usage naturally arising from the ordinary meaning of קנה (as shown in the analogous case of *κτάομαι*, and in the derivative מקנה), and recognized by the best authorities.‖ This is clearly the use of the word in Is. 1 : 3, *the*

---

*superbæ.* pr. vetustæ, i. e., intactæ et illibatæ. Lee (Heb. Lex.): הון עתק may signify *permanent, durable wealth.*

* As expressed by Gesenius (though not his own latest view; see footnote †, 2nd col.), Thes. II., p. 637: Pr. *substantiam, essentiam* alicujus; vel, quod præstaret, *quod* alicui *præsto est, id quod habet*, אֲשֶׁר יֵשׁ לוֹ. LXX.: *Ὕπαρξις.* Gr. Venet.: *Οὐσία.* Aben Esra: *Est* כנור *pro possessione perpetua acquisita in hereditatem æternam.* Also in his Hdwbch. (Dietrich's Ausg., 1857): Eig. Subst. *Sein, Dasein, Vorhandensein*, daher was vorhanden ist, *οὐσία*, Vermögen (vergl. עֲתִידוֹת), *Schätze.* So wahrscheinlich Spr. 8 : 21, *meinen Freunden Schätze zu verleihen.*

† Sept.: *Ἵνα μερίσω τοῖς ἐμὲ ἀγαπῶσιν ὕπαρξιν.* Vulg.: *Ut ditem diligentes me.*

‡ So, e. g., Ewald translates: *Dass ich meinen Freunden erbe Habe.*

C. B. Michaelis: יש verti posset, *est* mihi, ut sensus foret: Suppetit mihi quod amatoribus meis pro hereditate impertiar. Verum sic infinitivo præponi debuisset. Rectius ergo LXX. *ὕπαρξιν*, indeque Ar. *possessionem æternam*, quomodo et Aben Ezra exposuit, q. d., *bonum quod revera est* et constat, *bonum verum ac durabile.*

Rosenmüller: Præstat יש hic pro nomine capere, ut Græcus Alexandrinus, qui *ὕπαρξιν* vertit.... Sic et Aben-Esra exponit. Dathe: *Ut rem mei amantibus tradam possidendam.* Umbreit: יש ist *οὐσία*, wie es Vers. Venet. wörtlich giebt. Bertheau: יש muss Subst. sein, in ähnlicher Bedeutung wie תושיה, also etwa *wirkliches dauerndes Gut* bedeuten, Septuag. *ὕπαρξις.* De Wette: *Um denen, die mich lieben, Habe zu verleihen.*

Fürst (Hdwbch.): *Wesentliches*, d. h. *dauerndes Gut*, Spr. 8 : 21, wie bereits Ibn Esra übersetzt, und LXX. *ὕπαρξις*, gr. Ven. *οὐσία* haben.

* לְהַנְחִיל אֹהֲבַי יֵשׁ : יש אתי נחלה רבה

† Gesenius, Thes. II., p. 637 (formerly, as in footnote *, first col.): *Est* mihi quod *impertiar diligentibus me.*

To the objections to this construction he replies (*ibidem*): Sunt qui opponunt huic rationi, יש sic infinitivo præponendum fuisse, et deesse accusativum rei post הנחיל; sed illud refellitur loco 1 Sam. 21 : 5 לֶחֶם קֹדֶשׁ יֵשׁ, hoc verbis Deut. 32 : 8, ubi accusativus rei itidem omissus est.

‡ Hitzig: Erkläre mit Jarchi und Winer im WB.: *es ist etwas da, meinen Freunden es in Besitz zu geben.*

§ The true connection is well stated by Bertheau: As I walk in the way of righteousness, so must they who love me; but the righteous shall be prospered, and hence the case stands thus *I walk in the way of righteousness, that I may make*, etc., such being the necessary consequence. To the same effect Ewald.

‖ Gesenius (Thes. III., p. 1221): Qui emit rem, eam possidet inde (4) *possedit.* Winer (Simonis Lex.): 1. *acquisivit, comparavit sibi;* 2. *possedit.* Fürst (Heb. Concord.): *Emere, acquirere, comparare, possidĕre*, et *possidēre.*

So the earlier Christian hebraists (after their Jewish teachers). E. g., Pagnino (Thes. ling. sanct.): *Dominus* קנני *possedit me initium* (principium) *viæ ejus* (vel *initio viæ suæ;* Mercerus); and in his version: *Dominus possedit me principium viæ suæ.* Munster (*Dictionarium Heb.*, 1523): *Possedit, procuravit, emit,*

| KING JAMES' VERSION. | HEBREW TEXT. | | REVISED VERSION. | |
|---|---|---|---|---|
| 23 I was set up from everlasting, from the beginning, or ever the earth was. | מֵעוֹלָם נִסַּכְתִּי מֵרֹאשׁ<br>מִקַּדְמֵי־אָרֶץ׃ | 23 | From everlasting was I anointed, from the beginning,<br>from times before the earth. | 23 |

*ox knows his owner;* where the meaning is not (as asserted by Maurer) *knows his buyer,** as is evident from the nature of the case, and from the parallelism with בְּעָלָיו.

The marginal rendering, *possessed himself of me* (*comparavit sibi*),† gives by far the most common signification of the verb in the actual usage of the Heb. Scriptures, viz., *to get, to obtain*, in whatever manner. But the evidence of its appropriateness here does not seem to me sufficient to justify setting aside from the text the old vernacular rendering, found in all the earlier Eng. versions, and retained in the Common Version.

According to Gesenius and others, the word here means *created*, or *prepared.*‡ But the signification *to establish* (regarded by Gesenius as the primary one) would be more apposite. The sense would then be the same as in the parallel passage, Job 28 : 27, *he established it* (הֱכִינָהּ), viz., as the perpetual and unchanging law, both for the material and the moral world.

*In the beginning*, etc., the *adverbial accus.* (§ 118, 2, *a*), common in Hebrew. There is, therefore, no ground for the assertion : "To supply בְּ before רֵאשִׁית, and then translate *in the beginning*, is manifestly a departure from the text" (Stuart). Vulg.: *In initio viarum suarum.* So the Chald. and Syr.

Second member:—מֵאָז, *of old*, stands connected with מִפְעָלָיו (as by the accentuation) as an adverbial qualification (*works of old*), with the effect of an adjective.

V. 23. מֵאָז (end of v. 22) and מֵעוֹלָם stand in the same relation to each other in Ps. 93 : 2.

*Was I anointed*,§ a ceremony of consecration to some special service.

Gussett's objections to this use of נָסַךְ are unsatisfactory. Such a transfer as this (the remote object construed as the direct one, and the latter as the instrument or medium) is a common and natural phenomenon of language;* as, *to sprinkle water upon one*, and *to sprinkle one* (or, *to be sprinkled*) *with water*. In place of this happy and natural figure of speech, so facile in conception, and so common in language, is proposed the idea of *casting, founding* (a molten image), to express *forming, bringing into being*. So in Ps. 2 : 6, *I have formed my king on Zion, my holy hill;*† and here, *from everlasting was I formed* (prop. cast in a mould).

The objection made by Lengerke and others, that, with this sense of the verb, Ps. 2 : 6 can not be applied to David, because he was not anointed on Zion, is not valid; for the words "on Zion" do not denote the place of anointing, but the seat of the sovereignty to which it was the consecrating symbol. The anointing might be done where it was most convenient; but, wherever performed, its design and purport was to establish this divine sovereignty on Zion, as its earthly, visible seat.‡

Second member:—קַדְמֵי, plur. intensive of קֶדֶם (*id quod ante est*).§ Gesenius, and some others:‖ *From the first beginnings of*

*acquisivit;* (Proverbia Salomonis, 1524): *Dominus possedit me initium viæ suæ;* (Biblia Heb., 1546): *Dominus possedit me in initio viæ suæ.* Mercier (Pagnini Thes.): Utrumque significat hoc verbum, ut *κτᾶσθαι* Græcis, et *parare*, seu *comparare* labore, seu industria, vel pretio, et *in potestate sua habere*, quod et absolute dicimus *habere*.

So C. B. Michaelis: Recte Vulg. *possedit me*, vel *habuit me.* Le Clerc: *Jehova possedit me, initio viæ suæ.* Schultens: Tanquam peculium eximie carum vel *acquirere* vel *possidere.* Castellio: *Me Jova principio instituti habuit.* Dathe: *Me Jova possedit in prima mundi creatione.*

* Heb. u. chald. Hdwbch.: Part. *Käufer* Jes. 24 : 2, auch an Stellen wie Jes. 1 : 3.

† *Ἐκτήσατό με*, in the versions of Aquila, Symmachus, and Theodotion.

‡ Sept.: *Ἔκτισέ με.* So the Chald. and Syr.

Gesenius (Thes.): *Jova creavit me* sapientiam ut *primitias operum ejus.* Müntinghe: *Jehova schuf mich, das Erste seiner Werke.* Rosenmüller: *Jova me paravit* (formavit) *principium viæ suæ*, me omnium primam creavit. Ewald: *Jahve schuf mich als der Schöpfung Erstes.* Umbreit: *Jahve schuf mich, als den Anfang seines Weges.* Bertheau: *Schuf mich.* Maurer: *Jova creavit me primitias actionis suæ*, i. e., omnium primum me creavit. De Wette: *Jehova bereitete mich als den Anfang seines Handelns.* Hitzig: *Jahve erschuf mich als Erstling seines Thuns.*

§ As this verb is translated by Symmachus, Ps. 2 : 6, *κἀγὼ ἔχρισα τὸν βασιλέα μου.* So Gesenius (Thes. and Lex.). Winer (Simonis Lex.): *Perfudit oleo, unxit.* C. B. Michaelis: *Perfusa*, h. e., *uncta sum* in reginam ac principem, etc. Rosenmüller: *Inde ab æterno inuncta sum.* De Wette: *Von Alters her ward ich gesalbt.* Ewald: *Von Ur her ward ich gesalbt; . . .* zu ihrem ewigen Amte, als Ordnerin der Welt gesalbt oder eingeweiht. Umbreit: *Ward ich gesalbt.* Bertheau: *Von Alters her bin ich gesalbt*, zu meinem hohen königlichen Berufe. Maurer (Handwörterbuch): Niph. *gesalbt werden*, die Weisheit zu ihrem königlichen Berufe. So the earlier Christian hebraists. E. g., Mercier (Pagnini Thes.): Metaph. pro *constituere, ordinare, creare autorare, inaugurare*, quod id oleo fuso fieret. Cocceius (Lex.): *A seculo uncta sum*, h. e., constituta et declarata sum domina omnium. Fürst (Hdwbch.): *To consecrate, to install*, with the offering of a libation (נֶסֶךְ); übertr. *weihen, einsetzen*, unter Darbringung von נֶסֶךְ Ps. 2 : 6.

* Virgil, Æn. III. 625: Sanieque exspersa natarent limina.

† Lengerke: *Und Ich doch habe gebildet meinen König auf Zion. . . .* נסכתי erklärt man gemeinhin: *Ich habe gesalbt;* was dann wenigstens von David nicht gelten könnte, da dieser nicht auf Zion, sondern zu Bätlechem and Hebron gesalbt ist. So Hengstenberg (Kommentar, Ps. 2 : 6): *Und ich habe meinen König gebildet auf Zion.*

‡ Dr. Alexander's objection (The Psalms, Ps. 2 : 6) is obviated by the common use of the word ZION for the Messiah's universal kingdom, with reference always, at least in the Heb. Scriptures, to the local seat of this sovereignty under the Old Testament dispensation.

§ Schultens: In Hebræo est, *ab anterioritatibus terræ.* C. B. Michaelis: *A primordiis*, vel potius *ab anticipationibus terræ* h. e., inde ab eo quod terræ creationem prævertit. Dathe: *Ante ortum terræ.*

‖ Gesenius (Lex.): קַדְמֵי *primordia.* Ewald: *Von der Erde Uranfängen.* Umbreit: *Von der Erde Anfangszeiten.*

| KING JAMES' VERSION. | HEBREW TEXT. | | REVISED VERSION. |
|---|---|---|---|
| 24 When *there were* no depths, I was brought forth; when *there were* no fountains abounding with water. | בְּאֵין־תְּהֹמוֹת חוֹלָלְתִּי<br>בְּאֵין מַעְיָנוֹת נִכְבַּדֵּי־מָיִם׃ | 24 | When there were no deeps, I was brought forth; 24<br>when there were no fountains abounding in water. |
| 25 Before the mountains were settled, before the hills was I brought forth: | בְּטֶרֶם הָרִים הָטְבָּעוּ<br>לִפְנֵי גְבָעוֹת חוֹלָלְתִּי׃ | כה | Ere yet the mountains were sunken; 25<br>before the hills was I brought forth. |
| 26 While as yet he had not made the earth, nor the fields, nor the highest part of the dust of the world. | עַד־לֹא עָשָׂה אֶרֶץ וְחוּצוֹת<br>וְרֹאשׁ עַפְרוֹת תֵּבֵל׃ | 26 | While yet he had not made the earth nor the fields, 26<br>nor the first clods of the habitable world. |
| 27 When he prepared the heavens, I *was* there: when he set a compass upon the face of the depth: | בַּהֲכִינוֹ שָׁמַיִם שָׁם אָנִי<br>בְּחֻקוֹ חוּג עַל־פְּנֵי תְהוֹם׃ | 27 | When he founded the heavens, I was there; 27<br>when he traced a circle on the face of the deep. |
| 28 When he established the clouds above: when he strengthened the fountains of the deep: | בְּאַמְּצוֹ שְׁחָקִים מִמָּעַל<br>בַּעֲזוֹז עִינוֹת תְּהוֹם׃ | 28 | When he established the clouds above, 28<br>when the fountains of the deep became strong. |
| | V. 24. בנ"א חב׳ בפתח | | |

V. 26. the mass of clods

*the earth* (Stuart: *From the earliest period of the earth*); but this does not express the true force of the original word.

V. 24, second member. The form נכבדי is strictly in *apposition* with מעינות;* and, as suggested by Bertheau,† it takes the more naturally the masc. gender, as there is also a plural form, מעינים.

V. 25. *Were sunken.* The same word (הטבעו) is applied in Job 38 : 6, to the foundations of the earth. The meaning is: *were sunken*, till they rested firmly in the depths of the earth,‡ or on the bottom of the abyss. The same poetic conception is found in Jonah 2 : 6; properly, *I went down to the bases of the mountains.*

V. 26. *Fields*, etc. See the note on Job 5 : 10.

Second member:—Lit. *head* (i. e. first) *of the clods.* Bertheau,§ and others, as in the margin; but less pertinently in this connection. (עַד, Gesenius, Lex., C, 1.)

The word תבל is a poetic designation of the earth, expressive of its fertility or productive power, hence = *habitable earth*, ἡ οἰκουμένη.

V. 27, second member; compare Is. 40 : 22, and Job 26 : 10, where the expression is drawn, as it is here, from the apparent figure of the earth, and of the vault of heaven seeming to rest upon it.

V. 28. Gesenius (Thes. and Lex.): "*When the fountains of the deep waxed strong*; i. e., flowed with violence."* Hitzig paraphrases: "*When the fountains of the deep rushed wildly on*;" as also De Wette: "*And the fountains of the deep broke forth with violence.*"†

*Fountains of the deep*; refering to the outlets of the abyss of waters, through which it breaks forth to the earth's surface, forming streams and rivers. An instructive allusion to this is found in Ezek. 31 : 4; (Common Version): *The deep*‡ (תהום) *set him up on high with her rivers running about his plants, and sent out her little rivers unto all the trees of the field.* So in v. 15 it is said: *I covered the deep for him* (for his wickedness), *and I restrained the floods thereof, and the great waters were stayed*, etc. There is the same allusion in Gen. 49 : 25, *blessings of the deep that lieth under*; and in Deut. 33 : 13, *blessed of the Lord be his land, for the precious things of heaven, for the dew, and for the deep that coucheth beneath.* Compare also Gen. 7 : 11, and 8 : 2.

*Became strong*; pouring forth, in measureless abundance, the waters that fill the channels of mighty rivers.

By *fountains*, in this passage, some understand those from which the deep itself was originally poured forth.§ (Compare

* Hitzig: Daher die Apposition (*als keine Quellen waren, die befrachtet mit Wasser*).

† *Als noch nicht waren die Quellen, die wasserschwēren*; neben מעינות auch das Masc. מעינים, Ps. 104 : 10, wesshalb das Masc. des Adject. נכבדי um so weniger auffällt. So Rosenmüller: Participium masculinum (cum Dagesch euphonico in ד) refert se ad formam nominis masculinum מעינים, Ps. 104 : 10.

‡ Bertheau: *Ehe noch die Berge hineingesenkt waren* in der Erde Tiefen, Job 38 : 6.

§ *Und die Summe* (ראש, Ps. 139 : 17) oder die Masse *der Staubschollen des Erdkreises.*

* *Quum fontes maris invalescerent*, h. e., vehementer æstuarent. Winer (Simonis Lex.): *Cum valerent* (h. e., magna cum vi prorumperent) *fontes maris.*

† *Da die Quellen der Fluth anstürmten wild.* De Wette: *Und gewaltig hervorbrachen die Quellen der Tiefe.*

‡ As rightly understood by Rosenmüller (and Hitzig): תהום de laticibus subterraneis fontibusque, qui plantas alunt, dicitur et Gen. 49 : 25; Deut. 8 : 7, 33 : 13.

§ C. B. Michaelis (and Rosenmüller): *Fontes abyssi*, per quos aquæ Oceani ex terræ utero eruperunt et auctæ sunt, Gen 7 : 11 Cf. supra v. 24.

| KING JAMES' VERSION. | HEBREW TEXT. | | REVISED VERSION. | |
|---|---|---|---|---|
| 29 When he gave to the sea his decree, that the waters should not pass his commandment: when he appointed the foundations of the earth: | בְּשׂוּמוֹ לַיָּם ׀ חֻקּוֹ<br>וּמַיִם לֹא יַעַבְרוּ־פִיו<br>בְּחוּקוֹ מוֹסְדֵי אָרֶץ׃ | 29 | When he gave to the sea its bound,<br>that the waters should not pass his command;<br>when he appointed the foundations of the earth. | 29 |
| 30 Then I was by him, *as* one brought up *with him:* and I was daily *his* delight, rejoicing always before him; | וָאֶהְיֶה אֶצְלוֹ אָמוֹן<br>וָאֶהְיֶה שַׁעֲשֻׁעִים יוֹם ׀ יוֹם<br>מְשַׂחֶקֶת לְפָנָיו בְּכָל־עֵת׃ | ל | And I was one brought up at his side,<br>and was day by day a delight,<br>sporting always before him; | 30 |

V. 30. Then was I by him, an architect

note on Job 38 : 8.) But the above quotations make it clear, that these are not meant by *fountains of the deep;* nor is such an origin ascribed to the primeval ocean.

It is thought by others, with still less probability, that the writer refers to the mass of waters collected in the clouds above; and that by "*strong*" (or, "*firm*") is meant (as in Job 26 : 8) that "*the cloud is not rent under them.*" * But such a poetic use of חזוק (though possible, indeed) is arbitrarily assumed here, not only without support in usage, but against the clear and invariable use of the word, in numerous other passages. Moreover, "*became strong*" (or, "*firm*") is not properly predicated of *fountains*, in the sense of being restrained, hindered from pouring forth. Such a predicate belongs to the barrier or obstruction, by which the water is restrained.

V. 29. *Appointed*, etc., i. e., determined their extent and position; compare Job 38 : 4, 5.

V. 30. (ואהיה). The connection begins with the perfect (קנני, v. 22), implied also in the subsequent clauses, and is here continued with the imperfect and Vav consec.

*One brought up*, etc. Compare the use of the verbal root in Esth. 2 : 7, and 2 Kings 10 : 1, and of the passive part. in Lam. 4 : 5, to which this nominal form corresponds in its original consonant elements (like צָפוֹן).† This, Hitzig allows, must be conceded, if שעשועים is construed in the usual manner.‡ Gesenius' strongest objection * is obviated by the construction here given to the verb.

The Septuagint, taking אמון as = אָמָן (Cant. 7 : 1), renders it by *ἁρμόζουσα.*† So Gesenius (Thes. and Lex.), Dathe,‡ and most of the recent critics.§ But the common and familiar use of the root, and of this consonant form, gives a sense far more in harmony with the rest of the verse, as often pointed out,‖ and conceded by Gesenius.¶

Second member:—שעשועים, plur. intensive (like the Lat. *deliciæ*). Its true import and use are shown by Rödiger (Thes. fasc. poster., p. 1485).** The sense assumed by Bertheau †† is altogether unsuited to the word, in every other passage where it occurs (viz., Ps. 119 : 24, 77, 92, 143. 174; Jer. 31 : 20; Is. 5 : 7). The reference is made obvious by the words *before him*, in the next member.

* Ewald: *Als der Fluthen Quellen wurden fest.* . . . . Die *Quellen der Fluth* könnten die des Meeres auf der Erde sein, allein davon ist kaum erst zu sagen, dass sie fest wurden; wunderbar ist nur, dass die Quellen der obern Wasserfluth im lichten Himmel fest bleiben mit den Wolken, und so ist auch nach dem ersten Gliede bei חזוק an das himmlische Meer zu denken. Vergl. Ijob 26 : 8.

† So in the version of Aquila: *τιθηνουμένη.* Pagnino (Thes. ling. sanct.): *Et fui apud eum* אמן *nutritus* (sive *educatus*). Le Clerc: Aquilam bene vertisse ostendunt sequentia verba, quibus sapientia sub imagine alumni, quo delectabatur Deus, describitur. Schultens: Palmam tamen defero *alumno*, quod subnexa illuc trahat series. C. B. Michaelis: Sapientia se sistit ut *alumnum*, sive *filium ἐγκόλπιον* Joh. 1 : 18, adeoque Dei Patris delicium. Cocceius (Annott.): *Et eram filius in sinu gestatus apud ipsum.* Rosenmüller: Et id quidem [de infante, qui gestatur sive nutritur] omnium optime huc quadrat, ob epitheta, quæ proxime sequuntur, *deliciarum* et *ludentis*, quæ sunt puerorum. Müntinghe: *Da war ich schon bei ihm, sein liebes Pflegekind.* Schelling: *Parvulus tenerrime habitus.*

‡ Die Wurzel אמן konnte an שעשע denken lassen (vergl. Jes. 60 : 4, mit 66 : 12; und schon LXX. and Syr. fassen die Aussage ואהיה שעשועים so, als wäre die Weisheit eine Wonne Jahve's gewesen; wo alsdann אמון passend nach Aquila mit Schultens und Rosenmüller durch *alumnus* oder *nutritius* zu übersetzen, und billig אָמוּן (Klagl. 4 : 5) auszusprechen sein würde.

* Thes. I., p. 155: Ne dicam *parvuli* in sinu *gestati* imaginem ab hujus loci, qui est de sapientiæ munere *δημιουργικῷ* coll. Sir I., xxiv., contextu alieniorem esse.

† *Ἤμην παρ' αὐτῷ ἁρμόζουσα* (Itala: Eram penes illum disponens); followed by the Vulgate: *Cum eo eram cuncta componens.* So the Syr.

‡ *Ego ei artifex aderam.*

§ Umbreit: *Da war ich geschickte Künstlerin an seiner Seite.* Ewald: *Da war ich bei ihm als Künstlerin.* Fürst (Hdwbch.): *Werkmeisterin, Künstlerin.* Maurer: *Ego eram juxta eum* (ei aderam) *opifex.* Bertheau: *Und da ward ich an seiner Seite eine Künstlerin.* Hitzig: *Da war ich bei ihm Werkmeisterin.*

‖ Noldius (Concordant. Annott., 1884): שעשועים et משחקת non *artificum* sed *puerorum.* Gussett (Comment. ling. Heb., p. 131): In *alumno* est certe, quod ita venuste apteque possit *ἀλληγορίζεσθαι.*

¶ So formerly: "The rest of the verse agrees best with the idea of a child" (Lex., Dr. Gibbs' trans.); and he still admits (Thes. I., p. 115), aliquam quidem commendationem habet a reliquis hujus commatis imaginibus.

** *Deliciæ, oblectatio.* . . . ילד שעשעים proles qua gaudet aliquis et delectatur Jer. 31 : 20; נטע שעשעיו plantarium quod in deliciis habet Jes. 5 : 7.

†† *An entertaining sport*, and hence concr. *one joyously sporting* (*da ward ich ergötzliche Spielerei;* oder, wie wir sagen würden,

| KING JAMES' VERSION. | HEBREW TEXT. | | REVISED VERSION. | |
|---|---|---|---|---|
| 31 Rejoicing in the habitable part of his earth; and my delights *were* with the sons of men. | מְשַׂחֶקֶת בְּתֵבֵל אַרְצוֹ<br>וְשַׁעֲשֻׁעַי אֶת־בְּנֵי אָדָם׃ | 31 | sporting in his habitable earth,<br>and my delight was with the sons of men. | 31 |
| 32 Now therefore hearken unto me, O ye children: for blessed *are they that* keep my ways. | וְעַתָּה בָנִים שִׁמְעוּ־לִי<br>וְאַשְׁרֵי דְּרָכַי יִשְׁמֹרוּ׃ | 32 | Now then, children, hearken to me;<br>and happy they who keep my ways! | 32 |
| 33 Hear instruction, and be wise, and refuse it not. | שִׁמְעוּ מוּסָר וַחֲכָמוּ<br>וְאַל־תִּפְרָעוּ׃ | 33 | Hear instruction, and be wise,<br>and do not refuse. | 33 |
| 34 Blessed *is* the man that heareth me, watching daily at my gates, waiting at the posts of my doors. | אַשְׁרֵי אָדָם שֹׁמֵעַ לִי<br>לִשְׁקֹד עַל־דַּלְתֹתַי יוֹם ׀ יוֹם<br>לִשְׁמֹר מְזוּזֹת פְּתָחָי׃ | 34 | Happy the man who hearkens to me;<br>to watch at my doors day by day,<br>to keep the posts of my doorways. | 34 |
| 35 For whoso findeth me findeth life, and shall obtain favour of the LORD. | כִּי מֹצְאִי מָצָאי חַיִּים<br>וַיָּפֶק רָצוֹן מֵיְהֹוָה׃ | לה | For they that find me find life;<br>and he shall obtain favor from Jehovah. | 35 |

V. 35. מצ׳ יתיר י׳

Third member:—*Sporting*, the proper force of the word משחקת.* Stuart: "Lit. *laughing, sporting*, e. g., as an innocent and joyful child sports. The imagery is vivid; but the dignity of the agent seems to prohibit a literal version." But it did not prohibit the use of the Hebrew word, of which this is admitted to be the literal meaning. The expression is a part of the imagery of the original (which, of course, should be preserved); and, as such, it is pertinent and proper, whether in Hebrew or English, and needs no defense.

V. 31. *Sporting;* see remark on v. 30. *His habitable earth:* the suff. belongs to the complex idea תבל ארץ (§121, 6); the first word qualifying the second, his earth as habitable, and so fitted to be the abode of man.

Some suppose that wisdom here speaks of her own activity in the creation, as *her sport, her pastime;* "who, as a sporting favorite child, was allowed to do as she pleased; and who, as in sport (for a creation proceeds not from constraint or gloomy earnestness of purpose, but as from the spontaneous play of love), created the world according to God's will" (Ewald).† So Hitzig; who thinks to justify this acceptation of the verb, by reference to its use in 2 Sam. 2 : 14.‡ But the imagery, as the two verses are understood by these writers, is not in keeping with itself. As they translate, wisdom appears in the first member of v. 30 as the ARCHITECT of creation (*then was I with him, an architect*); an idea wholly incongruous with that of a sportive, indulged child, amusing itself without serious purpose or plan.

The two verses stand connected, by ואהיה, with the antecedent perfect as stated above (on v. 30); and the relation of time, in the particip. form (משחקת), is determind by the verb ואהיה to which it is subordinate.* Their import is: that WISDOM, before all time, was the favorite offspring of God, brought up at his side, and his continual delight; that even then she regarded, with sportive fondness, the future earth and its occupants, and her delight was with the sons of men.

Such is the beautiful imagery of these verses; expressing the relation which wisdom has always held, both to God and to his creature man, and thus forming an appropriate close to the paragraph.

V. 34. *To watch*, etc.; i. e., to be as attentive and observant, as if he were the watchman at my door, appointed to keep the posts of my doorway. There is an implied comparison, which often takes this form in Hebrew. Some suppose there is allusion to the attendance of courtiers, soliciting a favor, at the doors of princes, or of others in power.

V. 35. *They that find me*, etc.; according to the *Chethibh*, which is doubtless the true reading, and should be pointed

*da ward ich eine freudig spielende Tag für Tag*. Equally at variance with usage is Hitzig's: *und ich war in Herzensfreude Tag für Tag*.

* The signification *rejoice* (Am. Ed. of Gesenius' Lex.), is not recognized in the original work, nor in Rödiger's continuation of the Thesaurus.

† Als wäre sie bei der Schöpfung eine Werkmeisterin und Gehülfin gewesen, die Gott als spielendes Lieblingskind habe gewähren lassen, und die damals wie im Spiel (denn nicht aus Zwang oder finsterem Ernste geht eine Schöpfung hervor, sondern wie aus dem Spiel der freien Liebe) die Welt nach Gottes Willen geschaffen habe.

‡ Die Weisheit spielt ähnlich wie 2 Sam. 2 : 14 die Knappen, d. h. sie ist in heiterer Weise geschäftig, mühelos ihre Kunst zeigend in immer neuen Gebilden.

* Ewald arbitrarily refers the first משחקת to past, and the second to future time (*da war ich bei ihm als Künstlerin, . . . spielend vor ihm alle Zeit,—die ich spiele nun in seinem Erdkreis*). So Umbreit. This is justly condemned by Hitzig: Die Zeit darf nicht gewechselt, das Thun, v. 31, nicht mit Levi b. G., Mercer, Umbreit ff. als gegenwärtig gedacht werden.

| KING JAMES' VERSION. | HEBREW TEXT. | REVISED VERSION. |
|---|---|---|
| 36 But he that sinneth against me wrongeth his own soul: all they that hate me love death. | וְחֹטְאִי חֹמֵס נַפְשׁוֹ<br>כָּל־מְשַׂנְאַי אָהֲבוּ מָוֶת׃ 36 | 36 But he that fails of me wrongs his own soul; 36<br>all that hate me love death. |

מֹצְאַי, מֹצְאִי.* In the second member, the subject is individualized, by a construction frequent in Heb. poetry (*he*, i. e., every such one).† The monotony of form is broken, with happy effect, by the variation to the *sing.* in the next verse (*He that fails of me*).

V. 36. *That fails of me;* the primary signification of חטא (*to miss, to fail of*, a mark e. g.), and the proper meaning here, required by the construction, and by the contrast with *they that find me*, in the preceding verse. So Gesenius (Thes. and Lex.): "*Whosoever misseth me* (doth not find me). . . . opp. מצאי v. 35." So most of the leading Christian hebraists.‡

Ewald's objection to this, viz., that a comparison of ch. 20 : 2, and of the parallel שׂנא, requires here the purely moral sense,§ is groundless; for *to fail of* wisdom is to neglect seeking her (compare v. 17), and this strictly moral sense is parallel with שׂנא.

On the much contested point, whether by wisdom, in vv. 22–31, is meant the Word spoken of in John 1 : 1, and foll., I submit the following suggestions.

1. The same subject speaks here as at the beginning of the chapter. The fact, that *wisdom* and *understanding* are associated together, plainly shows that no reference is there made to a strict and literal personality. What is meant by this connection is clear from comparison with the second chapter; where *wisdom*, *understanding*, and *intelligence* (vv. 2, 3), *wisdom, knowledge*, and *understanding* (v. 6), *wisdom, knowledge, reflection*, and *understanding* (vv. 10, 11), are connected in the same manner. No one will pretend, that these words are not to be understood in their ordinary sense and acceptation in the Scriptures. The simple and natural figure in v. 10 (of ch. 2), *Wisdom shall come into thy heart*, is a clue (if one were needed) to the bolder personification in other passages; as of *wisdom* and *understanding* in ch. 3 : 13–18.

That there is no reference to a strict personality in v. 1 of this (eighth) chapter, is also evident from what follows; e. g., vv. 10, 11, where she exhorts to seek *knowledge* rather than wealth, on the ground that *wisdom* is of more worth than the costliest treasures; and in vv. 12, and foll., where she asserts her direct agency in the prudent and successful management of worldly interests.

2. Of this *wisdom*, thus identified with the spirit of wisdom inculcated throughout the book, the writer proceeds to say (vv. 22–31), *Jehovah possessed me*, etc.; *when he founded the heavens, I was there*, etc.; in accordance with the statements elsewhere made, e. g., *Jehovah by wisdom founded the earth, established the heavens by understanding* (ch. 3 : 19), *he has made the earth by his power, he has established the world by his wisdom* (Jer. 10 : 12). The dignity and worth of wisdom, and her consequent claims on the regard and obedience of man, are thus shown by her relation to Jehovah and to his work of creation. The whole representation, moreover, is highly poetic and figurative; and to base any doctrinal truth on single forms of expression, which are the mere drapery of the figure, is at variance with the best established principles of interpretation. One who should defend such a practice in general, as a principle of hermeneutics, would justly forfeit the character of a sober and judicious critic.

3. The representation here made, of the relation of wisdom to Jehovah in the work of creation, differs essentially from that given in John 1 : 1–3, and 10. It is there said, not only that the Word "*was in the beginning with God*" (v. 2), but that "*the Word was God*" (v. 1); that "*all things were made by him*" (v. 3), that "*the world was made by him*" (v. 10), not as the instrument, but as the personal agent, and by his own power. Compare Col. 1 : 16, "*by him were all things created*," and Eph. 3 : 9, Heb. 1 : 2, 1 Cor. 8 : 6.

4. The passage is nowhere directly quoted in the N. Test., as might have been expected, had it borne this important relation to the doctrine of the Messiah. The assumption, that the representation in John 1 : 1–10 was modeled after this passage, is without the shadow of probability; and the supposed tacit allusions to it (Col. 1 : 15, Rev. 3 : 14) do not sufficiently identify it for the purpose of argument.

---

* Maurer errs in saying: Quod singularis מֹצְאִי construitur cum plurali מֹצְאַי, causa est, quod in illo latet notio *omnis, quicunque*. Cf. 3 : 18, et 9 : 4, 5. The cases cited are not analogous to this, in which a *sing.* subject would be followed by its predicate in the *plural*. Elsewhere, only the reverse of this occurs, viz., the *plural* of the part. construed with the *singular* (§ 146, 4).

† Hitzig's assertion is, therefore, without just ground: Der Sing. מֹצְאִי ist gegen מֹצְאַי durch ויפק gesichert. On the contrary, it is correctly said by Bertheau: Nach solchen Particc. im Plural (die mich erfassenden = jeder der mich erfasst) in fortgesetzter Rede der Singular ויפק, *und trägt fort Gnade von Jahve*, nicht unerwartet ist.

‡ E. g. C. B. Michaelis: Opponitur *invenienti* v. 36, proprieque est *aberrat, non contingere scopum* aut rem quæsitam. Dathe: *Qui aberrat a me*. J. D. Michaelis (and Dœderlein): *Wer mich verfehlt*. Schelling: *Qui contra a me aberrat*. Müntinghe: Sprachkennern ist es bekannt, dass das heb. Wort, das gewöhnlich durch *sündigen* übersetzt wird, auch *abweichen, sich verirren* bedeuten kann; und diese Bedeutung ist hier auch schicklicher, weil das Abweichen von der Weisheit dem Finden derselben schnurgerade entgegen steht (v. 35). Umbreit: *Wer aber von mir abweicht*. Bertheau: *Und der mich verfehlt* (Job 5 : 24; vgl. den Hif. Richt. 20 : 16). Hitzig: *Und wer mich verfehlt*. . . . Der Sinn von חטא erhellt aus dem Gegensatze מצא (vgl. Hiob 5 : 24, Richter 20 : 16). Stuart: *But whosoever misseth me.*

§ Zu v. 36*a* vgl. 20 : 2, woraus, so wie aus dem entsprechenden שׂנא erhellt, dass חטא in rein sittlichem Sinne stehen muss. So Rosenmüller: Quum חטאי respondeat voci משׂנאי *qui me odio habent*, חטאי vix dubium est *qui in me peccat* significare, positum pro חטא בי sive חטא עלי, ut Ps. 18 : 40 קמי pro קמים עלי *qui contra me surgunt*. But the two cases are not analogous; the hostile movement, on which the construction in the one is founded, having nothing parallel in the other.

KING JAMES' VERSION.

CHAP. IX.

WISDOM hath builded her house, she hath hewn out her seven pillars:

2 She hath killed her beasts;
she hath mingled her wine; she hath also furnished her table.
3 She hath sent forth her maidens; she crieth upon the highest places of the city,
4 Whoso *is* simple, let him turn in hither: *as for* him that wanteth understanding, she saith to him,
5 Come, eat of my bread, and drink of the wine *which* I have mingled.
6 Forsake the foolish, and live;
and go in the way of understanding.
7 He that reproveth a scorner getteth to himself shame: and he that rebuked a wicked *man getteth* himself a blot.

HEBREW TEXT.

CHAP. IX.

א חָכְמוֹת בָּנְתָה בֵיתָהּ
חָצְבָה עַמּוּדֶיהָ שִׁבְעָה׃
2 טָבְחָה טִבְחָהּ מָסְכָה יֵינָהּ
אַף עָרְכָה שֻׁלְחָנָהּ׃
3 שָׁלְחָה נַעֲרֹתֶיהָ
תִקְרָא עַל־גַּפֵּי מְרֹמֵי קָרֶת׃
4 מִי־פֶתִי יָסֻר הֵנָּה
חֲסַר־לֵב אָמְרָה לּוֹ׃
ה לְכוּ לַחֲמוּ בְלַחֲמִי
וּשְׁתוּ בְּיַיִן מָסָכְתִּי׃
6 עִזְבוּ פְתָאיִם וִחְיוּ
וְאִשְׁרוּ בְּדֶרֶךְ בִּינָה׃
7 יֹסֵר ׀ לֵץ לֹקֵחַ לוֹ קָלוֹן
וּמוֹכִיחַ לְרָשָׁע מוּמוֹ׃

REVISED VERSION.

CHAP. IX.

WISDOM has builded her house; 1
she has hewn out her seven pillars.
She has slaughtered her beasts, mixed her wine, 2
yea, she has prepared her table.
She has sent out her maidens; 3
on the heights of the city she calls:
Whoso is simple, let him turn hither; 4
he that lacks understanding, she says to him:
Come, eat of my food, 5
and drink of the wine I have mixed.
Forsake follies, and live; 6
and go forward in the way of understanding.
He that reproves a scoffer gets himself reproach; 7
and he that rebukes the wicked, a blot to himself.

V. 6. Forsake the foolish

Ch. IX.—V. 1. חכמות, see note on ch. 1 : 20. *Her . . . . pillars*, the writer says, viz., of her own house, or those which she provides for its construction. The suff. pron., therefore, belongs appropriately to wisdom;* and there is no occasion for referring it to בית,† of which the *fem.* construction is by no means established (see note on ch. 2 : 18, and especially the footnote †). *Seven*, probably used as "a lesser round number" (Gesenius, Lex.).

V. 2. טבח means here a *beast for slaughter*, designed and prepared for it; not for *sacrifice*, for which זבח is the word. As a phrase, *slaughtered her beasts* expresses the precise import of the Hebrew. *Mixed her wine;* according to the ancient practice of diluting wine with water,‡ and perhaps with allusion to the use of *spices* (Gesenius, Thes. II., p. 808), which is doubtless meant in ch. 23 : 30.

V. 3. *She calls;* the imperfect (in contrast with the preceding perfect) expressing a continued action. This word belongs properly to the second member. *On the heights;* על גפי *on the back of* = *upon* (Gesenius, Lex.); or, perhaps, on the ridge or summit of the high places = the highest points.

V. 4. *Let him turn* (Jussive), is unquestionably the writer's meaning (comp. § 72, Rem. 4). *He that lacks;* חסר used absolutely, not with מי repeated from the first member.*

V. 6. פתאים, abstr. plur. of פתי as used in ch. 1 : 22, *simplicity, folly*, in all its forms.†

VV. 7–9. For the connection, see Expl. Notes. There is no ground to suppose (with Ewald‡), that wisdom here assigns her

* So Ewald (and Bertheau): *Ihre sieben Säulen.*

† Stuart: "The suff. in עמודיה may apply to בית (for this is sometimes fem.), and so I have applied it in the version. Bertheau, and others, refer it to *wisdom;* which, however, seems to be less appropriate."

‡ Anacreon, Od. XXXVI. 10, *Δὸς ὕδωρ, βάλ' οἶνον, ὦ παῖ· cede aquam* (ad vinum diluendum), *infunde vinum, O, puer!* Et Od. LV (LVII), 3, 4,

*Τὰ μὲν δέκ' ἔγχει*
*Ὕδατος, τὰ πέντε δ' οἴνου*
*Κυάθοις — — —*

*decem partes infunde aquæ, quinque vero vini cyathis* (Rosenmüller). Ælian. V. H. 2, 41, *προστιθέασιν αὐτῷ καὶ τοῦτο δήπου τὸ Σκυθικὸν κακὸν, ὅτι ἀκρατοπότης ἐγένετο.—Σκυθῶν γὰρ ἴδιον τὸ πίνειν ἄκρατον.* Vid. Chamæleon apud Athen., 10, 7, p. 427, C.: quo ipso auctore *ἀκρατέστερον πιεῖν* Lacones dixere *ἐπισκυθίζειν* (Fischer ad Anacr. Od. XXXVI. 10).

* Maurer: Verba חסר־לב, ante quæ Rosenmüllerus et Ewaldus haud apte repetunt מי, nominativum quem dicunt absolutum efficiunt.

† Sept.: *Ἀπολείπετε ἀφροσύνην.* Vulg.: *Relinquite infantiam.* Syr. and Chald.: *Want of thought.* Rosenmüller: Sunt qui reddant, *deserite fatuos;* . . . sed magis convenit ut nomen abstractum, *fatuitates*, capere quemadmodum singulare פתי supra 1 : 22. Bertheau: Die alten Uebersetzungen fassen פתאים mit Recht als Abstract-Bildung auf; vgl. פתיות v. 13, und פתי 1 : 22. Stuart: "פתאים, abstract plural here; lit. *simplicities.*"

‡ Mit verstockten Spöttern, erklärt sie dann vv. 7–9 eben so aufrichtig, wolle sie nichts gemein haben; . . . nur die, welche wenigstens schon im Zuge zur Weisheit und Gerechtigkeit seien,

| KING JAMES' VERSION. | HEBREW TEXT. | REVISED VERSION. |
|---|---|---|
| 8 Reprove not a scorner, lest he hate thee: rebuke a wise man, and he will love thee. | 8 אַל־תּוֹכַח לֵץ פֶּן־יִשְׂנָאֶךָּ הוֹכַח לְחָכָם וְיֶאֱהָבֶךָּ׃ | Rebuke not a scoffer, lest he hate thee; rebuke the wise, and he will love thee. 8 |
| 9 Give *instruction* to a wise *man*, and he will be yet wiser: teach a just *man*, and he will increase in learning. | 9 תֵּן לְחָכָם וְיֶחְכַּם־עוֹד הוֹדַע לְצַדִּיק וְיוֹסֶף לֶקַח׃ | Give to the wise, and he will be yet wiser; teach the just, and he will increase in learning. 9 |
| 10 The fear of the LORD *is* the beginning of wisdom: and the knowledge of the holy *is* understanding. | י תְּחִלַּת חָכְמָה יִרְאַת יְהוָה וְדַעַת קְדֹשִׁים בִּינָה׃ | The fear of Jehovah is the beginning of wisdom; and knowledge of the Holy is understanding. 10 |
| 11 For by me thy days shall be multiplied, and the years of thy life shall be increased. | 11 כִּי־בִי יִרְבּוּ יָמֶיךָ וְיוֹסִיפוּ לְּךָ שְׁנוֹת חַיִּים׃ | For by me shall thy days be multiplied; and years of life shall be added to thee. 11 |
| 12 If thou be wise, thou shalt by wise for thyself: but *if* thou scornest, thou alone shalt bear *it*. | 12 אִם־חָכַמְתָּ חָכַמְתָּ לָּךְ וְלַצְתָּ לְבַדְּךָ תִשָּׂא׃ | If thou art wise, thou art wise for thyself; and if thou scoffest, thou alone shalt bear it. 12 |
| 13 A foolish woman *is* clamorous; *she is* simple, and knoweth nothing. | 13 אֵשֶׁת כְּסִילוּת הֹמִיָּה פְּתַיּוּת וּבַל־יָדְעָה מָּה׃ | A foolish woman is clamorous, simple, and knows nothing. 13 |
| 14 For she sitteth at the door of her house, on a seat in the high places of the city, | 14 וְיָשְׁבָה לְפֶתַח בֵּיתָהּ עַל־כִּסֵּא מְרֹמֵי קָרֶת׃ | And she sits in the doorway of her house, on a seat in the high places of the city; 14 |

reasons for not including scoffers in her invitation, or implies in vv. 8*b*–10 that only those are invited who are already on the way to wisdom.

V. 7. מוּמוֹ *his blot* = מוּם לוֹ (as the same relation is expressed in the preceding member), *a blot to himself.* *

VV. 10–12. For the connection, see Expl. Notes. Second member:—קְדֹשִׁים, plur. intensive; † compare ch. 30 : 3, Hosea 12 : 1, and the use of קָדוֹשׁ in Job. 6 : 10, and elsewhere.

V. 11. *For*, etc., confirming the statement in the previous verse (see Expl. Notes). Bertheau is clearly mistaken in supposing this to be the ground of the remote requirement in v. 6. ‡

V. 12. Lit. *and scoffest thou* = *and if thou scoffest* (§ 155, 4, *a*), a frequent construction, especially in poetry; comp. Job 7 : 20.

V. 13. (See Expl. Notes.) The construction in the text is the one generally followed in the versions, * and is the most obvious and intelligible. The spirited construction followed by Ewald † is also allowable, but is less simple and plain. Against Hitzig's construction ‡ is the decisive objection, that פְּתַיּוּת is made to take the place of כְּסִילוּת in the usage of this book. *Folly*, the opposite of *wisdom*, is the proper subject here.

Second member:—פְּתַיּוּת (abstr. for concr.) is a second predicate. § מָה (Gesenius, Lex., A, 2), as in Job 13 : 13. *Knows nothing* is the proper rendering; a voluntary ignorance of all that most concerns man. ‖ *Cares for nothing* (Gesenius and others) weakens both the thought and expression.

V. 14. כִּסֵּא may be used for *a seat*, in the ordinary sense, as

---

lade sie ein und hoffe ihre Liebe zu verdienen; denn allerdings sei Furcht Jahve's der Weisheit Anfang, und den Heiligen kennen schon so gut als verständig sein (v. 10).

* Maurer: לֹקֵחַ pertinet etiam ad מוּמוֹ; hoc est pro מוּם לוֹ. Sept.: *Μωμήσεται ἑαυτόν*. Vulg.: *Sibi maculam generat.*

† Umbreit: קְדֹשִׁים ein plur. majest. für Gott, wie Hos. 12 : 1. Bertheau: *Und Erkenntniss des Heiligen;* קְדֹשִׁים im plural, wie אֱלֹהִים.

‡ V. 11 soll die Aufforderung in V. 6 begründen, und geht, nach der trennenden Zwischenbemerkung 7-10, auf V. 6 zurück; der Wechsel der zweiten Person Plur. in V. 6 mit der des Singul. in V. 11 stört nicht.

* Bertheau: *Das Weib der Thorheit* ist *lärmend*, etc. Rosenmüller: *Mulier stultitiæ*, i. e. stulta, est *strepera*. Maurer: *Mulier stultitiæ* est *impetuosa, Fatua, nec novit quidquam.* Umbreit: *Das Weib der Thorheit braust einher; ist Unvernunft und denkt an nichts.* Stuart: *A foolish woman is noisy.*

† *Das Weib der Thorheit, welche ohne Ruhe,*
*der Albernheit, und weiss nicht was;*
*die setzet sich*, u. s. w.

‡ *Eine stürmish erregte Närrin*
*ist die Unvernunft*, u. s. w.

§ Bertheau: Leichter ist es jedenfalls, mit Sept., Syr., Chald. . . . . das Abstractum für weiteres Prädicat zu nehmen: *ist lärmend, Thorheit* = thöricht, *und ganz unwissend*, insofern sie keine דַּעַת (z. B. 10 : 14) hat.

‖ Rosenmüller: *Et non novit quidquam;* eorum, quæ hominibus utilia et salutaria sunt, plane est ignara. (Compare Bertheau, footnote §.)

KING JAMES' VERSION.

15 To call passengers who go right on their ways:

16 Whoso *is* simple, let him turn in hither: and *as for* him that wanteth understanding, she saith to him,

17 Stolen waters are sweet, and bread *eaten* in secret is pleasant.

18 But he knoweth not that the dead *are* there; *and that* her guests *are* in the depths of hell.

CHAP. X.

THE proverbs of Solomon. A wise son maketh a glad father: but a foolish son *is* the heaviness of his mother.

2 Treasures of wickedness profit nothing: but righteousness delivereth from death.

3 The LORD will not suffer the soul of the righteous to famish: but he casteth away the substance of the wicked.

4 He becometh poor that dealeth *with* a slack hand: but the hand of the diligent maketh rich.

5 He that gathereth in summer *is* a wise son: *but* he that sleepeth in harvest *is* a son that causeth shame.

HEBREW TEXT.

טו לִקְרֹא לְעֹבְרֵי־דָרֶךְ
הַמְיַשְּׁרִים אֹרְחוֹתָם׃

16 מִי־פֶתִי יָסֻר הֵנָּה
וַחֲסַר־לֵב וְאָמְרָה לּוֹ׃

17 מַיִם־גְּנוּבִים יִמְתָּקוּ
וְלֶחֶם סְתָרִים יִנְעָם׃

18 וְלֹא יָדַע כִּי־רְפָאִים שָׁם
בְּעִמְקֵי שְׁאוֹל קְרֻאֶיהָ׃

CHAP. X.

מִשְׁלֵי שְׁלֹמֹה

א בֵּן חָכָם יְשַׂמַּח־אָב
וּבֵן כְּסִיל תּוּגַת אִמּוֹ׃

2 לֹא־יוֹעִילוּ אוֹצְרוֹת רֶשַׁע
וּצְדָקָה תַּצִּיל מִמָּוֶת׃

3 לֹא־יַרְעִיב יְהוָה נֶפֶשׁ צַדִּיק
וְהַוַּת רְשָׁעִים יֶהְדֹּף׃

4 רָאשׁ עֹשֶׂה כַף־רְמִיָּה
וְיַד חָרוּצִים תַּעֲשִׁיר׃

ה אֹגֵר בַּקַּיִץ בֵּן מַשְׂכִּיל
נִרְדָּם בַּקָּצִיר בֵּן מֵבִישׁ׃

REVISED VERSION.

to call to them that pass by the way, 15
who go right on their ways.

Whoso is simple, let him turn hither; 16
and he that lacks understanding, she says to him:

Stolen waters art sweet, 17
and bread of secrecy is pleasant.

And he knows not that the shades are there, 18
her guests in the depths of the underworld!

CHAP. X.

PROVERBS OF SOLOMON.

A WISE son makes a glad father; 1
but a foolish son is the grief of his mother.

Treasures of wickedness profit not; 2
but righteousness delivers from death.

Jehovah will not let the spirit of the righteous famish; 3
but he repels the longing of the wicked.

Poor is he that labors with a slothful hand; 4
but the hand of the diligent makes rich.

He that gathers in the summer is a wise son; 5
he that sleeps in the harvest is a son that brings shame.

in 2 Kings 4 : 10. מרמי the adverb. accus. (place where) § 118, 1, *b*. Dathe: *in elato urbis loco.*

V. 16. *Whoso is simple*, etc., is evidently the language of the writer, applying here the words employed by wisdom (v. 4). יסר, see note on v. 4. ואמרה, comp. § 126, Rem. 1, *b*, and § 129, 1, Rem. *b*. The implication is: *if one lacks—to him she says*, etc.

V. 17. *Bread of secrecy* (סתרים intensive plural), vicious and clandestine pleasures of every kind.

V. 18. *The shades;* the established term in English usage for the *bodiless spirit*, as being without substance; thus corresponding with the import (*weak, feeble*, compare Is. 14 : 10) of the Hebrew word. See note on Job 26 : 5.

Ch. X.—V. 1. *Proverbs of Solomon;* see Introduction, §

V. 3. *Longing* (eager desire, הוה) is the well established signification of the Heb. word.* So it was properly expressed by Tyndale: *But he putteth the ungodly from his desire.* The false rendering of the Syr. and Chald.* was followed by Cranmer (and the Bishops): *But he taketh away the rychesse of the ungodly;* and in the Genevan Version: *But he casteth away the substance of the wicked*, which was retained in the Common Version.

V. 5. *That brings shame;* that dishonors his father and mother

* Gesenius, Thes. I., p. 370): *Cupiditas, cupido*, a rad. no. 2, idem quod אִוָּה. Prov. X. 3: . . . *cupidinem malorum repellit.* Parall. נפש צדיק. Mich. 7 : 3, הות נפשו. LXX.: *Καταθύμιον ψυχῆς αὐτοῦ.* Vulg.: *Desiderium animæ suæ.* Ewald: *Des Frevler's Gier.* Umbreit: *Der Bösen Gier.* De Wette: *Der Frevler Gier weist er ab.* Bertheau: *Die Gier der Frevler.* Hitzig: *Die Gier der Frevler weist er zurück.* Stuart: *But the greedy desire of the wicked will he repel.*

* Rosenmüller: Interpretem C. B. Michaelis existimat הוה idem significare ratum esse quod הוֹן *opes.* Sed potuit הוה per metonymiam pro opibus cupide corrasis dictum sumere.

| KING JAMES' VERSION. | HEBREW TEXT. | | REVISED VERSION. | |
|---|---|---|---|---|
| 6 Blessings *are* upon the head of the just: but violence covereth the mouth of the wicked. | בְּרָכוֹת לְרֹאשׁ צַדִּיק<br>וּפִי רְשָׁעִים יְכַסֶּה חָמָס׃ | 6 | Blessings are for the head of the righteous;<br>but the mouth of the wicked covers violence. | 6 |
| 7 The memory of the just *is* blessed: but the name of the wicked shall rot. | זֵכֶר צַדִּיק לִבְרָכָה<br>וְשֵׁם רְשָׁעִים יִרְקָב׃ | 7 | The memory of the righteous is blessed;<br>but the name of the wicked shall rot. | 7 |
| 8 The wise in heart will receive commandments: but a prating fool shall fall. | חֲכַם־לֵב יִקַּח מִצְוֺת<br>וֶאֱוִיל שְׂפָתַיִם יִלָּבֵט׃ | 8 | The wise in heart will receive commands;<br>but a prating fool shall fall. | 8 |
| 9 He that walketh uprightly walketh surely: but he that perverteth his ways shall be known. | הוֹלֵךְ בַּתֹּם יֵלֶךְ בֶּטַח<br>וּמְעַקֵּשׁ דְּרָכָיו יִוָּדֵעַ׃ | 9 | He that walks in integrity will walk securely;<br>but he that perverts his ways will be known. | 9 |
| 10 He that winketh with the eye causeth sorrow: but a prating fool shall fall. | קֹרֵץ עַיִן יִתֵּן עַצָּבֶת<br>וֶאֱוִיל שְׂפָתַיִם יִלָּבֵט׃ | י | He that winks with the eye causes sorrow;<br>and a prating fool shall fall. | 10 |

V. 6. violence covers

V. 9. will be taught

instead of being their joy, as the wise son is said to be in v. 1. This justifies the use of the word *son*.

V. 6. *The mouth of the wicked covers violence;* as construed, according to the natural order of the words, by the best modern scholars,* and as they must necessarily be understood in v. 11. The relation of the two members is thus expressed by Ewald: "Whilst all bless the righteous as a counselor and benefactor, the wicked, who conceal within themselves only cruel words and thoughts, have no such blessings to hope for." Others construe the words as in the margin; e. g. Maurer, who supposes the meaning to be: His mouth is filled with violence, so as to be covered with it. But this is not what is meant by *covering the mouth*, which has a specific meaning and application. Others: His violence covers his mouth, so that he can say nothing in his own behalf; which is the proper import of the words so construed, but is not as pertinent here, and is still less so in v. 11.

V. 7. ברכה, concr. an object of blessing; לְ, with the subst. verb implied (Gesenius, Thes. and Lex., לְ, A, 2, *extr.*), *to be for* = *to become*, or *to be* such (comp. Is. 1 : 5).

V. 8. *A prating fool;* comp. *a man of lips* (Job 11 : 2), for a loquacious man.†

V. 9. *Will be known* is the most common signification of the word, and is pertinent here.* Gesenius,† and others: *Shall be made to know*, i. e., *shall be taught* = shall be chastised; compare the Hiph. in Judg. 8 : 16, and Niph. in Jer. 31 : 19.

V. 10. *A prating fool;* see note on v. 8. On the relation of the two members, see Expl. Notes,‡ and Maurer as quoted below, in footnote (§). There is no just ground, with Ewald, Bertheau, and others, to doubt the integrity of the Heb. text.§

---

* Ewald: *Der Frevler Mund birgt Grausamkeit.* Während Alle den Gerechten als Rathgeber und Wohlthäter segnen, haben Frevler, welche nur grausame Worte und Gedanken in sich bergen, nie solche Segnungen zu hoffen. Bertheau: *Und der Mund der Frevler verbirgt Gewaltthat*, um sie bei Gelegenheit auszuüben. Stuart: *But the mouth of the wicked concealeth injury.*

† Gesenius (Thes. III., p. 1336): Et sic איש שפתים *homo loquax, garrulus* Job 11 : 2, אויל שפתים *stultus garrulus* Prov. 10 : 8. Bertheau: *Der Thor der Lippen*, d. i., der Dumme, der auf Gebote nicht hört.

* So Ewald: *Wer seine Wege krümmt, der wird verrathen.* Umbreit: *Wird ertappt.* Bertheau: *Wird offenbar*, oder *wird ertappt*, 12 : 16. So the Sept.: *Ὁ δὲ διαστρέφων τὰς ὁδοὺς αὐτοῦ γνωσθήσεται.* Vulg.: *Manifestus erit.*

† Thesaurus, II., p. 572: Qui perverse vivit, pœnis *edocebitur.* Maurer: *Sentiet*, pœnas dabit; נודע ut Jer. 31 : 19. De Wette, *Wird* [durch Strafe] *gewitzigt werden.* Hitzig: *Wird gewitzigt.*

‡ Rosenmüller: Non vitium et virtutem, sed vitium cum vitio confert. Significatur, perniciosiorem esse eum qui dissimulanter malum agit, eo qui aperte, quod hic statim deprehendatur atque puniatur, ille negotium facessat sua dissimulatione, quia non statim dignoscitur.

§ Ewald: Im Masor. Text lautet das letzte Glied wie V. 8. *Wer dummer Lippen, kommt zu Fall.* Allein dann ist weder Vergleichung mit dem Gegensatze sichtbar, noch gute Zusammenstellung zweier ähnlicher Gedanken. Der Gegensatz und Sinn des Ganzen wird aber sofort deutlich, wenn man annimmt, dass hier eigentlich stand: וּמוֹכִיחַ בִּשְׂפָתַיִם שָׁלוֹם, worauf etwa das *ὁ δὲ ἐλέγχων μετὰ παῤῥησίας εἰρηνοποιεῖ* der LXX. führt.
Bertheau: *Wer mit den Augen blinzelt, verursacht Kränkung* . . .; dazu passt *b* bei den Septuag., *und wer mit Offenheit tadelt, schafft Frieden.* Unser *b* scheint durch irgend ein Versehen aus 8*b* hierher verschlagen zu sein.
To this it is well replied by Maurer: Qua mutatione facile profecto carebis, quum concinant membra, uti sunt, et optime quidem. Quod vult scriptor hoc est, periculosum esse et tecte loqui et temere loqui, quum prius qui faciat noceat aliis, qui posterius ipse sibi.

| KING JAMES' VERSION. | HEBREW TEXT. | | REVISED VERSION. | |
|---|---|---|---|---|
| 11 The mouth of a righteous *man is* a well of life: but violence covereth the mouth of the wicked. | מְקוֹר חַיִּים פִּי צַדִּיק<br>וּפִי רְשָׁעִים יְכַסֶּה חָמָס׃ | 11 | A well of life is the mouth of the righteous;<br>but the mouth of the wicked covers violence. | 11 |
| 12 Hatred stirreth up strifes: but love covereth all sins. | שִׂנְאָה תְּעֹרֵר מְדָנִים<br>וְעַל כָּל־פְּשָׁעִים תְּכַסֶּה אַהֲבָה׃ | 12 | Hatred stirs up strifes;<br>but love covers all offenses. | 12 |
| 13 In the lips of him that hath understanding wisdom is found: but a rod *is* for the back of him that is void of understanding. | בְּשִׂפְתֵי נָבוֹן תִּמָּצֵא חָכְמָה<br>וְשֵׁבֶט לְגֵו חֲסַר־לֵב׃ | 13 | In the lips of the discerning is found wisdom;<br>but a rod is for the back of him that lacks understanding. | 13 |
| 14 Wise *men* lay up knowledge: but the mouth of the foolish *is* near destruction. | חֲכָמִים יִצְפְּנוּ־דָעַת<br>וּפִי אֱוִיל מְחִתָּה קְרֹבָה׃ | 14 | The wise treasure up knowledge;<br>but the fool's mouth is a near downfall. | 14 |
| 15 The rich man's wealth *is* his strong city: the destruction of the poor *is* their poverty. | הוֹן עָשִׁיר קִרְיַת עֻזּוֹ<br>מְחִתַּת דַּלִּים רֵישָׁם׃ | טו | The rich man's wealth is his strong city;<br>the downfall of the needy is their poverty. | 15 |
| 16 The labour of the righteous *tendeth* to life: the fruit of the wicked to sin. | פְּעֻלַּת־צַדִּיק לְחַיִּים<br>תְּבוּאַת רָשָׁע לְחַטָּאת׃ | 16 | The wages of the righteous is life;<br>the gain of the wicked is sin. | 16 |
| 17 He *is in* the way of life that keepeth instruction: but he that refused reproof erreth. | אֹרַח לְחַיִּים שׁוֹמֵר מוּסָר<br>וְעֹזֵב תּוֹכַחַת מַתְעֶה׃ | 17 | A way of life is he who heeds correction;<br>but he who forsakes reproof leads astray. | 17 |

V. 11, second member:—See note on v. 6.

V. 14. *A near downfall;* מחתה, prop. *a breaking down*, and hence *ruin, destruction.** The form of the Sept. and Vulg. (*is near to*),† followed in all the early English (except the Genevan) and in some modern versions, is contrary to the only possible construction of the Hebrew.

V. 15. *The downfall of the needy.*‡ The other signification of מחתה, adopted in the Vulg.,§ and thence in Cranmer's, the Bishops', and the Genevan version (*the fear of the needy is their poverty*), is wholly out of place here.

V. 16. *Is life:* לְ, with the subst. verb implied; see the remark on v. 7. Strictly, *is for life*, i. e., is the same as life, life being inseparably connected with it. So in the second member; the gain of the wicked *is for sin*, i. e., constitutes sin, for the acquiring and holding it is sin. That פעלה means *wages* here (not *labor*), is evident from the parallel תבואה.

V. 17. *A way of life*, etc., is the only admissible construction of the Hebrew words. He is a way of life (as well stated by Bertheau), because he does not lead astray, and therefore conducts to life; for only he, who himself regards correction, can direct others aright.* So also Maurer.†

* Schultens: *propinqua destructio*, vel *ruina*, est jam jamque instans, et omni momento collapsura. Maurer: *Et* (at) *os stulti ruina propinqua* est; ædificio simile est cujus imminet strages, semper in eo est ut rumpat, nunquam non paratum est temere proferre cogitata animi.

Ewald: *Des Narren Mund ein naher Einsturz ist.* Umbreit (De Wette, Hitzig): *Ist naher Einsturz.* Bertheau: *Der Mund des Thoren ist ein naher*, jeden Augenblick bevorstehender, Schrecken und Verderben verursachender *Einsturz*, weil er mit seinen Einfällen rasch hervorplatzt.

† Sept.: *Στόμα δὲ προπετοῦς ἐγγίζει συντριβῇ.* Vulg.: *Os autem stulti confusioni proximum est.* Pagnino correctly: *Os stulti est contritio propinqua.* So the Genevan: *The mouth of the fool is a present destruction.* Bishops (after Tyndale and Cranmer): *But the mouth of the foolish is nigh destruction.*

‡ Ewald: *Der Dürft'gen Einsturz ihre Armuth.* Bertheau: *Einsturz der Dürftigen ist ihre Armuth;* während wenn sie Geld hätten, sie dem Einsturz ihrer Zustände, der Zertrümmerung ihrer Verhältnisse, oft genug vorbeugen könnten. Hitzig: *Der Dürftigen Bestürzung ist ihre Armuth.*

§ *Pavor pauperum egestas eorum.*

* *Ein Weg zum Leben ist wer bewahret Zucht; wer Warnung lässt*, ihrer nicht achtet und sie fahren lässt, 4, 2, *leitet irre;* ארח לחיים erhält durch מתעה seine Erklärung dahin: er ist ein Weg des Lebens weil er nicht irre leitet, also zum Leben hinführt; es wird darauf hingewiesen, dass nur der welcher Zucht bewahrt, andere recht unterweisen und somit zum Leben hinführen kann.

† *Via ad vitam* est i. e. viam quæ ducit ad salutem monstrat *qui servat disciplinam; Et*, sed, *qui relinquit reprehensionem, errare facit*, in errorem ducit. A quo facillimo, simplicissimo et aptissimo sensu vix credas potuisse interpretes aberrare. מתעה omnes intransitive capiunt. Prioribus autem verbis vim inferunt, suo quisque modo. Stuart: *A way of life is he who keepeth instruction; but he who forsaketh reproof, leadeth astray.*

Other constructions have been adopted, all of which are unnatural and forced. E. g., Schultens: *Iter ad viam est observans*

| KING JAMES' VERSION. | HEBREW TEXT. | | REVISED VERSION. | |
|---|---|---|---|---|
| 18 He that hideth hatred *with* lying lips, and he that uttereth a slander, *is* a fool. | מְכַסֶּה שִׂנְאָה שִׂפְתֵי־שָׁקֶר<br>וּמוֹצִא דִבָּה הוּא כְסִיל׃ | 18 | He that covers hatred with lying lips,<br>and he that publishes an ill report, the same is a fool. | 18 |
| 19 In the multitude of words there wanteth not sin: but he that refraineth his lips *is* wise. | בְּרֹב דְּבָרִים לֹא יֶחְדַּל־פָּשַׁע<br>וְחוֹשֵׂךְ שְׂפָתָיו מַשְׂכִּיל׃ | 19 | In the multitude of words there will not be wanting offense;<br>but he that restrains his lips is wise. | 19 |
| 20 The tongue of the just *is as* choice silver: the heart of the wicked *is* little worth. | כֶּסֶף נִבְחָר לְשׁוֹן צַדִּיק<br>לֵב רְשָׁעִים כִּמְעָט׃ | כ | Choice silver is the tongue of the righteous;<br>the heart of the wicked is of little worth. | 20 |
| 21 The lips of the righteous feed many: but fools die for want of wisdom. | שִׂפְתֵי צַדִּיק יִרְעוּ רַבִּים<br>וֶאֱוִילִים בַּחֲסַר־לֵב יָמוּתוּ׃ | 21 | The lips of the righteous feed many;<br>but fools die for lack of understanding. | 21 |
| 22 The blessing of the LORD, it maketh rich, and he addeth no sorrow with it. | בִּרְכַּת יְהוָה הִיא תַעֲשִׁיר<br>וְלֹא יוֹסִף עֶצֶב עִמָּהּ׃ | 22 | The blessing of Jehovah, that makes rich;<br>and he adds no sorrow therewith. | 22 |
| 23 *It is* as sport to a fool to do mischief: but a man of understanding hath wisdom. | כִּשְׂחוֹק לִכְסִיל עֲשׂוֹת זִמָּה<br>וְחָכְמָה לְאִישׁ תְּבוּנָה׃ | 23 | It is as mockery to a fool to execute counsel,<br>but wisdom to a man of understanding. | 23 |

V. 23. to act upon a plan

The intransitive sense of מתעה (second member), I do not think is sustained by reference to Jer. 42 : 20. The common English version (*ye dissembled in your hearts, when ye sent me*, etc.) gives the sense in effect, though not in form; for in their hearts they deceived and misled the prophet, when they deceptively sent him on a false errand. But however this may be, the usual causative sense is here the only admissible one, in connection with the first member.

V. 18. שפתי, accus. of the instrument, which is the natural construction of the words. In Bertheau's construction: *He that conceals hatred is of deceitful lips*, very little is expressed; for he who conceals hatred is, of course, a dissembler. In favor of the construction in the text, is the natural relation of the two members, and the use of הוא in the second, as an emphatic repetition of the subject in both.

V. 19. Simile Græcum illud apud Stobæum, Serm. XXXVI, 11, πολυλογία πολλὰ σφάλματα ἔχει (Rosenmüller).

V. 20. כמעט, *as little* = of little value.*

V. 21. The parallelism requires that חסר should be taken as a substantive. So it is expressed in all the ancient versions, and is so understood by most modern scholars.†

V. 23. *It is as mockery*, an object of derision and scorn, as the word is used in Job 12 : 4. זמה, *counsel*, or *plan*, in a good sense as in Job 17 : 11. That this is the true construction and meaning of the verse, is evident from the relation of לכסיל and לאיש in the two members.

Some construe and translate thus: *It is as sport to a fool to do mischief; but a man of understanding has wisdom* (Rosenmüller, Bertheau, Stuart); contrary to the obvious relation of לכסיל and לאיש. Others: *It is as sport to a fool to do mischief; but wisdom* is as sport (or, to exercise *wisdom* is as sport) *to the man*

*disciplinam.* Le Clerc: Calcat *viam ad vitam* . . . subaud. דורך, aut quid simile. Rosenmüller: *Semitam ad vitam* custodit, *qui custodit disciplinam*, ut שֹׁמֵר medium inter utrumque accusativum positum sit. Vel: *semitam ad vitam* est semita *custodientis disciplinam.* Umbreit: *Weg zum Leben dem, der Weisung wohl bewahrt.* De Wette: *Den Weg zum Leben* [wandelt] *wer Zucht bewahret.* Ewald: *Zum Leben wandelt wer da Zucht bewahret.* (ארח als Particip. אֹרֵחַ, oder ארח אֹרַח *Gang, Zug*, für *Reisegesellschaft, Reisende*, unbestimmt für einen Wanderer.) Hitzig: *Den Pfad zum Leben beachtet, wer Zucht.*

* Bertheau: *Gleich geringem*, d. i. von geringstem Werthe, im Gegensatze zu dem *auserwählten Silber.*

† Gesenius (Thes. and Lex., חָסֵר): "Subst. *want* of understanding. Prov. 10 : 21." Ewald: *Doch Narren sterben hin in Unverstand.* De Wette: *Die Thoren aber sterben aus Verstandes-Mangel.* Umbreit: *Die Thoren sterben selbst aus Mangel an Verstand.* Maurer: *Et* (sed) *stulti vecordia moriuntur*, non modo alios non juvant, sed sua vecordia pereunt ipsi. Hdwbch: חָסֵר nur als constr. Spr. 10 : 21, *Mangel.* Fürst (Hdwbch): חָסֵר (c. חֲסַר Spr. 10 : 21) *Mangel*, etc. Hitzig: *Aber die Thoren sterben durch Unverstand;* חסר ist hier nicht Stat. constr. von חסר wie Vs. 13, sondern von חֹסֶר. Richtig schon die Verss., nur dass den LXX לב ausfällt; falsch Bertheau: *Durch einen Unverständigen.* Stuart: *But fools die for lack of understanding.*

| KING JAMES' VERSION. | HEBREW TEXT. | | REVISED VERSION. | |
|---|---|---|---|---|
| 24 The fear of the wicked, it shall come upon him: but the desire of the righteous shall be granted. | מְגוֹרַת רָשָׁע הִיא תְבוֹאֶנּוּ<br>וְתַאֲוַת צַדִּיקִים יִתֵּן׃ | 24 | The dread of the wicked, that shall come upon him;<br>but the desire of the righteous He will grant. | 24 |
| 25 As the whirlwind passeth, so *is* the wicked no *more:* but the righteous *is* an everlasting foundation. | כַּעֲבוֹר סוּפָה וְאֵין רָשָׁע<br>וְצַדִּיק יְסוֹד עוֹלָם׃ | כה | As the whirlwind passes by, so the wicked is no more;<br>but the righteons is an everlasting foundation. | 25 |
| 26 As vinegar to the teeth, and as smoke to the eyes, so *is* the sluggard to them that send him. | כַּחֹמֶץ ׀ לַשִּׁנַּיִם וְכֶעָשָׁן לָעֵינָיִם<br>כֵּן הֶעָצֵל לְשֹׁלְחָיו׃ | 26 | As vinegar to the teeth, and as smoke to the eyes,<br>so is the sluggard to them that send him. | 26 |
| 27 The fear of the LORD prolongeth days: but the years of the wicked shall be shortened. | יִרְאַת יְהוָה תּוֹסִיף יָמִים<br>וּשְׁנוֹת רְשָׁעִים תִּקְצֹרְנָה׃ | 27 | The fear of Jehovah will prolong days;<br>but the years of the wicked shall be cut short. | 27 |
| 28 The hope of the righteous *shall be* gladness: but the expectation of the wicked shall perish. | תּוֹחֶלֶת צַדִּיקִים שִׂמְחָה<br>וְתִקְוַת רְשָׁעִים תֹּאבֵד׃ | 28 | The hope of the righteous is gladness;<br>but the expectation of the wicked shall perish. | 28 |
| 29 The way of the LORD *is* strength to the upright: but destruction *shall be* to the workers of iniquity. | מָעוֹז לַתֹּם דֶּרֶךְ יְהוָה<br>וּמְחִתָּה לְפֹעֲלֵי אָוֶן׃ | 29 | A stronghold for uprightness is the way of Jehovah;<br>but destruction to the workers of iniquity. | 29 |
| 30 The righteous shall never be removed: but the wicked shall not inhabit the earth. | צַדִּיק לְעוֹלָם בַּל־יִמּוֹט<br>וּרְשָׁעִים לֹא יִשְׁכְּנוּ־אָרֶץ׃ | ל | Forever, the righteous shall not be moved;<br>but the wicked shall not inhabit the land. | 30 |
| 31 The mouth of the just bringeth forth wisdom: but the froward tongue shall be cut out. | פִּי־צַדִּיק יָנוּב חָכְמָה<br>וּלְשׁוֹן תַּהְפֻּכוֹת תִּכָּרֵת׃ | 31 | The mouth of the righteous brings forth wisdom;<br>but the perverse tongue shall be cut out. | 31 |
| 32 The lips of the righteous know what is acceptable: but the mouth of the wicked *speaketh* frowardness. | שִׂפְתֵי צַדִּיק יֵדְעוּן רָצוֹן<br>וּפִי רְשָׁעִים תַּהְפֻּכוֹת׃ | 32 | The lips of the righteous know what is acceptable;<br>but the mouth of the wicked is perverseness. | 32 |
| CHAP. XI. | CHAP. XI. | | CHAP. XI. | |
| A FALSE balance *is* abomination to the LORD: but a just weight *is* his delight. | מֹאזְנֵי מִרְמָה תּוֹעֲבַת יְהוָה<br>וְאֶבֶן שְׁלֵמָה רְצוֹנוֹ׃ | א | A FALSE balance is the abomination of Jehovah;<br>but a full weight is his delight. | 1 |

*of understanding* (Umbreit,* De Wette, Ewald, Maurer,† Hitzig‡). A comparison of these constructions will, I think, be decisive in favor of the one I have given.

V. 24. *He will grant;* comp. chs. 3 : 35, 13 : 22, and the remark on 3 : 35.

V. 25. ואין; Lex. ו, 1, dd. *As the whirlwind passes by;* i. e., as when it passes, sweeping all before it. *So the wicked is no more;* he is swept away as by a whirlwind. The כְּ is strictly a particle of comparison; not of time, as understood by Ewald and Bertheau.

V. 30. *The land.* Compare, e. g., Ex. 20 : 12; Lev. 20 : 22; Deut. 11 : 8, 9; 25 : 15; Ps. 37 : 29. As there is, manifestly, the same allusion here, the word ארץ should be translated *land.*

V. 32. As the words פי and תהפכות stand, obviously, in the relation of subject and predicate, they should be connected only by the copula (the subst. verb) implied in the Hebrew by their juxtaposition.

Ch. XI.—V. 1. *A false balance.* See the note on ch. 16 : 11.

* In dem zweiten Hemistich muss vor לְאִישׁ תְּבוּנָה wieder כִּשְׂחוֹק hinzugedacht werden.

† *Pro ludo est stulto, patrare scelus; Et sapientia,* sapientia vero *viro* (homini) *intelligenti,* i. e. homini intelligenti vero pro ludo est sapientia, lusus est sapientia uti.

‡ Wahrscheinlich ist עשות vor חכמה zu wiederholen, diess fast zeugmatisch, da sonst nicht so gesprochen wird.

| KING JAMES' VERSION. | HEBREW TEXT. | | REVISED VERSION. | |
|---|---|---|---|---|
| 2 *When* pride cometh, then cometh shame: but with the lowly *is* wisdom. | בָּא זָדוֹן וַיָּבֹא קָלוֹן<br>וְאֶת־צְנוּעִים חָכְמָה׃ | 2 | When pride comes, there comes shame;<br>but with the lowly is wisdom. | 2 |
| 3 The integrity of the upright shall guide them: but the perverseness of transgressors shall destroy them. | תֻּמַּת יְשָׁרִים תַּנְחֵם<br>וְסֶלֶף בֹּגְדִים וְשָׁדֵּם׃ | 3 | The integrity of the upright will guide them;<br>but the perverseness of transgressors will destroy them. | 3 |
| 4 Riches profit not in the day of wrath: but righteousness delivereth from death. | לֹא־יוֹעִיל הוֹן בְּיוֹם עֶבְרָה<br>וּצְדָקָה תַּצִּיל מִמָּוֶת׃ | 4 | Riches profit not in the day of wrath;<br>but righteousness delivers from death. | 4 |
| 5 The righteousness of the perfect shall direct his way: but the wicked shall fall by his own wickedness. | צִדְקַת תָּמִים תְּיַשֵּׁר דַּרְכּוֹ<br>וּבְרִשְׁעָתוֹ יִפֹּל רָשָׁע׃ | ה | The righteousness of the perfect will make plain his way;<br>but the wicked will fall by his wickedness. | 5 |
| 6 The righteousness of the upright shall deliver them: but transgressors shall be taken in *their own* naughtiness. | צִדְקַת יְשָׁרִים תַּצִּילֵם<br>וּבְהַוַּת בֹּגְדִים יִלָּכֵדוּ׃ | 6 | The righteousness of the upright will deliver them;<br>but in the wickedness of transgressors shall they themselves be taken. | 6 |
| 7 When a wicked man dieth, *his* expectation shall perish: and the hope of unjust *men* perisheth. | בְּמוֹת אָדָם רָשָׁע תֹּאבַד תִּקְוָה<br>וְתוֹחֶלֶת אוֹנִים אָבָדָה׃ | 7 | When the wicked man dies, expectation shall perish;<br>yea, the hope of wickedness perishes. | 7 |
| 8 The righteous is delivered out of trouble, and the wicked cometh in his stead. | צַדִּיק מִצָּרָה נֶחֱלָץ<br>וַיָּבֹא רָשָׁע תַּחְתָּיו׃ | 8 | The righteous was delivered out of trouble;<br>and the wicked came into his place. | 8 |
| 9 A hypocrite with *his* mouth destroyeth his neighbour: but through knowledge shall the just be delivered. | בְּפֶה חָנֵף יַשְׁחִת רֵעֵהוּ<br>וּבְדַעַת צַדִּיקִים יֵחָלֵצוּ׃ | 9 | By the mouth the impure destroys his fellow;<br>but by knowledge the righteous are delivered. | 9 |
| 10 When it goeth well with the righteous the city rejoiceth: and when the wicked perish, *there is* shouting. | בְּטוּב צַדִּיקִים תַּעֲלֹץ קִרְיָה<br>וּבַאֲבֹד רְשָׁעִים רִנָּה׃ | י | When it is well with the righteous, the city rejoices;<br>and when the wicked perish, there is a shout of joy. | 10 |

V. 3. ישדם ק׳

V. 2. בא, ?155, 4, *a*.

V. 3. *Shall destroy them:* according to the *Keri*, which is, doubtless, the true reading.*

V. 5. *Will make plain* (not, *will direct*), the verb meaning properly, *to make even, plain—to level.*†

V. 6, second member:—the subject of the verb is suggested by the preceding genitive, as e. g. in Gen. 9 : 6.

* Bertheau: Dem Imperf. תנחם muss in *b* ein Imperf. entsprechen; daher ist mit dem Q'ri יְשָׁדֵּם zu lesen, von der Wurzel שָׁד. Hitzig: Das Ktib וְשַׁדָּם entstand, nach dem Targ. zu schliessen, daher, dass man וסלף für das Finit. ansah; es ist mit Syr. und Vulg. das Q'ri zu lesen.

† Bertheau: *Die Gerechtigkeit des Redlichen macht grade* oder *eben seinen Weg*, und schützt ihn so vor der Gefahr des Fallens, die hingegen die רשעה so nahe legt, dass der *Frevler* ihr nicht entgeht.

V. 7. אונים plur. intensive of אָוֶן. *The hope of wickedness* is the same as the hope of the wicked (of those who practice wickedness).* There is, therefore, no need (with Rosenmüller) to assume an adject. use of this noun;† nor (with Gesenius and others) to regard אונים as = אַנְשֵׁי אָוֶן.

Maurer suggests אוֹן as the sing., and translates: *The hope of riches perishes.* This is well, as to the sense and connection; but it has no support in the traditional exegesis, while the former has the authority of the Sept., Syr., and Chald.

V. 9. *The impure:* an appropriate designation of the godless, the impious, as *holy* is of the pious and devout man.

* As it is rendered in the Sept. ἀσεβῶν, Syr. ܥܘ̈ܠܐ, Chald. דְּעָבְדִין עַאְתָא.

† Cum Aben-Esra ex significatu nominis אָוֶן *vanitas, iniquitas* אוֹנִים capimus pro adjectivo, *iniqui*, formæ טוֹבִים *boni.*

| KING JAMES' VERSION. | HEBREW TEXT. | | REVISED VERSION. | |
|---|---|---|---|---|
| 11 By the blessing of the upright the city is exalted: but it is overthrown by the mouth of the wicked. | בְּבִרְכַּת יְשָׁרִים תָּרוּם קָרֶת<br>וּבְפִי רְשָׁעִים תֵּהָרֵס׃ | 11 | By the blessing of the upright<br>the city is raised up;<br>but by the mouth of the wicked<br>it is torn down. | 11 |
| 12 He that is void of wisdom despiseth his neighbour: but a man of understanding holdeth his peace. | בָּז לְרֵעֵהוּ חֲסַר־לֵב<br>וְאִישׁ תְּבוּנוֹת יַחֲרִישׁ׃ | 12 | He that despises his neighbor<br>is lacking in understanding;<br>but a man of intelligence holds<br>his peace. | 12 |
| 13 A talebearer revealeth secrets: but he that is of a faithful spirit concealeth the matter. | הוֹלֵךְ רָכִיל מְגַלֶּה־סּוֹד<br>וְנֶאֱמַן־רוּחַ מְכַסֶּה דָבָר׃ | 13 | He that goes talebearing is a<br>revealer of secrets;<br>but one of trusty spirit conceals<br>a matter. | 13 |
| 14 Where no counsel *is*, the people fall: but in the multitude of counsellors *there is* safety. | בְּאֵין תַּחְבֻּלוֹת יִפָּל־עָם<br>וּתְשׁוּעָה בְּרֹב יוֹעֵץ׃ | 14 | Where there is no direction the<br>people fall;<br>but in the multitude of counsel-<br>ors is safety. | 14 |
| 15 He that is surety for a stranger shall smart *for it:* and he that hateth suretiship is sure. | רַע יֵרוֹעַ כִּי־עָרַב זָר<br>וְשֹׂנֵא תוֹקְעִים בּוֹטֵחַ׃ | טו | Ill fares one when he is surety<br>for a stranger;<br>but he that hates sureties is<br>secure. | 15 |
| 16 A gracious woman retaineth honour: and strong *men* retain riches. | אֵשֶׁת חֵן תִּתְמֹךְ כָּבוֹד<br>וְעָרִיצִים יִתְמְכוּ־עֹשֶׁר׃ | 16 | A lovely woman obtains honor;<br>even as the violent obtain<br>riches. | 16 |

V. 12. *He that despises his neighbor,** with a vain conceit of his own superiority. Second member:—(See Expl. Notes).

V. 13. רכיל is the limiting accus., expressing the object of his going; to go on such an errand. Second member:—מכסה, lit. *is one that conceals;* but, as in many other instances, the part. is best expressed in English by the finite verb.

V. 14. תחבלות, see Job 37 : 12, and compare note on ch. 1 : 5.†

V. 15. רַע adverbial accus. prefixed to the verb with the same effect as the infin. absol.‡ *Sureties:* lit. *those who strike* (the hand, to wit) as sureties. He who hates sureties, and therefore will not be one, is the obvious meaning.

V. 16. The word חן respects not the person merely, but all which renders a woman lovely.* Hence אשת חן is not properly translated "*a beautiful woman.*" תתמך, *will obtain;*† it will be awarded her. *The violent*‡ (prop. formidable, inspiring terror), the only well established meaning of the word, and the appropriate one here. *Even as* (Lex. ו, 1, dd). For the force of the comparison, see Expl. Notes.

The true conception of the verse fully obviates Ewald's objections to the present form of the Heb. text: viz., 1. that עריצים is never used of men in a good sense (which is admitted); 2. that it is contrary to the spirit of the book, to regard riches as an enduring possession of the oppressor, as honor is of the meritorious woman.§ The *permanence* of the possession is not the point of comparison, but the effectiveness of the armory.

* Ewald: *Wer andere verachtet, ist sinnlos: doch ein verständ'ger Mann hält Schweigen.* Maurer: *Qui despicit alios,* fastuose in alios se gerit, *vecors* est; *vir intelligens* (prudens) *tacet.*

The Sept. reverses the subj. and pred., contrary to the natural construction of the words: *μυκτηρίζει πολίτας ἐνδεὴς φρενῶν.* Though such contempt for others always shows a want of understanding, it is not necessarily the way in which that want betrays itself. Vulgate (correctly as to the construction): *Qui despicit amicum suum, indigens corde est.*

† Ewald: *Wo keine Leitung, fällt das Volk dahin.* Bertheau: *Wenn keine Lenkung da ist, fällt das Volk.* Hitzig: *Wo keine Führung, kommt herunter ein Volk.*

‡ Gesenius (Thes. III., p. 1277): Prov. 11 : 15 . . . ubi רע more infinitivi absoluti ad augendam vim additur. Maurer: *Præmisso* רַע nomine vis verbi augetur. Wholly groundless is Bertheau's construction (followed by Stuart): Nimm רע als Substant., ירוע in seiner ursprünglich reflex. Bedeutung; *Ein Böser zeigt sich als Böser, wenn man vertritt* durch Bürgschaft *Fremden.*

* Gesenius (Thes. I., p. 500): *Gratia,* i. q. suavitas, venustas, pulchritudo (Anmuth) quæ gratiam conciliant. Prov. XI. 16: אֵשֶׁת חֵן *mulier venusta.* Maurer: Gratia vultus ac morum. Ewald: *Ein Weib von Anmuth.* Bertheau: *Das anmuthige Weib.* So the Sept., *γυνὴ εὐχάριστος.* Vulg., *mulier gratiosa;* hence, in all the English vernacular versions, *a gracious woman.*

† Rödiger (Thes. fasc. poster., p. 1508): *Assecutus est, consecutus est, accepit* v. c. honorem sq. acc. Prov. XI. 16; XXIX, 23. So the Vulg.: *Mulier gratiosa inveniet gloriam.*

‡ Ewald: In masor. Lesart, *wie Gewaltthätige.*

§ The Sept. rendering, which suggests (as he supposes) the true form of the Heb. text, is only one specimen among many of a disposition to develope and illustrate a thought, which is characteristic of this version of the book.

| KING JAMES' VERSION. | HEBREW TEXT. | | REVISED VERSION. |
|---|---|---|---|
| 17 The merciful man doeth good to his own soul: but *he that is* cruel troubleth his own flesh. | גֹּמֵל נַפְשׁוֹ אִישׁ חָסֶד<br>וְעֹכֵר שְׁאֵרוֹ אַכְזָרִי׃ | 17 | A merciful man does good to his own soul; 17<br>but the cruel afflicts his own flesh. |
| 18 The wicked worketh a deceitful work: but to him that soweth righteousness *shall be* a sure reward. | רָשָׁע עֹשֶׂה פְּעֻלַּת־שָׁקֶר<br>וְזֹרֵעַ צְדָקָה שֶׂכֶר אֱמֶת׃ | 18 | The wicked toils for deceptive hire; 18<br>but he who sows righteousness, for true wages: |
| 19 As righteousness *tendeth* to life: so he that pursueth evil *pursueth it* to his own death. | כֵּן־צְדָקָה לְחַיִּים<br>וּמְרַדֵּף רָעָה לְמוֹתוֹ׃ | 19 | so is righteousness for life, 19<br>and he follows evil for his death. |
| 20 They that are of a froward heart *are* abomination to the LORD: but *such as are* upright in *their* way *are* his delight. | תּוֹעֲבַת יְהוָה עִקְּשֵׁי־לֵב<br>וּרְצוֹנוֹ תְּמִימֵי דָרֶךְ׃ | כ | An abomination of Jehovah are the perverse in heart; 20<br>but those of blameless way are his delight. |
| 21 *Though* hand *join* in hand, the wicked shall not be unpunished: but the seed of the righteous shall be delivered. | יָד לְיָד לֹא־יִנָּקֶה רָּע<br>וְזֶרַע צַדִּיקִים נִמְלָט׃ | 21 | Hand to hand the evil will not be acquitted; 21<br>but the seed of the righteous is delivered. |

V. 17. The predicate stands, emphatically, first.* So the Sept. and Vulg.,† and most of the modern versions.‡

A preposterous sense is given to this verse by the other construction (Umbreit, Bertheau, Stuart): *He who does good to his own soul* (cares for himself) *is a benevolent man, and he who afflicts himself is a cruel one;* on the principle that as a man treats himself, so he will treat others.|| This certainly reverses all former ideas of benevolence and selfishness.¶

V. 18. *Toils* (עשׂה) as in ch. 31 : 13; Ruth 2 : 19, etc. *Deceptive hire* (that cheats the laborer with a false show of worth) is evidently the meaning, as shown by the parallel שׂכר אמת.§

* Hitzig: Was voransteht, sind offenbar die Prädicate; denn wer sich selber wohlthut, ist nicht nothwendig ein gütiger Mann (Umbreit, Bertheau), sondern vielleicht ein arger Egoist.

† Sept.: Τῇ ψυχῇ αὐτοῦ ἀγαθὸν ποιεῖ ἀνὴρ ἐλεήμων. Vulg.: *Benefacit animæ suæ misericors.*

‡ Ewald: *Dem eignen Selber thut wohl ein Mann von Liebe;*
*doch trübt sein Fleisch und Blut ein Grausamer.*

Maurer: *Benefacit suo animo* (sibi ipsi) *vir benignus; et affligit suam carnem* (se ipsum) *crudelis:* i. e., sibi ipsi benefacit, qui benefacit aliis; se ipsum affligit, qui affligit alios.

Hitzig: Sich selber thut Gutes der Liebreiche,
und seinen eigenen Leib betrübt der Mitleidlose.

§ Rödiger (Thes. fasc. poster.. p. 1479): *Impius mala fraude agit.* Ewald is near the truth, though he has not given the exact sense:

*Ein Frevler wohl ausbeutet Trugs-Gewinn;*
*doch wer da Recht aussäet, treuen Lohn.*

|| Bertheau: *Wer wohlthut seiner Seele,* für sich sorgt, *ist ein gütiger Mann, und wer sein Fleisch betrübt,* in der Weise wie Sir. 14 : 3, ff., beschrieben wird, *ist ein grausamer,* vgl. Sir. 14 : 5.

¶ Stuart: "*He who doeth good to himself, is a man of kindness; but he who troubleth his own flesh, is cruel.*

The design of this is not to recommend *selfishness,* in the proper sense of that word, but a wise and prudent care and solicitute for one's own real good. This is *kindness,* i. e., kindness to himself. On the contrary, he who vexes himself by an improper course of conduct, is cruel to himself." Not Solomon's meaning, surely!

V. 19. כֵּן, *so,* belongs to the second member of a comparison (demonstrative), not to the first (*as*), as given in the Common Version.

The true sense of this verse, and its relation to the preceding one, was seen by C. B. Michaelis;* and Bertheau admits this to be the proper sense of the Heb. text.† To construe כן as a subst. (Schultens, J. D. Michaelis), or as a particip. adjective (Ziegler, Umbreit, De Wette, Ewald, Maurer) is justly characterized by Bertheau‡ as a "mere make-shift."

The reading בן of the Sept., Syr., Arab., and one Cod. (De Rossi)§ has no sufficient support. Prof. Stuart too hastily adopts the opinion of some German critics, that the Heb. text is faulty. The only objection is to a connected quatrain, in this division of the book; but of this another example occurs in ch. 21 : 25, 26.

V. 21. *Hand to hand* (יד ליד) stands in immediate connection with the following subject and its verb, as an adverbial qualification; though standing hand to hand, for mutual support, they shall not go free. This phrase occurs again in ch. 16 : 5. The use there of the *sing.* (distributively) is no objection to this view; the reference being obviously to *all of the class,* as indicated by כל גבה in the first member. Less happily, C. B. Michaelis (fol-

* כֵּן *ita* nimirum. Respicit ad v. 18, ex quo hanc illationem auctor elicit per modum epiphonematis. Rosenmüller: *Sic justitia ad vitam* scil. ducit, sive prodest. Connectitur vero hic versus tanquam epiphonema cum superiore vocula כֵּן *sic,* q. d. *hac ratione,* uti jam dixi.

† Wenn כֵּן richtige Lesart ist, so soll sich unser Vers dem vorhergehenden anschliessen, in dieser Weise: so ist Gerechtigkeit zum Leben, u. s. w.

‡ Ist zu deutlich blosser Nothbehelf.

§ בן צדקה *Filius justitiæ* vel *justus,* cod. meus 368, LXX, Syrus, Arabs. R. Immanuel explicat per ישר *rectus,* deinde vero per בעל צדקה, seu in signif. nostri בן (De Rossi, Suppl. ad var. S. T. lect.).

| KING JAMES' VERSION. | HEBREW TEXT. | | REVISED VERSION. | |
|---|---|---|---|---|
| 22 *As* a jewel of gold in a swine's snout, *so is* a fair woman which is without discretion. | נֶזֶם זָהָב בְּאַף חֲזִיר<br>אִשָּׁה יָפָה וְסָרַת טָעַם׃ | 22 | A nose-ring of gold in a swine's snout,<br>is a woman fair and without discretion. | 22 |
| 23 The desire of the righteous *is* only good: *but* the expectation of the wicked *is* wrath. | תַּאֲוַת צַדִּיקִים אַךְ־טוֹב<br>תִּקְוַת רְשָׁעִים עֶבְרָה׃ | 23 | The desire of the righteous is only good;<br>the expectation of the wicked is wrath. | 23 |
| 24 There is that scattereth, and yet increaseth; and *there is* that withholdeth more than is meet, but *it tendeth* to poverty. | יֵשׁ מְפַזֵּר וְנוֹסָף עוֹד<br>וְחֹשֵׂךְ מִיֹּשֶׁר אַךְ־לְמַחְסוֹר׃ | 24 | There is that scatters, and is increased yet more;<br>and that withholds more than is meet, only to want. | 24 |
| 25 The liberal soul shall be made fat: and he that watereth shall be watered also himself. | נֶפֶשׁ־בְּרָכָה תְדֻשָּׁן<br>וּמַרְוֶה גַּם־הוּא יוֹרֶא׃ | כה | The liberal soul shall be enriched;<br>and he that waters shall himself be watered. | 25 |
| 26 He that withholdeth corn, the people shall curse him: but blessing *shall be* upon the head of him that selleth *it*. | מֹנֵעַ בָּר יִקְּבֻהוּ לְאוֹם<br>וּבְרָכָה לְרֹאשׁ מַשְׁבִּיר׃ | 26 | He that withholds corn, the people will curse him;<br>but blessing for the head of him that sells grain! | 26 |
| 27 He that diligently seeketh good procureth favour: but he that seeketh mischief, it shall come unto him. | שֹׁחֵר טוֹב יְבַקֵּשׁ רָצוֹן<br>וְדֹרֵשׁ רָעָה תְבוֹאֶנּוּ׃ | 27 | Him that seeks good will favor seek;<br>and he that seeks evil, it will come upon him. | 27 |

lowed by Stuart); though he join his hands, i. e., apply both hands, resisting with all his might. *

According to Gesenius, יד ליד = *generation to generation*, i. e., through all time.† But the evidence of such a usage is not made out. *From hand to hand*, in the examples referred to, means *from one to another*, i. e., by succession.

Ewald: *The hand for it;* i. e., my pledge for it (ch. 6 : 1; Job 17 : 3), I pledge myself for its truth.‡ So Hitzig,§ Bertheau, and others. But there is no other evidence of such a usage, as Ewald concedes.‖

V. 22. סרת טעם, part. construed with the genitive, as in some other instances where the verb itself is construed only with a preposition (§ 135, 1, Rem. *extr.*); comp. שָׁבֵי פֶשַׁע Is. 59 : 20.¶ Gesenius' Lex. (Am. ed.): "*Who departeth from discretion*, i. e., who is without discretion."

By טעם is here meant (as well explained by Hitzig *) a delicate sense of propriety, shown in modesty of look, speech, and demeanor.

V. 24. The three participles stand in the same relation to יֵשׁ, and the first two have obviously the same subject.† מִישֶׁר in its established Heb. use (with מִן of comparison) gives an apt and striking sense; much more so than *riches*, adopted by Schultens and Bertheau from the Arabic.‡

V. 25. *The liberal soul:* lit. *the soul of blessing* (of which this is characteristic), that delights in blessing, in imparting its bounty to others.

V. 26. *That sells grain:* the true sense of the Heb. word;§ see Gen. 42 : 6 (comp. 41 : 56, and 47 : 14–20); Deut. 2 : 28; Am. 8 : 5, 6. *That procureth grain* (Stuart) is a sense unknown in Heb. usage. The distinction is between the one who hoards it, for the purpose of enhancing the price, and the one who sells at the current price.

V. 27. The first three verbs agree in the general idea *to seek.* That they are used as synonyms of this leading idea, and are

---

* q. d. *Manum manui* licet jungat, h. e. ambas manus obvertat, immo manibus pedibusque obnixe omnia faciat, averruncet poenam.

† Thes. II., p. 566: *Manu in manum* (von Hand zu Hand), i. e., per omnes generationes et ætates, et cum negandi particula: *nunquam.*

‡ Hand der Hand! scheint eine alte Betheurung aus dem gemeinen Leben zu sein, wie wenn man für die Wahrheit der Sache einen Handschlag thun, sich verbürgen wolle.

§ Statt zu sagen: *ich verbürge es*, wird die Gebärde des Bürgens namhaft gemacht.

‖ So viel scheint der Zusammenhang als das Sicherste zu lehren.

¶ Umbreit: Wörtlich: eine zurückgewichene in Rücksicht des Geschmacks, d. i. vom Geschmack. Maurer (Hdwbch.: *Abweichend des Verstandes.* Bertheau: *Eine abweichende von klugem Urtheile.* Ewald (Lehrb., § 288, 3): סר טעם *geschmacklos*, Spr. 11 : 22.

* Ein zarter Sinn für das Schickliche, hauptsächlich hervortretend in Züchtigkeit des Blickes, der Rede, des ganzen Benehmens.

† Maurer: Verbi נוֹסָף Rosenmüllerus et Ewaldus non debebant subjectum facere opes. Est idem potius quod præcedentium.

‡ Ewald: *Und sparet mehr als billig.*

§ Gesenius (Thes. III., p. 1358): *Annonam vendidit.* Ewald: *Des Kornverkäufers.*

| KING JAMES' VERSION. | HEBREW TEXT. | | REVISED VERSION. | |
|---|---|---|---|---|
| 28 He that trusteth in his riches shall fall: but the righteous shall flourish as a branch. | בּוֹטֵחַ בְּעָשְׁרוֹ הוּא יִפֹּל<br>וְכֶעָלֶה צַדִּיקִים יִפְרָחוּ׃ | 28 | Whoso trusts in his riches, he shall fall;<br>but as the leaf shall the righteous flourish. | 28 |
| 29 He that troubleth his own house shall inherit the wind: and the fool *shall be* servant to the wise of heart. | עֹכֵר בֵּיתוֹ יִנְחַל־רוּחַ<br>וְעֶבֶד אֱוִיל לַחֲכַם־לֵב׃ | 29 | He that troubles his own house shall inherit wind;<br>and the fool is a servant to the wise in heart. | 29 |
| 30 The fruit of the righteous *is* a tree of life; and he that winneth souls *is* wise. | פְּרִי צַדִּיק עֵץ חַיִּים<br>וְלֹקֵחַ נְפָשׁוֹת חָכָם׃ | ל | The fruit of the righteous is a tree of life;<br>and he that wins souls is wise. | 30 |
| 31 Behold, the righteous shall be recompensed in the earth: much more the wicked and the sinner. | הֵן צַדִּיק בָּאָרֶץ יְשֻׁלָּם<br>אַף כִּי־רָשָׁע וְחוֹטֵא׃ | 31 | Lo, the righteous on earth shall be requited;<br>much more the wicked and the sinner. | 31 |
| CHAP. XII. | CHAP. XII. | | CHAP. XII. | |
| WHOSO loveth instruction loveth knowledge: but he that hateth reproof *is* brutish. | אֹהֵב מוּסָר אֹהֵב דָּעַת<br>וְשׂוֹנֵא תוֹכַחַת בָּעַר׃ | א | HE that loves correction loves knowledge;<br>but he that hates reproof is brutish. | 1 |
| 2 A good *man* obtaineth favour of the LORD: but a man of wicked devices will he condemn. | טוֹב יָפִיק רָצוֹן מֵיְהוָה<br>וְאִישׁ מְזִמּוֹת יַרְשִׁיעַ׃ | 2 | The good will obtain favor from Jehovah;<br>but the man of evil devices he will hold guilty. | 2 |

V. 31. If the righteous

interchangeable, appears from other passages, e. g., Ps. 38 : 21; * where דרשׁ (here joined with רע) is used with טוב (here joined with שׁחר) in the expression of the same idea. In English we have not synonyms by which we can thus vary the expression, without making distinctions not intended by the Hebrew, and so misleading the reader by diverting his attention from the thought itself to some incident in the expression of it.

*That seeks good* (the benevolent), in opposition to him *that seeks evil* (the malevolent), in the next member. For the first clause compare Ps. 122 : 9 (*I will seek thy good*), and Neh. 2 : 10 (prop. *to seek the good of*, etc.); for the second member, first clause, compare 1 Sam. 25 : 26 (*that seek evil to my lord*). *Will favor seek:* he will be the object of favor. The expression of the whole verse is singularly pointed and felicitous.

That רצון is the subject of the verb, in the second clause of the first member, is evident from the parallelism; *it will come upon him*, in the second member, answering to *favor will seek him*, in the first.

V. 30. There is no occasion, as well suggested by Maurer, for supplying פרי before עץ.† The counsels and example of the righteous are aptly compared, in their influence, to a tree of life. Second member:—See Expl. Notes.

In vv. 29 and 30, the two members aptly correspond, and make with each other a consistent and pertinent sense.* There is, therefore, no ground for supposing (with Ewald, Bertheau, and others) that the order of the Heb. text is disturbed, and that 29 *b* should be 30 *a*, and *vice versa*.

V. 31. *Requited* corresponds to ישׁלם in both its senses.† *Lo, behold*, the earlier and more common use of הן, is the most pertinent here, giving emphasis to the expression of the thought. The hypothetic form (*if*) is a comparatively feeble expression of the same sentiment. Second member:—The common use of אַף כי, in such a connection, gives a just and appropriate sense; and there is no ground for assuming any other use of this combination here.‡

* Literally: *And who requite evil in place of* (in return for) *good, and persecute me in place of my seeking good;* i. e., in return for my seeking their good. The Heb. expression is stronger than the English *in return for;* viz., that evil on their part *comes in place* of good on his.

† Commode probi hominis facta et consilia ipsi comparantur arbori vitæ.

* Maurer: Ceterum videt lector, quam bene concinant membra. Idem observavit in versu superiore. Valeat igitur festinantius proposita ab Ewaldo et aliis conjectura, qua turbato membrorum ordine פרי צדיק עץ חיים fieri jubetur membrum posterius versus 29, עבד אויל לחכם־לב hemistichium prius versus 30, et לקח נפשות חכם ejusdem posterius.

† "Shall be punished as he deserveth, 1 Pet. 4 : 18," is the comment of the Genevan version.

‡ As is done by Bertheau: אַף כי *und dass ein Frevler und Sünder!* der Ausruf muss etwa so ergänzt werden; im Lande belohnt werde, ist nimmer behauptet worden. So hat אַף כי hier im Gegensatze etwa die Bedeutung von: aber nicht.

| KING JAMES' VERSION. | HEBREW TEXT. | | REVISED VERSION. | |
|---|---|---|---|---|
| 3 A man shall not be established by wickedness: but the root of the righteous shall not be moved. | לֹא־יִכּוֹן אָדָם בְּרֶשַׁע<br>וְשֹׁרֶשׁ צַדִּיקִים בַּל־יִמּוֹט׃ | 3 | A man shall not be established by wickedness;<br>but the root of the righteous shall not be moved. | 3 |
| 4 A virtuous woman *is* a crown to her husband: but she that maketh ashamed *is* as rottenness in his bones. | אֵשֶׁת חַיִל עֲטֶרֶת בַּעְלָהּ<br>וּכְרָקָב בְּעַצְמוֹתָיו מְבִישָׁה׃ | 4 | A worthy woman is a crown to her husband;<br>and a base one is as rottenness in his bones. | 4 |
| 5 The thoughts of the righteous *are* right: *but* the counsels of the wicked *are* deceit. | מַחְשְׁבוֹת צַדִּיקִים מִשְׁפָּט<br>תַּחְבֻּלוֹת רְשָׁעִים מִרְמָה׃ | ח | The thoughts of the righteous are uprightness;<br>the guidance of the wicked is deceit. | 5 |
| 6 The words of the wicked *are* to lie in wait for blood: but the mouth of the upright shall deliver them. | דִּבְרֵי רְשָׁעִים אֱרָב־דָּם<br>וּפִי יְשָׁרִים יַצִּילֵם׃ | 6 | The words of the wicked are a lying in wait for blood;<br>but the mouth of the upright will deliver them. | 6 |
| 7 The wicked are overthrown, and *are* not: but the house of the righteous shall stand. | הָפוֹךְ רְשָׁעִים וְאֵינָם<br>וּבֵית צַדִּיקִים יַעֲמֹד׃ | 7 | The wicked are overthrown, and they are no more;<br>but the house of the righteous shall stand. | 7 |
| 8 A man shall be commended according to his wisdom: but he that is of a perverse heart shall be despised. | לְפִי שִׂכְלוֹ יְהֻלַּל־אִישׁ<br>וְנַעֲוֵה־לֵב יִהְיֶה לָבוּז׃ | 8 | According to his wisdom shall a man be praised;<br>but the perverse in heart shall be despised. | 8 |
| 9 *He that is* despised, and hath a servant, *is* better than he that honoureth himself, and lacketh bread. | טוֹב נִקְלֶה וְעֶבֶד לוֹ<br>מִמִּתְכַּבֵּד וַחֲסַר־לָחֶם׃ | 9 | Better is one despised, and that tills for himself,<br>than he who boasts himself, and lacks bread. | 9 |

V. 5. the plans V. 9. (V. R.) and that has a servant

Ch. XII.—V. 4. *A worthy woman:* a woman of true worth (as חיל is used in 1 Kings 1 : 52); not merely virtuous in the sense of a chaste wife, but one worthy of the relation in all respects. Second member:—מבישה intrans. (Lex., Hiph. 3), as sometimes used, e. g., ch. 14 : 35.

V. 6. *Will deliver them:* viz., those implied in the expression *lying in wait;* its intended victims. Such a reference of the pronoun to an implied subject is frequent in Hebrew.*

V. 7. Lit. *an overthrowing of the wicked* (scil. there is); comp. §131, 4, *b*.

V. 9. *And that tills for himself:*† as the text was read by the Seventy, the Syr. translator, and Jerome.‡ So it is read by Ziegler, Ewald,§ and Hitzig.‖ This is evidently the true reading; for it not only has the support of the oldest versions, but makes the most correct and consistent sense, in itself, and in connection with the parallel member. The proper contrast with the second member (as Ewald justly claims) is the man of humble condition and pretensions, who gets a sure livelihood by tilling the soil for himself (compare v. 11). In marked contrast with him (second member) is the man who prides himself on the show of wealth, or on his birth and connections, while he pines in want.

In the same sense, most of the modern versions translate (as the Genevan, for example): *He that is despised, and* [*is*] *his own servant, is better than he that boasteth himself and lacketh bread.** But this, though a possible construction of וְעֶבֶד לוֹ, will not be claimed as the most natural and probable one.

* Ewald: *Sie*, nämlich die einfältigen Unschuldigen, deren Blute und Leben die Frevler am leichtesten nachstellen zu können meinen: vergl. 1 : 11, ff.

† So עבד is used abs. in Deut. 15 : 19. Gesenius (Thes. II., p. 977): Omisso acc. Deut. XV, 19: *ne* agrum *colas cum* (בְּ) *primogenito bovis tui*, i. e. eo ad arandum eum adhibito.

‡ Sept.: *Κρείσσων ἀνὴρ ἐν ἀτιμίᾳ δουλεύων ἑαυτῷ.* Syr.: ܕܡܫܡܫ ܢܦܫܗ. Vulg.: *Melior est pauper et sufficiens sibi.*

§ Darum ist וְעֹבֵד, *und* den Acker *bauend für sich*, zu lesen.

‖ וְעֶבֶד fassen das Targum und Ibn Ezra, wie bei dieser Punctation am nächsten liegt, *et cui servus est;* dagegen, was im Parall. Forderung des Sinnes, Jarchi und Levi ben Gersom, *et servus sibi;* wo dann aber mit LXX., Syr., Vulg., das Particip zu punctiren sein wird.

* So Munster (Biblia Hebraica, 1546): *Melior est* (homo apud se) *despectus, et qui sui ipsius est servus, quam gloriosus aliquis qui eget pane.* Schultens: Hoc explicant; qui victum sibimet procurare valet, quo sensu et Hieronymus dedit *sufficiens sibi.* Dathe:

*Melior est ignobilis et sibimet ipse servus,*
*Quam is qui se jactat et pane caret.*

| KING JAMES' VERSION. | HEBREW TEXT. | | REVISED VERSION. | |
|---|---|---|---|---|
| 10 A righteous *man* regardeth the life of his beast: but the tender mercies of the wicked *are* cruel. | יוֹדֵעַ צַדִּיק נֶפֶשׁ בְּהֶמְתּוֹ<br>וְרַחֲמֵי רְשָׁעִים אַכְזָרִי׃ | י | The righteous cares for the life of his beast;<br>but the bowels of the wicked are cruel. | 10 |
| 11 He that tilleth his land shall be satisfied with bread: but he that followeth vain *persons is* void of understanding. | עֹבֵד אַדְמָתוֹ יִשְׂבַּע־לָחֶם<br>וּמְרַדֵּף רֵיקִים חֲסַר־לֵב׃ | 11 | He that tills his ground shall be satisfied with bread;<br>but he that follows vanities lacks understanding. | 11 |
| 12 The wicked desireth the net of evil *men:* but the root of the righteous yieldeth *fruit.* | חָמַד רָשָׁע מְצוֹד רָעִים<br>וְשֹׁרֶשׁ צַדִּיקִים יִתֵּן׃ | 12 | The wicked delights in the net of the evil;<br>but the root of the righteous will bring forth. | 12 |

V. 10. for the wants

Ib. but the compassions

*And has a servant** is the proper rendering of the Masoretic reading וְעֶבֶד לוֹ; and is defended by Rosenmüller, Bertheau, and others,† on the ground that he is thereby enabled to cultivate his land, and obtain his bread. But it could hardly be worth while to say of the man, who is able to own or hire laborers to earn a subsistence for him, that he is better off than the poor and proud starveling. At any rate, as an expression of what is admitted to be the writer's thought, this is not to be compared, in pertinency and point, with the other reading.

V. 10. *Cares for*, etc. It will hardly be claimed, that ידע נפש is to be understood in the same sense, whatever may be the subject of the latter; and that the phrase ידע נפש בהמתו must, therefore, be explained by Ex. 23 : 9, יְדַעְתֶּם אֶת־נֶפֶשׁ הַגֵּר. Margin: *the wants*, viz., of the animal life (as some understand נפש here); its capacity for suffering and enjoyment.

*The bowels of the wicked:*‡ the primary signification of the word, used here (like *heart*) for the seat of emotion.§ The *oxymoron* found in many versions, *the tender mercies of the wicked are cruel*, has very little probability.‖ אכזרי, properly *a cruel one* (as in ch. 5 : 9 : Jer. 6 : 23) = *cruel.*¶

V. 11. ריקים, *empty, vain* things, in which there is no substantial good. The word, by usage, is applied either to persons, or things; the parallelism here requires the latter.*

V. 12. *Net* (מצוד): as the word is used in Job 19 : 6, and Eccl. 7 : 26. There is no occasion for the assumed metonomy, *prey, gain.* For the relation of the two members, see Expl. Notes.

*Will bring forth* (יתן). The Hebrew verb, with the complement פְּרִי, means *to give fruit;* said of a *tree* (Ps. 1 : 3, Ezek. 34 : 27), and of the *earth* (Lev. 25 : 19); so with the complement כֹּחַ or יְבוּלָהּ, in Gen. 4 : 12, Ezek. 34 : 27. But the verbal idea *to give, to yield*, when said of a tree or its root, does not necessarily require a complement; and this is the more naturally omitted in the compressed brevity of style peculiar to these proverbial sayings.†

Other constructions are: *The root of the righteous He* (God) *will set;*‡ *the root of the righteous endures.*§ But the natural

* Chald.: טַב הוּא זְלִילָא וְעַבְדֵי אִית לֵיהּ. Genev. Fr. (1562): Mieux vaut l'homme abject, et qui ha serviteurs, que celui qui se glorifie, et ha faute de pain.

† Rosenmüller: *Et cui est servus*, qui vero tantum habet, ut servum alere possit, adeoque necessariis ad sustentandam vitam subsidiis non caret. Bertheau: Aber vielleicht ist er dadurch in den Stand gesetzt, etwa seinen Acker zu bebauen, und sich Brod zu schaffen.

‡ Gesenius (Thes. III., p. 1283): *Viscera, τὰ σπλάγχνα* . . . spec. ut sedes sensuum misericordiæ et caritatis. Prov. XII, 10, . . . *sed viscera improborum dura sunt.*

§ Maurer: רחמים hic significat *viscera*, affectuum sedem, *cor*, qui significatus primarius est vocis.

‖ Hitzig: Dass *das Mitleid der Frevler grausam sei* hat als Oxymoron geringere Wahrscheinlichkeit.

¶ Maurer: רחמים אכזרי est constructio quæ dicitur ad sensum. Umbreit: אכזרי, etwas Grausames.

* Sept.: *Οἱ δὲ διωκοντες μάταια ἐνδεεῖς φρενῶν.* Aq. and Theod.: *Κενά.* Sym.: *Ὁ δὲ ἐπισπεύδων εἰς ἀπραγίαν.* Vulg.: *Qui autem sectatur otium.* Rosenmüller: Malim ריקים neutraliter capere, ut intelligantur et vana et inania consilia, et res vanæ et inutiles, quibus quis studet, unde nihil lucri et utilitatis capit. Hitzig: Demnach bedeutet ריקים genauer: *Müssigkeiten*, windige Beschäftigungen, welche keine Arbeit sind.

† So the Syr. translator: ܘܥܩܪܐ ܕܙܕܝ̈ܩܐ ܢܩܘܡ. Gersonides correctly explains the second member as meaning, that they derive their strength from their own root. Mercer (Commentar. in Prov.): *radix autem justorum dabit* fructum suum. Eclipses hujusmodi in sententiis Salomonis sunt cræbræ, quia paucis verbis multa et gravia constringere voluit.

‡ Gesenius, Thes. II. p. 928: *sed radicem justorum* firmiter *figit* Deus. Bertheau: *Die Wurzel der Gerechten* (v. 3) *giebt er;* er bewirkt dass sie feststehen, nicht in Netze fallen, u. s. f. Rosenm.: *Dare* h. l. idem est ac *figere, firmare*, ut Ezech. 17 : 22, 37 : 26. Ad יתן subaudiendum est Dei nomen, ut 10 : 24, vel est impersonalis loquendi formula, *dabitur.*

§ Ewald (followed, in the essential point, by Stuart): *doch der Gerechten Wurzel dauert.* Da der Sinn schon an sich darauf führt, dass der Wurzel Dauer oder Nichtdauer zugeschrieben werde, . . . so scheint es am leichtesten, יתן als ein dem אֵיתָן gleichbedeutendes Adjectiv zu fassen, und darnach zu lesen יֵתָן.

| KING JAMES' VERSION. | HEBREW TEXT. | | REVISED VERSION. | |
|---|---|---|---|---|
| 13 The wicked is snared by the transgression of *his* lips: but the just shall come out of trouble. | בְּפֶשַׁע שְׂפָתַיִם מוֹקֵשׁ רָע<br>וַיֵּצֵא מִצָּרָה צַדִּיק׃ | 13 | In the transgression of the lips<br>is an evil snare;<br>but the righteous will go forth<br>out of trouble. | 13 |
| 14 A man shall be satisfied with good by the fruit of *his* mouth: and the recompense of a man's hands shall be rendered unto him. | מִפְּרִי פִי־אִישׁ יִשְׂבַּע־טוֹב<br>וּגְמוּל יְדֵי־אָדָם יָשׁוּב לוֹ׃ | 14 | Of the fruit of the mouth shall<br>a man be satisfied with good;<br>and the desert of one's hands<br>shall return to him. | 14 |
| 15 The way of a fool *is* right in his own eyes: but he that hearkeneth unto counsel *is* wise. | דֶּרֶךְ אֱוִיל יָשָׁר בְּעֵינָיו<br>וְשֹׁמֵעַ לְעֵצָה חָכָם׃ | טו | The way of a fool is right in his<br>own eyes;<br>but he that hearkens to counsel<br>is wise. | 15 |
| 16 A fool's wrath is presently known: but a prudent *man* covereth shame. | אֱוִיל בַּיּוֹם יִוָּדַע כַּעְסוֹ<br>וְכֹסֶה קָלוֹן עָרוּם׃ | 16 | The fool's anger is known the<br>same day;<br>but a shrewd man conceals an<br>affront. | 16 |
| 17 *He that* speaketh truth sheweth forth righteousness: but a false witness deceit. | יָפִיחַ אֱמוּנָה יַגִּיד צֶדֶק<br>וְעֵד שְׁקָרִים מִרְמָה׃ | 17 | He who breathes truth shows<br>the right,<br>but a false witness fraud. | 17 |
| 18 There is that speaketh like the piercings of a sword: but the tongue of the wise *is* health. | יֵשׁ בּוֹטֶה כְּמַדְקְרוֹת חָרֶב<br>וּלְשׁוֹן חֲכָמִים מַרְפֵּא׃ | 18 | There is that prates as with<br>thrusts of the sword;<br>but the tongue of the wise is a<br>healing. | 18 |
| 19 The lip of truth shall be established for ever: but a lying tongue *is* but for a moment. | שְׂפַת־אֱמֶת תִּכּוֹן לָעַד<br>וְעַד־אַרְגִּיעָה לְשׁוֹן שָׁקֶר | 19 | The truthful lip is established<br>forever,<br>and the lying tongue but for<br>a moment. | 19 |
| 20 Deceit *is* in the heart of them that imagine evil: but to the counsellors of peace *is* joy. | מִרְמָה בְּלֶב־חֹרְשֵׁי־רָע<br>וּלְיוֹעֲצֵי שָׁלוֹם שִׂמְחָה׃ | כ | Deceit is in the heart of them<br>that devise evil;<br>but to them that counsel peace<br>there is joy. | 20 |

V. 14. ישיב ק׳

relation of the verbal idea (*to give, to yield*) to that of a *root* is against the assumption of a *subject* not indicated in the connection. The other construction rests on a needless conjecture,* and weakens, moreover, the antithesis in the two members.

*Will bring forth:*† used in English, like the Hebrew word, with or without its complement.

V. 13. *An evil snare:* compare Eccl. 9 : 12, בִּמְצוֹדָה רָעָה. So in all critical works, till that of Bertheau (followed by Stuart), who translates, '*a snare to the evil.*'‡ But with this construction, the meaning must be, that "the צדיק in the second member is, according to the first, he who is not chargeable with the *transgression of the lips;*"§ which is not consistent with the language of the second member.

V. 14. *Shall return:* according to the *Chethibh* (יָשׁוּב), which is doubtless the true reading. *Qeri: He* (God) *will cause to return.*

V. 16. *The same day* (בַּיּוֹם) :* the literal and pointed expression of the Hebrew.

Second member: *a shrewd man* (ערום), see note on ch. 1 : 4, third paragraph), is the *subject*, as required by the contrast with '*fool,*' and not the predicate, as construed by some.†

V. 18. *As with* (כְּ) : see Gesenius' Gram., § 118, *Rem. c.*

V. 19, second member. *For a moment:* lit. *while I wink;* a form of expression established in Hebrew (compare Jer. 49 : 19), but not familiar to English usage.‡

V. 20. For the relation of the two members, see Expl. Notes.

---

* Gesenius, Thes. II. p. 928: Nil opus est conjectura יָתֵן *perennis*, quæ vox et ipsa conjecturalis est.

† As the Hebrew word is rendered in Ps. 1 : 3, in the Common Version.

‡ Nicht *böser Fallstrick*, sondern Fallstrick des Bösen, für den Bösen.

§ Der צדיק in *b* ist nach *a* der, welcher sich *des Vergehens der Lippen*, z. B. der trügerischen Rede 19 : 22 (?) nicht schuldig macht.

* Bertheau: *an demselben Tage*, d. i. sogleich nachdem er erregt ist. Ewald: *desselben Tags.*

† Rosenmüller: Tantum abest, ut ob illatam sibi injuriam turbas et contentiones excitet, et sese ulcisci studeat, ut potius ita se gerat, quasi offensam ne animadverteret quidem.

‡ Bertheau: ארגיעה ist der Voluntat. Hifil (Jerem. 49 : 19, 58 : 44), *ich will machen einen Wink* (רָגַע), doch hat sich diese ursprüngliche Bedeutung so weit abgeschliffen, dass die Form, als stände sie substantivish für רגע, mit der Präpos. עד verbunden wird: *bis ich mache einen Wink* = bis auf einen Augenblick.

| KING JAMES' VERSION. | HEBREW TEXT. | | REVISED VERSION. | |
|---|---|---|---|---|
| 21 There shall no evil happen to the just: but the wicked shall be filled with mischief. | לֹא־יְאֻנֶּה לַצַּדִּיק כָּל־אָוֶן<br>וּרְשָׁעִים מָלְאוּ רָע׃ | 21 | There shall no harm befall the just;<br>but the wicked are filled with evil. | 21 |
| 22 Lying lips *are* abomination to the LORD: but they that deal truly *are* his delight. | תּוֹעֲבַת יְהוָה שִׂפְתֵי־שָׁקֶר<br>וְעֹשֵׂי אֱמוּנָה רְצוֹנוֹ׃ | 22 | Lying lips are an abomination to Jehovah;<br>but they that deal truly are his delight. | 22 |
| 23 A prudent man concealeth knowledge: but the heart of fools proclaimeth foolishness. | אָדָם עָרוּם כֹּסֶה דָּעַת<br>וְלֵב כְּסִילִים יִקְרָא אִוֶּלֶת׃ | 23 | A shrewd man covers knowledge;<br>but the heart of fools proclaims folly. | 23 |
| 24 The hand of the diligent shall bear rule: but the slothful shall be under tribute. | יַד־חָרוּצִים תִּמְשׁוֹל<br>וּרְמִיָּה תִּהְיֶה לָמַס׃ | 24 | The hand of the diligent shall bear rule;<br>but the slothful shall be under tribute. | 24 |
| 25 Heaviness in the heart of man maketh it stoop: but a good word maketh it glad. | דְּאָגָה בְלֶב־אִישׁ יַשְׁחֶנָּה<br>וְדָבָר טוֹב יְשַׂמְּחֶנָּה׃ | כה | Heaviness in the heart of man bows it down;<br>but a good word makes it glad. | 25 |
| 26 The righteous *is* more excellent than his neighbour: but the way of the wicked seduceth them. | יָתֵר מֵרֵעֵהוּ צַדִּיק<br>וְדֶרֶךְ רְשָׁעִים תַּתְעֵם׃ | 26 | The righteous will guide his fellow;<br>but the way of the wicked leads them astray. | 26 |
| 27 The slothful *man* roasteth not that which he took in hunting: but the substance of a diligent man *is* precious. | לֹא־יַחֲרֹךְ רְמִיָּה צֵידוֹ<br>וְהוֹן־אָדָם יָקָר חָרוּץ׃ | 27 | The slothful will not roast his game;<br>but a precious treasure to one is the diligent. | 27 |
| 28 In the way of righteousness *is* life; and *in* the pathway *thereof there is* no death. | בְּאֹרַח־צְדָקָה חַיִּים<br>וְדֶרֶךְ נְתִיבָה אַל־מָוֶת׃ | 28 | In the path of righteousness is life,<br>even a beaten way, where is no death. | 28 |

V. 27. *Or*, will not snare his game

V. 21. *Shall—befall* (יאנה), as in Ps. 91 : 10.

V. 23. *Shrewd* (see note on ch. 1 : 4, second and third paragraphs). *Prudent* expresses more than is intended here by the Hebrew word.

V. 24, second member. *Slothful:* either an adject. referring to *hand*, as construed by some; or the subst. *slothfulness* (רמיה) is concr. = *the slothful*, as in v. 27*—*Under tribute* (לָמַס): as in Deut. 20 : 11.

V. 25. ישחנה (masc., with a fem. subj. *preceding* it, as in 29 : 25) is a very rare case; compare Gen. 15 : 17, וַעֲלָטָה הָיָה, and Gesen. Gram. § 147, *Rem.* 2. The remoteness of the subj. here makes the anomaly less strange. More difficult is the use of the *fem.* suff. (נה), with manifest reference to לב (perhaps as = נפש). That this is the construction of the sentence is admitted by nearly all critics of note.† Hitzig has not lightened the difficulty, by referring the Suff. to *hand*, in the preceding verse.

V. 26. *Will guide:* יתר, Hiph. of תור (or תרר), in the sense *to guide, to show the way.* So Gesenius, Umbreit, Ewald, Maurer, Bertheau.

*His fellow* (מרעהו). His *fellow-man* is meant; no nearer relation (*friend, companion,* or *neighbor*) obviously is intended here.

V. 27. *Will—roast:* the traditional Jewish explanation, and in accordance with Aramæan usage.*

*Will—snare* (margin) is preferred by some scholars. But it is a less attested signification. Moreover, it is not much to say, that the indolent will not snare his game; while there is point in the assertion, that he is too lazy to cook what is already provided.

V. 28, second member. Literally: *and a beaten way—no death.*

* Bertheau: *Die Trägheit*, d. i. der Träge, *wird sein zum Tribut*, = wird als Pflichtige arbeiten müssen.

† Bertheau: auf לב beziehen sich die beiden Suffixe des Femin., ausnahmsweise, da sonst לב immer Mascul. ist; es mochte dem Verf. etwa das Femin. נֶפֶשׁ vorschweben; auch fällt es etwas auf, dass דאגה mit dem Masc. des Verbi ישחנה verbunden ist. Doch verlangt der Sinn zu deutlich Annahme dieser Unregelmässigkeiten. So Ewald (*Kummer in Eines Herz drückt es danieder*), Maurer, Rosenmüller, and others.

* Ewald: Dass חרך nicht mit حرك *bewegen, jagen*, sondern mit حرق vergl. חרר zu vergleichen sei, lehrt schon die Richtigkeit des Bildes, welche fordert sich zu denken, wie der Träge eben das, was er schon hat, nicht fertig zu machen und anzuwenden Lust hat.

Bertheau: Das Wort bedeutet der jüdischen Ueberlieferung gemäss, die durch aramäischen Sprachgebrauch gesichert ist, *braten: nicht brät die Trägheit*, d. i. der Träge, *sein Wildpret.*

KING JAMES' VERSION.

CHAP. XIII.

A WISE son *heareth* his father's instruction: but a scorner heareth not rebuke.

2 A man shall eat good by the fruit of *his* mouth: but the soul of the transgressors *shall eat* violence.

3 He that keepeth his mouth keepeth his life: *but* he that openeth wide his lips shall have destruction.

4 The soul of the sluggard desireth, and *hath* nothing: but the soul of the diligent shall be made fat.

5 A righteous *man* hateth lying: but a wicked *man* is loathsome, and cometh to shame.

6 Righteousness keepeth *him that is* upright in the way: but wickedness overthroweth the sinner.

HEBREW TEXT.

CHAP. XIII.

א בֵּן חָכָם מוּסַר אָב
וְלֵץ לֹא־שָׁמַע גְּעָרָה׃
2 מִפְּרִי פִי־אִישׁ יֹאכַל טוֹב
וְנֶפֶשׁ בֹּגְדִים חָמָס׃
3 נֹצֵר פִּיו שֹׁמֵר נַפְשׁוֹ
פֹּשֵׂק שְׂפָתָיו מְחִתָּה־לוֹ׃
4 מִתְאַוָּה וָאַיִן נַפְשׁוֹ עָצֵל
וְנֶפֶשׁ חָרֻצִים תְּדֻשָּׁן׃
ה דְּבַר־שֶׁקֶר יִשְׂנָא צַדִּיק
וְרָשָׁע יַבְאִישׁ וְיַחְפִּיר׃
6 צְדָקָה תִּצֹּר תָּם־דָּרֶךְ
וְרִשְׁעָה תְּסַלֵּף חַטָּאת׃

REVISED VERSION.

CHAP. XIII.

A WISE son is one chastened of the father; 1
but a scoffer hears not rebuke.
Of the fruit of the mouth shall one feed on good. 2
but the spirit of the treacherous on violence.
He that keeps his mouth preserves his soul; 3
he that opens wide his lips, it is his destruction.
The spirit of the sluggard longeth, and has nothing; 4
but the spirit of the diligent shall be enriched.
Lying speech the righteous hates; 5
but base and shameful is the conduct of the wicked.
Righteousness will keep the blameless way; 6
but wickedness will pervert to sin.

---

*death!* i. e. *no death is there;* or more simply, in English, *where is no death.* The omission of the *relative* (in reference to place, as well as time, Gesen. Gram., § 123, 3, *b*) is a marked feature of poetical expression in Hebrew.

For the relation of the second member to the first, see Expl. Notes.

Other constructions lessen the significance of the striking expression דרך נתיבה.* E. g. Rosenmüller: *and the way of her path* (נְתִיבָה) is *not death;* Ewald: *and the way of her path—immortality;* Stuart: *and [in] her path-way is no death.*

The *Masoretic* pointing (ה without *Mappiq*, and אל) doubtless gives the true expression of the sense. A *beaten way*, moreover, can not be taken in a *bad sense*,† as one that leads to death.

Ch. XIII.—V. 1. *One chastened* · מוּסַר, *Hoph. part. constr.*;‡ or if regarded as the subst. מוּסָר (*chastening* = object of chastening §), the meaning and rendering will be the same. The older construction, which supplies here the *affirmative* side of the negative assertion '*hears not*,' in the second member, violates the laws of thought and speech.

V. 2. *Violence* (see Expl. Notes).—According to the most natural construction, the object in both members is governed by the verb (יאכל) in the first.* The objection made to this (that "the *spirit* does not *eat*"),† is mere trifling. The spirit of such has this for its reward; and in that sense is properly said to feed on it.

V. 4. *Shall be enriched* (compare 11 : 25), viz. with good. The figure is nearly the same in Hebrew and English.—*Spirit of the sluggard:* נפשׁו עצל, Gesenius, Heb. Gram., § 121, 5, *footnote.*‡

V. 5. יבאישׁ ויחפיר; comp. Ewald, Lehrb. § 122, *c*, 1; Gesen. Gram. § 53, 2, second paragraph, *extr.*§

V. 6. *Blameless way:* תָּם־דָּרֶךְ, prop. *innocence*, or *blamelessness, of way* = *blameless way.*—*Will keep*, in English, corresponds to the Heb. verb, in both its senses.

Second member. *Will pervert to sin:* as the words are con-

---

* Maurer: *Via trita*, i. e. recta et plana, in qua eunt probi, opposita deviis et inviis, in quas deflectunt improbi.

† Maurer: Nusquam, quod sciam, in malam partem accipitur via trita, quum hoc sensu via curva dicatur potius.

‡ So Ewald, correctly: מוסר muss ein passives *partic.* sein, also *Hof.*

§ Bertheau: *Zucht des Vaters* = Gegenstand der Zucht des Vaters, und sich ihr nicht entziehend.

* Bertheau: *Und die Gier der Treulosen* verzehrt (aus יאכל in *a* ist תאכל herauszunehmen) *Grausamkeit*, weil sein Thun ihm durch grausame Behandlung von anderen vergolten, somit seine Gier durch Grausamkeit gesättigt wird.

† Hitzig: Durch 26 : 7 sieht man sich versucht, חמס in *b* von תאכל abhängig zu machen, allein 'die Seele' isst nicht.

‡ Bertheau: Das Suff. in נפשׁו weiset schon auf עצל hin, welches Wort ganz so als wenn es in gewöhnlicher Weise dem stat. constr. untergeordnet wäre folgt; Ewald, Lehrb. 301, c. Hitzig's objections are not well founded.

§ Maurer: *Verbum mendax* (sermones fraudulentos) *odit justus; et* (sed) *improbus male et turpiter agit.* Bertheau: *Trügerisches Wort hasst . . . der Gerechte, und der Frevler handelt schmählich* (יבאישׁ in derselben Bedeutung als stände יביש, wie denn auch 19 : 16 statt מבאישׁ neben מחפיר wirklich מביש steht) *und handelt schändlich*, indem er Lug und Trug sich zu Schulden kommen lässt. Hitzig: *aber der Frevler handelt schlecht und schändlich.*

| KING JAMES' VERSION. | HEBREW TEXT. | | REVISED VERSION. | |
|---|---|---|---|---|
| 7 There is that maketh himself rich, yet *hath* nothing*; there is* that maketh himself poor, yet *hath* great riches. | יֵשׁ מִתְעַשֵּׁר וְאֵין כֹּל<br>מִתְרוֹשֵׁשׁ וְהוֹן רָב׃ | 7 | There is that makes himself rich, and has nothing at all;<br>that makes himself poor, and has great substance. | 7 |
| 8 The ransom of a man's life *are* his riches: but the poor heareth not rebuke. | כֹּפֶר נֶפֶשׁ־אִישׁ עָשְׁרוֹ<br>וְרָשׁ לֹא־שָׁמַע גְּעָרָה׃ | 8 | The ransom of a man's soul is his wealth;<br>and the poor hears not rebuke. | 8 |
| 9 The light of the righteous rejoiceth: but the lamp of the wicked shall be put out. | אוֹר־צַדִּיקִים יִשְׂמָח<br>וְנֵר רְשָׁעִים יִדְעָךְ׃ | 9 | The light of the righteous shall be joyous;<br>but the lamp of the wicked shall go out. | 9 |
| 10 Only by pride cometh contention: but with the well advised *is* wisdom. | רַק־בְּזָדוֹן יִתֵּן מַצָּה<br>וְאֶת־נוֹעָצִים חָכְמָה׃ | י | Only by pride comes contention;<br>but with those who take counsel there is wisdom. | 10 |
| 11 Wealth *gotten* by vanity shall be diminished: but he that gathereth by labour shall increase. | הוֹן מֵהֶבֶל יִמְעָט<br>וְקֹבֵץ עַל־יָד יַרְבֶּה׃ | 11 | Wealth vanishes more quickly than a vapor.<br>but he that gathers in hand will cause increase. | 11 |

V. 8. *Or*, of a man's life

V. 11. *Or*, Wealth from vanity vanishes away

strued by Hirzel.* Ewald justly distinguishes צדקה and רשעה as the inward activity and power, and תם־דרך and חטאת as the outward act.†

In the common explanation, חטאת is taken as the *abstract* for the *concrete* (*sin* for the *sinner*). But it will not be denied that the expression, '*wickedness will overthrow sin*' (i. e. '*the sinner*'), is a very harsh and improbable application of this principle. Gesenius, who favored it in the Thes.,‡ afterwards gave a different meaning to חטאת in this passage.§

V. 7. The "Poor rich man," and the "Rich poor man," have become common ideas; and illustrations of both have been seen in all ages.

Some translate: *there is that feigns himself rich*|| (i. e. pretends to more wealth than he has); *that feigns himself poor* (i. e. professes to be poorer than he is). Very true; but how shallow and trivial the reflection, compared with the profound and weighty observation of the sacred writer!

V. 8. For the meaning and relation of the two members, see Expl. Notes.*

V. 10. *Comes:* יתן, impers., like the Germ. *es giebt, es gab;* Gesenius, Lex. 1, h.

*Who take counsel* (נועצים). There is no necessity for assuming a *reflexive* use of this word,† its common *reciprocal* sense being pertinent here. In either case, however, the translation is correct; as '*to take counsel*' means either, to receive counsel from others, or to counsel with them.

V. 11. *More quickly* (מן of comparison) *than a vapor.* Gesenius, *more quickly than a breath;*‡ but the other signification, *vapor*, is more pertinent in this comparison.

A *vapor* (or a *breath*) is the favorite image, in Hebrew, of what is *unsubstantial*, and is therefore *insecure* or not to be relied on, and *fleeting* or rapidly passing away; and hence, to the Hebrew mind, it is a natural image of the proverbial instability of riches. But for this very reason, it is not the appropriate emblem of the *means* by which unstable riches are obtained ('*wealth gotten by vanity*'), or by which they are squandered ('*wealth is diminished by vanity,*' i. e. by vain pursuits).§

The relation of the two members is shown in the Explanatory Notes.

Second member. *That gathers in hand:* על יד, as in 1 Sam.

* *Rechtschaffenheit behütet unschuldigen Wandel; aber Frevelmuth führt abweges zur Sünde.* רשעה ist eigentlich die gottesvergessene schlechte Gesinnung, welche zur sündigen That antreibt. So also Schelling: *injustitia præcipites dat in peccatum.*

† Gerechtigkeit, Bosheit—die innere Thätigkeit und Kraft; Lebensunschuld, Sünde—die äussere That.

‡ Vol. II. p. 959. Multum vexatus est locus [Prov.] XIII. 6 . . . ita explicandus: *justitia tuetur integritatem* i. e. integros *sed improbitas dejicit peccatum* i. e. peccatores, אנשי חטאת, ut recte Aben Esra.

§ Communicated to Dr. Robinson, for the last American edition of the Manual Heb. Lexicon (see the Preface, p. vii.); and added in Hoffmann's Germ. ed. of the Latin work.

|| *To make* or *feign one's self* so and so, expressed by some verbs under this form, is not the proper meaning of the form itself, but lies in the nature of certain verbal ideas. So Ewald, Lehrb. § 124, 3, *a* (*extr.*): dass man den Hauptbegriff der Form bisweilen durch *sich stellen* übersetzen kann (welches Hitp. an sich gar nicht bedeutet), wie הִתְחַלָּה *sich krank machen*, d. i. *sich krank stellen*, 2 Sam. 13 : 5, liegt im Wesen einiger Begriffe.

* That I may not seem to have caricatured the common view, I subjoin here Hirzel's expression of it. Der Reiche *kann* nicht nur, sondern *muss*, z. B. wenn er Räubern in die Hände gefallen ist, sich mit Gelde loskaufen; der Arme dagegen ist taub gegen Drohung jeder Art, womit man Geld von ihm erpressen will.

† *Sibi consuli passus est*, i. e. *consilium admisit, consilio paruit* würde נועץ nur hier bedeuten (Hirzel).

‡ Lex. הֶבֶל, 1, *opes halitu citius evanescunt.* So Umbreit: *Reichthum verschwindet schneller als ein Hauch.*

§ De Wette: *Reichthum mindert sich durch Eitelkeit.*

| KING JAMES' VERSION. | HEBREW TEXT. | | REVISED VERSION. | |
|---|---|---|---|---|
| 12 Hope deferred maketh the heart sick: but *when* the desire cometh, *it is* a tree of life. | תּוֹחֶלֶת מְמֻשָּׁכָה מַחֲלָה לֵב<br>וְעֵץ חַיִּים תַּאֲוָה בָאָה׃ | 12 | Hope deferred makes the heart sick;<br>but desire attained is a tree of life. | 12 |
| 13 Whoso despiseth the word shall be destroyed: but he that feareth the commandment shall be rewarded. | בָּז לְדָבָר יֵחָבֶל לוֹ<br>וִירֵא מִצְוָה הוּא יְשֻׁלָּם׃ | 13 | He that despises the word shall be held accountable to it;<br>but whoso fears the command, he shall be rewarded. | 13 |
| 14 The law of the wise *is* a fountain of life, to depart from the snares of death. | תּוֹרַת חָכָם מְקוֹר חַיִּים<br>לָסוּר מִמֹּקְשֵׁי מָוֶת׃ | 14 | The law of the wise is a well of life,<br>to turn from the snares of death. | 14 |
| 15 Good understanding giveth favour: but the way of transgressors *is* hard. | שֵׂכֶל־טוֹב יִתֶּן־חֵן<br>וְדֶרֶךְ בֹּגְדִים אֵיתָן׃ | טו | Good understanding confers favor;<br>but the way of transgressors is hard. | 15 |
| 16 Every prudent *man* dealeth with knowledge: but a fool layeth open *his* folly. | כָּל־עָרוּם יַעֲשֶׂה בְדָעַת<br>וּכְסִיל יִפְרֹשׂ אִוֶּלֶת׃ | 16 | Every shrewd man acts with knowledge;<br>but a fool displays folly. | 16 |
| 17 A wicked messenger falleth into mischief: but a faithful ambassador *is* health. | מַלְאָךְ רָשָׁע יִפֹּל בְּרָע<br>וְצִיר אֱמוּנִים מַרְפֵּא׃ | 17 | A wicked messenger falls into mischief;<br>but a faithful ambassador is a healing. | 17 |
| 18 Poverty and shame *shall be to* him that refuseth instruction: but he that regardeth reproof shall be honoured. | רֵישׁ וְקָלוֹן פּוֹרֵעַ מוּסָר<br>וְשׁוֹמֵר תּוֹכַחַת יְכֻבָּד׃ | 18 | Poverty and shame to him who refuses correction;<br>but he who regards reproof shall be honored. | 18 |

17 : 22, 2 Kings 22 : 5.* It can not mean *'by hand'* as in the Common Version; nor does it mean 'by handfulls' (so much, at once, as may be held in the hand), i. e. by slow and gradual accumulation.—*Shall cause increase:* the Hiph. יַרְבֶּה.

V. 13. *Shall be held accountable to it* (יחבל לו), *Niph.* as passive of the common signification of *Kal* (e. g. chs. 20 : 16, 27 : 13).† Literally, *shall be pledged to it,* held by it in pledge.

V. 15. *Is hard.* So Maurer,‡ Ewald,§ Bertheau;‖ and this is the only sense of the word that suits the connection.

Gesenius, formerly (Lexicon manuale, 1833), from the ground-meaning, *enduring,* derived the sig. *firm, hard* (hence, poet., *a rock,* from its hardness).

Later, however (Thes., Vol. II. p. 644), he defined this word* as in Dr. Robinson's last edition of the Heb. Lexicon; where this passage is translated and explained thus: "*The way of transgressors is a perennial stream,* full of water, by which one may easily be borne away and overwhelmed." But, to the Hebrew mind, a '*perennial stream*' suggested far other ideas; nor could it be, in itself, an emblem of mischief, of something to be shunned as fraught with peril and disaster. In that climate, nothing was more desirable; and to say, '*the way of transgressors is a perennial stream,*' was comparing it to the greatest and most desired of temporal blessings.

V. 18. *To him who refuses,* is the proper expression of the thought in English.† Lit., *is he who refuses.*‡

* Maurer: *qui colligit in manum,* qui colligit semper et collecta curat et conservat.

† Schultens: Omnino לו non ad בז referendum, sed ad דבר *verbum* per excellentiam, *verbum Dei.* . . . Hoc *violans* . . . יחבל לו *oppignerabitur ei.* Tritissimus usus *pignerationis,* sub hoc radice; . . . sic infra cap. 20 : 16, et 27 : 13, ne plura citem. Hinc gravis figuratio assumsit *pignerationem ad pœnam.*

Ewald: *Wer das Wort verachtet, wird verpfändet ihm.* Wie der Gegensatz zwischen frecher Verachtung und scheuer Achtung klar ist, so der zwischen *verpfändet* und *bezahlt* oder belohnt sein. Das Bild ist also deutlich vom Schuldenwesen bei den Alten entlehnt. (Compare Lehrb. p. 684, footnote, 2.)

Maurer: *Qui contemnit verbum,* divinum puta, *ei* (verbo) *oppigneratur;* i. e. pœna tenetur quæ sumitur ab iis qui legem divinam violant.

‡ Nobis איתן, quum Num. 24 : 21 *firmum,* Jer. 5 · 15 *robustum* significat, hoc loco significare videtur *durum;* 'durum' vero aut pro *aspero* est positum, . . . aut pro *vasto, sterili.*

§ איתן *dauernd* nach dem was zu 12 : 12 gesagt ist; daher aber auch *hart.*

* *Via improborum* איתן est *fluvius perennis,* in quo progredi nequit viator, sed torrente abripitur.

† De Wette: *Armuth und Schande dem der Zucht verlässt.*

‡ Maurer: *Egestas et ignominia, qui rejicit disciplinam!* i. e. egestas et ignominia sunt ejus, ei, qui disciplinam respuit.

Bertheau: die Substant. *Armuth und Schmach* als Prädicate: *wer Zucht verwirft ist Armuth* = arm.

‖ Also ein steinigter Weg, auf dem es sich nicht bequem gehen lässt.

KING JAMES' VERSION.

19 The désire accomplished is sweet to the soul: but *it is* abomination to fools to depart from evil.

20 He that walketh with wise *men* shall be wise: but a companion of fools shall be destroyed.

21 Evil pursueth sinners: but to the righteous good shall be repaid.

22 A good *man* leaveth an inheritance to his children's children: and the wealth of the sinner *is* laid up for the just.

23 Much food *is in* the tillage of the poor: but there is *that is* destroyed for want of judgment.

HEBREW TEXT.

19 תַּאֲוָה נִהְיָה תֶּעֱרַב לְנָפֶשׁ
וְתוֹעֲבַת כְּסִילִים סוּר מֵרָע׃

כ הַלֹּוךְ אֶת־חֲכָמִים וְחֲכָם
וְרֹעֶה כְסִילִים יֵרוֹעַ׃

21 חַטָּאִים תְּרַדֵּף רָעָה
וְאֶת־צַדִּיקִים יְשַׁלֶּם־טוֹב׃

22 טוֹב יַנְחִיל בְּנֵי־בָנִים
וְצָפוּן לַצַּדִּיק חֵיל חוֹטֵא׃

23 רָב־אֹכֶל נִיר רָאשִׁים
וְיֵשׁ נִסְפֶּה בְּלֹא מִשְׁפָּט׃

V. 20. הולך ק׳ Ib. יחכם ק׳

REVISED VERSION.

Desire attained is sweet to the 19
soul;
and it is the abomination of
fools to depart from evil.

Walk with the wise, and be- 20
come wise;
but a companion of fools shall
come to harm.

Evil shall pursue sinners; 21
but good shall reward the
righteous.

The good will leave a heritage 22
to children's children;
but the sinner's wealth is laid
up for the righteous.

The ploughing of the poor is 23
food abundant;
but there is that is consumed
without measure.

V. 23. *Or*, that perishes by injustice

V. 20. *Walk* (הָלוֹךְ, *Kethibh*), *Infin. abs.* for the emphatic *Imperat.* (Gesenius, Gram., § 131, 4, *b*, *γ*).—*And be wise* (וַחֲכָם, *Kethibh*).* Here, as in most instances, the *Kethibh* is the true reading.†

Second member. *Shall come to harm:* ירוע, as in 11 : 15, *Niph. fut.* from רוּעַ, *to fare ill.*‡

V. 21. *Good shall reward.* The construction and order of the words being the same in both members, and the two antithetic words, רע and טוב, being in the same relative position, it is natural to suppose that they hold the same grammatical relation, namely as *subject* of the verb. So Gesenius§ (after C. B. Michaelis),‖ Umbreit,¶ Maurer.**

On the contrary, the verb in the second member is construed with an implied subject (*he*, namely God), by Rosenmüller,* Ewald,† Bertheau, Rödiger.‡

V. 22. *The good* (טוב), as in ch. 12 : 2.—*Will leave a heritage to* (*will cause to inherit*) : ינחיל, with only the *acc.* of *pers.*, as in Deut. 32 : 8.

Here again, as in the preceding verse, some assume an implied subject of ינחיל; *he* (God) *will cause to inherit.* But טוב is the natural subject of ינחיל, and the lot of '*the good*' is contrasted with that of '*the sinner*.'§

V. 23. *Ploughing:* ניר, in its primary sense, which is the appropriate one here.

*Without measure:* בלא משפט, the negative of למשפט, which is well translated '*in measure*' (comp. לִצְדָקָה, Joel 2 : 23) in Jer. 30 : 11.‖

The second member is commonly translated as in the margin;¶ but with a less obvious relation of the two members (see Expl. Notes, second paragraph).

* Masorethæ, mero conformandi studio ducti, legi *jubent* הוֹלֵךְ—יֶחְכָּם *qui it—sapiet* (Maurer).

† So Ewald: *Geh du mit Weisen um, und werde weise.* Bertheau: Ktib הָלוֹךְ Infin. abs. in der Bedeutung des nachdrücklichen Imperat. und וַחֲכָם, nicht wie Ewald will וְחָכָם, da als Fortsetzung des Infin. gleich der Imperat. eintritt.

‡ Ewald: Eigentlich, *wer zu Freunden nimmt Thoren, wird beschädigt werden.*

§ Lex. Man. (art. שָׁלֵם, *Pi.* 4, *extr.*) : *sed probos remuneratur* (pr. bezahlt) *felicitas*, proborum præmium est felicitas.

‖ Annott. uberior. (as an alternative rendering) : verti etiam potest *justos remunerabit bonum* ... Sic enim non solum ellipsis nulla erit, sed etiam hemistichium hoc posterius priori exactius conveniet, ut quemadmodum malum *persequi*, sic bonum ipsum *remunerare* dicatur.

¶ Eigentlich: die Guten bezahlet d. i. belohnet Glück.

** *Et* (sed) *justos remuneratur bonum*, felicitas; justorum vero præmium est felicitas.

* *Justos remunerabit bono*, is cujus est rependere, Deus.

† Bei ישלם ist das Subject Jahve zu ergänzen, 10 : 24, 12 : 12.

‡ Thes. fascic. poster., p. 1421 : *et probos remuneratur* (Deus) *felicitate.*

§ Bertheau: Doch kann ינחיל auch absolut ohne Accusativ dessen was man hinterlässt stehen (Deut. 32 : 8) so: *der Gute hinterlässt Erbschaft den Kindeskindern; . . .* auf diese Weise steht dem חוטא in *b* טוב in *a* scharf gegenüber.

‖ Fürst (Hebr. u. Chald. Hdwbch.) : *nach der Norm.* Some translate (in Jer. 30 : 11) *according to right;* which makes a false implication, as though the utter extinction, spoken of in the two preceding clauses, was not '*according to right.*'

¶ For example, Bertheau: *es giebt welche*, die, wiewohl reich, *fortgerafft sind durch Nicht-Recht.*

| KING JAMES' VERSION. | HEBREW TEXT. | | REVISED VERSION. | |
|---|---|---|---|---|
| 24 He that spareth his rod hateth his son: but he that loveth him chasteneth him betimes. | חוֹשֵׂךְ שִׁבְטוֹ שׂוֹנֵא בְנוֹ<br>וְאֹהֲבוֹ שִׁחֲרוֹ מוּסָר׃ | 24 | He that spares his rod hates his son;<br>but he that loves him gives him timely chastisement. | 24 |
| 25 The righteous eateth to the satisfying of his soul: but the belly of the wicked shall want. | צַדִּיק אֹכֵל לְשֹׂבַע נַפְשׁוֹ<br>וּבֶטֶן רְשָׁעִים תֶּחְסָר· | כה | The righteous eats to the satisfying of his spirit;<br>but the belly of the wicked shall want. | 25 |
| CHAP. XIV. | CHAP. XIV. | | CHAP. XIV. | |
| EVERY wise woman buildeth her house: but the foolish plucketh it down with her hands. | חַכְמוֹת נָשִׁים בָּנְתָה בֵיתָהּ<br>וְאִוֶּלֶת בְּיָדֶיהָ תֶהֶרְסֶנּוּ׃ | א | EVERY wise woman builds her house;<br>but the foolish plucks it down with her own hands. | 1 |
| 2 He that walketh in his uprightness feareth the LORD: but *he that is* perverse in his ways despiseth him. | הוֹלֵךְ בְּיָשְׁרוֹ יְרֵא יְהוָה<br>וּנְלוֹז דְּרָכָיו בּוֹזֵהוּ׃ | 2 | He that walks in his uprightness is one that fears Jehovah;<br>but he that is perverse in his ways despises him. | 2 |
| 3 In the mouth of the foolish *is* a rod of pride: but the lips of the wise shall preserve them. | בְּפִי־אֱוִיל חֹטֶר גַּאֲוָה<br>וְשִׂפְתֵי חֲכָמִים תִּשְׁמוּרֵם׃ | 3 | In the fool's mouth is a rod of pride;<br>but the lips of the wise will preserve them. | 3 |
| 4 Where no oxen *are*, the crib *is* clean: but much increase *is* by the strength of the ox. | בְּאֵין אֲלָפִים אֵבוּס בָּר<br>וְרָב־תְּבוּאוֹת בְּכֹחַ שׁוֹר׃ | 4 | Where there are no oxen, the crib is clean;<br>but by the strength of the ox is abundant increase. | 4 |
| 5 A faithful witness will not lie: but a false witness will utter lies. | עֵד אֱמוּנִים לֹא יְכַזֵּב<br>וְיָפִיחַ כְּזָבִים עֵד שָׁקֶר׃ | ה | A faithful witness will not lie;<br>but he that breathes falsehood is a lying witness. | 5 |
| 6 A scorner seeketh wisdom, and *findeth it* not: but knowledge *is* easy unto him that understandeth. | בִּקֶּשׁ־לֵץ חָכְמָה וָאָיִן<br>וְדַעַת לְנָבוֹן נָקָל׃ | 6 | The scoffer sought wisdom, but it came not;<br>but knowledge to the discerning is easy. | 6 |
| 7 Go from the presence of a foolish man, when thou perceivest not *in him* the lips of knowledge. | לֵךְ מִנֶּגֶד לְאִישׁ כְּסִיל<br>וּבַל־יָדַעְתָּ שִׂפְתֵי־דָעַת׃ | 7 | Go from the presence of a foolish man,<br>when thou perceivest not the lips of knowledge. | 7 |

V. 24. *Gives him timely chastisement.** The opinion of the Jewish teachers, that the primary idea of the Heb. word is that of *early, timely* attention to a thing, and hence that of *earnest seeking*, seems to be the correct one.† Comp. Rosenm. on Ps. 63 : 2.

To the rendering, '*seeks for him chastisement*,' Hirzel replies with some point by asking,‡ 'what there is in it to be long sought after?'

Ch. XIV.—V. 1. *The wise of women*,§ or (חָכְמוֹת, as some would point the word, see note on 1 : 20) *wisdom of women*;* in either case, the proper English expression is, *every wise woman.* Second member: *foolishness = the foolish.*

V. 4. *Crib* (אבוס). Gesenius, Lex.: "The signif. *stall* is also appropriate in Is. 1 : 3; where, however, Sept. and Vulg. render *præsepe*, i. e. *crib, manger*, which both here and in Job [39 : 9] is not less apt and probable."

V. 5. יפיח, *subj.* (not *predicate*), as in 12 : 17.

V. 6. *Sought* (בקש), *the Pret.* used here in its proper relation to the past.†

* Michaelis (Annott. uber.): q. d. *matutinat*, i. e. mature adhibet, *ei disciplinam.*

† Syr., [illegible]. Sept., ὁ δὲ ἀγαπῶν ἐπιμελῶς παιδεύει. Chald., וּדְרָחֵם לֵיהּ מְקַדֵּם לֵיהּ מַרְדוּתָא.

‡ Und was giebt es denn da lange zu suchen?

§ Rosenmüller: *Sapientes mulierum ædificat*, i. e. unaquæque sapientum mulierum *ædificat domum suam.*

* Aus בנתה geht hervor, dass חכמות hier nicht wie Judd. 5 : 29 der plur. fem. sein kann: *die Weisen der Frauen;* zu lesen ist חָכְמוֹת (Bertheau).

† So Ewald: *Ein Spötter suchte Weisheit.* Bertheau: *Der Spötter suchte Weisheit.*

| KING JAMES' VERSION. | HEBREW TEXT. | | REVISED VERSION. | |
|---|---|---|---|---|
| 8 The wisdom of the prudent *is* to understand his way: but the folly of fools *is* deceit. | חָכְמַת עָרוּם הָבִין דַּרְכּוֹ<br>וְאִוֶּלֶת כְּסִילִים מִרְמָה׃ | 8 | The wisdom of the shrewd is to understand his way;<br>but the folly of fools is deception. | 8 |
| 9 Fools make a mock at sin: but among the righteous *there is* favour. | אֱוִלִים יָלִיץ אָשָׁם<br>וּבֵין יְשָׁרִים רָצוֹן׃ | 9 | Guilt makes a mock of fools;<br>but among the upright there is favor. | 9 |
| 10 The heart knoweth his own bitterness; and a stranger doth not intermeddle with his joy. | לֵב יוֹדֵעַ מָרַּת נַפְשׁוֹ<br>וּבְשִׂמְחָתוֹ לֹא־יִתְעָרַב זָר׃ | י | The heart knows its own bitterness;<br>and a stranger intermeddles not with its joy. | 10 |
| 11 The house of the wicked shall be overthrown: but the tabernacle of the upright shall flourish. | בֵּית רְשָׁעִים יִשָּׁמֵד<br>וְאֹהֶל יְשָׁרִים יַפְרִיחַ׃ | 11 | The house of the wicked shall be destroyed;<br>but the dwelling of the upright shall prosper. | 11 |
| 12 There is a way which seemeth right unto a man; but the end thereof *are* the ways of death. | יֵשׁ דֶּרֶךְ יָשָׁר לִפְנֵי־אִישׁ<br>וְאַחֲרִיתָהּ דַּרְכֵי־מָוֶת׃ | 12 | There is a way right in the sight of a man;<br>but the end thereof—they are ways of death; | 12 |
| 13 Even in laughter the heart is sorrowful; and the end of that mirth *is* heaviness. | גַּם־בִּשְׂחֹק יִכְאַב־לֵב<br>וְאַחֲרִיתָהּ שִׂמְחָה תוּגָה׃ | 13 | Even by laughter may the heart become sad;<br>and of mirth the end is heaviness. | 13 |
| 14 The backslider in heart shall be filled with his own ways: and a good man *shall be satisfied* from himself. | מִדְּרָכָיו יִשְׂבַּע סוּג לֵב<br>וּמֵעָלָיו אִישׁ טוֹב׃ | 14 | From his own ways shall the backslidden in heart be filled,<br>and the good man from himself. | 14 |
| 15 The simple believeth every word: but the prudent *man* looketh well to his going. | פֶּתִי יַאֲמִין לְכָל־דָּבָר<br>וְעָרוּם יָבִין לַאֲשֻׁרוֹ׃ | טו | The simple believes every thing;<br>but the shrewd gives heed to his going. | 15 |
| 16 A wise *man* feareth, and departeth from evil: but the fool rageth, and is confident. | חָכָם יָרֵא וְסָר מֵרָע<br>וּכְסִיל מִתְעַבֵּר וּבוֹטֵחַ׃ | 16 | The wise fears, and turns from evil;<br>but a fool rages, and is confident. | 16 |
| 17 *He that is* soon angry dealeth foolishly: and a man of wicked devices is hated. | קְצַר־אַפַּיִם יַעֲשֶׂה אִוֶּלֶת<br>וְאִישׁ מְזִמּוֹת יִשָּׂנֵא׃ | 17 | He that is quick to anger deals foolishly;<br>but a man of plots is hated. | 17 |
| 18 The simple inherit folly: but the prudent are crowned with knowledge. | נָחֲלוּ פְתָאיִם אִוֶּלֶת<br>וַעֲרוּמִים יַכְתִּרוּ דָעַת׃ | 18 | The simple inherit folly;<br>but the shrewd are crowned with knowledge. | 18 |
| 19 The evil bow before the good; and the wicked at the gates of the righteous. | שַׁחוּ רָעִים לִפְנֵי טוֹבִים<br>וּרְשָׁעִים עַל־שַׁעֲרֵי צַדִּיק׃ | 19 | The evil bow down before the good,<br>and the wicked at the gates of the righteous. | 19 |
| 20 The poor is hated even of his own neighbour: but the rich *hath* many friends. | גַּם־לְרֵעֵהוּ יִשָּׂנֵא רָשׁ<br>וְאֹהֲבֵי עָשִׁיר רַבִּים׃ | כ | Even of his fellow is the poor man hated;<br>but the lovers of the rich are many. | 20 |

V. 9. The verb יליץ, in the *sing.*, has for its *subj.* אשם, meaning *guilt*, as in Gen. 26 : 10, Jer. 51 : 5.

V. 14, second member. Lit. *from with* (עַל = *by* or *with*) *himself.** The *suff.* in מעליו refers here to the *subj.*, as in 1 Sam. 17 : 22.

V. 16. *Rages* (the usual meaning of the Heb. verb) like a swollen stream, that defies all restraint; so is the blustering fool, in his self-confidence.

* Schelling: ad verbum, de viis suis satiabitur aversus corde, de iis quæ juxta eum sunt, s. de semet ipso vir probus; in quo nihil difficultatis est, ut ab recepta lectione מעליו discedendi, et cum *Capello* מִמַּעֲלָלָיו s. מַעֲלָלָיו legendi nulla necessitas sit.

| KING JAMES' VERSION. | HEBREW TEXT. | | REVISED VERSION. |
|---|---|---|---|
| 21 He that despiseth his neighbour sinneth: but he that hath mercy on the poor, happy *is* he. | בָּז לְרֵעֵהוּ חוֹטֵא<br>וּמְחוֹנֵן עֲנָיִים אַשְׁרָיו׃ | 21 | He that shows contempt for 21<br>his fellow sinneth;<br>but he that has compassion on<br>the poor, happy is he! |
| 22 Do they not err that devise evil? but mercy and truth *shall be* to them that devise good. | הֲלוֹא יִתְעוּ חֹרְשֵׁי רָע<br>וְחֶסֶד וֶאֱמֶת חֹרְשֵׁי טוֹב׃ | 22 | Do they not err who devise 22<br>evil?<br>but kindness and truth are<br>they that devise good. |
| 23 In all labour there is profit: but the talk of the lips *tendeth* only to penury. | בְּכָל־עֶצֶב יִהְיֶה מוֹתָר<br>וּדְבַר שְׂפָתַיִם אַךְ לְמַחְסוֹר׃ | 23 | In all labor there will be profit; 23<br>but talk of the lips is only to<br>penury. |
| 24 The crown of the wise *is* their riches: *but* the foolishness of fools *is* folly. | עֲטֶרֶת חֲכָמִים עָשְׁרָם<br>אִוֶּלֶת כְּסִילִים אִוֶּלֶת׃ | 24 | The crown of the wise is their 24<br>wealth;<br>the folly of fools—is folly. |
| 25 A true witness delivereth souls: but a deceitful *witness* speaketh lies. | מַצִּיל נְפָשׁוֹת עֵד אֱמֶת<br>וְיָפִחַ כְּזָבִים מִרְמָה׃ | כה | A true witness delivers souls; 25<br>but he that breathes lies is deception. |
| 26 In the fear of the LORD *is* strong confidence: and his children shall have a place of refuge. | בְּיִרְאַת יְהוָה מִבְטַח־עֹז<br>וּלְבָנָיו יִהְיֶה מַחְסֶה׃ | 26 | In the fear of Jehovah there is 26<br>strong trust;<br>and his children shall have a<br>refuge. |
| 27 The fear of the LORD *is* a fountain of life, to depart from the snares of death. | יִרְאַת יְהוָה מְקוֹר חַיִּים<br>לָסוּר מִמֹּקְשֵׁי מָוֶת׃ | 27 | The fear of Jehovah is a well 27<br>of life,<br>to turn from the snares of<br>death. |
| 28 In the multitude of people *is* the king's honour: but in the want of people *is* the destruction of the prince. | בְּרָב־עָם הַדְרַת־מֶלֶךְ<br>וּבְאֶפֶס לְאֹם מְחִתַּת רָזוֹן׃ | 28 | In the multitude of people is 28<br>the king's honor;<br>and in the want of people is<br>the prince's ruin. |
| 29 *He that is* slow to wrath *is* of great understanding: but *he that is* hasty of spirit exalteth folly. | אֶרֶךְ אַפַּיִם רַב־תְּבוּנָה<br>וּקְצַר־רוּחַ מֵרִים אִוֶּלֶת׃ | 29 | He that is slow to anger is of 29<br>great understanding;<br>but he that is hasty in spirit<br>exhibits folly. |
| 30 A sound heart *is* the life of the flesh: but envy the rottenness of the bones. | חַיֵּי בְשָׂרִים לֵב מַרְפֵּא<br>וּרְקַב עֲצָמוֹת קִנְאָה׃ | ל | The life of the body is a tran- 30<br>quil heart;<br>but envy is rottenness of the<br>bones. |
| 31 He that oppresseth the poor reproacheth his maker: but he that honoureth him hath mercy on the poor. | עֹשֵׁק דָּל חֵרֵף עֹשֵׂהוּ<br>וּמְכַבְּדוֹ חֹנֵן אֶבְיוֹן׃ | 31 | He that oppresses the weak 31<br>scorns his Maker;<br>but he that honors him has<br>compassion on the needy. |
| 32 The wicked is driven away in his wickedness: but the righteous hath hope in his death. | בְּרָעָתוֹ יִדָּחֶה רָשָׁע<br>וְחֹסֶה בְמוֹתוֹ צַדִּיק׃ | 32 | In his calamity the wicked is 32<br>driven away;<br>but the righteous has trust in<br>his death. |

V. 21. עֲנוּיִם ק׳

V. 22. *Kindness and truth:* the spirited conception of the original, which is admissible also in English. They are '*kindness and truth,*' being living representatives of these qualities.

V. 24. The literal rendering, in the ordinary sense of the words,* gives a just and striking sentiment; see Expl. Notes.

V. 28. *Prince:* רָזוֹן = רֹזֵן, as עָשׁוֹק = עֹשֵׁק.†

V. 29. *Exhibits folly:* strictly, *holds it up* to view.*

V. 32. *In his calamity,* corresponding to '*in his death,*' in the parallel member.

* Ewald: *aber der Thoren Narrheit—Narrheit ist.*

† Bertheau: רזון haben die alten Ueberss. durch *Fürst* übersetzt; die Form רזון statt der gewöhnlichen רוֹזֵן würde nur hier vorkommen, ist aber ohne weiteres zulässig. רָזוֹן kann sonst *Schwindsucht* heissen, hier hat das Wort diese Bedeutung nicht.

* Gesenius (Thes. vol. III. p. 1274): *impatiens offert,* in medium profert, *stultitiam.* Rosenmüller: stultitiam suam omnibus facit conspicuam, perinde ac si sublata manu palam eam ostentaret.

| KING JAMES' VERSION. | HEBREW TEXT. | | REVISED VERSION. | |
|---|---|---|---|---|
| 33 Wisdom resteth in the heart of him that hath understanding: but *that which is* in the midst of fools is made known. | בְּלֵב נָבוֹן תָּנוּחַ חָכְמָה<br>וּבְקֶרֶב כְּסִילִים תִּוָּדֵעַ׃ | 33 | Wisdom dwells in the heart of the discerning;<br>but in fools it shall be taught! | 33 |
| 34 Righteousness exalteth a nation: but sin *is* a reproach to any people. | צְדָקָה תְּרוֹמֵם גּוֹי<br>וְחֶסֶד לְאֻמִּים חַטָּאת׃ | 34 | Righteousness exalts a people;<br>but sin is the reproach of nations. | 34 |
| 35 The king's favour *is* toward a wise servant: but his wrath is *against* him that causeth shame. | רְצוֹן־מֶלֶךְ לְעֶבֶד מַשְׂכִּיל<br>וְעֶבְרָתוֹ תִּהְיֶה מֵבִישׁ׃ | לה | A wise servant has the king's favor;<br>but a base one has his wrath. | 35 |
| CHAP. XV. | CHAP. XV. | | CHAP. XV. | |
| A SOFT answer turneth away wrath: but grievous words stir up anger. | מַעֲנֶה־רַּךְ יָשִׁיב חֵמָה<br>וּדְבַר־עֶצֶב יַעֲלֶה־אָף׃ | א | A SOFT answer turns away wrath;<br>but a harsh word stirs up anger. | 1 |
| 2 The tongue of the wise useth knowledge aright: but the mouth of fools poureth out foolishness. | לְשׁוֹן חֲכָמִים תֵּיטִיב דָּעַת<br>וּפִי כְסִילִים יַבִּיעַ אִוֶּלֶת׃ | 2 | The tongue of the wise utters useful knowledge;<br>but the mouth of fools pours forth folly. | 2 |
| 3 The eyes of the LORD *are* in every place, beholding the evil and the good. | בְּכָל־מָקוֹם עֵינֵי יְהוָה<br>צוֹפוֹת רָעִים וְטוֹבִים׃ | 3 | The eyes of Jehovah are in every place,<br>beholding the evil and the good. | 3 |
| 4 A wholesome tongue *is* a tree of life: but perverseness therein *is* a breach in the spirit. | מַרְפֵּא לָשׁוֹן עֵץ חַיִּים<br>וְסֶלֶף בָּהּ שֶׁבֶר בְּרוּחַ׃ | 4 | A wholesome tongue is a tree of life;<br>but perverseness therein is a wound in the spirit. | 4 |
| 5 A fool despiseth his father's instruction: but he that regardeth reproof is prudent. | אֱוִיל יִנְאַץ מוּסַר אָבִיו<br>וְשֹׁמֵר תּוֹכַחַת יַעְרִם׃ | ה | A fool spurns his father's correction;<br>but he that regards reproof deals wisely. | 5 |
| 6 In the house of the righteous *is* much treasure: but in the revenues of the wicked is trouble. | בֵּית צַדִּיק חֹסֶן רָב<br>וּבִתְבוּאַת רָשָׁע נֶעְכָּרֶת׃ | 6 | In the house of the righteous is much treasure;<br>but in the gain of the wicked there is trouble. | 6 |
| 7 The lips of the wise disperse knowledge: but the heart of the foolish *doeth* not so. | שִׂפְתֵי חֲכָמִים יְזָרוּ דָעַת<br>וְלֵב כְּסִילִים לֹא־כֵן׃ | 7 | The lips of the wise disperse knowledge;<br>not so the heart of fools! | 7 |

V. 33. *It shall be taught* (the *impers. neut.*), a form of menace; compare the note on ch. 10 : 9.

V. 35. *A base one:* מביש *intrans.* (Lex., Hiph. 3).—*Has:* לְ of the first member being omitted before the parallel term in the second, as בְּ is in in Is. 48 : 14 (Gram,, § 154, 4).

Ch. XV.—V. 2. *Utters useful knowledge:* so Ewald,* Maurer,† Bertheau.‡ *Makes knowledge pleasant* (as some translate) is not antithetic to the other member.

V. 4. *A wholesome* (wholesomeness of) *tongue:* as מרפא is used in chs. 4 : 22, 12 : 18, 13 : 17, 16 : 24. The idea of *quietness* (comp. 14 : 30), *a gentle tongue*, is not as appropriate here.

* *Der Weisen Zunge gutes Wissen schafft.*

† *Lingua sapientum bonam* (rectam) *facit* (creat) *scientiam.*

‡ *Die Zunge macht gut Kenntniss* = verkündet *gute Kenntniss.*

V. 5. *Deals wisely* (prop. *callide agit*): compare the note on ch. 1 : 4, the last paragraph but one.

V. 7. *Not so!* לא כן, as in Ps. 1 : 4.* Its *position* here makes no difference; the thought being expressed in the Hebrew thus: *but the heart of fools—not so!*

The expression is certainly far from being feeble and tame, as asserted by Hirzel.† Gesenius: *and the heart of fools* (disperses) *vain* (foolish) *things.*‡ Ewald: *is not sure* (not trustworthy).§

* So Bertheau: לא כן *nicht so* wie die Lippen der Weisen streut das Herz der Thoren Kenntniss aus. In dieser am nächsten liegenden Bedeutung fassen Chald. und Vulg. לא כן auf.

† לא כן wie Ps. 1 : 4 gebraucht wäre unerträglich matt.

‡ Thes. vol. II. p. 667: *et cor stultorum* (spargit) *vana, stulta.*

§ *Der Thoren Herz unzuverlässig ist.*

| KING JAMES' VERSION. | HEBREW TEXT. | | REVISED VERSION. | |
|---|---|---|---|---|
| 8 The sacrifice of the wicked *is* an abomination to the LORD: but the prayer of the upright *is* his delight. | זֶבַח רְשָׁעִים תּוֹעֲבַת יְהוָה<br>וּתְפִלַּת יְשָׁרִים רְצוֹנוֹ׃ | 8 | The sacrifice of the wicked is an abomination to Jehovah;<br>but the prayer of the upright is his delight. | 8 |
| 9 The way of the wicked *is* an abomination unto the LORD: but he loveth him that followeth after righteousness. | תּוֹעֲבַת יְהוָה דֶּרֶךְ רָשָׁע<br>וּמְרַדֵּף צְדָקָה יֶאֱהָב׃ | 9 | An abomination to Jehovah is the way of the wicked;<br>but him who follows righteousness he loves. | 9 |
| 10 Correction *is* grievous unto him that forsaketh the way: *and* he that hateth reproof shall die. | מוּסָר רָע לְעֹזֵב אֹרַח<br>שׂוֹנֵא תוֹכַחַת יָמוּת׃ | י | A sore correction has he that forsakes the way;<br>he that hates reproof shall die. | 10 |
| 11 Hell and destruction *are* before the LORD: how much more then the hearts of the children of men? | שְׁאוֹל וַאֲבַדּוֹן נֶגֶד יְהוָה<br>אַף כִּי־לִבּוֹת בְּנֵי־אָדָם׃ | 11 | The underworld and destruction are before Jehovah;<br>how much more the hearts of the sons of men. | 11 |
| 12 A scorner loveth not one that reproveth him: neither will he go unto the wise. | לֹא־יֶאֱהַב לֵץ הוֹכֵחַ לוֹ<br>אֶל־חֲכָמִים לֹא יֵלֵךְ׃ | 12 | The scoffer loves not one that reproves him;<br>he will not go to the wise. | 12 |
| 13 A merry heart maketh a cheerful countenance: but by sorrow of the heart the spirit is broken. | לֵב שָׂמֵחַ יֵיטִב פָּנִים<br>וּבְעַצְּבַת־לֵב רוּחַ נְכֵאָה׃ | 13 | A glad heart makes a joyous countenance;<br>but by sorrow of heart the spirit is broken. | 13 |
| 14 The heart of him that hath understanding seeketh knowledge: but the mouth of fools feedeth on foolishness. | לֵב נָבוֹן יְבַקֶּשׁ־דָּעַת<br>וּפְנֵי כְסִילִים יִרְעֶה אִוֶּלֶת׃ | 14 | The heart of the discerning seeks for knowledge;<br>but the mouth of fools feeds on folly. | 14 |
| 15 All the days of the afflicted *are* evil: but he that is of a merry heart *hath* a continual feast. | כָּל־יְמֵי עָנִי רָעִים<br>וְטוֹב־לֵב מִשְׁתֶּה תָמִיד׃ | טו | All the days of the poor are evil;<br>but a cheerful heart is a continual feast. | 15 |
| 16 Better *is* little with the fear of the LORD, than great treasure and trouble therewith. | טוֹב־מְעַט בְּיִרְאַת יְהוָה<br>מֵאוֹצָר רָב וּמְהוּמָה בוֹ׃ | 16 | Better is a little with the fear of Jehovah,<br>than great treasure and trouble therewith. | 16 |
| 17 Better *is* a dinner of herbs where love is, than a stalled ox and hatred therewith. | טוֹב אֲרֻחַת יָרָק וְאַהֲבָה־שָׁם<br>מִשּׁוֹר אָבוּס וְשִׂנְאָה־בוֹ׃ | 17 | Better is a meal of herbs, when love is there,<br>than a stalled ox, and hatred therewith. | 17 |
| 18 A wrathful man stirreth up strife: but *he that is* slow to anger appeaseth strife. | אִישׁ חֵמָה יְגָרֶה מָדוֹן<br>וְאֶרֶךְ אַפַּיִם יַשְׁקִיט רִיב׃ | 18 | A wrathful man stirs up contention;<br>but he that is slow to anger appeases strife. | 18 |

V. 11. *Underworld:* compare the writer's note on Matt. 11 : 23, last paragraph.—*Destruction:* see the writer's notes (Philolog. and Expl.) on Job. 26 : 6.

V. 14. *Heart of the discerning* (not, '*a discerning heart,*' as construed by some), corresponding with the parallel member.* So Rosenmüller, Maurer, Bertheau.† Second member. *Mouth* (פִּי); the reading of many Mss.* and of the ancient versions (Sept., Syr., Chald., Vulg.).

V. 15, second member. *A cheerful heart,* is the writer's meaning, whatever construction we give to the words.

* De Rossi: V. 14, plures in textu ופי, etiam Toletanus meus 782 ex prima manu (Varr. Lectt. Vet. Test. vol. iv. p. 96). It is the reading of twenty-six of Kennicott's Mss.

* Michaelis (Annott. uber.): לב נבון posset exponi per syntaxim substantivi cum adjectivo, *cor prudens,* quomodo LXX. et Ar. (quamquam ex erronea lectione נבון pro נכון) *cor rectum;* sed ex analogia membri oppositi (*os stultorum*) malumus cum Vulg. et Chald. exponere, *cor sapientis* s. *prudentis,* per regimen (cf. 18 : 5).

† נבון muss, weil den כסילים entsprechend, so aufgefasst werden: *Herz des Kundigen.*

| KING JAMES' VERSION. | HEBREW TEXT. | REVISED VERSION. |
|---|---|---|
| 19 The way of the slothful *man is* as a hedge of thorns: but the way of the righteous *is* made plain. | 19 דֶּרֶךְ עָצֵל כִּמְשֻׂכַת חָדֶק<br>וְאֹרַח יְשָׁרִים סְלֻלָה. | The sluggard's way is like a thorn-hedge; 19<br>but the path of the upright is a highway. |
| 20 A wise son maketh a glad father: but a foolish man despiseth his mother. | כ בֵּן חָכָם יְשַׂמַּח־אָב<br>וּכְסִיל אָדָם בּוֹזֶה אִמּוֹ׃ | A wise son makes a glad father; 20<br>but a foolish man despises his mother. |
| 21 Folly *is* joy to *him that is* destitute of wisdom: but a man of understanding walketh uprightly. | 21 אִוֶּלֶת שִׂמְחָה לַחֲסַר־לֵב<br>וְאִישׁ תְּבוּנָה יְיַשֶּׁר־לָכֶת׃ | Folly is joy to him that lacks wisdom; 21<br>but the man of understanding walks uprightly. |
| 22 Without counsel purposes are disappointed: but in the multitude of counsellors they are established. | 22 הָפֵר מַחֲשָׁבוֹת בְּאֵין סוֹד<br>וּבְרֹב יוֹעֲצִים תָּקוּם׃ | Without counsel plans are frustrated; 22<br>but by the multitude of counsellors they are established. |
| 23 A man hath joy by the answer of his mouth: and a word *spoken* in due season, how good *is it!* | 23 שִׂמְחָה לָאִישׁ בְּמַעֲנֵה־פִיו<br>וְדָבָר בְּעִתּוֹ מַה־טּוֹב׃ | A man has joy in the answer of his mouth; 23<br>and a word in its season—how good! |
| 24 The way of life *is* above to the wise, that he may depart from hell beneath. | 24 אֹרַח חַיִּים לְמַעְלָה לְמַשְׂכִּיל<br>לְמַעַן סוּר מִשְּׁאוֹל מָטָּה׃ | The path of life is upward for the wise, 24<br>that he may turn from the underworld beneath. |
| 25 The LORD will destroy the house of the proud: but he will establish the border of the widow. | כה בֵּית גֵּאִים יִסַּח ׀ יְהוָה<br>וְיַצֵּב גְּבוּל אַלְמָנָה׃ | The house of the proud Jehovah will root out; 25<br>but he will establish the widow's bound. |
| 26 The thoughts of the wicked *are* an abomination to the LORD: but *the words* of the pure *are* pleasant words. | 26 תּוֹעֲבַת יְהוָה מַחְשְׁבוֹת רָע<br>וּטְהֹרִים אִמְרֵי־נֹעַם׃ | Evil devices are an abomination to Jehovah; 26<br>but pure are words of kindness. |
| 27 He that is greedy of gain troubleth his own house; but he that hateth gifts shall live. | 27 עֹכֵר בֵּיתוֹ בּוֹצֵעַ בָּצַע<br>וְשׂוֹנֵא מַתָּנֹת יִחְיֶה׃ | He that is greedy of gain is a troubler of his own house; 27<br>but he that hates bribes shall live. |
| 28 The heart of the righteous studieth to answer: but the mouth of the wicked poureth out evil things. | 28 לֵב צַדִּיק יֶהְגֶּה לַעֲנוֹת<br>וּפִי רְשָׁעִים יַבִּיעַ רָעוֹת׃ | The heart of the righteous meditates for an answer; 28<br>but the mouth of the wicked pours out mischiefs. |
| 29 The LORD *is* far from the wicked: but he heareth the prayer of the righteous. | 29 רָחוֹק יְהוָה מֵרְשָׁעִים<br>וּתְפִלַּת צַדִּיקִים יִשְׁמָע׃ | Jehovah is far from the wicked; 29<br>but the prayer of the righteous he will answer. |

V. 19. סללה, *cast up*, used substantively, and corresponding to our *highway*.

V. 22. Literally *a breaking* (is there) *of plans;* Gram. § 131, 4, b, *a*.*

Second member. *They are established.* Whether we regard the verb תקום as an *impers. neut.* (Bertheau), or as a singular referring to a *remote* plur. subj. (Maurer), the above translation is the proper expression of the writer's meaning in English. In this Hirzel agrees;* though he adopts (without good reason, as I think) another construction.†

V. 26, second member. *Kindness* comprehends (though not limited to it) the proper force of נעם.

V. 27. *He that is greedy of gain:* see the note on ch. 1 : 19.

* Der Infin. absol. הָפֵר nachdrücklich vorangestellt: *Brechen die Pläne*, d. i. ein Bruch der Pläne, ist (Bertheau)

* *Aber durch Menge der Berather kommen sie zu Stand.*

† Diese (LXX) und das Targ. ergänzen am Schlusse עֵצָה (vergl. 19 : 21), wogegen Berth. תקום wie Jes. 7 : 7 als Neutr. fassen will; vergl. aber vielmehr Jer. 51 : 29, 4 : 14, Jes. 66 : 18 (?).

| KING JAMES' VERSION. | HEBREW TEXT. | | REVISED VERSION. | |
|---|---|---|---|---|
| 30 The light of the eyes rejoiceth the heart: *and* a good report maketh the bones fat. | מְאוֹר־עֵינַיִם יְשַׂמַּח־לֵב<br>שְׁמוּעָה טוֹבָה תְּדַשֶּׁן־עָצֶם׃ | ל | The light of the eyes rejoices the heart;<br>a good report makes the bones fat. | 30 |
| 31 The ear that heareth the reproof of life abideth among the wise. | אֹזֶן שֹׁמַעַת תּוֹכַחַת חַיִּים<br>בְּקֶרֶב חֲכָמִים תָּלִין׃ | 31 | The ear that hears life-giving reproof<br>shall dwell among the wise. | 31 |
| 32 He that refuseth instruction despiseth his own soul: but he that heareth reproof getteth understanding. | פּוֹרֵעַ מוּסָר מוֹאֵס נַפְשׁוֹ<br>וְשׁוֹמֵעַ תּוֹכַחַת קוֹנֶה לֵּב׃ | 32 | He that refuses correction despises his own soul;<br>but he that hears reproof gets understanding. | 32 |
| 33 The fear of the LORD *is* the instruction of wisdom; and before honour *is* humility. | יִרְאַת יְהוָה מוּסַר חָכְמָה<br>וְלִפְנֵי כָבוֹד עֲנָוָה׃ | 33 | The fear of Jehovah is instruction in wisdom;<br>and humility is before honor. | 33 |
| CHAP. XVI. | CHAP. XVI. | | CHAP. XVI. | |
| THE preparations of the heart in man, and the answer of the tongue, *is* from the LORD. | לְאָדָם מַעַרְכֵי־לֵב<br>וּמֵיְהוָה מַעֲנֵה לָשׁוֹן׃ | א | OF man are the counsels of the heart;<br>but from Jehovah is the answer of the tongue. | 1 |
| 2 All the ways of a man *are* clean in his own eyes; but the LORD weigheth the spirits. | כָּל־דַּרְכֵי־אִישׁ זַךְ בְּעֵינָיו<br>וְתֹכֵן רוּחוֹת יְהוָה׃ | 2 | All a man's ways are pure in his own eyes;<br>but he that trieth spirits is Jehovah. | 2 |
| 3 Commit thy works unto the LORD, and thy thoughts shall be established. | גֹּל אֶל־יְהוָה מַעֲשֶׂיךָ<br>וְיִכֹּנוּ מַחְשְׁבֹתֶיךָ׃ | 3 | Commit thy works to Jehovah,<br>and thy purposes shall be established. | 3 |

V. 31. *Life-giving reproof* (חיים qualifying genitive), reproof that is connected with life; compare ch. 6 : 23, *instructive reproofs are the way of life.*

Ch. XVI.—V. 1. *Of man:* לְ in the sense of *belonging to* (Gram. § 115, 2). So Rosenmüller (*homini, s. hominis* sunt *ordinationes cordis*), Maurer,* Ewald,† Bertheau.

The clause was so construed in the ancient versions.‡ It was so rendered also by the early and later Christian Hebraists.§ The true sense was given in the vernacular versions of Reformed churches on the continent,* and also in the early English versions: *A man may well purpose a thing in his heart* (Coverdale, Matthews, Cranmer, Taverner, Bishops); so the Genevan, with still more precision: *The preparations of the heart [are] in man.*

The rendering of the Common version (found in no earlier one) can be justified by no construction of the Hebrew words.

Second member. *Answer of the tongue:* see Explanatory Notes. Some understand by this, the *answer to the tongue:* viz. the answer made to its expression of the purposes, or desires, of the heart.† (See Expl. Notes.)

V. 2. כל־זך (Ewald, Lehrb. p. 688 *ima.*).

* *Homini* (hominis) sunt *consilia animi;* hominis est apud animum statuere hoc vel illud. *Et* (sed) *a Jova* est *responsio* (exauditio) linguæ; i. e. sed Jova respondet precibus linguæ, sed qui cogitata (optata) hominum juvat eventu, deus est. Peragere proposita non possumus, nisi juvante deo.

† *Des Menschen sind des Herzens Anordnungen.*

‡ Syr., ܡܢ ܒܪܢܫܐ ܬܪܥܝܬܐ ܕܠܒܐ. Chald., מִן בַּר נְשׁ תַּרְעִיתָא דְלִבָּא. Vulg., *hominis est animum præparare.* The Sept. (though too paraphrastic) recognizes the same construction: *καρδία ἀνδρὸς λογιζέσθω δίκαια.*

§ Pagnino: *hominis sunt præparationes cordis.* Munster (Biblia Hebraica, 1546): *In potestate hominis sunt præparationes cordis.* Mercerus (Comment. in Job. et Salom. Prov.): *Hominis sunt præparationes cordis.* So Gussett (Comment. ling. Heb. ed. 2da, p. 1185): *penes hominem sunt præparationes cordis.* Cocceius (Annott. in Prov. Sol.): *Habeat homo dispositiones cordis: at a Domino est pronuntiatio linguæ.* Primo hoc versu docet, quam parvæ sint hominis vires, quippe qui ne profari quidem possit sine Deo, etiam si recte aut etiam non recte, sed tamen callide consilia in corde inierit.

* *Les préparations du cœur sont à l'homme* (Genev. Fr., 1562, and Martin). *Der Mensch setzt ihm wohl vor im Herzen* (Luther). *De mensche settet hem wat voor in der herten* (Belgic, first edition of the corrected version for the Reformed churches, 1562); *De mensche heeft schickingen des herten* (the same, as revised by order of the States-General, 1628–32).

† *Die Antwort der Zunge* ist die Gewährung der Wünsche, welche die Zunge ausspricht (Bertheau). Maurer (as above, note *). Ewald: *doch von Jahve Erhörung kommt der Zunge.*

| KING JAMES' VERSION. | HEBREW TEXT. | | REVISED VERSION. | |
|---|---|---|---|---|
| 4 The LORD hath made all *things* for himself: yea, even the wicked for the day of evil. | כֹּל פָּעַל יְהוָה לַמַּעֲנֵהוּ<br>וְגַם־רָשָׁע לְיוֹם רָעָה׃ | 4 | Jehovah made every thing for its purpose;<br>and even the wicked for the day of evil. | 4 |
| 5 Every one *that is* proud in heart *is* an abomination to the LORD: *though* hand *join* in hand, he shall not be unpunished. | תּוֹעֲבַת יְהוָה כָּל־גְּבַהּ־לֵב<br>יָד לְיָד לֹא יִנָּקֶה׃ | ח | An abomination to Jehovah is every one proud in heart;<br>hand to hand he shall not be acquitted. | 5 |
| 6 By mercy and truth iniquity is purged: and by the fear of the LORD *men* depart from evil. | בְּחֶסֶד וֶאֱמֶת יְכֻפַּר עָוֹן<br>וּבְיִרְאַת יְהוָה סוּר מֵרָע׃ | 6 | By kindness and truth is iniquity covered;<br>and by the fear of Jehovah is turning from evil. | 6 |
| 7 When a man's ways please the LORD, he maketh even his enemies to be at peace with him. | בִּרְצוֹת יְהוָה דַּרְכֵי־אִישׁ<br>גַּם־אוֹיְבָיו יַשְׁלִם אִתּוֹ׃ | 7 | When Jehovah delights in one's ways,<br>he causes even his enemies to be at peace with him. | 7 |
| 8 Better *is* a little with righteousness, than great revenues without right. | טוֹב מְעַט בִּצְדָקָה<br>מֵרֹב תְּבוּאוֹת בְּלֹא מִשְׁפָּט׃ | 8 | Better is a little with righteousness,<br>than great gains without right. | 8 |
| 9 A man's heart deviseth his way: but the LORD directeth his steps. | לֵב אָדָם יְחַשֵּׁב דַּרְכּוֹ<br>וַיהוָה יָכִין צַעֲדוֹ׃ | 9 | The heart of man devises his way;<br>but Jehovah directs his step. | 9 |
| 10 A divine sentence *is* in the lips of the king: his mouth transgresseth not in judgment. | קֶסֶם ׀ עַל־שִׂפְתֵי־מֶלֶךְ<br>בְּמִשְׁפָּט לֹא יִמְעַל־פִּיו׃ | י | An oracle is on the lips of the king;<br>in judgment his mouth shall not deal treacherously. | 10 |
| 11 A just weight and balance *are* the LORD'S: all the weights of the bag *are* his work. | פֶּלֶס ׀ וּמֹאזְנֵי מִשְׁפָּט לַיהוָה<br>מַעֲשֵׂהוּ כָּל־אַבְנֵי־כִיס׃ | 11 | A just scale and balance are of Jehovah;<br>all the weights of the bag are his work. | 11 |
| 12 *It is* an abomination to kings to commit wickedness: for the throne is established by righteousness. | תּוֹעֲבַת מְלָכִים עֲשׂוֹת רֶשַׁע<br>כִּי בִצְדָקָה יִכּוֹן כִּסֵּא׃ | 12 | It is the abomination of kings to do wickedness;<br>for by righteousness is the throne established. | 12 |
| 13 Righteous lips *are* the delight of kings; and they love him that speaketh right. | רְצוֹן מְלָכִים שִׂפְתֵי־צֶדֶק<br>וְדֹבֵר יְשָׁרִים יֶאֱהָב׃ | 13 | Righteous lips are the delight of kings;<br>and him that speaks right things he loves. | 13 |

V. 4. *For its purpose:* the *suff.* referring to כֹּל, as now generally understood by scholars.*

*Purpose:* either מַעַן, *object, purpose,*† or מַעֲנֶה in the same sense. The latter, moreover, in its common signification *answer*, may mean that which answers to the nature of a thing (its fitting destiny, the purpose of its being), or which answers to an act, as the end or object to be attained.‡

* Gesenius (Thes. vol. II. p. 1051): *omnia fecit Jova suum in finem.* Ewald: *Alles hat Gott gemacht zu seinem Zweck.* Fürst (Heb. u. Chald. Hdwbch., art. מַעַן): *alles hat Gott gemacht zu seinem* (des כֹּל) *Zwecke.* Bertheau: das Suffix geht auf כֹּל zurück. Rosenmüller: Melius tamen cum altero hemistichio conveniet hoc, si Suffixum ad כֹּל referatur. Umbreit: Wir müssen jeden Falls das Suffix הוּ auf כֹּל beziehen. Maurer: *Omnia fecit Jova suum in finem*, ut fini suo respondeant.

† Fürst (as above): eig. das *Sichhinneigen nach, das Hinzielen auf* etwas, daher *Absicht, Zweck*, consilium, propositum.

The rendering of the Common Version ('*for himself*') follows that of the Vulgate, *propter se ipsum;* but there can be no doubt, that the true sense is given by the Masoretic punctuation,* as now admitted by all scholars.

V. 5. *Hand to hand:* see the note on ch. 11 : 21.

V. 9. *Directs,* יכין, as in Jer. 10 : 23, Ps. 119 : 133.

V. 11. *Scale,* whatever may be its etymology (a contested point), is now in common use for the graduated bar of the Roman balance, corresponding to the Heb. פלס.

* Der Artikel scheint in לַמַּעֲנֵהוּ (vergl. §501) deswegen beibehalten, um eine Verwechslung mit dem gewöhnlichen לְמַעֲנֵהוּ '*seinetwegen*' zu vermeiden (Ewald).

‡ Bertheau: מענה ist die Antwort z. B. 15 : 1, 23, 16 : 1; sofern diese einer Frage entspricht, ist sie das Entsprechende; was dem Thun jemandes entspricht, ist der Zweck den er durch das Thun erreichen will.

| KING JAMES' VERSION. | HEBREW TEXT. | | REVISED VERSION. | |
|---|---|---|---|---|
| 14 The wrath of a king *is as* messengers of death: but a wise man will pacify it. | חֲמַת־מֶלֶךְ מַלְאֲכֵי־מָוֶת<br>וְאִישׁ חָכָם יְכַפְּרֶנָּה׃ | 14 | The king's wrath is as messengers of death;<br>but a wise man will appease it. | 14 |
| 15 In the light of the king's countenance *is* life; and his favor *is* as a cloud of the latter rain. | בְּאוֹר־פְּנֵי־מֶלֶךְ חַיִּים<br>וּרְצוֹנוֹ כְּעָב מַלְקוֹשׁ׃ | טו | In the light of the king's countenance is life;<br>and his favor is as a cloud of the latter rain. | 15 |
| 16 How much better *is it* to get wisdom than gold! and to get understanding rather to be chosen than silver! | קְנֹה־חָכְמָה מַה־טּוֹב מֵחָרוּץ<br>וּקְנוֹת בִּינָה נִבְחָר מִכָּסֶף׃ | 16 | To get wisdom—how much better than gold!<br>and to get understanding is choicer than silver. | 16 |
| 17 The highway of the upright *is* to depart from evil: he that keepeth his way preserveth his soul. | מְסִלַּת יְשָׁרִים סוּר מֵרָע<br>שֹׁמֵר נַפְשׁוֹ נֹצֵר דַּרְכּוֹ׃ | 17 | The highway of the upright is a turning from evil;<br>he that keeps his way preserves his soul. | 17 |
| 18 Pride *goeth* before destruction, and a haughty spirit before a fall. | לִפְנֵי־שֶׁבֶר גָּאוֹן<br>וְלִפְנֵי כִשָּׁלוֹן גֹּבַהּ רוּחַ׃ | 18 | Pride is before destruction,<br>and a haughty spirit before a fall. | 18 |
| 19 Better *it is to be* of an humble spirit with the lowly, than to divide the spoil with the proud. | טוֹב שְׁפַל־רוּחַ אֶת־עֲנִיִּים<br>מֵחַלֵּק שָׁלָל אֶת־גֵּאִים׃ | 19 | Better is the humble in spirit with the lowly,<br>than to divide the spoil with the proud. | 19 |
| 20 He that handleth a matter wisely shall find good: and whoso trusteth in the LORD, happy *is* he. | מַשְׂכִּיל עַל־דָּבָר יִמְצָא־טוֹב<br>וּבוֹטֵחַ בַּיהוָה אַשְׁרָיו׃ | כ | He that gives heed to the word will find good;<br>and he that trusts in Jehovah, happy is he! | 20 |
| 21 The wise in heart shall be called prudent: and the sweetness of the lips increaseth learning. | לַחֲכַם־לֵב יִקָּרֵא נָבוֹן<br>וּמֶתֶק שְׂפָתַיִם יֹסִיף לֶקַח׃ | 21 | The wise in heart shall be called discerning;<br>and learning adds sweetness to the lips. | 21 |
| 22 Understanding *is* a wellspring of life unto him that hath it: but the instruction of fools *is* folly. | מְקוֹר חַיִּים שֵׂכֶל בְּעָלָיו<br>וּמוּסַר אֱוִלִים אִוֶּלֶת׃ | 22 | A well of life is understanding to its possessor;<br>but the correction of fools is folly. | 22 |
| 23 The heart of the wise teacheth his mouth, and addeth learning to his lips. | לֵב חָכָם יַשְׂכִּיל פִּיהוּ<br>וְעַל־שְׂפָתָיו יֹסִיף לֶקַח׃ | 23 | The heart of the wise instructs his mouth,<br>and increases learning on his lips. | 23 |
| 24 Pleasant words *are as* a honey-comb, sweet to the soul, and health to the bones. | צוּף־דְּבַשׁ אִמְרֵי־נֹעַם<br>מָתוֹק לַנֶּפֶשׁ וּמַרְפֵּא לָעָצֶם׃ | 24 | Words of kindness are as the honey-comb,<br>sweetness to the soul, and a healing to the bones. | 24 |

V. 19. עֲנוים ק׳ V. 22. בנ״א אוילים

V. 17. *Highway* (מסלה); one that is cast up and leveled. This is always the meaning of the Heb. word;* though the compound form of the English word might, in some instances, give too emphatic an expression of it. Compare the Expl. Notes.

V. 18. *Before destruction:* close upon it, and just ready to plunge into it. '*Goes before*' (Common Version), i. e. is in advance of it, is not the meaning.

V. 21. לחכם—יקרא, as in Gen. 2 : 23.—Those who adopt the construction (second member), '*sweetness of the lips increases learning*,' suppose the writer to mean, that a persuasive manner attracts listeners, and thus increases learning; which is not at all pertinent in connection with the parallel member.

V. 22. *To its possessor:** the *constr. st.* (Gram. § 116) expressing the relation in a general manner (in reference to).†

V. 24. *Kindness* (נעם); see the note on ch. 15 : 26.—מתוק *neut.* used substantively, corresponding to מרפא.‡

* Bertheau: מסלה ist immer der gebahnte Weg. *Der gebahnte Weg der Redlichen ist fernbleiben vom Bösen;* womit gemeint ist, dass ihnen wirklich auf solcher Bahn, also ohne Anstoss, zu wandeln gestattet ist, so lange sie Böses vermeiden.

* Gesenius (Thes. vol. I. p. 224): *fons felicitatis est prudentia domino suo*, i. e. huic qui ea præditus est.

† Ewald: Eigentlich "die Einsicht seines Herrn," d. i. dessen, der sie hat, besitzt, also allerdings des Klugen. Diess so kürzer gesagt für: הַשֵּׂכֶל לִבְעָלָיו.

‡ Maurer: *Dulcedo* (dulcia) *animo, et sanatio* (salubria) *ossibus* (corpori). מתוק neutr., vim substantivi habens.

KING JAMES' VERSION.

25 There is a way that seemeth right unto a man; but the end thereof *are* the ways of death.

26 He that laboureth laboureth for himself; for his mouth craveth it of him.

27 An ungodly man diggeth up evil: and in his lips *there is* as a burning fire.

28 A froward man soweth strife: and a whisperer separateth chief friends.

29 A violent man enticeth his neighbour, and leadeth him into the way *that is* not good.

30 He shutteth his eyes to devise froward things: moving his lips he bringeth evil to pass.

31 The hoary head *is* a crown of glory, *if* it be found in the way of righteousness.

32 *He that is* slow to anger *is* better than the mighty: and he that ruleth his spirit than he that taketh a city.

33 The lot is cast into the lap; but the whole disposing thereof *is* of the LORD.

HEBREW TEXT.

כה יֵשׁ דֶּרֶךְ יָשָׁר לִפְנֵי־אִישׁ
וְאַחֲרִיתָהּ דַּרְכֵי־מָוֶת׃

26 נֶפֶשׁ עָמֵל עָמְלָה לּוֹ
כִּי־אָכַף עָלָיו פִּיהוּ׃

27 אִישׁ בְּלִיַּעַל כֹּרֶה רָעָה
וְעַל־שְׂפָתָיו כְּאֵשׁ צָרָבֶת׃

28 אִישׁ תַּהְפֻּכוֹת יְשַׁלַּח מָדוֹן
וְנִרְגָּן מַפְרִיד אַלּוּף׃

29 אִישׁ חָמָס יְפַתֶּה רֵעֵהוּ
וְהוֹלִיכוֹ בְּדֶרֶךְ לֹא־טוֹב׃

ל עֹצֶה עֵינָיו לַחְשֹׁב תַּהְפֻּכוֹת
קֹרֵץ שְׂפָתָיו כִּלָּה רָעָה׃

31 עֲטֶרֶת תִּפְאֶרֶת שֵׂיבָה
בְּדֶרֶךְ צְדָקָה תִּמָּצֵא׃

32 טוֹב אֶרֶךְ אַפַּיִם מִגִּבּוֹר
וּמֹשֵׁל בְּרוּחוֹ מִלֹּכֵד עִיר׃

33 בַּחֵיק יוּטַל אֶת־הַגּוֹרָל
וּמֵיְהוָה כָּל־מִשְׁפָּטוֹ׃

V. 27. שפתו ק׳

REVISED VERSION.

There is a way right in the 25
sight of a man;
but the end thereof—they are
ways of death.

The laborer's appetite labors 26
for him;
for his mouth has laid a burden
on him.

A vile man is he that devises 27
mischief;
and on his lips is as burning
fire.

A perverse man sends forth 28
contention;
and a talebearer separates a
near friend.

A man of violence seduces his 29
friend,
and leads him in a way that is
not good.

When he shuts his eyes, he is 30
devising perverseness;
when he bites his lips, he has
perfected mischief.

The hoary head is a crown of 31
glory,
if it is found in the way of
righteousness.

The slow to anger is better 32
than the mighty,
and he that rules his spirit than
he that takes a city.

The lot is cast into the lap; 33
but its decision is all of Jehovah.

---

V. 26. אכף in its proper sense *to load, to lay on a load*;* compare the subst. אֶכֶף, *a burden*, Job 33 : 7.†

V. 27. *Devises mischief* (כרה רעה) is the writer's meaning, expressed in a literal form; the image (of *digging*, viz. *a pitfall*) can not be preserved in English.‡

V. 28. *Talebearer* (נרגן); prop. one who talks much, an idle prater, and hence a gossiping go-between, a *talebearer*.

V. 29. *Seduces his friend* (Lex. *Piel*, 1): by practicing on his open-heartedness and simplicity, for his own evil ends.*

V. 30. *Shutting* = *when he shuts*, etc.—*Is devising* (לחשב): Gram. § 132, 3, *Rem.* 1.—*Has perfected:* as expressed by the change to the *Pret.*†

V. 31. *If it is found* (תמצא): Gram. § 155, 4, *a*

V. 33. *The lot is cast* (יוטל את־ה'): Gram. § 143, 1, *a.*—*Its decision* (משפט as in Numb. 27 : 21); namely, the decision which *the lot makes*, that is of Jehovah,—he appoints and directs it; not *gen. obj.* (Maurer), *the decision concerning it.*‡

---

* Ewald: *weil Bürden ihm hat aufgelegt sein Mund.*

† Out of this naturally arose the later Syr. usage (Bernstein, Lex. Chrestom. Kirsch. p. 21: ܐܟܦ, . . . . I. intrans. *sedulus fuit, operam dedit, studium impendit* rei, *curæ fuit* alicui alqd. II. transit. *studium* alcuis *commovit, instigavit, sollicitavit, pressit, compulit*, seq. ܒ vel ܠ pers. *alqm.* ad alqd.); but which we are not to regard, with Bertheau, as the primary meaning of the Heb. word found here.

‡ Gesenius (Thes. vol. II. p. 711): Imagine a fovea petita paulo audacius dictum est Prov. XVI. 27, . . . *homo nequam perniciam fodit*, i. e. struit.

* Ewald: *bethöret seinen Freund.*

† Maurer: *perfecit*, i. e. jamjam excogitavit, paratum habet *malum* alteri inferendum.

‡ *Doch von Jahve kommt seine ganze Entscheidung* (Bertheau). *Doch von Jahve kommt all sein Urtheil* (Ewald).

| KING JAMES' VERSION. | HEBREW TEXT. | | REVISED VERSION. | |
|---|---|---|---|---|
| CHAP. XVII. | CHAP. XVII. | | CHAP. XVII. | |
| BETTER *is* a dry morsel, and quietness therewith, than a house full of sacrifices *with* strife. | טוֹב פַּת חֲרֵבָה וְשַׁלְוָה־בָהּ<br>מִבַּיִת מָלֵא זִבְחֵי־רִיב׃ | א | BETTER is a dry morsel, and quietness therewith,<br>than a house full of slaughtered beasts, with strife. | 1 |
| 2 A wise servant shall have rule over a son that causeth shame, and shall have part of the inheritance among the brethren. | עֶבֶד מַשְׂכִּיל יִמְשֹׁל בְּבֵן־מֵבִישׁ<br>וּבְתוֹךְ אַחִים יַחֲלֹק נַחֲלָה׃ | 2 | A wise servant shall rule over a base son,<br>and shall share the inheritance among brethren. | 2 |
| 3 The fining pot *is* for silver, and the furnace for gold: but the LORD trieth the hearts. | מַצְרֵף לַכֶּסֶף וְכוּר לַזָּהָב<br>וּבֹחֵן לִבּוֹת יְהוָה׃ | 3 | A refining pot for silver, and a furnace for gold;<br>but the trier of hearts is Jehovah. | 3 |
| 4 A wicked doer giveth heed to false lips; *and* a liar giveth ear to a naughty tongue. | מֵרַע מַקְשִׁיב עַל־שְׂפַת־אָוֶן<br>שֶׁקֶר מֵזִין עַל־לְשׁוֹן הַוֺּת׃ | 4 | An evil-doer gives heed to the deceitful lip;<br>falsehood listens to the pernicious tongue. | 4 |
| 5 Whoso mocketh the poor reproacheth his Maker: *and* he that is glad at calamities shall not be unpunished. | לֹעֵג לָרָשׁ חֵרֵף עֹשֵׂהוּ<br>שָׂמֵחַ לְאֵיד לֹא יִנָּקֶה׃ | ה | He that mocks at the poor scorns his Maker;<br>he that rejoices at calamity shall not be acquitted. | 5 |
| 6 Children's children *are* the crown of old men; and the glory of children *are* their fathers. | עֲטֶרֶת זְקֵנִים בְּנֵי בָנִים<br>וְתִפְאֶרֶת בָּנִים אֲבוֹתָם | 6 | Children's children are the crown of old men;<br>and the glory of children are their fathers. | 6 |
| 7 Excellent speech becometh not a fool: much less do lying lips a prince. | לֹא־נָאוָה לְנָבָל שְׂפַת יֶתֶר<br>אַף כִּי־לְנָדִיב שְׂפַת־שָׁקֶר׃ | 7 | Excellent speech is not suitable for a fool;<br>much less is a lying lip for the noble. | 7 |
| 8 A gift *is as* a precious stone in the eyes of him that hath it: whithersoever it turneth, it prospereth. | אֶבֶן־חֵן הַשֹּׁחַד בְּעֵינֵי בְעָלָיו<br>אֶל־כָּל־אֲשֶׁר יִפְנֶה יַשְׂכִּיל׃ | 8 | A gift is a precious stone in the eyes of its possessor;<br>to whomsoever it turns, it prospers. | 8 |
| 9 He that covereth a transgression seeketh love; but he that repeateth a matter separateth *very* friends. | מְכַסֶּה־פֶּשַׁע מְבַקֵּשׁ אַהֲבָה<br>וְשֹׁנֶה בְדָבָר מַפְרִיד אַלּוּף׃ | 9 | He that covers a fault seeks love;<br>but he that repeats a matter separates a near friend. | 9 |
| 10 A reproof entereth more into a wise man than a hundred stripes into a fool. | תֵּחַת גְּעָרָה בְמֵבִין<br>מֵהַכּוֹת כְּסִיל מֵאָה׃ | י | A reproof sinks deeper in a man of understanding,<br>than beating a fool a hundred times. | 10 |

Ch. XVII.—V. 1. *With strife:* the *constr. st.* denoting connection or accompaniment.

V. 2. *Base:* מביש *intrans.* as in ch. 14 : 35.

V. 4. *Pernicious tongue:* הות in its most usual signification.*

V. 7. *Excellent speech:* the natural import of the words, and the appropriate sense in the connection; see Expl. Notes.—*The noble:* see the note on Job 21 : 28.

V. 8, second member. *To whomsoever:* אל כל־אשר, evidently used of *persons.**

The sentiment of the verse is expressed by Euripides (Medea, 960): *πείθειν δῶρα καὶ θεοὺς λόγος.*

V. 9. *Repeats a matter* (שנה בדבר): compare Gram. §138, 1, *Rem.* 3, foot-note (*).†

* Maurer: *Mendacium* i. e. mendax *aurem præbet linguæ perniciosæ*, quæ alios perdere studet. Bertheau: Da neben שקר das Partic. מזין steht, . . . so muss *Trug hört* soviel bedeuten als: *wer trügerisch ist hört auf Verderben bringende Zunge.*

* Bertheau: *zu wem es auch gelangt.*

† Ewald: Eigentlich: wer wiederkommt, mit einem Worte, es aus böser Absicht wiederholt, statt es mit Liebe und Nachsicht zu verbergen.

| KING JAMES' VERSION. | HEBREW TEXT. | | REVISED VERSION. | |
|---|---|---|---|---|
| 11 An evil *man* seeketh only rebellion: therefore a cruel messenger shall be sent against him. | אַךְ מְרִי יְבַקֶּשׁ־רָע<br>וּמַלְאָךְ אַכְזָרִי יְשֻׁלַּח־בּוֹ׃ | 11 | An evil man seeks only rebellion;<br>and a cruel messenger will be sent against him. | 11 |
| 12 Let a bear robbed of her whelps meet a man, rather than a fool in his folly. | פָּגוֹשׁ דֹּב שַׁכּוּל בְּאִישׁ<br>וְאַל־כְּסִיל בְּאִוַּלְתּוֹ׃ | 12 | Let a bear robbed of her young meet a man,<br>and not a fool in his folly. | 12 |
| 13 Whoso rewardeth evil for good, evil shall not depart from his house. | מֵשִׁיב רָעָה תַּחַת טוֹבָה<br>לֹא־תָמִישׁ רָעָה מִבֵּיתוֹ׃ | 13 | Whoso returns evil for good,<br>evil shall not depart from his house. | 13 |
| 14 The beginning of strife *is as* when one letteth out water: therefore leave off contention, before it be meddled with. | פּוֹטֵר מַיִם רֵאשִׁית מָדוֹן<br>וְלִפְנֵי הִתְגַּלַּע הָרִיב נְטוֹשׁ׃ | 14 | The beginning of contention is the breaking forth of water;<br>desist then, before the strife is embittered. | 14 |
| 15 He that justifieth the wicked, and he that condemneth the just, even they both *are* abomination to the LORD. | מַצְדִּיק רָשָׁע וּמַרְשִׁיעַ צַדִּיק<br>תּוֹעֲבַת יְהוָה גַּם־שְׁנֵיהֶם׃ | טו | He that justifies the wicked, and that condemns the righteous,<br>are both of them alike an abomination to Jehovah. | 15 |
| 16 Wherefore *is there* a price in the hand of a fool to get wisdom, seeing *he hath* no heart *to it?* | לָמָּה־זֶּה מְחִיר בְּיַד־כְּסִיל<br>לִקְנוֹת חָכְמָה וְלֶב־אָיִן׃ | 16 | Wherefore is a price in the hand of a fool,<br>to get wisdom, when there is no heart! | 16 |
| 17 A friend loveth at all times, and a brother is born for adversity. | בְּכָל־עֵת אֹהֵב הָרֵעַ<br>וְאָח לְצָרָה יִוָּלֵד | 17 | The friend loves at all times;<br>and a brother is born for adversity. | 17 |

V. 13. תמוש ק׳

V. 11. The position of מרי in immediate connection with אך, and the obvious propriety of the thought, show that מרי is the *object* (not the *subj.*), as in the Sept. and Vulg.*

V. 12. *Let a bear—meet*, etc.: פָּגוֹשׁ, *Infin. abs.* as an emphatic *Imperat.* (Gram. §131, 4, *b*, *γ*).

*Meet a man* (פגוש . . . באיש).† Umbreit‡ and Bertheau (who is followed by Stuart§) give the false construction, '*meet a bear robbed of her young.*'||

Second member. *And not* (וְאַל) is the emphatic form of the Hebrew; strictly, *let not*, the proper use of אל.

* Des אך wegen liegt es am nächsten, das Wort [מרי] mit Septuag. und Vulg. für das Obj. zu halten (Bertheau).

† Ewald: *Mag ein verwaister Bär auf Einen stossen.* Maurer: *incidat ursus orbatus* (i. e. ursa orbata catulis) *in aliquem.* Hirzel: *Ein verwaister Bär möge stossen auf einen Mann, aber nicht ein Narr in seiner Thorheit.*

‡ Gewöhnlich übersetzt man das בְּאִישׁ *contra virum*.... Einfacher und klarer scheint aber die Construction des Verses, wenn wir בְּאִישׁ von שַׁכּוּל abhängig sein lassen, und אִישׁ für *masculus* oder *ein Junges* überhaupt nehmen, wie es 1 Mos. 4 : 1 von dem Neugebornen steht.

On the contrary, Ewald asserts with truth: unstreitig steht איש in derselben Bedeutung, die es so oft in diesen allgemein zu fassenden Sprüchen hat.

§ Who mistakes, however, his construction of באיש, and translates '*robbed of her whelps by a man*,' as though that were the point.

|| *Stosse auf eine ihrer Jungen beraubte Bärin.*

V. 14. *The breaking forth* (פוטר): as correctly understood by Ewald* and Maurer.†

Second member. *Before it is embittered:* so Gesenius,‡ Maurer,§ Umbreit,|| and, to the same effect, Ewald¶ and Hitzig.**

Bertheau: *Before its rolling on* (before the violent outbreak) *give up strife.* But this rests only on an uncertain etymology, without any support in the traditional exegesis.

V. 15. *Both of them alike:* גַּם gives emphasis to שְׁנֵי, '*they both*,' i. e. the one as well as the other = *both alike.*

V. 16. For the meaning, see Expl. Notes. The idea that "all is not to be bought with gold," and that "a man can not purchase wisdom for any price, who is without understanding" (Bertheau and Stuart), and that "it avails nothing for a fool to obtain wisdom, when he has not understanding to use it" (Maurer), are all foreign to the intent of the writer.

V. 17. The *true* friend, and the *true* brother, of course are

* *Ein Wasserdurchbruch.* פוטר ist eigentlich *was* Wasser *durchlässt.*

† פוטר, quod præter Ewaldum omnes pro Participio habent, nomen est formæ יוֹתֵר, significans *fissionem*, hinc *proruptionem.*

‡ Thes. (vol. I. p. 290): *priusquam exacerbatur lis, desiste.*

§ *Et* (itaque) *priusquam* fervidius *exardescat lis, dimitte.*

|| *Eh' sich der Streit erhitzt, lass ab davon.*

¶ Von offen ausbrechender, höhnender Erbitterung gesagt; ... daher, wie alle Begriffe der Erbitterung, des Zorns, möglicherweise mit ב verbunden (18 : 1).

** *Bevor der Streit die Zähne bleckt, lass ab!*

| KING JAMES' VERSION. | | HEBREW TEXT. | REVISED VERSION. | |
|---|---|---|---|---|
| 18 A man void of understanding striketh hands, *and* becometh surety in the presence of his friend. | 18 | אָדָם חֲסַר־לֵב תֹּקֵעַ כָּף<br>עֹרֵב עֲרֻבָּה לִפְנֵי רֵעֵהוּ׃ | A man lacking understanding<br>is he that strikes hands,<br>that becomes surety in presence<br>of his friend. | 18 |
| 19 He loveth transgression that loveth strife: *and* he that exalteth his gate seeketh destruction. | 19 | אֹהֵב פֶּשַׁע אֹהֵב מַצָּה<br>מַגְבִּיהַּ פִּתְחוֹ מְבַקֶּשׁ־שָׁבֶר׃ | He loves sin that loves contention;<br>he that makes high his gate<br>seeks ruin. | 19 |
| 20 He that hath a froward heart findeth no good: and he that hath a perverse tongue falleth into mischief. | כ | עִקֶּשׁ־לֵב לֹא יִמְצָא־טוֹב<br>וְנֶהְפָּךְ בִּלְשׁוֹנוֹ יִפּוֹל בְּרָעָה׃ | The perverse in heart shall not<br>find good;<br>and one changeful with his<br>tongue falls into mischief. | 20 |
| 21 He that begetteth a fool *doeth it* to his sorrow: and the father of a fool hath no joy. | 21 | יֹלֵד כְּסִיל לְתוּגָה לוֹ<br>וְלֹא יִשְׂמַח אֲבִי נָבָל׃ | One begets a fool to his own<br>sorrow;<br>and the father of the foolish<br>shall not have joy. | 21 |
| 22 A merry heart doeth good *like* a medicine: but a broken spirit drieth the bones. | 22 | לֵב שָׂמֵחַ יֵיטִב גֵּהָה<br>וְרוּחַ נְכֵאָה תְּיַבֶּשׁ־גָּרֶם׃ | A joyous heart makes happy<br>cure;<br>but a broken spirit dries up<br>the bones. | 22 |
| 23 A wicked *man* taketh a gift out of the bosom to pervert the ways of judgment. | 23 | שֹׁחַד מֵחֵק רָשָׁע יִקָּח<br>לְהַטּוֹת אָרְחוֹת מִשְׁפָּט׃ | The wicked takes a gift out of<br>the bosom,<br>to pervert the ways of justice. | 23 |
| 24 Wisdom *is* before him that hath understanding; but the eyes of a fool *are* in the ends of the earth. | 24 | אֶת־פְּנֵי מֵבִין חָכְמָה<br>וְעֵינֵי כְסִיל בִּקְצֵה־אָרֶץ׃ | Wisdom is present with the<br>discerning;<br>but the fool's eyes are at the<br>end of the earth. | 24 |
| 25 A foolish son *is* a grief to his father, and bitterness to her that bare him. | כה | כַּעַס לְאָבִיו בֵּן כְּסִיל<br>וּמֶמֶר לְיוֹלַדְתּוֹ׃ | A foolish son is a grief to his<br>father,<br>and bitterness to her that bore<br>him. | 25 |

V. 22. בנ"א וייטיב

meant; and there is no reason why the *Imperf.* (יוּלָּד) should not be understood in its ordinary use.*

Other constructions. (Umbreit, Maurer): *and he* (the friend) *in adversity is born a brother*, will become a brother to thee in adversity. (Bertheau†): *and a brother for adversity*, one who shows himself such in the hour of need, *is to be born* (must then be born).‡ (Hitzig): *but as brother is he born of adversity.*§

V. 18. *To strike the hand* is the Heb. form here, our usage requiring the plural, *to strike hands.*

V. 20. *One changeful with his tongue:* now saying this and now that, one on whose word there is no dependence; hence in the Arab. *lying.**

V. 21. *To his own sorrow:* lit. *for a grief to himself;* a better construction than, *whoso begets a fool, it is a grief to him.*

V. 22. *Cure* (i. e. the completed process of healing) is the sense naturally drawn from the use of the verbal form in Hos. 5 : 13. So Gesenius,† Ewald,‡ Hitzig,§ and others. The signification *body* (Bertheau, Stuart) is not as well sustained, nor is it as appropriate here.

V. 24. *Is present with:* Gesenius, Lex. אֵת II. 1, and פָּנֶה (with preps.) B.‖

* So Ewald: *ein Bruder wird für Drangsal erst geboren.* Compare his remark (p. 20), so dass man sagen könne, ein Bruder werde gleichsam für Drangsale geboren.

† After C. B. Michaelis (Annott. uber.): *sed frater ad angustiam, nascitur,* seu adhuc *nasciturus est.*

‡ *Und ein Bruder für die Noth,* welcher sich in der Noth als Bruder bewährt, *soll erst geboren werden.* Das Imperf. יוּלָּד weist darauf hin, dass er noch nicht geboren, noch nicht vorhanden ist.

§ *Aber als Bruder wird er von der Noth geboren.* Als 'Bruder' ist er dann eine *καινὴ κτίσις.*

* Gesenius (Thes. and Lex.): *qui versutæ linguæ est.* Bertheau: *Wer sich umwendet mit seiner Zunge,* bald so bald so redet. Hitzig: *Wer sich windet mit seiner Zunge.*

† Thes. vol. I. p. 269: *remotio ligaturæ* i. e. *sanatio* vulneris. Prov. 17 : 22, . . . *cor lætum felicem dat sanationem.*

‡ *Ein frohes Herze gute Heilung schafft.*

§ *Ein fröhliches Herz fördert Genesung.*

‖ Bertheau: את פני *bei dem Antlitze* muss nach *b dicht* **vor,** *in nächster Nähe bezeichnen.*

KING JAMES' VERSION.

26 Also to punish the just *is* not good, *nor* to strike princes for equity.

27 He that hath knowledge spareth his words: *and* a man of understanding is of an excellent spirit.

28 Even a fool, when he holdeth his peace, is counted wise: *and* he that shutteth his lips *is esteemed* a man of understanding.

CHAP. XVIII.

THROUGH desire a man, having separated himself, seeketh *and* intermeddleth with all wisdom.

2 A fool hath no delight in understanding, but that his heart may discover itself.

3 When the wicked cometh, *then* cometh also contempt, and with ignominy reproach.

4 The words of a man's mouth *are as* deep waters, *and* the wellspring of wisdom *as* a flowing brook.

5 *It is* not good to accept the person of the wicked, to overthrow the righteous in judgment.

6 A fool's lips enter into contention, and his mouth calleth for strokes.

7 A fool's mouth *is* his destruction, and his lips *are* the snare of his soul.

HEBREW TEXT.

גַּם עֲנוֹשׁ לַצַּדִּיק לֹא־טוֹב 26
לְהַכּוֹת נְדִיבִים עַל־יֹשֶׁר׃

חוֹשֵׂךְ אֲמָרָיו יוֹדֵעַ דָּעַת 27
וְקַר־רוּחַ אִישׁ תְּבוּנָה׃

גַּם אֱוִיל מַחֲרִישׁ חָכָם יֵחָשֵׁב 28
אֹטֵם שְׂפָתָיו נָבוֹן׃

CHAP. XVIII.

לְתַאֲוָה יְבַקֵּשׁ נִפְרָד א
בְּכָל־תּוּשִׁיָּה יִתְגַּלָּע׃

לֹא־יַחְפֹּץ כְּסִיל בִּתְבוּנָה 2
כִּי אִם־בְּהִתְגַּלּוֹת לִבּוֹ׃

בְּבוֹא רָשָׁע בָּא גַם־בּוּז 3
וְעִם־קָלוֹן חֶרְפָּה׃

מַיִם עֲמֻקִּים דִּבְרֵי פִי־אִישׁ 4
נַחַל נֹבֵעַ מְקוֹר חָכְמָה׃

שְׂאֵת פְּנֵי־רָשָׁע לֹא־טוֹב ח
לְהַטּוֹת צַדִּיק בַּמִּשְׁפָּט׃

שִׂפְתֵי כְסִיל יָבֹאוּ בְרִיב 6
וּפִיו לְמַהֲלֻמוֹת יִקְרָא׃

פִּי כְסִיל מְחִתָּה־לוֹ 7
וּשְׂפָתָיו מוֹקֵשׁ נַפְשׁוֹ׃

REVISED VERSION.

Also it is not good to lay a 26
fine on the righteous,
to smite the noble for uprightness.

He that has knowledge is sparing 27
of his words;
and a man of understanding is cool in spirit.

Even a fool when he is silent 28
may pass for wise,
while he shuts his lips, for a man of discernment.

CHAP. XVIII.

HE that separates himself 1
seeks his own pleasure;
against all good counsel he is embittered.

The fool has no pleasure in 2
understanding,
but in his heart's disclosure of itself.

When the wicked comes, then 3
comes also contempt,
and reproach along with shame.

The words of a man's mouth 4
are deep waters;
the well-spring of wisdom is a gushing stream.

It is not good to regard the 5
person of the wicked,
to turn aside the righteous in judgment.

The fool's lips enter into 6
strife,
and his mouth calls for blows.

The fool's mouth is his destruc- 7
tion;
and his lips are a snare to his soul.

V. 26. *Also* (גם): *this too* (as well as others) is not good, noting it as worthy of marked distinction.*

*To lay a fine upon* (ענוש): here absol. with לְ; compare its use in Deut. 22 : 19; elsewhere, simply *to inflict a penalty, to punish.*

*To smite the noble*, is the natural construction, and accords with the parallel terms (*to lay a fine on the righteous*) in the other member.

*For uprightness*: Lex. עַל, A, 2, d; יֹשֶׁר, 2, b.†

V. 28, second member; אטם evidently holds the same grammatical relation as מחריש.

Ch. XVIII.—V. 1. *Seeks his own pleasure:* lit. *seeks for pleasure*, that is, for what pleases himself.*—יְבַקֵּשׁ לְ, as in Job 10 : 6. *Is embittered:* see ch. 17 : 14.

V. 2. *In his heart's disclosure of itself:*† compare ch. 12 : 23, 15 : 2.

* Rosenmüller: Inter alia, quæ nequaquam bene et laudabiliter fiunt, est et hoc.

† Thes. (vol. II. p. 642): עַל יֹשֶׁר *propter probitatem*, Prov. 17 : 26 (non, ut alii, *ultra id quod fas est*).

* *Nach Lust*, nach Befriedigung eigner Lust, *sucht wer sich absondert* (Bertheau). Saadias, . . . *qui sese separat* ab aliorum consortio (suum ipsius consilium non aliorum sequi vult) *quærit desiderium*, cupiditatem suam (Rosenmüller).

† Bertheau: *an dem sich offenbaren seines Herzens.* **Ewald**: *an seines Herzens Offenbarung.*

| KING JAMES' VERSION. | HEBREW TEXT. | | REVISED VERSION. |
|---|---|---|---|
| 8 The words of a talebearer *are* as wounds, and they go down into the innermost parts of the belly. | דִּבְרֵי נִרְגָּן כְּמִתְלַהֲמִים<br>וְהֵם יָרְדוּ חַדְרֵי־בָטֶן׃ | 8 | The words of a tale-bearer are as dainty morsels; 8<br>and it is they that go down to the inmost parts of the belly. |
| 9 He also that is slothful in his work is brother to him that is a great waster. | גַּם מִתְרַפֶּה בִמְלַאכְתּוֹ<br>אָח הוּא לְבַעַל מַשְׁחִית׃ | 9 | Also he that shows himself slack in his service, 9<br>the same is brother to the wasteful. |
| 10 The name of the LORD *is* a strong tower: the righteous runneth into it, and is safe. | מִגְדַּל־עֹז שֵׁם יְהוָה<br>בּוֹ־יָרוּץ צַדִּיק וְנִשְׂגָּב׃ | י | The name of Jehovah is a strong tower; 10<br>the righteous runs into it and is safe. |
| 11 The rich man's wealth *is* his strong city, and as a high wall in his own conceit. | הוֹן עָשִׁיר קִרְיַת עֻזּוֹ<br>וּכְחוֹמָה נִשְׂגָּבָה בְּמַשְׂכִּיתוֹ׃ | 11 | The rich man's wealth is his strong city, 11<br>and as a high wall in his own conceit. |
| 12 Before destruction the heart of man is haughty; and before honour *is* humility. | לִפְנֵי־שֶׁבֶר יִגְבַּהּ לֵב־אִישׁ<br>וְלִפְנֵי כָבוֹד עֲנָוָה׃ | 12 | The heart of man is lifted up before destruction; 12<br>and humility is before honor. |
| 13 He that answereth a matter before he heareth *it*, it *is* folly and shame unto him. | מֵשִׁיב דָּבָר בְּטֶרֶם יִשְׁמָע<br>אִוֶּלֶת הִיא־לוֹ וּכְלִמָּה׃ | 13 | Whoso gives answer before he hears, 13<br>it is folly to him and shame. |
| 14 The spirit of a man will sustain his infirmity; but a wounded spirit who can bear? | רוּחַ אִישׁ יְכַלְכֵּל מַחֲלֵהוּ<br>וְרוּחַ נְכֵאָה מִי יִשָּׂאֶנָּה׃ | 14 | The spirit of a man will sustain his sickness; 14<br>but a broken spirit, who can bear it! |
| 15 The heart of the prudent getteth knowledge; and the ear of the wise seeketh knowledge. | לֵב נָבוֹן יִקְנֶה־דָּעַת<br>וְאֹזֶן חֲכָמִים תְּבַקֶּשׁ־דָּעַת׃ | טו | The heart of the discerning will get knowledge; 15<br>and for knowledge the ear of the wise will seek. |
| 16 A man's gift maketh room for him, and bringeth him before great men. | מַתָּן אָדָם יַרְחִיב לוֹ<br>וְלִפְנֵי גְדוֹלִים יַנְחֶנּוּ׃ | 16 | A man's gift makes room for him, 16<br>and leads him before the great. |
| 17 *He that is* first in his own cause *seemeth* just; but his neighbour cometh and searcheth him. | צַדִּיק הָרִאשׁוֹן בְּרִיבוֹ<br>יָבָא רֵעֵהוּ וַחֲקָרוֹ׃ | 17 | The first in his suit is right; 17<br>his fellow comes and searches him out. |
| 18 The lot causeth contentions to cease, and parteth between the mighty. | מִדְיָנִים יַשְׁבִּית הַגּוֹרָל<br>וּבֵין עֲצוּמִים יַפְרִיד׃ | 18 | The lot makes contentions cease, 18<br>and parts between the strong. |
| 19 A brother offended *is harder to be won* than a strong city: and *their* contentions *are* like the bars of a castle. | אָח נִפְשָׁע מִקִּרְיַת־עֹז<br>וּמִדְוָנִים כִּבְרִיחַ אַרְמוֹן׃ | 19 | A brother estranged is harder to win than a strong city; 19<br>and contentions are as the bar of a fortress. |

V. 8. *As dainty morsels* (lit. *as things eagerly swallowed**). This is the only signification of the Heb. word, that has any good foundation in Semitic etymology and usage (Schultens, *in loc.* Gesenius, Thes. vol. II. p. 724).

*It is they* (הֵם emphatic, Gram. § 137, 3, *Rem.* 2), namely these things (the talebearer's words),† that 'go down to the inner parts of the belly,'—that make a lodgment deep within.

* *Tanquam avide inglutita* (Schultens).

† Ewald is mistaken, therefore, in saying that והם, on this construction of the words, is superfluous (auch wäre im letzten Falle וְהֵם überflüssig.

V. 9. *Also* (גַּם), as in ch. 17 : 26.

V. 13. *Gives answer.* שׁוּב, when followed by דָּבָר, must have its literal meaning (*to return word = to give answer*).

V. 17. *Comes,* יָבֹא, is doubtless the true reading (*Qeri* וּבָא, *then comes*).

V. 19. Whether we construe נפשׁע as a *particip. adj.* with אח (Gesenius and others), or, according to the Jewish accentuation, as the *predicate* (Ewald, Bertheau), the form of the text is required to give in English the full import of the compressed form in the Hebrew.

In either case מִן denotes an *excess*, the nature of which is implied in the meaning of נפשׁע; viz., that he is more persistent in

| KING JAMES' VERSION. | HEBREW TEXT. | REVISED VERSION. |
|---|---|---|
| 20 A man's belly shall be satisfied with the fruit of his mouth; *and* with the increase of his lips shall he be filled. | כ מִפְּרִי פִּי־אִישׁ תִּשְׂבַּע בִּטְנוֹ<br>תְּבוּאַת שְׂפָתָיו יִשְׂבָּע׃ | With the fruit of a man's mouth 20<br>shall his belly be filled;<br>he shall be filled with the produce of his lips. |
| 21 Death and life *are* in the power of the tongue: and they that love it shall eat the fruit thereof. | 21 מָוֶת וְחַיִּים בְּיַד־לָשׁוֹן<br>וְאֹהֲבֶיהָ יֹאכַל פִּרְיָהּ׃ | Death and life are in the power 21<br>of the tongue;<br>and he who loves it shall eat its fruit. |
| 22 *Whoso* findeth a wife findeth a good *thing*, and obtaineth favour of the LORD. | 22 מָצָא אִשָּׁה מָצָא טוֹב<br>וַיָּפֶק רָצוֹן מֵיְהוָה׃ | He found a wife—he found 22<br>good,<br>and obtained favor from Jehovah. |
| 23 The poor useth entreaties; but the rich answereth roughly. | 23 תַּחֲנוּנִים יְדַבֶּר־רָשׁ<br>וְעָשִׁיר יַעֲנֶה עַזּוֹת׃ | The poor utters entreaties; 23<br>but the rich makes harsh answers. |
| 24 A man *that hath* friends must shew himself friendly; and there is a friend *that* sticketh closer than a brother. | 24 אִישׁ רֵעִים לְהִתְרוֹעֵעַ<br>וְיֵשׁ אֹהֵב דָּבֵק מֵאָח׃ | A man given to friends is bent 24<br>on self-ruin;<br>but there is a lover, that cleaves closer than a brother. |
| CHAP. XIX. | CHAP. XIX. | CHAP. XIX. |
| BETTER *is* the poor that walketh in his integrity, than *he that is* perverse in his lips, and is a fool. | א טוֹב רָשׁ הוֹלֵךְ בְּתֻמּוֹ<br>מֵעִקֵּשׁ שְׂפָתָיו וְהוּא כְסִיל׃ | BETTER is a poor man walk- 1<br>ing in his integrity,<br>than one perverse in his lips, and he a fool. |
| 2 Also, *that* the soul *be* without knowledge, *it is* not good; and he that hasteth with *his* feet sinneth. | 2 גַּם בְּלֹא־דַעַת נֶפֶשׁ לֹא־טוֹב<br>וְאָץ בְּרַגְלַיִם חוֹטֵא׃ | Also that the soul be without 2<br>knowledge is not good;<br>and he that is hasty with the feet mis-steps. |
| 3 The foolishness of man perverteth his way: and his heart fretteth against the LORD. | 3 אִוֶּלֶת אָדָם תְּסַלֵּף דַּרְכּוֹ<br>וְעַל־יְהוָה יִזְעַף לִבּוֹ׃ | A man's folly subverts his way; 3<br>and his heart is angry against Jehovah. |

his estrangement, more difficult to win back, 'than a strong city.'*

The sacred writer does not say of a brother, that he "is more rebellious," or that he is "more refractory," than a strong city. This is not the character which he ascribes to this relation.

*Estranged* is preferable to 'offended' (Common Version), as admitting the *reflexive* sense.

V. 22. *He found*, etc. The proper use of the *Pret.* (followed by another *Pret.*) gives the true sense.† (See Expl. Notes.)

Second member: ויפק, see the note on ch. 3 : 13.

V. 24. *A man given to friends:* the qualifying genitive (*a man of friends*, one of whom this is characteristic) is evidently to be taken in this sense.‡ (See Expl. Notes.)

*Is bent on self-ruin:* להתרועע, Gram. § 132, 3, *Rem.* 1, 1).* So (after Gersonides) Schultens, Gesenius, Rosenmüller, Umbreit, Maurer, De Wette, in accordance with the use of the word in Is. 24 : 19.

The rendering, '*will show himself as a base one*' (Bertheau,† Stuart), is etymologically correct, but has not, like the other, the support of actual usage.

Ch. XIX.—V. 2. *Mis-steps:*‡ Gesenius, Lex. ("also of the feet, *to miss, to make a false step*") and Thes.

V. 3. *Subverts his way* (Gesenius,§ Bertheau‖); the rendering, *perverts his way* (De Wette, Maurer, and others), is not as pertinent in connection with the other member.

* So Maurer (who, in his Commentary, adopted Ewald's view, but rejects it in his Lexicon) well explains (Lex., art. פשע) the force of the construction first given (and the second, literally translated, implies the same thing): *Ein Bruder* ist . . . *abtrünniger als eine feste Stadt*, d. h. ein Bruder, der dem andern einmal abtrünnig geworden ist, ist beharrlicher, hartnäckiger als eine abgefallene feste Stadt.

† As correctly expressed by Ewald:
*Er fand ein Weib—er fand ein Gut,*
*gewann so Gunst von Jahve sich.*

‡ Rosenmüller: אִישׁ cum alio nomine constructum indicat eum, qui alicui rei operam dat. Maurer: *vir sodalium* est *ad sese perdendum*, qui multis gaudet sodalibus gaudet in sui perniciem.

* The rendering, '*must show himself a friend*,' followed in the Common Version, is now admitted to be without any support in etymology or usage.

† *Wird als einen schlechten sich erweisen.*

‡ "Mis-step, *v. n.* to take a false step" (Worcester's Dict.).

§ Thes. vol. II. p. 959: 2) *evertit, subvertit; . . . stultitia hominis subvertit viam ejus.*

‖ *Die Thorheit des Menschen bringt zu Fall seinen Weg.*

KING JAMES' VERSION.

4 Wealth maketh many friends; but the poor is separated from his neighbour.
5 A false witness shall not be unpunished; and *he that* speaketh lies shall not escape.

6 Many will entreat the favour of the prince: and every man *is* a friend to him that giveth gifts.
7 All the brethren of the poor do hate him: how much more do his friends go far from him? he pursueth *them with* words, *yet* they *are* wanting *to him*.

8 He that getteth wisdom loveth his own soul: he that keepeth understanding shall find good.

9 A false witness shall not be unpunished; and *he that* speaketh lies shall perish.

10 Delight is not seemly for a fool; much less for a servant to have rule over princes.

11 The discretion of a man deferreth his anger; and *it is* his glory to pass over a transgression.
12 The king's wrath *is* as the roaring of a lion; but his favour *is* as dew upon the grass.

13 A foolish son *is* the calamity of his father: and the contentions of a wife *are* a continual dropping.

HEBREW TEXT.

הוֹן יֹסִיף רֵעִים רַבִּים 4
וְדָל מֵרֵעֵהוּ יִפָּרֵד׃

עֵד שְׁקָרִים לֹא יִנָּקֶה ה
וְיָפִיחַ כְּזָבִים לֹא יִמָּלֵט׃

רַבִּים יְחַלּוּ פְנֵי־נָדִיב 6
וְכָל־הָרֵעַ לְאִישׁ מַתָּן׃

כָּל אֲחֵי־רָשׁ ׀ שְׂנֵאֻהוּ 7
אַף כִּי מְרֵעֵהוּ רָחֲקוּ מִמֶּנּוּ
מְרַדֵּף אֲמָרִים לֹא־הֵמָּה׃

קֹנֶה־לֵּב אֹהֵב נַפְשׁוֹ 8
שֹׁמֵר תְּבוּנָה לִמְצֹא־טוֹב׃

עֵד שְׁקָרִים לֹא יִנָּקֶה 9
וְיָפִיחַ כְּזָבִים יֹאבֵד׃

לֹא־נָאוֶה לִכְסִיל תַּעֲנוּג י
אַף כִּי־לְעֶבֶד ׀ מְשֹׁל בְּשָׂרִים׃

שֵׂכֶל אָדָם הֶאֱרִיךְ אַפּוֹ 11
וְתִפְאַרְתּוֹ עֲבֹר עַל־פָּשַׁע׃

נַהַם כַּכְּפִיר זַעַף מֶלֶךְ 12
וּכְטַל עַל־עֵשֶׂב רְצוֹנוֹ׃

הַוֹּת לְאָבִיו בֵּן כְּסִיל 13
וְדֶלֶף טֹרֵד מִדְיְנֵי אִשָּׁה׃

V. 7. לו ק׳

REVISED VERSION.

Wealth adds many friends; 4
but the poor is separated from his friend.
A false witness shall not be acquitted; 5
and he that breathes lies shall not escape.
Many make court to a noble; 6
and every one is friend to a liberal man.

All the poor man's brethren hate him, 7
much more do his friends keep far from him;
he follows after words—them he has!
He that gets wisdom loves his own soul; 8
he that lays up understanding finds good.
A false witness shall not be acquitted; 9
and he that breathes lies shall perish.
Delicate living is not suitable for a fool; 10
much less for a servant to rule over princes.
A man's wisdom makes him slow to anger; 11
and it is his glory to pass over a fault.
A growl as of the young lion is the anger of a king; 12
but as dew on the grass is his favor.
A foolish son is a calamity to his father; 13
and the bickerings of a wife are a continual dripping.

V. 6. *Make court to* (יחלו פני): see the note on Job 11 : 19 (by mistake, included in the note on v. 18).

Second member: *every one is friend* (without the *art.*) is the proper English expression.*

V. 7. *His friends:* מרע, as *abstr.* used collectively with the *plur.*

*He follows after words:* so De Wette (who construes לא as the particle of negation) and Gesenius.†

* Bertheau: *Und Gesammtheit des Freundes* = Masse von Freunden *ist dem Geschenke spendenden Manne.*

† De Wette: Er folgt [ihren] Worten—sie sind nicht da!

*Them he has:* הֵמָּה, emphatic. Lit. *his are they;* לא being loosely written, as in some other instances, for לו (Gesenius, Lex., Note to art. לא).*

V. 13. *A continual dripping:* one drop *thrusting* another forward, i. e. following close upon it.†

Gesenius (Thes. vol. III. p. 1267): *verba sectatur,* iis delectatur et confidit.

* Bertheau: Statt לא will Qri לו lesen, welche Lesart in den Text aufzunehmen unnöthig ist, da לא andere wiewohl immerhin seltene Schreibart für לו sein kann.

† Bertheau: *eine beständige Traufe;* טרד *treiben,* eine treibende Traufe ist die, bei welcher ein Tropfen den andern drängt.

| KING JAMES' VERSION. | HEBREW TEXT. | | REVISED VERSION. |
|---|---|---|---|
| 14 House and riches *are* the inheritance of fathers: and a prudent wife *is* from the LORD. | בַּיִת וָהוֹן נַחֲלַת אָבוֹת<br>וּמֵיְהוָה אִשָּׁה מַשְׂכָּלֶת׃ | 14 | House and wealth are a paternal inheritance; 14<br>but a prudent wife is from Jehovah. |
| 15 Slothfulness casteth into a deep sleep; and an idle soul shall suffer hunger. | עַצְלָה תַּפִּיל תַּרְדֵּמָה<br>וְנֶפֶשׁ רְמִיָּה תִרְעָב׃ | טו | Sloth brings down a deep sleep; 15<br>and the spirit of the idle shall hunger. |
| 16 He that keepeth the commandment keepeth his own soul; *but* he that despiseth his ways shall die. | שֹׁמֵר מִצְוָה שֹׁמֵר נַפְשׁוֹ<br>בּוֹזֵה דְרָכָיו יוּמָת׃ | 16 | He that keeps a command keeps his own soul; 16<br>he that slights his ways shall be put to death. |
| 17 He that hath pity upon the poor lendeth unto the LORD; and that which he hath given will he pay him again. | מַלְוֵה יְהוָה חוֹנֵן דָּל<br>וּגְמֻלוֹ יְשַׁלֶּם־לוֹ׃ | 17 | He that has pity on the poor lends to Jehovah; 17<br>and he will repay him his desert. |
| 18 Chasten thy son while there is hope, and let not thy soul spare for his crying. | יַסֵּר בִּנְךָ כִּי־יֵשׁ תִּקְוָה<br>וְאֶל־הֲמִיתוֹ אַל־תִּשָּׂא נַפְשֶׁךָ׃ | 18 | Correct thy son while there is hope; 18<br>but lift not up thy soul to slay him. |
| 19 A man of great wrath shall suffer punishment: for if thou deliver *him*, yet thou must do it again. | גְּרָל־חֵמָה נֹשֵׂא עֹנֶשׁ<br>כִּי אִם־תַּצִּיל וְעוֹד תּוֹסִף׃ | 19 | He that is rough in anger suffers punishment; 19<br>for if thou deliver, then thou must do it again. |
| 20 Hear counsel, and receive instruction, that thou mayest be wise in thy latter end. | שְׁמַע עֵצָה וְקַבֵּל מוּסָר<br>לְמַעַן תֶּחְכַּם בְּאַחֲרִיתֶךָ׃ | כ | Hear counsel, and receive correction; 20<br>that thou mayest be wise in thy after years. |
| 21 *There are* many devices in a man's heart; nevertheless the counsel of the LORD, that shall stand. | רַבּוֹת מַחֲשָׁבוֹת בְּלֶב־אִישׁ<br>וַעֲצַת יְהוָה הִיא תָקוּם׃ | 21 | Many are the devices in the heart of man; 21<br>but the counsel of Jehovah, that shall stand. |
| 22 The desire of a man *is* his kindness: and a poor man *is* better than a liar. | תַּאֲוַת אָדָם חַסְדּוֹ<br>וְטוֹב רָשׁ מֵאִישׁ כָּזָב׃ | 22 | The charm of a man is his kindness; 22<br>and better is the poor than a man of falsehood. |
| 23 The fear of the LORD *tendeth* to life: and *he that hath it* shall abide satisfied; he shall not be visited with evil. | יִרְאַת יְהוָה לְחַיִּים<br>וְשָׂבֵעַ יָלִין בַּל־יִפָּקֶד רָע׃ | 23 | The fear of Jehovah is unto life; 23<br>and sated shall one repose, nor be visited with evil. |

V. 16. ימות ק׳

V. 15. *Brings down:* יפיל (*causes to fall*), the verb used in Gen. 2 : 21.

V. 16. *Shall be put to death* (יוּמָת, *Kethibh*): a common formula.*

V. 17. *His desert* (גמלו): as in ch. 12 : 14.

V. 18. *Lift not up*, etc.: the strong and expressive image of the original.

V. 19. *He who is rough in anger* (whose anger breaks out in rough and violent expression): גרל, *rough, stern,* as defined (after Schultens) by Gesenius.* Other definitions, *prone* (Maurer), *frequent* (*häufig*, Ewald), are without sufficient evidence.

It is quite clear, that the *Qeri* ('*of great wrath,*' as in the Common Version) arose from the early loss of the signification of the true reading.†

V. 22. *The charm*, etc. (see Expl. Notes).

V. 23. The implied *subject*, in the second member, is as readily suggested in English as in Hebrew.—רע *adverb accus.* (Gram. §118, 3).

* In textu est יוּמָת *perimetur*, a magistratu puta; nam de capite plectendis a magistratu יוּמָת usurpari solet in formula illa satis frequente מוֹת יוּמָת, v. c. Gen. 26 : 11, Exod. 19 : 12, 21 : 12 (Rosenmüller).

* The preference for the *Qeri*, which was intimated (fortasse pro vera habenda est) in the Thes. (1829), was afterwards corrected in the Lexicon manuale (1833).

† Maurer: Quod Keri legi jubet גְּרָל־ manifesta emendatio est verbi non intellecti.

KING JAMES' VERSION.

24 A slothful *man* hideth his hand in *his* bosom, and will not so much as bring it to his mouth again.

25 Smite a scorner, and the simple will beware: and reprove one that hath understanding, *and* he will understand knowledge.

26 He that wasteth *his* father, *and* chaseth away *his* mother, *is* a son that causeth shame, and bringeth reproach.

27 Cease, my son, to hear the instruction *that causeth* to err from the words of knowledge.

28 An ungodly witness scorneth judgment: and the mouth of the wicked devoureth iniquity.

29 Judgments are prepared for scorners, and stripes for the back of fools.

CHAP. XX.

WINE *is* a mocker, strong drink *is* raging: and whosoever is deceived thereby is not wise.

2 The fear of a king *is* as the roaring of a lion: *whoso* provoketh him to anger sinneth *against* his own soul.

3 *It is* an honour for a man to cease from strife: but every fool will be meddling.

HEBREW TEXT.

24 טָמַן עָצֵל יָדוֹ בַּצַּלָּחַת
גַּם־אֶל־פִּיהוּ לֹא יְשִׁיבֶנָּה׃

כח לֵץ תַּכֶּה וּפֶתִי יַעְרִם
וְהוֹכִיחַ לְנָבוֹן יָבִין דָּעַת׃

26 מְשַׁדֶּד־אָב יַבְרִיחַ אֵם
בֵּן מֵבִישׁ וּמַחְפִּיר׃

27 חֲדַל־בְּנִי לִשְׁמֹעַ מוּסָר
לִשְׁגּוֹת מֵאִמְרֵי־דָעַת׃

28 עֵד בְּלִיַּעַל יָלִיץ מִשְׁפָּט
וּפִי רְשָׁעִים יְבַלַּע־אָוֶן׃

29 נָכוֹנוּ לַלֵּצִים שְׁפָטִים
וּמַהֲלֻמוֹת לְגֵו כְּסִילִים׃

CHAP. XX.

א לֵץ הַיַּיִן הֹמֶה שֵׁכָר
וְכָל־שֹׁגֶה בּוֹ לֹא יֶחְכָּם׃

2 נַהַם כַּכְּפִיר אֵימַת מֶלֶךְ
מִתְעַבְּרוֹ חוֹטֵא נַפְשׁוֹ׃

3 כָּבוֹד לָאִישׁ שֶׁבֶת מֵרִיב
וְכָל־אֱוִיל יִתְגַּלָּע׃

REVISED VERSION.

The sluggard hides his hand in 24
the dish;
he will not even bring it back
to his mouth.

If thou smite a scoffer, even 25
the simple will deal wisely;
and admonish the discerning,
he will learn knowledge.

A father's destroyer, a mother's 26
persecutor,
is the son that causes shame
and disgrace.

Cease, my son, to hear instruc- 27
tion,
so as to err from the words of
knowledge.

A vile witness mocks at jus- 28
tice;
and the mouth of the wicked
swallows down iniquity.

Judgments are prepared for 29
the scoffers,
and stripes for the back of
fools.

CHAP. XX.

WINE is a mocker, strong 1
drink is raging;
and none that errs therein shall
be wise.

A growl as of the young lion 2
is the terror of a king;
he that provokes him to anger
sins away his life.

It is an honor to a man to 3
dwell apart from strife;
but every fool will get angry.

V. 25. *Will deal wisely* (יערם): see the note on ch. 1:4, third paragraph.

V. 26. Lit. *one that destroys a father, that persecutes*, etc. (transition from the particip. form, to that of the finite verb, Gram. § 134, *Rem.* 2).—*Causes to flee* from him (יבריח) by acts of unkindness = *persecutes.**

V. 27. *So as to err* (*for erring*, gerundial form) is the simplest construction, and is doubtless the true sense.†

Ch. XX.—V. 2. *Provokes him to anger*:‡ as the *Mid.* sense of *Hithp.* is correctly understood by Maurer,* Ewald,† Bertheau.‡

*Sins away his life* (forfeits it by sin). Gesenius (Thes. and Lex. 3): "*to sin away* any thing, i. e. *to forfeit* by sinning." So חטא is used with the *accus.* (with לְ, *to sin against*).

V. 3. The form שֶׁבֶת in its common use (as *Infin.* of יָשַׁב) makes a more pertinent sense here, than as a derivative from שָׁבַת (Gesenius and others). The honor meant is, *to keep aloof* from strife

* Others reverse the *subj.* and *pred.* Stuart: "*he that doeth violence to his father, or chaseth away his mother, is a son who acteth shamefully and putteth to the blush.*" Very true; but to say this would not require the wisdom of a Solomon.

† *Ad aberrandum a dictis scientiæ*, i. e. doctrinam, quæ te a præceptis sapientiæ avocet (Maurer).

‡ So the ancient versions: Sept. ὁ δὲ παροξύνων αὐτὸν. Syr. ܘܡܚܡܬ ܠܗ. Chald. וּמַן דְּמַחְמֵית לֵיהּ. Vulg. *qui provocat eum.*

* Heb. u. Chald. Hdwbch.: auch mit dem *Acc.*, *sich* (sibi) Jemanden *erzürnen*, ihn gegen sich reizen, Spr. 20 : 2.

† Auch dasselbe Verbum kann so seine Verbindung ändern, wie הִתְעַבֵּר mit בְּ der Person, *sich gegen jem. erzürnen*, aber auch mit dem Accusativ, *sich einen erzürnen*, Spr. 20 : 2 (Lehrb. § 124, b).

‡ מתעבר ist hier mit dem Suffix verbunden; die gewöhnliche Bedeutung dieses Hitpoel, *sich erzürnen* gegen Jemanden (Ps. 78 : 62, vgl. Prov. 26 : 17), hat hier also den activen Begriff *sich einen erzürnen* erhalten, vgl. Ewald, Lehrb. 124, b.

| KING JAMES' VERSION. | HEBREW TEXT. | | REVISED VERSION. | |
|---|---|---|---|---|
| 4 The sluggard will not plough by reason of the cold; *therefore* shall he beg in harvest, and *have* nothing. | מֵחֹרֶף עָצֵל לֹא יַחֲרֹשׁ<br>יִשְׁאַל בַּקָּצִיר וָאָיִן׃ | 4 | Because of cold the sluggard will not plough;<br>he shall beg in the harvest, and have nothing. | 4 |
| 5 Counsel in the heart of man *is like* deep water; but a man of understanding will draw it out. | מַיִם עֲמֻקִּים עֵצָה בְלֶב־אִישׁ<br>וְאִישׁ תְּבוּנָה יִדְלֶנָּה׃ | ה | Counsel in the heart of man is deep water;<br>but a man of understanding will draw it out. | 5 |
| 6 Most men will proclaim every one his own goodness: but a faithful man who can find? | רָב־אָדָם יִקְרָא אִישׁ חַסְדּוֹ<br>וְאִישׁ אֱמוּנִים מִי יִמְצָא׃ | 6 | Many a man will proclaim his good-will;<br>but a faithful man who shall find? | 6 |
| 7 The just *man* walketh in his integrity: his children *are* blessed after him. | מִתְהַלֵּךְ בְּתֻמּוֹ צַדִּיק<br>אַשְׁרֵי בָנָיו אַחֲרָיו׃ | 7 | He that walks in his integrity, a righteous man,<br>happy are his children after him! | 7 |
| 8 A king that sitteth in the throne of judgment scattereth away all evil with his eyes. | מֶלֶךְ יוֹשֵׁב עַל־כִּסֵּא־דִין<br>מְזָרֶה בְעֵינָיו כָּל־רָע׃ | 8 | A king, sitting on the throne of judgment,<br>searches out all evil with his eyes. | 8 |
| 9 Who can say, I have made my heart clean, I am pure from my sin? | מִי־יֹאמַר זִכִּיתִי לִבִּי<br>טָהַרְתִּי מֵחַטָּאתִי׃ | 9 | Who can say, I have cleansed my heart,<br>I am pure from my sin? | 9 |
| 10 Divers weights, *and* divers measures, both of them *are* alike abomination to the LORD. | אֶבֶן וָאֶבֶן אֵיפָה וְאֵיפָה<br>תּוֹעֲבַת יְהוָה גַּם־שְׁנֵיהֶם׃ | י | Divers weights, divers measures,<br>are both an abomination to Jehovah. | 10 |
| 11 Even a child is known by his doings, whether his work *be* pure, and whether *it be* right. | גַּם בְּמַעֲלָלָיו יִתְנַכֶּר־נָעַר<br>אִם־זַךְ וְאִם־יָשָׁר פָּעֳלוֹ׃ | 11 | Even a child is known by his acts,<br>whether pure and whether right his deed. | 11 |
| 12 The hearing ear, and the seeing eye, the LORD hath made even both of them. | אֹזֶן שֹׁמַעַת וְעַיִן רֹאָה<br>יְהוָה עָשָׂה גַם־שְׁנֵיהֶם׃ | 12 | The hearing ear and the seeing eye,<br>Jehovah has made them both. | 12 |
| 13 Love not sleep, lest thou come to poverty: open thine eyes, *and* thou shalt be satisfied with bread. | אַל־תֶּאֱהַב שֵׁנָה פֶּן־תִּוָּרֵשׁ<br>פְּקַח עֵינֶיךָ שְׂבַע־לָחֶם׃ | 13 | Love not sleep, lest thou become poor;<br>open thine eyes, thou shalt be satisfied with bread. | 13 |
| 14 *It is* naught, *it is* naught, saith the buyer: but when he is gone his way, then he boasteth. | רַע רַע יֹאמַר הַקּוֹנֶה<br>וְאֹזֵל לוֹ אָז יִתְהַלָּל׃ | 14 | It is naught, it is naught, says the buyer;<br>but he goes his way, then boasteth. | 14 |

V. 4. ושאל ק׳

not merely *to cease* from it), in distinction from the fool, who is ever ready to get angry.—יתגלע, see the note on ch. 17 : 14.

V. 4. *He shall beg:* the *Kethibh* יִשְׁאַל.*

V. 7. Evidently, צדיק is here subordinate to the subject, as understood by Ewald, and (as an alternative rendering) by Maurer.

V. 8. *Searches out.* From the signification *to winnow* (זרה, *Kal, and Piel*), comes that of *sifting, searching out*, as in Ps. 139 : 3, and below v. 26.

A king does not sit on the throne of judgment "*to scatter evil*," but to search out and punish it.

V. 11. The force of גם here applies to the whole statement in the clause to which it is prefixed, viz. that *by his doings the child is known.* Gesenius' suggestion (Thes.* and Lex.), that "in the beginning of a clause it refers not to the nearest but a more remote word," is the same in effect; but we can express it by the word *even* only in connection with the subject.

* Ewald: יִשְׁאַל K'tib ist hier sprechender und stärker als das blosse וְשָׁאַל und *wird bitten.*

* Vol. I. p. 293: Nonnunquam .. ab initio enuntiationis ponitur, etsi non ad vocabulum proximum, sed ad alium quoddam in medio aut fine ejus refertur. Prov. ... 20 : 11, *etiam juvenis ex operibus suis cognoscitur.*

| KING JAMES' VERSION. | HEBREW TEXT. | | REVISED VERSION. | |
|---|---|---|---|---|
| 15 There is gold, and a multitude of rubies: but the lips of knowledge *are* a precious jewel. | יֵשׁ זָהָב וְרָב־פְּנִינִים<br>וּכְלִי יְקָר שִׂפְתֵי־דָעַת׃ | טו | There is gold, and abundance of pearls;<br>but a precious furnishing are lips of knowledge. | 15 |
| 16 Take his garment that is surety *for* a stranger: and take a pledge of him for a strange woman. | לְקַח־בִּגְדוֹ כִּי־עָרַב זָר<br>וּבְעַד נָכְרִיִּם חַבְלֵהוּ׃ | 16 | Take his garment, when he is surety for an alien;<br>and for strangers take a pledge of him. | 16 |
| 17 Bread of deceit *is* sweet to a man; but afterwards his mouth shall be filled with gravel. | עָרֵב לָאִישׁ לֶחֶם שָׁקֶר<br>וְאַחַר יִמָּלֵא־פִיהוּ חָצָץ׃ | 17 | Sweet to a man is the bread of deceit;<br>but afterward, his mouth shall be filled with gravel. | 17 |
| 18 *Every* purpose is established by counsel: and with good advice make war. | מַחֲשָׁבוֹת בְּעֵצָה תִכּוֹן<br>וּבְתַחְבֻּלוֹת עֲשֵׂה מִלְחָמָה׃ | 18 | Every purpose is established by counsel;<br>and with wise direction thou shalt make war. | 18 |
| 19 He that goeth about *as* a talebearer revealeth secrets: therefore meddle not with him that flattereth with his lips. | גּוֹלֶה־סּוֹד הוֹלֵךְ רָכִיל<br>וּלְפֹתֶה שְׂפָתָיו לֹא תִתְעָרָב׃ | 19 | He that goes talebearing is a revealer of secrets;<br>then meddle not with one of open lips. | 19 |
| 20 Whoso curseth his father or his mother, his lamp shall be put out in obscure darkness. | מְקַלֵּל אָבִיו וְאִמּוֹ<br>יִדְעַךְ נֵרוֹ בֶּאֱישׁוּן חֹשֶׁךְ׃ | כ | He that curses his father and his mother,<br>his light shall go out in midnight darkness. | 20 |
| 21 An inheritance *may be* gotten hastily at the beginning; but the end thereof shall not be blessed. | נַחֲלָה מְבֹחֶלֶת בָּרִאשׁוֹנָה<br>וְאַחֲרִיתָהּ לֹא תְבֹרָךְ׃ | 21 | A heritage abhorred in the beginning,<br>its end shall not be blessed. | 21 |
| 22 Say not thou, I will recompense evil; *but* wait on the LORD, and he shall save thee. | אַל־תֹּאמַר אֲשַׁלְּמָה־רָע<br>קַוֵּה לַיהוָה וְיֹשַׁע לָךְ׃ | 22 | Say not, I will repay evil;<br>wait on Jehovah, and he shall help thee. | 22 |
| 23 Divers weights *are* an abomination unto the LORD; and a false balance *is* not good. | תּוֹעֲבַת יְהוָה אֶבֶן וָאָבֶן<br>וּמֹאזְנֵי מִרְמָה לֹא־טוֹב׃ | 23 | Divers weights are an abomination to Jehovah;<br>and deceptive balances are not good. | 23 |
| 24 Man's goings *are* of the LORD; how can a man then understand his own way? | מֵיְהוָה מִצְעֲדֵי־גָבֶר<br>וְאָדָם מַה־יָּבִין דַּרְכּוֹ׃ | 24 | Of Jehovah are a man's steps;<br>and man, how shall he understand his way? | 24 |

V. 16. נכרית ק׳ V. 20. יתיר ר׳

V. 15. *Pearls:* see the note on ch. 3 : 15.—*Furnishing* (כלי) as used with reference to *garments* (Deut. 22 : 5), *bridal array* (Is. 61 : 10), etc. For the signification '*jewel*' (Common Version) there is no foundation.

V. 16. *When he is surety for* (כי ערב), as in ch. 11 : 15. For the meaning, see Expl. Notes.

*An alien:* זר is here, in connection with נכרי, to be understood in the sense of *foreigner, alien,* one of another nation (Lex. a), in distinction from נכרי one of another family (Lex. b).

Second member: *strangers* (*Kethibh* נכרים) is doubtless the true reading.

V. 18. *Every purpose,* etc.: the verb in the *sing.* individualizes the *plur.* subject.

*With wise direction:* תחבלות, *guidance, direction,* as in Job 37 : 12, Prov. 1 : 5, 11 : 14, 12 : 5; hence emphatically (by implication) *wise direction,* as here and in ch. 24 : 6.

*Thou shalt make war* (*Imperat.* as an emphatic assurance, Gram. § 130, 1); i. e. thou shalt be able to do it.

V. 20. *In midnight darkness.* Literally, *in the eye-ball of darkness;* either, in its central point, *in midnight darkness,* when it is deepest, or with reference to the intense blackness of the eyeball (pupil of the eye), from which no ray of light is returned.

V. 21. *Abhorred,* מבחלת, as in Zech. 11 : 8. (See Expl. Notes.)

*Its end* (ואחריתה), *Vav* of the apodosis, the first member being hypothetical in effect = *if a heritage is abhorred,* etc.

V. 22. *Shall help* (וישע): the *Jussive* expressing the speaker's subjective assurance of its certainty.

KING JAMES' VERSION.

25 *It is* a snare to the man *who*
devoureth *that which is* holy, and
after vows to make inquiry.
26 A wise king scattereth the
wicked, and bringeth the wheel
over them.
27 The spirit of man *is* the
candle of the LORD, searching all
the inward parts of the belly.

28 Mercy and truth preserve
the king: and his throne is up-
holden by mercy.

29 The glory of young men *is*
their strength: and the beauty of
old men *is* the gray head.

30 The blueness of a wound
cleanseth away evil: so *do* stripes
the inward parts of the belly.

CHAP. XXI.

THE king's heart *is* in the hand
of the LORD, *as* the rivers of water: he turneth it whithersoever
he will.
2 Every way of a man *is* right
in his own eyes: but the LORD
pondereth the hearts.

3 To do justice and judgment
*is* more acceptable to the LORD
than sacrifice.

4 A high look, and a proud
heart, *and* the ploughing of the
wicked, *is* sin.
5 The thoughts of the diligent
*tend* only to plenteousness; but
of every one *that is* hasty only to
want.

HEBREW TEXT.

כח מוֹקֵשׁ אָדָם יָלַע קֹדֶשׁ
וְאַחַר נְדָרִים לְבַקֵּר׃
26 מְזָרֶה רְשָׁעִים מֶלֶךְ חָכָם
וַיָּשֶׁב עֲלֵיהֶם אוֹפָן׃
27 נֵר יְהוָה נִשְׁמַת אָדָם
חֹפֵשׂ כָּל־חַדְרֵי־בָטֶן׃
28 חֶסֶד וֶאֱמֶת יִצְּרוּ־מֶלֶךְ
וְסָעַד בַּחֶסֶד כִּסְאוֹ׃
29 תִּפְאֶרֶת בַּחוּרִים כֹּחָם
וַהֲדַר זְקֵנִים שֵׂיבָה׃
ל חַבֻּרוֹת פֶּצַע תַּמְרִיק בְּרָע
וּמַכּוֹת חַדְרֵי־בָטֶן׃

CHAP. XXI.

א פַּלְגֵי־מַיִם לֶב־מֶלֶךְ בְּיַד־יְהוָה
עַל־כָּל־אֲשֶׁר יַחְפֹּץ יַטֶּנּוּ׃
2 כָּל־דֶּרֶךְ אִישׁ יָשָׁר בְּעֵינָיו
וְתֹכֵן לִבּוֹת יְהוָה׃
3 עֲשֹׂה צְדָקָה וּמִשְׁפָּט
נִבְחָר לַיהוָה מִזָּבַח׃
4 רוּם עֵינַיִם וּרְחַב־לֵב
נֵר רְשָׁעִים חַטָּאת׃
ה מַחְשְׁבוֹת חָרוּץ אַךְ־לְמוֹתָר
וְכָל־אָץ אַךְ־לְמַחְסוֹר׃

V. 30. תמרוק ק׳

REVISED VERSION.

It is a snare to a man, when he 25
utters rashly what is sacred,
and after vows makes inquiry.
A wise king sifts out the wick- 26
ed,
and turns over them the wheel.
A lamp of Jehovah is the spirit 27
of man,
searching all the inmost parts
of the belly.
Kindness and truth will pre- 28
serve a king;
and by kindness he upholds his
throne.
The glory of young men is their 29
strength;
and the honor of old men is the
gray head.
Wounding stripes are a cleans- 30
ing for the wicked,
and strokes in the inmost parts
of the belly.

CHAP. XXI.

CHANNELS of water is the king's 1
heart in Jehovah's hand;
he turns it whithersoever he
will.
Every way of a man is right in 2
his own eyes;
but the trier of hearts is Jehovah.
To do righteousness and jus- 3
tice,
is more acceptable to Jehovah
than sacrifice.
Lofty eyes, and pride of heart, 4
the light of the wicked, is
sin.
The plans of the diligent tend 5
only to plenty;
but of every one that is hasty,
to want.

V. 25. *When he utters rashly* (Lex. יָלַע) is the true rendering, whether ילע is accented as the *third Perf.* (*utters he* = *if he utters*) or as the shortened *Imperf.* from לוּע (*should he utter*).

V. 26. *Sifts out* (see the remark on v. 8) is the proper expression here, in connection with the allusion in the second member. (See Expl. Notes.)

V. 29, *Honor* (הדר), as in Ps. 149 : 9.

V. 30. *Stripes of wounding* = stripes that wound, *wounding stripes.*—*A cleansing for the wicked:* בְּ with reference to the primary meaning, *a rubbing* (or *scouring*) *upon.*

The second member should be so expressed, that its relation to the subject and predicate of the first may be open to the same difference of construction as in the Hebrew.

Ch. XXI.—V. 4. *Light* (נֵר *defect.* for נִיר; in many Mss. pointed נִר), as in all the ancient versions, and as required by the imagery in the first member.

| KING JAMES' VERSION. | HEBREW TEXT. | | REVISED VERSION. | |
|---|---|---|---|---|
| 6 The getting of treasures by a lying tongue *is* a vanity tossed to and fro of them that seek death. | פֹּעַל אֹצָרוֹת בִּלְשׁוֹן שָׁקֶר<br>הֶבֶל נִדָּף מְבַקְשֵׁי־מָוֶת׃ | 6 | Treasures gotten with a lying tongue,<br>are a vapor driven away, seekers of death! | 6 |
| 7 The robbery of the wicked shall destroy them; because they refuse to do judgment. | שֹׁד־רְשָׁעִים יְגוֹרֵם<br>כִּי מֵאֲנוּ לַעֲשׂוֹת מִשְׁפָּט׃ | 7 | The violence of the wicked shall sweep them away,<br>because they refuse to do right. | 7 |
| 8 The way of man *is* froward and strange: but *as for* the pure, his work *is* right. | הֲפַכְפַּךְ דֶּרֶךְ אִישׁ וָזָר<br>וְזַךְ יָשָׁר פָּעֳלוֹ׃ | 8 | A man of crooked way turns aside;<br>but the pure, his work is straight. | 8 |
| 9 *It is* better to dwell in a corner of the housetop, than with a brawling woman in a wide house. | טוֹב לָשֶׁבֶת עַל־פִּנַּת־גָּג<br>מֵאֵשֶׁת מִדְוָנִים וּבֵית חָבֶר׃ | 9 | It is better to dwell in a corner of the house-top,<br>than with a brawling woman and a house in common. | 9 |
| 10 The soul of the wicked desireth evil: his neighbour findeth no favor in his eyes. | נֶפֶשׁ רָשָׁע אִוְּתָה־רָע<br>לֹא־יֻחַן בְּעֵינָיו רֵעֵהוּ׃ | י | The soul of the wicked desires evil;<br>his neighbor finds no favor in his eyes. | 10 |
| 11 When the scorner is punished, the simple is made wise: and when the wise is instructed, he receiveth knowledge. | בַּעֲנָשׁ־לֵץ יֶחְכַּם־פֶּתִי<br>וּבְהַשְׂכִּיל לְחָכָם יִקַּח דָּעַת׃ | 11 | When the scoffer is punished, the simple becomes wise;<br>and when the wise is instructed he receives knowledge. | 11 |
| 12 The righteous *man* wisely considereth the house of the wicked: *but God* overthroweth the wicked for *their* wickedness. | מַשְׂכִּיל צַדִּיק לְבֵית רָשָׁע<br>מְסַלֵּף רְשָׁעִים לָרָע׃ | 12 | The Just One considers the wicked man's house;<br>he that plunges the wicked into ruin. | 12 |
| 13 Whoso stoppeth his ears at the cry of the poor, he also shall cry himself, but shall not be heard. | אֹטֵם אָזְנוֹ מִזַּעֲקַת־דָּל<br>גַּם־הוּא יִקְרָא וְלֹא יֵעָנֶה׃ | 13 | He that shuts his ear from the cry of the weak,<br>he too shall call and not be heard. | 13 |
| 14 A gift in secret pacifieth anger: and a reward in the bosom, strong wrath. | מַתָּן בַּסֵּתֶר יִכְפֶּה־אָף<br>וְשֹׁחַד בַּחֵק חֵמָה עַזָּה׃ | 14 | A gift in secret subdues anger,<br>and a present in the bosom violent rage. | 14 |
| 15 *It is* joy to the just to do judgment: but destruction *shall be* to the workers of iniquity. | שִׂמְחָה לַצַּדִּיק עֲשׂוֹת מִשְׁפָּט<br>וּמְחִתָּה לְפֹעֲלֵי אָוֶן׃ | טו | It is joy to the righteous that justice be done;<br>but destruction to the workers of iniquity. | 15 |

V. 6. *The making* (getting) *of treasures* = *treasures gotten*.

*Vapor* (הבל) is the appropriate sense here; comp. the remark on ch. 13 : 11.

*Seekers of death* (Maurer*) makes a good sense (see Expl. Notes), and there is no occasion for adopting (with Ewald and Bertheau) a conjectural emendation (מוקשי) of the Heb. text.

V. 8. *Of crooked way:* literally, *crooked in way* = *of crooked way.*

*Turns aside:* וָזָר *third Perf.* of זור (used as in Ps. 58 : 4), and וְ of the *apodosis* (Gram. § 145, 2, *Rem.*).† The way of rectitude is conceived as a straight and onward path, from which the wicked turns aside.

The resort to Arabic etymology and usage (suggested by Lud. Capellus, and followed by many others, e. g. Gesenius, Thes. vol. I. p. 399), is unnecessary, the usage of the Heb. furnishing a clear and pertinent rendering.

V. 9. *Than with:* compare מֵעֵת Ps. 4 : 8, *above the time,* for *more than in the time.*—*A house in common:* as the Sept. and Vulg.*

V. 15. *That justice be done* (lit. *the doing of justice*), viz. by the magistrate.

* *Petentes mortem,* i. e. in perniciem rapientes eos, qui hoc modo illos corradunt.

† Maurer: *tortuosus viæ vir, is recedit,* i. e. qui tortuosæ viæ est vir, recedit; . . . וזר Prædicatum, . . compositum ex copula Prædicati indice, ut infra 23 : 24, 31 : 28, al., et זָר.

De Wette: *Wer krumme Wege geht, der weicht ab.*

* Sept. *καὶ ἐν οἴκῳ κοινῷ.* Vulg. *et in domo communi.*

| KING JAMES' VERSION. | HEBREW TEXT. | | REVISED VERSION. | |
|---|---|---|---|---|
| 16 The man that wandereth out of the way of understanding shall remain in the congregation of the dead. | אָדָם תּוֹעֶה מִדֶּרֶךְ הַשְׂכֵּל<br>בִּקְהַל רְפָאִים יָנוּחַ׃ | 16 | A man who wanders from the way of wisdom,<br>shall abide in the congregation of the shades. | 16 |
| 17 He that loveth pleasure *shall be* a poor man: he that loveth wine and oil shall not be rich. | אִישׁ מַחְסוֹר אֹהֵב שִׂמְחָה<br>אֹהֵב יַיִן וָשֶׁמֶן לֹא יַעֲשִׁיר׃ | 17 | A needy man is he that loves pleasure;<br>he that loves wine and oil shall not be rich. | 17 |
| 18 The wicked *shall be* a ransom for the righteous, and the transgressor for the upright. | כֹּפֶר לַצַּדִּיק רָשָׁע<br>וְתַחַת יְשָׁרִים בּוֹגֵד׃ | 18 | The wicked is a ransom for the righteous,<br>and the treacherous in place of the upright. | 18 |
| 19 *It is* better to dwell in the wilderness, than with a contentious and an angry woman. | טוֹב שֶׁבֶת בְּאֶרֶץ מִדְבָּר<br>מֵאֵשֶׁת מִדְיָנִים וָכָעַס׃ | 19 | Better is it to dwell in a desert land,<br>than with a brawling and fretful woman. | 19 |
| 20 *There is* treasure to be desired and oil in the dwelling of the wise; but a foolish man spendeth it up. | אוֹצָר ׀ נֶחְמָד וָשֶׁמֶן בִּנְוֵה חָכָם<br>וּכְסִיל אָדָם יְבַלְּעֶנּוּ׃ | כ | Precious treasure, and oil, are in the abode of the wise;<br>but the foolish man swallows it down. | 20 |
| 21 He that followeth after righteousness and mercy findeth life, righteousness, and honour. | רֹדֵף צְדָקָה וָחָסֶד<br>יִמְצָא חַיִּים צְדָקָה וְכָבוֹד׃ | 21 | He that follows after righteousness and kindness,<br>shall find life, righteousness, and honor. | 21 |
| 22 A wise *man* scaleth the city of the mighty, and casteth down the strength of the confidence thereof. | עִיר גִּבֹּרִים עָלָה חָכָם<br>וַיֹּרֶד עֹז מִבְטֶחָה׃ | 22 | A wise man scaled a city of the mighty,<br>and threw down its trusted strength. | 22 |
| 23 Whoso keepeth his mouth and his tongue, keepeth his soul from troubles. | שֹׁמֵר פִּיו וּלְשׁוֹנוֹ<br>שֹׁמֵר מִצָּרוֹת נַפְשׁוֹ׃ | 23 | He that keeps his mouth and his tongue,<br>keeps his soul from troubles. | 23 |
| 24 Proud *and* haughty scorner *is* his name, who dealeth in proud wrath. | זֵד יָהִיר לֵץ שְׁמוֹ<br>עוֹשֶׂה בְּעֶבְרַת זָדוֹן׃ | 24 | An inflated proud one, scoffer is his name;<br>acting in the insolence of pride. | 24 |
| 25 The desire of the slothful killeth him; for his hands refuse to labour. | תַּאֲוַת עָצֵל תְּמִיתֶנּוּ<br>כִּי־מֵאֲנוּ יָדָיו לַעֲשׂוֹת׃ | כה | The sluggard's longing slays him;<br>because his hands refuse to work. | 25 |
| 26 He coveteth greedily all the day long: but the righteous giveth and spareth not. | כָּל־הַיּוֹם הִתְאַוָּה תַאֲוָה<br>וְצַדִּיק יִתֵּן וְלֹא יַחְשֹׂךְ׃ | 26 | All the day he has longing desire;<br>but the righteous shall give, and not spare. | 26 |
| 27 The sacrifice of the wicked *is* abomination: how much more, *when* he bringeth it with a wicked mind? | זֶבַח רְשָׁעִים תּוֹעֵבָה<br>אַף כִּי־בְזִמָּה יְבִיאֶנּוּ׃ | 27 | The sacrifice of the wicked is abomination;<br>how much more when it is brought with evil purpose. | 27 |
| 28 A false witness shall perish: but the man that heareth speaketh constantly. | עֵד־כְּזָבִים יֹאבֵד<br>וְאִישׁ שֹׁמֵעַ לָנֶצַח יְדַבֵּר׃ | 28 | A lying witness shall perish;<br>but a man that hears shall always speak. | 28 |

V. 16. *Shades:* see ch. 2 : 18, and the note on Job 26 : 5.

V. 22. *Scaled—and threw down:* the *Perf.* followed by the *consec. Imperf.*, as in ch. 22 : 3.—Lit. strength of its confidence (§ 121, 6) = strength in which it confides, *its trusted strength.*

V. 24. *An inflated proud one,* etc., is the only construction which the words, in their order and accentuation in Hebrew, will bear. So Ewald, Bertheau, and others.*

V. 27. *When one brings it* (Gram. § 137, 3, *a*) = *when it is brought.*

* Ewald: *ein Uebermüthiger, der sich bläht, heisst Spötter.* Bertheau: *ein sich blähender Stolzer, Spötter ist sein Name.*

| KING JAMES' VERSION. | HEBREW TEXT. | | REVISED VERSION. | |
|---|---|---|---|---|
| 29 A wicked man hardeneth his face: but *as for* the upright, he directeth his way. | הֵעֵז אִישׁ רָשָׁע בְּפָנָיו<br>וְיָשָׁר הוּא ׀ יָכִין דַּרְכּוֹ׃ | 29 | A wicked man hardens his face;<br>but the upright, he shall establish his ways. | 29 |
| 30 *There is* no wisdom nor understanding nor counsel against the LORD. | אֵין חָכְמָה וְאֵין תְּבוּנָה<br>וְאֵין עֵצָה לְנֶגֶד יְהוָה׃ | ל | There is no wisdom, and no understanding,<br>and no counsel, before Jehovah. | 30 |
| 31 The horse *is* prepared against the day of battle: but safety *is* of the LORD. | סוּס מוּכָן לְיוֹם מִלְחָמָה<br>וְלַיהוָה הַתְּשׁוּעָה׃ | 31 | A horse is prepared for the day of battle;<br>but the deliverance is of Jehovah. | 31 |
| CHAP. XXII. | CHAP. XXII. | | CHAP. XXII. | |
| A *good* name *is* rather to be chosen than great riches, *and* loving favour rather than silver and gold. | נִבְחָר שֵׁם מֵעֹשֶׁר רָב<br>מִכֶּסֶף וּמִזָּהָב חֵן טוֹב׃ | א | MORE choice is a name than great riches,<br>loving favor than silver and gold. | 1 |
| 2 The rich and poor meet together: the LORD *is* the maker of them all. | עָשִׁיר וָרָשׁ נִפְגָּשׁוּ<br>עֹשֵׂה כֻלָּם יְהוָה׃ | 2 | Rich and poor meet together;<br>the maker of them all is Jehovah. | 2 |
| 3 A prudent *man* foreseeth the evil, and hideth himself: but the simple pass on, and are punished. | עָרוּם ׀ רָאָה רָעָה וְיִסָּתֵר<br>וּפְתָיִים עָבְרוּ וְנֶעֱנָשׁוּ׃ | 3 | The shrewd saw evil, and hid himself;<br>but the simple passed on, and were punished. | 3 |
| 4 By humility *and* the fear of the LORD *are* riches, and honour, and life. | עֵקֶב עֲנָוָה יִרְאַת יְהוָה<br>עֹשֶׁר וְכָבוֹד וְחַיִּים׃ | 4 | The reward of humility, of the fear of Jehovah,<br>is wealth, and honor, and life. | 4 |
| 5 Thorns *and* snares *are* in the way of the froward: he that doth keep his soul shall be far from them. | צִנִּים פַּחִים בְּדֶרֶךְ עִקֵּשׁ<br>שׁוֹמֵר נַפְשׁוֹ יִרְחַק מֵהֶם׃ | ה | Thorns, snares, are in the way of the perverse;<br>he that keeps his soul shall be far from them. | 5 |
| 6 Train up a child in the way he should go: and when he is old, he will not depart from it. | חֲנֹךְ לַנַּעַר עַל־פִּי דַרְכּוֹ<br>גַּם כִּי־יַזְקִין לֹא־יָסוּר מִמֶּנָּה׃ | 6 | Train the child according to his way;<br>even when he is old he will not turn from it. | 6 |
| 7 The rich ruleth over the poor, and the borrower *is* servant to the lender. | עָשִׁיר בְּרָשִׁים יִמְשׁוֹל<br>וְעֶבֶד לֹוֶה לְאִישׁ מַלְוֶה׃ | 7 | The rich rules over the poor;<br>and the borrower is servant to the man that lends. | 7 |

V. 3. ונסתר ק׳

V. 29. *Hardens* (lit. *makes strong*) *his face:* that is, he puts on a strong and unyielding expression of countenance.—בפניו (Gram. § 138, 1, *Rem.* 3, foot-note).

*Shall establish his ways:* the reading of the *Kethibh*, יָכִין דְּרָכָיו.

Ch. XXII.—V. 1. *Loving favor.* The adj. טוב is here added to חן, to strengthen the expression (comp. Gesenius, Lex. טוֹב, 1, c, *extr.*); and its effect is best represented by the rendering of the Common Version.

Many (e. g. Ewald, Maurer, Hitzig) construe טוב as *pred.* (*better than*); but its *position* in the sentence is against this view.

V. 3. *The shrewd* (ערום): see the note on ch. 1 : 4, second and third paragraphs.

*Saw*, etc. (the *concr.* instead of the *abstr.* statement), followed here by the *consec. Imperf.* (*Kethibh* וַיִּסָּתֵר). In the next member, the two *Perfects* stand in the same relation, expressing contemporaneous events.*

V. 6. *According to* (על פי) *his way*, i. e. his way of life, the way he is to pursue in life (as I understand it); not "according to his disposition and habits" (pro ratione morum et indolis, Gesenius, Lex. חָנַךְ), for then the second member, though not without force, would be far less significant.

The Common Version, "*in the way he should go*," expresses more than the Hebrew; and this beautiful sentiment is, at most, only implied in the more general truth.†

* Das Perf. ונענשו steht, weil das Unglück sie auf dem Wege überfiel, so dass ונענשו nicht Folge von עברו, sondern gleichzeitig mit diesem ist (Bertheau).

† Stuart (*in locum*) justly says: "As דַּרְכּוֹ can mean only *the way of the child*, the *morale* couched under the phrase *he should*

| KING JAMES' VERSION. | HEBREW TEXT. | | REVISED VERSION. | |
|---|---|---|---|---|
| 8 He that soweth iniquity shall reap vanity: and the rod of his anger shall fail. | זוֹרֵעַ עַוְלָה יִקְצוֹר־אָוֶן<br>וְשֵׁבֶט עֶבְרָתוֹ יִכְלֶה׃ | 8 | He that sows iniquity shall reap mischief;<br>and the rod for his pride shall be ready. | 8 |
| 9 He that hath a bountiful eye shall be blessed; for he giveth of his bread to the poor. | טוֹב־עַיִן הוּא יְבֹרָךְ<br>כִּי־נָתַן מִלַּחְמוֹ לַדָּל׃ | 9 | The man of kindly eye, he shall be blest;<br>for he gives of his bread to the poor. | 9 |
| 10 Cast out the scorner, and contention shall go out; yea, strife and reproach shall cease. | גָּרֵשׁ לֵץ וְיֵצֵא מָדוֹן<br>וְיִשְׁבֹּת דִּין וְקָלוֹן׃ | י | Drive out the scoffer, and contention will go forth;<br>and litigation and reproach will cease. | 10 |
| 11 He that loveth pureness of heart, *for* the grace of his lips the king *shall be* his friend. | אֹהֵב טְהוֹר־לֵב<br>חֵן שְׂפָתָיו רֵעֵהוּ מֶלֶךְ׃ | 11 | He that loves the pure in heart,<br>his lips are grace, the king is his friend. | 11 |
| 12 The eyes of the LORD preserve knowledge; and he overthroweth the words of the transgressor. | עֵינֵי יְהוָה נָצְרוּ דָעַת<br>וַיְסַלֵּף דִּבְרֵי בֹגֵד׃ | 12 | The eyes of Jehovah kept knowledge;<br>and he overthrew the words of the treacherous. | 12 |
| 13 The slothful *man* saith, *There is* a lion without, I shall be slain in the streets. | אָמַר עָצֵל אֲרִי בַחוּץ<br>בְּתוֹךְ רְחֹבוֹת אֵרָצֵחַ׃ | 13 | The sluggard says, There is a lion without;<br>I shall be slain in the streets. | 13 |
| 14 The mouth of strange women *is* a deep pit: he that is abhorred of the LORD shall fall therein. | שׁוּחָה עֲמֻקָּה פִּי זָרוֹת<br>זְעוּם יְהוָה יִפּוֹל־שָׁם׃ | 14 | The mouth of strange women is a deep pit;<br>he that is hated of Jehovah shall fall therein. | 14 |
| 15 Foolishness *is* bound in the heart of a child; *but* the rod of correction shall drive it far from him. | אִוֶּלֶת קְשׁוּרָה בְלֶב־נָעַר<br>שֵׁבֶט מוּסָר יַרְחִיקֶנָּה מִמֶּנּוּ׃ | טו | Folly is bound in the heart of a child;<br>the rod of correction will put it far from him. | 15 |
| 16 He that oppresseth the poor to increase his *riches, and* he that giveth to the rich, *shall* surely *come* to want. | עֹשֵׁק דָּל לְהַרְבּוֹת לוֹ<br>נֹתֵן לְעָשִׁיר אַךְ לְמַחְסוֹר׃ | 16 | He that oppresses the weak, to make increase for himself,<br>is one that gives to the rich, only to want. | 16 |
| 17 Bow down thine ear, and hear the words of the wise, and apply thine heart unto my knowledge. | הַט אָזְנְךָ וּשְׁמַע דִּבְרֵי חֲכָמִים<br>וְלִבְּךָ תָּשִׁית לְדַעְתִּי׃ | 17 | Incline thine ear, and hear the words of the wise;<br>and apply thy heart to my knowledge. | 17 |

VV. 8. 11. 14. יתיר ו׳

V. 8. *Rod for his pride* (עברה = *ὕβρις*, Lex. 2), for the chastisement of his pride.*

V. 9. *The man of kindly eye:* טוֹב עַיִן, the *art.* defining the *compound idea* (Gram. §111, 1).†

V. 10. *Litigation:* contending *at law*, in distinction from ריב, *strife* in a more general (as well as this specific) sense.

V. 11. *That loves the pure in heart:* that delights in such, because such is his own nature. There is no necessity, therefore, for regarding טהור (with Maurer, Bertheau, and others), as a *subst.*

*Are grace:* comp. Eccl. 10 : 12, *the words of a wise man's mouth are grace.*

V. 16. The pointed contrast, of להרבות לו with למחסור, shows that this construction and relation of the two members is the true one.*

go, finds in reality no proper place here, although the sentiment in itself is excellent, and agreeable to the tenor of the Scriptures."

* Maurer: *Et virga insolentiæ ejus* (virga qua insolentia ejus castigabitur) *parata est.*

† Gesenius (Thes. vol. I. p. 545): טוֹב עַיִן qui benigni oculi est, qui benignitatem vultu prodit (cf. חוס) i. e. benignus, misericors.

* So, I find, it is understood by Bertheau. Ich meine so: *wer den Armen bedrückt um zu nehmen für sich* = um noch reicher zu werden, *giebt einem Reichen—nur zum Mangel.* Die Spitze der Rede liegt darin, dass der Reiche eben derselbe ist der die Armen bedrückt; weil aber solches Thun ihm nicht zum Segen gereicht, ... so kann gleich gesagt werden, dass er es erwirbt—**nur** zum Mangel.

| KING JAMES' VERSION. | HEBREW TEXT. | | REVISED VERSION. | |
|---|---|---|---|---|
| 18 For *it is* a pleasant thing if thou keep them within thee; they shall withal be fitted in thy lips. | נְעִים כִּי־תִשְׁמְרֵם בְּבִטְנֶךָ<br>יִכֹּנוּ יַחְדָּו עַל־שְׂפָתֶיךָ׃ | 18 | For it is pleasant, if thou keep them in thy breast;<br>if they are ready all of them on thy lips. | 18 |
| 19 That thy trust may be in the LORD, I have made known to thee this day, even to thee. | לִהְיוֹת בַּיהוָה מִבְטַחֶךָ<br>הוֹדַעְתִּיךָ הַיּוֹם אַף־אָתָּה׃ | 19 | That thy trust may be in Jehovah,<br>I have taught thee this day, yea thee. | 19 |
| 20 Have not I written to thee excellent things in counsels and knowledge, | הֲלֹא כָתַבְתִּי לְךָ שָׁלִשׁוֹם<br>בְּמֹעֵצוֹת וָדָעַת׃ | כ | Have I not written to thee heretofore,<br>with counsels and knowledge; | 20 |
| 21 That I might make thee know the certainty of the words of truth; that thou mightest answer the words of truth to them that send unto thee? | לְהוֹדִיעֲךָ קֹשְׁטְ אִמְרֵי אֱמֶת<br>לְהָשִׁיב אֲמָרִים אֱמֶת לְשֹׁלְחֶיךָ׃ | 21 | to teach thee the rightness of words of truth,<br>that thou mayest answer truth to them that send thee? | 21 |
| 22 Rob not the poor, because he *is* poor: neither oppress the afflicted in the gate: | אַל־תִּגְזָל־דָּל כִּי דַל־הוּא<br>וְאַל־תְּדַכֵּא עָנִי בַשָּׁעַר׃ | 22 | Rob not the weak because he is weak;<br>and oppress not the poor in the gate. | 22 |
| 23 For the LORD will plead their cause, and spoil the soul of those that spoiled them. | כִּי־יְהוָה יָרִיב רִיבָם<br>וְקָבַע אֶת־קֹבְעֵיהֶם נָפֶשׁ׃ | 23 | For Jehovah will plead their cause,<br>and despoil of life those who despoil them. | 23 |
| 24 Make no friendship with an angry man; and with a furious man thou shalt not go; | אַל־תִּתְרַע אֶת־בַּעַל אָף<br>וְאֶת־אִישׁ חֵמוֹת לֹא תָבוֹא׃ | 24 | Make no friendship with a passionate man,<br>and go not with a man given to anger; | 24 |
| 25 Lest thou learn his ways, and get a snare to thy soul. | פֶּן־תֶּאֱלַף אֹרְחֹתָו<br>וְלָקַחְתָּ מוֹקֵשׁ לְנַפְשֶׁךָ׃ | כה | lest thou learn his ways,<br>and bring a snare to thy soul. | 25 |
| 26 Be not thou *one* of them that strike hands, *or* of them that are sureties for debts. | אַל־תְּהִי בְתֹקְעֵי־כָף<br>בַּעֹרְבִים מַשָּׁאוֹת׃ | 26 | Be not of those who strike hands,<br>of those who become surety for debts. | 26 |
| 27 If thou hast nothing to pay, why should he take away thy bed from under thee? | אִם־אֵין־לְךָ לְשַׁלֵּם<br>לָמָּה יִקַּח מִשְׁכָּבְךָ מִתַּחְתֶּיךָ׃ | 27 | If thou hast nothing to pay,<br>why should he take thy bed from under thee! | 27 |
| 28 Remove not the ancient landmark, which thy fathers have set. | אַל־תַּסֵּג גְּבוּל עוֹלָם<br>אֲשֶׁר עָשׂוּ אֲבוֹתֶיךָ׃ | 28 | Remove not the ancient landmark,<br>which thy fathers made. | 28 |

V. 20. שלשים ק׳ V. 25. ארחתיו ק׳

V. 20. *Heretofore: Kethibh* שִׁלְשׁוֹם, which is doubtless the true reading.*

V. 21. *The rightness:* קֹשְׁטְ, properly the *right measure*, and hence *right* or *just* in the abstract.† This is the only English word that will express the meaning.

*Answer:* comp. the note on ch. 18 : 13.*

V. 22. *Poor:* עָנִי, as in Deut. 24 : 12, 14, 15.

V. 24. *Given to anger:* lit. *a man of angers* (plur., viz. of frequent anger).

V. 26. *Strike hands:* literally, *the hand* (see the note on ch. 17 : 18).

* Bertheau: Da in der That V. 21 der Zweck des Schreibens auf andere Weise bestimmt wird wie der der heutigen Belehrung in V. 19, so passt שלשום durchaus.

† Maurer (Hdwbch.): קֹשְׁטְ das rechte Maass, dah. *Richtigkeit* (vgl. arab. قسط das rechte Maass u. Gerechtigkeit). Bertheau: *um dich zu lehren die Richtigkeit wahrer Worte.*

* Ewald: אמרים אמת könnten nach §481, 502 verbunden sein; doch scheint man leichter חשיב אמרים als ein Ganzes in der Bedeutung "zurückmelden" so zu verstehen, dass אמת davon abhängt.

KING JAMES' VERSION.

29 Seest thou a man diligent in his business? he shall stand before kings; he shall not stand before mean *men*.

HEBREW TEXT.

29 חָזִיתָ אִישׁ ׀ מָהִיר בִּמְלַאכְתּוֹ
לִפְנֵי־מְלָכִים יִתְיַצָּב
בַּל־יִתְיַצֵּב לִפְנֵי חֲשֻׁכִּים׃

REVISED VERSION.

Seest thou a man diligent in his business? 29
he shall stand before kings;
he shall not stand before the mean.

### CHAP. XXIII.

WHEN thou sittest to eat with a ruler, consider diligently what *is* before thee:
2 And put a knife to thy throat, if thou *be* a man given to appetite.
3 Be not desirous of his dainties: for they *are* deceitful meat.

4 Labor not to be rich: cease from thine own wisdom.

5 Wilt thou set thine eyes upon that which is not? for *riches* certainly make themselves wings; they fly away as an eagle toward heaven.

6 Eat thou not the bread of *him that hath* an evil eye, neither desire thou his dainty meats:
7 For as he thinketh in his heart, so *is* he: Eat and drink, saith he to thee; but his heart *is* not with thee.

### CHAP. XXIII.

א כִּי־תֵשֵׁב לִלְחוֹם אֶת־מוֹשֵׁל
בִּין תָּבִין אֶת־אֲשֶׁר לְפָנֶיךָ׃
2 וְשַׂמְתָּ שַׂכִּין בְּלֹעֶךָ
אִם־בַּעַל נֶפֶשׁ אָתָּה׃
3 אַל־תִּתְאָו לְמַטְעַמּוֹתָיו
וְהוּא לֶחֶם כְּזָבִים׃
4 אַל־תִּיגַע לְהַעֲשִׁיר
מִבִּינָתְךָ חֲדָל׃
ה הֲתָעוּף עֵינֶיךָ ׀ בּוֹ וְאֵינֶנּוּ
כִּי עָשֹׂה יַעֲשֶׂה־לּוֹ כְנָפַיִם
כְּנֶשֶׁר וְעָיִף הַשָּׁמָיִם׃
6 אַל־תִּלְחַם אֶת־לֶחֶם רַע עָיִן
וְאַל־תִּתְאָו לְמַטְעַמֹּתָיו׃
7 כִּי ׀ כְּמוֹ־שָׁעַר בְּנַפְשׁוֹ כֶּן־הוּא
אֱכוֹל וּשְׁתֵה יֹאמַר לָךְ
וְלִבּוֹ בַּל־עִמָּךְ׃

V. 5. התעיף ק׳ Ib. ועוף ק׳

### CHAP. XXIII.

WHEN thou sittest to eat with a ruler, 1
mark well what is before thee;
and put a knife to thy throat, 2
if thou art given to appetite.
Long not for his dainties; 3
for it is treacherous food.

Labor not to become rich; 4
cease from thine own understanding.
Shall thine eye flit over it, and it be gone! 5
for it will surely make itself wings,
as the eagle, and the birds of heaven.

Eat not the bread of the evil-eyed; 6
and long not for his dainties.
For as he thinks in his soul, so is he; 7
eat and drink, will he say to thee,
but his heart is not with thee.

V. 2. for thou puttest

V. 5. as the eagle flies toward heaven (V. R.)

V. 29. חשכים, *obscure* in position and rank, of low condition, *mean*.

Ch. XXIII.—V. 1. *What is before thee:* the whole scene, including the ruler himself.

V. 2. *And put* (ושמת), Gram. § 126, 6, *c*.* *For thou puttest* (Ewald and others) is not the natural construction of this familiar combination.

V. 5. *Flit over it*, etc. (see Expl. Notes), according to the *Kethibh* (comp. Gram. § 147, *a*),† which is doubtless the correct reading.

The constructions, *wilt thou let thine eyes flit* (Gesenius), which is not an authorized use of *Kal*, and *shall thy glance flit* (Ewald, *constr. ad sensum*), and *wilt thou flit with thine eyes* (Maurer's commentary, as an alternative rendering), are not grammatically necessary.

*And birds:* ועוף, as in many Mss. and printed editions.* This reading is also the most pertinent in the connection.†

V. 7. *As he thinks.* So Gesenius (Lex.), Rödiger,‡ Maurer, Bertheau. As he is, in heart; not as he professes to be, in looks and words.

* Maurer: וְשַׂמְתָּ manifesto est Præteritum relativum, quo qui præcedit Jussivus continuetur.

† Maurer (Heb. u. Chald. Hdwbch., *art.* עוּף): *sollen fliegen deine Augen?* was die Differenz des Num. bei vorgesetztem Verb. nicht hindert.

* Non minori alii numero ועוף, inter quos hisp. mei 4, 782, 941, pluresque editiones, etiam cum cholem ועוֹף *et volucre*, ut Biblia Brix., et triplex. Prov. editio Basil. heb.-lat. 1520, 1524, 1548. (*De Rossi, Var. Lectt. Vet. Test. Vol. iv. p.* 100.)

† Ubi alæ, ibi volatus. Nihil igitur desiderabis. Observa etiam sæpe alias memoratas עוף השמים *aves cœli* (Maurer).

‡ Thes. fasc. poster. p. 1459: *nam quemadmodum æstimat* s. cogitat *animo suo ita* ille *est* (non qualem se esse vultu et verbis simulat).

| KING JAMES' VERSION. | HEBREW TEXT. | | REVISED VERSION. | |
|---|---|---|---|---|
| 8 The morsel *which* thou hast eaten shalt thou vomit up, and lose thy sweet words. | פִּתְּךָ־אָכַלְתָּ תְקִיאֶנָּה<br>וְשִׁחַתָּ דְּבָרֶיךָ הַנְּעִימִים | 8 | The morsel thou hast eaten,<br>thou shalt vomit it up,<br>and lose thy pleasant words. | 8 |
| 9 Speak not in the ears of a fool: for he will despise the wisdom of thy words. | בְּאָזְנֵי כְסִיל אַל־תְּדַבֵּר<br>כִּי־יָבוּז לְשֵׂכֶל מִלֶּיךָ׃ | 9 | Speak not in the ears of a<br>fool;<br>for he will despise the wisdom<br>of thy words. | 9 |
| 10 Remove not the old landmark; and enter not into the fields of the fatherless: | אַל־תַּסֵּג גְּבוּל עוֹלָם<br>וּבִשְׂדֵי יְתוֹמִים אַל־תָּבֹא׃ | י | Remove not an old land-<br>mark;<br>and enter not into the orphans'<br>fields. | 10 |
| 11 For their redeemer *is* mighty; he shall plead their cause with thee. | כִּי־גֹאֲלָם חָזָק<br>הוּא־יָרִיב אֶת־רִיבָם אִתָּךְ׃ | 11 | For their deliverer is strong;<br>he will plead their cause with<br>thee. | 11 |
| 12 Apply thine heart unto instruction, and thine ears to the words of knowledge. | הָבִיאָה לַמּוּסָר לִבֶּךָ<br>וְאָזְנֶךָ לְאִמְרֵי־דָעַת | 12 | Bring thy heart to instruc-<br>tion,<br>and thy ears to words of knowl-<br>edge. | 12 |
| 13 Withhold not correction from the child: for *if* thou beatest him with the rod, he shall not die. | אַל־תִּמְנַע מִנַּעַר מוּסָר<br>כִּי־תַכֶּנּוּ בַשֵּׁבֶט לֹא יָמוּת׃ | 13 | Withhold not correction from<br>a child;<br>for if thou smite him with the<br>rod, he shall not die. | 13 |
| 14 Thou shalt beat him with the rod, and shalt deliver his soul from hell. | אַתָּה בַּשֵּׁבֶט תַּכֶּנּוּ<br>וְנַפְשׁוֹ מִשְּׁאוֹל תַּצִּיל | 14 | Thou with the rod wilt smite<br>him;<br>but his soul thou shalt deliver<br>from the underworld. | 14 |
| 15 My son, if thine heart be wise, my heart shall rejoice, even mine. | בְּנִי אִם־חָכַם לִבֶּךָ<br>יִשְׂמַח לִבִּי גַם־אָנִי׃ | טו | My son, if thy heart be wise,<br>my heart shall rejoice, yea<br>mine; | 15 |
| 16 Yea, my reins shall rejoice, when thy lips speak right things. | וְתַעְלֹזְנָה כִלְיוֹתָי<br>בְּדַבֵּר שְׂפָתֶיךָ מֵישָׁרִים׃ | 16 | and my reins shall exult,<br>when thy lips speak things that<br>are right. | 16 |
| 17 Let not thine heart envy sinners; but *be thou* in the fear of the LORD all the day long. | אַל־יְקַנֵּא לִבְּךָ בַּחַטָּאִים<br>כִּי אִם־בְּיִרְאַת יְהוָֹה כָּל־הַיּוֹם׃ | 17 | Let not thy heart be envious<br>at sinners,<br>but be ever in Jehovah's fear. | 17 |
| 18 For surely there is an end; and thine expectation shall not be cut off. | כִּי אִם־יֵשׁ אַחֲרִית<br>וְתִקְוָתְךָ לֹא תִכָּרֵת׃ | 18 | For if there is an end,<br>then thy expectation shall not<br>be cut off. | 18 |
| 19 Hear thou, my son, and be wise, and guide thine heart in the way. | שְׁמַע־אַתָּה בְנִי וַחֲכָם<br>וְאַשֵּׁר בַּדֶּרֶךְ לִבֶּךָ׃ | 19 | Hear thou, my son, and be<br>wise;<br>and guide thy heart aright in<br>the way. | 19 |
| 20 Be not among winebibbers; among riotous eaters of flesh: | אַל־תְּהִי בְסֹבְאֵי־יָיִן<br>בְּזֹלֲלֵי בָשָׂר לָמוֹ׃ | כ | Be not among wine-drinkers,<br>among those who are prodigal<br>of their own flesh. | 20 |
| 21 For the drunkard and the glutton shall come to poverty: and drowsiness shall clothe *a man* with rags. | כִּי־סֹבֵא וְזוֹלֵל יִוָּרֵשׁ<br>וּקְרָעִים תַּלְבִּישׁ נוּמָה׃ | 21 | For the drunkard and the prod-<br>igal shall be impoverished,<br>and drowsiness will clothe with<br>rags. | 21 |

V. 18. *For if* (כי אם). So Gesenius (Thes. and Lex. כי אם, 2), Rosenmüller, and Bertheau. *Nay but* (De Wette, Maurer) is not so pertinent here. (See Expl. Notes.)

VV. 20, 21. *The prodigal*: the squanderer, the spendthrift; not in the specific sense of '*the glutton*,' as in the Common Version.

*Of their own flesh* (see Expl. Notes): לְ (in בשר למו) expressing *possession, belonging to*.*

* Gesenius (Thes. and Lex. זלל): *qui corporis sui prodigi sunt*, voluptuosi, voluptatibus dediti. Ewald: *die ihren eignen Leib verwüsten.*

KING JAMES' VERSION.

22 Hearken unto thy father
that begat thee, and despise not
thy mother when she is old.

23 Buy the truth, and sell *it*
not; *also* wisdom, and instruction,
and understanding.
24 The father of the righteous
shall greatly rejoice: and he that
begetteth a wise *child* shall have
joy of him.
25 Thy father and thy mother
shall be glad, and she that bare
thee shall rejoice.
26 My son, give me thine heart,
and let thine eyes observe my
ways.
27 For a whore *is* a deep ditch;
and a strange woman *is* a narrow
pit.
28 She also lieth in wait as *for*
a prey, and increaseth the transgressors among men.

29 Who hath woe? who hath
sorrow? who hath contentions?
who hath babbling? who hath
wounds without cause? who hath
redness of eyes?

30 They that tarry long at the
wine; they that go to seek mixed
wine.

31 Look not thou upon the
wine when it is red, when it giveth his colour in the cup, *when* it
moveth itself aright.

HEBREW TEXT.

22 שְׁמַע לְאָבִיךָ זֶה יְלָדֶךָ
וְאַל־תָּבוּז כִּי־זָקְנָה אִמֶּךָ׃

23 אֱמֶת קְנֵה וְאַל־תִּמְכֹּר
חָכְמָה וּמוּסָר וּבִינָה׃

24 גִּיל יָגִיל אֲבִי צַדִּיק
יוֹלֵד חָכָם וְיִשְׂמַח בּוֹ׃

כה יִשְׂמַח־אָבִיךָ וְאִמֶּךָ
וְתָגֵל יוֹלַדְתֶּךָ׃

26 תְּנָה בְנִי לִבְּךָ לִי
וְעֵינֶיךָ דְּרָכַי תִּרְצֹנָה׃

27 כִּי־שׁוּחָה עֲמוּקָּה זוֹנָה
וּבְאֵר צָרָה נָכְרִיָּה׃

28 אַף־הִיא כְּחֶתֶף תֶּאֱרֹב
וּבוֹגְדִים בְּאָדָם תּוֹסִף׃

29 לְמִי אוֹי לְמִי אֲבוֹי
לְמִי מִדְיָנִים ׀ לְמִי־שִׂיחַ
לְמִי פְּצָעִים חִנָּם
לְמִי חַכְלִלוּת עֵינָיִם׃

ל לַמְאַחֲרִים עַל־הַיָּיִן
לַבָּאִים לַחְקֹר מִמְסָךְ׃

31 אַל־תֵּרֶא יַיִן כִּי יִתְאַדָּם
כִּי־יִתֵּן בַּכִּיס עֵינוֹ
יִתְהַלֵּךְ בְּמֵישָׁרִים׃

V. 24. גיל ק׳ Ib. יגיל ק׳ Ib. ישמח ק׳
V. 26. תצרנה ק׳ V. 31. בכוס ק׳

REVISED VERSION.

Hearken to thy father that 22
begat thee;
and despise not thy mother
when she is old.
Buy truth, and sell it not; 23
wisdom, and instruction, and
understanding.
The father of the righteous 24
shall greatly exult;
he that begets one that is wise
shall rejoice in him.
Let thy father and thy mother 25
rejoice;
and let her exult that bore thee.
My son, give me thy heart; 26
and let thine eyes delight in
my ways.
For a harlot is a deep pit; 27
and a strange woman is a
narrow well.
Yea, as for prey, she lies in 28
wait;
and multiplies them that deal
perfidiously with men.
Who has wailing? who has 29
want?
who has contentions? who has
complaining?
who has wounds without cause?
who has dimness of the eyes?
They that tarry long over the 30
wine,
that come to make trial of mixed wine.
Look not on the wine how it 31
reddens,
how it makes its bead in the
cup,
moves itself aright.

---

Bertheau's objection to this is not well taken. Their *prodigality* shows itself in the unrestrained indulgence of every appetite; and this to their own physical injury and ruin.

V. 24. וְיִשְׂמַח (*Kethibh*), *Vav* with *apodosis*, Gram. §145, 2.

V. 26. *Delight in my ways:* תִּרְצֶנָה (*Kethibh*) with the *accus.*, as in Ps. 102:15, and elsewhere.*

V. 28. *As for prey.* So the subst. with כְּ may be construed (Gram. §118, 3, *Rem.* third paragr.), and there is no necessity for taking חתף as *concr.* for *robber.*

*Deal perfidiously with:* בוגדים, construed with בְּ, as in Is. 33:1. So Ewald.†

* Maurer: תִּרְצֶנָה defective scriptum (ut תְּעַשֶּׁנָה, Job 15:12) a רָצָה, quod constat etiam cum Acc. construi.

† Ita ut בְּ non sit *inter*, sed ad ipsum pertineat בגד verbum; non male (Maurer).

V. 29. *Want:* אבוי, *abstr.* from the same root (אבה), as אֶבְיוֹן, *needy.** The signification, *alas*, has no sufficient ground.

V. 31. Other renderings: *Goes easily down* (Lud. de Dieu†); *flows smoothly* (Gesenius, Lex.‡), *goes straight down* (Ewald

* Gesenius (Thes. vol. I. p. 12): Rarius hoc vocabulum, abstractum τοῦ אֶבְיוֹן, formæ קְטוֹל, h. l. videtur adhibitum esse propter paronomasiam cum voce אוֹי. E veteribus LXX. *θόρυβος tumultus, turbæ* [molestia?], rectius Chald. דְּוָיָא *miseria, afflictio*, Syr. ܕܘܘܕܐ *agitatio, molestia*, nisi legundum ܕܘܘܢܐ *miseria, ærumna*, cum alibi Chaldæus et Syrus in Proverbiis concinere soleant. Recte Abulwalid, cujus sententiam etiam laudat Kimchius, ad paupertatis et miseriæ notionem illud retulit.

† Crit. Sac. p. 176: Verte, *subit facillime*, ad verbum, *in facilitatibus*, aut *in rectitudinibus.*

‡ But in the Thes. (vol. II. p. 643): hinc במישרים recta via; . . . *vinum.* . . . *recta descendit* in guttur.

KING JAMES' VERSION.

32 At the last it biteth like a serpent, and stingeth like an adder.
33 Thine eyes shall behold strange women, and thine heart shall utter perverse things.

34 Yea, thou shalt be as he that lieth down in the midst of the sea, or as he that lieth upon the top of a mast.
35 They have stricken me, *shalt thou say, and* I was not sick; they have beaten me, *and* I felt *it* not: when shall I awake? I will seek it yet again.

CHAP. XXIV.

Be not thou envious against evil men, neither desire to be with them:
2 For their heart studieth destruction, and their lips talk of mischief.

3 Through wisdom is a house builded; and by understanding it is established:

4 And by knowledge shall the chambers be filled with all precious and pleasant riches.

5 A wise man *is* strong; yea, a man of knowledge increaseth strength.
6 For by wise counsel thou shalt make thy war: and in multitude of counsellors *there is* safety.

7 Wisdom *is* too high for a fool: he openeth not his mouth in the gate.

8 He that deviseth to do evil shall be calleth a mischievous person.

HEBREW TEXT.

32 אַחֲרִיתוֹ כְּנָחָשׁ יִשָּׁךְ
וּכְצִפְעֹנִי יַפְרִשׁ׃
33 עֵינֶיךָ יִרְאוּ זָרוֹת
וְלִבְּךָ יְדַבֵּר תַּהְפֻּכוֹת׃

34 וְהָיִיתָ כְּשֹׁכֵב בְּלֶב־יָם
וּכְשֹׁכֵב בְּרֹאשׁ חִבֵּל׃

לה הִכּוּנִי בַל־חָלִיתִי
הֲלָמוּנִי בַּל־יָדָעְתִּי
מָתַי אָקִיץ
אוֹסִיף אֲבַקְשֶׁנּוּ עוֹד׃

CHAP. XXIV.

א אַל־תְּקַנֵּא בְּאַנְשֵׁי רָעָה
וְאַל־תִּתְאָו לִהְיוֹת אִתָּם׃
2 כִּי־שֹׁד יֶהְגֶּה לִבָּם
וְעָמָל שִׂפְתֵיהֶם תְּדַבֵּרְנָה׃

3 בְּחָכְמָה יִבָּנֶה בָּיִת
וּבִתְבוּנָה יִתְכּוֹנָן׃

4 וּבְדַעַת חֲדָרִים יִמָּלְאוּ
כָּל־הוֹן יָקָר וְנָעִים׃

ה גֶּבֶר־חָכָם בַּעוֹז
וְאִישׁ דַּעַת מְאַמֶּץ־כֹּחַ׃
6 כִּי בְתַחְבֻּלוֹת תַּעֲשֶׂה־לְּךָ מִלְחָמָה
וּתְשׁוּעָה בְּרֹב יוֹעֵץ׃

7 רָאמוֹת לֶאֱוִיל חָכְמוֹת
בַּשַּׁעַר לֹא יִפְתַּח־פִּיהוּ׃

8 מְחַשֵּׁב לְהָרֵעַ
לוֹ בַּעַל מְזִמּוֹת יִקְרָאוּ׃

REVISED VERSION.

32 In its end it will bite like a serpent, 32
and sting like a viper.
33 Thine eyes will look on strange women, 33
and thy heart will utter perverse things.

34 And thou wilt be as one lying asleep in the heart of the sea, 34
and as one that lies sleeping on the top of a mast.

35 They smite me, I feel no pain; 35
they beat me, I know it not;
when shall I awake?
I will seek it yet again.

CHAP. XXIV.

Be not envious of evil men; 1
and long not to be with them.
2 For their heart meditates violence, 2
and their lips talk of mischief.

3 By wisdom is a house builded; 3
and by understanding it is established;

4 and by knowledge the store-rooms are filled, 4
with all precious and pleasant treasures.

5 A wise man is strong; 5
and a man of knowledge increases strength.
6 For with wise direction thou shalt make war; 6
and in the multitude of counselors is safety.

7 Wisdom is too high for a fool; 7
he shall not open his mouth in the gate.

8 Whoso plans to do evil, 8
he shall be called mischief-maker.

---

and Bertheau). But '*down*' is not in the Hebrew, though it could readily have been expressed; and the writer is describing the tempting aspect of wine *in the cup*.

Ch. XXIV.—V. 5. *Is with strength* (בעוז) = *is strong;* Lex. ב, B, 2, d.—*With wise direction:* see the note on ch. 20 : 18.

*Thou shalt make* (תעשה לך): for לְּךָ, compare Gram. § 154, 3, 2, *e*.

V. 7. חכמות (comp. the note on ch. 1 : 20).

V. 8. *He shall be called:* comp. ch. 16 : 21, and the reference there given.

| KING JAMES' VERSION. | HEBREW TEXT. | | REVISED VERSION. | |
|---|---|---|---|---|
| 9 The thought of foolishness *is* sin: and the scorner *is* an abomination to men. | זִמַּת אִוֶּלֶת חַטָּאת<br>וְתוֹעֲבַת לְאָדָם לֵץ׃ | 9 | The purpose of folly is sin;<br>and the scoffer is an abomination to men. | 9 |
| 10 *If* thou faint in the day of adversity, thy strength *is* small. | הִתְרַפִּיתָ בְּיוֹם צָרָה<br>צַר כֹּחֶכָה׃ | 10 | If thou faint in the day of adversity,<br>thy strength is small. | 10 |
| 11 If thou forbear to deliver *them that are* drawn unto death, and *those that are* ready to be slain; | הַצֵּל לְקֻחִים לַמָּוֶת<br>וּמָטִים לַהֶרֶג אִם־תַּחְשׂוֹךְ׃ | 11 | To rescue those taken away to death,<br>and those tottering to the slaughter, wilt thou forbear? | 11 |
| 12 If thou sayest, Behold, we knew it not; doth not he that pondereth the heart consider *it?* and he that keepeth thy soul, doth *not* he know *it?* and shall *not* he render to *every* man according to his works? | כִּי־תֹאמַר הֵן לֹא־יָדַעְנוּ זֶה<br>הֲלֹא־תֹכֵן לִבּוֹת ׀ הוּא־יָבִין<br>וְנֹצֵר נַפְשְׁךָ הוּא יֵדָע<br>וְהֵשִׁיב לְאָדָם כְּפָעֳלוֹ׃ | 12 | For if thou say, Lo, we knew not this;<br>shall not he, the trier of hearts, perceive,<br>and the keeper of thy soul, shall not he know?<br>and he renders back to man according to his deed. | 12 |
| 13 My son, eat thou honey, because *it is* good; and the honeycomb, *which is* sweet to thy taste: | אֱכָל־בְּנִי דְבַשׁ כִּי טוֹב<br>וְנֹפֶת מָתוֹק עַל־חִכֶּךָ׃ | 13 | Eat honey, my son, for it is good;<br>and honey-drippings, sweet to thy palate. | 13 |
| 14 So *shall* the knowledge of wisdom *be* unto thy soul: when thou hast found *it*, then there shall be a reward, and thy expectation shall not be cut off. | כֵּן ׀ דְּעֶה חָכְמָה לְנַפְשֶׁךָ<br>אִם־מָצָאתָ וְיֵשׁ אַחֲרִית<br>וְתִקְוָתְךָ לֹא תִכָּרֵת׃ | 14 | So learn wisdom for thy soul;<br>if thou find it, then there is an end,<br>and thy expectation shall not be cut off. | 14 |

V. 10. *Faintest thou* = *if thou faintest* (Gram. § 155, 4, *a*). *Small:* lit. *strait, narrow*, i. e. of small compass or extent, limited or small in amount. The adj. צַר* (not *third perf.* of צָרַר, as Stuart, after Bertheau) is selected for the paronomasia with צָרָה.

A wholly false turn is given by some to this verse. Thus Stuart translates it, "*If thou hast become relaxed in the day of distress, thy strength is straitened;*" and says in explanation of it: "*Relaxation* is the opposite of strenuous *exertion;* and for the latter the day of distress calls. In such a state, viz., one in which a man feels but little power to make effort when much is needed, that small power is of course *reduced to straits.*"

Of course it is; no one need be told this, nor is the lesson of much value. On the contrary, the lesson of the wise man is, that *adversity tests the moral strength of men;* that to faint in the day of adversity is a proof of moral weakness.

V. 11. *Wilt thou forbear* (אִם interrogative, as understood by Rosenmüller) seems to me the most natural construction of this clause, in connection with the two following. הצל, as הכר v. 23.

*O that thou wouldst hold back*† (viz. from death; אִם optantis, *if thou wouldst*, for wouldst thou but do it = O that thou wouldst), seems quite out of place after the positive form of the *Imperative.*

*Forbear not* (אִם after an implied *formula jurantis**) *to rescue*, etc. So Gesenius, formerly, Thes. vol. I. p. 530 (but later, as in the following paragraph).

*If thou forbear* (אִם conditional) *to rescue*, etc. So the clause was construed by Gussett;† and this is Gesenius' latest view.‡

But then the clause, 'shall not he the *trier of hearts* perceive,' is not a pertinent apodosis; unless we include the intervening member as part of the conditional protasis, which is contrary to the usual relation of the particles אם and כִּי (see Lex. כִּי, B, 4).

V. 12. *For if thou say:* כִּי, with *Imperf.* as *Subj.*, as in ch. 23:13, second member.

V. 13. *Honey-drippings* (*sing. collect.*): נֹפֶת צוּפִים = נפת (Ps. 19:11), the word being appropriated, by special usage, to the dropping of honey from the comb.

* Gesenius (Thes. III. p. 1188, *art.* צַר, adj.): *angustum est robur tuum* (deine Kraft ist beschränkt), i. e. angustis terminis inclusum.

† Maurer: *Eripe eos qui* injuste *abripiuntur ad mortem; et eos qui vacillant* (nutant) *ad occisionem, utinam retineas*, cohibeus a morte. Bertheau: *O* (?) *rette zum Tode geschleppte und zur Erwürgung wankende, o halte sie zurück!*

* Umbreit: אם steht hier schwörend und betheuernd für *ja nicht.*

† Comment. Ling. Heb. p. 552: Prov. 24:11, . . . *liberare captos ad mortem, et lapsos ad jugulationem, si detinueris;* ibi *liberare* est infinitivus instar nominis, liberationem illorum si detinueris, cum ea erat in manu tua, ita ut liberationem illis non dares, cum ad tale in illos officium te ipsorum periculum movebat.

‡ Communicated to Dr. Robinson, for the last American edition of the Manual Heb. Lexicon (see Dr. R's. preface, p. VII).

KING JAMES' VERSION.

15 Lay not wait, O wicked *man*, against the dwelling of the righteous; spoil not his resting place:

16 For a just *man* falleth seven times, and riseth up again: but the wicked shall fall into mischief.

17 Rejoice not when thine enemy falleth, and let not thine heart be glad when he stumbleth:

18 Lest the LORD see *it*, and it displease him, and he turn away his wrath from him.

19 Fret not thyself because of evil *men*, neither be thou envious at the wicked;

20 For there shall be no reward to the evil *man;* the candle of the wicked shall be put out.

21 My son, fear thou the LORD and the king: *and* meddle not with them that are given to change:

22 For their calamity shall rise suddenly; and who knoweth the ruin of them both?

23 These *things* also *belong* to the wise. *It is* not good to have respect of persons in judgment.

24 He that saith unto the wicked, Thou *art* righteous; him shall the people curse, nations shall abhor him:

25 But to them that rebuke *him* shall be delight, and a good blessing shall come upon them.

HEBREW TEXT.

טו אַל־תֶּאֱרֹב רָשָׁע לִנְוֵה צַדִּיק
אַל־תְּשַׁדֵּד רִבְצוֹ׃

16 כִּי שֶׁבַע ׀ יִפּוֹל צַדִּיק וָקָם
וּרְשָׁעִים יִכָּשְׁלוּ בְרָעָה׃

17 בִּנְפֹל אוֹיִבְךָ אַל־תִּשְׂמָח
וּבִכָּשְׁלוֹ אַל־יָגֵל לִבֶּךָ׃

18 פֶּן־יִרְאֶה יְהוָה וְרַע בְּעֵינָיו
וְהֵשִׁיב מֵעָלָיו אַפּוֹ׃

19 אַל־תִּתְחַר בַּמְּרֵעִים
אַל־תְּקַנֵּא בָּרְשָׁעִים׃

כ כִּי ׀ לֹא־תִהְיֶה אַחֲרִית לָרָע
נֵר רְשָׁעִים יִדְעָךְ׃

21 יְרָא־אֶת־יְהוָה בְּנִי וָמֶלֶךְ
עִם־שׁוֹנִים אַל־תִּתְעָרָב׃

22 כִּי־פִתְאֹם יָקוּם אֵידָם
וּפִיד שְׁנֵיהֶם מִי יוֹדֵעַ׃

23 גַּם־אֵלֶּה לַחֲכָמִים
הַכֵּר־פָּנִים בְּמִשְׁפָּט בַּל־טוֹב׃

24 אֹמֵר ׀ לְרָשָׁע צַדִּיק אָתָּה
יִקְּבֻהוּ עַמִּים יִזְעָמוּהוּ לְאֻמִּים׃

כה וְלַמּוֹכִיחִים יִנְעָם
וַעֲלֵיהֶם תָּבוֹא בִרְכַּת־טוֹב׃

V. 17. יתיר י׳.

REVISED VERSION.

Lie not in wait, wicked man, 15
at the dwelling of the righteous;
despoil not his resting-place.
For seven times shall the right- 16
eous fall, and arise;
but the wicked stumble into ruin.

When thy enemy falls rejoice 17
not;
when he stumbles let not thy heart exult;
lest Jehovah see, and it be evil 18
in his eyes,
and he turn away his anger from him.

Be not angry against evil- 19
doers;
be not envious at the wicked.
For there shall not be an end 20
for the evil;
the light of the wicked shall go out.

Fear Jehovah, my son, and 21
the king;
meddle not with those given to change.
For their calamity shall rise 22
suddenly;
and who knows the ruin of them both?

THESE ARE ALSO OF THE WISE. 23
To regard the person in judgment is not good.
He that says to the wicked, 24
Thou art righteous,
peoples shall curse him, nations shall abhor him.
But to them that rebuke there 25
shall be delight;
and on them shall come the blessing of the good.

V. 22. *Of them both:* of him who fears not God, and of him who fears not the king (the *novarum rerum avidi* of the preceding verse). So שניהם is correctly explained by Rosenmüller, Ewald, Maurer.* Bertheau (and after him Stuart) erroneously refer it to *God* and the *king* (*gen. auct.*), as authors of the 'calamity' and 'ruin' (*their calamity*, for the calamity they inflict).

* Rosenmüller: *Et exitium utriusque eorum*, qui vel Deum vel regem non veretur, *quis novit?* Ewald: *Beider*, die entweder Gott oder den König nicht fürchten.

V. 23. *Are also of the wise:* לְ, either *Lam. auct.* or simply meaning *theirs, belonging to them*, as their sayings. This the connection requires; for the meaning, '*for* the wise' (for their use and benefit) is out of place here.*

*To regard*, etc. This member stands in connection with the following verse.

* Rosenmüller: Sed malim cum Grotio et aliis ל nomini חכמים præmissum pro nota Genitivi sive auctoris habere, . . . ut vertendum sit: *hæc quoque sapientum* scil. sunt dicta, s. sententiæ.

| KING JAMES' VERSION. | HEBREW TEXT. | | REVISED VERSION. | |
|---|---|---|---|---|
| 26 *Every man* shall kiss *his* lips that giveth a right answer. | שְׂפָתַיִם יִשָּׁק<br>מֵשִׁיב דְּבָרִים נְכֹחִים׃ | 26 | He kisses the lips,<br>who answers with right words. | 26 |
| 27 Prepare thy work without, and make it fit for thyself in the field; and afterwards build thine house. | הָכֵן בַּחוּץ ׀ מְלַאכְתֶּךָ<br>וְעַתְּדָהּ בַּשָּׂדֶה לָךְ<br>אַחַר וּבָנִיתָ בֵיתֶךָ׃ | 27 | Prepare thy work abroad,<br>and make it ready for thee in the field;<br>then, afterward, build thy house. | 27 |
| 28 Be not a witness against thy neighbour without cause; and deceive *not* with thy lips. | אַל־תְּהִי עֵד־חִנָּם בְּרֵעֶךָ<br>וַהֲפִתִּיתָ בִּשְׂפָתֶיךָ׃ | 28 | Be not witness without cause against thy neighbor;<br>for wouldst thou deceive with thy lips? | 28 |
| 29 Say not, I will do so to him as he hath done to me: I will render to the man according to his work. | אַל־תֹּאמַר כַּאֲשֶׁר עָשָׂה־לִי<br>כֵּן אֶעֱשֶׂה־לּוֹ<br>אָשִׁיב לָאִישׁ כְּפָעֳלוֹ׃ | 29 | Say not, As he has done to me, so will I do to him;<br>I will render to a man according to his deed. | 29 |
| 30 I went by the field of the slothful, and by the vineyard of the man void of understanding; | עַל־שְׂדֵה אִישׁ־עָצֵל עָבַרְתִּי<br>וְעַל־כֶּרֶם אָדָם חֲסַר־לֵב׃ | ל | I passed by the field of the sluggard,<br>and by the vineyard of a man lacking understanding. | 30 |
| 31 And, lo, it was all grown over with thorns, *and* nettles had covered the face thereof, and the stone wall thereof was broken down. | וְהִנֵּה עָלָה כֻלּוֹ ׀ קִמְּשׂוֹנִים<br>כָּסּוּ פָנָיו חֲרֻלִּים<br>וְגֶדֶר אֲבָנָיו נֶהֱרָסָה׃ | 31 | And lo, it was all grown up with nettles;<br>its face was covered with brambles;<br>and its stone wall was torn down. | 31 |
| 32 Then I saw, *and* considered *it* well: I looked upon *it, and* received instruction. | וָאֶחֱזֶה אָנֹכִי אָשִׁית לִבִּי<br>רָאִיתִי לָקַחְתִּי מוּסָר׃ | 32 | Then I looked, I considered well;<br>I saw, I received instruction. | 32 |
| 33 *Yet* a little sleep, a little slumber, a little folding of the hands to sleep: | מְעַט שֵׁנוֹת מְעַט תְּנוּמוֹת<br>מְעַט ׀ חִבֻּק יָדַיִם לִשְׁכָּב׃ | 33 | A little sleep, a little slumber,<br>a little folding of the hands to rest; | 33 |
| 34 So shall thy poverty come *as* one that travelleth; and thy want as an armed man. | וּבָא־מִתְהַלֵּךְ רֵישֶׁךָ<br>וּמַחְסֹרֶיךָ כְּאִישׁ מָגֵן׃ | 34 | and prowling comes thy poverty,<br>and thy wants as an armed man! | 34 |

V. 26. Lit. *Returns right words,* viz. in answer, = *answers with right words.*

V. 27. *Then, afterward, build,* expresses the emphatic form אחר ובנית (lit. *afterward, then build,* Gram. § 155, 1, *a,* third paragraph).

V. 28. The ו (second member) is commonly regarded as *Vav consec.* with the *Perf.* after an *Imperat.*; the consecutive clause, in this one instance,* taking the form of a question.

The ו may be the simple *copulative;* and then the *Perf.* expresses the *abstr. Pres.* (Gram. § 126, 3, *b*), *dost thou deceive* = art thou one that deceives, one that would willingly practice deception?

In either case, the second member implies that there is no will to deceive; and thus confirms the caution, in the first member, to shun the temptation to it. The version in the text expresses the meaning, according to either construction.

V. 31. *Was grown up with* (Gram. § 138, 1, *Rem.* 2).*—*Nettles* (old English versions), as now generally understood. '*Thorns*' (Kimchi), of the Common Version, is a false rendering.†

V. 34. *Prowling:*‡ מתהלך as the *part.*, not *substantively,* as מהלך is used, (ch. 6 : 11) with the sign of comparison כְּ.

*Thy wants* (*plur.* מחסריך), as one in want of all things.‖

* Ewald (Lehrb. p. 735, foot-note): das einzige Beispiel wäre וַהֲפִתִּיתָ Spr. 24 : 28.

* Ewald (Lehrb. § 281, *b*): *Der Boden* עָלָה סִירִים *steigt auf* (nach optischer Täuschung) *von Dornen.*

† Comp. Celsius, Hierobot. II. pp. 206–208; Winer, Rlwbch. I. p. 274.

‡ See the note on ch. **6 : 11.**

‖ Ewald: *all dein Mangel.*

| KING JAMES' VERSION. | | HEBREW TEXT. | REVISED VERSION. | |
|---|---|---|---|---|
| CHAP. XXV. | | CHAP. XXV. | CHAP. XXV. | |
| THESE *are* also proverbs of Solomon, which the men of Hezekiah king of Judah copied out. | א | גַּם־אֵלֶּה מִשְׁלֵי שְׁלֹמֹה<br>אֲשֶׁר הֶעְתִּיקוּ אַנְשֵׁי ׀ חִזְקִיָּה<br>מֶלֶךְ־יְהוּדָה׃ | THESE ALSO ARE PROVERBS OF SOLOMON, WHICH THE MEN OF HEZEKIAH KING OF JUDAH COPIED OUT. | 1 |
| 2 *It is* the glory of God to conceal a thing: but the honour of kings *is* to search out a matter. | 2 | כְּבֹד אֱלֹהִים הַסְתֵּר דָּבָר<br>וּכְבֹד מְלָכִים חֲקֹר דָּבָר׃ | It is the glory of God to conceal a thing;<br>but the glory of kings is to search a thing out. | 2 |
| 3 The heaven for height, and the earth for depth, and the heart of kings *is* unsearchable. | 3 | שָׁמַיִם לָרוּם וָאָרֶץ לָעֹמֶק<br>וְלֵב מְלָכִים אֵין חֵקֶר׃ | The heavens for height, and the earth for depth,<br>and the heart of kings, are unsearchable. | 3 |
| 4 Take away the dross from the silver, and there shall come forth a vessel for the finer. | 4 | הָגוֹ סִיגִים מִכָּסֶף<br>וַיֵּצֵא לַצֹּרֵף כֶּלִי׃ | Take away the dross from the silver,<br>and there shall come forth a vessel for the founder. | 4 |
| 5 Take away the wicked *from* before the king, and his throne shall be established in righteousness. | ה | הָגוֹ רָשָׁע לִפְנֵי־מֶלֶךְ<br>וְיִכּוֹן בַּצֶּדֶק כִּסְאוֹ׃ | Take away the wicked before a king,<br>and his throne shall be established in righteousness. | 5 |
| 6 Put not forth thyself in the presence of the king, and stand not in the place of great *men:* | 6 | אַל־תִּתְהַדַּר לִפְנֵי־מֶלֶךְ<br>וּבִמְקוֹם גְּדֹלִים אַל־תַּעֲמֹד׃ | Do not bear thyself proudly before the king;<br>and stand not in the place of the great. | 6 |
| 7 For better *it is* that it be said unto thee, Come up hither; than that thou shouldest be put lower in the presence of the prince whom thine eyes have seen. | 7 | כִּי טוֹב אֲמָר־לְךָ עֲלֵה הֵנָּה<br>מֵהַשְׁפִּילְךָ לִפְנֵי נָדִיב<br>אֲשֶׁר רָאוּ עֵינֶיךָ׃ | For it is better that one say to thee, Come up hither,<br>than that thou be put lower in presence of the prince,<br>whom thine eyes have seen. | 7 |
| 8 Go not forth hastily to strive, lest *thou know not* what to do in the end thereof, when thy neighbour hath put thee to shame. | 8 | אַל־תֵּצֵא לָרִב מַהֵר<br>פֶּן מַה־תַּעֲשֶׂה בְּאַחֲרִיתָהּ<br>בְּהַכְלִים אֹתְךָ רֵעֶךָ׃ | Go not forth hastily to contend at law;<br>lest thou do aught in the end of it,<br>when thy neighbor has put thee to shame. | 8 |
| 9 Debate thy cause with thy neighbour *himself;* and discover not a secret to another: | 9 | רִיבְךָ רִיב אֶת־רֵעֶךָ<br>וְסוֹד אַחֵר אַל־תְּגָל׃ | Plead thy cause with thy neighbor;<br>and reveal not another's secret. | 9 |
| 10 Lest he that heareth *it* put thee to shame, and thine infamy turn not away. | י | פֶּן־יְחַסֶּדְךָ שֹׁמֵעַ<br>וְדִבָּתְךָ לֹא תָשׁוּב׃ | Lest he that hears reproach thee,<br>and thine evil report turn not away. | 10 |

Ch. XXV.—V. 1. העתיק, *to remove, to transfer* (from one place to another); and hence (of things written) *to transcribe, to copy out*, as the Sept. ἐξεγράψαντο.

V. 2. *Are unsearchable:* lit. *there is no searching* (of them), as in Job 5 : 9.*

V. 3. *The founder* (צֹרֵף), as in Judg. 17 : 4.

V. 8. *To contend at law:* the special meaning of ריב. So the old English versions: *Be not hasty to go to the law.—Lest thou do aught* (see Expl. Notes).*

V. 9. *Plead thy cause,* etc. (See Expl. Notes.)

V. 10. *Thine evil report:* the *passive* use of the *suff. pron.*, as in Gen. 37 : 2; where, as in Num. 13 : 32, 14 : 37, the Heb.

* Bertheau: *Himmel in Beziehung auf Höhe, Erde in Beziehung auf Tiefe, . . . . und Herz der Könige* sind ohne *Erforschung.*

* Maurer: *Ne quid facias in fine ejus* (litis); ne in fine ejus quid facias, quod tibi haudquaquam salutare aut honorificum sit futurum.

| KING JAMES' VERSION. | HEBREW TEXT. | | REVISED VERSION. | |
|---|---|---|---|---|
| 11 A word fitly spoken *is like* apples of gold in pictures of silver. | תַּפּוּחֵי זָהָב בְּמַשְׂכִּיּוֹת כָּסֶף<br>דָּבָר דָּבֻר עַל־אָפְנָיו׃ | 11 | Apples of gold in gravings of silver,<br>is a word spoken in its season. | 11 |
| 12 *As* an earring of gold, and an ornament of fine gold, *so is* a wise reprover upon an obedient ear. | נֶזֶם זָהָב וַחֲלִי־כָתֶם<br>מוֹכִיחַ חָכָם עַל־אֹזֶן שֹׁמָעַת׃ | 12 | An ear-ring of gold, and a necklace of fine gold,<br>is a wise reprover, to a listening ear. | 12 |
| 13 As the cold of snow in the time of harvest, *so is* a faithful messenger to them that send him: for he refresheth the soul of his masters. | כְּצִנַּת־שֶׁלֶג ׀ בְּיוֹם קָצִיר׃<br>צִיר נֶאֱמָן לְשֹׁלְחָיו<br>וְנֶפֶשׁ אֲדֹנָיו יָשִׁיב׃ | 13 | As the coolness of snow in time of harvest,<br>is a trusty messenger to them that send him;<br>for he restores the spirit of his master. | 13 |
| 14 Whoso boasteth himself of a false gift *is like* clouds and wind without rain. | נְשִׂיאִים וְרוּחַ וְגֶשֶׁם אָיִן<br>אִישׁ מִתְהַלֵּל בְּמַתַּת־שָׁקֶר׃ | 14 | Clouds and wind, and no rain,<br>is a man that boasts of a deceptive gift. | 14 |
| 15 By long forbearing is a prince persuaded, and a soft tongue breaketh the bone. | בְּאֹרֶךְ אַפַּיִם יְפֻתֶּה קָצִין<br>וְלָשׁוֹן רַכָּה תִּשְׁבָּר־גָּרֶם׃ | טו | By long forbearing a prince is persuaded;<br>and the soft tongue will break a bone. | 15 |
| 16 Hast thou found honey? eat so much as is sufficient for thee, lest thou be filled therewith, and vomit it. | דְּבַשׁ מָצָאתָ אֱכֹל דַּיֶּךָּ<br>פֶּן־תִּשְׂבָּעֶנּוּ וַהֲקֵאתוֹ׃ | 16 | Hast thou found honey, eat what suffices thee;<br>lest thou be sated with it, and vomit it up. | 16 |
| 17 Withdraw thy foot from thy neighbour's house; lest he be weary of thee, and *so* hate thee. | הֹקַר רַגְלְךָ מִבֵּית רֵעֶךָ<br>פֶּן־יִשְׂבָּעֲךָ וּשְׂנֵאֶךָ׃ | 17 | Restrain thy foot from the house of thy friend;<br>lest he become weary of thee and hate thee. | 17 |

word is correctly rendered '*evil report*', in the Common Version.

V. 11. *Gravings*, משכיות, in the original sense of *cutting, carving*. The signification, *baskets*, is contrary to etymology and usage.* Old English Versions, *graved work*.

*In* (not '*with*,' Gesenius, De Wette, Ewald) *gravings of silver*. (See Expl. Notes.)

*In its season*, על אפניו (Gesenius, Thes. and Lex. אֹפֶן), as Symmachus, and the Vulgate.† Properly, *its seasons*, which we express by the *collect. sing.* For this form of the *Plur.* with *light suff.*, see Lehrgeb. § 133, VII. 17.

Some (as Bertheau) refer this *Plur.* to the *Sing.* אוֹפָן, *wheel.*‡ But this word has an *immutable Cholem*, and doubles its final radical; and the rendering, *on its wheels* ('quickly spoken'*) gives no pertinent sense.

V. 17. The rendering of the Common Version, '*withdraw thy foot*,' is derived from the Latin Vulgate,† and misrepresents the sacred writer's meaning; for he only enjoins that one should make his visits *rare*‡ (should put restraint on them), not that he should wholly discontinue them.

* Gesenius (Thes. vol. III. p. 1330): Alii, *in calathis argenteis* (Luth. *goldene Aepfel in silbernen Schalen*), coll. شَكِيكَةٌ *sporta fructuaria:* sed משכית non potest referri ad rad. שכך.

Ewald: Die gewöhnliche Uebersetzung, *goldene Aepfel in silbernen Schalen*, lässt sich nicht als richtig denken.

† Symm. ἐν καιρῷ αὐτοῦ. Vulg. *in tempore suo*.

‡ Rosenmüller: Alii *sermonem dictum super rotas suas* volunt esse eum, qui procedit recte, facile, feliciter, quasi rotas haberet. Verum quo minus אָפְנָיו ad אֹפֶן referamus, illud vetat, quod id nomen in Plurali est אֳפַנִּים. Erit igitur ad Singularem אֹפֶן referendum, quod significatu cum harmonicis Arabum افان et ابان comparandum, quæ *tempus opportunum* denotant; unde recte Vulgatus *in tempore suo* interpretatus est.

* Bertheau: *ein rasch gesprochenes treffendes* (?) *Wort*.

† *Substrahe pedem tuum de domo proximi tui*.

‡ Compare the Sept.: σπάνιον εἴσαγε σὸν πόδα πρὸς σεαυτοῦ φίλον.

| KING JAMES' VERSION. | HEBREW TEXT. | | REVISED VERSION. |
|---|---|---|---|
| 18 A man that beareth false witness against his neighbour *is* a maul, and a sword, and a sharp arrow. | מֵפִיץ וְחֶרֶב וְחֵץ שָׁנוּן<br>אִישׁ־עֹנֶה בְרֵעֵהוּ עֵד שָׁקֶר׃ | 18 | A war-club, and a sword, 18<br>and a sharp arrow,<br>is a man that bears false witness against his neighbor. |
| 19 Confidence in an unfaithful man in time of trouble *is like* a broken tooth, and a foot out of joint. | שֵׁן רֹעָה וְרֶגֶל מוּעָדֶת<br>מִבְטָח בּוֹגֵד בְּיוֹם צָרָה׃ | 19 | A broken tooth, and an unsteady foot, 19<br>is trust in the faithless in time of trouble. |
| 20 *As* he that taketh away a garment in cold weather, *and as* vinegar upon nitre, so *is* he that singeth songs to a heavy heart. | מַעֲדֶה־בֶּגֶד ׀ בְּיוֹם קָרָה<br>חֹמֶץ עַל־נָתֶר<br>וְשָׁר בַּשִּׁרִים עַל לֶב־רָע׃ | כ | One that puts off a garment 20<br>in time of cold;<br>vinegar upon nitre;<br>so is he that sings songs to a sad heart! |
| 21 If thine enemy be hungry, give him bread to eat; and if he be thirsty, give him water to drink: | אִם־רָעֵב שֹׂנַאֲךָ הַאֲכִלֵהוּ לָחֶם<br>וְאִם־צָמֵא הַשְׁקֵהוּ מָיִם׃ | 21 | If thy enemy hungers, give 21<br>him bread to eat;<br>and if he thirsts, give him water to drink. |
| 22 For thou shalt heap coals of fire upon his head, and the LORD shall reward thee. | כִּי גֶחָלִים אַתָּה חֹתֶה עַל־רֹאשׁוֹ<br>וַיהוָה יְשַׁלֶּם־לָךְ׃ | 22 | For thou heapest burning coals 22<br>on his head;<br>and Jehovah will requite thee. |
| 23 The north wind driveth away rain: so *doth* an angry countenance a backbiting tongue. | רוּחַ צָפוֹן תְּחוֹלֵל גָּשֶׁם<br>וּפָנִים נִזְעָמִים לְשׁוֹן סָתֶר׃ | 23 | The north wind brings forth 23<br>rain,<br>and a covert tongue an angry countenance. |
| 24 *It is* better to dwell in the corner of the housetop, than with a brawling woman and in a wide house. | טוֹב שֶׁבֶת עַל־פִּנַּת־גָּג<br>מֵאֵשֶׁת מִדְוָנִים וּבֵית חָבֶר׃ | 24 | It is better to dwell in a 24<br>corner of the house-top,<br>than with a brawling woman and a house in common. |
| 25 *As* cold waters to a thirsty soul, so *is* good news from a far country. | מַיִם קָרִים עַל־נֶפֶשׁ עֲיֵפָה<br>וּשְׁמוּעָה טוֹבָה מֵאֶרֶץ מֶרְחָק׃ | כה | Cold water to the fainting 25<br>spirit;<br>so is good news from a far country! |
| 26 A righteous man falling down before the wicked *is as* a troubled fountain, and a corrupt spring. | מַעְיָן נִרְפָּשׂ וּמָקוֹר מָשְׁחָת<br>צַדִּיק מָט לִפְנֵי רָשָׁע׃ | 26 | A fountain trampled, and a 26<br>well defiled,<br>is a righteous man, ready to fall before the wicked. |

V. 19. *An unsteady foot.* The sense is the same, whether (with Gesenius) we regard מועדת as *Kal Part.* (ו, Gram. § 27, *Rem.* 1), or (with Rosenmüller and Ewald, after Kimchi) as *Pual Part.* for מְמוּעֶדֶת, or (with Winer) as a noun, *pes vacillationis.*

V. 20. *So is he,* etc. Lit. *And he;* the *Vav copulative* connecting this act with the two preceding ones, as being a third of the same nature and character as the other two. It may, therefore, be expressed either in connection with the particle of comparison, or by the *copulative* alone, as is done in ch. 27 : 21.

There are but four examples of this structure of the proverb, viz. this verse, v. 25, and chs. 26 : 21, 27 : 21. In all, the וְ might properly be expressed by the simple *copulative;* but this would here, perhaps, be too harsh and unusual a construction in English.

V. 22. *Burning coals* (גחלים), in distinction from פֶּחָם (ch. 26 : 21).

V. 23. *Brings forth:* compare Ps. 90 : 2.* The rendering in the Common Version follows the Vulg. *dissipat pluvias,* for which there is no ground.†

*A covert tongue* (לשון סתר), that seeks a cover or disguise, for some evil purpose, in distinction from one that is open and frank in its utterances. There is a manifest allusion to the etymological meaning of צפון.

V. 24. See the note on ch. 21 : 9.

V. 25. *So is,* etc. See the note on v. 20.

V. 26. מָט, *tottering, ready to fall.* (See Expl. Notes.)

* So the oldest versions: Sept. *ἄνεμος βοῤῥᾶς ἐξεγείρει νέφη.* Chald. בִּטְנָא מִטְרָא. Aquila, *ὠδίνει ὄμβρον.* Syr. ܡܘܠܕܐ ܡܛܪܐ.

† Rosenmüller: Nostro loco intelligendus ille ventus, qui inter aquilonem et occasum flat, Thrascias sive Caurus, qui a Seneca in *Hippol* vs. 1130 *imbrifer* dicitur.

| KING JAMES' VERSION. | HEBREW TEXT. | REVISED VERSION. |
|---|---|---|
| 27 *It is* not good to eat much honey: so *for men* to search their own glory *is not* glory. | 27 אָכֹל דְּבַשׁ הַרְבּוֹת לֹא־טוֹב<br>וְחֵקֶר כְּבֹדָם כָּבוֹד׃ | To eat honey in excess is not good; 27<br>and their searching after honor is not honor. |
| 28 He that *hath* no rule over his own spirit *is like* a city *that is* broken down, *and* without walls. | 28 עִיר פְּרוּצָה אֵין חוֹמָה<br>אִישׁ אֲשֶׁר ׀ אֵין מַעְצָר לְרוּחוֹ׃ | A city broken down, without a wall, 28<br>is a man whose spirit is without restraint. |
| CHAP. XXVI. | CHAP. XXVI. | CHAP. XXVI. |
| As snow in summer, and as rain in harvest, so honour is not seemly for a fool. | א כַּשֶּׁלֶג ׀ בַּקַּיִץ וְכַמָּטָר בַּקָּצִיר<br>כֵּן לֹא־נָאוֶה לִכְסִיל כָּבוֹד׃ | As snow in summer, and rain in harvest, 1<br>so honor is not seemly for a fool. |
| 2 As the bird by wandering, as the swallow by flying, so the curse causeless shall not come. | 2 כַּצִּפּוֹר לָנוּד כַּדְּרוֹר לָעוּף<br>כֵּן קִלְלַת חִנָּם לֹא תָבֹא׃ | As the sparrow in wandering, as the swallow in flying, 2<br>so a curse causeless shall not come. |
| 3 A whip for the horse, a bridle for the ass, and a rod for the fool's back. | 3 שׁוֹט לַסּוּס מֶתֶג לַחֲמוֹר<br>וְשֵׁבֶט לְגֵו כְּסִילִים׃ | A whip for the horse, a bridle for the ass, 3<br>and a rod for the back of fools. |
| 4 Answer not a fool according to his folly, lest thou be also like unto him. | 4 אַל־תַּעַן כְּסִיל כְּאִוַּלְתּוֹ<br>פֶּן־תִּשְׁוֶה־לּוֹ גַם־אָתָּה׃ | Answer not a fool according to his folly, 4<br>lest thou also be like to him. |
| 5 Answer a fool according to his folly, lest he be wise in his own conceit. | ח עֲנֵה כְסִיל כְּאִוַּלְתּוֹ<br>פֶּן־יִהְיֶה חָכָם בְּעֵינָיו׃ | Answer a fool according to his folly, 5<br>lest he become wise in his own eyes. |
| 6 He that sendeth a message by the hand of a fool cutteth off the feet, *and* drinketh damage. | 6 מְקַצֶּה רַגְלַיִם חָמָס שֹׁתֶה<br>שֹׁלֵחַ דְּבָרִים בְּיַד־כְּסִיל׃ | He cuts off the feet, drinks in damage, 6<br>that sends a message by the hand of a fool. |
| 7 The legs of the lame are not equal: so *is* a parable in the mouth of fools. | 7 דַּלְיוּ שֹׁקַיִם מִפִּסֵּחַ<br>וּמָשָׁל בְּפִי כְסִילִים׃ | The legs hang down from the lame; 7<br>so is a proverb in the mouth of fools. |

V. 27. *Is not:* the force of לא continued from the first member (Gram. § 152, 3).

*Their searching after honor* (the *Suff.* referring to the complex idea). So Gesenius, Thes. (art. חקר), and Lex. (art. כבוד).*

This is the proper meaning of the Masoretic punctuation of the common Heb. text. The latter is given in all the Mss. of Kennicott and De Rossi; and the former is confirmed by the reading (כבודם) of fifty-nine of Kennicott's Mss.

The only objection to this rendering, see Gesenius, foot-note (*), is the use of the possess. pron., *their*, without an antecedent. But of this there are other examples,† where the reference naturally and readily suggests itself without being expressed. *Their searching*, viz. of any and all who make the search. There is no occasion, therefore, for the proposed conjectural changes of the Heb. text (Arnoldi and others, more recently Bertheau), without any authority of Mss.

V. 28. Whose spirit (אשר—לרוחו, Gram. § 123, 1).*

Ch. XXVI.—V. 7. *Hang down.* This is the true meaning, whether (with Gesenius, Thes. and Lex. דָּלַל, 1) we regard the Heb. form as = דַּלּוּ, or (with Maurer†) as an irregular punctuation of דליו (Gram. § 75, *Rem.* 4) from דָּלָה.‡ The meaning,

* Thes. vol. I. p. 515: וְחֵקֶר כְּבוֹדָם כָּבוֹד, quæ ad verbum esse possint *et investigatio honoris* i. e. nimium honoris studium (cf. rad. חָקַר Job 28 : 3, et similem usum Job 3 : 21) non est *honor* (negandi particula ex superioribus repetita, v. Lgb. p. 832). Sed molestum est Suffixum in כְּבֹדָם, *etc.*

† As in ch. 20 : 16, *Take his garment when he is surety for an alien.*

* Bertheau: *Eine durchbrochene* (2 Chron. 32 : 5) *Stadt ohne Mauer ist ein Mann dessen Geiste keine Schranke ist.*

† Heb. Hdwbch. (art. דלה): Pl. 3, einmal דַּלְיוּ, Spr. 26 : 7, für דַּלּוּ analog den Fällen bei Ges. § 74, Anm. 4 u. 11.

‡ "But it is easier with R. Judah, R. Jonah, and several Mss. to read דַּלְיוּ i. q. דַּלּוּ from r. דָּלָה" (Gesenius, Lex. דָּלַל, 1, *extr.*).

| KING JAMES' VERSION. | HEBREW TEXT. | | REVISED VERSION. | |
|---|---|---|---|---|
| 8 As he that bindeth a stone in a sling, so *is* he that giveth honour to a fool. | כִּצְרוֹר אֶבֶן בְּמַרְגֵּמָה<br>כֵּן־נוֹתֵן לִכְסִיל כָּבוֹד׃ | 8 | As binding a stone in a sling,<br>so is he that gives honor to a fool. | 8 |
| 9 *As* a thorn goeth up into the hand of a drunkard, so *is* a parable in the mouth of fools. | חוֹחַ עָלָה בְיַד־שִׁכּוֹר<br>וּמָשָׁל בְּפִי כְסִילִים׃ | 9 | A thorn came up into a drunkard's hand;<br>so is a proverb in the mouth of fools. | 9 |
| 10 The great *God* that formed all *things* both rewardeth the fool, and rewardeth transgressors. | רַב מְחוֹלֵל־כֹּל<br>וְשֹׂכֵר כְּסִיל וְשֹׂכֵר עֹבְרִים׃ | י | A master-workman forms all things;<br>but he that hires a fool,<br>is as he that hires passers-by. | 10 |
| 11 As a dog returneth to his vomit, *so* a fool returneth to his folly. | כְּכֶלֶב שָׁב עַל־קֵאוֹ<br>כְּסִיל שׁוֹנֶה בְאִוַּלְתּוֹ׃ | 11 | As a dog returning to his vomit,<br>is a fool repeating his folly. | 11 |
| 12 Seest thou a man wise in his own conceit? *there is* more hope of a fool than of him. | רָאִיתָ אִישׁ חָכָם בְּעֵינָיו<br>תִּקְוָה לִכְסִיל מִמֶּנּוּ׃ | 12 | Seest thou a man wise in his own eyes?<br>there is more hope of a fool than of him. | 12 |
| 13 The slothful *man* saith, *There is* a lion in the way; a lion *is* in the streets. | אָמַר עָצֵל שַׁחַל בַּדָּרֶךְ<br>אֲרִי בֵּין הָרְחֹבוֹת׃ | 13 | The sluggard says, There is a lion in the way;<br>there is a lion in the streets. | 13 |
| 14 *As* the door turneth upon his hinges, so *doth* the slothful upon his bed. | הַדֶּלֶת תִּסּוֹב עַל־צִירָהּ<br>וְעָצֵל עַל־מִטָּתוֹ׃ | 14 | The door turns on its hinge,<br>and the sluggard on his couch. | 14 |
| 15 The slothful hideth his hand in *his* bosom; it grieveth him to bring it again to his mouth. | טָמַן עָצֵל יָדוֹ בַּצַּלָּחַת<br>נִלְאָה לַהֲשִׁיבָהּ אֶל־פִּיו׃ | טו | The sluggard hides his hand in the dish;<br>it wearies him to bring it back to his mouth. | 15 |
| 16 The sluggard *is* wiser in his own conceit than seven men that can render a reason. | חָכָם עָצֵל בְּעֵינָיו<br>מִשִּׁבְעָה מְשִׁיבֵי טָעַם׃ | 16 | The sluggard is wiser in his own eyes,<br>than seven men that can render a reason. | 16 |
| 17 He that passeth by, *and* meddleth with strife *belonging* not to him, *is like* one that taketh a dog by the ears. | מַחֲזִיק בְּאָזְנֵי־כָלֶב<br>עֹבֵר מִתְעַבֵּר עַל־רִיב לֹּא־לוֹ׃ | 17 | He lays hold of a dog by the ears<br>who, passing by, gets angry in a quarrel that is not his. | 17 |
| 18 As a mad *man* who casteth fire-brands, arrows, and death, | כְּמִתְלַהְלֵהַּ הַיֹּרֶה זִקִּים חִצִּים<br>וָמָוֶת׃ | 18 | As a madman that hurls fiery darts, arrows, and death; | 18 |

*take away* (Bertheau, Stuart, and others), does not follow from the signification *to draw out* (as from a well), fig. *to deliver*.

V. 8. *As binding a stone in a sling.* So the Sept., *he who binds a stone in a sling*, and also (for the only word in dispute) the Syr., *as a stone in a sling.** So Ewald† and Bertheau.

V. 10. *A master-workman:* רַב (Thes. and Lex., 2, d), one who is a *master* in his art.‡ Others (on uncertain grounds, see the writer's note on Job 16 : 13) *an arrow*, or *an archer*.

Third member. The *Vav* connects the subject of this member with that of the preceding one, as being both of the same class (comp. the remark on ch. 25 : 20). Hirzel: *But he who hires a fool, is as he who hires vagrants.**

V. 17. *Lays hold of* expresses the proper force of מחזיק ב, to grasp with a firm hand, to hold fast, as in Job 8 : 15, and (metaph.) 2 : 3, 27 : 6.*

V. 18. *A madman* (מתלהלה): as shown by Gesenius, Thes. vol. II. p. 744. Bertheau, *a foolish jester* (Stuart, *a silly jester*), on an uncertain etymology, without any historical support. Moreover, he who *hurls fiery darts, arrows, and death*, is somewhat more in earnest than 'a silly jester.'

* Sept. ὃς ἀποδεσμεύει λίθον ἐν σφενδόνῃ (where ἀπὸ adds the idea of holding back *from* the object aimed at, by binding the missile fast). Syr. ܐܝܟ ܟܐܦܐ ܒܩܠܥܐ.

† Der Sinn des Spruches ist höchst klar, und schon die LXX haben ihn richtig gefasst. מרגמה ist unstreitig *Schleuder*, von رجم *schleudern*.

‡ Gesenius, Thes. 1. p. 453: *magister creat omnia* (opp. qui stultum conducit, conducit transeuntes); i. e. artifex peritus omnia bene perficit, *ein Meister bringt Alles zu Stande*.

* The use of על (in the second member) is owing to the figurative form of the conception (*poured himself out*) upon, or *over*.

| KING JAMES' VERSION. | HEBREW TEXT. | REVISED VERSION. |
|---|---|---|
| 19 So *is* the man *that* deceiveth his neighbour, and saith, Am not I in sport? | כֵּן־אִישׁ רִמָּה אֶת־רֵעֵהוּ<br>וְאָמַר הֲלֹא־מְשַׂחֵק אָנִי׃ 19 | so is a man that deceives his neighbor, 19<br>and says, Am not I in sport? |
| 20 Where no wood is, *there* the fire goeth out: so where *there is* no talebearer, the strife ceaseth. | בְּאֶפֶס עֵצִים תִּכְבֶּה־אֵשׁ<br>וּבְאֵין נִרְגָּן יִשְׁתֹּק מָדוֹן׃ כ | Where there is no more wood, 20<br>the fire goes out;<br>and where there is no tale-bearer, contention ceases. |
| 21 *As* coals *are* to burning coals, and wood to fire; so *is* a contentious man to kindle strife. | פֶּחָם לְגֶחָלִים וְעֵצִים לְאֵשׁ<br>וְאִישׁ מִדְוָנִים לְחַרְחַר־רִיב׃ 21 | A coal to burning coals, and 21<br>wood to fire;<br>so is a contentious man to the kindling of strife. |
| 22 The words of a talebearer *are* as wounds, and they go down into the innermost parts of the belly. | דִּבְרֵי נִרְגָּן כְּמִתְלַהֲמִים<br>וְהֵם יָרְדוּ חַדְרֵי־בָטֶן׃ 22 | The words of a tale-bearer are 22<br>as dainty morsels;<br>and it is they that go down to the inmost parts of the belly. |
| 23 Burning lips and a wicked heart *are like* a potsherd covered with silver dross. | כֶּסֶף סִיגִים מְצֻפֶּה עַל־חָרֶשׂ<br>שְׂפָתַיִם דֹּלְקִים וְלֶב־רָע׃ 23 | Dross-silver, spread over pot- 23<br>tery,<br>are ardent lips and an evil heart. |
| 24 He that hateth dissembleth with his lips, and layeth up deceit within him; | בִּשְׂפָתוֹ יִנָּכֵר שׂוֹנֵא<br>וּבְקִרְבּוֹ יָשִׁית מִרְמָה׃ 24 | He that hates dissembles with 24<br>his lips;<br>but in his breast he lays up deceit. |
| 25 When he speaketh fair, believe him not: for *there are* seven abominations in his heart. | כִּי־יְחַנֵּן קוֹלוֹ אַל־תַּאֲמֶן־בּוֹ<br>כִּי שֶׁבַע תּוֹעֵבוֹת בְּלִבּוֹ׃ כה | When he makes his voice gra- 25<br>cious, believe him not;<br>for seven abominations are in his heart. |
| 26 *Whose* hatred is covered by deceit, his wickedness shall be shewed before the *whole* congregation. | תִּכַּסֶּה שִׂנְאָה בְּמַשָּׁאוֹן<br>תִּגָּלֶה רָעָתוֹ בְקָהָל׃ 26 | Hatred covers itself with de- 26<br>ception;<br>his wickedness will be disclosed in the congregation. |
| 27 Whoso diggeth a pit shall fall therein: and he that rolleth a stone, it will return upon him. | כֹּרֶה שַׁחַת בָּהּ יִפֹּל<br>וְגֹלֵל אֶבֶן אֵלָיו תָּשׁוּב׃ 27 | He that digs a pit shall fall 27<br>therein;<br>and he that rolls a stone, it shall return upon him. |
| | V. 24. בשפתיו ק׳ | |

V. 20. *No more:* אפס, prop. a *cessation,* or *end;* when the supply ceases, is meant.

V. 21, second member; compare (on וְ) the note on ch. 25 : 20, and the same usage in ch. 27 : 21.

V. 22. Zöckler translates (Lange's Bibelwerk, Am. ed.): "The words of a slanderer are words of sport." So Bertheau, after C. B. Michaelis (Annott. uber.) followed by Stuart and others. But the words of a slanderer are not commonly looked upon as "words of sport," either in his intention, or in their effect. For this rendering there is no better support than the assumed identity in meaning of לחח (26 : 10) and לחם.

The only thing reasonably certain, on philological grounds, is the Arabic usage (see on ch. 18 : 8) on which Schultens and Gesenius base their definition of the Heb. word. Ewald's objection, that the corresponding form in Arabic has an active and not a passive sense, is not decisive against it; the verbal idea being variously modified, in different dialects, by variations of form in expressing it.

That the words of the tale-bearer (or slanderer) are to many "as dainty morsels," is too sadly attested in human experience.

V. 23. *Dross-silver* (כֶּסֶף סיגים): silver that is not freed from its impurities, unrefined silver; not *silver dross,* which is another thing, and is not the meaning of the combination, *silver of dross.**

V. 25. The English form, "*when he speaks fair,*" does not give the true meaning (referring rather to *matter* than *manner*), and falls far below the descriptive power of the Hebrew expression.

V. 26. *Covers itself* (תכסה, Hithp.; Ges. Gram. § 54, 2, b, Ewald Lehrb. 8th ed. § 124, 2, e, Böttcher Lehrb. § 291, *β*, § 1014, 2 †), not *is covered,* as renderd by Umbreit and many others in which the graphic force of the expression is lost. *Covers itself;* puts on this disguise.‡

* *Schlackensilber* (Umbreit, Ewald). כֶּסֶף סיגים ist das Silber, welches noch nicht von den Schlacken gereinigt worden (Umbreit).

† Est Hithp. pro תתכסה, cf. הכונן pro התכונן (Maurer)

‡ Tegit se odium simulatione (Maurer).

| KING JAMES' VERSION. | HEBREW TEXT. | | REVISED VERSION. | |
|---|---|---|---|---|
| 28 A lying tongue hateth *those that are* afflicted by it; and a flattering mouth worketh ruin. | לְשׁוֹן־שֶׁקֶר יִשְׂנָא דַכָּיו<br>וּפֶה חָלָק יַעֲשֶׂה מִדְחֶה׃ | 28 | A false tongue hates its victims;<br>and a smooth mouth will work ruin. | 28 |
| CHAP. XXVII. | CHAP. XXVII. | | CHAP. XXVII. | |
| BOAST not thyself of to-morrow; for thou knowest not what a day may bring forth. | אַל־תִּתְהַלֵּל בְּיוֹם מָחָר<br>כִּי לֹא־תֵדַע מַה־יֵּלֶד יוֹם׃ | א | MAKE not thy boast of to-morrow;<br>for thou knowest not what a day may bring forth. | 1 |
| 2 Let another man praise thee, and not thine own mouth; a stranger, and not thine own lips. | יְהַלֶּלְךָ זָר וְלֹא־פִיךָ<br>נָכְרִי וְאַל־שְׂפָתֶיךָ׃ | 2 | Let an alien praise thee, and not thine own mouth;<br>a stranger, and not thine own lips. | 2 |
| 3 A stone *is* heavy, and the sand weighty; but a fool's wrath *is* heavier than them both. | כֹּבֶד אֶבֶן וְנֵטֶל הַחוֹל<br>וְכַעַס אֱוִיל כָּבֵד מִשְּׁנֵיהֶם׃ | 3 | A stone is heavy, and the sand is weighty;<br>but a fool's anger is heavier than both of them. | 3 |
| 4 Wrath *is* cruel, and anger *is* outrageous; but who *is* able to stand before envy? | אַכְזְרִיּוּת חֵמָה וְשֶׁטֶף אָף<br>וּמִי יַעֲמֹד לִפְנֵי קִנְאָה׃ | 4 | Wrath is cruel, and anger is impetuous;<br>but who can stand before jealousy? | 4 |
| 5 Open rebuke *is* better than secret love. | טוֹבָה תּוֹכַחַת מְגֻלָּה<br>מֵאַהֲבָה מְסֻתָּרֶת׃ | ה | Better is open rebuke,<br>than secret love. | 5 |
| 6 Faithful *are* the wounds of a friend; but the kisses of an enemy *are* deceitful. | נֶאֱמָנִים פִּצְעֵי אוֹהֵב<br>וְנַעְתָּרוֹת נְשִׁיקוֹת שׂוֹנֵא׃ | 6 | Faithful are the wounds of a friend;<br>and plentiful are the kisses of an enemy. | 6 |
| 7 The full soul loatheth a honey-comb; but to the hungry soul every bitter thing is sweet. | נֶפֶשׁ שְׂבֵעָה תָּבוּס נֹפֶת<br>וְנֶפֶשׁ רְעֵבָה כָּל־מַר מָתוֹק׃ | 7 | A sated spirit tramples the dripping honey;<br>but a famished spirit—every bitter thing is sweet. | 7 |

V. 28. *A false tongue hates;* לשון construed as *masc.*, as in Ps. 22 : 16; here perhaps (as suggested by Gesenius, lex. s. v.) by "metonomy for a lying person."*

*Its victims:* literally, *its crushed ones;* the proper passive sense of דך, as in the other three passages (Pss. 9 : 10, 10 : 18, 74 : 21) where it occurs. So Umbreit (correctly as to form, *ihre Zerriebenen*), Rosenmüller (*contritos suos*), Bertheau (*ihre Zermalmten*). Gesenius (Thes. and Lex.) assumes here an active signification, "crushing, *i. e.* chastising; *a lying tongue* (person) *hateth them that chastise it.*" This is not only contrary to usage,† but seems quite unnecessary; for the usual meaning yields a more pointed and significant sense, and one which common observation approves.‡ There seems, therefore, to be no difficulty to be evaded by change of reading or punctuation, as Ewald and Böttcher propose.

* Fürst, Hdwbch: masc. Ps. 22 : 16, und Spr. 26 : 28 nach besonderer Auffassung.

† Sed דך alias constanter passive *attritum, oppressum* significare constat (Rosenmüller).

‡ Compare Miss Seward's celebrated retort on Dr. Johnson: "Sir, this is an instance, that we are always most violent against those whom we have injured."

Ch. XXVII.—V. 2. *An alien:* see the note on ch. 20 : 16, second paragraph; and for the point of the admonition see Explanatory Notes.——*Another* is less pertinent in connection with נכרי in the other member, (comp. ch. 20 : 16), and gives a less pointed sense.

V. 4. *Impetuous* (שטף), like an overflowing flood, or a rushing torrent.—*Jealousy* (קנאה) is the meaning here, as in ch. 6 : 34.

V. 6. *Plentiful*, a sense grounded in Heb. usage; see Ezek. 35 : 13, and Maurer's just reduction (Comment. and Hdwbch.) of all the uses of the verb to one radical signification. For the rendering *deceitful*, only Arabic usage can be cited; and it is hardly necessary to say, that an enemy's kisses are *deceitful*, though he may be very *profuse* in such tokens of pretended friendship.*

V. 7. *Spirit:* the vital spirit, *anima*, as in chs. 6 : 30, 10 : 3, 25 : 25; to which "is ascribed whatever has respect to the sustenance of life by food and drink" (Gesenius, Heb. lex., נפש). "Here the English version often renders it by *soul*, but improperly" (Robinson, *ibidem*).

* Bertheau: נעתרות, deutlich nicht von ... عثر, wiewohl diesem Worte der Begriff des Täuschens eignet, da an كثر *reichlich sein* zu denken näher liegt.

KING JAMES' VERSION.

8 As a bird that wandereth from her nest, so *is* a man that wandereth from his place.

9 Ointment and perfume rejoice the heart: so *doth* the sweetness of a man's friend by hearty counsel.

10 Thine own friend, and thy father's friend, forsake not; neither go into thy brother's house in the day of thy calamity: *for* better *is* a neighbour *that is* near than a brother far off.

11 My son, be wise, and make my heart glad, that I may answer him that reproacheth me.

12 A prudent *man* foreseeth the evil, and hideth himself; *but* the simple pass on, *and* are punished.

13 Take his garment that is surety for a stranger, and take a pledge of him for a strange woman.

14 He that blesseth his friend with a loud voice, rising early in the morning, it shall be counted a curse to him.

HEBREW TEXT.

8 כְּצִפּוֹר נוֹדֶדֶת מִן־קִנָּהּ
כֵּן אִישׁ נוֹדֵד מִמְּקוֹמוֹ׃

9 שֶׁמֶן וּקְטֹרֶת יְשַׂמַּח־לֵב
וּמֶתֶק רֵעֵהוּ מֵעֲצַת־נָפֶשׁ׃

י רֵעֲךָ ׀ וְרֵעַה אָבִיךָ אַל־תַּעֲזֹב
וּבֵית אָחִיךָ אַל־תָּבוֹא בְּיוֹם אֵידֶךָ
טוֹב שָׁכֵן קָרוֹב מֵאָח רָחוֹק׃

11 חֲכַם בְּנִי וְשַׂמַּח לִבִּי
וְאָשִׁיבָה חֹרְפִי דָבָר׃

12 עָרוּם ׀ רָאָה רָעָה נִסְתָּר
פְּתָאִים עָבְרוּ נֶעֱנָשׁוּ׃

13 קַח־בִּגְדוֹ כִּי־עָרַב זָר
וּבְעַד נָכְרִיָּה חַבְלֵהוּ׃

14 מְבָרֵךְ רֵעֵהוּ ׀ בְּקוֹל גָּדוֹל
בַּבֹּקֶר הַשְׁכֵּים
קְלָלָה תֵּחָשֶׁב לוֹ׃

V. 10. יתיר ה׳

REVISED VERSION.

As a bird wandering from her nest, 8
so is a man that wanders from his place.

Oil and perfume gladden the heart; 9
but sweeter is one's friend than fragrant wood.

Thy friend and thy father's friend do not forsake; 10
and do not go to thy brother's house in the day of thy calamity;
better is a neighbor near than a brother afar off.

Be wise, my son, and make my heart glad; 11
that I may answer him that reproaches me.

The shrewd saw evil, he hid himself; 12
the simple passed on,——they were punished.

Take his garment, when he is surety for an alien; 13
and for a strange woman, take a pledge of him.

He that blesses his neighbor with loud voice, 14
rising early in the morning,
it shall be accounted to him as cursing,

V. 9. *One's friend:* indefinite use of the *suff. pron.*; his friend, for the friend one has.* Compare its use in an assumed or supposed case, ch. 20: 16, *Take his garment, when he is surety for an alien.* The principle applicable to אדוני is misapplied by Böttcher Heb. Lehrb. § 876, c, (as referred to by Dr. Aiken on this passage, Lange's Bible-work, Am. ed.), and Exeget. Krit. Aehrenlese, 3te Abth. p. 29, to this case and to some others, which are readily explained, either in conformity with the proper use of the *suff. pron.*, or on the ground of a somewhat careless freedom in its reference.

*Fragrant wood:* עצה, as in Jer. 6 : 6: נפש, as in Is. 3 : 20.† Others understand by עצת נפש *counsel of the soul;* either the friend's counsel, proceeding from the soul, sincere and kindly (Ewald, *doch Freundes Süsse stammt aus Seelenrath;* Bertheau, *und Süsse seines Freundes aus Rathschluss der Seele* erfreut das Herz; Böttcher, Aehrenlese, 3te Abth. p. 29, *Süssigkeit seines Freundes*=Süsses vom Freunde [ist ihm] *Rath der seele,* d. i. sorglicher, eifriger, wohlgemeinter Rath, — מִ partitive); or, counsel of one's own soul (Lange, *und Süssigkeit des Freundes ist besser als Rath der* [eignen] *Seele*).

In neither of these constructions does the sentiment of the 2d member appear very just or pointed in itself, or to have any proper relation to the preceding member. On the contrary, the sentiment expressed in the text is both just and pointed, and is pertinent in its relation to the first member. Compare Explanatory Notes.

V. 10. רעה, pointed for the *Qeri;* here the full form, Ges. Gram. § 85, V. 11.

V. 12. Compare the note on ch. 22 : 3. The reader will observe here the more spirited expression of the sense by the *asyndote* construction.

The word ערום should be carefully distinguished from those expressing the more generic idea of *wisdom, prudence.* See the remarks on ch. 1 : 4.

V. 13. Compare the note on ch. 20 : 16.

V. 14. השכים, *infin. abs.* as adverbial accusative (Ges. Gram. § 131, 2)=with rising early.

* Ewald (*in loc.*): *die Süsse seines Freundes,* des Freundes den man hat So Bertheau, Elster, Kamphausen, and others.

† Gesenius (Thes. vol. II. p. 1057): עֵצָה .. collect. *ligna* i. q. עֵצִים, de materia Jer. 6 : 6, de lignis odoratis (עצת נפש) Prov. 27 : 9. Fürst (Heb. Hdwbch): *coll.* s. v. a. עצים *Holz* Jer. 6 : 6. . . . Spr 27 : 9 (die liebliche Rede der Freundschaft ist) *mehr als Holz des Wohlgeruchs.*

| KING JAMES' VERSION. | HEBREW TEXT. | REVISED VERSION. |
|---|---|---|
| 15 A continual dropping in a very rainy day and a contentious woman are alike. | טו דֶּלֶף טוֹרֵד בְּיוֹם סַגְרִיר<br>וְאֵשֶׁת מִדְוָנִים נִשְׁתָּוָה׃ | A continual dripping in a time of heavy rain, 15<br>and a contentious woman, are alike. |
| 16 Whosoever hideth her hideth the wind, and the ointment of his right hand, *which* bewrayeth *itself*. | 16 צֹפְנֶיהָ צָפַן־רוּחַ<br>וְשֶׁמֶן יְמִינוֹ יִקְרָא׃ | He that confines her confines the wind, 16<br>and his right hand encounters oil. |
| | V. 15. מדינים ק׳ | |

V. 15. Compare (on דלף טורד) the note on ch. 19 : 13. נשתוה, *Nithp.* of שָׁוָה, as shown by Rödiger, Thes. fasc. poster. p. 1376. Compare Addenda, p. 114, where he examines Hitzig's suggestion, that it is a Niphal form (for נשותה) 3d pers. sing. fem. Ewald (*in loc.* and Lehrb. 8th ed. § 132, c, d) regards it as a blending of two forms, by prefixing the characteristic of *Niph.* to that of *Hithp.* (נשתוה *sich ausgleichen*) and translates, *das gleicht sich aus.*

V. 16. *He that:* צפניה, *plur.* construed distributively with a sing. verb ; Gesenius, Lehrgeb. § 184, *a*, Gram. § 146, 4 ; comp ch. 3 : 18,—*Confines* (Gesenius, Lex., and Fürst, Hdwbch.) is more suited to this connection than the signification *hides.** The object is not to *hide* a contentious woman, but to restrain her violence.

Second member. Nonnihil difficilis, as was said by Mercer three hundred years ago, and the case is little better now.† The following are possible constructions and renderings of this clause :

1. שמן may be (a) *accus.* after צפן implied from the first member, or (b) *nom.* to יקרא, or (c) *accus.* after it.

2. ימינו may be (a) *gen.* after שמן, or (b) *nom.* to יקרא, or (c) *accus.* after it.

3. יקרא may have for its *nom.* (a) the subject of צפן in the first member, or (b) שמן, or (c) may stand in a relative clause.

4. יקרא may mean (a) *calls for*, (b) *proclaims*, (c) *meets, encounters* (=יקרה), or (d) *grasps*, or *grasps after* (as assumed).

Hence the following renderings :

1. No. 1, b, *and the oil of his right hand will proclaim* (itself) ‡

2. No. 1, a, with 2, a, and 3, c, *and* [hides] *the oil of his right hand, which proclaims* (by its fragrance betrays) itself. §

3. No. 2, b, with 4, c, *and his right hand meets oil* (which it cannot hold fast, and he labors in vain) ||

4. No. 3, a, with 1, c, *and shall call for the oil of his right hand.**

5. No. 2, b, with 4, d, and 1, c, *and his right hand grasps after oil.*†

6. No. 2, b, with 4, a, and 1, c, *and his right hand calls for oil,*—as a medicament, for healing his bruises.‡

In Nos. 1 and 2, the distinction of the *right* hand is without significance. Nos. 3 and 5 are essentially the same. The latter is not translation, as the meaning *to grasp, to grasp after,* does not belong to קרא (קרה),§ and is only assumed here as the intent of the act expressed by the Heb. verb (*meeting*, for the purpose of holding). Zöckler || can only say in behalf of this rendering : "grasps after something, meets a thing, . . . seeks to hold something fast ;" which is far from justifying it as a translation.

No aid can be obtained from the ancient versions, none of which represent the Heb. text.¶

It cannot be disguised, that some disappointment is felt in reading the second member. The first spontaneously, and almost of necessity, suggests the idea of rude violence, in the resistless force of the wind ; in the second, this image is exchanged for the soft and smoothly gliding oil (compare ch. 5 : 3, and Ps. 55 : 21), or even for its subtile fragrance ; a marked anticlimax. If to escape this, we correct our impression of the first member, and understand by " the wind " an element so fine and subtile as to

* Berthеau : *Jeder der solches Weib birgt, birgt Wind.*

† Auch die neueren Ausleger finden hier grosse Schwierigkeit, und gehen vielfach auseinander (Umbreit).

‡ Pagnino (Thes. Heb. 1529) : *oleum* (aut *unguentum*) *dextræ suæ prædicabit.* Seb. Münster (Biblia Heb. 1546) : *et oleum de dextra ejus clamabit.* Vatablus : quod se suo odore velut clamore prodet (annotation).

§ Mercer (Comment. in Prov. Sal., 1573) : abscondit *unguentum dextræ suæ, quod clamat ;* quasi dicat : Perinde est ac si unguentum quo dextram suam perfudit, occultare vellet, quod suo se ipsum odore prodit, ac velut clamat, ut latere non possit (in his annotations). So Rosenmüller, and the common English version.

|| Ewald, Hirzel. Hitzig. So also Stuart (but with a different application), *cometh upon oil*, which makes the object so slippery that it cannot be held fast.

* Rabbi Isaac Eichel (1790), as quoted by Rosenmüller *in locum : sed oleum* (i. e. medullam, vim) *dexteræ suæ advocet ;* i. e. rixosae mulieris os verberibus esse compescendum.

† Umbreit : *und seine Rechte fasst nach Oel.* So Elster, Bertheau, Zöckler (Lange's Bibelwerk, Am. ed. *and his right hand grasps after oil*), Kamphausen (Bunsen's Bibelwerk).

‡ Maurer : *et oleum dextra ejus provocat,* arcessit . . . i. e. ejus dextra brevi se sentiet unguibus laceratam rixosae mulieris ; oleo enim mitigantur vulnera (Jes. 1 : 6).

§ Quod קרא nusquam significat (Maurer).

|| Greift nach etwas, begegnet einer Sache . . . sucht etwas festzuhalten.

¶ The Versio Veneta (ed. Villoison) verbally conforms to it : *καὶ ἔλαιον δεξιᾶς αὐτοῦ καλέσει.*

The following are the renderings of the old English versions. Coverdale, Matthews, Cranmer, and Taverner : *He that refraineth her refraineth the wind, and holdeth oil fast in his hand.* (Cranmer, *the oil*). Genevan : *He that hideth her hideth the wind, and* [she is as] *the oil in his right hand, that uttereth itself.* Bishops' : *He that stilleth her stilleth the wind, and stoppeth the smell of the ointment in his hand.*

| KING JAMES' VERSION. | | HEBREW TEXT. | REVISED VERSION. | |
|---|---|---|---|---|
| 17 Iron sharpeneth iron; so a man sharpeneth the countenance of his friend. | 17 | בַּרְזֶל בְּבַרְזֶל יָחַד<br>וְאִישׁ יַחַד פְּנֵי־רֵעֵהוּ׃ | Iron is sharpened on iron;<br>and a man sharpens the face of his fellow. | 17 |
| 18 Whoso keepeth the fig tree shall eat the fruit thereof: so he that waiteth on his master shall be honoured. | 18 | נֹצֵר תְּאֵנָה יֹאכַל פִּרְיָהּ<br>וְשֹׁמֵר אֲדֹנָיו יְכֻבָּד׃ | He that keeps a fig-tree shall eat its fruit;<br>and he who regards his master shall be honored. | 18 |
| 19 As in water face *answereth* to face, so the heart of man to man. | 19 | כַּמַּיִם הַפָּנִים לַפָּנִים<br>כֵּן לֵב הָאָדָם לָאָדָם׃ | As face to face in water,<br>so is the heart of man to man. | 19 |
| 20 Hell and destruction are never full: so the eyes of man are never satisfied. | כ | שְׁאוֹל וַאֲבַדֹּה לֹא תִשְׂבַּעְנָה<br>וְעֵינֵי הָאָדָם לֹא תִשְׂבַּעְנָה׃ | The underworld and destruction are not satisfied;<br>and the eyes of man are not satisfied. | 20 |
| 21 *As* the fining pot for silver, and the furnace for gold, so *is* a man to his praise. | 21 | מַצְרֵף לַכֶּסֶף וְכוּר לַזָּהָב<br>וְאִישׁ לְפִי מַהֲלָלוֹ׃ | A refining pot for silver, and a furnace for gold;<br>so is a man to the mouth that praises him. | 21 |
| 22 Though thou shouldest bray a fool in a mortar among wheat with a pestle, *yet* will not his foolishness depart from him. | 22 | אִם־תִּכְתּוֹשׁ אֶת־הָאֱוִיל ׀ בַּמַּכְתֵּשׁ<br>בְּתוֹךְ הָרִיפוֹת בַּעֱלִי<br>לֹא־תָסוּר מֵעָלָיו אִוַּלְתּוֹ׃ | Though thou shouldst bray a fool in the mortar,<br>among the pounded grain with a pestle,<br>his folly will not depart from him. | 22 |
| | | V. 20. ואבדון ק' | | |

elude any attempt at repression, we then lose altogether the image of a "contentious," woman, in one whose gentle persistence is irresistible.

Maurer objects to the renderings given by others, as weak, or forced, or unmeaning.* His own (see above, as quoted in the foot-note on No. 6), implies more than is pleasant to admit. To the rendering of Eichel (No. 4) Rosenmüller objects, that שמן does not express *force;* which may possibly be true in such a connection as this. But with the stem שמן, in several of its forms, is connected the idea of physical force; as of a well-fed ox, Is. 10 : 27, *the yoke is broken off by reason of fatness*, of lusty strength;† of well-nourished men, strong and robust, Judges 3 : 29, common English version, "all *lusty* " (Vulgate, *robustos*); ‡ Ps. 78 : 31, *their stout ones*=the stoutest of them.§

V. 17. *Iron is sharpened on iron.* So Gesenius, Thes. and Lex.‖ Rödiger, to the same effect (with a different construction of the first verb*): *Iron one sharpens on iron, and a man sharpens*, etc.

V. 19. *As—in water* (כמים), *accus.* of place; Gesenius, Gram. § 118, 1, *b*, and Rem. *a*.

V. 21. How the terms in the second member are related to each other seems quite clearly settled by the relation of the "refining pot" to "silver," and of "the furnace" to "gold," in the first. For this reason Gesenius (Thes. Vol. I. p. 382†) justly objects to all constructions which do not recognize this relation, taking לפי here in the sense of *according to.* So, with many others, Eichel, Böttcher (Proben alttest. Schrifterkl. and Neue Aehrenl.), Zöckler (Lange's Bibelwerk). The latter translates and explains thus (Am. ed.): "*The fining pot is for silver and the furnace for gold, But man according to his glorying;* that is, one is judged according to the standard of that of which he makes his boast." Böttcher: "One is known by that which he praises in himself, or in other persons and things, for that shows his inclinations and tendencies." Stuart, understanding by "praise" the praise of others: "*So is a man in respect to his praise;* a man's praise will disclose his true character. Praise is apt to puff up men, and make them self-conceited. If it does, or does not, in either alternative it makes their true character known."

It must be admitted that, in either of these views, the expectation raised by the first member is hardly realized in the second. That a man is judged by that of which he boasts or which he

* Superiorum interpretationes aliæ jejunæ, contortæ aliæ, aliæ omni carentes sensu.

† Gesenius, Lex. שמן, *and the yoke* (of Israel) *is broken from fatness*, the figure being taken from a fat ox, which breaks and casts off his yoke." Fürst (Hdwbch. s. v.) *und abgeschüttelt wird das Joch vom Gesichte* (Kopfe) *des starken Thieres.*

‡ Fürst (Hdwbch. שָׁמֵן) kräftig. Bachmann (Buch der Richter), fett, d. i. vollsaftig, wohlgenährt, starke, . . . Männer von strotzender Körperkraft.

§ Fürst (Hdwbch. מִשְׁמָן) *die Starken, . . . kräftige Jugend.* Gesenius (Lex. s. v.) "*fat ones*, i. e. stout, robust warriors."

‖ Thes. חדד, *Hiph.*; *ferrum acuitur in ferro, et vir acuit vultum*, i. e. obtutum, aciem mentis et ingenii *socii sui.*

* Append. to Thes. p. 88. Prov. locum verto: *ferrum acuit aliquis in ferro. et vir acuit*, etc. Pg. 6 (Index gram. et analyt.), ego malim scribi יַחַד fut. Hiph. rad. חדד, *acuit* (aliquis).

† Quem [sententiarum parallelismum] negligunt quicunque לפי h. l. *pro ratione* reddunt.

KING JAMES' VERSION.

23 Be thou diligent to know the state of thy flocks, *and* look well to thy herds:

24 For riches *are* not for ever: and doth the crown *endure* to every generation?

25 The hay appeareth, and the tender grass sheweth itself, and herbs of the mountains are gathered.

26 The lambs *are* for thy clothing, and the goats *are* the price of the field.

27 And *thou shalt have* goats' milk enough for thy food, for the food of thy household, and *for* the maintenance for thy maidens.

CHAP. XXVIII.

THE wicked flee when no man pursueth: but the righteous are bold as a lion.

2 For the transgression of a land many *are* the princes thereof: but by a man of understanding *and* knowledge the state *thereof* shall be prolonged.

HEBREW TEXT.

23 יָדֹעַ תֵּדַע פְּנֵי צֹאנֶךָ
שִׁית לִבְּךָ לַעֲדָרִים׃
24 כִּי לֹא לְעוֹלָם חֹסֶן
וְאִם־נֵזֶר לְדוֹר ׀ דוֹר׃
כה נִגְלָה חָצִיר וְנִרְאָה־דֶשֶׁא
וְנֶאֶסְפוּ עִשְּׂבוֹת הָרִים׃
26 כְּבָשִׂים לִלְבוּשֶׁךָ
וּמְחִיר שָׂדֶה עַתּוּדִים׃
27 וְדֵי ׀ חֲלֵב עִזִּים לְלַחְמְךָ
לְלֶחֶם בֵּיתֶךָ
וְחַיִּים לְנַעֲרוֹתֶיךָ׃

CHAP. XXVIII.

א נָסוּ וְאֵין־רֹדֵף רָשָׁע
וְצַדִּיקִים כִּכְפִיר יִבְטָח׃
2 בְּפֶשַׁע אֶרֶץ רַבִּים שָׂרֶיהָ
וּבְאָדָם מֵבִין יֹדֵעַ כֵּן יַאֲרִיךְ׃

V. 24. ודור ק׳

REVISED VERSION.

Look well to the appearance of 23
thy flock;
give heed to the herds.
For wealth is not forever, 24
nor is a crown to generation
and generation.
The hay is gone, and the ten- 25
der grass appears,
and the mountain herbs are
gathered.
There are lambs for thy cloth- 26
ing;
and he-goats, the worth of a
field;
and goats' milk enough for thy 27
food,
for the food of thy house,
and sustenance for thy maidens.

CHAP. XXVIII.

THE wicked flee, when no 1
one pursues;
but the righteous are bold as
the young lion.
When a land revolts, its 2
princes are many;
but, with discerning and knowing men, there may be permanence.

V. 24. And is a crown to generation and generation?

commends, and how a man bears praise, has little resemblance to the effect of the refining pot and the furnace. Their office is to separate the dross from the genuine metal. With this accords the construction of the second member adopted from Schultens by Gesenius; and it admits of two applications, for which see Explanatory Notes.

V. 24. אם, a form of asseveration; Gesenius, lex., C, 1, c, Fürst, lex, 1, d. So Bertheau,* Ewald† According to others (Rosenmüller, Umbreit, Maurer, Kamphausen, Zöckler) a particle of interrogation.

V. 25. *The hay* (חציר, as distinguished from דשא), grass full grown, and ready for mowing.—*The tender grass* (דשא) as it first shoots up from the root (Gen. 1:11) springing out of the earth under the warm sun after a shower (2 Sam. 23:4). The use of both elsewhere in the general sense of *grass* is entirely consistent with the distinction made here, where the two are contrasted.

Ch. XXVIII.—V. 1. יבטח may be taken as the distributive *sing.* after a *plur.* subject (as in ch. 3:18) with reference to each individual of the number (Ges. Gr. § 146, 4). But the form, *are as a young lion is bold*, is a correct Heb. construction (though it cannot be retained in English), and expresses the same sense. There is no necessity for making יבטח a relative clause, as is done by Ewald and Zöckler.

V. 2. Whether we read (as in the Masoretic text) *in the rebellion of a land*, or with Hitzig בְּפֶשַׁע *in the rebelling of a land*, the sense is the same,—namely, when a land rebels. As פשע implies a moral wrong, the want of right moral perception, it has in the second member its proper antithesis,—discernment and knowledge.

Second member; literally, *with men discerning*, etc., בְּ expressing accompaniment, connection with, (German, *bei*) and by implication, when such are found. Gesenius (Thes. כֵּן, B), *ubi homines sapiunt*. Ewald: *doch sind die Menschen weise*.*

Literally, *one may prolong*, indeterminate third pers. The construction, he.=some one of its princes, is constrained.

* In dem Versicherungssatze zum Ausdruck der stärksten Negation, *gewiss nicht*.

† Sprüche Salomo's, and Lehrb. (8te Ausg) § 361.

* Strictly, *with man* (die Mannschaft). The construction with בְּ (adopted to conform with בפשע, and point the antithesis) expresses in one way what בהיות would express in another, and in effect is equivalent to it; and by אדם is meant, collectively, the men. Hitzig's objections, therefore, to the Heb. text as it now stands, are without just ground.

| KING JAMES' VERSION. | | HEBREW TEXT. | REVISED VERSION. | |
|---|---|---|---|---|
| 3 A poor man that oppresseth the poor *is like* a sweeping rain which leaveth no food. | 3 | גֶּבֶר רָשׁ וְעֹשֵׁק דַּלִּים<br>מָטָר סֹחֵף וְאֵין לָחֶם׃ | A man, poor and oppressing the weak,<br>is a sweeping rain, when there is no bread. | 3 |
| 4 They that forsake the law praise the wicked: but such as keep the law contend with them. | 4 | עֹזְבֵי תוֹרָה יְהַלְלוּ רָשָׁע<br>וְשֹׁמְרֵי תוֹרָה יִתְגָּרוּ בָם׃ | They that forsake the law praise the wicked;<br>but such as keep the law contend with them. | 4 |
| 5 Evil men understand not judgment: but they that seek the LORD understand all *things*. | ה | אַנְשֵׁי־רָע לֹא־יָבִינוּ מִשְׁפָּט<br>וּמְבַקְשֵׁי יְהוָה יָבִינוּ כֹל׃ | Evil men understand not judgment;<br>but they that seek Jehovah understand all. | 5 |
| 6 Better *is* the poor that walketh in his uprightness, than *he that is* perverse *in his* ways, though he *be* rich. | 6 | טוֹב־רָשׁ הוֹלֵךְ בְּתֻמּוֹ<br>מֵעִקֵּשׁ דְּרָכַיִם וְהוּא עָשִׁיר׃ | Better is the poor that walks in his integrity,<br>than one of perverse ways, though he be rich. | 6 |
| 7 Whoso keepeth the law *is* a wise son: but he that is a companion of riotous *men* shameth his father. | 7 | נוֹצֵר תּוֹרָה בֵּן מֵבִין<br>וְרֹעֶה זוֹלְלִים יַכְלִים אָבִיו׃ | He that keeps the law is a discreet son;<br>but a companion of the prodigal brings his father to shame. | 7 |
| 8 He that by usury and unjust gain increaseth his substance, he shall gather it for him that will pity the poor. | 8 | מַרְבֶּה הוֹנוֹ בְּנֶשֶׁךְ וּבְתַרְבִּית<br>לְחוֹנֵן דַּלִּים יִקְבְּצֶנּוּ׃ | He that adds to his wealth by interest and increase,<br>shall gather it for him that has pity on the weak. | 8 |
| | | V. 8. ותרבית ק׳ | | |

כן emphasizes the relation of the apodosis to the preceding conditional clause,=*so*, in that case.*

V. 3. *When there is no bread*, is the proper rendering. The relation of the two members is partially lost in the renderings (all essentially the same), *so that bread fails* (Ewald), *so that there is no bread* (Bertheau), *without bringing bread* (Hitzig, Zöckler), *without giving bread* (Kamphausen). As thus rendered, "the weak," the main point of comparison, have nothing answering to them in the second member. (See Expl. Notes.)

V. 6. Perverse in ways=of perverse ways. The Masoretic punctuation of דרכים as a dual (here and in v. 18), the correctness of which is at least doubtful,† may have been suggested by what is implied in עקש, namely, that the tortuous course of such is not always one and the same.‡ This is well. But no explanation of the dual form, which supposes two ways to be meant, is strictly consistent. Thus according to Rabbi Levi, as there are but two ways, the good and the bad, he who leaves the former must follow the latter. But how then does he walk in *two* ways? Zöckler (Lange's Bibelwerk) is not more successful: * "Literally, 'than one who is crooked in the two ways,' or, 'than one who is perverse in a double way;' . . . that is, one who unskilfully and waywardly passes from one way to another, one who, with divided heart, stands midway between the right path and the bypath of immorality." If he is "midway between the right path and the bypath," then he walks in neither; if he "passes from one to the other," he is only partly wrong. So understood the dual form is, at least, an inapt expression of the thought. Stuart's conception of it is better, though his rendering, "perverse by double-dealing," is not an expression of the Hebrew.†

V. 8. *Interest:* namely, on money loaned. *Increase:* what was paid in kind, for a loan of produce, in addition to the amount loaned, the Roman *fænus reale;* ‡ as when three and a half kors of wheat were required in payment of the three loaned.

The attentive reader of the English Bible is already familiar with this use of the word *increase*, in such passages as Lev. 25 : 36. 37. "Take thou no usury [interest §] of him, or increase;

* Gesenius (Thes. כן, B). כן h. l. proprie valet, *si sic est*, et ad signi apodoseos potestatem prope accedit, ut alibi אז. Ewald (*in loc.*), כן kann unstreitig wie unser *so* zur schärfern Ausschliessung des Nachsazes dienen; . . . *sind die Menschen einsichtsvoll—so*, unter solchen Bedingung. *lebt er lange.*

† Hitzig: Der Dual דְּרָכַיִם nur hier und v. 18, von den Versionen nicht anerkannt, lässt keine wahrscheinliche Deutung zu. Kamphausen: Statt der Mehrzahl "Wege" will die Punctation nach Vs. 18 die Zweizahl; aber die alten Uebersezer haben wohl mit Recht von einem Doppelwege hier und V. 18 nichts gefunden.

‡ Bertheau: *Der Verkehrte des Doppelweges* ist der welcher nicht auf dem einen graden Wege bleibt, und eben desshalb ein עקש ist.

* In his translation, he sinks the peculiarity of the dual form: "he that walks in crooked ways" (wer krumme Wege geht).

† "*Two ways*, because such a man now pursues this course, and then that, in order that he may deceive."

‡ Rosenmüller (on Lev. 25 : 36): נשך est *foenus pecuniarium* quod pro *pecunia* mutuo accepta solvitur; . . . תרבית *foenus reale*, pro rebus commodatis, ut frumento, musto, oleo pendendum.

§ The Heb. Scriptures knew no such thing as usury, in the modern sense of the word. See Smith's Bible Dictionary, American edition, art. Usury.

KING JAMES' VERSION.

9 He that turneth away his ear from hearing the law, even his prayer *shall be* abomination.

10 Whoso causeth the righteous to go astray in an evil way, he shall fall himself into his own pit: but the upright shall have good *things* in possession.

11 The rich man *is* wise in his own conceit; but the poor that hath understanding searcheth him out.

12 When righteous *men* do rejoice, *there is* great glory: but when the wicked rise, a man is hidden.

13 He that covereth his sins shall not prosper: but whoso confesseth and forsaketh *them* shall have mercy.

14 Happy *is* the man that feareth alway: but he that hardeneth his heart shall fall into mischief.

15 *As* a roaring lion, and a ranging bear; *so is* a wicked ruler over the poor people.

16 The prince that wanteth understanding *is* also a great oppressor: *but* he that hateth covetousness shall prolong *his* days.

HEBREW TEXT.

9 מֵסִיר אָזְנוֹ מִשְּׁמֹעַ תּוֹרָה
גַּם־תְּפִלָּתוֹ תּוֹעֵבָה׃
י מַשְׁגֶּה יְשָׁרִים׀ בְּדֶרֶךְ רָע
בִּשְׁחוּתוֹ הוּא־יִפּוֹל
וּתְמִימִים יִנְחֲלוּ־טוֹב׃
11 חָכָם בְּעֵינָיו אִישׁ עָשִׁיר
וְדַל מֵבִין יַחְקְרֶנּוּ׃
12 בַּעֲלֹץ צַדִּיקִים רַבָּה תִפְאָרֶת
וּבְקוּם רְשָׁעִים יְחֻפַּשׂ אָדָם׃
13 מְכַסֶּה פְשָׁעָיו לֹא יַצְלִיחַ
וּמוֹדֶה וְעֹזֵב יְרֻחָם׃
14 אַשְׁרֵי אָדָם מְפַחֵד תָּמִיד
וּמַקְשֶׁה לִבּוֹ יִפּוֹל בְּרָעָה׃
טו אֲרִי־נֹהֵם וְדֹב שׁוֹקֵק
מוֹשֵׁל רָשָׁע עַל עַם־דָּל׃
16 נָגִיד חֲסַר תְּבוּנוֹת וְרַב מַעֲשַׁקּוֹת
שֹׂנֵא בֶצַע יַאֲרִיךְ יָמִים׃

V. 16. יתיר ר׳

REVISED VERSION.

He that turns away his ear 9
from hearing the law,
even his prayer is abomination.
He that misleads the upright 10
in an evil way,
shall himself fall into his own pit;
but the blameless shall inherit good.
A rich man is wise in his 11
own eyes;
but the poor who has understanding will search him out.
When the righteous triumph, 12
great is the glory;
but when the wicked rise, a man hides himself.
He that covers his transgres- 13
sion shall not prosper;
but he that confesses and forsakes shall find mercy.
Happy the man that fears 14
always;
but he that hardens his heart shall fall into evil.
A growling lion, and a rang- 15
ing bear,
is a wicked ruler over a feeble people.
A prince lacking in under- 16
standing and abundant in oppressions;
such as hate plunder shall have length of days.

thou shall not give him thy money upon usury [interest], nor lend him thy victuals for increase." Compare Ezek. 18 : 8. "He that hath not given forth upon usury [interest], neither hath taken any increase;" v. 13, "and hath taken increase;" v. 17, "hath not received usury [interest] nor increase;" 22 : 12, "thou hast taken usury [interest] and increase."

In all these passages the term *increase* is required in a translation, and is already familiar. No other English word expresses the meaning of the Hebrew.

V. 10, third member, *shall inherit:* see Explanatory Notes.

V. 15. *A ranging bear*, is the true rendering of שוקק.* The idea of *ravening*, in the proper sense of that word, does not lie in the Heb. root.—*Growling*, נהם, in distinction from שאג, and more illustrative of the case presented here.

V. 16. *A prince lacking in understanding and abundant in oppressions:* meaning, such there are; and implying, that as one trait is lacking the other abounds. The Heb. form simply presents the two traits in their connection and relation, and is equally admissible in English. So Hitzig,* and Kamphausen † It is quite unnecessary to suppose an appeal in the form of address ("O prince," Ewald,‡ Bertheau, Elster, Zöckler), or to assume a disjunctive relation of the second member, as in the common English version (and Luther's and De Wette's versions), or a synecdoche in the first, "as to a prince" (Stuart).

Second member. *Plunder:* namely, of the people by an oppressive ruler,§ as implied from the first member. The renderings, "covetousness" (com. Eng. version), "unjust gain ("Gesenius, Thes. and Lex., Hitzig, Zöckler, Kamphausen), do not properly connect the subject of this member with the oppressive rule in the first.

*Such as hate* expresses the generalization of the subject in שנאי (properly, שֹׂנְאֵי).

* Bertheau: *Ein* nach Beute suchender *umherscheifender Bär.*

* Man betrachte das Glied als abgerissenen Nominativ, der ein suffix in *b* nicht aufnimmt.

† Ein Fürst, arm an Vernunft und reich an Erpressung.

‡ O Häuptling, arm an Gut, reich an Erpressung.

§ Gesenius, Thes. vol. I. p. 229. Transfertur ad regum optimatumque populum spoliantium rapinas, Jer. 22 : 17, Ezek. 22 : 13.

| KING JAMES' VERSION. | HEBREW TEXT. | | REVISED VERSION. | |
|---|---|---|---|---|
| 17 A man that doeth violence<br>o the blood of *any* person shall<br>lee to the pit; let no man stay<br>iim. | אָדָם עָשֻׁק בְּדַם־נָפֶשׁ<br>עַד־בּוֹר יָנוּס אַל־יִתְמְכוּ־בוֹ׃ | 17 | A man oppressed with life-<br>blood,<br>will flee even to the pit, that<br>they may not lay hold on<br>him. | 17 |
| 18 Whoso walketh uprightly<br>hall be saved: but *he that is* per-<br>verse *in his* ways shall fall at once. | הוֹלֵךְ תָּמִים יִוָּשֵׁעַ<br>וְנֶעְקַשׁ דְּרָכַיִם יִפּוֹל בְּאֶחָת׃ | 18 | He that walks uprightly shall<br>be saved;<br>but he whose ways are perverse<br>shall fall at once. | 18 |
| 19 He that tilleth his land shall<br>iave plenty of bread: but he that<br>'olloweth after vain *persons* shall<br>iave poverty enough. | עֹבֵד אַדְמָתוֹ יִשְׂבַּע־לָחֶם<br>וּמְרַדֵּף רֵיקִים יִשְׂבַּע־רִישׁ׃ | 19 | He that tills his ground shall<br>be satisfied with bread;<br>but he that follows after vanities<br>shall be sated with poverty. | 19 |
| 20 A faithful man shall abound<br>with blessings: but he that maketh<br>iaste to be rich shall not be inno-<br>:ent. | אִישׁ אֱמוּנוֹת רַב־בְּרָכוֹת<br>וְאָץ לְהַעֲשִׁיר לֹא יִנָּקֶה׃ | כ | A trusty man has many bless-<br>ings;<br>but he that hastes to be rich<br>shall not be held innocent. | 20 |
| 21 To have respect of persons<br>'s not good: for, for a piece of<br>oread *that* man will transgress. | הַכֵּר־פָּנִים לֹא־טוֹב<br>וְעַל־פַּת־לֶחֶם יִפְשַׁע־גָּבֶר׃ | 21 | To regard the person is not<br>good;<br>and for a morsel of bread a man<br>will transgress. | 21 |

V. 18. *Or*, he that is perverse in a double way shall fall in one.

V. 17. *Oppressed:* stronger than *laden, burdened.** The expression, דם נפש may mean either *blood of life* (compare Gen. 9 : 5)=*life-blood* (Robinson, Heb. lex.), or *blood of a soul* (person), as it is generally understood. But the former sense seems to be more appropriate here, being a more pointed expression of the guilt of blood-shedding, inasmuch as "the life is in the blood" (Lev. 17 : 14), and this is recognized in the form, *life-blood.*

Second member. *That they may not lay hold on him:* אל expressing the subjective feeling of the homicide, his dread of apprehension.† The rendering, *let them not lay hold on him.*‡ accords with the more usual force of אל, but, as objected by Maurer,§ is far-fetched and is inappropriate here.

V. 18. *Whose ways are perverse.*|| See the note on v. 6.—*At once* (that is, suddenly and utterly). So Gesenius, Thes. vol. I. p. 63, subito l. prorsus, *auf einmal*; Lex. man. *Subito, repente* (*mit einem Male*).

Many translate: *But he who is perverse in two ways will fall in one.* So Umbreit, Rosenmüller, Maurer, Ewald, Bertheau, Hitzig, Zöckler (Lange's Bibelwerk¶), Kamphausen.

But the phrase, "in one," has little significance,* unless as referring to the difficulty and hazards of walking in two ways at once,† which will hardly be claimed to be its import.‡—Umbreit finds a pointed irony in the words, *he who walks in two ways will fall in one.* But there is more point in the expression than in the thought.

V. 20. *Trusty,*—"that may be safely trusted, fit to be confided in" (*Worcester*, and *Webster*),—accords with the etymological meaning of the root, *to* (safely) *rest on.* It is not, as Hitzig justly says, exactly the same (ist nicht genau das Selbe) as איש אמונים in 20 : 6. His own rendering (*der redliche Mann*) expresses rather the characteristic that makes a man trusty, a man to be confided in.—Fürst (lex.): "calmness, repose (Gelassenheit, Ruhe) opposed to haste in order to get gain;" a definition invented to suit this passage, and without support from etymology or usage.

*A man will transgress:* in such a case is meant (namely, where there is regard for the person) as is readily understood. There is no need, therefore, of interposing "yet" ("and [yet] for a

* Homicida dicitur *oppressus*, quem profusus a se sanguis angit, velut sub furiarum verbere eum agitans (Rosenmüller).

† Maurer: *ne se prehendant*, ne prehendatur *verens* . . . . אל est negativ subjectiva ipsius fugientis, ejusque verentis ne prehendatur.

‡ Namely, for punishment, that being unnecessary, since the horror of his crime is its own sufficient punishment (Umbreit); or, to hold him back from his destined fate, that being impossible (Ewald, Zöckler).

§ Quaesita, et minus commoda est.

|| Gesenius, Thes. II. p. 1062, Cujus viæ sunt perversæ.

¶ *Auf Einem fällt er;* Am. edition, "*shall fall suddenly,*" which is not in accordance with the original German rendering, or with the explanation given in the exegetical notes.

* Schultens: dilutiuscule.

† If this is not meant, then the verb "will fall" expresses all that can be intended. Prof Stuart translates, "*shall fall in one* [of them]," but gives as the sense, "double dealing will end in a fall," which certainly expresses the whole.

‡ The most that can be made of this view is well stated by C. B. Michaelis (Annott. uber.): Ut viatori, oculis suis diversas contuenti vias, lapsus sive in hac sive in illa metuendus est; ita qui modo sic modo in contrarium agit, factisque alium se præbet ac verbis ac gestibus, detecta sive hic sive illic malitia sua, cadet.

| KING JAMES' VERSION. | HEBREW TEXT. | REVISED VERSION. |
|---|---|---|
| 22 He that hasteth to be rich *hath* an evil eye, and considereth not that poverty shall come upon him. | 22 נִבְהָל לַהוֹן אִישׁ רַע עָיִן<br>וְלֹא־יֵדַע כִּי־חֶסֶר יְבֹאֶנּוּ׃ | He that is eager for wealth 22<br>is a man of evil eye,<br>and knows not when want shall<br>come upon him. |
| 23 He that rebuketh a man, afterwards shall find more favour than he that flattereth with the tongue. | 23 מוֹכִיחַ אָדָם אַחֲרַי חֵן יִמְצָא<br>מִמַּחֲלִיק לָשׁוֹן׃ | He that reproves a man shall 23<br>afterward find favor,<br>more than he that flatters with<br>the tongue. |
| 24 Whoso robbeth his father or his mother, and saith, *It is* no transgression; the same *is* the companion of a destroyer. | 24 גּוֹזֵל ׀ אָבִיו וְאִמּוֹ<br>וְאֹמֵר אֵין־פָּשַׁע<br>חָבֵר הוּא לְאִישׁ מַשְׁחִית׃ | He that robs his father and 24<br>his mother,<br>and says, It is no trespass;<br>the same is a companion for a<br>destroyer. |
| 25 He that is of a proud heart stirreth up strife: but he that putteth his trust in the LORD shall be made fat. | כח רְחַב־נֶפֶשׁ יְגָרֶה מָדוֹן<br>וּבוֹטֵחַ עַל־יְהוָה יְדֻשָּׁן׃ | The proud in spirit stirs up 25<br>contention;<br>but he that trusts in Jehovah<br>shall be enriched. |
| 26 He that trusteth in his own heart is a fool: but whoso walketh wisely, he shall be delivered. | 26 בּוֹטֵחַ בְּלִבּוֹ הוּא כְסִיל<br>וְהוֹלֵךְ בְּחָכְמָה הוּא יִמָּלֵט׃ | Whoso trusts in his own 26<br>heart, he is a fool;<br>but one that walks in wisdom,<br>he shall be delivered. |

morsel of bread"), as is is done by Schultens (et tamen) and by Ewald, Bertheau, and Zöckler.*

V. 22. The construction usually followed in the first member is that expressed by Gesenius in his Thes.† and Lex. (art. בהל), namely: "*the man of evil eye hastes after riches*, i. e. anxiously seeks to be rich." But haste to be rich is not the special and distinctive characteristic of an evil eye,—that is, of the envious. Hence it is found necessary to supplement this idea with that of *avaricious* (C. B. Michaelis, *avarus*, Bertheau, *habsüchtig*), which is not included in the Heb. phrase, *an evil eye*.

The construction given in the text is certainly favored by the greater propriety and justness of the sentiment (compare remarks in Expl. Notes), as Hitzig has clearly shown, in case the first member is taken as a proposition by itself; and this, he allows, is in itself admissible.‡ His objection to this construction, that איש should not stand next before the predicate, is less valid; for it is emphatically a part of the predicate, just as the phrase, "is a man of evil eye," is more emphatic than, "is evil-eyed."

Zöckler takes note of the fact, that the reading of the LXX (חסד, to be understood as in ch. 14 : 34) is found in the Edit. Bomberg. of 1525, and in the Plantin., 1566. It is the reading of the Edit. Bomberg. of 1521, lying before me. But the reading of the Masoretic text is found in the Syr. (ܚܣܝܪܘܬܐ) and Targ. (חוסרנא), and in the majority of Heb. Mss.; only six (or at most seven, and two others by the first hand) of Kennicott's Codd, having חסד.

V. 23. *Afterward*:* אַחֲרַי, a prolonging of אַחֲרֵי standing independently by itself.† Böttcher compares לִפְנַי, 1 K. 6 : 17.

V. 25. *Proud in spirit:* corresponding to "proud in heart," Ps. 101 : 5. So Gesenius, Thes. and Lex. (רחב): "רחב לבב Ps. 101 : 5, רחב נפש Prov. 28 : 5, of a tumid, inflated heart, or spirit, i. e. *proud, arrogant*;" and Fürst, Hdwbch (רחב): רחב לבב Ps. 101 : 5 *aufgeblasen, hochmüthig*, wie רחב נפש Spr. 28 : 25. So Rosenmüller, Maurer, Bertheau.

Since נפש, as well as לבב, is in Heb. usage the seat of the emotions, Hitzig's objection to the above rendering ‡ is not well grounded. It is as proper to say רחב נפש *proud in spirit*, as רחב לבב *proud in heart*. The phrase quoted against this rendering from Is. 5 : 14, Hab. 2 : 5, הרחיבה נפשה *has enlarged her desire* § (has become insatiably greedy), is not decisive against it, as the word נפש may be taken here in a different sense.

Those who take נפש here in the sense of *desire* ‖ (appealing to Is. 5 : 14, Hab. 2 : 5) translate, *the covetous*; except Ewald, who translates, *wer schwellender Seele*, and by inflation of spirit understands *selfishness*, inordinate self-love, as being nearly related to a perverted self-confidence.

* Kamphausen says justly: Löst man mit "Und doch" auf, so ist der Zusammenhang schwieriger als bei der Fassung, dass Einer, der nicht unparteiisch ist, durch den geringsten Vortheil (Ezek. 13 : 19) zu einem falschen Richterspruch, also zu einem grossen Verbrechen, verleitet werden kann.

† *Festinat ad divitias vir invidiosus*, i. e. anxie petit divitias.

‡ Man könnte zur Noth den נבהל להון als Subject zu איש רע עין betrachten; dagegen geht in keiner Weise an mit LXX und SYR. dieses Verhältniss von Subj. und Präd. umzudrehen.

* Ewald (*wird später Gnade finden*), Maurer, Bertheau, Hitzig, Kamphausen, Böttcher (Aehrenl. 3te Abth. p. 33), Zöckler, Fürst (Hdwbch. אחר, 4, b).

† Ewald, Lehrb. § 220, a (extr.): אַחֲרַי *nachher* oder *zuletzt*, welches noch den *st. constr.* אַחֲרֵי reiner darstellt, und als einzelwort nur etwas gedehnter *-ái* für *ae* am Ende spricht.

‡ Da נפש nicht mit לב das Selbe ist.

§ Not, as Gesenius (נפש, 2, 2d paragr.) "her throat."

‖ Umbreit (der Habsüchtige), Hitzig, Kamphausen, Zöckler.

KING JAMES' VERSION.

27 He that giveth unto the poor shall not lack: but he that hideth his eyes *shall have* many a curse.

28 When the wicked rise, men hide themselves: but when they perish, the righteous increase.

CHAP. XXIX.

He, that being often reproved hardeneth *his* neck, shall suddenly be destroyed, and that without remedy.

2 When the righteous are in authority, the people rejoice: but when the wicked beareth rule, the people mourn.

3 Whoso loveth wisdom rejoiceth his father: but he that keepeth company with harlots spendeth *his* substance.

4 The king by judgment establisheth the land: but he that receiveth gifts overthroweth it.

HEBREW TEXT.

27 נוֹתֵן לָרָשׁ אֵין מַחְסוֹר
וּמַעְלִים עֵינָיו רַב־מְאֵרוֹת׃

28 בְּקוּם רְשָׁעִים יִסָּתֵר אָדָם
וּבְאָבְדָם יִרְבּוּ צַדִּיקִים׃

CHAP. XXIX.

א אִישׁ תּוֹכָחוֹת מַקְשֶׁה־עֹרֶף
פֶּתַע יִשָּׁבֵר וְאֵין מַרְפֵּא׃

2 בִּרְבוֹת צַדִּיקִים יִשְׂמַח הָעָם
וּבִמְשֹׁל רָשָׁע יֵאָנַח עָם׃

3 אִישׁ־אֹהֵב חָכְמָה יְשַׂמַּח אָבִיו
וְרֹעֶה זוֹנוֹת יְאַבֶּד־הוֹן׃

4 מֶלֶךְ בְּמִשְׁפָּט יַעֲמִיד אָרֶץ
וְאִישׁ תְּרוּמוֹת יֶהֶרְסֶנָּה׃

REVISED VERSION.

He that gives to the poor is 27
without want;
but he that hides his eyes has
many a curse.
When the wicked rise, a man 28
hides himself;
but when they perish, the righteous multiply.

CHAP. XXIX.

A MAN often reproved, who 1
hardens his neck,
shall suddenly be destroyed,
and without remedy.
When the righteous multiply, 2
the people rejoice;
but when the wicked rule, the
people mourn.
One that loves wisdom re- 3
joices his father;
but a companion of harlots
squanders wealth.
A king by judgment estab- 4
lishes a land;
but a man that exacts tribute
overthrows it.

The question must be determined by the connection, and that is not clearly decisive. On the one hand, the proud, arrogant, overbearing man is the one who is most likely to provoke resistance and contention; who, in his self-confidence and self-sufficiency, stands directly opposed to him who humbly trusts in Jehovah, and patiently commits his cause to Him. The proud and litigious man is also less likely to prosper, than he who trusts to the righteousness of his cause and commits it to him who judges righteously. According to the other rendering, the antitheses are: inordinate greed on the one hand, patient trustfulness on the other; contention on the one hand, prosperity on the other.

Ch. XXIX.—V. 1. *A man of reproofs* (איש תוכחות), who has received reproofs, has been often reproved. Ewald refers, for a parallel case, to Deut. 25 : 2, בן הכות; Zöckler, more pertinently, to Is. 53 : 8 (8 by mistake for 3, as in the Am. ed.) איש מכאבות. Gesenius (Thes. vol. II. p. 593, and Lex. תוכחת) less well, "*a man of arguments*, who when censured defends himself." In the Thes. he quotes the other rendering as also admissible.*

V. 2. *When the righteous multiply;* implying a condition favorable to them in the affairs of State; antithetic, therefore, to the first clause of the parallel member. There is no good ground for rendering, with Hitzig, *zur macht gelangen*, for the sake of correspondence with משל.

V. 4. Compare Ezek. 45 : 9, and what is there enjoined upon a ruler, almost in the form used here; namely, "execute judgment and justice, take away your exactions."

* Alii, *qui reprehenditur et pervicax est*, quod etiam ferri potest.

Second member, תרומה (literally, *oblation;* see Ges. Lex. רום, Hiph. 3, and compare ἀνάθημα); in the Mosaic laws the portion of one's goods required as an oblation to the Lord (Ex. 25 : 2; 30 : 13, 14; Lev. 7 : 14); hence not unfitly expressing what might be required of one's possessions as an offering (tribute) to the ruler of the country,* as it is used in Ezek. 45 : 7, 16 (Ges. lex. תרומה, 2). So it is understood by Rosenmüller, Hitzig, and by Kamphausen, who pertinently refers to 1 K. 12 : 4, "Thy father made our yoke grievous,"† etc.

The above use of the word is the only one recognized in the seventy-one passages where it occurs, unless this be an exception. The sense of a private *gift* or *present*, as a bribe, though sanc-

* For this offering, legal provision was to be made in the new kingdom (Ezek. ch. xlv.), that arbitrary exaction (גרשה, v. 9) might be unnecessary in the future.—It is noteworthy, that the like provision was made for relieving the common people of Egypt from the burdens of taxation, by setting apart a portion of the territory for the expenses of the government. *Τὴν δὲ δευτέραν μοῖραν οἱ βασιλεῖς παρειλήφασιν εἰς προσόδους ἀφ' ὧν εἰς τε τοὺς πολέμους χορηγοῦσι, καὶ τὴν περὶ αὑτοὺς λαμπρότητα διαφυλάττουσι· καὶ τοὺς μὲν ἀνδραγαθήσαντας δωρεαῖς κατὰ τὴν ἀξίαν τιμῶσι, τοὺς δὲ ἰδιώτας διὰ τὴν ἐκ τούτων εὐπορίαν οὐ βαπτίζουσι ταῖς εἰσφοραῖς.* (Diodorus Sic. Lib. I. c. 73).

† That the onerous tribute was the "grievous yoke" complained of, is shown by the stoning of the king's officer, "Adoram who was over the tribute" (v. 18).

| KING JAMES' VERSION. | HEBREW TEXT. | | REVISED VERSION. | |
|---|---|---|---|---|
| 5 A man that flattereth his neighbour spreadeth a net for his feet. | גֶּבֶר מַחֲלִיק עַל־רֵעֵהוּ<br>רֶשֶׁת פּוֹרֵשׂ עַל־פְּעָמָיו׃ | 5 | A man that flatters his neighbor,<br>spreads a net for his steps. | 5 |
| 6 In the transgression of an evil man *there is* a snare: but the righteous doth sing and rejoice. | בְּפֶשַׁע אִישׁ רָע מוֹקֵשׁ<br>וְצַדִּיק יָרוּן וְשָׂמֵחַ׃ | 6 | In the wicked man's transgression is a snare;<br>but the righteous shall exult and rejoice. | 6 |
| 7 The righteous considereth the cause of the poor: *but* the wicked regardeth not to know *it*. | יֹדֵעַ צַדִּיק דִּין דַּלִּים<br>רָשָׁע לֹא־יָבִין דָּעַת׃ | 7 | The righteous regards the cause of the weak;<br>the wicked will not discern knowledge. | 7 |
| 8 Scornful men bring a city into a snare: but wise *men* turn away wrath. | אַנְשֵׁי לָצוֹן יָפִיחוּ קִרְיָה<br>וַחֲכָמִים יָשִׁיבוּ אָף׃ | 8 | Scoffers enkindle a city;<br>but the wise turn away anger. | 8 |
| 9 *If* a wise man contendeth with a foolish man, whether he rage or laugh, *there is* no rest. | אִישׁ־חָכָם נִשְׁפָּט אֶת־אִישׁ אֱוִיל<br>וְרָגַז וְשָׂחַק וְאֵין נָחַת׃ | 9 | When a wise man goes to law with a foolish man,<br>whether he be angry or laugh, there is no rest. | 9 |
| 10 The bloodthirsty hate the upright: but the just seek his soul. | אַנְשֵׁי דָמִים יִשְׂנְאוּ־תָם<br>וִישָׁרִים יְבַקְשׁוּ נַפְשׁוֹ׃ | 10 | Men of blood hate the upright;<br>but the just will care for his soul. | 10 |

tioned by distinguished names,* is not grounded in etymology or usage.

V. 5. Commonly, לשון (28 : 23), or אמרים (2 : 16, 7 : 5), is supposed to be implied in מחליק, but without accounting for the use of על. Ewald better: *über einen streicheln*, החליק על, im schlimmen geistigen Sinne soviel seyn kann als *ihm schmeicheln*, Spr. 29 : 5 (Lehrbuch, § 217, I., 4, *i*).

V. 6. Ewald (and Böttcher, Neue Aehrenl. p. 33), regarding רע as superfluous when taken with איש (though by position, as he admits, properly belonging there †), connects it with מוקש, *an evil snare*. Until snares are discovered that are not evil (evil to the ensnared) not much is thus gained in point of superfluity. But, in truth, it is not superfluous in connection with איש. The idea is: The righteous escapes the snare into which the wicked falls in transgression, and rejoices in his safety. The wicked man and the righteous as thus contrasted, and "wicked" is by no means superfluous.

The thought is clearly expressed in the text as it stands, and Hitzig's conjectural emendation (יִוָּקֵשׁ), approved by Kamphausen, is quite unnecessary.‡

V. 9. The leading subject in the first member is most naturally the subject of the second. So the two members are constructed by Ewald, and by Umbreit, Rosenmüller, De Wette, Maurer, and the earlier Hebraists, Mercier, Schultens, C. B. Michaelis, and others. Hitzig's objection, that the action expressed in the second member is unsuited to the wise man, is not well founded. The case is well stated by Mercier: Nunc asperius cum eo agit, nunc mitius, et velut cum eo jocatur; . . . omnibus modis stultum lucrifacere conatur, sed nil tamen proficit.*

Bertheau (followed by Stuart), Kamphausen, Zöckler, make the "foolish man" antecedent to the implied pronominal subject of the second member, the import of which is best stated by Stuart: "He will at one time be agitated with rage, at another with scornful laughter; a quiet and considerate state of mind he will not come to." The grammatical construction, in the version, as in the Hebrew, allows either interpretation.

*Whether—or.* Ewald, on the passage, and Jahrbb. der Bibl. Wiss. XI. p. 28.

V. 10. *Will care for his soul;* will have a tender regard for him, in contrast to the hatred of "men of blood."—*Care for:* strictly, make it an object of inquiry and solicitude. So Kamphausen,† who compares the use of the synonym דרש in Ps. 142 : 5.

The verb בקש may be taken, as suggested by Böttcher,‡ in the sense of *require*, as it is used in Gen. 43 : 9 (compare 31 : 39),

---

* Gesenius Thes. and Lex., Ewald, Fürst Hdwbch, Umbreit, Maurer, Bertheau, Zöckler.

† *Böser Fallstrick* (Ew.) lauft der Wortstellung zuwider (Hitzig.)

‡ The form ירון is explained by the near relation of verbs עע and עו. "On account of this relation, they have sometimes borrowed forms from each other, e. g. יָרֹן for יָרוֹן Prov. 29 : 6" (Ges. Gram. § 68, Rem. 9).

* So C. B. Michaelis (Annott. uber.): Quomodocunque cum eo egerit, *sive irascatur sive rideat* (uti Vulg. reddidit), h. e. sive asperis sive mollibus utatur verbis.

† Dem Hass der Blutmenschen (Ps. 5 : 7) die sich durch den Frommen abgestossen (vgl. vs. 27) fühlen, entspricht die herzliche (vgl. 27 : 9) Liebe der Redliche zu ihm; s. z. Ps. 142 : 5.

‡ Neue Aehrenl. p 34. *Redliche suchen sein Leben* (vindicant, beanspruchen es) in diesem sonst ungewohnten guten Sinn durch Gen. 9 : 5 (?) 1 Sam. 20 : 16, Ezek. 3 : 18, ff. Baruch 6 : 7 [Epist. Jerem. 6] (vgl. LXX. Pr. 29 [29 : 10]) gesichert.

| KING JAMES' VERSION. | HEBREW TEXT. | REVISED VERSION. |
|---|---|---|
| 11 A fool uttereth all his mind: but a wise *man* keepeth it in till afterwards. | 11 כָּל־רוּחוֹ יוֹצִיא כְסִיל<br>וְחָכָם בְּאָחוֹר יְשַׁבְּחֶנָּה׃ | A fool utters all his mind; 11<br>but the wise restrains [and keeps] it back. |
| 12 If a ruler hearken to lies, all his servants *are* wicked. | 12 מֹשֵׁל מַקְשִׁיב עַל־דְּבַר־שָׁקֶר<br>כָּל־מְשָׁרְתָיו רְשָׁעִים׃ | A ruler that gives heed to 12<br>words of falsehood,—<br>all his servants are wicked. |
| 13 The poor and the deceitful man meet together: the LORD lighteneth both their eyes. | 13 רָשׁ וְאִישׁ תְּכָכִים נִפְגָּשׁוּ<br>מֵאִיר־עֵינֵי שְׁנֵיהֶם יְהוָה׃ | The poor and the oppressor 13<br>meet together;<br>He that gives light to the eyes of them both is Jehovah. |
| 14 The king that faithfully judgeth the poor, his throne shall be established for ever. | 14 מֶלֶךְ שׁוֹפֵט בֶּאֱמֶת דַּלִּים<br>כִּסְאוֹ לָעַד יִכּוֹן׃ | A king that truthfully judges 14<br>the weak,—<br>his throne shall stand forever firm. |
| 15 The rod and reproof give wisdom: but a child left *to himself* bringeth his mother to shame. | טו שֵׁבֶט וְתוֹכַחַת יִתֵּן חָכְמָה<br>וְנַעַר מְשֻׁלָּח מֵבִישׁ אִמּוֹ׃ | The rod and reproof give 15<br>wisdom;<br>but a child left to itself shames its mother. |

"of my hand shalt thou require him,*" and its synonym דרש in Gen. 9 : 5, "I will require the life of man." But this idea, though pertinent, is not so strictly antithetic to "hate" in the first member.

Another rendering, "will seek his life [to deliver it]," adopted by many,† may perhaps be justified by such examples as Ps. 122 : 9, "I will seek thy good," Neh. 2 : 10, "to seek the welfare of the children of Israel;" but the cases are not exactly parallel. Ps. 142 : 5, referred to by Rosenmüller and Maurer, is a different construction.

V. 11. *All his mind:* specially said of the feelings, passions, and consequent purposes, as indicated by the idea of *restraint* in the antithetic clause.

*Restrains [and keeps] it back.* So Umbreit, Rosenmüller,‡ De Wette, Maurer,§ Kamphausen.‖

Some understand by רוח *rage, wrath*,¶ others, more generally, *mind, spirit*, as the seat of all the emotions and passions.**

By some the *suf. pron.* is referred to the fool's rage, to which he gives hasty and inconsiderate utterance, and which the wise man appeases or restrains. So Gesenius,* Ewald, Bertheau, Zöckler. Others, with more reason, refer it to the mind, or feeling, of the wise man, who restrains the expression of it (etym. *strokes it back*). So Umbreit, *hält es zurück;* Rosenmüller and Maurer (as above); Hitzig;† Kamphausen, *hält beschwichtigend damit zurück.*

The form באחור, occurring only here, is treated by Gesenius (Thes. and Lex.) as=לאחור, *retrorsum;* Hitzig (in notes) *nach hinten;* Kamphausen (in notes) *in den Hintergrund.* Others, less pertinently, render it *afterward*‡ *at last;* Ewald and Zöckler, *später;* Bertheau, *zulezt,* nachdem der Zorn ausgeschüttet ist,—which seems here to be plane otiosum. When his rage has spent itself, it does not require to be appeased.

V. 13. *The oppressor* (man of oppressions). Ewald and Zöckler, without any substantial ground,§ take the phrase in the sense of *usurer.* But this is a groundless limitation of the sense. The "man of oppressions" is one who uses any of the various modes of oppression, which are many.——Second member. *He that gives light:* see Explanatory Notes.

V. 14. *Truthfully. Mit Wahrheit,* d. h. getreu dem Sachverhalte, so dass er ihnen משפט אמת (Sach. 7 : 9) angedeihen lässt; nicht bloss *mit Gewissenhaftigkeit,* treu seiner Ueberzeugung, denn diese könnte auch irren (Hitzig).

V. 15. *Left to itself:* as well expressed by the Vulgate, qui dimittitur voluntati suae.

* Namely, should harm befall him, and I fail to return him safely. So here, the just "will require his life," should it suffer harm at the hands of "men of blood." They will hold such men to a strict account.

† Gesenius, Thes. and Lex., "Once in a good sense, *to seek to preserve one's life,* Prov. 29 : 10; so Rosenmüller, Maurer, Bertheau.

‡ *Retrorsum reprimit eum:* spiritum suum, i. e. animi sensus, studia et motus prudenter novit moderari et celare.

§ Compescit eum [animum], ut retrorsum eat, ad se redeat, i. e. reprimit eum. Sensus: homo stultus temere promit omnes animi sensus, motus et studia; . . . sapiens vero caute ea reprimit et celat

‖ Der Thor schüttet aus seinen ganzen Geist, und ein Weiser—zurück (eig. in den Hintergrund, vgl. Ps. 114 : 3) beschwichtigt er ihn, d. h. seinen eigenen Geist.

¶ Gesenius *iram,* Thes. and Lex. אחור, and שבח *Piel.* 1; Ewald *Gluthauch;* Hitzig *shnauben;* Bertheau and Zöckler *Zorn;* Kamphausen (paraphrastically) *Alles, was ihn bewegt.*

** Probabilior eadem mihi videtur ob praemissum כל (Maurer). So Rosenmüller, *animum* (in notes, *spiritum*); Umbreit and De Wette, *Gemüth.*

* Thes. אחור, 1, c, iram stulti quasi retrorsum agit, ut ad se redeat.

† Die Meinung ist nicht: der Weise sänftige später (?) den Zorn des Narren; vielmehr den eigenen beherrscht er.

‡ Quod plane ineptum (Maurer).

§ Ewald nimmt ohne weiteres תך in der Bedeutung *Zins* (Bertheau).

| KING JAMES' VERSION. | HEBREW TEXT. | | REVISED VERSION. |
|---|---|---|---|
| 16 When the wicked are multiplied, transgression increaseth: but the righteous shall see their fall. | בִּרְבוֹת רְשָׁעִים יִרְבֶּה־פָּשַׁע<br>וְצַדִּיקִים בְּמַפַּלְתָּם יִרְאוּ׃ | 16 | When the wicked increase, 16<br>transgression increases;<br>but the righteous shall look on<br>their fall. |
| 17 Correct thy son, and he shall give thee rest; yea, he shall give delight unto thy soul. | יַסֵּר בִּנְךָ וִינִיחֶךָ<br>וְיִתֵּן מַעֲדַנִּים לְנַפְשֶׁךָ׃ | 17 | Correct thy son, and he will 17<br>give thee rest,<br>and will give delight to thy<br>soul. |
| 18 Where *there is* no vision, the people perish: but he that keepeth the law, happy *is* he. | בְּאֵין חָזוֹן יִפָּרַע עָם<br>וְשֹׁמֵר תּוֹרָה אַשְׁרֵהוּ׃ | 18 | When there is no vision, the 18<br>people are unrestrained;<br>but he that keeps the law,—<br>happy is he. |
| 19 A servant will not be corrected by words: for though he understand he will not answer. | בִּדְבָרִים לֹא־יִוָּסֶר עָבֶד<br>כִּי־יָבִין וְאֵין מַעֲנֶה׃ | 19 | By words a servant is not 19<br>corrected;<br>for he will understand,—but<br>there is no answer. |
| 20 Seest thou a man *that is* hasty in his words? *there is* more hope of a fool than of him. | חָזִיתָ אִישׁ אָץ בִּדְבָרָיו<br>תִּקְוָה לִכְסִיל מִמֶּנּוּ׃ | כ | Seest thou a man hasty in 20<br>his words?<br>there is more hope of a fool<br>than of him. |
| 21 He that delicately bringeth up his servant from a child shall have him become *his* son at the length. | מְפַנֵּק מִנֹּעַר עַבְדּוֹ<br>וְאַחֲרִיתוֹ יִהְיֶה מָנוֹן׃ | 21 | One brings up his servant 21<br>tenderly from childhood,<br>and in the end he will be as a<br>son. |
| 22 An angry man stirreth up strife, and a furious man aboundeth in transgression. | אִישׁ־אַף יְגָרֶה מָדוֹן<br>וּבַעַל חֵמָה רַב־פָּשַׁע׃<br>V. 21. he will be a refractory one in the end | 22 | A man given to anger stirs 22<br>up contention;<br>and a wrathful man abounds in<br>transgression. |

V. 16. *Shall look upon:* See Expl. Notes, and compare Gesenius, Lex. ראה, 2, a, and בְּ, B, 4, a.

V. 18. *Vision.* The literal, etymological meaning of the word should be retained here, both for comparison with other passages where it must be so rendered, and because Divine communications were usually made in vision. Compare Gen. 46 : 2; 2 Sam. 7 : 17; Job 4 : 13; Dan. 2 : 19. The rendering *revelation*, by Gesenius and others, is untrue to the Hebrew conception here, and corresponds rather to the verbal idea expressed in גלה.

V. 19. *Will understand.* So Gesenius, Thes. בין, 1, b, [*animadvertere*] auribus, i. q. *audire*, auribus percipere. Job 23 : 5, Prov. 29 : 19.

Second member. כי causal (LXX. γάρ, Vulg. *quia*); not conditional, as understood by Rosenmüller and Maurer, *si intelligat.**

Bertheau misses the point in rendering, *He will perceive it*, namely, that there is nothing but words. Still more wide of the mark is Ewald's conception: But, on the contrary, he will be made to understand without answering,—without first making a prolix justification of himself, impairing the effect of the discipline.

V. 21. *In the end he will be as a son:* a free expression of the sense. Strictly, his end, it will be the condition of a son † (the verb conforming to the predicate),—or, in his end will be the condition of a son.*

The form מנון most probably denotes the abstract, the relation or condition of a son, rather than a son.†

Fürst (Hdwbch), with a much less certain derivation, both as to form and relation to the verbal idea, from the stem מנן, translates as in the margin, "he will be a refractory one in the end." So the Vulgate, *sentiet eum contumacem;* Symmachus, *ἔσται γογγυσμός*.

The rendering of the LXX., *ὀδυνηθήσεται*, and of the Syr. ܢܬܬܢܚܣ, and Chald. מנסח, have no certain ground in etymology.‡ Hitzig makes an unsuccessful attempt to show that the two former have a common origin in the stem נוד §—Ewald's rendering, *undankbar*, is also without sure support.

V. 22. *A man given to anger.* A man of anger, איש אף, of whom anger is the characteristic and distinguishing trait.

* Das Verstehen, die Regel, darf nicht als ein bloss möglicher Fall gesetzt werden (Hitzig.)

† *Finis ejus*, servi, *erit filius* . . . Suffixum in אחריתו respicit servum (Maurer).

* *Et in extremo ejus*, servi, *erit conditio filii*, sese tandem tanquam heri filium . . . geret (Rosenmüller).

† *Nomen* מנון, hoc solo loco obvium, a נין *filius* Gen. 21 : 23, Job 18 : 19. Jes. 14 : 22, unde verbum Ps. 72 : 17 ינון *sobolescet*, hoc loco *statum, conditionem filii* denotare vix dubium (Rosenmüller).

‡ Sine solido etymologiae fundamento (C. B. Michaelis, Annott, uber.).

§ Vereinigen sich in der Wurzel נוד.

| KING JAMES' VERSION. | HEBREW TEXT. | REVISED VERSION. |
| --- | --- | --- |
| 23 A man's pride shall bring him low: but honour shall uphold the humble in spirit. | גַּאֲוַת אָדָם תַּשְׁפִּילֶנּוּ 23<br>וּשְׁפַל־רוּחַ יִתְמֹךְ כָּבוֹד׃ | A man's pride will bring him low; 23<br>but the humble in spirit shall retain honor. |
| 24 Whoso is partner with a thief hateth his own soul: he heareth cursing, and bewrayeth *it* not. | חוֹלֵק עִם־גַּנָּב שׂוֹנֵא נַפְשׁוֹ 24<br>אָלָה יִשְׁמַע וְלֹא יַגִּיד׃ | He that divides with a thief 24<br>hates his own soul;<br>he hears the curse, but does not inform. |
| 25 The fear of man bringeth a snare: but whoso putteth his trust in the LORD shall be safe. | חֶרְדַּת אָדָם יִתֵּן מוֹקֵשׁ כה<br>וּבוֹטֵחַ בַּיהוָה יְשֻׂגָּב׃ | Fear of man brings a snare; 25<br>but he that trusts in Jehovah shall be set on high. |
| 26 Many seek the ruler's favour; but *every* man's judgment *cometh* from the LORD. | רַבִּים מְבַקְשִׁים פְּנֵי־מוֹשֵׁל 26<br>וּמֵיְהוָה מִשְׁפַּט־אִישׁ׃ | Many seek the face of the 26<br>ruler;<br>but from Jehovah is man's judgment. |
| 27 An unjust man *is* an abomination to the just: and *he that is* upright in the way *is* abomination to the wicked. | תּוֹעֲבַת צַדִּיקִים אִישׁ עָוֶל 27<br>וְתוֹעֲבַת רָשָׁע יְשַׁר־דָּרֶךְ׃ | An abomination to the right- 27<br>eous is the unjust man;<br>and an abomination to the wicked is he whose way is right. |
| CHAP. XXX. | CHAP. XXX. | CHAP. XXX. |
| THE words of Agur the son of Jakeh, *even* the prophecy: the man spake unto Ithiel, even unto Ithiel and Ucal. | דִּבְרֵי אָגוּר בִּן־יָקֶה הַמַּשָּׂא א<br>נְאֻם הַגֶּבֶר לְאִיתִיאֵל<br>לְאִיתִיאֵל וְאֻכָל׃ | WORDS OF AGUR, SON OF JAKEH; 1<br>THE ORACLE.<br>The saying of the man to Ithiel,<br>to Ithiel and Ucal. |
| | V. 1. בנ"א רפה | |

V. 23. *Shall retain* (יתמוך), rather than *obtain* (which the word may also mean) as being more strictly antithetic to "will bring him low," in the first member.

V. 24. *Divides with a thief;* as well illustrated by C. B. Michaelis (Annott. uber.); *Dividens,* 1 Sam. 30 : 24, hoc est, partem ablati capiens, *cum fure;* socius furis, si non furando, tamen occultando ac suscipiendo.

Hitzig obtains the same general sense * from a different construction of the verse; treating the first member as predicate of the second, and the last clause of the former as neither predicate of its first clause nor in apposition with it, but as equally correct.†

He objects to the usual construction, on the ground that the second member does not so directly hold good of the concealer of a theft.‡ The objection is more ingenious than sound. Every man is supposed to "hear the curse," in the sense of the proverb, who knows the law and its penalties; and every man, under the law, is presumed to know them.

His other objection,—that the offender does not hate his own life, inasmuch as death was not the penalty of the offense,—is founded on a misconception of the meaning. He "hates his own soul," inasmuch as he brings on himself the curse,—whatever that may be.

V. 25. *Shall be set on high:* above the reach of danger; a common Hebrew image of security, and a characteristic conception, which should be preserved in a translation. Compare Pss. 59 : 1; 69 : 29; 91 : 14; 107 : 41.

V. 26. Some translate the second member, *from Jehovah is each one's right,*—therefore commit your cause to him.* Both renderings are antithetic to the first member; but the rendering of the text is more directly so, and is favored by the occurrence of the same sentiment under other forms, as in ch. 21 : 1.

Ch. XXX. On this portion of the book, see Introd. § ***

V. 1. *Words of Agur, son of Jakeh; the oracle.* So Gesenius (Thes. and Lex.), Fürst (Hdwbch), Rosenmüller, Maurer, Bertheau (if the Masoretic punctuation is followed); and so Kamphausen,† De Wette (die heilige Schrift). So also Umbreit and Ewald, except that they connect המשא with the following words in a relative clause.‡

The word משא, *an utterance*, a thing spoken, in itself is

* Wer solche Sünde, welche Sühnung heischt (3 Mos. 5 : 1 ff.), nicht zur Anzeige bringt, sondern das Geheimniss derselben mit dem Sünder theilt, ist nicht besser, als ff.

† He claims to have been the first to perceive the right construction of the verse, and translates:

Mit dem Diebe theilt, sich selber hasst,
wer einen Fluch hört und zeigt nicht an.

‡ Von Diebshehler nicht so geradezu gültig ist.

* Maurer: *A Jova est,* proficiscitur, *jus cujusque.* Itaque, ante omnia causam tuam committe deo.

† Worte Agur's, des Sohnes Jakeh, der Ausspruch.

‡ Der Gottesspruch, den der Mann geredet (Umbreit).—Der Hochspruch welchen sprach der Held (Ewald).

| KING JAMES' VERSION. | HEBREW TEXT. | | REVISED VERSION. | |
|---|---|---|---|---|
| 2 Surely I *am* more brutish than *any* man, and have not the understanding of a man. | כִּי בַעַר אָנֹכִי מֵאִישׁ<br>וְלֹא־בִינַת אָדָם לִי׃ | 2 | Yea, I am more stupid than any ;<br>and I have not the understanding of a man. | 2 |

without limitation of the nature or source of that which is uttered. But in all the numerous passages where it has this sense, it is used exclusively of a Divine utterance, a Divine communication, or what professed to be such (Lam. 2 : 14) ; and this, in the nature of the case, might be prophetic or didactic.

The remainder of the verse is construed as it is here by Gesenius, Fürst, Umbreit (except the immaterial relative construction), Rosenmüller, Maurer, De Wette. It has in its favor the weighty authority of the Masoretic punctuation ; which, though occasionally at fault, is the product of the ablest Hebrew scholarship that has come down to us, and as a commentary on the Hebrew text is not to be set aside without very cogent reasons.

According to this construction, המשא is a common noun with the *art.* ; Jakeh, Ithiel, and Ucal are proper names ; the two latter, of persons to whom the words of Agur, at least the first division of them (vv. 1—6), are addressed.

The objections to the Masoretic construction of the text are the following :*

1. Occurrence of proper names (יקה and אכל) not found elsewhere, and of uncertain etymology.

2. Repetition of the name *Ithiel*, in the second member of the parallelism.

3. Address of the message, or discourse, to two persons, otherwise unknown, and not afterward referred to.

4. Use of כי affirmatively, at the beginning of a discourse.

5. Use of the *article* with a noun in the *constr. st.*, in case המשא and נאם are in apposition (Stuart).

6. Use of the *article* with משא, followed not by one single discourse, but by many sayings of dissimilar purpose and tenor.—Moreover, it is not elsewhere used with the *art.*, unless followed by the demonstrative pronoun (Is. 14 : 28 ; Ezek. 12 : 10), or by a relative clause (Hab. 1 : 1 ; Is. 22 : 25).

7. The dative of the one addressed, after נאם, which is nowhere else followed by the indirect object.†

8. Unauthorized use of משא, elsewhere meaning a *Divine utterance*, an oracle, in the special sense of a prophecy.

9. Use of the *article*, without significance, in הגבר (Muehlau).

10. משא must be used here as in ch. 31 : 1, where it can only be a proper name, and the genitive after מלך ; since " Lemuel the king " must in Hebrew be either למואל המלך, or המלך למואל.

To these objections it may be answered :

1. It ought not to be accounted strange, that two proper names should occur but once, and that a third should occur but twice. Doubtless there were proper names among the Hebrews, that do not occur even once in our Scriptures.—The etymology of such names is sometimes quite obscure and uncertain, on account of the comparatively meagre remains of the ancient language. It is an unsafe ground for conjectural emendation of the traditional text.

*Jakeh*, according to Gesenius (by comparison with the Arabic) means *devout, pious.* The etymology of *Ucal* is less satisfactory (Thes. I. p. 91, formae כומז, nisi est i. q. אוכל, *possum*).

2. The repetition is sufficiently accounted for on the ground of parallelism alone ;* and there is a possible, though not very probable, ground for it in the personal relations of the parties.†

3. There is as good reason for addressing two unknown persons here, as for addressing one, also unknown, in ch. 31 : 1 ; and they need not be mentioned twice in one short discourse.

4. כי is here put affirmatively at the beginning of a discourse, by an ellipsis of the formula of affirmation ‡ A like ellipsis, by which the particle serves for " a wider introduction to direct discourse even at the beginning of a new section," is conceded by Fürst (Lex. כי, c), and by Muehlau (p. 9) ; and this is all that need be claimed for it here.

5. The words המשא and נאם are not in apposition.

6. המשא is probably used only with reference to the first discourse which follows ; certainly there is no necessity for including more.—That in every other passage it happens to require the *demon. pron.* or is followed by a relative clause, when it takes the *art.*, is no proof that it may not, in a different connection, take the *art.* alone.§ With the heading, " Words of Agur," *the oracle* means the one imparted to or through him, in what immediately follows.

7. The exception is not well taken ; both subject and indirect object being thus used after נאם in Ps. 110 : 1, נאם יהוה לאדני.

8. משא, by etymology an *utterance*, by usage what is divinely uttered or communicated, in the nature of the case may be either prophetic or didactic. Here it may include only what is strictly connected with it (vv. 1—6), and in matter and manner is appropriate to it.

9. The *article* is not without significance, indicating one noted for superior wisdom.

* Hitzig (Zeller's theolog. Jahrbb. 1844 ; die Sprüche Salomo's) ; Bertheau (die Sprüche Salomo's, Einleit. § 2. 5) ; Stuart (Commentary on the Book of Proverbs) ; Zöckler (Lange's Bibelwerk, 1867) ; Muehlau (de proverbiorum quae dicuntur Aguri et Lemuelis origine atque indole, 1869).

† Nusquam enim hic reperitur dicendi modus (Muehlau, p. 8).

* Repetitur לאיתיאל . . . in parallelismi gratiam (Maurer).

† Quod forsan et ipse illis temporibus vel ob sapientiam celebris, vel primariae tum dignitatis vir esset (Rosenmüller).

‡ Gesenius (Lex. כי, 1, a), " by an ellipsis of a like formula, כי is put affirmatively even at the beginning of an oracle, Is. 15 : 1."

§ Such reasoning, common with some German writers, is quite illogical.

**KING JAMES' VERSION.**

3 I neither learned wisdom, nor have the knowledge of the holy.
4 Who hath ascended up into heaven, or descended? who hath gathered the wind in his fists? who hath bound the waters in a garment? who hath established all the ends of the earth? what *is* his name, and what *is* his son's name, if thou canst tell?

**HEBREW TEXT.**

וְלֹא־לָמַדְתִּי חָכְמָה 3
וְדַעַת קְדֹשִׁים אֵדָע׃
מִי עָלָה־שָׁמַיִם ׀ וַיֵּרַד 4
מִי אָסַף־רוּחַ ׀ בְּחָפְנָיו
מִי צָרַר־מַיִם ׀ בַּשִּׂמְלָה
מִי הֵקִים כָּל־אַפְסֵי־אָרֶץ
מַה־שְּׁמוֹ וּמַה־שֶּׁם־בְּנוֹ כִּי תֵדָע׃

V. 4. That thou shouldst know

**REVISED VERSION.**

I have not learned wisdom, 3
nor have I knowledge of the Holy.
Who has ascended to heaven, 4
and come down?
Who has gathered the wind in his fists?
Who has bound the waters in a mantle?
Who has founded all the ends of the earth?
What is his name, and what his son's name?
For thou knowest!

10. משא is not necessarily used here as in ch. 31 : 1.—Nor in ch. 31 : 1 is it necessarily a proper name, on account of the absence of the *art.* with מלך. The anarthrous construction is there appropriate to the brevity of a superscription, and to the abstract expression of official dignity * in distinction from the actual relation of reigning monarch.—In saying that "king Lemuel" must necessarily be in Hebrew המלך למואל, Muehlau overlooked Zech. 14 : 16, 17, למלך יהוה צבאות.

Of the different constructions and renderings of the passage, the following are examples:

1. Retaining the Masoretic punctuation, and treating the proper names as symbolical of different classes of thinkers, represented under fictitious and significant names. Ewald; "Said to God-with-me,—to God-with-me-and-I-am-strong." Keil regards אכל, "I-am-strong," as representing still another class, the strong spirits.

2. Rejecting the punctuation, but retaining the Masoretic text. Hitzig: "Words of Agur, son of the Mistress of Massa" (after the pointing, בְּן־יִקְהָה מַשָּׂא *son of her* whom *Massa obeys*); "I have wearied myself about God,—wearied myself about God, and became dimmed" (in mental vision), with the division לאיתי אל, as in one cod. of Kennicott and two of De Rossi,† and the pointing. לָאִיתִי אֵל לָאִיתִי אֵל וָאֵכֶל; Bertheau, *and fainted* (fut. Kal of כלל=כלה), Stuart, *and have failed* (fut. apoc. of כלה), Böttcher (Neue Aehrenl. p. 35) *and made an end.*—Davidson (Introd. to the Old Testament, Vol. II. p. 338), with the same division and pointing, "I am weary, O God. I am weary, O God and am become weak." So Delitzsch (Herzog's Realencyklop., art. Sprüche Salomo's, p. 702).

3. Rejecting the Masoretic punctuation, and re-writing the consonant text. Davidson (as above) and Delitzsch (as above). "Agur, son of Jakeh of Massa" (מִמַּשָּׂא instead of המשא). Böttcher, Neue Aehrenl. p. 34 (changing המשא to הַמַּשָּׂאִי) *son of Jakeh, the Massaite.* Muehlau (changing both the consonants and the order of words), "Saying of the man of Massa" (*or*, הַמַּשָּׂאִי) נאם הגבר מִמַּשָּׂא.

Others might be added. But these may suffice to show where we are, or rather where we might not be, after abandoning the only trustworthy traditional exegesis, with which the Chaldee and partially the Syriac coincide. See the Introd. § ***, and compare the articles *Agur*, *Jakeh*, *Ucal*, in Smith's Bible Dictionary, and the art. *Massa*, with Dr. Hackett's addition in the American edition of that work.

V. 2. *Yea.* Gesenius, Lex. 1, a: "By an ellipsis of a like formula [of asseveration] כי is put affirmatively even at the beginning of an oracle, Is. 15 : 1." *Sane* (Rosenmüller and Maurer); *Ja* (Umbreit, De Wette, Ewald).

The supposition, that we have here a dialogue between Ithiel and Agur, as assumed by Doederlein * and Ewald, has no foundation in the structure of the discourse, and only mars its beauty and significance.

*Than any.*† Hitzig's construction, "I am a beast and not a man," barely possible in itself (compare Gesenius' reference to Is. 53 : 14, lex. מן, 6, b), is not justified by his appeal to Is. 44 : 11; and its pertinency here, admitted by Zöckler, is rightly questioned by Dr. Aiken (Lange's Biblework, Am. ed.).

V. 3. *The Holy.* See the note on ch. 9 : 10.

V. 4. *Who has ascended to heaven, and come down?* By Zöckler (Lange's Biblework) this question, like those which follow, is understood to express "an activity belonging exclusively to God, and characteristic of him in his supermundane nature" (Am. edition, p. 248). This certainly is possible. But the

* Noch leichter sind Fälle wie למואל מלך, was eben so gut möglich ist wie unser *könig Lemôel*, Spr. 31 : 1 (Ewald, Lehrb. § 277, b, extr).

† לאיתי אל separatim, ut legit Michaelis, *defatigatus sum Deo*, Kenn. 147, mei 380, 607 (De Rossi Var. Lect. V. T. Vol. IV. p. 103).

* Itaque dialogici carminis formam imitari videtur hic locus, qui primum Ithielis meliora edoceri optantis sensus et dicta refert, dein Aguri vatis divini institutionem, brevem quidem sed aptam huic argumento, atque sic institutam ut aditum ad verae religionis mysteria monstret menti docili et ingenuae, recenset. Doederlein, Scholia in libros V. T. Poet. (Grotii annotationum in Vet. Test. auctarium).

† *Bardus ego* sum *prae viro*, i. e. stupidior sum alio quoque. (Rosenmüller). So Maurer, and Kamphausen; *than a man*, Ewald and Bertheau.

| KING JAMES' VERSION. | HEBREW TEXT. | REVISED VERSION. |
|---|---|---|
| 5 Every word of God *is* pure:<br>he *is* a shield unto them that put<br>their trust in him. | 5 כָּל־אִמְרַת אֱלוֹהַּ צְרוּפָה<br>מָגֵן הוּא לַחֹסִים בּוֹ׃ | 5 Every word of God is pure; 5<br>a shield is he to them that trust<br>in him. |
| 6 Add thou not unto his words,<br>lest he reprove thee, and thou be<br>found a liar. | 6 אַל־תּוֹסְףְּ עַל־דְּבָרָיו<br>פֶּן־יוֹכִיחַ בְּךָ וְנִכְזָבְתָּ׃ | 6 Add not thou to his words; 6<br>lest he reprove thee, and thou<br>be found a liar. |
| 7 Two *things* have I required<br>of thee; deny me *them* not before<br>I die: | 7 שְׁתַּיִם שָׁאַלְתִּי מֵאִתָּךְ<br>אַל־תִּמְנַע מִמֶּנִּי בְּטֶרֶם אָמוּת׃ | 7 Two things have I asked of 7<br>thee;<br>withhold them not from me be-<br>fore I die. |
| 8 Remove far from me vanity<br>and lies; give me neither poverty<br>nor riches; feed me with food<br>convenient for me: | 8 שָׁוְא ׀ וּדְבַר־כָּזָב הַרְחֵק מִמֶּנִּי<br>רֵאשׁ וָעֹשֶׁר אַל־תִּתֶּן־לִי<br>הַטְרִיפֵנִי לֶחֶם חֻקִּי׃ | 8 Put far from me vanity and 8<br>lies;<br>give me not poverty, nor riches;<br>feed me with food sufficient for<br>me. |
| 9 Lest I be full, and deny *thee*,<br>and say, Who *is* the LORD? or<br>lest I be poor, and steal, and take<br>the name of my God *in vain*. | 9 פֶּן אֶשְׂבַּע ׀ וְכִחַשְׁתִּי<br>וְאָמַרְתִּי מִי יְהוָה<br>וּפֶן־אִוָּרֵשׁ וְגָנַבְתִּי<br>וְתָפַשְׂתִּי שֵׁם אֱלֹהָי׃ | 9 Lest I be full, and deny, 9<br>and say, Who is Jehovah;<br>and lest I be poor, and steal,<br>and impugn the name of my<br>God. |

words, "has ascended to heaven, and come down," expressing ascent from a lower sphere and return to it, seem not to be characteristic of Him "in his supermundane nature." They imply, rather, one belonging to the lower sphere, and his ascent to the higher, for something with which he revisits the sphere to which he belongs. This, moreover, is pertinent in the connection. After professing his own imperfect knowledge of "the Holy," and as a preliminary to his rebuke of arrogant pretensions to it, he pertinently demands, whether any has ascended where that knowledge can be gained, and has brought it back to earth;* following this question with others, significant of our ignorance of all that might thus have been known.

*His fists:* dual because existing in pairs. Zöckler's fanciful supposition, that by "his two fists" is intimated the alternation of "two opposing currents of wind," is justly objected to by Dr. Aiken.

*A mantle.* According to the punctuation, *the mantle,* in which the punctators have been true to the Hebrew conception, designating by the article the garment of that peculiar shape, as is done in the consonant text itself in Gen. 9 : 23

*Has founded all the ends of the earth:* has laid its foundations, in all its length and breadth.—Zöckler, less in accordance with the use of the terms, "fixeth all the ends of the earth;" referring to "the bounds of the continents against the sea" (Am. edition).

*For thou knowest!* Gesenius (Lex. כי, 2, a, extr.), "ironically, Prov. 30 : 4, *what is his name and what his son's name?* כי תדע *for thou knowest* it of course."—*That thou shouldst know it* (Ewald, Bertheau, Kamphausen) is a proper rendering of the phrase in such a connection as Job 38 : 5, and may be here; though an act there takes after it the demonstrative conjunction indicating its sequence, which is not the case here.—*If thou knowest* (Rosenmüller, Maurer, Hitzig, Delitzsch, Zöckler) is a very questionable use of כי in such a connection as this.

* *Quis ascendit in coelum,* ut quid illic agatur intelligeret, *et descendit,* ut edoceret mortales quid viderit? (Maurer).

V. 7. *Withhold them not:* the pronominal object of the verb implied, as is often the case (Gesenius, Gram. § 121, Rem. 2).

V. 8. *Vanity* is the proper rendering,*—that which deceives, and disappoints expectation, by its empty and unsubstantial seeming. His prayer is, that he may seek only the true and substantial good.† If he was not above temptation to the practice of deception and lying, as the words are sometimes understood, he was on a very low moral plane.

*Food of my allotment* ‡=my allotted food; my allowance of food,—an amount sufficient for me. Compare the use of חק in Gen. 47 : 22, "the priests had a portion from Pharaoh, and they ate their portion (חקם) which Pharaoh gave them" (the writer's revised version).

V. 9. *And deny:* namely, make the denial implied in the following question—"Who is Jehovah?"—refusing to own his relation to me, and my dependence on him. Compare the passages referred to in the Explanatory Notes.

There is no propriety in supplying an object of the verb *deny.* So De Wette, Ewald, Kamphausen.§ So Zöckler, Lange's

* Ewald, correctly, Eitles; though his general conception of the thought is below its moral tone.

† So Maurer rightly understands the words: *Quidquid vanum est et verba mendacia remove a me. . . .* Unum igitur animi, alterum corporis bonum petit. Prius est, ut procul absit a sectandis rebus vanis.

‡ Eig.: mein Brod des חק, d. h. des Deputates, zugemessenen Theiles, 1 Mos. 47 : 22, Spr. 31 : 15 (Hitzig).

§ Damit ich nicht, übersättiget, verleugne, und spreche: Wer ist Jehovah? (De Wette). Damit ich nicht, zu satt geworden, längne—und sage: Wer ist Jahve? (Ewald). Dass ich nicht satt werde, und verleugne und spreche, Wer ist der Ewige? (Kamphausen, in notes).

| KING JAMES' VERSION. | | HEBREW TEXT. | REVISED VERSION. |
|---|---|---|---|
| 10 Accuse not a servant unto his master, lest he curse thee, and thou be found guilty. | י | אַל־תַּלְשֵׁן עֶבֶד אֶל־אֲדֹנָו<br>פֶּן־יְקַלֶּלְךָ, וְאָשָׁמְתָּ׃ | Slander not a servant to his 10<br>master;<br>lest he curse thee, and thou be<br>held guilty. |
| 11 *There is* a generation *that* curseth their father, and doth not bless their mother. | 11 | דּוֹר אָבִיו יְקַלֵּל<br>וְאֶת־אִמּוֹ לֹא יְבָרֵךְ׃ | A generation,—that curse 11<br>their father,<br>and bless not their mother! |
| 12 *There is* a generation *that are* pure in their own eyes, and *yet* is not washed from their filthiness. | 12 | דּוֹר טָהוֹר בְּעֵינָיו<br>וּמִצֹּאָתוֹ לֹא רֻחָץ׃ | A generation,—pure in their 12<br>own eyes,<br>and not washed from their filthiness! |
| 13 *There is* a generation, oh how lofty are their eyes! and their eyelids are lifted up. | 13 | דּוֹר מָה־רָמוּ עֵינָיו<br>וְעַפְעַפָּיו יִנָּשֵׂאוּ׃ | A generation,—how lofty are 13<br>their eyes,<br>and their eye lids are lifted up! |
| 14 *There is* a generation, whose teeth *are as* swords, and their jaw teeth *as* knives, to devour the poor from off the earth, and the needy from *among* men. | 14 | דּוֹר ׀ חֲרָבוֹת שִׁנָּיו<br>וּמַאֲכָלוֹת מְתַלְּעֹתָיו<br>לֶאֱכֹל עֲנִיִּים מֵאֶרֶץ<br>וְאֶבְיוֹנִים מֵאָדָם׃ | A generation,—their teeth 14<br>are swords,<br>and their fangs are knives;<br>to devour the poor from the<br>earth,<br>and the needy from among men! |

V. 10. אדניו ק'

Bibelwerk, in the original German edition.* In the American edition the object is supplied,—"Lest I, being full, deny (God),"—obscuring the true relation of the two members, though expressing the general sentiment.

*Impugn.* Properly, *to lay hold of*, with violence. Fürst (Lex.), "*to lay hold upon*, i. e. *to do violence to*, with the accus. שם יי׳ Prov. 30 : 9."† So De Wette and Kamphausen.‡ So also Zöckler (Lange's Bibelwerk, in the original German edition §); who justly says that it is the "wicked profanation of the Divine name, by mockery, cursing, and reviling" [or simply, angry reproach, which is all that is necessarily implied] "and not merely false swearing by the name of God in denying the guilt of theft."

V. 10. *Slander:* after the analogy of other denominatives in Hiphil, like האזין for example, *to ear*, to use the ear, to hearken; hence הלשין *to tongue*, to make free use of the tongue, to slander. Some would express the Hiph. form by *cause to slander*. But the idea of slander is itself communicated to the stem by the Hiph. form,‖ expressing the active use of the member (Gesenius, Gr. § 53, 2, Rem. 2d paragr.). With the rendering, "cause not the servant to slander his master," there is little need of the caution, "lest he curse thee." That might well be expected. Not more happy is the attempted escape from this, by supposing the subject (he) of the second member to be the servant himself; and that one may chance to hit upon the wrong person, a faithful servant, who will only curse the instigator for his pains. The risk would be considerable; but hardly a just ground of moral dissuasion.* In any view of this rendering, there is no congruity between the two members.

V. 11. *A generation*, without the substantive verb (Hitzig, Zöckler in the original German) is the proper expression of the writer's conception. The form of address, "O generation" (Ewald), is quite remote from it. Compare ch. 28 : 16.

That the traits enumerated in this and the three following verses are not merely "four forms of ungodliness" of one and the same generation (Zöckler), seems pretty clearly indicated by the repetition of the word, otherwise quite unnecessary, with each one of them. More consistent is the view of C. B. Michaelis,† followed by Umbreit, Rosenmüller, Maurer, Bertheau.

V. 14. *From the earth . . . from among men.* Not simply, *poor of the earth . . . needy among men* (Stuart, "wretched of the land . . . needy among men"), which in itself is grammatically correct, but is feeble in this connection. Of course they belong to the earth (or land) and are a part of men. The idea is, the utter consumption of the poor and needy from the earth and from among men, leaving no vestige of them. For the same

* Auf dass ich nicht satt geworden verleugne
und spreche: Wer ist Jehovah?

† Gesenius (Lex.), "*to lay hold upon the name of Jehovah*, sc. unlawfully and wrongfully, to do violence to the name of God, by falsehood and perjury;" a limitation not required by the connection. Maurer, more correctly, Dei mei nomen violem, vel pejerando (Exod. 20 : 7), vel deo injustitiæ insimulando, aut quomodocunque ex impatientia irreverenter de eo loquendo.

‡ Und mich vergreife am Namen meines Gottes.

§ Und antasten den Namen meines Gottes.

‖ Veri tamen similius est, Hiph. hic idem esse quod Po. Ps. 101 : 5, proprie *linguam facere*, exercere, hinc *calumniari* (Maurer).

* Not better is Bertheau's assumption (adopted by Stuart), that the servant, on finding how ill it turns out for himself, curses the instigator of his offense. Both suppositions interpret more into the passage than they interpret out of it.

† Sextum apophthegma, sistens quatuor detestabilia. Est *generatio*, h. e. genus hominum (Annott. uber.).

KING JAMES' VERSION.

15 The horseleech hath two daughters, *crying*, Give, give. There are three *things that* are never satisfied, *yea*, four *things* say not, *It is* enough :

HEBREW TEXT.

טו לַֽעֲלוּקָה ׀ שְׁתֵּי בָנוֹת הַב הַב
שָׁלוֹשׁ הֵנָּה לֹא תִשְׂבַּעְנָה
אַרְבַּע לֹא־אָמְרוּ הוֹן

REVISED VERSION.

The leech has two daughters, 15
Give, Give.
Three things there are that are not satisfied ;
four say not, Enough !

reason we should translate *earth* (not "land"), as the stronger expression.*

V. 15. *Leech* (עלוקה). So in all the ancient versions, and in the cognate dialects, as shown by Gesenius and Fürst.

The only questions to be considered are: 1st, whether the sacred writer means simply a *leech* in the literal sense; 2d, whether under this term there is allusion to a popular superstition of a "female blood-sucking monster," and two "female demons" her daughters; and 3d, whether the saying, here attributed to Agur, is of Indian origin.

On the point, whether the *leech* may be properly accepted as "personified insatiableness" (Bertheau), I think popular sentiment may be taken as a very fair test, in which the leech has become the proverbial representative of remorseless craving.

The assumption, by Gesenius and others,† of such a popular superstition among the Hebrews, under the name לילית Is. 34 : 14, is fully refuted by Dr. Alexander, on the passage.‡

The Indian origin attributed to this saying § (Hitzig, Bertheau, Zöckler, Delitzsch) rests on very slender grounds of probability. The simplicity, naturalness, and consistency of the Hebrew conception, are very decisive proofs of its originality. In all these it is superior to the Indian saying, of which it is taken by some to be the copy. It has, therefore, no appearance of an imitation, which always falls below the original, and betrays itself by dilution and tameness, in place of the vigor and compression which we see here. There is little in the Indian saying that resembles this of Agur ; and in the little which they have in common, there is nothing so unusual, or so unlikely to occur to more than one, as to subject either to the suspicion of borrowing from the other.‖

The case stands thus :

1. It is conceded, that the word is purely Semitic, of Semitic etymology and meaning* (Gesenius, Fürst, Ewald, Delitzsch).

2. It is assumed that a *foreign idea* is naturalized under this indigenous word (Gesenius, Delitzsch).

3. Of this, it is admitted, there is no proof in the sacred writings, nothing to show any other application of this word than that suggested by its etymology and recognized meaning.

4. The assumption of a popular superstition among the Hebrews, to which there may be allusion here, is not exegetically sustained.

5. The assumption of such an allusion does not facilitate the interpretation of this passage. Its requirements are fully met when the term is taken in its literal sense ; and it is needless to look for illustration to popular superstitions not native to the Hebrews, and of which there is no certain indication in their earlier or contemporary literature.†

The relation of the several members of this passage to each other is very simple, and suggests itself. To the *leech*, representing appetite, passion, greed, every inordinate desire, there are *two daughters, Give, Give,* representing their insatiable demands ; for however much is given, there is a twofold cry for more. The thought is further illustrated, in the following members, by four significant and striking parallels.‡

On the contrary, the elaborate arrangement and combinations, devized by Hitzig and Bertheau, and approved by others, are

* *Die Dulder zu verzehren aus der Erde—und die hülflosen aus den Menschen* (Ewald). *Zu fressen die Dulder hinweg von der Erde, und die Armen aus der Menschheit weg* (Hitzig). *Hinweg zu fressen die Elenden von der Erde und die Armen aus der Zahl der menschen* (Zöckler).

† Delitzsch (Commentar über den Proph. Jes. 34 : 10) holds this view.

‡ Prof. Lee (Heb. Lex., לילית) says on Is. 34 : 14, "The context, however, evidently speaks of real beings." So here, the term in question is associated in the context with others representing real existences.

§ Namely, in the Hitopadaeça (ed. Lassen, p. 66) as quoted by Hitzig :

> Fire is not sated with wood, nor the great sea with the streams,
> Nor the Death-god with all the living, nor the fair-eyed with men.

‖ Dagegen kann ich die Aehnlichkeit zwischen dem Spruche welcher v. 15 bleiben würde, und dem im Hitôpadaeça ed. Lassen p. 66, nicht so gross und bedeutsam finden wie Hitzig, noch weniger aus der sehr geringen Aehnlichkeit zwischen beiden solche Folgerungen ziehen wie Hitzig (Ewald, Jahrbb. der Wiss., 1848, p. 112).

* Hitzig thinks it may have a Sanskrit etymology (עלוקה sankrit. Etymologie zu bekennen scheint). On the contrary, the alliteration in the sanskrit *galukâ* is only accidental (Fürst, Lex. ; Ewald, Jahrbb. der Bibl. Wiss., 1848, p. 112).

† Dr. Aiken justly says (Lange's Biblework, Am. ed., p. 250) : "Only the most unnatural theory of inspiration can take exception [on that ground] to the suggestion of a possible Indian origin for the substance and the external form of this proverb ; its place and form here being secured by an appropriate and adequate influence of the Holy Spirit." It may be added, that the Holy Spirit is not limited as to his instruments or modes of action. We only need that his teachings shall be duly attested.

‡ The natural and commendable desire for offspring (compare the only too passionate expression of it, Gen. 30 : 1, "Give me children, or else I die"), is certainly all that is here meant by the unsatisfied craving of the barren womb. It is not just to the sacred writer to impute to him any other thought.

| KING JAMES' VERSION. | HEBREW TEXT. | REVISED VERSION. |
|---|---|---|
| 16 The grave; and the barren womb; the earth *that* is not filled with water; and the fire *that* saith not, *It is* enough. | שְׁאוֹל וְעֹצֶר רָחַם<br>אֶרֶץ לֹא־שָׂבְעָה מַּיִם<br>וְאֵשׁ לֹא־אָמְרָה הוֹן׃ 16 | 16 The underworld, and the barren womb;<br>the earth, that is not satisfied with water,<br>and fire, that says not, Enough! |
| 17 The eye *that* mocketh at *his* father, and despiseth to obey *his* mother, the ravens of the valley shall pick it out, and the young eagles shall eat it. | עַיִן ׀ תִּלְעַג לְאָב<br>וְתָבוּז לִיקֲּהַת־אֵם<br>יִקְּרוּהָ עֹרְבֵי־נַחַל<br>וְיֹאכְלוּהָ בְנֵי־נָשֶׁר׃ 17 | 17 The eye that mocks at a father,<br>and scorns obedience to a mother;<br>the ravens of the valley shall pick it out,<br>and the young of the vulture shall eat it. |
| 18 There be three *things which* are too wonderful for me, yea, four which I know not: | שְׁלֹשָׁה הֵמָּה נִפְלְאוּ מִמֶּנִּי<br>וְאַרְבָּעָ לֹא יְדַעְתִּים׃ 18 | 18 Three things there are, too difficult for me;<br>and four, which I understand not. |
| 19 The way of an eagle in the air; the way of a serpent upon a rock; the way of a ship in the midst of the sea; and the way of a man with a maid. | דֶּרֶךְ הַנֶּשֶׁר ׀ בַּשָּׁמַיִם<br>דֶּרֶךְ נָחָשׁ עֲלֵי־צוּר<br>דֶּרֶךְ־אֳנִיָּה בְלֶב־יָם<br>וְדֶרֶךְ גֶּבֶר בְּעַלְמָה׃ 19 | 19 The way of the eagle in the heavens;<br>the way of the serpent on a rock;<br>the way of a ship in the midst of the sea;<br>and the way of a man with a maid. |
| 20 Such *is* the way of an adulterous woman; she eateth, and wipeth her mouth, and saith, I have done no wickedness. | כֵּן ׀ דֶּרֶךְ אִשָּׁה מְנָאָפֶת<br>אָכְלָה וּמָחֲתָה פִיהָ<br>וְאָמְרָה לֹא־פָעַלְתִּי אָוֶן׃ כ | 20 So is the way of an adulterous woman;<br>she eats, and wipes her mouth,<br>and says, I have done no iniquity. |

V. 17. בנ״א ק׳ רפה V. 18. וארבעה ק׳

unnatural and inconsistent. For example, by the *two daughters* (imaginary "female demons") are meant the underworld and the barren womb. But with what propriety can they be represented by two female demons; and in what proper sense can the mother "female monster," though personifying insatiableness, be made to hold this relation of maternity to the underworld and the barren womb? The conception is simply monstrous. Quite as ingenious, and more instructive, would be the supposition of Jephet Ben Eli, that the two daughters are المعدة والفرج* (representing the two animal appetites most indulged), and that the following four instances (as he says further on) are the Creator's illustrations of inordinate appetites, which are never sated with indulgence.†

V. 17 is to be taken by itself, and not in connection with vv. 15, 16, as fancifully suggested by Ewald.‡ See further remarks in Explanatory Notes.

*Vulture* is probably meant here, under the general term נשר, which includes several species. See Smith's Bible Dictionary, art. Eagle, and Wood's Bible Animals, art. Griffon Vulture, p. 344 and following.

VV. 18–20. The writer's view of this very difficult passage may be seen in the Explanatory Notes. It only remains here to consider other views which seem to me less tenable.

And first I remark, that as only physical relations are taken into account in the first three instances, many think that such is the case in the remaining two. This may seem most natural; but only to an outward and superficial view. To give the fourth and fifth instances any moral significance, or any proper significance whatever, they must be taken in a higher sense. Understood in a merely physical sense, they are weak and irrelevant trifling.

It is common to assume, as the point of comparison in all the five instances, that *no trace* of the act remains. The eagle cleaves the air, leaving no track behind him by which his course may be traced. So of the serpent on a rock, of a ship in the sea. But is there anything wonderful in this, or difficult to understand? Is it not true of everything that moves through air or water, or over solid rock? What other animal, any more than the serpent, leaves its track on a rock? Plainly, something more is intended.*

* *Stomachus et verenda.*

† Jepheti Ben Eli Karaitae in Prov. Sal. cap. xxx. commentarius, quem nunc primum Arabice ed. Z. Auerbach. 1866.

‡ Die Unersättlichkeit der Raubvögel tritt gar nicht hervor, während doch bei einer Verbindung mit V. 15 f. grade diese nachdrücklichst hervorgehoben werden müsste (Bertheau).

* Since the above was in type, I observe that Jephet Ben Eli, in his commentary (see above, on v. 15) says of the serpent,

| KING JAMES' VERSION. | HEBREW TEXT. | | REVISED VERSION. | |
|---|---|---|---|---|
| 21 For three *things* the earth is disquieted, and for four *which* it cannot bear: | תַּחַת שָׁלוֹשׁ רָגְזָה אֶרֶץ<br>וְתַחַת אַרְבַּע לֹא־תוּכַל שְׂאֵת׃ | 21 | Under three things the land is disquieted;<br>and under four it can not bear up. | 21 |
| 22 For a servant when he reigneth; and a fool when he is filled with meat; | תַּחַת עֶבֶד כִּי יִמְלוֹךְ<br>וְנָבָל כִּי יִשְׂבַּע־לָחֶם׃ | 22 | Under a servant, when he reigns,<br>and a fool when he is sated with food; | 22 |
| 23 For an odious *woman* when she is married; and an handmaid that is heir to her mistress. | תַּחַת שְׂנוּאָה כִּי תִבָּעֵל<br>וְשִׁפְחָה כִּי־תִירַשׁ גְּבִרְתָּהּ׃ | 23 | under a hated woman, when she is married,<br>and a maidservant when she is heir to her mistress. | 23 |
| 24 There be four *things which are* little upon the earth, but they *are* exceeding wise: | אַרְבָּעָה הֵם קְטַנֵּי־אָרֶץ<br>וְהֵמָּה חֲכָמִים מְחֻכָּמִים׃ | 24 | Four things there are, the smallest of the earth,<br>and they wise, instructed in wisdom. | 24 |
| 25 The ants *are* a people not strong, yet they prepare their meat in the summer; | הַנְּמָלִים עַם לֹא־עָז<br>וַיָּכִינוּ בַקַּיִץ לַחְמָם׃ | כה | The ants, a people not strong;<br>and they prepare their food in summer. | 25 |

V. 22. *Or*, becomes king.

V. 23, 2d member. *Or*, has dispossessed

Moreover, this utterly fails in its application to the fourth instance, as is admitted by Zöckler (Lange's Biblework, Am. ed. p. 251), and the force of the admission is not lessened by his subsequent explanation; for as he himself justly claims, it is the marriageable maiden (עלמה), the bride in her first intercourse with the bridegroom, that is here spoken of;* and in any case, what might be true "of the night following" is not to the purpose. Bertheau's plea (in which he is followed by Stuart) that only "the man" comes into account here, is not valid. It might as well be said, that only the eagle, serpent, and ship come into account, without reference to air, rock, and sea.

The whole theory of "*leaving no trace*" is interpreted into the passage.† It is not suggested in any form of expression.‡ is trivial in all the five instances, and of some of them untrue, and leaves the passage without moral significance.§

V. 21. *The land* (rather than *earth*, Zöckler), as properly rendered in Am. 7 : 10.

V. 22 (margin). *Becomes king* (begins to reign), as the Hebrew word is correctly rendered in the common English version, in 2 Sam. 2 : 10; 1 Kings 16 : 23, 29; 22 : 41; 2 Kings 3 : 1. De Wette, Kamphausen, *wenn er König wird.* Zöckler, *wenn er Herrscher wird.*

V. 23. See Explanatory Notes.—*Hated:* Zöckler, correctly, *Gehassten.* De Wette, correctly as to the sense, *Verschmäheten.* Not *hateful;* though unlovely (Kamphausen, *Unliebsam*) seems implied, as the ground of the designation.

Second member. *Is heir to.* De Wette, *ihre Gebieterin beerbt.* Bertheau, Zöckler, *ihre Herrin beerbt.*—(Margin), *has dispossessed.* So Gesenius (Lex.). Kamphausen, *wenn sie ihre Frau verdrängt.*

V. 24. *Smallest of the earth* (Gesenius, Gram. § 119, 2).—*Instructed in wisdom,*—taught wisdom,—added to the simple epithet *wise,* for more emphatic expression. Kamphausen, *weise und gewitzigt.* Zöckler, *weise, wohlgewitzigt.* Others, less happily, and with a less natural construction of the Hebrew, *the wise made wise;* that is, wiser than the commonly wise, wisest of all. So Ewald, *allerweisesten;* Bertheau, *die weise gewordenen Weisen,* die allerweisesten.

V. 25. See Explanatory Notes.—*Prepare their food in summer,* can mean only, that in summer they make provision for the coming winter. To say that in summer they provide food for the season, would be simply nonsense; for when should they provide it, except when it is wanted and is to be had? And what animal neglects to do this?

that its track is apparent only when it moves on the ground. وانما يبين اثرها اذا مشت على التراب. That it leaves a track on the ground, but not on a rock, is equally true of other animals; and in this view there is no reason for selecting the serpent as an example. In all other points also he accords with the views opposed in the text.

* Puris honestisque verbis, venerandum illud concubii pudici secretum (Aulus Gellius, Noctes Atticae, lib. ix. c. 10, 4).

† So Ewald understands the writer to mean, namely that he does not comprehend how the eagle, with its heavy body, flies through the air, how the serpent without feet moves on a rock, and the ship with its heavy burden traverses remote seas.

‡ "Wipes her mouth," which Bertheau thinks interprets back into all the preceding instances, only indicates with what careless levity she regards a crime, of which she can so easily remove the evidence.

§ The lesson deduced from this view by Stuart, namely "a caution against unlimited credulity in first appearances," will not be thought an exception to the statement in the text.

| KING JAMES' VERSION. | HEBREW TEXT. | REVISED VERSION. |
| --- | --- | --- |
| 26 The conies *are but* a feeble folk, yet make they their houses in the rocks; | 26 שְׁפַנִּים עַם לֹא־עָצוּם. <br> וַיָּשִׂימוּ בַסֶּלַע בֵּיתָם׃ | The conies, a people not powerful; 26 <br> and they make their abode in the cliff. |
| 27 The locusts have no king, yet go they forth all of them by bands; | 27 מֶלֶךְ אֵין לָאַרְבֶּה <br> וַיֵּצֵא חֹצֵץ כֻּלּוֹ׃ | The locusts have no king; 27 <br> and they go forth all of them in bands. |
| 28 The spider taketh hold with her hands, and is in kings' palaces. | 28 שְׂמָמִית בְּיָדַיִם תְּתַפֵּשׂ <br> וְהִיא בְּהֵיכְלֵי מֶלֶךְ׃ | The lizard takes hold with the hands; 28 <br> and she is in kings' palaces. |
| 29 There be three *things* which go well, yea, four are comely in going: | 29 שְׁלֹשָׁה הֵמָּה מֵיטִבֵי צָעַד <br> וְאַרְבָּעָה מֵטִבֵי לָכֶת׃ <br> V. 29 בנ"א מטיבי | Three things there are, graceful in step, 29 <br> and four are graceful in going. |

V. 26. *Conies.* The Biblical name of an animal now known to be the *Hyrax Syriacus*, a small, timid, and wary animal, inhabiting the rocky cliffs of Palestine.* We have no exactly corresponding name in English, and the Biblical name is used here, as defined in Webster's English Dictionary, art. *Coney.*

*Cliff:* not simply "rock," as in the common English version, but a lofty rock or cliff, and hence difficult of access.† This is its proper specific meaning, and is usually indicated more or less clearly in the connection.‡ See, for example, Judg. 15 : 8, properly, *dwelt in the top of the cliff Etam;* v. 11, *went to the top of the cliff Etam;* 2 Chr. 25 : 12, properly, *brought them to the top of the cliff, and cast them down from the top of the cliff.*

V. 27. *Locust:* ארבה, the name of the locust as most generally known, namely in its last and full stage of developement, the winged or migratory locust, in which state it commences its ravaging march over remote regions.

Second member. *In bands.* Ewald, Hitzig, Bertheau, Kamphausen, Zöckler, *geordnet.* More exactly, Gesenius (Lex). "*divided*, that is, in divisions, bands"; Fürst (Lex.), "*forming ranks, lines* (i. e. arranged divisions), *in bands.*"

V. 28. The word שממית, improperly rendered "spider" in the common English version, is now known to denote some species of lizard, of which several were common in Palestine. Smith's Bible Dictionary, arts, Spider and Lizard. Wood's Bible Animals, arts. Spider, p. 643; Lizard, p. 529; Ferret, p. 69.

For the habits of the Lizard supposed to be here referred to, see Explanatory Notes. Ewald supposes the writer to mean, that though she only feels with the hands, yet she knows how to provide for herself such beautiful dwellings as palaces; § a possible construction of the writer's words, but not the most obvious and natural one.

Böttcher's suggestion (Neue Aehrenl. 1371) that בידים תתפש means *is held fast with the hands,** being so small and powerless, is anticipated by Jephet Ben Eli, p. 40 (as above, on v. 15).

V. 29. זרזיר מתנים, *girded about the loins,* or *contracted in the loins.* It is not the name of an animal, but a descriptive designation of one, *loin-begirt,*† or *slender-loined.* Only this is known with certainty; all else is conjecture.

But whatever may be thus designated, it is almost certain that a natural trait, something belonging to itself, is the ground of the designation, and not some foreign addition, which is no part of itself, and therefore does not necessarily characterize it.

Hence the meaning *war-horse,*‡ so called because belted about the loins with military trappings, as represented in the sculptures of Persepolis, may well be questioned, as not corresponding with the proper application of the phrase. There is the same objection to Maurer's rendering, *wrestler,* approved by the writer of the art. Greyhound, in Smith's Bible Dictionary. The passage quoted by Maurer from Buxtorf's Chald. and Rab. Lex. would show (if there were need of showing it, as Maurer justly thinks is not the case) that *girded one* might be a descriptive designation of a wrestler, "his girded one" (זרזירו) meaning one girded to contend with him. But Maurer's statement, that this signification *viget in Talmude,* is hardly justified by its single occurrence in a tract of the Jerusalem Talmud, where a *gloss* is required to explain it. It might naturally denote any athlete, a

* Diese [Steinklüften] sind grade aber der immerwährende Aufenthalt und Schlupfwinkel des Wubbr. (Seetzen's Reise, Vol. II. p. 230).

† Stanley, Sinai and Palestine (Appendix, § 29): "סֶלַע, a cliff, from סָלַע to be lifted up; hence here the leading idea is that of height, and the allusions are continually to 'the top of the cliff,' as for instance, Judg. 15 : 8; 2 Kings 14 : 7; Is. 2 : 21.'

‡ "Came down into a rock," 1 Sam. 23 : 25, is a mistranslation; properly, *went down the cliff,* descended it.

§ Die kleine nur mit den Händen tastende Eidechse weiss sich doch so schöne Wohnungen zu verschaffen wie Paläste sind.

* תתפש *wird Jefast mit Händen,* nämlich so klein und ohnmächtig ist sie, vgl. v. 24 ff.

† Sym. *περιεσφραγισμένος* (*περιεσφιγμένος?* Sophocles' Lex.) *τὴν ὀσφυήν.*

‡ Gesenius, Thes. (Vol. II. p. 435), and his Lexicon Manualis, where he gives the preference to *war-horse;* but in his later and maturer view, communicated to Dr. Robinson for the Am. ed. of the Manual Lexicon (Dr. Robinson's preface, p. vii), he does not decide between *war-horse, greyhound,* and *wrestler.*

Aber זרזיר verräth sich schon durch seine verstärkte Adjectivform als natürliche Eigenschaft (Böttcher, Neue Aehrenl. 1372).

| KING JAMES' VERSION. | HEBREW TEXT. | | REVISED VERSION. | |
|---|---|---|---|---|
| 30 A lion, *which is* strongest among beasts, and turneth not away for any ; | לַיִשׁ גִּבּוֹר בַּבְּהֵמָה<br>וְלֹא־יָשׁוּב מִפְּנֵי־כֹל׃ | ל | A lion, mighty among beasts,<br>and he turns not back before any. | 30 |
| 31 A greyhound ; a he goat also ; and a king, against whom *there is* no rising up. | זַרְזִיר מָתְנַיִם אוֹ־תָיִשׁ<br>וּמֶלֶךְ אַלְקוּם עִמּוֹ׃ | 31 | A greyhound, or a he-goat ;<br>and a king, with whom are the people. | 31 |
| 32 If thou hast done foolishly in lifting up thyself, or if thou hast thought evil, *lay* thine hand upon thy mouth. | אִם־נָבַלְתָּ בְהִתְנַשֵּׂא<br>וְאִם־זַמּוֹתָ יָד לְפֶה׃ | 32 | If thou hast been foolish in exalting thyself,<br>and if thou hast thought evil,—the hand to the mouth! | 32 |
| 33 Surely the churning of milk bringeth forth butter, and the wringing of the nose bringeth forth blood : so the forcing of wrath bringeth forth strife. | כִּי מִיץ חָלָב יוֹצִיא חֶמְאָה<br>וּמִיץ־אַף יוֹצִיא דָם׃<br>וּמִיץ אַפַּיִם יוֹצִיא רִיב׃ | 33 | For pressing of milk brings forth cheese ;<br>and pressing of the nose brings forth blood ;<br>and pressing of anger brings forth strife. | 33 |

wrestler, runner, etc., but there is no evidence that it was the special designation of one.

There is no special ground for the rendering *stag*, suggested by Fürst (Lex.) as perhaps intended. Still less applicable is this phrase to the *cock* (LXX. *ἀλέκτωρ ἐμπεριπατῶν θηλείαις εὔψυχος ;* Aquila, Theodotion, *ἀλέκτρυὼν νώτῳ*), the *eagle*, or the *bee* (in Aben Ezra), or the *zebra* (Ludolph, Simonis).

On the whole, there seems to be no sufficient ground for changing the rendering of the common English version, *Greyhound* (Kimchi, Rabbi Ben Gersom, Versio Veneta, ed. Villoison. *λαγωοκύων ψοιῶν*), approved by Ewald,* Bertheau,† and retained from Luther's version, and defended on good grounds by Zöckler.

Second member. The word אלקום, as in the common Masoretic text, is understood to be an Arabic form, meaning *the people*. So Gesenius,‡ Umbreit, Rosenmüller and others, and more recently Muehlau.

By others the form is divided, and is read אל קום, as in four codd. of Kennicott and fourteen of De Rossi ; § and is construed like אל־מות in ch. 12 : 28. So the Hebrew interpreters generally,|| and the earlier christian scholars,¶ and some of the more

* Nach diesem Zusammenhange kann זרזיר מתנים, eigentlich der lendenenge oder -schmächtige (vgl. § 158, *a*), sehr gut vom Windspiele verstanden werden.

† *Der magere, schmächtige an den Lenden*, nach judischen Erklärern *das Windspiel*, welches hier ganz herpasst.

‡ Thes. vol. I. p. 93. Idem quod arab. القوم *populus*. . . . *Rex, quocum populus* i. e. populo suo stipatus, in media populi corona incedens.

§ Kennicott, אל קום, 98, 155, 188, 226.—De Rossi, אל קום *cui resisti nequit* [enumerates the four of Kennicott, and fourteen of his own].

|| Jephet Ben Eli Karaitae (see last paragraph of remarks on v. 15, and foot-note) gives this first, and the other as an alternative rendering ; وملك لا قيام معه وقيل القوم معه.

¶ Münster (Biblia Hebraica, 1546), *atque rex contra quem nemo consurgit*. (Note). אלקום componitur ab לא קום — Mercier (In Prov. Comment.), *et rex in quem nemo insurgit*.

recent ones. Ewald, *ein König, der unwiderstehlich ;** Maurer ;† Bertheau, *ein König bei welchem Nicht-Widerstand ist ;* Kamphausen ;‡ Zöckler, who with Hitzig and Bertheau objects, that an Arabic form is not to be looked for here.—For this use of עמי a parallel expression, referred to by Hitzig, is found in Ps. 94 : 16.

More recently Muehlau,§ who has more minutely examined this portion of the book, defends the Arabic form, on the ground of the frequent occurrence of such forms in the "Words of Agur." He claims, that the Arabic word does not properly mean *the people* of the country (Freytag), but specifically those who are called out for its defense, who *rise up* in defense of the land.—On the contrary, compare Gesenius, Manual Lex., art. אלקום and the verb קום, 3, the Samar. קום *to live*, and the Heb. noun יקום, Gen. 7 : 4, 23.

V. 32. *The hand to the mouth !* The spirited expression of the sacred writer should not be toned down to common-place tameness, by supplying the ellipsis with "*put*" or "*lay*," as is sometimes done.

V. 33. *Pressing of milk :* of coagulated milk, to expel the serum, and separate it from the caseine. A different process, in the making of *butter*, is described by Robinson, Researches in Palestine, Vol. II. p. 180, and by Thompson, The Land and the Book, Vol. I. p. 393.

*Anger :* naturally expressed by אפים (the nostrils, *dual* as

(Note). Cui nemo resistat, cum quo ut pugnet, et adversus quem ut stet, nemo sese offerre ausit, rex invictus, quem nemo ausit aggredi.

* אל קום ist unstreitig (vgl. 12 : 28 und § 286 *g*) so zu verstehen, wie man hier *μή* gebrauchen könnte.

† Qui אלקום statuunt significare *non surgere*, significatus habent usitatos et formam compositionis, quae firmetur illo אל־מות 12 : 28.

‡ Da unser Spruchbuch nicht arabisch, sondern hebräisch abgefasst ist, kann 'alqûm unmöglich "sein Volk" heissen.

§ De proverbiorum quae dicuntur Aguri et Lemuelis origine atque indole, 1869.

**KING JAMES' VERSION.**

**CHAP. XXXI.**

THE words of king Lemuel, the prophecy that this mother taught him.

2 What, my son? and what, the son of my womb? and what, the son of my vows?

3 Give not thy strength unto women, nor thy ways to that which destroyeth kings.

4 *It is* not for kings, O Lemuel, *it is* not for kings to drink wine; nor for princes strong drink:

5 Lest they drink, and forget the law, and pervert the judgment of any of the afflicted.

6 Give strong drink unto him that is ready to perish, and wine unto those that be of heavy hearts.

**HEBREW TEXT.**

**CHAP. XXXI.**

א דִּבְרֵי לְמוּאֵל מֶלֶךְ
מַשָּׂא אֲשֶׁר־יִסְּרַתּוּ אִמּוֹ׃
2 מַה־בְּרִי וּמַה־בַּר בִּטְנִי
וּמֶה בַּר־נְדָרָי׃
3 אַל־תִּתֵּן לַנָּשִׁים חֵילֶךָ
וּדְרָכֶיךָ לַמְחוֹת מְלָכִין׃
4 אַל לַמְלָכִים ׀ לְמוֹאֵל
אַל לַמְלָכִים שְׁתוֹ־יָיִן
וּלְרוֹזְנִים אֵו שֵׁכָר׃
ה פֶּן־יִשְׁתֶּה וְיִשְׁכַּח מְחֻקָּק
וִישַׁנֶּה דִּין כָּל־בְּנֵי־עֹנִי׃
6 תְּנוּ־שֵׁכָר לְאוֹבֵד
וְיַיִן לְמָרֵי נָפֶשׁ׃

V. 4. בנ"א בשורק Ib. אי ק'

**REVISED VERSION.**

**CHAP. XXXI.**

THE words of king Lemuel. 1
An oracle, with which his
mother instructed him.
What, my son? 2
And what, son of my womb?
And what, son of my vows?
Give not thy strength to women, 3
nor thy ways to that which destroys kings.
It is not for kings, O Lemuel, 4
it is not for kings to drink wine,
nor for princes, or strong drink.
Lest he drink, and forget the law, 5
and pervert the cause of any of the sons of want.
Give strong drink to the perishing, 6
and wine to the sorrowful in spirit.

always existing in pairs), the dilating of the nostrils,* and quickened breathing through them, being the most marked physical indication of it. Zöckler's fanciful suggestion, that the two parties to the strife are intended by the dual form (as though the two nostrils could be conceived as pitted against each other in strife) is properly corrected by Dr. Aiken (Lange's Bible-work, Am. ed. p. 252).

Ch. XXXI. 1-10. See Introd. § *⁎*

V. 1. *King Lemuel.* See the note on ch. 30 : 1, No. 10 (of answers to objections) p. 129.†—*Oracle* (משא); see the note on ch. 30 : 1, second paragraph.

V. 2. *What, my son?* Some translators and interpreters interpolate the words, "shall I say,"—what [shall I say] my son? But this by no means exhausts, or rather is far from truly expressing, the import of the question; and it would be better to leave the reader to his own reflections, than thus limit him to a single point of view, and that not the true one. See Explanatory Notes.—בר, as in Ps. 2 : 12.

V. 3. למחות (for להמחות, *Hiph. Infin.*) *to the destroying* = destroying influence, that which destroys; ‡ namely, a course of conduct that is destructive in its effects, a life of licentious indulgence.§ This sense of the word, with the pointing לַמְחוֹת, is well expressed by Ewald;* though he prefers to read לְמֹחוֹת (מֹחוֹת the *plur.* of the *part.* מֹחָה, formed from מֹחַ *marrow*), *to those who enervate.* So Fürst, in his lexicon. Böttcher (Neue Aehrenl. 1372) with the same reading, but with the sense *to stroke, to caress,*† would translate, *those who caress kings* (die liebkosende Schmeichlerinnen. Hitzig, on quite uncertain grounds, renders, *who leer after kings.*‡

Fourth member. *Nor:* the force of the negative continued from the first member, as often in such connections.—*Or:* או pointed as אַו, its distributive use being too nearly allied to the ground meaning to be justly questioned.§ See the passages referred to by Hitzig, ch. 30 : 31, and Job 22 : 1, improperly objected to by Muehlau, p. 57. Some, with the pointing אַו, make it the subject nominative, *nor for princes the desire of strong drink* (Gesenius, Lex. אַו, 1).||

The reading of the *Keri, Nor for princes* (to say) *where is strong drink,* as in the majority of cases, is not to be preferred.

V. 5. מחקק (*Pual part*) *what is prescribed*=statute, or law.

* Compare its expression in the Apollo Belvedere; and Shakspeare (King Henry V. iii. 1) "Now set the teeth, and stretch the nostril wide."

† Kamphausen: Worte von König Lemuel; ein Ausspruch womit ihn seine Mutter unterwies.

‡ Ewald: *zum Vernichten von Königen* = so dass Könige vernichtet werden, also auch du.

§ The reference which some make to destructive wars, is out of place in this connection.

* Eigentlich: *und* (gib oder *mache* nicht) *deine Wege* oder Handlungen *zum Vernichten von Königen* = so dass Könige vernichtet werden, also auch du; welches eben am meisten durch Wollust geschiet.

† Denn das semitische מחה (מחא) umfasst deutlich latein. mulcere und mulcare. He fails, however, to make out his case, and does not even justify his *wohl auch.*

‡ Die blinzen nach Königen.

§ Maurer: Quum vero quae viget significatio *aut* a loco non abhorreat, eam hic quoque tenendam putamus.

|| Fürst (Lex.), with the pointing אַו, takes it interrogatively (*Keri* אֵי, *where?*), *nor for princes* (to say) *where is strong drink?*

| KING JAMES' VERSION. | HEBREW TEXT. | | REVISED VERSION. | |
|---|---|---|---|---|
| 7 Let him drink, and forget his poverty, and remember his misery no more. | יִשְׁתֶּה וְיִשְׁכַּח רִישׁוֹ<br>וַעֲמָלוֹ לֹא יִזְכָּר־עוֹד׃ | 7 | Let him drink, and forget his poverty,<br>and remember his misery no more. | 7 |
| 8 Open thy mouth for the dumb in the cause of all such as are appointed to destruction. | פְּתַח־פִּיךָ לְאִלֵּם<br>אֶל־דִּין כָּל־בְּנֵי חֲלוֹף׃ | 8 | Open thy mouth for the dumb;<br>for the cause of all orphan children. | 8 |
| 9 Open thy mouth, judge righteously, and plead the cause of the poor and needy. | פְּתַח־פִּיךָ שְׁפָט־צֶדֶק<br>וְדִין עָנִי וְאֶבְיוֹן׃ | 9 | Open thy mouth, judge righteously;<br>and judge the poor and needy. | 9 |
| 10 ¶ Who can find a virtuous woman? for her price *is* far above rubies. | אֵשֶׁת־חַיִל מִי יִמְצָא<br>וְרָחֹק מִפְּנִינִים מִכְרָהּ׃ | י | A capable woman who shall find?<br>for far above pearls is her worth. | 10 |
| 11 The heart of her husband doth safely trust in her, so that he shall have no need of spoil. | בָּטַח בָּהּ לֵב בַּעְלָהּ<br>וְשָׁלָל לֹא יֶחְסָר׃ | 11 | The heart of her husband confides in her;<br>and he shall not lack for gain. | 11 |
| 12 She will do him good and not evil all the days of her life. | גְּמָלַתְהוּ טוֹב וְלֹא־רָע<br>כֹּל יְמֵי חַיֶּיהָ׃ | 12 | She will render to him good, and not evil,<br>all the days of her life. | 12 |
| 13 She seeketh wool, and flax, and worketh willingly with her hands. | דָּרְשָׁה צֶמֶר וּפִשְׁתִּים<br>וַתַּעַשׂ בְּחֵפֶץ כַּפֶּיהָ׃ | 13 | She seeks for wool and flax;<br>and works with her willing hands. | 13 |
| 14 She is like the merchants' ships; she bringeth her food from afar. | הָיְתָה כָּאֳנִיּוֹת סוֹחֵר<br>מִמֶּרְחָק תָּבִיא לַחְמָהּ׃ | 14 | She is like the merchants' ships;<br>she brings her food from afar. | 14 |
| 15 She riseth also while it is yet night, and giveth meat to her household, and a portion to her maidens. | וַתָּקָם ׀ בְּעוֹד לַיְלָה<br>וַתִּתֵּן טֶרֶף לְבֵיתָהּ<br>וְחֹק לְנַעֲרֹתֶיהָ׃ | טו | And she rises while it is yet night,<br>and gives nourishment to her household,<br>and a task to her maids. | 15 |

V. 8. *Orphan children:* Gesenius Thes. and Lex.; Fürst Lex.

V. 10. *A capable woman:* as the meaning is well expressed by Dr. Robinson, Heb. lex., חיל, 4. The phrase is so used in Gen. 47 : 6, properly, "if thou knowest that there are capable men among them;" common English version, less accurately, "men of activity."* So it is used in Ex. 18 : 21, 25, well rendered in the common English version, "able men."†

A "virtuous woman" (common version) is not meant. The reference here is not to moral excellences alone, as would now be understood by the term *virtuous*, but to all the qualities natural and acquired, which fit one for the station of a wife and mother, and mistress of a household. So she is described in the following verses.

Second member. *Pearls.* See the note on ch. 3 : 15.

V. 11. *Gain* (שלל). See Roediger, Ges. Thes., p. 1420, 2nd col. *ima.*

V. 13. *With her willing hands;* strictly, *with the delight of her hands,* Gesenius, Thes. Vol. II. p. 1075 (עשה, 1): *et laborat lubenti manu* (Sie schaffet mit Lust ihrer Hände). Ewald: *mit ihrer Hände Lust.*

Another construction is admissible, namely: *works cheerfully* (strictly, with pleasure) *with her hands* (§ 118, 3). Böttcher (Neue Aehrenl. 1376): *und schaffet mit Lust eigenhändig;* כפיה, wie das häufige ידיו, in Supposition.

V. 15, third member. *A task:* חק as in Ex. 5 : 14. חקכם *your task,* your appointed work. At early dawn, while it is yet night, she rises and dispenses food to her household, and to each maid her daily task. Thus both duties of a mistress are fulfilled, of providing nourishment for all, and assigning their several tasks.

Another rendering is admissible; namely, *a portion* (חק) *for*

* Men of capacity is the meaning; men able to perform the duties required, as the phrase is used in Ex. 18 : 21, 25.

† It may interest the reader to trace the rendering of this phrase in the early English versions. Coverdale: Gen. 47 : 6, *men of activity;* Ex. 18 : 21, 25, *honest men;* Prov. 31 : 10, *an honest, faithful woman.* Matthews, Cranmer, Taverner, Bishops: Gen. 47 : 6, *men* (Cr. and Bish. *man*) *of activity;* Ex. 18 : 21, *men of activity,* v. 25, *active men;* Prov. 31 : 10 (as Cov.). Genevan: Gen. 47 : 6, *men of activity;* Ex. 18 : 21, 25, *men of courage;* Prov. 31 : 10, *a virtuous woman.* Common English version: Gen. 47 : 6, *men of activity;* Ex. 18 : 21, 25, *able men;* Prov. 31 : 10, *a virtuous woman.*

It will be seen that King James' revisers abandoned all the early English versions for their own better rendering in Ex. 18 : 21, 25, and for that of the Puritan exiles in Prov. 31 : 10.

| KING JAMES' VERSION. | HEBREW TEXT. | REVISED VERSION. |
|---|---|---|
| 16 She considereth a field, and buyeth it; with the fruit of her hands she planteth a vineyard. | 16 זָמְמָה שָׂדֶה וַתִּקָּחֵהוּ<br>מִפְּרִי כַפֶּיהָ נָטְעָ כָּרֶם׃ | 16 She considers a field, and obtains it;<br>with the fruit of her hands she plants a vineyard. |
| 17 She girdeth her loins with strength, and strengtheneth her arms. | 17 חָגְרָה בְעוֹז מָתְנֶיהָ<br>וַתְּאַמֵּץ זְרוֹעֹתֶיהָ׃ | 17 She girds her loins with strength,<br>and strengthens her arms. |
| 18 She perceiveth that her merchandise *is* good: her candle goeth not out by night. | 18 טָעֲמָה כִּי־טוֹב סַחְרָהּ<br>לֹא־יִכְבֶּה בַלַּיְל נֵרָהּ׃ | 18 She perceives that her gains are good;<br>her lamp goes not out by night. |
| 19 She layeth her hands to the spindle, and her hands hold the distaff. | 19 יָדֶיהָ שִׁלְּחָה בַכִּישׁוֹר<br>וְכַפֶּיהָ תָּמְכוּ פָלֶךְ׃ | 19 She puts forth her hands to the distaff,<br>and her hands lay hold on the spindle. |
| | V. 16. נטעה ק׳ V. 18. בלילה ק׳ | |

*her maids.** See the note on ch. 30 : 8, 2d paragraph. But in this rendering one important duty of a mistress is omitted, and the former sense of חק seems more appropriate in this connection.

V. 16. *With the fruit of her hands she plants a vineyard*, is the true sense and the best expression of it, whether we read (as *Kethib*) נְטַע in the constr. st., *from the fruit of her hands is the planting of a vineyard* (Bertheau†), or with the *Qeri*, נטעה *she plants* (Böttcher).

Less well, Hitzig and Zöckler take נטע כרם as = a vineyard (*Rebenpflanzung*), making it a second object of the verb תקח in the first member.‡

V. 18, first member. See explanatory notes. Another view of the sense (with the same rendering) is taken by Bertheau § and others; namely, she perceives that her gain is good in the sense of pleasant, acceptable (*wie lieblich ihr Erwerb*, Ewald), that her activity has good results, is gainful (guten Erfolg hat, Kamphausen; vortheilhaft, gewinnbringend ist, Hitzig), and by this is encouraged and spurred on (was zu noch grösserer Thätigkeit ansporut, Kamphausen) to continued diligence,—"her lamp goes not out by night." This has the merit of showing a connection between the two members, which is certainly desirable; but it is gained at the sacrifice of significance and point in the first member. It is not much to say of her, that she finds her diligence agreeably rewarded, and is thereby encouraged to persevere in it. The relation of parallel members in this alphabetic poem is not so rigidly exact, as to require such a sacrifice to show a connection here.—*She perceives*, טעמה; properly *tests* (Ps. 34 : 9, *taste, and see*), and perceives by testing.

V. 19. *The distaff—the spindle.* "I saw a woman sitting at the door of her hut on Zion, spinning woolen yarn with a spindle, while another near her was twirling nimbly the ancient distaff" (Thomson, The Land and the Book, II. 572.)

Wilkinson (Manners and Customs of the Ancient Egyptians) on page 136 of Vol. III. shows the different forms of spindles used by the Egyptians, and on page 134, and page 60 of Vol. II., the manner of using them, as exhibited in the ancient sculptures. But none of the sculptures there copied show the manner of disposing the material from which the thread was drawn in spinning. On the frieze of the Forum Palladium at Rome, a woman is represented in the act of spinning, holding in her left hand the distaff to which the material is attached, while with the thumb and finger of her right hand she twirls the spindle for twisting the thread. (Smith's Dict. of Greek and Rom. Antiq., p. 565). Some similar device for supporting the material seems to have been necessary in the oriental process of spinning.*

On the spindle in Egyptian sculptures is a disc, or a ring, attached to the upper (not the lower) part, to give it a more rapid and steadier rotary motion. This, called the *whorl*, is supposed by some to be the כישור in the second member. So Gesenius (after Kimchi, and the earlier christian Hebraists, Vatable, Mercier, and others), Hitzig, Zöckler in his note. But neither the parallelism nor the expression is very happy; repeating the thought, and designating the instrument by its name in the first member, and by one of its parts in the second.

*Her hands lay hold on*; strictly, her bended hands, closing on the object held. We have no corresponding term, answering to *hand* as the Hebrew כף does to יד. There is the same difficulty in distinguishing these terms in the following verse; where, in

* Bertheau: טֶרֶף *die Zehrung*, . . . die, weil sie nach bestimmtem Masse jedem zugetheilt wird, חק . . . genannt werden kann.

† *Von der Frucht seiner Hände ist Bepflanzung* (ketib נְטַע stat. constr. von נֶטַע Jes. 5 : 7) *des Weinbergs;* den Gewinn verwendet es den Grundbesitz zu vermehren.

‡ Böttcher: nach Jes. 5 : 7 es als Nomen נֶטַע zu fassen, wofür doch eher מַטַּע stehen müsste (Mi. 1 : 6), ist keinem alten Uebersetzer eingefallen, und giebt einen schwerfälligen, durch so viele Beispiele, die כרם mit Vb. fin. zeigen, gar nicht empfohlenen Sinn. Vgl. Gen. 9 : 20. Dt. 6 : 11. 2 R. 19 : 29. Am. 9 : 14. Ec. 2 : 4, u. a. (Neue Aehrenl., 1377.)

§ *Es schmeckt dass gut ist sein Erwerb*, und das schmeckend arbeitet es unverdrossen ganze Nächte hindurch um noch mehr zu gewinnen.

* "The ordinary distaff does not occur in these subjects, but we may conclude they had it; and Homer mentions one of gold, given to Helen by 'Alcandra the wife of Polybus,' who lived in Egyptian Thebes. Od. iv. 131." (Wilkinson, as above, Vol. III p. 137).

| KING JAMES' VERSION. | HEBREW TEXT. | | REVISED VERSION. |
|---|---|---|---|
| 20 She stretcheth out her hand to the poor; yea, she reacheth forth her hands to the needy. | כַּפָּהּ פָּרְשָׂה לֶעָנִי<br>וְיָדֶיהָ שִׁלְּחָה לָאֶבְיוֹן׃ | כ | She stretches out her hand to the poor, 20<br>and reaches forth her hands to the needy. |
| 21 She is not afraid of the snow for her household: for all her household *are* clothed with scarlet. | לֹא־תִירָא לְבֵיתָהּ מִשָּׁלֶג<br>כִּי כָל־בֵּיתָהּ לָבֻשׁ שָׁנִים׃ | 21 | She fears not for her household on account of snow; 21<br>for all her household are clothed in crimson. |
| 22 She maketh herself coverings of tapestry; her clothing *is* silk and purple. | מַרְבַדִּים עָשְׂתָה־לָּהּ<br>שֵׁשׁ וְאַרְגָּמָן לְבוּשָׁהּ׃ | 22 | Coverlets she makes for herself; 22<br>fine linen and purple are her clothing. |
| 23 Her husband is known in the gates, when he sitteth among the elders of the land. | נוֹדָע בַּשְּׁעָרִים בַּעְלָהּ<br>בְּשִׁבְתּוֹ עִם־זִקְנֵי־אָרֶץ׃ | 23 | Her husband is known in the gates, 23<br>when he sits with the elders of the land. |
| 24 She maketh fine linen, and selleth *it;* and delivereth girdles unto the merchant. | סָדִין עָשְׂתָה וַתִּמְכֹּר<br>וַחֲגוֹר נָתְנָה לַכְּנַעֲנִי׃ | 24 | Fine undergarments she makes and sells, 24<br>and delivers girdles to the merchant. |
| 25 Strength and honour *are* her clothing; and she shall rejoice in time to come. | עוֹז־וְהָדָר לְבוּשָׁהּ<br>וַתִּשְׂחַק לְיוֹם אַחֲרוֹן׃ | כה | Dignity and honor are her clothing; 25<br>and she laughs at the time to come. |
| 26 She openeth her mouth with wisdom; and in her tongue *is* the law of kindness. | פִּיהָ פָּתְחָה בְחָכְמָה<br>וְתוֹרַת־חֶסֶד עַל־לְשׁוֹנָהּ׃ | 26 | She opens her mouth with wisdom, 26<br>and the law of kindness is on her tongue. |
| 27 She looketh well to the ways of her household, and eateth not the bread of idleness. | צוֹפִיָּה הֲלִיכוֹת בֵּיתָהּ<br>וְלֶחֶם עַצְלוּת לֹא תֹאכֵל׃ | 27 | She watches the ways of her household, 27<br>and eats not the bread of idleness. |
| 28 Her children arise up, and call her blessed; her husband *also*, and he praiseth her. | קָמוּ בָנֶיהָ וַיְאַשְּׁרוּהָ<br>בַּעְלָהּ וַיְהַלְלָהּ׃ | 28 | Her children rise up and call her happy; 28<br>her husband, and he praises her: |

V. 27. הליכות ק'

the first member, the bended (hollowed) hand contains the gift for the poor. The distinction is not necessary, however, to the expression of the sense, but only of the writer's manner. Here כַּף might be rendered (though not accurately) by "fingers;" but not in the following verse.

V. 21. *In crimson:* the most luxurious and expensive apparel; compare 2 Sam. 1 : 24, *who clothed you in scarlet* [crimson]. There was therefore no lack of means to provide all needful clothing; and it is no just objection to this rendering, that *crimson* is not a protection against cold. The LXX and the Vulgate treat the Heb. form as a *Dual.* שְׁנַיִם, *double clothing* (*zweifach*, Böttcher), which is preferred by Rosenmüller, and by Böttcher (Neue Aehrenl. 1378). But this falls below the tone of the description.

V. 24. *Fine undergarments.* See the lexicons of Gesenius and Fürst. The latter properly remarks, that comparison with the Coptic *shendo* (*fine linen*), the Sanscrit *sindhu*, and the Greek *σινδών*, is probably incorrect, the *n* of the first syllable being there essential.*

V. 25. *Dignity;* as in the lexicons of Gesenius and Fürst. Not *strength*,* as some translate. "Strength and honor" are not a very apt association. Laughable is the reference by Bertheau and Zöckler to v. 17, as though the "strength" with which she clothes herself were the strength of her loins! With more reason it is said by Hitzig: Hier in *a* tritt nunmehr bildliches Gewand an die Stelle des eigentlichen 22, *b*.

V. 27. *She watches:* is on the watch, to see that all goes on rightly, and to provide for every exigency. The significance and emphasis of the Hebrew word is lost in the common rendering, "looks well to."

V. 28. *Happy.* See explanatory notes.† Here, as in many

* Mihi quidem haec incerta videntur, quum in Semiticis *n* et *l* in tertia sede radicalia sint, in *σινδών* *ν* extremum a Graecis adjectum (Gesenius, Thes., סדין).

* Nicht 'kraft,' die gar wunderlich zur 'kleidung' passt, sondern *Würde*, urspr. Steife (Böttcher, Neue Aehrenl. 1380).—Ewald: *Ruhm Pracht und Glanz war ihr Gewand.*

† Kamphausen*: preisen sie glückselig.*

| KING JAMES' VERSION. | HEBREW TEXT. | | REVISED VERSION. | |
|---|---|---|---|---|
| 29 Many daughters have done virtuously, but thou excellest them all. | רַבּוֹת בָּנוֹת עָשׂוּ חָיִל<br>וְאַתְּ עָלִית עַל־כֻּלָּנָה׃ | 29 | Many daughters have done worthily;<br>but thou surpassest them all. | 29 |
| 30 Favour *is* deceitful, and beauty *is* vain: *but* a woman *that* feareth the LORD, she shall be praised. | שֶׁקֶר הַחֵן וְהֶבֶל הַיֹּפִי<br>אִשָּׁה יִרְאַת־יְהוָה הִיא תִתְהַלָּל׃ | ל | Comeliness is a deception, and beauty is a vain thing;<br>a woman that fears Jehovah, she shall be praised. | 30 |
| 31 Give her of the fruit of her hands; and let her own works praise her in the gates. | תְּנוּ־לָהּ מִפְּרִי יָדֶיהָ<br>וִיהַלְלוּהָ בַשְּׁעָרִים מַעֲשֶׂיהָ׃ | 31 | Give to her of the fruit of her hands;<br>and let her works praise her in the gates. | 31 |
| | V. 29 בנ״א מטיבר | | | |

other passages, the Hebrew ברך and אשר are improperly confounded in the common English version.

V. 29. *Worthily:* as the Hebrew is well rendered in the common English version, in Ruth 4 : 11.*

* Ewald; *have shown capacity* (Tüchtigkeit) which is not amiss; Gesenius and Fürst, *have acquired wealth*, which is quite aside from the point.—*Daughters*. See explanatory notes.

V. 30. *Is a deception*, is the proper rendering. "Is deceitful" does not express the writer's thought. He means to say, that mere external beauty, an outward show representing no inward traits, is a ground or source of deception, whereby men impose upon themselves, and are deceived and disappointed. See explanatory notes.—*A vain thing*, is the meaning. "Vanity" is ambiguous.—The *article* (החן , היפי) with the subject, preceded by the predicate substantive; that quality so much admired.

THE END.

# PROVERBS.

---

## REVISED VERSION

WITH

## EXPLANATORY NOTES.

THE

# BOOK OF PROVERBS.

THE COMMON VERSION REVISED

FOR

THE AMERICAN BIBLE UNION

WITH

AN INTRODUCTION AND EXPLANATORY NOTES.

BY THOMAS J. CONANT.

NEW YORK:
SHELDON AND COMPANY, NO. 677 BROADWAY.
LONDON: TRÜBNER & CO., 60 PATERNOSTER ROW.
1872.

T. Holman, Printer and Stereotyper, New York.

# INTRODUCTION.

## § 1.

### DIVINE AUTHORITY AND INSPIRATION OF THE BOOK.*

THE claim of this book to a place in the divine canon rests on the attestation of Christ and his inspired Apostles. It was a part of that collection of sacred writings,† known as the Oracles of God, with the care of which the Jewish people were intrusted (Rom. 3 : 2). Of these writings, collectively, the Savior and his Apostles often speak as the word of God; recognizing, and directly asserting, their divine authority and inspiration. See, for example, such passages as Matt. 5 : 17–19 ; John 5 : 39 ; Rom. 3 : 2 ; Matt. 22 : 43, and Mark 12 : 36 ; 2 Tim. 3 : 16 ; 1 Pet. 1 : 10–12 ; 2 Pet. 1 : 21. This book was, therefore, as a part of these divine writings (called in the New Testament the Scriptures, the Holy Scriptures, the Oracles of God) expressly recognized by the Savior and his Apostles as of divine authority, and was declared to be "profitable for teaching, for reproof, for correction, for instruction in righteousness" (2 Tim. 3 : 16).

In this character, as a book of divine instruction, it is often expressly quoted by the inspired writers of the New Testament. Compare, for example, Prov. 3 : 11, 12, with Heb. 12 : 5, 6 ; Prov. 3 : 34, with James 4 : 6 ; Prov. 10 : 12, with 1 Pet. 4 : 8 ; Prov. 25 : 21, 22, with Rom. 12 : 20 ; Prov. 26 : 11, with 2 Pet. 2 : 22. Clear allusions are found in other passages ; as in Rom. 2 : 6, compared with Prov. 24 : 12 ; Rev. 3 : 19, compared with Prov. 3 : 12.

The genuineness of the book (in other words, that it is a DIVINE BOOK, that in this sense it is not a spurious production) is thus established by the highest authority. To prove its claim to this character, it is not necessary that the writers of the several portions of the book (§§ 3 and 5) should be ascertained with certainty, and their relation to other writers of the Old Testament clearly known. This, if satisfactorily shown, would not of itself establish their claim to be regarded as divinely commissioned and inspired teachers. The authority of a writing, claimed to be divine, does not in any case rest on the particular writer or human instrumentality, but on the divine attestation given to it. The HOLY SPIRIT was not restricted in his choice of instruments, or in his methods of originating and communicating instruction.

* The remarks in this section are in part repeated here from the writer's Introduction to the Book of Job, Part Second, and to the Book of Genesis, revised version, with explanatory notes

† The proofs, that it was a part of that collection, belong to a general Introduction to the Old Testament.

## § 2.

## RELIGIOUS CHARACTER AND TEACHINGS.

This portion of the Holy Scriptures is a book of practical wisdom. Its instructions are all practical; maxims for the conduct of life. It is the *Œconomics* of the Bible. The literature of the world may be searched in vain for its parallel, in the variety and completeness of its applications to all the relations and phases of human life, in the certainty of its foundation principles, and in the strength and effectiveness of its sanctions. It goes to the depths of man's moral nature, and arraigns him face to face with his Maker and Judge.

As the basis of its instructions, the ground of obligation to obey them, and their moral and penal sanctions, it recognizes the following points: 1st, A moral government of the universe by its Maker and Sovereign; 2nd, His will as the supreme law of his creatures, and their only safe guide in duty; 3rd, An intelligent filial love for him, and dread of his displeasure, as the highest and purest motive to virtuous action; 4th, His unerring justice, as a pledge of ultimate reward for obedience, and of punishment for transgression.

That God has a witness for himself, in the sense of moral accountability inseparable from man's nature, is everywhere presupposed. It thus appeals to the purest, noblest, and the strongest and most effective motives that can influence a moral being. The whole effect is to elevate and ennoble the life of man, while giving practical instructions for its proper direction.

Accordingly, we are taught (ch. 1 : 7), that the fear of God is the seminal principle of which the whole moral life is the outgrowth, and is the central law of all our moral relations; that in this all true knowledge has its beginning; whatever is called knowledge, without this its primal element, being essentially ignorance, a false perversion of the truth, serving only to misdirect the inquirer, and lead him further from it. The book begins (ch. 1 : 7), and ends (ch. 31 : 30), with the FEAR OF JEHOVAH as the ground of moral excellence, and the guide of practical duty.

Having laid down this elemental law, the book proceeds to develope its practical applications to human life. The instructions that follow never lose sight of it. It is the basis of all. But its too frequent repetition, with brief practical rules of conduct, would be wearisome as well as needless. In the explanatory notes, it has not been thought necessary or desirable to interpose strictly religious considerations, where they are not suggested by the text. It has rather been the interpreter's aim, to adopt everywhere the tone of the sacred writer, and to develope his thought in his own spirit and manner.

Practical precepts, for regulating what may be called the secular concerns of life, are an essential part of a divine revelation. It would be incomplete without them. Men need to know what divine wisdom approves in the management of worldly affairs. They should not be left to guide themselves by the maxims of worldly policy, or even of worldly prudence. So divine wisdom has judged; and accordingly, it has provided a code of practical œconomics, more comprehensive and more minute in its moral and prudential elements and applications, than is to be found in any other literature. Whoever masters its principles and rules of life, and intelligently applies them, can not fail to be a wise, a prosperous, and a happy man.

To treat such a book as intended for doctrinal religious instruction is to interpret it falsely, and to obscure its true aim and value. Every part of divine revelation has its appropriate object. It is no true conception of the divine word, to regard it as setting no value on the present life, and as leaving it without proper guidance. God's wisdom and goodness are as apparent in needful directions for man's earthly and temporal welfare, as in the provisions for his higher spiritual life. It is not therefore wise to say, for example, as has often been done, and as though it were a commendation of the Divine Book, that "CHRIST may be found anywhere in it, if one will but look for him." Wherever his wisdom and goodness are seen, in his word or in his works, there the devout spirit will find him. According to those beautiful lines of Cowper:

> "Happy who walks with Him! Whom what he finds,
> Of flavor or of scent in fruit or flower,
> Or what he views of beautiful or grand
> In nature, from the broad, majestic oak
> To the green blade that twinkles in the sun,
> Prompts with remembrance of a present God."

But we should not wisely interpret, if we treat this book as intended to teach our special relations to Him, so fully and clearly revealed in their appropriate place. To assume in ch. 18 : 24, for example, a reference to him in the sacred writer's mind, is to unsettle all just rules of interpretation applicable to this book. In itself the reference is certainly true; and the text may properly be made the occasion of directing the human spirit to one who alone knows all its wants, and is able and ever ready to supply them all.

Many have supposed that ch. 8 : 22–31 is to be interpreted doctrinally, as relating to one of the profoundest mysteries of the divine nature. But WISDOM, the divine attribute that guides the purposes, and is seen in all the works and ways of the Divine Being, there claims to be the friend and guide of his creature, man. As such she is personified, speaking with divine authority, and demanding obedience to her will, as being the will of God. The reasons for this view of the passage are briefly stated in the concluding remarks on the chapter, and more fully in the critical and philological notes of Part First. The following remark, made in that connection, is appropriate here: The whole representation is highly poetic and figurative; and to base any doctrinal truth on single forms of expression, which are the mere drapery of the figure, is at variance with the best established principles of interpretation. One who should defend such a practice in general, as a principle of hermeneutics, would justly forfeit the character of a sober and judicious critic.

The book recognizes the obligation of every man to use wisely the talents intrusted to him; in other words, to develope and train his intellectual and moral powers, so far as his means and opportunities will allow. The neglect of this duty, through self-indulgent indolence, is not spared. This is a just as well as a marked feature of the book. For it is undeniable, that miscarriage in worldly affairs is oftener owing to indolent neglect of the powers given for our guidance, or to culpable misdirection of them, than to any original deficiency in them. Hence the *simple*, who indolently accept things as they may appear, without taking the trouble to look sharply into their real nature, and thus suffer themselves to be imposed upon, are properly rebuked; while the *shrewd*, who make diligent use of their powers of discernment and observation, are commended. It is not supposed that one will go through life with his eyes shut; or that, having them open, he will see nothing. The men who honestly prosper in worldly affairs are they who give themselves the trouble to think and observe, and who cultivate the power of thinking and observation.

Wit and humor are here made to serve a good purpose. No weapon is more effective against certain vices than well-directed ridicule. Indeed every vice has its ludicrous aspect. Crime, when properly viewed, is a hideous absurdity; and vice, in all its forms, is intellectually and morally a monstrous blunder. As such, it is as much a matter of derision and scorn, as it is of a profounder moral reprobation; and there are those who have a far keener sense of the former than of the latter, and dread it more. To make vice ridiculous, and raise the laugh against it, is the surest way to discountenance and check it. Many who care nothing for serious admonition, however just, can not stand before the shafts of ridicule. In this book, a grave oriental humor, a polished irony, witty turns, and grotesque description, sometimes give point to the exposure of folly and vice.

## § 3.

## DIVISIONS AND CONTENTS.

In these there is much variety, both as to form and spirit, in different parts of the book. In all of them, however, there is one principle of unity, the object of all being practical instruction. Strictly doctrinal teaching, as already observed, is not the object in any portion of the book; though in all, correct doctrinal views are the recognized groundwork of the instructions given.

The following are clearly marked divisions of the book; indicated partly by its contents, and partly by appropriate introductory headings.

First division. Chapters i.—ix. Short continuous discourses, ten in number, chiefly for the guidance of the young, imparting practical principles of religion and morals for the conduct of life.

The aim of these beautiful discourses is to bring the human spirit into immediate consciousness of the Divine ; to show with what tender solicitude the Infinite Father seeks the welfare of his children, both by holding out the rewards of piety and virtue, and by showing the fearful penalties of disobedience.

The perils that beset the unwary feet of the young, in the temptations to which that period of life is specially exposed ; the obligation of the law of chastity, and the tendency of its violation to destroy both body and soul; the pure and chaste enjoyments of the connubial relation, and their healthful and refining influences ; the value of truth and uprightness, of kindness and fidelity, in all the relations of life; the duty and necessity of industry, of prudent foresight, of thoughtful provision for the wants of the body, and for the higher and nobler aspirations of the soul; these and other kindred topics are pressed on the mind and heart of the reader, with a tender and earnest warmth, and with the charms of poetic conception and imagery. In no other part of the sacred writings do we find moral painting so delicate, so glowing, so charming in its pictures of virtue and its rewards, so startling in vivid delineation of the allurements to vice, and their fatal snares.

Second division. Chapters x.—xxii. 16. This division bears the heading, Proverbs of Solomon, and differs essentially, in form and in its general spirit and manner, from the preceding one. It consists of single, disconnected sayings or maxims, mostly expressed in two lines closely related in substance and form, and containing the choicest treasures of practical wisdom.

Third division. Chapters xxii. 17—xxiv. 22. Very brief continuous discourses for practical direction in life, less extended than those of the first division, from which they differ much in general tone and manner, and distinguished by continuity of discourse in each from the single isolated sentences in the preceding division.

Fourth division. Chapter xxiv. 23–34. A distinct collection of a few sayings of the wise, distinguished by the separate heading, These also are of the Wise ; closing with the spirited description of indolent unthriftiness and its results.

Fifth division. Chapters xxv.—xxix. Another and distinct collection of Solomon's proverbs, copied out by the men of king Hezekiah ; differing somewhat, in form and spirit, from the preceding collection of his proverbs.

Sixth division. Chapter xxx. Words of Agur. These consist, 1st, of an Oracle, apparently intended to expose the vain pretensions of those who assume to be wise above what is written, and to comprehend the mysteries of the universe ; 2nd, a prayer, containing a brief summary of daily wants and desires ; 3rd, spirited and instructive sketches of various characters, typical forms of humanity, that appear in every age.

It is thought by some, that among the instances in the third class are specimens of grave oriental sportiveness, in the form of ingenious enigmas, with a moral purport. Three things being proposed, to find a fourth of similar traits or qualities, with a moral lesson ; or one being proposed, to find three others like it ; the task being, to find out not only the similitudes, but an ingenious and pointed expression, for them and for the moral. If this was intended merely for diversion, as a trial of wit and ingenuity, it was certainly an instructive and profitable one, and well suited to the oriental mind. It is to be presumed, that the Orientals needed amusement as well as we ; and there could not be a more innocent or instructive one. Compare Samson's riddle and its solution, Judges 14 : 12–18.

Seventh division. Chapter xxxi. 1–9. The words of king Lemuel ; an Oracle with which his mother instructed him. The wisest cautions and counsels on the dangers and duties of royalty.

Eighth division. Chapter xxxi. 10–31. Delineation of the ideal Hebrew matron ; not to be taken as a literal guide for all times and circumstances (see explanatory notes), but as showing that woman has equal capacities with man for the practical duties of life, and is thereby fitted for any to which the exigencies of life may call her.

It will be seen, from this brief analysis, how comprehensive and various are the contents of this wonderful book ; embodying the accumulated wisdom of ages of observation and experience, to which the Holy Spirit, "from whom all good counsels and just works proceed," has set the seal of his own sanction, "as profitable for teaching, for reproof, for correction, for instruction in righteousness" (2 Tim. 3 : 16).

## § 4.

## POETIC FORM. VARIETIES OF PARALLELISM.

The Hebrew word (*mâshâl*) which we express by *Proverb*, and from which the book is named, properly means *similitude*, *resemblance*, or *comparison*. Primarily, it denoted an apt illustration of a spiritual or moral truth by some apparent resemblance in physical nature. Its original and normal form, answering to the primary meaning of the name, is seen in such examples as the following :

Ch. 10 : 26. As vinegar to the teeth, and as smoke to the eyes,
so is a sluggard to them that send him.

The idea is, that one is as irritating and vexatious to the spirit, as the other is to the bodily senses.

Ch. 26 : 1. As snow in summer, and rain in harvest,
so honor is not seemly for a fool.

One is as misapplied as the other.—The reader will readily find other examples, though this original form is comparatively unfrequent. The particles expressing comparison are sometimes omitted. For example :

Ch. 25 : 11. Apples of gold in gravings of silver,
is a word spoken in its season.

Ch. 25 : 19. A broken tooth, and an unsteady foot,
is trust in the faithless in time of trouble.

Ch. 25 : 14. Clouds and wind, and no rain,
is a man that boasts of a deceptive gift.

And without the copula:

Ch. 26 : 3. A whip for the horse, a bridle for the ass,
and a rod for the back of fools.

Or the verb in the first member is implied in the second:

Ch. 26 : 14. The door turns on its hinge,
and the sluggard on his couch.

Ch. 25 : 23. The north wind brings forth rain,
and a covert tongue an angry countenance.

Besides these minor variations, the modifications of this original and normal form are numerous. One, the least frequent, takes the form technically called the *synonymous parallelism** in Hebrew poetry; consisting of two lines, the sentiment of the first being repeated in the second, with some slight and pleasing variation of the expression. For example:

Ch. 11 : 25. The liberal soul shall be enriched;
and he that waters shall himself be watered.

Here the parallel synonymous terms are, "the liberal soul" in the first member, "he that waters" in the second; "shall be enriched" in the first, "shall be watered" in the second.

Ch. 16 : 32. The slow to anger is better than the mighty,
and he that rules his spirit than he that takes a city.

Less exact forms are more frequent. For example:

Ch. 16 : 15. In the light of the king's countenance is life;
and his favor is as the latter rain.

Ch. 16 : 20. He that gives heed to the word will find good;
and he that trusts in Jehovah, happy is he!

More frequent, as being better adapted for the pointed expression of sayings to be treasured in memory, is the *antithetic parallelism* of Hebrew poetry; the correspondence of the two parallel members consisting in an opposition of sentiment and of the parallel terms. Examples abound in the second division of the book, where this form is the prevailing one. The following will serve as illustrations:

Ch. 10 : 1. A wise son makes a glad father;
but a foolish son is the grief of his mother.

Here the antithesis is perfect; the contrasted terms being, "a wise son" in the first member, "a foolish son" in the second; "makes a glad father" in the first, "is the grief of his mother" in the second.

Ch. 13 : 9. The light of the righteous shall be joyous;
but the lamp of the wicked shall go out.

Contrasted terms, light of the righteous—lamp of the wicked; shall be joyous—shall go out. Other examples are:

Ch. 16 : 1. Of man are the counsels of the heart;
but from Jehovah is the answer of the tongue.

* See the writer's Introduction to the revised version of the Book of Psalms, § 7.

Ch. 17 : 22. A joyous heart makes happy cure;
but a broken spirit dries up the bones.

The constant repetition of this regular form would be monotonous and wearisome, and ill adapted to the expression of some closely related truths, and still less suitable where the relation is more remote. Hence there are many variations, and looser forms, of this species of parallelism. The following are examples :

Ch. 18 : 14. The spirit of a man will sustain his sickness;
but a broken spirit, who can bear it!

Ch. 20 : 6. Many a man will proclaim his good will;
but a faithful man who shall find?

Still more varied in form are the following :

Ch. 16 : 3. Better is a little with righteousness,
than great gains without right.

Ch. 19 : 1. Better is a poor man walking in his integrity,
than one perverse in his lips, and he a fool.

Another form, frequent in other divisions of the book, is the *synthetic* or *constructive* parallelism, the construction of the members being the same or very similar. Such are the following :

Ch. 16 : 3. Commit thy works to Jehovah,
and thy purposes shall be established.

Ch. 18 : 16. A man's gift makes room for him,
and leads him before the great.

Ch. 20 : 20. He that curses his father and his mother,
his light shall go out in midnight darkness.

Ch. 21 : 13. He that shuts his ear to the cry of the weak,
he too shall call and not be heard.

Ch. 22. : 9. The man of kindly eye, he shall be blessed;
for he gives of his bread to the poor.

Stanzas of four lines, or more, are constructed by variously combining these several forms. As in the following example of the illustration of moral truths by physical resem blances; the physical resemblance being expressed in one parallelism, and the corresponding moral truth in another.

Ch. 25 : 4, 5. Take away the dross from the silver,
and there shall come forth a vessel for the founder.
Take away the wicked before a king,
and his throne shall be established in righteousness.

A favorite stanza of four lines consists of the synonymous followed by the synthetic parallelism. For example:

Ch. 24 : 3, 4. By wisdom is a house builded,
and by understanding it is established;
and by knowledge the store-rooms are filled,
with all precious and pleasant treasures.

Ch. 22 : 26, 27. Be not of those who strike hands,
of those who become surety for debts.
If thou hast nothing to pay,
why should he take thy bed from under thee!

Ch. 24 : 17, 18. When thy enemy falls rejoice not;
when he stumbles let not thy heart exult.
Lest Jehovah see, and it be evil in his eyes,
and he turn away his anger from him.

The synonymous followed by the antithetic:

Ch. 24 : 15, 16. Lie not in wait, wicked man, at the dwelling of the righteous;
despoil not his resting-place.
For seven times shall the righteous fall and arise;
but the wicked stumble into ruin.

The synthetic followed by the synonymous:

Ch. 24 : 1, 2. Be not envious of evil men;
and long not to be with them.
For their heart meditates violence,
and their lips talk of mischief.

The synthetic or constructive parallelism is much employed in continuous discourse. Of this an interesting specimen is found in ch. 22 : 17–21; and many examples may be seen in the twenty-third and twenty-fourth chapters. The continuous discourses of the first division of the book are beautiful illustrations of these several forms.

## § 5.

## WRITERS OF THE BOOK. ARRANGEMENT OF IT.

We learn from the book itself, as shown in the two preceding sections, that it is a collection of writings from different sources, all having a common object, practical instruction, but showing very considerable diversity of manner.

From the statements of the book, we also learn that Solomon was the principal writer. His name is prefixed to it in the superscription to the whole book, "Proverbs of Solomon, son of David, king of Israel" (ch. 1 : 1). His name is also prefixed to the second division of the book (chs. 10–22 : 16), which bears the heading, "Proverbs of Solomon;" its contents having the peculiar and normal form of the Hebrew *mâshâl*, or proverbial saying (§ 3). He is again named as the writer of the proverbs contained in the fifth division (chs. 25–29), which "the men of king Hezekiah copied out." Hence the whole book properly bears his name as the principal writer. It is not improbable that all was written by Solomon, except what is expressly ascribed to others; namely, the collection of a few sayings of the Wise in ch. 24 : 23–34, and chs. 30–31 : 9.

It has been objected, that the several portions here ascribed to Solomon could not all have been written by the same person, on the ground of the very marked difference of manner, both in the structure of the discourse, and in the style of expression. The former is clearly observable in the version; as is also the latter in some of its peculiarities, of which specimens may be seen in the preceding section.

The objection, however, is not a valid one. The difference in structure is explained by the different objects of the writer. The same man may express himself, at one time in connected discourses, and at another in single unconnected maxims. The style of expression also, and even the choice of words, will vary considerably in the full and free flow of continuous discourse, and in the short, compact, and abrupt form of sententious maxims, the parts of which are studiously adjusted to each other for artificial effect.

The slight differences of manner, observable in the different divisions consisting of short connected discourses, are not inconsistent with the supposition that all proceeded from the same writer. The lofty themes of the first division naturally take a higher tone of conception and expression, than we should expect to find in the humbler, and for the most part more business-like teachings of the third and fourth divisions. It should also be considered, that in different periods of life there are marked variations of manner in the same writer.

Such objections are, therefore, entitled to little weight, when urged against strong external testimony, to which there is no counter evidence of the same kind.

The collections of strictly proverbial sayings, in divisions second and fifth, are both ascribed to Solomon. A difference, both of object and manner, is observable in these two collections. But the difference is no proof that they are incorrectly ascribed to one person. The same writer may have different objects in uttering such sayings, and a manner adapted to each. Moreover, in the expression of single truths in isolated maxims, a man is not always bound to one and the same form. He may at different times use all the varieties of form exhibited in the preceding section.

An interesting portion of the book, the thirtieth chapter, is ascribed to Agur as the writer. Of him nothing is known, except that his utterances have been recognized as a part of the divine word by the attestation of Christ and his inspired Apostles. (See § 1.) The same is true of the counsels of the prophet sage, the mother of king Lemuel (ch. 31 : 1–9). In both these divisions the language of the original Hebrew has characteristic peculiarities, leading to the conclusion that the writers, though Israelites and of the chosen seed, were not natives of Palestine; showing that the Divine being, as remarked in § 1, is not restricted in his choice of instruments or means for communicating instruction.

Of the sources of the few sayings of the Wise, contained in ch. 24 : 23–34, nothing seems to have been known when the contents of the book were arranged in the form it now bears. Hence it is only said of them, "These also are of the Wise."

Respecting the writer of the beautiful description of the model Hebrew matron (ch. 31 : 10–31) nothing certain is known. It is in the acrostic form found in psalms as early as the age of David; and is not therefore, on account of its form, to be referred to a later age than that of Solomon, as some have assumed.

The arrangement of the book is not methodical, with one very marked and important exception. The more extended discourses, unfolding at some length the ground principles on which all its teachings are based, occupy the first place, and are impressively urged on the attention of the reader, preparing him for all that follows. The remaining portions, consisting of collections already made, having no logical relation to each other, are inserted without definite rule of arrangement, each collection standing by itself. As a natural incident of such a process, the same proverb will be found to have been repeated in different collections, and retained in both when brought together. The attentive reader will also observe, that forms of earlier proverbs are occasionally models of others in subsequent collections.

The book could not have received its present form earlier than the time of king Hezekiah; one collection contained in it (chs. 25–29) having been made by his direction. At what time, and by whose authority, its several parts were collected and arranged as they now stand, is not definitely known. It was done by an authority which was recognized by the Jews, to whose care the sacred writings were intrusted; and the whole is authenticated to the christian believer by the testimony of Christ and his Apostles.

# TO THE READER.

The preceding introduction, showing the general object of the book, its structure, peculiarities of form in its different sections, and the characteristics of its various teachings, contains all that seems necessary to prepare the common English reader for the intelligent and profitable study of its contents. Without such a general survey of its several parts, and of their proper relation to each other, it presents only a confused combination of various materials, without any intelligible relation, or uniformity of design.

The arrangement of the translation in the form intended by the sacred writer,—namely, that of continuous discourse where he employs it, and of short proverbial maxims in isolated couplets or brief stanzas where such are used,—while it clearly exhibits the varieties of form in the several parts, assists the reader to follow the course of thought where it is continuous, and to distinguish the single and separate thoughts in their isolation. The mischievous device of breaking up the whole text into minute fragments, first adopted in the Genevan version of 1560, effaces to the eye all that is peculiar in the structure of the book, the varieties of form in its contents, and the continuity and beautiful symmetry in its more extended discourses. All these are readily perceived, when the sacred text is properly arranged in paragraphs, in accordance with the sense and connection, and the poetic relation of parallel members is preserved.

The notes accompanying the revised version in the following pages are strictly expository; intended to assist the reader in apprehending the sacred writer's thought as expressed in the revised version, and giving the reasons, where it seems necessary, for my own views of the connection and meaning. The critical and philological notes, stating the grounds for the renderings in the revised version, are printed for the use of scholars in connection with the Hebrew text.

In the following notes the writer has not drawn from commentaries already before the public; preferring that his work should be a contribution to the literature of the subject, rather than repeat what others have written. His own observation of life, and reflection upon it, have been his guide in unfolding and applying the teachings of this wonderful book. With its religious principles his own mind and heart are in full accord and sympathy. But he has not sought for religious instruction where the sacred writer has not chosen to furnish it, nor to find everywhere material for a religious homily. His aim has been to bring out the original thought, and to make the intended application of it; only in special cases tracing its more remote and indirect bearings, not contemplated by the sacred writer.

# THE BOOK OF PROVERBS.

---

MARGINAL TRANSLATIONS AND READINGS.

PROVERBS of Solomon, son of David, king of Israel: 1
for knowing wisdom and instruction, 2
for understanding sagacious words;
for receiving instruction in prudence, 3
in righteousness, and justice, and rectitude;
for giving shrewdness to the simple, 4
to youth knowledge and reflection.
The wise will hear, and shall increase knowledge, 5
and guidance the discerning will obtain;
for understanding a proverb and a byword, 6
the words of the wise and their dark sayings.

The fear of Jehovah is the beginning of knowledge; 7
wisdom and instruction fools despise.
Hear, my son, the instruction of thy father, 8
and reject not the law of thy mother.
For a garland of grace are they to thy head, 9
and chains for thy neck.

---

VV. 1–6, a brief introductory paragraph. In this the design and uses of the book are set forth: viz.. 1. in general, to give lessons in practical moral wisdom, and in all the social virtues (vv. 2, 3); 2. specially, to instruct the young, and the weak and inexperienced, imbuing them with knowledge and discretion (v. 4); 3. the wise and discerning will gain knowledge and direction, so as to understand for themselves proverbial maxims, and the dark and difficult sayings of the wise (vv. 5, 6).

V. 4. *The simple;* properly, those who lie open to every impression, taking every thing upon trust, and having no inward strength to repel influences from without, and no control over them. This is well illustrated by ch. 14 : 15, where the same class is spoken of, and contrasted with the opposite character.

Second member. The object is not only to give knowledge to the young, but what is far more important, to form the habit of *reflection*, of *consideration*, without which all else is valueless for the formation of character.

V. 6. *By-word;* a current, proverbial saying, but properly taunting and satirical in its character (as in Hab. 2 : 6), exposing folly and wickedness by just scorn and derision. *Dark sayings;* vailing deep instruction under a form intelligible only to the thoughtful and discerning; applied also to subjects in themselves deep and mysterious (Ps. 49 : 4, and 78 : 2).

VV. 7–9 set forth the grounds for giving earnest heed to the admonitions which follow.

All true knowledge has its beginning in the fear of God, the central law of all our moral relations. Without it, other knowledge is unavailing, even for the security of earthly and temporal interests; and, as daily observation shows, may only serve to ensure and hasten the ruin of its possessor. Only fools despise this heavenly wisdom, and the means of gaining it.

To parental instruction and training is committed, primarily, the formation of the principles and habits of the young. The precept in v. 8 is given in the spirit of another Divine command: Children, obey your parents IN THE LORD (Eph. 6 : 1); for obedience is here required to those who themselves fear and honor God.

V. 9. *Garland of grace,* expresses both its beauty, and the

MARGINAL TRANSLATIONS AND READINGS.

10 My son, if sinners entice thee,
do not thou consent.
11 If they say: Go with us;
let us lie in wait for blood;
let us lurk for the innocent, without cause. (*for the innocent in vain*)
12 Let us swallow them up alive, as the underworld,
and whole, as those who go down to the pit.
13 All precious substance shall we find;
we will fill our houses with spoil.
14 Cast in thy lot among us;
let there be one purse for us all.
15 My son, go not in the way with them;
withhold thy foot from their path.
16 For their feet run to evil,
and haste to shed blood.
17 For surely, in vain is the net spread
in the sight of any bird.
18 And they, for their own blood they lie in wait,
and lurk for their own lives.
19 So are the ways of every one greedy of gain; (*greedy of spoil*)
it takes its possessor's life.

20 Wisdom cries abroad;
in the streets she utters her voice.
21 At the head of the thronged ways she calls,
at the openings of the gates;
in the city she utters her words:

favor it obtains for its possessor. Second member; compare Dan. 5 : 29.

The first division of the book (ch. 1 : 10—ch. 9) commences here, and consists of a series of continuous discourses on different topics.

VV. 10–19. Admonition to resist the enticements to criminal gains; fatal influence of a spirit of covetousness.

*If sinners entice thee,*—to any course of evil. One is specified in the following verses, and stands as the representative of all aggression on the rights of others, whether by violence or fraud.

V. 12. *Let us swallow them up alive,* etc., is figurative language, expressing the insatiable rapacity of those who give themselves up to the pursuit of unlawful gain.

V. 17. I understand this of the snare thus laid (as described in the preceding verses), for the youth enticed into such dangerous companionship. As the net is vainly spread in the sight of the bird, so it would seem that a snare so fatal, and so openly laid, would not entrap even the most unwary.

It is differently understood by some, however, who suppose that the youth is warned against such seducers, by the certainty of their failure; they spread their snares for their victims in vain; they fail of their object, and perish in their wickedness.

But to this there are two objections. First, it assumes more, unhappily, than is too often true of their ill success; secondly, it is not the design, nor would it be quite to the point, to warn against such ill contrived schemes as are sure to fail. *A net spread in the sight of the bird,* is not an image of well concerted villainy. It is in the next verse, not here, that we find their fate described.

V. 19. *So are the ways of all;* so fares it with all such, is the meaning. *Greedy of gain;* in whom the love of gain is the ruling principle and passion. The same class is spoken of in Jer. 6 : 13, and 8 : 10 (com. vers., "given to covetousness"). Compare 1 Tim. 6 : 9, 10.

Second member:—*It takes its possessor's life;* sooner or later, this spirit of covetousness (or the gain it seeks) will "drown men in destruction and perdition" (1 Tim. 6 : 9).

VV. 20–33. The second discourse. Wisdom is here represented as a person speaking, uttering her warnings and threatenings in public places and the crowded thoroughfares of the city. Such personification is frequent in the Scriptures, and occurs again in this book in chs. 8 and 9. The implied instruction here is, that men need this heavenly monitor in all the transactions of life; and that they can not safely stifle her warning voice within them, even in the tumult of business or of pleasure. That she speaks by divine authority, and in the name of Jehovah, is evident from vv. 26, and foll.

V. 21. *Openings of the gates;* the broad spaces within or be-

MARGINAL TRANSLATIONS AND READINGS.

22 How long, ye simple, will ye love simplicity!
and scoffers delight themselves in scoffing,
and fools hate knowledge!
23 Turn ye at my reproof; — *to my reproof*
lo, I will pour out to you my spirit,
I will make known to you my words.
24 Because I have called, and ye refused;
I have stretched out my hand, and no one regarded;
25 and ye have refused all my counsel,
nor would receive my reproof:
26 I also will laugh in your calamity, — *at your calamity*
I will mock when your fear comes;
27 when your fear comes as a tempest,
and your calamity shall come as a whirlwind;
when distress and anguish come upon you.
28 Then shall they call on me, but I will not answer;
they shall seek me early, but shall not find me.
29 For that they hated knowledge,
and chose not the fear of Jehovah;
30 they consented not to my counsel,
they despised all my reproof;
31 therefore shall they eat of the fruit of their way,
and be filled with their own devices.
32 For the turning away of the simple shall slay them,
and the security of fools shall destroy them.
33 But he that hearkens to me shall dwell in safety,
and be at rest, without fear of evil.

1 My son, if thou wilt receive my words,
and treasure up with thee my commands;
2 so as to direct thine ear to wisdom,
incline thy heart to understanding;
3 yea, if thou criest out for intelligence,
for understanding utterest thy voice;
4 if thou search for her as silver,
and as hidden treasures dig for her;
5 then shalt thou understand the fear of Jehovah,
and find the knowledge of God.

---

fore the city-gates, used as market-places, for holding courts of justice, and for other public and private business. See note on Job 5 : 4.

V. 23. *I will pour out*,—as from a refreshing, life-giving fountain; imparting to you of my own nature, the spirit of wisdom.

V. 32. *The turning away*, from the right; or, from the voice of wisdom. *Security;* the false trust of those who feel themselves secure in their careless neglect of God and his requirements. Such false security will prove their ruin.

Ch. II.—The third discourse. Wisdom will be bestowed on those who earnestly seek it; its advantages to its possessor.

In this beautifully constructed discourse, the statement of the conditions (vv. 1–4) is followed by a twofold expression of the result of compliance with them; viz., one in v. 5, and another in v. 9, each confirmed and illustrated by the verses immediately following it. It is also to be observed, that vv. 12, 16, 20, all stand in the same relation; each expressing an end or object to be attained, of which the principal and the sum of all is given in v. 20.

VV. 5–8. The first result of this earnest search for

MARGINAL TRANSLATIONS AND READINGS.

6 For Jehovah gives wisdom;
from his mouth are knowledge and understanding;
7 and has help in store for the upright,
a shield for those who walk in integrity;
8 to keep the paths of rectitude,
and the way of his pious ones he guards.
9 Then shalt thou understand righteousness and justice,
and equity, every good way.

every way of the good

10 For wisdom shall come into thy heart,
and knowledge shall be sweet to thy soul:
11 reflection shall watch over thee,
understanding shall keep thee:
12 to preserve thee from the evil way,
from the man that speaks perverseness;
13 who forsake the paths of rectitude,
to walk in ways of darkness;
14 who rejoice to do evil,
exult in the perverseness of the wicked;
15 whose paths are crooked,
and they are perverse in their ways:
16 to preserve thee from the strange woman,
from the stranger that flatters with her words;
17 who forsakes the partner of her youth,
and forgets the covenant of her God:
18 for her house inclines to death,
and her ways to the shades:
19 none that go unto her return again,
nor attain to the paths of life:
20 to the end that thou mayest walk in the way of the good,
and keep the paths of the righteous.

V. 5 means: thou shalt understand what is true religion—in what it consists; and shalt find (attain to) the knowledge of God. V. 6 shows the ground of this assertion. Such knowledge comes only from the eternal source of wisdom, from Jehovah himself; and his help is ever ready for those who uprightly and sincerely seek him.

V. 9. Another result, viz., the right understanding of the duties of practical religion, in all the relations of life.

VV. 10 and 11. *Wisdom* is this divine principle, coming from God, taking possession of the heart, and controlling all the springs of moral action; *reflection* is the habit of circumspection, and of cautious regard to all external relations; *understanding* is the power of correctly estimating those relations, that they may not be violated through ignorance and misconception.

VV 12–20 show the practical working of this divine armory; viz., to preserve from the influence of evil men (vv. 12–15); especially, from the enticements of the adulteress, and the certain ruin of all who become her victims (vv. 16–19); and in general, to direct in the way of the good, in the paths of the righteous (v. 20).

V. 16. *To preserve thee* (see preceding remark). *Strange*, as belonging to another, the wife of another man, not thine own; and also, in general, one who is not thy wife, who is strange or foreign to thee, as one in whom thou hast no right. The word is used only when unlawful intercourse with her is the subject.

V. 17. *Forgets the covenant of her God:* viz., in forsaking the partner of her youth (the husband, who espoused her in her youth); such conduct being a violation of God's law, and hence of the covenant obligation binding on all his people. *Of her youth;* compare Joel 1 : 8, and Prov. 5 : 18, Is. 54 : 6, Mal. 2 : 14, 15.

V. 18. *Inclines*,—tends downward; it is the entrance on the downward way to death and hell.

Second member:—*The shades*, the term by which disembodied spirits are represented in Hebrew. See the remarks on Job 26 : 5, and the references there given.

V. 20. *To the end that* (see remark on vv. 12–20), sums up all in one comprehensive view.

| | | MARGINAL TRANSLATIONS AND READINGS. |
|---|---|---|
| For the upright shall dwell in the land, | 21 | |
| and the perfect shall remain in it. | | |
| But the wicked shall be cut off from the land, | 22 | |
| and transgressors shall be rooted out of it. | | |
| My son, forget not my law, | 1 | |
| and let thy heart keep my commands. | | |
| For length of days, and years of life, | 2 | |
| and peace, shall they add to thee. | | |
| Kindness and truth, let them not leave thee: | 3 | |
| bind them on thy neck; | | |
| write them on the tablet of thy heart. | | |
| So shalt thou find favor, and good understanding, | 4 | good repute |
| in the eyes of God and man. | | |
| Trust in Jehovah, with all thy heart, | 5 | |
| and lean not on thine own understanding. | | |
| In all thy ways acknowledge him, | 6 | |
| and he will make plain thy paths. | | |
| Be not wise in thine own eyes; | 7 | |
| fear Jehovah, and turn from evil. | | |
| It shall be health to thy sinews, | 8 | Let it be |
| and moisture to thy bones. | | |
| Honor Jehovah from thy substance, | 9 | with thy substance |
| and from the first fruits of all thine increase. | | with the first fruits |
| So shall thy barns be filled with plenty, | 10 | |
| and thy presses shall burst out with new wine. | | |

V. 21. The *perfect* man is one, in whom no trait is wanting that is essential to the character of the good man. Compare Matt. 19 : 21.

V. 22. *Shall be rooted out.* The allusion is to plucking up a plant by the roots, so that nothing is left of it in the soil where it grew. In like manner, they shall be rooted out from the land of their birth, leaving no remnant behind them.

Ch. III.—The fourth discourse, in several parts, containing various instructions and admonitions. VV. 1–4. Blessings promised to the obedient, and to the kind and truthful.

V. 3. *Kindness and truth* are foundation principles, in all social relations. Hence they often occur in connection; as in Gen. 24 : 49; 47 : 29; Josh. 2 : 14. *Let them not depart from thee* is the same as, *part not with them;* in other words, cease not to cherish and practice them.

Second and third members. The language is figurative. Let them be thy outward adorning (1 Pet. 3 : 3), as ornaments worn on the neck; and an inward law, as if written on the tablet of the heart.

V. 4. *And good understanding,* viz., in the eyes of God and man; as one who rightly understands his own relation to others and its obligations. The possession of this trait of character is said, in ch. 13 : 15, to "confer favor." Comp. also Ps. 111 : 10.

VV. 5–8. Admonition to trust in God, and not in one's own wisdom; and in all things to acknowledge him, and to fear his displeasure.

V. 6. *In all thy ways acknowledge him;* act with conscious reference to him in all things, recognizing his rightful authority, and the duty of obedience to it in every act of life.

Second member:—Sentiment: thy ways shall be made plain, leading directly and plainly onward to the object sought; not crooked, winding, difficult to follow, and uncertain where they will end, as are the ways of all who refuse God's authority and guidance, and trust to their own understanding. Compare Ps. 27 : 11; 5 : 8.

V. 8. It shall be to thy soul what healthful and refreshing influences are to the body, imparting firmness and strength.

VV. 9, 10. *First fruits;* viz., the first of its kind, whether of the products of the earth (both solid and liquid, Ex. 22 : 29; Deut. 18 : 4), or of the increase of flocks and herds by propagation (Ex. 22 : 30; Deut. 15 : 19), or of their annual product, as wool, etc. (Deut. 15 : 19; 18 : 4). Of these an offering was to be made to Jehovah (Lev. 2 : 12). Compare Lev. 23 : 10–14; Deut. 26 : 1–11.

The principle here laid down is universal and unalterable; and its application, as here stated, is the general law of Providence. But divine love, guided by that wisdom which sees the end from

MARGINAL TRANSLATIONS AND READINGS.

than corals

in wisdom

11 Spurn not, my son, the chastening of Jehovah,
and loathe not his rebuke.
12 For whom Jehovah loves he rebukes,
even as a father the son he delights in.

13 Happy the man who finds wisdom,
and the man who obtains understanding.
14 For her gain is better than the gain of silver,
and her increase than gold.
15 More precious is she than pearls;
and all thy delights can not compare with her.
16 Length of days is in her right hand;
in her left hand riches and honor.
17 Her ways are ways of pleasantness,
and all her paths are peace.
18 A tree of life is she to them that lay hold on her,
and blest is every one that retains her.
19 Jehovah by wisdom founded the earth;
established the heavens by understanding.

the beginning, may seek the highest good of its object by varying the application. The highest earthly reward of the pious man may be found, in the end, to be the good wrought out for others, in various ways, by what he has been made to suffer. Moreover, "whom Jehovah loves he corrects," is also a law of his kingdom. But there is still another law, which distinguishes him who honors, and him who honors not God from his substance. To the former, all things, whether prosperity or adversity, work together for good; to the latter, for evil. "I will curse your blessings" is written against every one, who lays up treasures for himself, and is not rich toward God.

Finally, he who truly seeks to honor God, and not himself in the gratification of his own will, submits the direction and disposal of all to infinite wisdom and love.

*New wine:* the juice of the grape, as it flowed from the winepress, which continued to be so called till the vinous fermentation was completed, when it became *wine.* * Preserved in its natural state, it was a nutritious and healthful article of diet, † and is often mentioned as one of the chief blessings granted to the husbandman. See, e. g., Deut. 7 : 13, 11 : 14; Joel 2 : 19 (com. version in all, *wine*). But if exposed to the first stages of the vinous fermentation, it becomes a highly exhilarating drink; which accounts for the expression in Hos. 4 : 11; 7 : 14.

Compare Is. 65 : 8, *as the new wine is found in the cluster.* In numerous passages of the common version, it is improperly rendered *wine;* as, e. g., in Gen. 27 : 28; Num. 18 : 12; Deut. 14 : 23, 18 : 4, 33 : 28; Jer. 31 : 12; Joel 2 : 19, and many others.

* See Micah 6 : 15 (com. version 'sweet wine'), where it is distinguished from wine. Compare Is. 65 : 8.

† Hence, it is mentioned along with breadstuffs, as an article of sustenance; Gen. 27 : 37 (com. version 'wine'); Hosea 9 : 2; Zech. 9 : 17, where the true sense is lost in the com. version.

VV. 11, 12. This admonition is set over against the preceding one; showing that, to the trustful and submissive spirit, God is equally gracious in his blessings and his chastisements.

VV. 13–26. The blessedness of those who attain to true wisdom. According to chs. 1 : 7, 9 : 10; Ps. 111 : 10, this has its beginning in the fear of JEHOVAH, the seminal germ, of which the whole moral life is the growth. Its worth and its blessings, as described in these verses, need no further development.

V. 14. *Her gain,* the gain which she brings to one. *Better than the gain of silver,* etc., means that wisdom without wealth is of more value than wealth without wisdom; and should teach us that the riches, promised in v. 16, are nothing more than one of the incidental benefits of this priceless treasure.

V. 16. *Length of days.* Compare Ps. 91 : 16; 1 K. 3 : 14. It is true, moreover, that God has laid the ground for this in his own laws of nature; for what chiefly shortens life is the indulgence of propensities and passions, which are forbidden by the fear of God. *Riches and honor.* These also she has to bestow, and of these her favor is the surest pledge; for true wisdom is the only policy that never defeats itself. But these too, like all other temporal good, are at the disposal of the Sovereign Arbiter, bestowed or withheld as he may see best for the welfare of all. Compare on v. 14.

V. 18. *Tree of life.* Compare Gen. 2 : 9; Rev. 2 : 7; 22 : 2, 14.

VV. 19, 20, refer briefly to the wonders wrought by wisdom, in the structure of the material universe, and in its adaptation to the physical wants of its occupants. To the knowledge and skill displayed by the Architect of Nature, allusion is often made in the Scriptures; e. g. Ps. 136 : 5; Jer. 10 : 12.

It thus appears, that God effects his own beneficent ends by the exercise of those attributes, of which human reason and understanding are the reflection. Man, created in the divine image,

20 By his knowledge the deeps were broken open, (the deeps broke forth)
and vapors distil the dew.
21 My son, let them not depart from thine eyes;
keep true wisdom and reflection;
22 and they will be life to thy soul,
and grace to thy neck.
23 Then shalt thou go thy way securely,
and thy foot shall not stumble.
24 When thou liest down, thou shalt not fear;
yea, thou shalt lie down, and sweet shall be thy sleep.
25 Be not dismayed at sudden fear,
nor at the destruction of the wicked when it comes;
26 for Jehovah shall be thy confidence;
and he will keep thy foot from being taken.

27 Withhold not good from them to whom it is due,
when it is in the power of thy hands to do it.
28 Say not to thy neighbor: Go, and come again,
and to-morrow I will give, when it is by thee.
29 Devise not evil against thy neighbor,
when he dwells securely by thee.
30 Strive not with a man without cause,
when he has done thee no evil.
31 Envy not the man of violence,
and choose none of his ways;
32 for the perverse is the abomination of Jehovah,
but his favor is with the upright.

was allied to the Supreme Intelligence; capable of intelligent moral action, and of directing all his powers to the wisest, noblest ends. To regain this is the great problem of his destiny; and the first step is the fear of Jehovah, that moral element, which brings him into harmony with the Divine.

V. 20. *The deeps were broken open* (margin: *broke forth*); i. e. were opened, and made to flow forth in natural fountains, for watering the surface of the earth. This is referred to in Gen. 49 : 25 (properly, *blessings of the deep that lies beneath*, i. e. of the underlying deep), and Deut. 33 : 13 (properly, *for the deep that lies beneath*); where the waters reposing in the bosom of the earth are meant.

Second member:—another provision for this object. During the warm season, in those countries, vegetation is almost wholly dependent on the copious and refreshing dews of night. Hence the numerous allusions to this, as one of the chief blessings of heaven. Compare, e. g., ch. 19 : 12; Deut. 33 : 13, 28; Zech. 8 : 12.

VV. 21, 22. *True wisdom;* that which is really such, in distinction from what often falsely claims to be wisdom among men. *Thy soul;* the spiritual nature of man, of which truth is the aliment and life. *Grace;* by this is not meant beauty, merely, but such as wins the favor of the beholder. *To thy neck;* where ornaments were worn (ch. 1 : 9).

VV. 23–26 describe the security of such as walk by these precepts, with divine wisdom for their guide, and divine power for their protection. Let the young, especially, ponder well these truths, in making their choice of principles and maxims for the government of life.

VV. 27, 28. Against a selfish and niggardly spirit; which, if it can not decently refuse a favor, makes a shift to delay it, in the hope of avoiding it altogether. Compare Matt. 5 : 42. *To whom it is due;* by this is meant every one who is in need of that, which is in thy power to do. Two things are implied: *need* on one side, and *ability* on the other. Wherever these two conditions exist, there is a moral claim and a moral obligation, that can not be disregarded without violating the law of love, which is the law of God.

V. 29. Against treachery to that mutual trust, on which all social security rests. He who can be plotting evil against an unsuspecting and confiding neighbor, has the heart of a Judas in his bosom.

V. 30. Against the spirit of contention, the mere love of strife, that seeks it for its own sake, and is uneasy so long as there is peace and quietude.

VV. 31, 32. *The man of violence,* one who uses his superior force or power, in whatever form, to deprive others of their just

MARGINAL TRANSLATIONS AND READINGS.

but fools bear away shame | *Or*, but shame lifts fools on high

The chief thing | *Or*, The beginning of wisdom is to get wisdom

33 The curse of Jehovah is in the house of the wicked;
but the habitation of the righteous he will bless.
34 Though he mocks at those who mock,
yet gives he favor to the lowly.
35 The wise shall inherit honor;
but fools he exalts to shame.

1 HEAR, children, the instruction of a father;
and attend, to know understanding.
2 For I give you good instruction;
forsake ye not my law.
3 For a son was I to my father;
tender, and an only child, in the sight of my mother.
4 And he taught me, and said to me:
let thy heart retain my words;
keep my commands, and live.
5 Get wisdom; get understanding;
forget not, and turn not from the words of my mouth.
6 Forsake her not, and she will keep thee;
love her, and she will preserve thee.
7 The first thing is wisdom; get wisdom,
and with all thy getting, get understanding.
8 Exalt her, and she will promote thee;
will honor thee, when thou dost embrace her.
9 She will give a garland of grace for thy head;
a crown of beauty will she deliver to thee.

10 Hear, my son, and receive my words;
and years of life shall be multiplied to thee.

rights; here contrasted with the *upright* (v. 32), the just man, who exacts only what is rightfully his, and renders to all their due. The former is not to be envied or imitated, however successful he may seem to be.

V. 34. The proud scoffer, who mocks at all things serious, will receive in return the scorn his folly deserves at the hand of God. (Compare ch. 1 : 26; Ps. 2 : 4.) The parallelism is by contrast; notwithstanding this sternness to the impious scorner, yet he is gracious to the humble.

V. 35. A sarcastic irony points the expression of the second member. First, there is the honorable distinction of the wise; and set over against it, is exaltation to shame, to public ignominy and scorn, which is the deserved promotion of fools.

Ch. IV.—Fifth discourse in three parts. VV. 1—9. Admonition to give heed to instruction; to seek wisdom; its advantages.

V. 1. *Children*; an appropriate form of address for a senior religious teacher, especially in speaking to the young. Compare 1 John 4 : 4. Whether this, or the paternal relation, is intended, must be determined by the reader from the circumstances of the case.

Second member:—*To know understanding;* to know what it is, to distinguish true understanding from false pretensions to it. Or it may mean, to learn, to acquire, the power of understanding.

V. 3. *For a son*, etc. For I was myself nurtured with tender care, and early taught the value of the truths which I impart to you. *An only child.* The words, *in the sight of my mother*, show that he was not literally an only child; but was regarded with the tenderness felt for such.

V. 7. Compare the Saviour's injunction, Matt. 6 : 33. Margin: *The chief thing*, to the same effect.

Second member:—*With all thy getting*, etc. Neglect not, in all thy acquisitions, the attainment of understanding; let this have its place with all of them, in thy desires and efforts.

VV. 10–19. Admonition to heed instruction, repeated; to keep the way of wisdom, and avoid the path of the wicked; their ways contrasted.

MARGINAL TRANSLATIONS AND READINGS.

11 I have taught thee in the way of wisdom;
have led thee in paths of rectitude.
12 When thou walkest, thy step shall not be straitened;
and when thou runnest, thou shalt not stumble.
13 Lay hold on instruction, let not go; — *let her not go*
keep her, for she is thy life.
14 Enter not into the path of the wicked,
nor go onward in the way of the evil.
15 Avoid it, pass not over it;
turn off from it, and pass on.
16 For they sleep not unless they do evil;
and their sleep is taken away, if they cause none to fall.
17 For they eat the bread of wickedness,
and wine of violence they drink.
18 But the way of the righteous is as the clear light,
shining more and more, to the noon-day.
19 The way of the wicked is as thick darkness;
they know not at what they stumble.

20 My son, attend to my words;
incline thine ear to my sayings.
21 Let them not depart from thine eyes;
keep them within thy heart.
22 For life are they to every one that finds them,
and healing to all his flesh.
23 Above every care, keep thy heart; — *Above all that is kept,*
for out of it are the issues of life.
24 Put away from thee frowardness of the mouth;
and perverseness of the lips put far from thee.
25 Let thine eyes look right forward,
and thine eye-lids be straight before thee.
26 Ponder the path of thy foot;
and let all thy ways be established.
27 Turn not to right or left;
remove thy foot from evil.

V. 17. By *bread of wickedness*, and by *wine of violence*, is meant such as are the gains of wrong doing and of violence.

VV. 18, 19. The way of the righteous, and the way of the wicked, are presented here in beautiful and striking contrast. The one is like the light from a cloudless sky, shining clear and unobstructed, and increasing in brightness from early dawn to the splendors of noon-day. The way of the other is as the deepest gloom of night; in which they stumble at they know not what, unable to shun it, or to recover from it.

VV. 20–27. Admonition to heed and treasure up instruction, repeated; to the keeping of the heart; to avoid falsehood, and all side pretenses; to consider well one's own ways, and shun every deviation from the right.

V. 22. They are to the moral nature, what healing influences are to the physical frame, imparting health and vigor.

V. 23. Compare the Saviour's words (in Matt. 15 : 19); *out of the heart proceed evil thoughts, murders, adulteries, fornications, thefts, false witness, blasphemies.* From the heart, then, are the issues of life; that is, man's outward life proceeds from the heart, and hence the keeping of the heart is his first and highest concern.

Others understand by life, *happiness, felicity;* for which it is sometimes used in the Scriptures. Others, again, suppose that by *issues of life* is meant its *exit* or *issue*, i. e. the end or termination of it. But neither is as pertinent as the one first given.

V. 25. Pursue directly the object desired, and not seek it by indirect and side pretenses.

V. 26. *Established;* opposed to unstable and vacillating, from which nothing sure and permanent can result. In order to this, it is necessary (first member), to *ponder the path of the foot;* to take no step, without due caution and deliberation.

| MARGINAL TRANSLATIONS AND READINGS | | |
|---|---|---|
| | 1 | My son, give heed to my wisdom;<br>to my understanding incline thine ear: |
| | 2 | so as to regard counsels,<br>and that thy lips may keep knowledge. |
| | 3 | For the lips of a strange woman drop with honey,<br>and her mouth is smoother than oil. |
| | 4 | But her end is bitter as wormwood,<br>sharp as a twoedged sword. |
| | 5 | Her feet go down to death,<br>her steps take hold on the underworld; |
| That she may not ponder the way of life,<br>her paths waver, ere she is aware. | 6 | that thou mayest not ponder the way of life:<br>her paths waver, ere thou knowest. |
| | 7 | Now then, children, hearken to me;<br>and turn not away from the words of my mouth. |
| | 8 | Remove thy way far from her,<br>and come not nigh the door of her house: |
| thy bloom. | 9 | that thou give not thy strength to others,<br>and thy years to the cruel; |
| and thy labors be in | 10 | that strangers may not sate themselves on thy wealth,<br>and on thy labors, in the house of a stranger: |
| | 11 | and thou groan in thy latter end,<br>when thy flesh and thy fullness are consumed; |
| | 12 | and say: How have I hated instruction,<br>and my heart despised reproof; |
| | 13 | and I hearkened not to the voice of my teachers,<br>nor inclined my ear to my instructors. |
| | 14 | Almost was I in all evil,<br>in the midst of the congregation and assembly. |
| | 15 | Drink waters from thine own cistern,<br>and streams out of thine own well. |

Ch. V.—Sixth discourse, in three parts.

VV. 1–6. Admonition to heed and retain instruction, repeated; fatal seductiveness of the strange woman.

V. 3. *Strange woman;* see remarks on ch. 2 : 16.

V. 5. The path in which she leads is the way to death. Her steps already take hold on the realm of death; they cleave fast to it, with a firm and unyielding hold.

V. 6. *That thou mayest not ponder*, etc.; such is their influence, viz., to turn off the thoughts from the way of life. He who follows her steps is led further and further from that way, and from all reflection upon it.

Second member:—Her ways lead down to death; and the victim, ere he is aware, finds the path shaking and giving way beneath his feet.

The form of the Hebrew allows also the translation given in the margin. This is thought preferable by some, but erroneously; for it is not the writer's object to describe the fate of the adulteress, but that of her victim.

VV. 7–14. Admonition to beware of her, and of the fate of her victims.

V. 7. *Children;* see remark on ch. 4 : 1.

V. 9. *Give not thy strength*, etc. Compare ch. 31 : 3. *The cruel;* as selfish, mercenary, and reckless of all consequences to those ensnared by her. *Thy years*, the same as thy life, a prey to the cruel and insatiable consumer of thy youthful strength.

V. 10. That others, not of thy own household but in the house of a stranger, may not revel on thy earnings, the fruits of thy labor. *Labor*, used here for fruit of labor, as in Deut. 28 : 33, Ps. 78 : 46.

V. 14. Another aggravation of this guilt and folly. All this wickedness has been wrought in the midst of God's chosen people, whereby that holy relation was profaned and his name dishonored. Compare Gen. 34 : 7; Deut. 22 : 21; Judg. 20 : 6.

VV. 15–23. Divinely instituted relation of the sexes (Gen. 2 : 24; Mark 10 : 7–9); severity of God's displeasure toward those who violate it (vv. 20–23).

V. 15. By *waters from thine own cistern* are meant the pure and healthful influences of connubial love. With these are contrasted, in the next verse, the impure and unwholesome streams, the corrupt and unsatisfying pleasures, of unlawful connections.

Shall thy fountains spread abroad, 16
streams of water in the streets?
Let them be for thee, by thyself, 17
and not for strangers with thee.
Let thy fountain be blest; 18
and have joy of the wife of thy youth.
The lovely hind, and graceful roe! 19
let her breasts satisfy thee at all times,
and be thou always ravished with her love.
And why wilt thou, my son, be ravished with a strange woman, 20
and embrace the bosom of a stranger?
For a man's ways are before the eyes of Jehovah, 21
and all his paths He ponders.
His own iniquities ensnare him, the offender, 22
and in the toils of his own sin shall he be holden.
He shall die, without instruction; 23
and shall reel with the abundance of his folly.

My son, if thou hast become surety for thy friend, 1
hast struck thy hands for a stranger;
thou art snared with the words of thy mouth, 2
art taken with the words of thy mouth.
Do this now, my son, and deliver thyself, 3
for thou art come into the power of thy friend;
go humble thyself, and be urgent with thy friend.
Give not sleep to thine eyes, 4
nor slumber to thine eyelids;

MARGINAL TRANSLATIONS AND READINGS.

and shall perish in the

thy neighbor

V. 16. *Thy fountains,* at which thou drinkest. Shall they be such (i. e. wilt thou seek such) as are common to all, streams of water in the streets, where all may drink who will?

V. 18. *Let thy fountain* (that at which thou drinkest) be blest,—be one which God has made so, the relation ordained and blest by him; all other lies under his ban and curse.

V. 19. The sentiment is: Let thy love for her be unchanging; let her ever be "the joy of thy heart and the delight of thy eyes," and let no enticement allure thee from her.

V. 20. *Of a stranger.* The point of the remonstrance is: forsaking her whom God has made one with thee in interest and affection, for the mercenary and heartless embrace of a stranger, who has neither affection nor interest in common with thee.

V. 21. The admonition is enforced by reference to the Supreme Judge, in whose sight are the ways of all, and who will bring every work into judgment, with every secret thing.

V. 23 *Without instruction:* in voluntary ignorance, as one who refuses instruction, and resists every means of correction. Compare the remark on Job 4 : 21, at the end.

The second member continues this thought, and represents him as already the helpless victim of his own folly, reeling as one giddy with an intoxicating drug. Such is the fatal spell of an overmastering passion! The text and margin are the same in effect; but the version of the text is now preferred.

Ch. VI.—Seventh discourse, in five parts.

VV. 1–5. Against becoming surety for another.

V. 1. *Striking hands* was the customary form of confirming a contract, or a promise of any kind. The borrower or debtor, e. g., confirmed the promise to pay at the appointed time by giving his hand; the surety bound himself for the fulfillment of the promise, by giving also his hand to the lender or creditor.

The surety thus became subject, in his property and person, to the same liabilities as his principal, in case the latter was unable to make payment, or neglected to do it. The power of the creditor over property and person is shown in ch. 22 : 26, 27, and 2 Kings 4 : 1. Compare Lev. 25 : 39–43.

By *stranger* here is meant *one of another family* (as in Deut. 25 : 5); one who has not, therefore, the natural rights and claims of a kinsman.

V. 2. There is an emphatic repetition of the principal thought, *with the words of thy mouth.* Thou art ensnared with thine own words; and hast done thyself an injury, which no other could have done thee.

V. 3. *Art come into the power of thy friend;* since it depended wholly on his fidelity and promptness in making payment, whether the sponsor should be held to his liability for the debt.

VV. 6–11. Against slothfulness in business. Compare Rom. 12 : 11.

MARGINAL TRANSLATIONS AND READINGS.

5 deliver thyself as the roe from the hand,
and as the bird from the hand of the fowler.

6 Go to the ant, sluggard;
observe her ways, and be wise;
7 who, having no prince,
overseer, or ruler,
8 provides her meat in the summer,
gathers her food in the harvest.
9 How long, sluggard, wilt thou lie;
when wilt thou arise from thy sleep?
10 A little sleep, a little slumber,
a little folding of the hands to rest!
11 and as a prowler comes thy poverty,
and thy want as an armed man.

12 A vile man, a base man,
is he who walks in falsehood;
13 winking with his eyes, talking with his feet,
pointing with his fingers;
14 in whose heart is perverseness;
devising evil at all times;
who scatters discords.

who sends out

15 Therefore shall his calamity come suddenly;
in a moment shall he be destroyed without remedy.

16 Six things there are Jehovah hates;
and seven are the abomination of his soul.

the abominations (V. R.)

17 Lofty eyes, a lying tongue,
and hands that shed innocent blood;
18 a heart devising wicked counsels,
feet running with haste to evil;
19 who breathes out falsehoods, a lying witness,
and who scatters discords between brethren.

V. 7. Her industry and providence are not compulsory, and enforced by authority. *Overseer:* properly, the one who registered the amount of labor performed by each, and was held responsible for the full amount required. Such were set over the children of Israel by Pharaoh's taskmasters; see Ex. 5 : 6, 10, 14, 15, 19, common version, *officers*.—See note on ch. 30 : 25.

V. 10 is thought by some to be the language of the sluggard, pleading for a little longer rest; but more probably (in connection with the following verse), the taunting expostulation of the writer, exposing his folly and its consequences.

V. 11. *Prowler:* one who has no settled abode or regular occupation, but roves about in search of opportunities for plunder. Poverty and want will come upon the sluggard like armed banditti, and leave him nothing.

VV. 12–15. A covert and insidious mode of communication is the characteristic of this class. They " walk in falsehood," for their life is a deception. By sly winks, by significant gestures, they covertly convey their insidious meaning; so as to incur no danger of detection, or of being held to the just responsibility which no honest man shuns. The crafty intriguer thus screens himself, while he " devises evil," and " scatters discords." The dastardly defamer securely aims his poisoned shaft at the unconscious victim;

" Willing to wound, and yet afraid to strike;
Just hints a fault, and hesitates dislike."

There is nothing new under the sun. The types of humanity, depicted in this ancient book, are repeated with every generation; and though sketched three thousand years ago, are still as true to nature as if now drawn from their living representatives. The one here described is the most odious and infamous of them all; and hence it is stigmatized with double emphasis.

VV. 16–19. An enumeration of seven things abhorred by Jehovah. They require no comment.

20 Keep, my son, the command of thy father,
and reject not the law of thy mother.
21 Bind them on thy heart continually;
fasten them on thy neck.
22 When thou walkest, she will guide thee;
when thou liest down, she will watch over thee;
and when thou wakest, she will talk with thee.
23 For the command is a lamp, and the law is a light;
and instructive reproofs are the way of life:
24 to keep thee from the evil woman,
from the flattery of the strange woman's tongue.
25 Covet not her beauty in thy heart,
nor let her take thee with her eyelids.
26 For for a harlot is but a round of bread;
but the married woman hunts for the precious life.
27 Can a man take up fire into his bosom,
and his clothes not be burned?
28 Or can a man walk on the hot coals,
and his feet not be scorched?
29 So he that goes in to his neighbor's wife;
no one shall be innocent that touches her.
30 They slight not the thief, when he steals,
to satisfy his spirit when he is hungry;
31 and if found, he shall restore seven-fold,
all the substance of his house shall he give.
32 He that commits adultery with a woman is without understanding;
a destroyer of his own soul is he that does it.
33 Blows and shame shall he get;
and his reproach shall not be wiped away.

MARGINAL TRANSLATIONS AND READINGS.

22 it will
it will
23 corrective reproofs

VV. 20–35. Renewed admonition to filial obedience, and its advantages (vv. 20–24); to shun the snare of the adulteress (vv. 25–35).

V. 22. *She will guide thee* (margin, in the same sense, *it will guide thee*); referring, as some think, to the words *command* and *law*, in v. 20. More probably, it is a simple and natural personification of that parental instruction, obedience to which is here enjoined, and will be thus rewarded.

The language is, of course, figurative. These precepts, so loved and obeyed, will guide the steps securely, will banish fear from the couch of repose, and will give to the waking thoughts themes of pleasing and profitable reflection.

V. 24. *Strange woman.* See ch. 2 : 16, and the remarks on it. She is here called *the evil woman*, in a special and emphatic sense, as one regardless of all obligations to her husband, and of all consequences to the victim of her fatal allurements.

V. 26. Uncleanness, in every form, is strenuously forbidden and severely punished by the divine law. But adultery, with a married woman, as being a violation of the most sacred of all earthly relations, was treated with the greatest severity, the life of both the guilty parties being required (Lev. 20 : 10; Deut. 22 : 22). Hence, the victim of the adulteress was exposed, not only to the immediate vengeance of the injured husband (v. 33), but to the severest penalty of the law. She therefore "hunts for the precious life." But the common harlot seeks only her guilty subsistence; for her a round of bread suffices.

VV. 30, 31. The assertion in the preceding verse (*shall not be innocent*) is here confirmed by an argument from the less to the greater. If the thief, who steals to satisfy his hunger, is not slighted as unworthy of notice and punishment; how much more deserving of punishment is he, who is guilty of so much greater wrong, and with no such mitigation of his crime!

*Shall restore sevenfold.* By the Mosaic law, he who stole an ox was compelled to restore five-fold, and he who stole a sheep fourfold (Ex. 22 : 1); if he had not the means to do this, he was to be sold for the theft (Ex. 22 : 3). It is not improbable, therefore, that *sevenfold* is here put indefinitely for a great number (manifold); unless there is reference here to a private adjustment, in order to escape public exposure, which is less probable.

*All the substance of his house shall he give;* in case that should be necessary, in order to make the required restitution.

VV. 33–35. The consequences of detection. Jealousy, the

MARGINAL TRANSLATIONS AND READINGS.

and call understanding, Friend!

behind my lattice

in the midst

Now in the street, now in the broad ways

34 For jealousy is the husband's rage;
and he will not spare in the day of vengeance.
35 He will regard no ransom;
nor consent, though thou make many gifts.

1 My son, keep my sayings;
and treasure up with thee my commands.
2 Keep my commands and live,
and my law as the apple of thine eye.
3 Bind them on thy fingers;
write them on the tablet of thy heart.
4 Say to wisdom: My sister art thou!
and call understanding, Kinswoman!
5 to guard thee from the strange woman,
from the stranger who flatters with her words.
6 For at the window of my house,
through my lattice I looked forth;
7 and saw among the simple,
I discerned among the youths,
a young man without understanding,
8 passing along the street by her corner,
and he went the way to her house;
9 at twilight, in the evening of the day,
in the depth of night and gloom.
10 And lo, a woman meeting him,
with harlot's attire, and deceitful in heart.
11 She is loud and stubborn;
her feet abide not in her house.
12 Now before the house, now in the streets;
and by every corner she lies in wait.
13 And she laid hold on him, and kissed him;
with impudent face she said to him:
14 There are peace-offerings by me;
to-day I have paid my vows:

husband's rage, is proverbial in every age and nation, as the most violent and inexorable of all the passions. What then may not the culprit expect from its unbridled fury?

*Blows,* etc. (v. 33); the private vengeance taken by the husband in the moment of detection. But this does not appease his wrath. No ransom will be accepted; no amount of gifts will purchase exemption from the utmost rigor of the law. See the remark on v. 26, and the references to Lev. 20 : 10; Deut. 22 : 22.

Ch. VII.—Eighth discourse. Admonition renewed to filial obedience, and to the love of wisdom and understanding; especially as a security against the wiles of the adulteress (vv. 1–5). Her seductive and fatal arts (vv. 6–23); warning to beware of her (vv 24–27).

V. 3. *Bind them on thy fingers;* compare Deut. 6 : 8, 11 : 18. The meaning is: Let them be ever in remembrance, as if written on scrolls and bound on the fingers, where they may be always seen.

VV. 6–23. The need of this heavenly monitor is here shown by an example of the dangers to which the heedless and unguarded are exposed.

VV. 11, 12. *She is loud,* etc., is descriptive of her general character and deportment, not of her manner on this particular occasion.

V. 14. *Peace-offerings;* described Lev. ch. 3. The blood of the animal was sprinkled on the altar (Lev. 3 : 2, 8, 13), and an offering was made by fire of the fat, kidneys, caul, etc. (see vv. 3, 4, 9, 10, 14, 15.) The flesh was required to be eaten within one, or at most two days, including the day of the offering (Lev. 7 : 15, 16). Thus it was made the occasion of a religious festival; compare 1 Kings 3 : 15. If the offering was made in fulfillment of a vow (as professed in this case), all except the portion burned on

therefore came I forth to meet thee, 15
to seek thy face, and have found thee.
With coverings I have spread my couch, 16
with embroideries of Egyptian thread.
I have sprinkled my bed, 17
with myrrh, aloe-wood, and cinnamon.
Come, let us drink our fill of love till the morning, 18
let us delight ourselves with love.
For the goodman is not at home; 19
he has gone on a journey far away.
The purse of silver he has taken in his hand; 20
at the day of the full moon he will come home.
With her much ensnaring art she inclines him, 21
impels him with the flattery of her lips.
He goes after her straightway; 22
as an ox comes to the slaughter,
and as a fool to the gyves for correction:
till an arrow cleave his liver; 23
as a bird hastes to the snare,
and knows not that it is for his life.
  Now then, children, hearken to me, 24
and attend to the words of my mouth.
Let not thy heart turn aside to her ways; 25
go not astray in her paths.
For many has she cast down wounded, 26
and numerous are all her slain.
Ways to the underworld—is her house, 27
going down to the chambers of death!

MARGINAL TRANSLATIONS AND READINGS.

embroidered with

with her smooth speech she impels him

and as to the gyves, to the correction of a fool

wander not into her paths

---

the altar was required to be eaten on the same day, or, at furthest, on the day following (see Lev. 7 : 16). Hence the import of her language is: *I have a banquet prepared at my house;* but expressed under the form of a religious observance.

V. 16. *Embroideries of Egyptian thread.* Egypt was celebrated for its fabrics of cotton and linen. Compare, e. g., Ezek. 27 : 7, *Fine linen with broidered work from Egypt;* Is. 19 : 9, *They* (of Egypt) *that work in fine flax* (prop. *in combed flax*).

V. 17. *Aloe-wood:* a highly fragrant substance, produced by age or disease in the *aloe-tree* (Num. 24 : 6, properly *aloe-trees*, Common Version, *trees of lignaloes*). It was brought from India (and, as said by some, from Arabia); and was so much prized and so extremely rare, as to be worth its weight in gold.

V. 19. *The goodman:* meaning the master of the house, and expressing also his relation to herself as her husband.

V. 20. *The purse,* etc. That he would not speedily return, is indicated by the provision made for a long journey. *At the day of the full moon* may mean, on the next coming full moon. It is quite probable, however, that the full moon of the seventh month is meant, the time of the great convocation of the whole people at the *feast of tents* (Lev. 23 : 34–36), which would naturally be so designated; compare Ps. 81 : 3.

VV. 26, 27. *She,* namely such as she, the class she belongs to and represents. The truth of these warning words is attested by the records of all ages and nations. Her house may be termed *ways to the underworld;* for there meet and combine all the corrupting and destroying influences, that ruin body and soul, and lead down to endless perdition.

*Chambers of death:* the mansions of the dead, in the realm of death; so called from the mystery and gloom resting on those dreaded abodes. But as death is the lot of all, of the good and the evil, there is something special intended in the application of such language to the wicked. It is well illustrated in Ps. 49 : 14, 15, 19. The wicked are there said to be "laid in the grave like sheep;" like brute beasts, having no hope beyond it. "But God," says the righteous, "will redeem my soul from the power of the grave" (certainly not from subjection to physical death, as some absurdly interpret, for this no one can claim); while of the wicked it is said (v. 19), "they shall never see light," they shall lie forever under the frown of God!

| MARGINAL TRANSLATIONS AND READINGS. | | |
|---|---|---|
| | 1 | Does not wisdom call,<br>and understanding utter her voice? |
| | 2 | At the head of the high places, by the way,<br>in the cross-ways, she takes her stand. |
| | 3 | By the gates, at the mouth of the city,<br>at the entering of the gateways, she cries aloud: |
| | 4 | Unto you, O men, I call;<br>and my voice is to the sons of men. |
| | 5 | Learn shrewdness, ye simple,<br>and fools, be wise in heart. |
| of princely things | 6 | Hear, for of noble things I speak;<br>and the opening of my lips is with right things. |
| | 7 | For my mouth shall utter truth;<br>and wickedness is the abomination of my lips. |
| | 8 | In righteousness are all the words of my mouth;<br>there is nothing crooked and perverse in them. |
| are all right<br>and just | 9 | They are all plain to him that has understanding,<br>and straight to them that find knowledge. |
| | 10 | Take my instruction, and not silver;<br>and knowledge rather than choice gold. |
| all precious things | 11 | For wisdom is better than pearls;<br>and all objects of delight will not compare with it. |
| | 12 | I, wisdom, dwell in prudence,<br>and find out the knowledge of wise counsels. |

Ch. VIII.—Ninth discourse. Wisdom calls on men to receive her admonitions and instructions (vv. 1–11); their priceless value (vv. 12–21); her own exalted worth, and her love to the human race (vv. 22–31); blessedness of those who hear and obey her (vv. 32–36).

*Wisdom* and *Understanding* are here represented under the idea of a person (as in ch. 1 : 20–33), addressing her invitations and reproofs to all classes of men, wherever to be found.

A true understanding of our relations to God, of necessity, underlies the right understanding of all other relations; and, consequently, without it there can be no wise direction of our powers, for securing either present or future well-being. (Compare remarks on ch. 1 : 7.) No man is safe, even as to his worldly interests, in whose heart is not firmly rooted that "fear of Jehovah which is the beginning of wisdom," and which is proof against all temptation to wrong-doing, however secure it may seem from human detection. He who denies his accountability to the Judge of all, whatever may be his natural shrewdness, or his mastery of the maxims of worldly prosperity, is ever liable to some fatal error, which in a moment may plunge him, and all dependent on him, in irretrievable ruin.

Accordingly, this divine book, in all its practical precepts, recognizes this ground principle of human welfare. Hence, wisdom and understanding here urge their united appeals, with the earnestness and tender sympathy, with which divine love has always sought to reclaim the erring and lost.

VV. 1–3. The importance and urgency of this divine message are set forth, by representing it as proclaimed from the highest elevations, and in the most public and crowded thoroughfares. (V. 3. *By the gates;* comp. the remarks on Job 5 : 4; 31 : 21.)

This, perhaps, exhausts the true import and design of these words. But it may be proper to consider, how far they are strictly and literally fulfilled. Does not wisdom call, and understanding utter her voice? Are they not heard, wherever God has bestowed the power of reflection, and opened to it the volume of his works? The Heathen, we are told by an inspired apostle (Rom. 2 : 14, 15), are a law to themselves, and show the work of the law written in their hearts; and of the visible heavens it is said: "Their line is gone out through all the earth, and their words to the end of the world" (Ps. 19 : 4). Moreover, the written Word of God, in this and other passages, proclaims these truths, and his spirit bears testimony to them in every human heart (Gen. 6 : 3).

V. 5. The meaning of this verse is made clear by comparison with ch. 14 : 15. (Compare the remark on ch. 1 : 4.) It asserts the moral obligation, to make diligent and unwearied use of the powers of discrimination and judgment which God has bestowed, in all the concerns of life. The *simple* is one who yields himself, without resistance, to outward impressions and influences; making the example of others and the current maxims of the place and time his guide, without testing them by the principles and precepts of God's word. This is, perhaps, the most common form of what is called *folly* in the Scriptures. Of the opposite character, it is said (ch. 14 : 15), he "*gives heed to his going.*"

V. 12. *I, wisdom, dwell in prudence;* make her my abode. In other words: prudence is the practical virtue, in which wisdom

13 The fear of Jehovah is to hate evil;
pride, and haughtiness, and an evil way,
and a perverse mouth, do I hate.
14 Counsel is mine, and true wisdom;
I am understanding; strength is mine.
15 By me kings reign,
and princes decree justice.
16 By me princes rule,
and nobles, all the judges of the earth.
17 Them that love me I love;
and they that early seek me shall find me.
18 Wealth and honor are with me;
enduring riches and righteousness.
19 My fruit is better than gold, yea than refined gold;
and my increase than choice silver.
20 I walk in the way of righteousness,
within the paths of rectitude;
21 to make those who love me inherit substance,
and their storehouses I will fill.

22 Jehovah possessed me in the beginning of his way,
before his works of old.
23 From everlasting was I anointed, from the beginning,
from times before the earth.
24 When there were no deeps, I was brought forth;
when there were no fountains abounding in water.
25 Ere yet the mountains were sunken;
before the hills was I brought forth.

MARGINAL TRANSLATIONS AND READINGS.

17 that love her (V. R.)

21 There is to bestow on those who love me

22 possessed himself of me | *Or*, established me the beginning of his way (*or*, in the beginning of his way). *Others:* created me

manifests herself. Where there is not prudent management, there is no true wisdom. Second member:—She alone can devise those counsels, by which life may be rightly and safely governed.

V. 13. It follows, from the statements in this verse, that to wisdom belongs the fear of Jehovah; and by her it is imparted.

VV. 14–16. *True wisdom;* what is really such, in distinction from false pretensions to it; such as the vile cunning and craft, that too often usurp its place in the conduct of human affairs.

*By me kings reign;* in the true and proper sense of the word is meant. To exercise power over men, for other ends and by other means than wisdom dictates, is to tyrannize and oppress, not to reign. Moreover, such an exercise of authority has no sure and permanent basis; and hence she claims (v. 14), that to her belongs *strength* as well as *counsel* and *understanding.*

V. 17. The marginal reading (*love her*) refers to wisdom herself, as an object already before the mind of the reader.

VV. 18–21. They who obey the dictates of wisdom, and follow in the paths of rectitude, have the surest pledge of success in all their worldly interests. What is here promised, is the stated and ordinary course of Providence; though sometimes varied, as might be expected, in the present state of trial and discipline. See remarks on ch. 3 : 9, 10, and 16.

*Riches and righteousness* (v. 18); their union alone giving a real and permanent value to the former; for without the latter there can be no *enduring riches,* they perish with the using.

VV. 22–31. The exalted worth of WISDOM, and her claims on man's attention and obedience, are here shown by her relation to Jehovah before time began, by her connection with the work of creation, and by her regard for the race of man.

V. 22. *Possessed me,* had me in possession; terms used in speaking of a valued treasure, of something prized for its intrinsic worth. (Marginal renderings:—see remarks at the end of the chapter. *Established,* as the law of the material and moral world; Job 28 : 27.)

*His way:* his course of action; the way which he has taken in creation and providence. *Beginning of his way;* comp. Gen. 1 : 1.

V. 23. *Anointing* was a rite of consecration to an office (e. g., of *priests,* Ex. 28 : 41, 29 : 7, 40 : 15; Lev. 8 : 12; of kings, 1 Sam. 9 : 16, 10 : 15, 15 : 1, 17; 16 : 12, 13; 2 Sam. 2 : 4, 5 : 3; 1 Kings 1 : 34, 39; 2 Kings 9 : 3, 6; 11 : 12; 23 : 30). The word also expressed the designation to an office, and the communication of extraordinary endowments for it (Is. 61 : 1).

V. 24. *Were no deeps;* compare Gen. 1 : 2. Second member:—compare the remark on ch. 3 : 20, and below, on v. 28.

V. 25. *Were sunken,* to their foundations in the depths of the earth or sea. Compare Jonah 2 : 6.

MARGINAL TRANSLATIONS AND READINGS.
nor the mass of clods

26 While yet he had not made the earth nor the fields,
nor the first clods of the habitable world.
27 When he founded the heavens, I was there;
when he traced a circle on the face of the deep.
28 When he established the clouds above;
when the fountains of the deep became strong.
29 When he gave to the sea its bound,
that the waters should not pass his command;
when he appointed the foundations of the earth.
30 And I was one brought up at his side;
and was day by day a delight,
31 sporting always before him;
sporting in his habitable earth,
and my delight was with the sons of men.
32 Now then, children, hearken to me;
and happy they who keep my ways!
33 Hear instruction, and be wise,
and do not refuse.
34 Happy the man who hearkens to me;
to watch at my doors day by day,
to keep the posts of my doorways.
35 For they that find me find life;
and he shall obtain favor from Jehovah.
36 But he that fails of me wrongs his own soul;
all that hate me love death.

---

V. 27. *Founded the heavens;* established the beautiful structure of the visible heavens. The expression is drawn from the appearance of the celestial dome, that seems suspended over the earth. Comp. remarks at the end of ch. 26 of Job. *I was there;* compare ch. 3 : 19. Second member:—compare Job 26 : 10, and the remark on it.

V. 28. Compare the remark on Job 37 : 16. Second member:—*Became strong;* began to break forth in exhaustless abundance, forming streams and mighty rivers on the surface of the earth. Compare the remark on ch. 3 : 20.

V. 29. Compare Job 38 : 8, 10, 11. Third member:—compare Job 38 : 6; Ps. 102 : 25.

V. 30. *One brought up,* etc. Margin: *an architect;* but the authority for this version is doubtful, and it is less suited to the remainder of the verse. Third member:—*Sporting;* as a child, in accordance with the imagery of this verse (*brought up at his side*), and of v. 24 (*I was brought forth*). Those who translate *architect,* in the first member, suppose that creation is here represented as the infantile sport and pastime of wisdom; a view hardly worthy of serious notice.

V. 31 refers to the same period as the preceding verse (*and I was one brought up at his side*), expressing the anticipated delight of wisdom in the habitable earth, and in man its future occupant.

V. 34. *To watch,* etc., i. e., to be as attentive and observant as the watchman, whose hourly business it is to keep the doors of my house.

V. 36. *He that fails of me:* neglects to seek me, and thus fails of finding me; for "they that early seek me shall find me" (v. 17). This character is distinguished from that in the preceding verse: *They that find me find life.*

---

Wisdom is shown in the intelligent direction of one's powers to the best and noblest ends. Any other than such a direction of them is folly. The creative power of God was under its guidance. Of his works the divinely inspired Psalmist says: IN WISDOM HAST THOU MADE THEM ALL. This would not be true, if they had not been made for the best and worthiest ends, and with an intelligent adaptation to those ends. He is said, moreover (Job 28 : 27), to have "*established it;*" i. e., settled it for ever, as the universal and unchanging law of his physical and moral world. Its ground element and beginning in man is the "*fear of Jehovah*" (Job 28 : 28), the germ of all that moral development which is essential to true wisdom.

WISDOM, therefore, speaks by the authority of God; for she personates a principle, which he has established as the law of his universe, and to which all things created are subjected by him. The delight of Jehovah, and the guide of his work, she here claims to be the guide and friend of his creature man. Were her

1 WISDOM has builded her house;
she has hewn out her seven pillars.
2 She has slaughtered her beasts, mixed her wine,
yea, she has prepared her table.
3 She has sent out her maidens;
on the heights of the city she calls:
4 Whoso is simple, let him turn hither;
he that lacks understanding, she says to him:
5 Come, eat of my food,
and drink of the wine I have mixed.
6 Forsake follies, and live;
and go forward in the way of understanding.
7 He that reproves a scoffer gets himself reproach;
and he that rebukes the wicked, a blot to himself.
8 Rebuke not a scoffer, lest he hate thee;
rebuke the wise, and he will love thee.
9 Give to the wise, and he will be yet wiser;
teach the just, and he will increase in learning.
10 The fear of Jehovah is the beginning of wisdom;
and knowledge of the Holy is understanding.

MARGINAL TRANSLATIONS AND READINGS.

6 Forsake the foolish

admonitions heeded by all, how soon would earth become as Eden, and her deserts like the garden of Jehovah!

In the language of vv. 22–31 (compared with John 1 : 1–3, 10, 14; Rev. 3 : 14; Col. 1 : 15), many interpreters, from the early ages of the church, have thought they saw a direct reference to HIM who was the divine impersonation of this wisdom, and through whom it has expressed itself, in the beautiful order and harmony of the material and moral worlds, as they were created by him.

It should be observed, however, that the representation is not the same here as in John 1 : 1–3, and 10. It is there said that "*the Word was God*" (v. 1); that "*all things were made by him*" (v. 3), that "*the world was made by him*" (v. 10), not as the instrument merely, but as the agent and doer. (Compare Col. 1 : 16, "*by him were all things created*," and Eph. 3 : 9, Heb. 1 : 2, 1 Cor. 8 : 16.) Neither of these is here affirmed of wisdom.

It should also be observed, that there can be no reference to a literal person in vv. 1–21; for the writer there speaks of *wisdom* and *understanding* in connection, just as he does in chapter second of *wisdom, understanding*, and *intelligence* (vv. 2, 3), of *wisdom, knowledge*, and *understanding* (v. 6), and of *wisdom, knowledge, reflection*, and *understanding* (vv. 10, 11). No one can doubt that these words, in all these passages, are to be understood in their ordinary sense and application in the Scriptures. Moreover, the ground of the exhortation to seek *knowledge*, in vv. 10, 11, is the high value of *wisdom;* and in vv. 12 and following, the writer asserts its immediate agency in the skillful direction of worldly affairs.

Interpreters have differed widely in their opinions on this passage. A faithful version enables the reader to judge of it for himself, as well as can be done by the reader of the original, if equally practiced and skillful in interpreting the divine word.

Ch. IX.—Tenth discourse. WISDOM invites to her feast (vv. 1–6); the scoffer spurns reproof, which the wise gratefully accepts; advantages of wisdom, and folly of rejecting it (vv. 7–12); contrast of the foolish woman and of the fate of her victims (vv. 13–18).

Under the idea of a feast, wisdom here invites all, without distinction, to partake of her bounty. A place of entertainment has been prepared by her, befitting her own exalted worth, and the dignity of her mission. Already she has slaughtered her beasts, has mixed her wine, yea, has prepared her table; in other words, "*all things are now ready*." Accordingly, she has sent out her servants, and invites all to her banquet. What this consists of, is shown in vv. 4–6.

V. 2. *Mixed her wine;* viz. with water and spices, to make it a pleasant and nourishing drink, and prevent its intoxicating effect. It is mentioned here, as being a customary part of a feast. Compare Is. 25 : 6; 55 : 1, 2.

V. 4. *Simple;* compare the remarks on chs. 8 : 5, and 1 : 4.

VV. 7–9. Occasion is here taken, from the admonition to the simple and foolish, to add a caution on the subject of administering reproof; showing how differently it is received by the scoffer, and by the truly wise.

V. 8. It is useless to rebuke the scoffer; it will not benefit him, and the well meant kindness will only incur his hatred. Compare the Saviour's precept: *Neither cast ye your pearls before swine* (Matt. 7 : 6). We are not to infer that there are no occasions, when fidelity to truth and right requires the rebuke of a scoffer, though to him it may do no good. The meaning is: One should not rebuke a scoffer, expecting to retain his good will.

V. 9. *Give to the wise:* what is to be given is shown by the connection, viz., counsel and instruction.

VV. 10–12. In contrast with the spirit of the scoffer (who

MARGINAL TRANSLATIONS AND READINGS.

11 For by me shall thy days be multiplied;
and years of life shall be added to thee.
12 If thou art wise, thou art wise for thyself;
and if thou scoffest, thou alone shalt bear it.

13 A foolish woman is clamorous,
simple, and knows nothing.
14 And she sits in the doorway of her house,
on a seat in the high places of the city;
15 to call to them that pass by the way,
who go right on their ways.
16 Whoso is simple, let him turn hither;
and he that lacks understanding, she says to him:
17 Stolen waters are sweet,
and bread of secrecy is pleasant.
18 And he knows not that the shades are there,
her guests in the depths of the underworld!

## PROVERBS OF SOLOMON.

1 A WISE son makes a glad father;
but a foolish son is the grief of his mother.
2 Treasures of wickedness profit not;
but righteousness delivers from death.

mocks at all things serious and sacred) is *the fear of Jehovah.* This is the very beginning of wisdom, and true understanding consists in the knowledge of the Holy. Compare remarks on ch. 8, third paragraph.

V. 11 (*For by me,* etc.) confirms the statement in the preceding verse, by one of the most obvious and often repeated of the many advantages of wisdom, standing here as the representative of them all. Compare ch. 3 : 16, *Length of days is in her right hand.*

V. 12 sums up the whole with a direct, individual appeal. Each is here acting for himself, and in a matter that concerns his own highest welfare. If wise, it is for thyself; if a scoffer, the peril is all thine own!

VV. 13-18. In marked contrast with wisdom and her votaries, appears the representative of folly, with the victims of its delusion. She also is ever on the alert; watching in public places for her prey, ready to decoy the simple and unwary from their ways. But it is not to a free and public banquet she invites. It is to "stolen waters," and "bread of secrecy;" pleasures that shun the light, and are near the abodes of death.

V. 13. *Knows nothing;* as those who desire not the knowledge of God (Rom. 1 : 28), and are voluntarily and willfully ignorant of all that most concerns them.

V. 15. *Who go right on their ways* (pursuing their own business), and whom she seeks to divert into the paths of sin and ruin.

V. 17. *Bread of secrecy;* the enjoyment of which is forbidden, and must be cautiously concealed.

V. 18. *The shades;* the spirits of the dead. The Hebrew Scriptures distinguish the *dead* from the *disembodied spirit,* by appropriate terms; which, however, the Common English Version confounds (rendering both by the same term *dead*), thus obliterating from the Old Testament this striking evidence of an existence after death. See the proofs of this in the references given on Job 26 : 5. *Shades* is the proper English term answering to the import of the original word, and is applied in the same way by English writers.

*Her house* is called (ch. 7 : 27) *ways to the underworld,* and *her steps* (it is said, ch. 5 : 5) *take hold on it;* so near to its abodes, that the shades of the dead are there, and her guests are already as in the depths of hell! (Compare the remarks on ch. 7 : 27, second paragraph.)

Ch. X.—Here commences the second division of the book, extending as far as ch. 22 : 16. It consists of single sentences, unconnected with each other, conveying in few words the choicest treasures of practical wisdom.

V. 2. While riches gained by wickedness are of no profit, serving no really valuable purpose, *righteousness* delivers from all evil; for death itself is no evil to him who has nothing to fear from it. Compare 1 Tim. 4 : 8.

MARGINAL TRANSLATIONS AND READINGS.

3 Jehovah will not let the spirit of the righteous famish;
but he repels the longing of the wicked.

4 Poor is he that labors with a slothful hand;
but the hand of the diligent makes rich.

5 He that gathers in the summer is a wise son;
he that sleeps in the harvest is a son that brings shame.

6 Blessings are for the head of the righteous;
but the mouth of the wicked covers violence. — *Margin:* violence covers

7 The memory of the righteous is blessed;
but the name of the wicked shall rot.

8 The wise in heart will receive commands;
but a prating fool shall fall.

9 He that walks in integrity will walk securely;
but he that perverts his ways will be known. — *Margin:* will be taught

10 He that winks with the eye causes sorrow;
and a prating fool shall fall.

11 A well of life is the mouth of the righteous;
but the mouth of the wicked covers violence.

12 Hatred stirs up strifes;
but love covers all offenses.

13 In the lips of the discerning is found wisdom;
but a rod is for the back of him that lacks understanding.

14 The wise treasure up knowledge;
but the fool's mouth is a near downfall.

V. 5. *A son that brings shame;* one that is a reproach to his father and mother, instead of being their joy, as the wise son is represented in v. 1.

V. 6. *The mouth* is the organ that makes known, or conceals, the workings of the heart. The mouth of the wicked covers (that is, hides from view) the violence which his heart meditates. It is the office of his mouth to conceal his evil thoughts. On the contrary, the just man has nothing to conceal, and he is the object of blessing.

The words are by some translated as in the margin, meaning: His violence (his own wrong doing) covers his mouth, that is, puts him to silence; he can say nothing for himself. The sentiment is just; but the version in the text is doubtless the true one.

V. 8. The wise seeks to know his duty, and he is consequently secure from harm; but the prating fool, less intent to hear than be heard, is always liable to mistake and ruin.

V. 9. *That perverts his way;* that is, who makes his ways perverse, in other words, walks in perverse ways. *Will be known.* His only safety is in concealment; but his perverseness will betray itself, and he will be exposed to just punishment. Margin: *will be taught*, as is said in Judg. 8 : 16, *with them he taught the men of Succoth;* that is, he chastised them. Or the meaning here may be simply: shall be taught better, shall be made to know the folly of such a course. Compare the same expression in Jer 31 : 19 (Common Version, *I was instructed*).

V. 10. *That winks with the eye;* compare remarks on ch. 6 :13 *A prating fool* (second member) represents folly of another class; and the relation of the two members is not at first obvious. But the same mischiefs are caused by the malicious artifices of the sly intriguer, and by the careless gossip of the prating fool. Hence the two are here classed together; and the declared fate of the one is, by implication, the fate of both. Or the meaning may be, that covert insinuations and foolish prating are both to be avoided; for by the former one injures others, and by the latter he harms himself.

V. 11. The mouth of the just is like a well of living water, pure, wholesome, and refreshing, the source of life and joy to all who partake of it. Second member:—Compare remarks on v. 6.

V. 13. The man of true discernment is not liable to speak rashly with his lips, and is safe from the correction to which the ignorant exposes himself.

V. 14. A sentiment similar to the preceding one, expressed with great point and force. The fool's mouth is a *near* downfall; for he can not open it without imminent risk of a blunder, which may do him serious harm. But the wise treasure up knowledge;

| MARGINAL TRANSLATIONS AND READINGS. | | |
|---|---|---|
| | 15 | The rich man's wealth is his strong city;<br>the downfall of the needy is their poverty. |
| | 16 | The wages of the righteous is life;<br>the gain of the wicked is sin. |
| | 17 | A way of life is he who heeds correction;<br>but he who forsakes reproof leads astray. |
| | 18 | He that covers hatred with lying lips,<br>and he that publishes an ill report, the same is a fool. |
| | 19 | In the multitude of words there will not be wanting offense;<br>but he that restrains his lips is wise. |
| | 20 | Choice silver is the tongue of the righteous;<br>the heart of the wicked is of little worth. |
| | 21 | The lips of the righteous feed many;<br>but fools die for lack of understanding. |
| | 22 | The blessing of Jehovah, that makes rich;<br>and he adds no sorrow therewith. |
| to execute a plan | 23 | It is as mockery to a fool to execute counsel,<br>but wisdom to a man of understanding. |
| | 24 | The dread of the wicked, that shall come upon him;<br>but the desire of the righteous He will grant. |
| | 25 | As the whirlwind passes by, so the wicked is no more;<br>but the righteous is an everlasting foundation. |
| | 26 | As vinegar to the teeth, and as smoke to the eyes,<br>so is the sluggard to them that send him. |
| | 27 | The fear of Jehovah will prolong days;<br>but the years of the wicked will be cut short. |

so that what they have to utter is well considered, and is profitable to others and themselves.

By treasuring up what they know (first member) may possibly be meant, that they are not eager to exhibit it on every occasion. Compare ch. 12 : 23.

V. 15. Wealth furnishes means of protection against many of the calamities of life; while for want of it, the needy sink under them, and perish.

V. 16. *The wages of the righteous* (what he earns by his industry) *is life;* because it is acquired by a course of uprightness, to which life is promised. LIFE here means all that is comprehended in the favor of God (*in his favor is life*, Ps. 30 : 5). On the contrary, *the gain of the wicked is sin.* It is gained by wickedness, and is a sinful possession; the acquiring and the holding it is a sin.

V. 17. Only he who himself heeds correction is a safe guide to others; and in this sense he is to them *a way of life*, his example and precepts being a way which they may safely follow.

V. 18. *He that covers*, etc. He that cloaks his secret enmity under false professions; of sorrow, e. g., for a slander, which he helps to spread more widely, by telling all how much he laments it.

V. 20. Compare ch. 8 : 19. The parallelism of the second member is by contrast; and on the principle, that "out of the abundance of the heart the mouth speaketh."

V. 21. Many are fed (with instruction and knowledge) from the lips of the righteous man; but fools, so far from helping others, perish themselves for want of understanding.

V. 23. *To execute counsel;* that is, to act upon a well considered plan. He never counsels (with himself, or others) before he acts. He accounts this a mockery, a thing to be scoffed at; but to the man of understanding, it is the part of wisdom.

V. 25. The wicked is suddenly swept away, as by a whirlwind; but the righteous is a foundation that can not be moved.

V. 26. As vinegar only sets the teeth on edge, and as smoke only blinds and offends the eye, so a sluggish messenger serves only to annoy and vex his employer.

MARGINAL TRANSLATIONS AND READINGS.

28 The hope of the righteous is gladness;
but the expectation of the wicked shall perish.

29 A stronghold for uprightness is the way of Jehovah;
but destruction to the workers of iniquity.

30 Forever, the righteous shall not be moved;
but the wicked shall not inhabit the land.

31 The mouth of the righteous brings forth wisdom;
but the perverse tongue shall be cut out.

32 The lips of the righteous know what is acceptable;
but the mouth of the wicked is perverseness.

1 A FALSE balance is the abomination of Jehovah;
but a full weight is his delight.

2 When pride comes, there comes shame;
but with the lowly is wisdom.

3 The integrity of the upright will guide them;
but the perverseness of transgressors will destroy them.

4 Riches profit not in the day of wrath;
but righteousness delivers from death.

5 The righteousness of the perfect will make plain his way;
but the wicked will fall by his wickedness.

6 The righteousness of the upright will deliver them; [be taken.
but in the wickedness of transgressors shall they themselves

7 When the wicked man dies, expectation shall perish;
yea, the hope of wickedness perishes.

8 The righteous was delivered out of trouble;
and the wicked came into his place.

V. 28. *The hope of the righteous is gladness.* There is gladness in his hope; a joyful confidence that all shall be well, for he knows in whom he trusts. The wicked also has his expectation; but it is full of trembling and uncertainty (for he knows he has no sure ground of confidence), and will fail him in the end.

V. 29. *The way of Jehovah* is his way of acting; the course which he takes, in the government of the world. This *is a stronghold* (a perfect security) for uprightness, for all who walk uprightly; but a destruction to evildoers.

V. 30. *Forever.* It shall never be otherwise, is the meaning; this is the perpetual and unchanging law of the divine government. *Shall not be moved:* he shall remain firm and unshaken, on a secure and immovable foundation. Compare v. 25.

*Shall not inhabit the land.* The form of expression is taken from the promises and threatenings made to those who occupied the land of Canaan, and to whom these words were first addressed. See, for example, Ex. 20 : 12; Lev. 20 : 22; Deut. 11 : 8, 9; 25 : 15; Ps. 37 : 29. The principle, however, is universal in its application, and is intended for all.

V. 32. *What is acceptable:* in the sight of God, is meant; what he is pleased with, and will accept. They are able to utter it, from the dictation of a heart that is right with God; and hence, by a happy figure, are said to *know it.*

Ch. XI.—V. 1. *A false balance;* compare Lev. 19 : 35, 36; Deut. 25 : 13–15.

V. 2. Compare ch. 16 : 18, and 29 : 23.

V. 3. A just man's integrity is a sure and faithful guide, and will never mislead him into the difficulties and perplexities in which the transgressor is involved by his perverseness, and which sooner or later will end in total ruin.

V. 4. *Day of wrath;* of any manifestation of God's anger against sin, as the Flood, the final Judgment. Comp. ch. 10 : 2.

V. 5. *Will make plain his way;* will make for him a level and even way, without obstruction, where there shall be no danger of a fall, to which the wicked is continually exposed. *Perfect:* ch. 2 : 21.

V. 8. *Came into his place;* was himself overtaken by the calamity, which he had prepared for the righteous. Compare Ps. 9 : 15; 57 : 6.

MARGINAL TRANSLATIONS AND READINGS.

Generation to generation (v. 21)

9 By the mouth the impure destroys his fellow;
but by knowledge the righteous are delivered.

10 When it is well with the righteous, the city rejoices;
and when the wicked perish, there is a shout of joy.

11 By the blessing of the upright the city is raised up;
but by the mouth of the wicked it is torn down.

12 He that despises his neighbor is lacking in understanding;
but a man of intelligence holds his peace.

13 He that goes talebearing is a revealer of secrets;
but one of trusty spirit conceals a matter.

14 Where there is no direction the people fall;
but in the multitude of counselors is safety.

15 Ill fares one when he is surety for a stranger;
but he that hates sureties is secure.

16 A lovely woman obtains honor;
even as the violent obtain riches.

17 A merciful man does good to his own soul;
but the cruel afflicts his own flesh.

18 The wicked toils for deceptive hire;
but he who sows righteousness, for true wages:
19 so is righteousness for life,
and he follows evil for his death.

20 An abomination of Jehovah are the perverse in heart;
but those of blameless way are his delight.

21 Hand to hand the evil will not be acquitted;
but the seed of the righteous is delivered.

22 A nose-ring of gold in a swine's snout,
is a woman fair and without discretion.

23 The desire of the righteous is only good;
the expectation of the wicked is wrath.

---

V. 9. *The impure* (the godless man), by "evil communication," spreads his infecting poison, to the destruction of those around him. But true knowledge is an effectual antidote; and by this the righteous escape the contagion.

V. 12. *That despises his neighbor:* with a vain conceit of his own superiority.

*Holds his peace.* Whatever weakness he may detect in another, he gives no indication of conscious superiority, by which the vain-glorious is so apt to betray his own emptiness.

V. 13. Compare Lev. 19 : 16 (properly, *thou shalt not go tale-bearing among thy people*). Such a character *is a revealer of secrets,* and therefore not to be confided in. A man of trusty spirit will carefully guard what is committed to him.

V. 14. What calamities are brought upon a people, where there is no wise direction of public affairs, may be seen in the history of every nation. The lesson is especially important for all those, to whom Divine Providence has committed the choice of their own rulers and public counselors.

V. 16. The qualities of mind and person, which render a woman lovely, will secure honor to their possessor. They are her strength, and her means of influence; and these gentle weapons are as sure of conquest, as the physical force and energy of will which are the strength of man.

V. 21. *Hand to hand:* that is, linked together for mutual support. In themselves or their offspring (Ps. 37 : 28), or in both, they shall receive due punishment. But the righteous shall be blessed in his seed, as well as in himself (Ps. 69 : 36; 102 : 28). Some translate as in the margin; but the text gives the true meaning.

V. 23. What the righteous desires is bestowed as a good, with-

24 There is that scatters, and is increased yet more;
and that withholds more than is meet, only to want.

25 The liberal soul shall be enriched;
and he that waters shall himself be watered.

26 He that withholds corn, the people will curse him;
but blessing for the head of him that sells grain!

27 Him that seeks good will favor seek;
and he that seeks evil, it will come upon him.

28 Whoso trusts in his riches, he shall fall;
but as the leaf shall the righteous flourish.

29 He that troubles his own house shall inherit wind;
and the fool is a servant to the wise in heart.

30 The fruit of the righteous is a tree of life;
and he that wins souls is wise.

31 Lo, the righteous on earth shall be requited;
much more the wicked and the sinner.

MARGINAL TRANSLATIONS AND READINGS.

31 If the righteous

1 He that loves correction loves knowledge;
but he that hates reproof is brutish.

2 The good will obtain favor from Jehovah;
but the man of evil devices he will hold guilty.

---

out any admixture of evil from the hand of God; and hence it is "*only good.*" The expectation of the wicked (what he expects) is granted in just anger; and hence it is wrath, the expression of the divine displeasure. "*I will curse your blessings*" (Mal. 2 : 2) is the key to the dealings of a righteous God with the wicked.

V. 26. *He that withholds corn:* that is, who hoards it up for the purpose of increasing the price, without adding to the value. This is very questionable morality, in regard to any article of commerce. He who has not added to the value of a thing, has no moral right to demand a price for what he has not rendered. It is robbery. He, especially, who deals thus with breadstuffs and other necessaries of life, enriches himself on the necessities and sufferings of the poor, and is the cause of untold misery—untold but to the eye and ear of God, the judge of both.

*That sells grain:* that is, takes the current price for it; which, without monopolies and other means of controlling the market, is always an expression of the true value of a thing.

V. 27. *Him that seeks good.* The meaning of this will be seen by comparing Ps. 122 : 9 (*I will seek thy good*), Neh. 2 : 10 (properly, *to seek the good of*, etc.). Such an one *favor will seek;* he will be an object of favor. *He that seeks evil:* compare 1 Sam. 25 : 26 (*that seek evil to my lord*).

V. 28. This verse teaches, that the righteous is not one whose trust is in his riches.

*Shall flourish as the leaf* means, shall be as the green leaf. This is a common emblem of prosperity; compare Jer. 17 : 8; Ps. 1 : 3.

V. 29. *That troubles his own house:* that afflicts, distresses his own household, by neglecting or mismanaging his worldly affairs, so as not to make suitable provision for them (1 Tim. 5 : 8); or by involving them in the consequences of his criminal love of gain (15 : 27). *Shall inherit wind:* shall have nothing else to live on; a common expression for what is unsubstantial and valueless (Hos. 12 : 1; Eccl. 5 : 16).

Second member:—The consequence of such folly is subjection to the superior judgment and forecast of another. He who neglects his business, or conducts it unwisely, becomes servant to the more diligent and skillful manager of his affairs.

V. 30. *The fruit of the righteous* (his wise counsels and holy example) *is a tree of life;* a healthful influence, imparting life to all who partake of it.

The influence of such a man wins the soul; it reaches and sways the intellectual and moral nature. He who can do this is wise. This language may properly be applied to all, who, in any manner, win men from error to the truth.

V. 31. If the righteous shall be so dealt with, how much more the wicked and the sinner! Compare Jer. 25 : 29; 1 Peter 4 : 17, 18.

| MARGINAL TRANSLATIONS AND READINGS. | | |
|---|---|---|
| | 3 | A man shall not be established by wickedness;<br>but the root of the righteous shall not be moved. |
| | 4 | A worthy woman is a crown to her husband;<br>and a base one is as rottenness in his bones. |
| | 5 | The thoughts of the righteous are uprightness;<br>the guidance of the wicked is deceit. |
| | 6 | The words of the wicked are a lying in wait for blood;<br>but the mouth of the upright will deliver them. |
| | 7 | The wicked are overthrown, and they are no more;<br>but the house of the righteous shall stand. |
| | 8 | According to his wisdom shall a man be praised;<br>but the perverse in heart shall be despised. |
| that has a servant | 9 | Better is one despised, and that tills for himself,<br>than he who boasts himself, and lacks bread. |
| for the wants<br>but the compassions | 10 | The righteous cares for the life of his beast;<br>but the bowels of the wicked are cruel. |
| | 11 | He that tills his ground shall be satisfied with bread;<br>but he that follows vanities lacks understanding. |
| | 12 | The wicked delights in the net of the evil;<br>but the root of the righteous will bring forth. |
| | 13 | In the transgression of the lips is an evil snare;<br>but the righteous will go forth out of trouble. |
| | 14 | Of the fruit of the mouth shall a man be satisfied with good;<br>and the desert of one's hands shall return to him. |

Ch. XII.—V. 5. Even the thoughts of the righteous, what he plans in his secret soul, are uprightness; he has no covert ends to gain in the directions he gives to others. On the contrary, *the guidance of the wicked* (the counsels he gives) *is deceit;* and is intended to mislead others for his own advantage.

V. 6. *The words of the wicked* are often intended (as said in v. 5) to misguide others to their ruin; from which the mouth of the upright (their sincere and honest counsels) will rescue them.

*Will deliver them:* namely, those exposed to the *lying in wait* of the wicked. *Lying in wait* necessarily implies an intended victim, or victims; and a pronoun in Hebrew often refers to a subject not expressed, but merely implied in the preceding words.

V. 9. The man of low condition, who subsists by his own industry, will not lack bread (compare v. 11); while he who makes a mere show of wealth, or prides himself on his birth and connections, may pine in want.

Margin: *that has a servant* (according to an ancient manner of reading of the Heb. text); namely, to aid him in earning his subsistence. But this is a far less happy expression of what is obviously the writer's thought; and the version in the text is believed to be the true sense of the Hebrew. *And is his own servant:* in the same sense as above given. So the Genevan version: *He that is despised, and is his own servant, is better than he that boasteth himselfe and lacketh bread.*

V. 10. *For the life of his beast:* for all the wants of its animal life. For this he makes careful provision, so as to minister to its enjoyment, and prevent needless suffering.

V. 11. *Vanities:* what is empty and unsubstantial; frivolous and trifling pursuits, with no earnest and well-directed purpose; or empty theories, unsubstantiated by observation and experience.

V. 12. In striking contrast with the chance gains of the wicked, is here shown the sure and natural increase of the righteous. The former is likened to a net, stealthily spread for the prey, that may take little or much, or perchance nothing; the latter is the natural and certain growth from the root, planted in the earth, that will not fail to bear fruit.

V. 13. '*The transgression of the lips*' (the utterance of an envious or malicious tongue) proves a '*snare,*' to its author often, as well as to its intended victim; but the innocent will escape out of it. Such is certainly the general law; and its exceptions only show what is incident to the imperfect moral condition of the race.

MARGINAL TRANSLATIONS AND READINGS.

15 The way of a fool is right in his own eyes;
but he that hearkens to counsel is wise.

16 The fool's anger is known the same day;
but a shrewd man conceals an affront.

17 He who breathes truth shows the right,
but a false witness fraud.

18 There is that prates as with thrusts of the sword;
but the tongue of the wise is a healing.

19 The truthful lip is established forever,
and the lying tongue but for a moment.

20 Deceit is in the heart of them that devise evil;
but to them that counsel peace there is joy.

21 There shall no harm befall the just;
but the wicked are filled with evil.

22 Lying lips are an abomination to Jehovah;
but they that deal truly are his delight.

23 A shrewd man covers knowledge;
but the heart of fools proclaims folly.

24 The hand of the diligent shall bear rule;
but the slothful shall be under tribute.

25 Heaviness in the heart of man bows it down;
but a good word makes it glad.

26 The righteous will guide his fellow;
but the way of the wicked leads them astray.

27 The slothful will not roast his game;
but a precious treasure to one is the diligent.

(27) will not snare his game

V. 16. The truly wise man, instead of resenting an affront, and thereby making it public, conceals such injuries as being unworthy of notice and retaliation, while the 'fool's anger' divulges them to his own dishonor.

V. 17. *Who breathes truth:* one whose breath is truth, or to whom truth is as his breath. The testimony of such a witness shows what is right; but as for the false witness, what he shows, what his testimony proves, is fraud.

Human testimony is one of the chief agencies of society. Without it, the social organization could not be sustained, nor its machinery kept in motion. Much of what must necessarily be known, in conducting the affairs of life, we owe to the veracity of witnesses. Hence the many precepts respecting it in this book; enforcing the obligation of a strict observance of the ninth commandment in the Decalogue.

V. 18. Imprudent and thoughtless prating is like sword-thrusts; often inflicting most serious mischiefs, on society as well as on individuals. In nothing is wisdom more needed than in the use of the tongue. Compare what is said in James, 3 : 5–8.

V. 19. As truth is always consistent with itself, and is in harmony with the eternal laws of Providence, so he whose reliance is on truth can never fail. On the contrary, falsehood may succeed for a time; but it has no basis of permanence in itself, or in the principles of the divine government, and will fail him who puts his trust in it.

V. 20. The contrast, in the two members, is between the *root* in one case, and the *fruit* in the other. The *root* of evil counsel is a deceitful heart, and only harm can come of it; but peaceful counsel has joy for its *fruit*.

V. 23. This accords with the common observation, that the most sagacious and discerning are also the most reserved and silent; while the shallow and superficial are always prating.

V. 26. *Will guide his fellow:* that is, will show him the right way; he walks in it himself, and his example will guide his fellow in it; but the wicked themselves forsake it, as do all who follow them.

MARGINAL TRANSLATIONS AND READINGS.

28 In the path of righteousness is life,
even a beaten way, where is no death.

1 A WISE son is one chastened of the father;
but a scoffer hears not rebuke.

2 Of the fruit of the mouth will one feed on good;
but the spirit of the treacherous on violence.

3 He that keeps his mouth preserves his soul;
he that opens wide his lips, it is his destruction.

4 The spirit of the sluggard longeth, and has nothing;
but the spirit of the diligent shall be enriched.

5 Lying speech the righteous hates;
but base and shameful is the conduct of the wicked.

6 Righteousness will keep the blameless way;
but wickedness will pervert to sin.

7 There is that makes himself rich, and has nothing at all,
that makes himself poor, and has great substance.

8 The ransom of a man's soul is his wealth; (Marginal: of a man's life)
and the poor hears not rebuke.

9 The light of the righteous shall be joyous;
but the lamp of the wicked shall go out.

V. 28, second member. The '*path of righteousness*' is a '*beaten way*,' trodden and made plain and safe; in distinction from a pathless wild, where one wanders without knowing on what he treads, or whither he is going.

Ch. XIII.—V. 2. No gift of God is more potent, for good or evil, than SPEECH; and its possessor may so use this power of influencing others, as to confer blessings that will return upon himself.

Second member. *Violence:* to themselves, is the meaning. The fruit of such a spirit (which also manifests itself in *words*) is violence and injury to its possessor; it works his own hurt.

V. 3. Compare James 3 : 2–8.—Second member. *That opens wide his lips:* the inconsiderate prater, whose mouth is always open, ready to utter whatever thought is uppermost.

V. 4. *Shall be enriched:* namely, with good; he shall be abundantly supplied.

V. 5. "The basis of all excellence" (it may as justly be said in the moral as in the æsthetic sense) "is truth;" and hence the conduct of the wicked, who has no regard for truth, is 'base and shameful;' his word can not be relied on.

V. 6. *Righteousness* (the inward love of rectitude, and delight in it) *will keep*, i. e. will adhere to, the way that is blameless; but *wickedness* (an evil disposition of heart) will pervert to open sin.

V. 7. We have here, first the "Poor rich man," and next, the "Rich poor man."

That man is poor, however rich he may be in worldly goods, who knows not the true uses of wealth; and he is truly rich, who impoverishes himself in ministering to others.

V. 8. '*The ransom of the soul*,' its redemption from the power of ignorance and sin, is the true riches; and poor is he who heeds not rebuke, since "instructive reproofs" (ch. 6 : 23) "are the way of life."

Many translate as in the margin: *the ransom of a man's life is his wealth.* They suppose the writer to mean, that the rich man can purchase his own safety (for example, when accused before a corrupt magistrate, or taken by robbers) with his wealth; while the poor, since it is known that nothing can be extorted from him, hears no rebuke, i. e. is not chided for the purpose of exacting money.

But in that case, the pronoun (*his*) and its substantive (*man's*) should change places, *a man's wealth is the ransom of his life;* and the word '*rebuke*' is not the appropriate one, since money is extorted by *threats*, not by *rebuke*. Moreover, as this is a rather doubtful advantage of poverty (wealth being accounted a convenience in such a case), the second member has been explained thus: 'The poor man, notwithstanding this great advantage of wealth, will not listen to those who rebuke him for his lack of diligence in acquiring it.' But *poverty*, as such (and nothing else is expressed or implied here), is not made the subject of rebuke in the Scriptures; and if the writer had meant *the slothful, the indolent*, he could easily have said so, as he has elsewhere.

V. 9. *Shall be joyous* is said, by a beautiful figure, of the *light of the righteous;* that is, it shall burn with a bright and cheerful flame.

| | | MARGINAL TRANSLATIONS AND READINGS. |
|---|---|---|
| Only by pride comes contention;<br>but with those who take counsel there is wisdom. | 10 | |
| Wealth vanishes more quickly than a vapor;<br>but he that gathers in hand will cause increase. | 11 | Wealth from vanity vanishes away |
| Hope deferred makes the heart sick;<br>but desire attained is a tree of life. | 12 | |
| He that despises the word shall be held accountable to it;<br>but whoso fears the command, he shall be rewarded. | 13 | |
| The law of the wise is a well of life,<br>to turn from the snares of death. | 14 | |
| Good understanding confers favor;<br>but the way of transgressors is hard. | 15 | |
| Every shrewd man acts with knowledge;<br>but a fool displays folly. | 16 | The shrewd does all things with knowledge. |
| A wicked messenger falls into mischief;<br>but a faithful ambassador is a healing. | 17 | |
| Poverty and shame to him who refuses correction;<br>but he who regards reproof shall be honored. | 18 | |
| Desire attained is sweet to the soul;<br>and it is the abomination of fools to depart from evil. | 19 | |
| Walk with the wise, and become wise;<br>but a companion of fools shall come to harm. | 20 | |
| Evil shall pursue sinners;<br>but good shall reward the righteous. | 21 | |
| The good will leave a heritage to children's children;<br>but the sinner's wealth is laid up for the righteous. | 22 | |
| The ploughing of the poor is food abundant;<br>but there is that is consumed without measure. | 23 | <br>that perishes by injustice |

V. 10. The spirit of humility is the spirit of peace; where that spirit is, there is no strife. The writer says truly, therefore, that contention comes 'only by pride.'

Second member. Wisdom dwells with those who seek counsel, which the foolish self-sufficiency of pride disdains.

V. 11. This verse contrasts the instability of wealth, in the first member, with the sure gains of industry, in the second. It is a general truth (and hence is expressed here without qualification) that riches are unstable; but '*he who gathers in hand*,' that is, who carefully lays up his earnings, '*shall cause increase*,' he shall add more and more to his stores.

V. 12, second member. *A tree of life:* reviving and refreshing the spirit, sickened by 'hope deferred.'

V. 13. *Shall be held accountable to it:* he shall be held answerable to the divine law, which he has despised, and by it shall be judged. So the Saviour says (John 12 : 48): *The word that I have spoken, the same shall judge him in the last day.*

V. 14. *Law of the wise:* either what he enjoins, or what he follows; what his counsel prescribes as a law of conduct to others, or what he obeys as a law for himself. This is a '*well of life;*' he who drinks of it shall live, for its office and effect is, to '*turn from the snares of death.*'

V. 16. *Displays folly:* he is content with nothing less; what others despise as folly is wisdom to him, and he makes a display of it on all occasions.

V. 17. *A wicked messenger*, one who delights in promoting mischief, involves himself in it; but a *faithful ambassador*, one who is true to his employer, seeking only the best ends, exerts a healing influence.

V. 19. The attainment of the soul's desire is sweet; and the fool, whose desires are set on evil, abhors to depart from it.

V. 23, second member. *Without measure:* that is, in undue quantity, with a lavish consumption, beyond our real wants.

The poor, by his humble toil, is supplied with what nature

MARGINAL TRANSLATIONS AND READINGS.

24 He that spares his rod hates his son;
but he that loves him gives him timely chastisement.

25 The righteous eats to the satisfying of his spirit;
but the belly of the wicked shall want.

1 EVERY wise woman builds her house;
but the foolish plucks it down with her own hands.

2 He that walks in his uprightness is one that fears Jehovah;
but he that is perverse in his ways despises him.

3 In the fool's mouth is a rod of pride;
but the lips of the wise will preserve them.

4 Where there are no oxen, the crib is clean;
but by the strength of the ox is abundant increase.

5 A faithful witness will not lie;
but he that breathes falsehood is a lying witness.

6 The scoffer sought wisdom, but it came not;
but knowledge to the discerning is easy.

7 Go from the presence of a foolish man,
when thou perceivest not the lips of knowledge.

8 The wisdom of the shrewd is to understand his way;
but the folly of fools is deception.

9 Guilt makes a mock of fools;
but among the upright there is favor.

10 The heart knows its own bitterness;
and a stranger intermeddles not with its joy.

11 The house of the wicked shall be destroyed;
but the dwelling of the upright shall prosper.

---

requires. How much then, that is consumed on artificial wants of our own creation, might be husbanded for the needy and perishing!

According to the marginal reading, this verse contrasts the security of humble and honest industry, with the dangers that attend on all wrong-doing. By the former, even the poor laborer has enough for nature's necessities; while the latter often ends in irretrievable ruin.

Ch. XIV.—V. 3. The boastful tongue of the fool is 'a rod of pride,' "speaking great things," and effecting nothing, except to his own harm. Humility is the only wisdom; and the truly wise is one whose acts go before his words, and whose lips keep his counsel and preserve him.

V. 4. No oxen no fodder,—is the meaning; but (second member) he that would thrive by tillage must add to his productive force.

V. 5, second member. *That breathes falsehoods:* one whose breath is falsehood, or to whom falsehood is as his breath (ch. 12 : 17), an habitual liar. Such a man is a '*lying witness;*' and hence the rule of courts, excluding the testimony of one who is not "a man of common truth and veracity."

V. 6. There are occasions, when the worst of men see the advantages of the true wisdom, and would gladly possess it. What it is, is shown in the introductory remarks on ch. 8, third paragraph. But this wisdom comes not at will; it is the result of habits of mind, of an intellectual and moral training, producing a power of discernment to which 'knowledge is easy.'

V. 8. *To understand his way.* In this his wisdom consists; namely, to mark well, and fully comprehend, the way he should go.

Second member. *Is deception:* his folly, which to him is wisdom, and of which he makes his boast (ch. 13 : 16), 'is deception,' serving only to mislead him.

V. 9. Guilt has no rewards for its votaries; they are deluded and mocked in their expectations of advantage from it. On the contrary, the upright enjoy true favor (the favor of God), and receive their reward.

MARGINAL TRANSLATIONS AND READINGS.

12 There is a way right in the sight of a man;
but the end thereof—they are ways of death.

13 Even by laughter may the heart become sad;
and of mirth the end is heaviness.

14 From his own ways shall the backslidden in heart be filled,
and the good man from himself.

15 The simple believes every thing;
but the shrewd gives heed to his going. (Marginal: the shrewd does all things with knowledge)

16 The wise fears, and turns from evil;
but a fool rages, and is confident.

17 He that is quick to anger deals foolishly;
but a man of plots is hated.

18 The simple inherit folly;
but the shrewd are crowned with knowledge.

19 The evil bow down before the good,
and the wicked at the gates of the righteous.

20 Even of his fellow is the poor man hated;
but the lovers of the rich are many.

21 He that shows contempt for his fellow sinneth;
but he that has compassion on the poor, happy is he!

22 Do they not err who devise evil?
but kindness and truth are they that devise good.

23 In all labor there will be profit;
but talk of the lips is only to penury.

V. 13. Frivolous mirth leaves the heart vacant, and open to self-inflicted reproach. Such unsubstantial joy always tends to reaction; leaving the mind unsatisfied, and a prey to bitter reflection.

V. 14. *The backslidden in heart:* he whose heart is turned back from following after God (Ps. 44 : 18), and no longer delights in his ways; such shall be sated with his own ways, and have more than enough of them.

Second member. *From himself:* in the same sense in which it is said, in ch. 12 : 14, '*the desert of one's hands shall return to him.*'

V. 15. *The simple:* see the remark on ch. 1 : 4.—*Believes every thing:* that is, he distrusts nothing, and hence is easily imposed upon, and led away into error and sin. Such weakness, and such criminal neglect to use the powers given for one's own direction, are often sharply reproved in this book.

V. 17. It is weakness and folly to give way to sudden bursts of anger, and such conduct is pitied and despised; but the man is hated, who conceals his malice, only to plot schemes of revenge.

V. 18. Compare ch. 1 : 4, where it is said to be one of the objects of this book '*to give shrewdness to the simple.*'

*The simple* (as already remarked, on ch. 1 : 4) are those who indolently and criminally neglect the proper use of their own powers of reflection and observation; who hence never attain to true knowledge, and have only folly for their inheritance. But the *shrewd* man, the keen observer, who allows nothing to escape his attention, 'is crowned with knowledge.'

V. 20. The parasite, it seems, is a creature of all times and places.

V. 21. *That shows contempt for his fellow:* that does not acknowledge in him a fellow-man and a brother, and as such entitled to sympathy and aid, to the full extent of his wants. To withhold this is to 'show contempt' for that common nature, which unites all in one brotherhood.

V. 22. *Do they not err:* that is, do they not mistake, and fail of their desired object?

Second member. They are (so to speak) kindness and truth itself, of which they are the living representatives.

V. 23. *Talk of the lips* is that which has no deeper source; which is uttered without principle or reflection, and to effect no worthy end. Such trifling tends only to penury; while in all earnest effort 'there will be profit.'

MARGINAL TRANSLATIONS AND READINGS.

24 The crown of the wise is their wealth;
the folly of fools—is folly.

25 A true witness delivers souls;
but he that breathes lies is deception.

26 In the fear of Jehovah there is strong trust;
and his children shall have a refuge.

27 The fear of Jehovah is a well of life,
to turn from the snares of death.

28 In the multitude of people is the kings honor;
and in the want of people is the prince's ruin.

29 He that is slow to anger is of great understanding;
but he that is hasty in spirit exhibits folly.

30 The life of the body is a tranquil heart;
but envy is rottenness of the bones.

31 He that oppresses the weak scorns his Maker;
but he that honors him has compassion on the needy.

32 In his calamity the wicked is driven away;
but the righteous has trust in his death.

33 Wisdom dwells in the heart of the discerning;
but in fools it shall be taught!

34 Righteousness exalts a people;
but sin is the reproach of nations.

35 A wise servant has the king's favor;
but a base one has his wrath.

1 A SOFT answer turns away wrath;
but a harsh word stirs up anger.

2 The tongue of the wise utters useful knowledge;
but the mouth of fools pours forth folly.

3 The eyes of Jehovah are in every place,
beholding the evil and the good.

---

V. 24. By '*the crown of the wise*' is meant their wisdom, or the honor in which they are held on account of it; and this is their wealth. As to the '*folly of fools*' (of which they themselves make so much account, compare ch. 13 : 16) it '*is folly*,'—neither more nor less, and nothing else need be said of it.

V. 25. Compare the remarks on ch. 12 : 17. Life itself is often staked on the veracity of witnesses; and he who habitually disregards truth will only deceive and mislead.

V. 27. Compare the remark on ch. 13 : 14.

V. 28. The strength of a nation and of its government (other things being equal) is in the number of its effective population. The security, which good government affords to the welfare of a people, promotes its increase in numbers, and thus adds to the national strength. In this consists 'the king's honor;' the want of this is 'the prince's ruin.'

V. 30. Nothing is more necessary, even to the health of the body, than a heart at peace with itself and with all others. Many a man becomes the victim of physical disease, and of premature decay in body and mind, through jealousy, envy, and other malignant passions, that gnaw at the heart and poison the springs of life.

V. 32. When evil overtakes the wicked, he is abandoned a helpless victim to its power, having no deliverer. But the righteous has a trust, that does not fail him, even in death.

V. 33. The 'heart of the discerning' is the home of wisdom; there is its proper dwelling-place, and there it constantly abides. Even fools are sometimes 'taught' a lesson in wisdom; but it is much after the manner described in Judges 8 : 16 (where the same Hebrew word is used): "he took thorns of the wilderness, and briers, and with them he taught the men of Succoth."

MARGINAL TRANSLATIONS AND READINGS.

4 A wholesome tongue is a tree of life;
but perverseness therein is a wound in the spirit.

5 A fool spurns his father's correction;
but he that regards reproof deals wisely.

6 In the house of the righteous is much treasure;
but in the gain of the wicked there is trouble.

7 The lips of the wise disperse knowledge;
not so the heart of fools!

8 The sacrifice of the wicked is an abomination to Jehovah;
but the prayer of the upright is his delight.

9 An abomination to Jehovah is the way of the wicked;
but him who follows righteousness he loves.

10 A sore correction has he that forsakes the way;
he that hates reproof shall die.

11 The underworld and destruction are before Jehovah;
how much more the hearts of the sons of men.

12 The scoffer loves not one that reproves him;
he will not go to the wise.

13 A glad heart makes a joyous countenance;
but by sorrow of heart the spirit is broken.

14 The heart of the discerning seeks for knowledge;
but the mouth of fools feeds on folly.

15 All the days of the poor are evil;
but a cheerful heart is a continual feast.

16 Better is a little with the fear of Jehovah,
than great treasure and trouble therewith.

17 Better is a meal of herbs, when love is there,
than a stalled ox, and hatred therewith.

18 A wrathful man stirs up contention;
but he that is slow to anger appeases strife.

19 The sluggard's way is like a thorn-hedge;
but the path of the upright is a highway.

Ch. XV.—V. 4. *Is a tree of life:* compare the remark on ch. 11 : 30.

Second member. Whilst the discreet use of the tongue is a healthful influence, a perverse use of it 'is a wound in the spirit,' often the most deadly and incurable.

V. 6. The prosperity of the righteous is a blessing to them; but even the gain of the wicked is increase of trouble.

V. 11. *The underworld:* see the writer's note on Matt. 11 : 23, last paragraph.—*Destruction:* compare the note on Job 26 : 6.

V. 14, second member. The sentiment is perhaps similar (expressed in another form) to that of v. 33 in the preceding chapter. Fools are in love with folly; and with that they are fed! But the meaning may be merely, that they delight in folly, and that it is as savory food to them.

V. 15. In the humblest condition, and under all privations, a cheerful heart provides an unfailing feast. What a lesson to those, all whose abundance, in comforts and luxuries, can not stop their murmurs!

V. 16. *The fear of Jehovah* shuts out all causes of disquietude, dread, anger, jealousy, hate, repining; but all these are the natural attendants of 'great treasure,' when unsanctified by acknowledgment of the Giver.

V. 19. The sluggard's way is beset with hindrances, which become more and more formidable by his indolence and neglect, till

MARGINAL TRANSLATIONS AND READINGS.

20 A wise son makes a glad father;
but a foolish man despises his mother.

21 Folly is joy to him that lacks wisdom;
but the man of understanding walks uprightly.

22 Without counsel plans are frustrated;
but by the multitude of counselors they are establised.

23 A man has joy in the answer of his mouth;
and a word in its season—how good!

24 The path of life is upward for the wise,
that he may turn from the underworld beneath.

25 The house of the proud Jehovah will root out;
but he will establish the widow's bound.

26 Evil devices are an abomination to Jehovah;
but pure are words of kindness.

27 He that is greedy of gain is a troubler of his own house;
but he that hates bribes shall live.

28 The heart of the righteous meditates for an answer;
but the mouth of the wicked pours out mischiefs.

29 Jehovah is far from the wicked;
but the prayer of the righteous he will answer.

30 The light of the eyes rejoices the heart;
a good report makes the bones fat.

31 The ear that hears life-giving reproof,
it shall dwell among the wise.

32 He that refuses correction despises his own soul;
but he that hears reproof gets understanding.

at length they are as impassable as a thorn-hedge. (Compare ch. 24 : 30, 31.) But to the upright man, one who conscientiously and resolutely does each appointed duty in its season, his path is as a highway, cast up and leveled, and cleared of all obstructions.

V. 20, second member. *Despises his mother:* inasmuch as he shows no regard for the relation, and for its obligations; thus practically despising it.

V. 21. A comparison with the remarks made on vv. 10 and 11 of the second chapter, will make the relation of the two members clear.

V. 23. A fitting answer, seasonably given, is just ground of joy and gratulation to him who makes it.

V. 24. *Is upward for the wise:* that is, it directs his steps upward, so that he shall not take the downward way to final ruin.

V. 25, second member. *He will establish the widow's bound:* he asserts, and will vindicate, her rights; for he is the "*widow's judge*" (Ps. 68 : 5).

V. 26, second member. *Pure:* the Levitical sense, figuratively applied here, in distinction from '*an abomination*,' or what is unclean and offensive in his sight.

V. 27. Against greediness of gain, and its temptations to the use of unlawful means of indulgence (see second member), which often leads to the ruin of a household.

But even short of this, the devotee of gain is in many ways 'a troubler of his own house;' sacrificing to this sordid passion every domestic and social interest.

V. 28. The conscientious man is careful in forming the opinions he is to utter, knowing that what has once passed his lips is beyond his control; but the wicked cares not for consequences, and pours out his evil thoughts without reflection or restraint.

V. 30. *Cheerfulness* is one of the most contagious of social influences; nor can we estimate the social value of a uniformly happy temperament, that sees the bright side of every thing, and always puts the best construction on it, and turns it to the best account. It is like *good news*, making 'the bones fat;' while its opposite dries them away to a shriveled and marrowless skeleton.

V. 31. *Life-giving reproof:* compare ch. 6 : 23, *instructive reproofs are the way of life.*

V. 32. *Despises his own soul:* treats with contempt all that makes him a man, and raises him above the brute; to the level of which he thus tries to sink himself, and too often successfully.

MARGINAL TRANSLATIONS AND READINGS.

33 The fear of Jehovah is instruction in wisdom;
and humility is before honor.

1 Of man are the counsels of the heart;
but from Jehovah is the answer of the tongue.

2 All a man's ways are pure in his own eyes;
but he that trieth spirits is Jehovah.

3 Commit thy works to Jehovah,
and thy purposes shall be established.

4 Jehovah made every thing for its purpose;
and even the wicked for the day of evil.

5 An abomination to Jehovah is every one proud in heart;
hand to hand he shall not be acquitted.

6 By kindness and truth is iniquity covered;
and by the fear of Jehovah is turning from evil.

7 When Jehovah delights in one's ways,
he causes even his enemies to be at peace with him.

8 Better is a little with righteousness,
than great gains without right.

9 The heart of man devises his way;
but Jehovah directs his step.

10 An oracle is on the lips of the king;
in judgment his mouth shall not deal treacherously.

---

V. 33. *The fear of Jehovah.* Compare the remarks on ch. 1 : 7–9, second paragraph, and the introductory remarks on ch. 8, third paragraph.

This is true humility, and this spirit is before honor and leads to it; compare the remark on ch. 18 : 12.

Ch. XVI.—V. 1. *The answer of the tongue* may mean, either the answer it makes, or the answer made to it.

If it means the former, then the sense of the verse is: whatever man may devise in his heart, on any matter proposed for his consideration, the appropriate answer of the tongue comes only from Jehovah; just as (according to v. 9) 'man's heart devises his way,' but Jehovah alone can 'direct his step.' According to this view, we are taught in these two verses, that man is unable by his own counsels and plans, to give a right decision on any matter, or to direct his way, without Jehovah's aid. This is probably the correct view.

Many take this expression in the second sense, *the answer made to the tongue;* viz., to its utterance of the counsels of the heart. By this is meant, that the answer to the tongue's expression of the counsels or purposes of the heart is from Jehovah, that the final decision rests with him; in other words, "man proposes, God disposes." The sentiment is a just and important one; but this is not the natural construction and meaning.

V. 2. Compare the remark on ch. 21 : 2.

V. 4. *For its purpose:* what it is fitted for, and what is suited to its nature and character.

Second member. *For the day of evil:* inasmuch as that is the destiny appointed for the wicked, and is suited to his deserts.

V. 5. *Every one:* that is, all such; nor shall any be acquitted, however linked together in interest, and for mutual support. Though joined hand to hand, namely, with others of like spirit, he shall not go free. Compare the remark on 11 : 21.

V. 6. *Is covered:* namely, from the sight of God; it is not remembered and visited with punishment, when temporal judgments overtake the hard-hearted and perfidious.

Second member. *The fear of Jehovah* is the root of the whole matter; for it is by this one is enabled to turn from evil, and escape the calamities that overtake others.

V. 9. See the remarks on v. 1, second paragraph.

V. 10. *An oracle is on the lips of the king;* because "he is the minister of God" (Rom. 13 : 4) and speaks with authority from God; and hence it is here enjoined on him, that he 'shall not deal treacherously in judgment.'

MARGINAL TRANSLATIONS AND READINGS.

11 A just scale and balances are of Jehovah;
all the weights of the bag are his work.

12 It is the abomination of kings to do wickedness;
for by righteousness is the throne established.

13 Righteous lips are the delight of kings;
and him that speaks right things he loves.

14 The king's wrath is as messengers of death;
but a wise man will appease it.

15 In the light of the king's countenance is life;
and his favor is as a cloud of the latter rain.

16 To get wisdom—how much better than gold!
and to get understanding is choicer than silver.

17 The highway of the upright is a turning from evil;
he that keeps his way preserves his soul.

18 Pride is before destruction,
and a haughty spirit before a fall.

19 Better is the humble in spirit with the lowly,
than to divide the spoil with the proud.

20 He that gives heed to the word will find good;
and he that trusts in Jehovah, happy is he!

21 The wise in heart shall be called discerning;
and learning adds sweetness to the lips.

22 A well of life is understanding to its possessor;
but the correction of fools is folly.

23 The heart of the wise instructs his mouth,
and increases learning on his lips.

V. 11. *Are of Jehovah:* that is, are appointed by him. They are his requirement; see Lev. 19 : 36, *just balances, just weights—shall ye have.* In the same sense it is said (second member) that 'the weights of the bag are his work' (Deut. 25 : 13, 15); and hence, he who falsifies them falsifies God's own work, and perverts his ordinance to fraud and robbery.

*Of the bag:* in which the weights are kept for use. See Deut. 25 : 13, *thou shalt not have in thy bag divers weights, a great and a small;* Micah 6 : 11, *with the bag of deceitful weights.*

V. 12. Nothing is more to be abhorred by kings than wrong-doing; for it undermines the throne itself, which is established only 'by righteousness.'

V. 14. Compare ch. 17 : 11. 'The king's wrath is as messengers of death,' for his commands are such; but the wise man, by his prudent management, will appease it.

V. 15. *The latter rain:* see the note on Job 29 : 23.

V. 17. *The highway of the upright:* compare ch. 15 : 19, and the remark on it. This '*highway of the upright,*' the leveled, unobstructed path which they tread, consists in '*turning from evil.*'

V. 18. *Before destruction:* that is, just before it, and ready to plunge into it.

V. 19. Better off, is the meaning; he fares better in his humble lot with the lowly, than if he shared in the spoils of the proud. By 'spoils' is meant their wicked gains, however obtained.

V. 20. Compare ch. 13 : 13.

V. 21. He is the man of real discernment, who possesses the true wisdom; and learning (in this sense) '*adds sweetness to the lips,*' gives a charm to discourse.

V. 22. *A well of life:* compare ch. 10 : 11.—The second member, taken by itself, might mean, that it is folly to correct a fool, since it answers no good purpose. But a comparison with the first member shows, that the other sense of the words is the true one; namely, that *folly is the correction of fools;* their own folly is their chastisement, just as understanding is a well of life to its possessor.

V. 23. Compare Matt. 12 : 34, *out of the abundance of the heart the mouth speaks.*

MARGINAL TRANSLATIONS AND READINGS.

24 Words of kindness are as the honey-comb,
sweetness to the soul, and a healing to the bones.

25 There is a way right in the sight of a man;
but the end thereof—they are ways of death.

26 The laborer's appetite labors for him;
for his mouth has laid a burden on him.

27 A vile man is he that devises mischief;
and on his lips is as burning fire.

28 A perverse man sends forth contention;
and a talebearer separates a near friend.

29 A man of violence seduces his friend,
and leads him in a way that is not good.

30 When he shuts his eyes, he is devising perverseness;
when he bites his lips, he has perfected mischief.

31 The hoary head is a crown of glory,
if it is found in the way of righteousness.

32 The slow to anger is better than the mighty,
and he that rules his spirit than he that takes a city.

33 The lot is cast into the lap;
but its decision is all of Jehovah.

1 Better is a dry morsel, and quietness therewith,
than a house full of slaughtered beasts, with strife.

2 A wise servant shall rule over a base son,
and shall share the inheritance among brethren.

3 A refining pot for silver, and a furnace for gold;
but the trier of hearts is Jehovah.

4 An evil-doer gives heed to the deceitful lip;
falsehood listens to the pernicious tongue.

V. 25. A man's own conviction is no sure warrant to him, that the way of his choice is the right one; nor does the sincerity of his conviction make any difference. Only the divine testimony clearly and correctly apprehended, can be safely relied on.

V. 26. *Appetite* stimulates the laborer's toil, which its gratification rewards, and is properly said to labor for him; since without the necessities of his mouth, there would be no labor of his hands.

V 28. It is a perverse disposition that delights in and foments contention; and none does this more effectually than the talebearer, whose officious intermeddling often alienates a near friend.

V. 29. *Seduces his friend:* as described in ch. 1 : 10–19.

V. 30 describes a man of this character, in the act of contriving and perfecting his plots. When he *shuts his eyes* (the outward sign of abstraction and reflection), it is certain that he is concocting some scheme of villainy; for what else should such a man be meditating? When he *compresses his lips* (the expression of decision and determination), be sure he has perfected his plan of mischief, and is ready for action!

V. 33. Compare Num. 26 : 55, 1 Sam. 14 : 41, Jonah 1 : 7, and similar passages. See the remark on ch. 18 : 18.

Ch. XVII.—V. 2. *A wise servant* was the one, to whose prudent management a father would then naturally commit the estate and the direction of a worthless son; giving him, as the reward of his fidelity, an inheritance among his children.

V. 3. As the 'refining pot is to silver, and the furnace to gold,' detecting and consuming what is counterfeit and worthless, so is Jehovah to the heart of man.

V. 4. Honest, truthful, and salutary counsel is not what the evil-minded seek. The lips to which they give heed are 'deceitful;' and 'falsehood' (he of whom falsehood is the characteristic) seeks direction from the tongue that leads to ruin.

MARGINAL TRANSLATIONS AND READINGS.

5 He that mocks at the poor scorns his Maker;
he that rejoices at calamity shall not be acquitted.

6 Children's children are the crown of old men;
and the glory of children are their fathers.

7 Excellent speech is not suitable for a fool;
much less is a lying lip for the noble.

8 A gift is a precious stone in the eyes of its possessor;
to whomsoever it turns, it prospers.

9 He that covers a fault seeks love;
but he that repeats a matter separates a near friend.

10 A reproof sinks deeper in a man of understanding,
than beating a fool a hundred times.

11 An evil man seeks only rebellion;
and a cruel messenger will be sent against him.

12 Let a bear robbed of her young meet a man,
and not a fool in his folly.

13 Whoso returns evil for good,
evil shall not depart from his house.

14 The beginning of contention is the breaking forth of water;
desist then, before the strife is embittered.

V. 5. *Scorns his Maker*, whose image he mocks in his workmanship. Compare the noble sentiment, so beautifully and strikingly expressed in Job 31 : 15;

> Did not he, who made me in the womb, make him?
> and has not One formed us in the womb?

Second member: compare Job 31 : 29;

> If I rejoiced in my enemy's calamity,
> and triumphed when evil befell him; *etc.*

V. 7. By '*fool*' is here meant the same character as is expressed by the same Hebrew word in Ps. 14 : 1, where he is thus described: *The fool has said in his heart, there is no God. They are corrupt*, etc.

Unsuitable for such a man is 'excellent speech;' namely, to talk well on noble themes, such as wisdom, virtue, and the like.

V. 8. *A gift*, however humble in pecuniary value, is prized and cherished as an expression of affectionate regard from the giver; and in this sense it '*prospers*,' or effects its purpose, on whomsoever bestowed.

But the second member indicates, that the gift here intended is a mercenary one, designed to win favor, rather than to express it. The sacred writer states a truth to which there is no exception, when he says, that such a gift '*prospers*' (attains its end) on whomsoever it is bestowed; for no man can *receive* a gift intended to influence his judgment or action, without being demoralized by it.

It is, moreover, too commonly true (as expressed by one of the shrewdest observers of the class of whom this is here said) that "every man has his price." This may be gold, or office, or civil honors, or literary distinctions, or last and subtlest bait of al *be let alone* in the coveted enjoyment of an elegant and graceful ease, while others wage the rough conflict for truth and right. In our own age, we see the talent, learning, and moral influence of whole countries, *bought* into the service of the government, by the judicious distribution of such rewards.

V. 9. The spirit of peace, that 'seeks love' and not ill-will, 'covers a fault' and forgets it; while the opposite spirit 'repeats a matter' (brings it up again and again), and thus alienates the nearest friend. Some men can never let a matter rest; once offended, they are never pacified.

V. 10. If the reader doubts this saying, let him make trial of the second part of it; those who have done so are satisfied with the first experiment, and have no desire to make another.

V. 11. *A cruel messenger:* one dispatched by government to execute the penalty for disobedience or opposition to its authority; see examples in 1 Kings 2 : 25, and 29 (compare 1 : 5–7).

V. 12. A fool, in a paroxysm of folly, is more to be dreaded than a raging bear, robbed of her young.

V. 14. The 'breaking forth of water,' so slight at first that a handful of earth might check it, yet wears its channel deeper and deeper, till it becomes a mighty rushing stream, which no force can confine.

So it is with strife. Small in its beginnings, and then easily subdued by moderation and forbearance, it gradually gathers strength by enlisting various interests and passions, till it is beyond control. Then heed the wise man's counsel; and desist, while you may!

MARGINAL TRANSLATIONS AND READINGS.

15 He that justifies the wicked, and that condemns the righteous,
are both of them alike an abomination to Jehovah.

16 Wherefore is a price in the hand of a fool,
to get wisdom, when there is no heart!

17 The friend loves at all times;
and a brother is born for adversity.

18 A man lacking understanding is he that strikes hands,
that becomes surety in presence of his friend.

19 He loves sin that loves contention;
he that makes high his gate seeks ruin.

20 The perverse in heart shall not find good;
and one changeful with his tongue falls into mischief.

21 One begets a fool to his own sorrow;
and the father of the foolish shall not have joy.

22 A joyous heart makes happy cure;
but a broken spirit dries up the bones.

23 The wicked takes a gift out of the bosom,
to pervert the ways of justice.

24 Wisdom is present with the discerning;
but the fool's eyes are at the end of the earth.

25 A foolish son is a grief to his father,
and bitterness to her that bore him.

26 Also it is not good to lay a fine on the righteous,
to smite the noble for uprightness.

V. 15. It is the same hatred of right, and love of wrong, that leads one to 'justify the wicked,' and another 'to condemn the righteous;' and, therefore, both are alike abhorred by Jehovah.

V. 16. The meaning is: to what purpose is it, or what avails it, that means are put into the hand of the fool to get wisdom, when he has no heart to seek it? He has in hand the price to be paid for it; namely the means, given to all, for the pursuit and attainment of the true wisdom. But he has no heart to pay the price; in other words, to make the exertion, and to practice the self-denial, which it costs.

V. 17. The brother should show himself to be such in *adversity;* he is born, as it were, for the hour of need.

V. 18. *Strikes hands:* see the remarks on ch. 6 : 1, and on Job 17 : 1–3, second paragraph.

*In presence of his friend:* the surety being executed in presence of the one, on whose behalf it was given.

V. 19. The love of contention abides only in the heart that is in love with sin; for the love of holiness is the spirit of peace and good-will to all.

*Makes high his gate:* that is, builds a lofty mansion, for the gratification of his pride. This, and the spirit of contention, are one (ch. 13 : 10); and he who lives for its indulgence, seeks his own ruin (ch. 18 : 12).

V. 20. *Changeful with his tongue:* saying now this now that, without regard to truth or consistency, and exposing himself to all the evils of detection.

V. 22. Physicians testify to the happy influence of a cheerful spirit on remedies administered for the cure of bodily disease. On the contrary, grief renders them ineffectual, and dries up the springs of life.

V. 23. The secreted gift is opportunely drawn from the bosom, and deposited where it will turn the scale against the right!

V. 24. To the discerning, wisdom is nigh at hand; for his heart is her abode (ch. 14 : 33), and he need not go in search of her; but the fool, whose 'eyes are at the end of the earth,' sees not what is 'straight before him' (ch. 4 : 25).

V. 26. The righteous have often suffered grievous wrongs, in person and property, at the hands of ungodly magistrates; and the noblest spirits have been 'smitten' for their devotion to right and truth.

*'Also,'* the writer says, implying that this is to be added to other like sentiments, and distinguished among them by this special mark.

MARGINAL TRANSLATIONS AND READINGS.

27 He that has knowledge is sparing of his words;
and a man of understanding is cool in spirit.

28 Even a fool when he is silent may pass for wise,
while he shuts his lips, for a man of discernment.

1 He that separates himself seeks his own pleasure;
against all good counsel he is embittered.

2 The fool has no pleasure in understanding,
but in his heart's disclosure of itself.

3 When the wicked comes, then comes also contempt,
and reproach along with shame.

4 The words of a man's mouth are deep waters;
the well-spring of wisdom is a gushing stream.

5 It is not good to regard the person of the wicked,
to turn aside the righteous in judgment.

6 The fool's lips enter into strife;
and his mouth calls for blows.

7 The fool's mouth is his destruction;
and his lips are a snare to his soul.

8 The words of a talebearer are as dainty morsels;
and it is they that go down to the inmost parts of the belly.

9 Also he that shows himself slack in his service,
the same is brother to the wasteful.

---

V. 27. Compare ch. 12 : 23.—*Cool in spirit:* not of a hasty temper, and therefore not hasty in speech (compare the first member).

V. 28. The fool has one refuge, namely in silence; where, however, he seldom seeks it.

Ch. XVIII.—V. 1. *He that separates himself* (namely, from sympathy and concert with others) *seeks his own pleasure;* that is, he regards only his own will, and seeks what pleases himself. Such a spirit is at variance with the social laws of our nature, and makes a man a useless and even an unwholesome member of any community.

Such is the general truth; and the language is applicable to most of the cases, in which a man 'separates himself' from fellowship and co-operation with others.

V. 2, second member. *In his heart's disclosure of itself:* that is, in betraying whatever is in his heart.

He has no pleasure in adding to his stock (such as it is) of knowledge and ideas, but only in showing off what he has, betraying his poverty in both. The reason was long since taught, "why men have two ears and one tongue;" but it will be much longer, before those who most need the lesson will have learned it.

V. 3. The wicked, wherever he comes, brings contempt on his connections and associates; and with shame (the disgrace attending base conduct) comes reproach.

V. 4. *Are deep waters.* The corresponding member shows, that the writer means speech in its proper use, and put to its right purpose, namely the utterance of a mind stored with wisdom and reflection. Such utterances are 'deep waters;' 'a gushing stream' from 'the well-spring of wisdom.'

V. 5. *To regard the person of the wicked:* see the notes on Job 13 : 8 and 10; and below, on chs. 24 : 23, 28 : 21.

Second member. *To turn aside the righteous:* see the remarks on Job 24 : 4.

V. 6. His lips are ready to enter into every controversy; and his mouth, by its senseless and insolent clamor, provokes severe castigation.

V. 7. Compare ch. 10 : 14, and the remark on it.—*His lips,* instead of 'preserving him' (like the 'lips of the wise,' ch. 14 : 3), by their careless and indiscreet use ensnare his soul, often leading him into difficulty and danger.

V. 8. By too many, unhappily, the 'words of a talebearer' are eagerly swallowed; and these are the things that find deepest lodgment within, and are there retained and "inwardly digested."

V. 9. *Also:* prefixed to many of these sayings, as an emphatic

10 The name of Jehovah is a strong tower;
the righteous runs into it and is safe.

11 The rich man's wealth is his strong city,
and as a high wall in his own conceit.

12 The heart of man is lifted up before destruction;
and humility is before honor.

13 Whoso gives answer before he hears,
it is folly to him and shame.

14 The spirit of a man will sustain his sickness;
but a broken spirit, who can bear it!

15 The heart of the discerning will get knowledge;
and for knowledge the ear of the wise will seek.

16 A man's gift makes room for him,
and leads him before the great.

17 The first in his suit is right;
his fellow comes and searches him out.

18 The lot makes contentions cease,
and parts between the strong.

19 A brother estranged is harder to win than a strong city;
and contentions are as the bar of a fortress.

MARGINAL TRANSLATIONS AND READINGS.

intimation, namely that this also is worthy of note. (Compare ch. 17 : 26, 19 : 2.)

He that is 'slack (remiss) in his service,' and 'the wasteful,' are of the same kindred; they are blood-relations, and one is as bad as the other.

VV. 10, 11, contrast the secure refuge of the righteous, the strong tower where harm can never reach him, with the rich man's vain trust in his wealth.

V. 12. Compare Matt. 23 : 12, "*whoever shall exalt himself shall be humbled, and he that shall humble himself shall be exalted.*"

In the nature of the case, this self-exaltation, this proud and presumptuous self-confidence, is full of peril to him who indulges it; and all experience shows its insecurity, and that there is but a step between it and the headlong plunge in ruin.

On the contrary, as self-exaltation is just before destruction, so 'humility is before honor,' and leads directly to it.

V. 13 rebukes the too common fault, of carelessly giving an opinion before a full hearing of the case.

V. 14. Bodily infirmities are lightly borne, while the spirit is strong to endure them. But when the spirit is crushed, and the sustaining power itself needs support, how shall this be borne!

V. 15. *The discerning.* Moral discernment is meant; and 'the discerning' are those who make a right use of the powers of discrimination and judgment bestowed on all, but properly used by few. Such 'will get knowledge;' namely, a true understanding of their moral relations and duties, without which all other knowledge is not only valueless, but is often mischievous and destructive, to its possessor and to others. For this knowledge the wise will seek, and his ear is ever open to receive it.

V. 16. *Makes room*, etc.: that is, procures a favorable reception for him, and gives him access to men of power and influence.

V. 17. *Is right:* in his own view, and so far as appears from his own showing. *His fellow*, the other party in the suit, follows and 'searches him out,' detecting and exposing the weak points in his case.

V. 18. In cases where God has himself directed the use of the lot (see references on ch. 16 : 33), its decision is the expression of his will.

But cases also arise, in the common affairs of life, which can be determined on no principle and by no evidence; and then the decision of the lot is a *fair one*, and as such may, without superstition, be regarded as according with the divine will.

In ancient times, *the decision of the lot* was a common resort in matters of dispute. It put an end to contentions; and 'the strong,' by mutual agreement, could thus settle their difficulties without resort to force.

V. 19. Personal estrangement, and especially between those who are most nearly related, is as hard to overcome as the defenses of 'a strong city.' The admonition is, *to shun 'contention;'* for it is like 'the bar of a fortress,' in the obstacles it opposes to conciliation.

MARGINAL TRANSLATIONS AND READINGS.

20 With the fruit of a man's mouth shall his belly be filled;
he shall be filled with the produce of his lips.

21 Death and life are in the power of the tongue;
and he who loves it shall eat its fruit.

22 He found a wife—he found good,
and obtained favor from Jehovah.

23 The poor utters entreaties;
but the rich makes harsh answers.

24 A man given to friends is bent on self-ruin;
but there is a lover, that cleaves closer than a brother.

1 BETTER is a poor man walking in his integrity,
than one perverse in his lips, and he a fool.

2 Also that the soul be without knowledge is not good;
and he that is hasty with the feet mis-steps.

3 A man's folly subverts his way;
and his heart is angry against Jehovah.

4 Wealth adds many friends;
but the poor is separated from his friend.

---

VV. 20, 21. Admonitions to the discreet use of the power of speech, expressed with singular point and force.

*The fruit of the mouth* is its utterances, and these are the *produce of the lips.* The point of the expression is, that 'the belly is filled,' not only by what enters in at the mouth, but (in a far more important sense) by what proceeds out of it.

It is by speech, chiefly, that we communicate with others, unfolding ourselves and influencing them. Hence the tongue (or the mouth, in the same sense) is the man's representative, by which he is known and held to account.

*Death and life* (whatever most concerns a man, even to the extent of life and death) are, therefore, in its power; and 'he who loves it' (who delights in indulging it) 'shall eat its fruit.' In whose power, then, should be the tongue?

V. 22. The proverb simply asserts a fact, namely that this has been; and consequently, it may be again. The admonition to the reader is: see to it, that your choice of a wife be such, that this may be your own lot.

*Obtained favor from Jehovah:* namely, in the enjoyment of so great a blessing; for such a wife is his gift (ch. 19 : 14).

V. 23. The poor, in his dependence and helplessness, can only entreat; and the rich, as is too often the case, makes a rough and unfeeling answer.

The object is, to characterize the two, in this relation of weakness and dependence on one side, and of haughty domination on the other; and this for the purpose of rebuking the abuse of a power conferred for beneficent ends.

V. 24. *A man given to friends:* one of whom this is the special characteristic.

The expression may mean, either one who has a passion for companionship, and gives up himself and his time to a host of comrades, which is probably intended; or, one who is *every body's friend,* without discrimination or regard to desert, and hence is every body's prey. The expression may include both.

In marked distinction from the many who go by the vague name of 'friend,' is the *lover,* the one who truly loves, the real friend, who 'cleaves closer than a brother.'

*There is a lover:* that is, there are such.

Ch. XIX.—V. 1. The contrast of the two members shows, that in the second is meant one, who by the perverse use of 'his lips' escapes the humble lot of the upright poor, and yet is himself a fool; for integrity is the true wisdom, and honest poverty is better than wealth basely acquired. Compare the form given to the expression of this sentiment in ch. 28 : 6.

V. 2. A man should know his way, and walk with considerate and heedful steps. A 'soul without knowledge' has no power of self-direction, and is the victim of outward influences foreign to itself, being at the mercy of every stronger and better informed mind.

*Also:* compare ch. 18 : 9, and ch. 17 : 26, and the remark made on the latter.

V. 3. Men are prone, when suffering the effects of their own folly, to lay the blame on divine Providence. It is amazing, how many thus suddenly become believers in the special providence of God; who might have fared better if they had believed it sooner.

V. 4. Compare ch. 14 : 20.

MARGINAL TRANSLATIONS AND READINGS.

5 A false witness shall not be acquitted;
and he that breathes lies shall not escape.

6 Many make court to a noble;
and every one is friend to a liberal man.

7 All the poor man's brethren hate him;
much more do his friends keep far from him;
he follows after words—them he has!

8 He that gets wisdom loves his own soul;
he that lays up understanding finds good.

9 A false witness shall not be acquitted;
and he that breathes lies shall perish.

10 Delicate living is not suitable for a fool;
much less for a servant to rule over princes.

11 A man's wisdom makes him slow to anger;
and it is his glory to pass over a fault.

12 A growl as of the young lion is the anger of a king;
but as dew on the grass is his favor.

13 A foolish son is a calamity to his father;
and the bickerings of a wife are a continual dripping.

14 House and wealth are a paternal inheritance;
but a prudent wife is from Jehovah.

V. 5. Compare the remarks on ch. 12 : 17.

V. 6. Rank, and the liberal use of wealth, gather crowds of obsequious flatterers and professed 'friends;' whose selfish adulation is as little honorable to the object of it, as it is to themselves.

V. 7. *Hate him:* as one whose natural claims to regard and kindness are rather annoying, considering how little return he can make for being burdensome.

There is a polished irony in the concluding member. The favors he is encouraged to hope for from 'friends' he finds to be empty talk, and that in seeking them he has 'followed after words'—which he gets!

V. 8. *Loves his own soul:* since he makes provision for its highest necessities and demands. Compare v. 2, and the remark on it. This is the opposite of the character described in ch. 15 : 32.

V. 9. Nearly as v. 5; compare the reference there made to ch. 12 : 17.

V. 10. If an easy and luxurious life is beyond the fool's desert, and unsuitable for him, much more unseemly is it, that the servant should rule over his master; as is the case, when through love of pleasure or aversion to business, a prince neglects affairs of state, and abandons himself and his kingdom to the management of his servants. Against such imbecility and folly the proverb is directed.

V. 11. It will be seen, by comparison of the two members, that *forbearance towards an offender* is the trait here ascribed to wisdom.

Nothing shows the superiority of the truly wise man more than his treatment of personal offenses. If forbearance does not disarm hostility, and convert ill-will to kindness and esteem (which it scarcely ever fails to do) it will at least secure his own peace of mind, and make all attempts to disturb it harmless.

While many glory in resenting and punishing an offense, the wise man glories in forgiving and forgetting it. Which of these traits shows true nobility of spirit, as well as wisdom?

V. 12. Of the truth, here set forth in striking and beautiful imagery, the Apostle gives a literal expression: *Dost thou wish not to be afraid of the power? Do that which is good, and thou shalt have praise of the same.... But if thou do that which is evil, be afraid; for he beareth not the sword in vain* (Rom. 13 : 3, 4).

V. 13. The proverb groups together, for the admonition of all concerned, the two relations on which temporal happiness chiefly depends, and the evils which turn them both to bitterness.

The husband is here supposed to be the aggrieved party. But the 'bickerings' show that another party claims to be aggrieved. To her the Scriptures point out an armory (ch. 11 : 16, Tit. 2 : 4, 5) better suited to her nature, because furnished from it; if that does not avail, nothing will.—*Dripping:* as in 27 : 15.

V. 14. The implication is, that while inherited wealth is an accident of birth, enjoyed by some and denied to others without respect to their choice or seeking, a prudent wife is *no accident.* On the contrary, she is Jehovah's gift; to be sought and ob-

MARGINAL TRANSLATIONS AND READINGS.

15 Sloth brings down a deep sleep;
and the spirit of the idle shall hunger.

16 He that keeps a command keeps his own soul;
he that slights his ways shall be put to death.

17 He that has pity on the poor lends to Jehovah;
and he will repay him his desert.

18 Correct thy son while there is hope;
but lift not up thy soul to slay him.

19 He that is rough in anger suffers punishment;
for if thou deliver, then thou must do it again.

20 Hear counsel, and receive correction;
that thou mayest be wise in thy after years.

21 Many are the devices in the heart of man;
but the counsel of Jehovah, that shall stand.

22 The charm of a man is his kindness;
and better is the poor than a man of falsehood.

23 The fear of Jehovah is unto life;
and sated shall one repose, nor be visited with evil.

24 The sluggard hides his hand in the dish;
he will not even bring it back to his mouth.

25 If thou smite a scoffer, even the simple will deal wisely;
and admonish the discerning, he will learn knowledge.

tained, as all his other blessings are, by careful search and intelligent choice.

The connection of this proverb with the preceding one is not without its admonition.

V. 15. The effect of sloth is like some mysterious influence, settling down upon the spirit; a stupor as of a 'deep sleep,' locking up the faculties of the soul. That he who indulges it should 'hunger,' is no hardship; but it is hard that others must often starve with him.

V. 16. A priceless trust is committed to every man, the *keeping of his soul;* and he fulfills the trust, by keeping God's command.

To be unfaithful to this trust, and to incur the fearful penalty, it is enough that he merely *slights his ways,* neglects to give heed to them, making light of God's requirements.

V. 17. *Lends to Jehovah,* is his own acknowledgment of the debt; *he will repay,* is his bond to refund it.

"If you like the security" (said Dean Swift, after reading this verse as a text for a charity sermon), "down with your dust!" He said no more; and nothing more need be said.

V. 18. *While there is hope:* implying that the correction may be deferred (as it too often is) till it will be unavailing.

Second member: against excessive and cruel punishment, to which unnatural passion often leads, as it sometimes does even to fatal severity.

This may seem to us an unnecessary caution. But past history shows that it may be needed; nor are there wanting examples of its necessity (happily, few) in our own time.

V. 19. *Rough in anger:* the man of ungovernable temper, whose passion bursts over all bounds of propriety and decency. Such a temper will not go unpunished; for if one offense is overlooked, it will soon be followed by another.

V. 20. This admonition is addressed to the young; who, if they would be wise in after life, must give heed to counsel and correction in youth.

V. 21. It matters not who "proposes" (according to the homely saying), or what is proposed, so long as God "disposes" and what he purposes shall stand.

This is said, both as an encouragement to the believer, who trusts in an overruling Providence, and as a warning to the unbeliever, that his best devised schemes are vain, if not in harmony with God's revealed purpose.

V. 22. *The charm of a man:* that which makes him the delight of others, which causes them to delight in him.

*His kindness* means his sincere and genuine good-will; not the mere profession of what he is able but has no will to do; for the poor, who has nothing, is better than a man of false professions.

V. 23. Compare Job 11:18, 19.

V. 24. *Hides,* etc. He sluggishly lets fall his hand into the dish, and there it remains hidden from sight, because he is too lazy to bring the morsel to his mouth!

V. 25. A rebuke, "well laid on," is not without its fruit, even

MARGINAL TRANSLATIONS AND READINGS.

26 A father's destroyer, a mother's persecutor,
is the son that causes shame and disgrace.

27 Cease, my son, to hear instruction,
so as to err from the words of knowledge.

28 A vile witness mocks at justice;
and the mouth of the wicked swallows down iniquity.

29 Judgments are prepared for the scoffers,
and stripes for the back of fools.

1 WINE is a mocker, strong drink is raging;
and none that errs therein shall be wise.

2 A growl as of the young lion is the terror of a king;
he that provokes him to anger sins away his life.

3 It is an honor to a man to dwell apart from strife;
but every fool will get angry.

4 Because of cold the sluggard will not plough;
he shall beg in the harvest, and have nothing.

5 Counsel in the heart of man is deep water;
but a man of understanding will draw it out.

6 Many a man will proclaim his good-will;
but a faithful man who shall find?

7 He that walks in his integrity, a righteous man,
happy are his children after him!

when administered to 'the simple;' but for 'the discerning,' a milder admonition is quite sufficient.

V. 26. *A father's destroyer! A mother's persecutor!* Such, in the eye of God, is 'the son that causes shame and disgrace;' and to this fearful charge he must answer at the bar of God.

V. 27. The reader is admonished to cease from hearing such instruction, as causes one to err from the words that convey true knowledge. Such are the words of God, and of those who speak in accordance therewith.

V. 28. The testimony of a false witness is a mockery of justice, since it thwarts the very purpose for which he is presumed to testify.

Second member. The iniquitous falsehoods he utters are as delicious morsels, which he eagerly swallows. This compressed figurative expression means, when literally analyzed: *Iniquity* (*lying*, in this case) is as sweet to his palate, as dainty morsels that are eagerly swallowed down.

Ch. XX.—V. 1. *Wine is a mocker;* and well may it make sport and mockery of those, who are weak enough to "put an enemy in their mouths, to steal away their brains!"

V. 2. Compare the remark on ch. 19 : 12.

V. 3. *To dwell apart from strife:* to keep away from it, to have nothing to do with it, giving no occasion for it, and taking no part in it.

A contentious, quarrelsome temper is as sure an index of folly, as 'coolness of spirit' is of true understanding (ch. 17 : 27).

V. 4. *In the harvest,* the season when industry receives its reward, and the diligent have plenty, he shall beg—and have nothing!

V. 5. As water that lies deep in the earth is not easily reached, and is drawn out with difficulty, so it is with *counsel, in the heart of man.* It is only the 'man of understanding,' who can fathom its depths, and avail himself of it.

The man of counsel, of practical wisdom, sees things in all their relations; and his views can be drawn out, and comprehended, only by one of like spirit.

V. 6. Distrust professions of attachment and regard. There are many that make them; but the man of tried fidelity is rarely found.

V. 7. *Happy are his children:* in the precious legacy of a good name, better than riches; in the priceless treasure of an example of purity and uprightness. 'Of good parentage' is a recommendation the world over; and no better heritage can be left to a child.

MARGINAL TRANSLATIONS AND READINGS.

8 A king, sitting on the throne of judgment,
searches out all evil with his eyes.

9 Who can say, I have cleansed my heart,
I am pure from my sin?

10 Divers weights, divers measures,
are both an abomination to Jehovah.

11 Even a child is known by his acts,
whether pure and whether right his deed.

12 The hearing ear and the seeing eye,
Jehovah has made them both.

13 Love not sleep, lest thou become poor;
open thine eyes, thou shalt be satisfied with bread.

14 It is naught, it is naught, says the buyer;
but he goes his way, then boasteth.

15 There is gold, and abundance of pearls;
but a precious furnishing are lips of knowledge.

16 Take away his garment, when he is surety for an alien;
and for strangers, take a pledge of him.

17 Sweet to a man is the bread of deceit;
but afterward his mouth shall be filled with gravel.

18 Every purpose is established by counsel;
and with wise direction thou shalt make war.

V. 8. The duty of the sovereign power, here personated by the 'king,' whether executed by himself or through the representatives of his authority.

V. 9. Compare Job 9 : 2 (and the remark on it) and Rom. 3 : 26.

V. 10, first member, is explained by Deut. 25 : 13, 14, "thou shalt not have in thine house divers measures (v. 13, "divers weights"), a great and a small;" 'a great' for what is *bought*, 'a small' for what is *sold*.

V. 11. Even in the conduct of a child, though not the result of thought and reflection, the moral character of the act is discernible, and by it the disposition of the child is known.

V. 12. For the sentiment expressed by this proverb, see Ps. 94 : 9.

V. 13. *Open thine eyes:* that is, keep thine eyes open, be wakeful and diligent.

V. 14. The tricks of trade, it seems, are no new thing; they are nearly as old as the sun, and it is to be feared will endure as long.

V. 15. The implication is,—there is no want of the cheap adorning of gold and pearls, which any one may sport who has the trash to buy it with; but there is a more precious 'furnishing,' which all the mines of earth can not supply, and which no wealth can purchase.

V. 16. If one is so wanting in prudence as to become surety for an alien, he incurs the rigorous exaction of the forfeiture.

*Take away his garment:* exact the amount of the indebtedness for which he is surety, even to the taking of his garment.

Second member. *Take a pledge of him:* require of him a pledge, as security for the debt.

The law forbade the creditor to take in pledge the poor debtor's garment, and retain it over night. This was for the protection of *the poor;* as is expressly said in Deut. 24 : 12, 13, and implied in Ex. 22 : 25–27.

But it was different with one who would be accepted (as in the case here supposed) as surety for another's debt; and who thus exposed himself to the exaction of the given pledge, whatever it might be, even to the "bed from under him" (ch. 22 : 27).

V. 17. *Bread of deceit,* obtained by deception, like 'stolen waters' (ch. 9 : 17), *is sweet;* for to the depraved appetite it has a double relish, as being won by successful fraud, and against the chances of detection. But how many such find their mouths filled with gravel, and how few of them fare better!

V. 18, second member; an illustration of the principle stated in the first. *With wise direction,* even the most difficult of all undertakings, and one requiring the skillful combination of the greatest number and variety of forces, *a war,* may be successfully conducted.

19 He that goes talebearing is a revealer of secrets;
then meddle not with one of open lips.

20 He that curses his father and his mother,
his light shall go out in midnight darkness.

21 A heritage abhorred in the beginning,
its end shall not be blessed.

22 Say not, I will repay evil;
wait on Jehovah, and he shall help thee.

23 Divers weights are an abomination to Jehovah;
and deceptive balances are not good.

24 Of Jehovah are a man's steps;
and man, how shall he understand his way?

25 It is a snare to a man, when he utters rashly what is sacred,
and after vows makes inquiry.

26 A wise king sifts out the wicked,
and turns over them the wheel.

27 A lamp of Jehovah is the spirit of man,
searching all the inmost parts of the belly.

28 Kindness and truth will preserve a king;
and by kindness he upholds his throne.

29 The glory of young men is their strength;
and the honor of old men is the gray head.

MARGINAL TRANSLATIONS AND READINGS.

V. 19. *One of open lips* is one whose mouth will hold nothing; and who therefore keeps nothing intrusted to him.

Such a character is he who *goes talebearing;* one who goes about repeating all he hears. He is branded here as *a revealer of secrets;* for he discloses whatever is confided to him, however sacred the trust.

V. 20. *Light* is the Scriptural symbol of prosperity and joy; compare Job 18 : 5, 6, 21 : 17, 22 : 28. In this sense, *his light shall go out,* leaving him *in midnight darkness!*

V. 21. A heritage so obtained, as to be abhorred by all in its beginning, shall not be blest in its end; its end shall be as disastrous, as its beginning was odious.

V. 22. Compare ch. 24 : 29, and Rom. 12 : 19, *vengeance is mine; I will repay, saith the Lord.*

V. 23. Compare the reference on v. 10.

V. 24. *Of Jehovah are a man's steps:* compare ch. 16 : 9, second member, and the note on v. 1 of that chapter, the second paragraph.

*Man, how shall he understand his way;* the doubtful, intricate, and perilous way, where human wisdom is baffled, and "like folly shows!"

V. 25. *What is sacred* means, as the second member shows, whatever utterance has a sanctity that may not be violated, as a *vow* or an *oath.* As examples of the rashness here condemned, see Judges 11 : 30, 31, 34, 35, and 1 Sam. 14 : 24–30, 36–44.

V. 26. See the remark on v. 8.—*Turns over them the wheel:* the wheel of the threshing-machine is meant. The expression is figurative; implying, that the 'sifting' is the result of a process, as effectual as is the action of the threshing-machine in severing the wheat and the chaff.*

This statement obviates, I think, the only objection to this view; namely, that the 'sifting' is mentioned first, as though prior to the 'turning of the wheel.' It is mentioned first, because it is the leading idea in the sentence, the other act being only subordinate and instrumental to this; and each is to be understood in its well-known order.

V. 27. The spirit of man is itself a light within him, placed there by Jehovah, that he may search out and thoroughly know himself. Woe to him, who, having such a light from God, neglects its use!

V. 28. *Truth,* or fidelity to the rights of all, and *kindness,* or regard for the good of each, are the elements of a wise and successful government.

V. 29. *Strength,* and *wisdom* (of which the 'gray head' is the symbol), are respectively the glory of the young and the old.

* For a brief description of this instrument, see the writer's note on Job 41 : 30, the third paragraph. The common opinion, that it is here spoken of as an instrument of punishment, is there incidentally expressed; but the writer desires the above statement to be taken as his own maturer view of the case.

MARGINAL TRANSLATIONS AND READINGS.

30 Wounding stripes are a cleansing for the wicked,
and strokes in the inmost parts of the belly.

1 CHANNELS of water is the king's heart in Jehovah's hand;
he turns it whithersoever he will.

2 Every way of a man is right in his own eyes;
but the trier of hearts is Jehovah.

3 To do righteousness and justice,
is more acceptable to Jehovah than sacrifice.

4 Lofty eyes, and pride of heart,
the light of the wicked, is sin.

5 The plans of the diligent tend only to plenty;
but of every one that is hasty, to want.

6 Treasures gotten with a lying tongue,
are a vapor driven away, seekers of death!

7 The violence of the wicked shall sweep them away,
because they refuse to do right.

8 A man of crooked way turns aside;
but the pure, his work is straight.

9 It is better to dwell in a corner of the house-top,
than with a brawling woman and a house in common.

V. 30. *A cleansing*. The same word is used (in Hebrew) for the cleansing of metals from rust, by rubbing and scouring (Jer. 46 : 4, '*furbish the spears*'); and similar to this is the moral effect of timely and appropriate chastisement.

*And strokes:* that is, so are strokes in the inward parts. As corporeal chastisement is an instrument of reformation, so is the severe discipline of faithful admonition and rebuke,—of strokes inflicted within.

Or the meaning may be (as understood by many) that *wounding stripes are a cleansing for the wicked, and are strokes in the inmost parts of the belly;* that is, they are felt within. But this is less probable.

Ch. XXI.—V. 1. *Channels of water*. In those tropical climates, where rain is wholly withheld through the long hot season, it is necessary to sustain vegetation by conveying water to plants through small channels scraped in the earth; and these the cultivator turns in whatever direction he pleases.*

V. 2. There is an eye that penetrates beyond the outward and apparent, and searches out the secret springs of action, and detects their moral character. However right a man's ways may be, in his own eyes, only he who looks on the heart can determine their real character and desert.

V. 3. Compare 1 Sam. 15 : 22, Mic. 6 : 7, 8, Hos. 6 : 6, Matt. 23 : 23.

V. 4. *Light of the wicked* (compare the note on ch. 20 : 20) is a comprehensive expression for all that constitutes their joy and pride. In all this God is not acknowledged nor honored; and hence, like their ungodly gains (ch. 10 : 16), it is sin.

V. 5. The diligent lays his plans for slow and sure increase, by steady and constant effort. But the *hasty*, seeking for more rapid gains, disregards the fixed laws of production and increase, and his plans end in want.

V. 6. *Treasures, gotten with a lying tongue*, have no more stability than a vapor driven by the wind; and *death* is the end they seek, for all who seek them, and trust in them.

V. 7. *The violence of the wicked* is the ground of their destruction; because they refuse *to do right*, they are swept away.

V. 8. The way of rectitude is a straight and onward path, from which he who is crooked or perverse in his way, turns aside.

The *pure*, on the contrary, goes straight forward in his work; his dealings are all open and plain, and he never turns aside, to right or left, from the direct path of probity and honor.

V. 9. Dr. Hackett, in his Illustrations of Scripture, p. 75, says: "On the roof of the house in which I lodged at Damascus, were chambers and rooms along the side and at the corners of the open

* "Just before leaving the cultivated part of Egypt, we halted one day in the vicinity of some gardens of vegetables, through which the water was conveyed by means of little channels or trenches, two or three inches deep. They could be formed in the soft earth very easily and expeditiously; and were carried in this direction or that, as the wants of the plantation required. Thus the gardener had the streams which flowed in these trenches entirely under his control, and could turn them this way or that, as he pleased." (*Dr. Hackett's Illustrations of Scripture, ch. iv.*)

MARGINAL TRANSLATIONS AND READINGS.

10 The soul of the wicked desires evil;
his neighbor finds no favor in his eyes.

11 When the scoffer is punished the simple becomes wise;
and when the wise is instructed he receives knowledge.

12 The Just One considers the wicked man's house;
he that plunges the wicked into ruin.

13 He that shuts his ear from the cry of the weak,
he too shall call and not be heard.

14 A gift in secret subdues anger,
and a present in the bosom violent rage.

15 It is joy to the righteous that justice be done;
but destruction to the workers of iniquity.

16 A man who wanders from the way of wisdom,
shall abide in the congregation of the shades.

17 A needy man is he that loves pleasure;
he that loves wine and oil shall not be rich.

18 The wicked is a ransom for the righteous,
and the treacherous in place of the upright.

19 Better is it to dwell in a desert land,
than with a brawling and fretful woman.

20 Precious treasure, and oil, are in the abode of the wise;
but the foolish man swallows it down.

space or terrace, which constitutes often a sort of upper story. I observed the same thing in connection with other houses."

Such a retreat, *in a corner of the house-top*, would be better, than to have the whole house in common with a brawling woman!

V. 10. So intent is the wicked on his own selfish and evil ends, that he regards no interest of another, and spares no one who stands in the way of his own. Contrast the law of love, as declared by the Apostle, Philip. 2 : 4, 1 Cor. 10 : 24.

V. 11. Compare the remark on ch. 19 : 25.

V. 12. *Considers the wicked man's house:* he marks it well, attentively considers it. What the wicked most dreads, the eye of 'the Just One,' is ever upon him and on his house; for what purpose, and to what end, is shown by the second member, *he that plunges the wicked in ruin.* In his own time, he will perform this his own work.

"Jehovah will not see, the God of Jacob will not heed" (Ps. 94 : 7) is the practical infidelity of all wicked men. Against this unbelief the proverb is directed.

V. 13. The point of the expression is: how can he, who is deaf to the cry of the weak, hope to be heard in his own weakness and distress!

V. 14. Compare the remarks on ch. 17, vv. 8 and 23.

V. 15 shows the different relations, held by the righteous and the wicked, towards a government justly administered. In the maintenance of right is the safety of the one, and the destruction of the other.

V. 16. *Shall abide in the congregation of the shades.* That shall be the end of his wanderings; there he shall find his abode, though not the one he seeks. See the remarks on ch. 7 : 26, 27, second paragraph.

*Shades:* disembodied spirits; see ch. 2 : 18, and the remarks on ch. 9 : 18, and on Job 26 : 5, with the references there given.

V. 17. The man who lives for pleasure only, for the gratification of his animal appetites, who 'swallows down' his substance (as said in v. 20), soon becomes himself *a needy man*, with not enough to satisfy the demands of nature.

V. 18. *A ransom for the righteous:* compare Is. 43 : 3, 4.

When divine judgments are brought upon a people, and *the wicked* and *the treacherous* are cut off, they may properly be said to be a *ransom for the righteous* who is spared; and this is the direct application of the language. Compare, for example, Ps. 91 : 5–8.

V. 19. Compare the same sentiment, in v. 9.

V. 20. *Swallows it down:* consumes all that he gets, and as fast as he gets it; all goes to feed an insatiable appetite, and nothing is laid up (as by the wise) for the future.

MARGINAL TRANSLATIONS AND READINGS.

21 He that follows after righteousness and kindness,
shall find life, righteousness, and honor.

22 A wise man scaled a city of the mighty,
and threw down its trusted strength.

23 He that keeps his mouth and his tongue,
keeps his soul from troubles.

24 An inflated proud one, scoffer is his name;
acting in the insolence of pride.

25 The sluggard's longing slays him;
because his hands refuse to work.

26 All the day he has longing desire;
but the righteous shall give, and not spare.

27 The sacrifice of the wicked is abomination;
how much more when it is brought with evil purpose.

28 A lying witness shall perish;
but a man that hears shall always speak.

29 A wicked man hardens his face;
but the upright, he shall establish his ways.

30 There is no wisdom, and no understanding,
and no counsel, before Jehovah.

31 A horse is prepared for the day of battle;
but the deliverance is of Jehovah.

1 MORE choice is a name than great riches,
loving favor than silver and gold.

V. 21. Observe the happy effect of the twofold use of the word righteousness; in the first member, *follows after righteousness* (what is pleasing to God), in the second, *shall find righteousness* (acceptance with God).

V. 22. *Wisdom* (knowledge, and the skill to use it) is an overmatch for material strength and brute force.

V. 23. Compare the remarks on ch. 18 : 20, 21.

V. 24. He who is swollen with pride is a scoffer, in spirit and name; for, *in the insolence of pride*, he contemns all authority, human and divine.

VV. 25, 26. *Slays him.* He is the victim of his own unsatisfied longings, and even starves rather than labor to supply nature's wants.

While the sluggard pines all the day in want, *the righteous* has more than enough for himself, and can freely give to the needy.

For the word *righteous*, and the reason why he is here contrasted with the *sluggard*, see the remarks on ch. 15 : 19.

V. 27. *The sacrifice of the wicked* (by which he hopes to avert God's displeasure against him for unrepented sin) is always an abomination; how much more, when it is brought with a *conscious* evil purpose (comp. Mal. 1 : 13, 14, and Lev. 22 : 19–25).

V. 28, first member; compare the remarks on ch. 12 : 17.

*A man that hears shall always speak;* that is, a man that hears shall have a hearing. This is as it should be; it is a fair principle, and at once commends itself.

As *a witness* (and this is the special application here) such a man should never be denied a hearing. The attentive, observant listener is the man who can tell what he has heard and seen; but the *lying witness* cares not what he reports.

V. 29. The wicked puts on a hard and unyielding expression of countenance; either to hide his own sense of shame from others, or to brave and out-face their just reproaches; or, perhaps, to cover and conceal from them his guilty designs, under the mask of a face that betrays nothing.

But, harden his face as he may, it is only the upright *who shall establish his ways,*—whose plans shall not be overthrown.

V. 30. *Before Jehovah.* In his presence, all finite *wisdom,* and *understanding,* and *counsel* are nothing, and all are of no avail against him.

V. 31. Compare Ps. 20 : 7, 33 : 16, 17.

Ch. XXII.—V. 1. *A name:* of course an honorable name, in which sense this word is often used; as in Eccl. 7 : 1, where the proper translation is, *better* (that is, of richer fragrance) *is a name*

2 Rich and poor meet together;
the maker of them all is Jehovah.

3 The shrewd saw evil, and hid himself;
but the simple passed on, and were punished.

4 The reward of humility, of the fear of Jehovah,
is wealth, and honor, and life.

5 Thorns, snares, are in the way of the perverse;
he that keeps his soul shall be far from them.

6 Train the child according to his way;
even when he is old he will not turn from it.

7 The rich rules over the poor;
and the borrower is servant to the man that lends.

8 He that sows iniquity shall reap mischief;
and the rod for his pride shall be ready.

9 The man of kindly eye, he shall be blest;
for he gives of his bread to the poor.

10 Drive out the scoffer, and contention will go forth;
and litigation and reproach will cease.

11 He that loves the pure in heart,
his lips are grace, the king is his friend.

MARGINAL TRANSLATIONS AND READINGS.

*than precious ointment;* compare 2 Sam. 8 : 13, and 23 : 18, 22, (properly, *had a name*).

The second member (*loving favor*, etc.) shows that here is meant a name for probity and kindness, and for all that endears a man to his fellow-men.

V. 2. *Meet together:* in the *grave* is meant, where all are gathered alike; *small and great, both are there* (Job 3 : 19).

As their destiny is one, so is their origin; *the maker of them all is Jehovah.* What a vain pretense is the distinction of wealth, the accident of an hour! See further, on ch. 29 : 13.

V. 3. *The shrewd—the simple:* see the remarks on ch. 14 : vv. 15 and 18.

*Were punished:* as the simple often are, for their negligence and folly, in failing to exercise the forethought, and take the precautions, necessary for their safety.

V. 4. The spirit of *humility*, and of *the fear of Jehovah*, is the spirit of caution, of self-distrust, and of conscious dependence on the divine guidance and blessing. It is therefore, in itself, the surest way to *wealth, and honor, and life.*

V. 5. *That keeps his soul.* For the meaning of this, see ch. 19 : 16, and the remark on it.

V. 6. *According to his way:* his way in life. Whatever course he is to take in after-life, train him for it when a child, and *even when old he will not turn from it.*

This is the great law of education, to form right habits at the beginning; and it applies to the intellectual and moral training, no less than to a preparation for the business of life.

V. 7, in both members, only states as *a fact* the natural and necessary relation of the two parties; but without justifying the use which is too often made of it.

For the first member, compare the remarks on ch. 18 : 23, the second paragraph.

V. 8, first member, is one of the unchanging laws of the divine economy (Gal. 6 : 7); and the strange neglect of it only proves the wide prevalence of practical infidelity, of 'an evil heart of unbelief,' even where it would be least looked for.

*For his pride:* his insolent defiance of law, divine and human; for such is this unbelief, and its practical working, whatever outward mask it may put on.

*Is ready:* however he may deceive himself, by present appearances, yet *it lingers not*, and *it slumbers not* (2 Pet. 2 : 3).

V. 9. *Of kindly eye:* one beaming with kindness and good-will; that looks with pity on every object of want and suffering.

*For he gives:* he is one whose "eye affects his heart" (Lam. 3 : 51), and is the expression of it.

V. 10. *The scoffer* is one who contemns all authority, divine and human; one whose influence, therefore, promotes insubordination and strife.

*Contention* is a fruitful source of *reproach*, which finds no root where there is peace and good-will.

V. 11. *That loves the pure in heart*, such as he is himself; in such he delights, because such is his own nature.

*His lips are grace:* there is a charm in his discourse; for his heart is free from guile, and his words are truth and sincerity.

*The king is his friend:* for 'righteous lips are the delight of kings' (ch. 16 : 13).

MARGINAL TRANSLATIONS AND READINGS.

12 The eyes of Jehovah kept knowledge;
and he overthrew the words of the treacherous.

13 The sluggard says, There is a lion without;
I shall be slain in the streets.

14 The mouth of strange women is a deep pit;
he that is hated of Jehovah shall fall therein.

15 Folly is bound in the heart of a child;
the rod of correction will put it far from him.

16 He that oppresses the weak, to make increase for himself,
is one that gives to the rich, only to want.

---

17 Incline thine ear, and hear the words of the wise;
and apply thy heart to my knowledge.
18 For it is pleasant, if thou keep them in thy breast;
if they are ready all of them on thy lips.
19 That thy trust may be in Jehovah,
I have taught thee this day, yea thee.
20 Have I not written to thee heretofore,
with counsels and knowledge;
21 to teach thee the rightness of words of truth,
that thou mayest answer truth to them that send thee?

V. 12. *The eyes of Jehovah* (his ever-watchful oversight and care) *kept knowledge;* that is, upheld and defended it from overthrow.

By *knowledge* is meant, here as elsewhere in this book, a true understanding and strict observance of one's relations and duties to God and his fellow-men. See the remarks on ch. 1 : 7–9, second paragraph, and on ch. 8, third paragraph.

This knowledge Jehovah *kept;* he upheld and defended it, while he *overthrew the words of the treacherous.* Such is the law of the divine government, and so it has ever proved in the end.

V. 13. A spice of grave Oriental humor. So great is the sluggard's aversion to activity, that any, even the least effort is as formidable to him as encountering a beast of prey.

Or the thought may be this. The excuses, by which the sluggard seeks to justify his inaction, and quiet his conscience, are as frivolously absurd, as is the apprehension of meeting a lion in the open streets!

V. 14. *The mouth,* etc.: with reference to her ensnaring words, with which she lures her victim to his ruin (compare ch. 2 : 16, 6 : 24, 7 : 21).

The enticements of such a mouth are a deep pit; and to fall therein is proof that one has already turned from Jehovah, and incurred his severe displeasure. None but such can be so ensnared.

V. 15. The writer means to say, that *folly* is the common trait of childhood; it *is bound* (so to speak) *in the heart of a child.*

*The rod of correction* is sometimes necessary, as an auxiliary to moral influence, and where that fails must be applied.

V. 16. The oppression of *the weak,* for the sake of *increase,* defeats its own purpose, tending only *to want.* It is a possession unblessed while it is held; and the longer one holds it, the poorer he will be in the end.

*Is one that gives to the rich* (meaning himself); a pointed expression of this grievous wrong, of taking from him who has not, for the benefit of him who has.

PART THIRD. Chs. 22 : 17—24 : 22.

Here commences the third division of the book, extending to the twenty-second verse of the twenty-fourth chapter. It consists, mostly, of short continuous discourses, differing in form from the preceding collection of single, unconnected sayings.

VV. 17–21. An introductory paragraph, admonishing to a diligent and heedful consideration of the words of the wise.

V. 17. *My knowledge:* that which I have, and am able to impart.

V. 18. *For it is pleasant,* etc. He who *keeps them in his breast,* and has them *ready on his lips,* will never want agreeable companionship in solitude, or what he may utter acceptably in social intercourse.

V. 19. *That thy trust may be in Jehovah.* This is the noblest end of teaching, and the evidence of the highest and purest knowledge; for he who *trusts in Jehovah* is one who knows and obeys him.

V. 21. *The rightness of words of truth:* as the ground of the obligation *to answer truth,* to make a truthful return, on whatever mission or service one may be sent.

MARGINAL TRANSLATIONS AND READINGS.

22 Rob not the weak because he is weak;
and oppress not the poor in the gate.
23 For Jehovah will plead their cause,
and despoil of life those who despoil them.

24 Make no friendship with a passionate man,
and go not with a man given to anger;
25 lest thou learn his ways,
and bring a snare to thy soul.

26 Be not of those who strike hands,
of those who become surety for debts.
27 If thou hast nothing to pay,
why should he take thy bed from under thee!

28 Remove not the old landmark,
which thy fathers made.

29 Seest thou a man diligent in his business?
He shall stand before kings;
he shall not stand before the mean.

1 When thou sittest to eat with a ruler,
mark well what is before thee;
2 and put a knife to thy throat, — *Margin:* for thou puttest
if thou art given to appetite.
3 Long not for his dainties;
for it is treacherous food.

---

VV. 22, 23. Against robbery and oppression of the weak and poor.

V. 22. *Because he is weak,* and thou art strong; the very reason, why thy excess of strength should supply his want of it.

*In the gate:* see the writer's notes on Job 5 : 4, and 31 : 21.

V. 23. They are not so defenseless as might seem. 'Their deliverer is strong' (23 : 11), and life and death are in his hands.

VV. 24, 25. Against companionship with the passionate, and the influence of his evil example.

VV. 26, 27. Against becoming surety for another's indebtedness; the risks thereby incurred. Compare the remarks on ch. 20 : 16.

V. 28. See the note on Job 24 : 2, and the passages there referred to.

The removal of a *landmark* destroyed the only evidence, by which one's rightful boundary could then be ascertained. By such an act of perfidy, the criminal not only wronged the injured party, but violated the sacred faith which his own fathers had pledged. Hence it was looked upon as the most heinous of offenses against human rights. Compare Hos. 5 : 10.

V. 29. Such (it is meant) *shall stand before kings;* such men are sought by a wise and prudent monarch, as his counselors and executive officers.

*Shall stand before,* etc.: the customary term for expressing official attendance on one in authority, to receive his commands. Compare, for example, 1 Kings 10 : 8, Dan. 1 : 5.

Ch. XXIII.—VV. 1–3. Moderation in eating and drinking was an essential point, in the Oriental sense of propriety; and the coarse indulgence of appetite would have been a marked affront, in presence of a ruler. Pity, that it should not be so regarded everywhere!

*Mark well,* etc. Carefully note what is before thee, where thou art, and in whose presence thou sittest.

V. 2. The idea is: Better put a knife to thy throat, than indulge its cravings.

Margin: *for thou puttest,* etc., is a possible though not the probable rendering; meaning, thou puttest thy life in peril, if thou yield to the demands of appetite.

V. 3. *Treachery* may lurk, under many forms, in such an entertainment; and one who is thrown off his guard, by excessive indulgence, may easily be betrayed into improprieties, or disclosures, to his own injury or ruin. He who loses his self-command, puts himself in another's power.

MARGINAL TRANSLATIONS AND READINGS.

the eagle flies toward heaven (V. R.)

4 Labor not to become rich;
cease from thine own understanding.
5 Shall thine eye flit over it, and it be gone!
For it will surely make itself wings.
as the eagle, and the birds of heaven.

6 Eat not the bread of the evil-eyed;
and long not for his dainties.
7 For as he thinks in his soul, so is he;
eat and drink, will he say to thee,
but his heart is not with thee.
8 The morsel thou hast eaten, thou shalt vomit it up,
and lose thy pleasant words.

9 Speak not in the ears of a fool;
for he will despise the wisdom of thy words.

10 Remove not an old landmark;
and enter not into the orphans' fields.
11 For their deliverer is strong;
he will plead their cause with thee.

12 Bring thy heart to instruction,
and thy ears to words of knowledge.

13 Withhold not correction from a child;
for if thou smite him with the rod, he shall not die.
14 Thou with the rod wilt smite him;
but his soul thou shalt deliver from the underworld.

---

VV. 4, 5. The folly of setting one's heart upon riches.—*Cease from* (cease to follow) *thine own understanding:* which, according to the current maxims of the world, would make riches the great aim of life, and its chief blessing.

*Shall thine eye flit over it, and it be gone!* It is gone, as in a glance of the eye. What was seen but an instant before, has disappeared forever. It makes itself wings, like *the eagle and the birds of heaven;* and its flight can no more be restrained, or followed, than theirs; it is gone, and no one knows where.

V. 6. *Evil-eyed:* grudging, envious; in contrast with the *kindly-eyed* (ch. 22 : 9), the generous and bountiful. Compare Deut. 15 : 9, and Matt. 20 : 15.

V. 7. His outward bearing, however bland and courteous, is no index of the man; *as he thinks in his soul, so is he.*

V. 8. No true enjoyment can be found in such entertainment. It breeds only disgust. What thou hast eaten shall prove as offensive, as a morsel that one vomits up; and *thy pleasant words* (thy fair speeches, and compliments) shall be lost.

V. 9. *Speak not,* etc.: on the principle (Matt 7 : 6), *nor cast your pearls before the swine.* His own folly to him is wisdom (compare the remark on ch. 13 : 16); and hence thy wisdom he would account folly.

V. 10. *Remove not an old landmark.* Compare the remarks on ch. 22 : 28.

V. 11. As already remarked (on ch. 22 : 23), they are not as helpless as they may seem to be. *Their deliverer is strong;* and has himself said, 'I will surely hear their cry' (Ex. 22 : 23).

*He will plead their cause with thee.* And what canst thou plead with him, except that thou wast strong, and they were weak? But now, thou art weak, and their deliverer strong.

He who would have God on his side, must be on the side of the orphan.

V. 12. The *heart* must seek instruction, and the *ears* be opened to words that convey it,—to *words of knowledge.*

There are many teachers, in our time, and many that wait on their teaching. But rare are the *words of knowledge,* from which the heart, that seeks instruction, can obtain it.

VV. 13, 14. Compare the remark on ch. 22 : 15. Better smite with the rod (painful as the duty may be) than, through neglect of timely chastisement, expose the soul to endless death.

*Shalt deliver,* etc. Compare the remarks on ch. 7 : 26, 27, the second paragraph.

15 My son, if thy heart be wise,
my heart shall rejoice, yea mine;
16 and my reins shall exult,
when thy lips speak things that are right.
17 Let not thy heart be envious at sinners,
but be ever in Jehovah's fear.
18 For if there is an end,
then thy expectation shall not be cut off.

19 Hear thou, my son, and be wise;
and guide thy heart aright in the way.
20 Be not among wine-drinkers,
among those who are prodigal of their own flesh.
21 For the drunkard and the prodigal shall be impoverished,
and drowsiness will clothe with rags.

22 Hearken to thy father that begat thee;
and despise not thy mother when she is old.
23 Buy truth, and sell it not;
wisdom, and instruction, and understanding.
24 The father of the righteous shall greatly exult;
he that begets one that is wise shall rejoice in him.
25 Let thy father and thy mother rejoice;
and let her exult that bore thee.

26 My son, give me thy heart;
and let thine eyes delight in my ways.
27 For a harlot is a deep pit;
and a strange woman is a narrow well.

MARGINAL TRANSLATIONS AND READINGS.

18 an after-time

VV. 15–18. A parent's joy in a wise and discreet son (vv. 15, 16); the sinner is not to be envied, for he who fears Jehovah shall in the end be prospered (vv. 17, 18).

V. 17. *Envious at sinners:* to which the righteous is sometimes tempted; compare Ps. 73 : 3.

V. 18. *For if there is an end* (as thou knowest there is). *An end,* namely of this state of things, which (while it lasts) seems to make the sinner an object of envy. Compare Ps. 73 : 3, and vv. 17–20.

Margin: *An after-time* (as the Heb. word sometimes means) in the same sense; namely, the promised time, when the righteous shall receive his just expectation, and the sinner his reward.

VV. 19–21. Warning against companionship with the dissolute.

V. 20. *Prodigal of their own flesh:* as is the voluptuary and debauchee, who wastes and destroys the energies of his physical nature, *his own flesh,* in a round of guilty and exhausting pleasures. Compare ch. 5 : 9 and 11.

VV. 22–25. Regard due to parents (v. 22); value of truth, etc. (v. 23); the blessing, to parents, of righteous and wise offspring, and their right to this joy (vv. 24, 25).

V. 22. *Who begat thee:* that sacred relation, let it never be disregarded!

*When she is old:* when age and infirmities, so often the ground of inattention and neglect, should render her far more an object of affection and reverence.

VV. 24, 25. How blest the son, over whose birth the father may rejoice, and the mother exult! Alas that so many make the day of their birth one of humiliation and anguish!

VV. 26–28. A parent's plea for the love and obedience of a son; especially as a preservative from the most fatal of the many snares that tempt the young.

V. 26. *Give me thy heart,* in confiding affection; *and delight in my ways,* in which I walk as a safe example for thee. Happy the parent, who can thus claim the confidence and imitation of his child!

This is evidently the writer's meaning, for so this address (*My son*) must be understood in this connection; compare its use in vv. 15–18, and 22–25.

But these words may properly be applied, as they often are, as the language of Him who is the spiritual father of all, and who claims the heart by a still higher right than that of the earthly parent.

V. 27. *A harlot is a deep pit,* into which the unwary falls, and sinks beyond help; *a narrow well,* out of which he can not extricate himself.

MARGINAL TRANSLATIONS AND READINGS.

28 Yea, as for prey, she lies in wait;
and multiplies them that deal perfidiously with men.

29 Who has wailing? who has want?
who has contentions? who has complaining?
who has wounds without cause?
who has dimness of the eyes?
30 They that tarry long over the wine,
that come to make trial of mixed wine.

31 Look not on the wine how it reddens,
how it makes its bead in the cup,
moves itself aright.
32 In the end it will bite like a serpent,
and sting like a viper.
33 Thine eyes will look on strange women,
and thy heart will utter perverse things.
34 And thou wilt be as one lying asleep in the heart of the sea,
and as one that lies sleeping on the top of a mast.
35 They smite me, I feel no pain;
they beat me, I know it not;
when shall I awake?
I will seek it yet again.

1 Be not envious of evil men;
and long not to be with them.
2 For their heart meditates violence,
and their lips talk of mischief.

V. 28. *As for prey, she lies in wait:* lurking, as do those who watch for one whom they may plunder.

*Multiplies*, etc. Her haunts are the school of vice, and she leads her victims into the practice of every crime. Compare ch. 7 : 26, 27, and the remarks, first paragraph.

VV. 29–35. Miseries caused by the intoxicating cup; warnings against its fatal spell.

V. 29. A spirited description of the evils attending the habit of intoxication.

*Wounds without cause:* in groundless quarrels, engendered by the mere spirit of contention in those who are heated with wine.

V. 30. *That come to make trial*, etc.: to test the skill and the excellence of the mixture.—*Mixed wine:* wine prepared with spices.

V. 31. *Look not on the wine, how it reddens*, etc. Shun the sight of the tempting draught. Let not thine eye gloat on its ruddy and sparkling glow, its pearly beads, as it moves aright in the cup.

V. 32. This delicious draught, so tempting to the eye and palate, will in the end be the serpent's bite, the viper's sting!

V. 33. It corrupts the moral sense, and breaks down every moral restraint. The eye will learn to look with immodest gaze on the abandoned, and the heart will give utterance to impure thoughts and desires.

VV. 34, 35. A lively, and withal humorous, description of the drunken man's helplessness and exposure. All his senses, given to warn of outward danger, are locked up by the power of the intoxicating cup, and are bound as with a spell. He lies unconscious of all around him; as helpless and exposed as one sleeping in the midst of the sea, or on the top of a mast. When smitten, he does not feel it; when beaten, he knows it not. If he has any dreamy consciousness, it is of a longing to awake, and take another draught; he will seek it yet again!

And yet this now senseless brute was made in the image of God. No wonder, that the Scriptures rank drunkenness with the worst crimes against human nature and social order.

Ch. XXIV.—VV. 1, 2. *Be not envious of evil men:* on account of the occasional and temporary success of their wicked designs. Compare the remarks on ch. 3 : 31, 32.

*Their heart* and *their lips*, the fountain of moral action and its outlet, are both polluted; their thoughts and their words are only of evil. Who then can *be with them*, without becoming like them? 1 Cor. 15 : 33.

MARGINAL TRANSLATIONS AND READINGS.

3 By wisdom is a house builded;
and by understanding it is established;
4 and by knowledge the store-rooms are filled,
with all precious and pleasant treasures.

5 A wise man is strong;
and a man of knowledge increases strength.
6 For with wise direction thou shalt make war;
and in the multitude of counselors is safety.

7 Wisdom is too high for a fool;
he shall not open his mouth in the gate.

8 Whoso plans to do evil,
he shall be called mischief-maker.

9 The purpose of folly is sin;
and the scoffer is an abomination to men.

10 If thou faint in the day of adversity,
thy strength is small.

11 To rescue those taken away to death,
and tottering to the slaughter, wilt thou forbear?

VV. 3, 4. In marked distinction from the precarious successes of evil men, referred to in the two preceding verses, is here presented the sure and certain prosperity of the truly wise.

V. 3. Practical WISDOM and UNDERSTANDING are here meant, as exhibited in the pursuit of the best ends by means best adapted to secure them. Of course, the *moral* element is included, as being the ground of all true wisdom and understanding. Compare the remarks on *wisdom* at the close of the notes on ch. viii., the first and second paragraphs, and on *wisdom* and *understanding*, ch. 2 : 10, 11.

By Scriptural usage, the word *house* includes the idea of the *family* or *household*. See, for example, Gen. 7 : 1, 12 : 17; Ex. 1 : 21; 2 Sam. 7 : 11.

The nature of the *parallelism*,* in this verse, shows that the two members are to be taken as one statement; as though the writer had said: *By wisdom and understanding a house is builded and established.*

V. 4. *Knowledge* means, in this connection, that acquaintance with material and industrial laws, and with the relations of business, which results from the faithful use of the faculties given to man for his direction; the diligent application of which, as the moral duty of every man, is so often and so earnestly enjoined in this book.

VV. 5, 6. *Is strong:* both in the power of right, as one who will undertake nothing at variance with it, and in the skillful adaptation of means to ends.—*Increases strength:* adds to his strength, makes it more and more effective.

V. 6. *Shalt make war:* compare the remark on ch. 20 : 18.

V. 7. *In the gate:* the open area, by the gate of the city, where assemblies were held for deliberation on public affairs, and for the administration of justice. Compare ch. 8 : 3, and the references given on Job 5 : 4.

*Shall not open his mouth.* A summary way of dealing with the impertinence of folly.

V. 8. The intriguing plotter is meant; one whose employment it is, to *plan evil.* As his object is mischief, he is justly branded, by common consent, with the name his occupation suggests.

V. 9. *Folly*, in this connection (see second member), seems to be that careless levity about serious things, which virtually makes a mock of them, and the subject of which ranks with *the scoffer*, who is *an abomination to men.*

Even *the purpose* of such folly, its whole spirit and tendency, *is sin.*

V. 10. *Adversity* is the test of one's moral strength. *To faint*, in the day of adversity, is a proof of moral weakness.

Adversity, therefore, is not necessarily an evil. It is sometimes needful, to show one the weakness of that on which he leans for support, and to point out to him the source of true moral strength.

VV. 11, 12. In this remarkable passage, there are several things to be noted.

First, the class here represented as in need of sympathy and help. They are *those taken away to death, and* (to make the case more definite still) *tottering to the slaughter;* that is, going helplessly to a violent death, not as the just punishment of crime (implied in the whole passage), but through mere weakness and inability to protect themselves.

Secondly, the duty of *rescuing* such from their undeserved doom.

* See the Introduction, § 4.

MARGINAL TRANSLATIONS AND READINGS.

12 For if thou say, Lo, we knew not this;
shall not he, the trier of hearts, perceive,
and the keeper of thy soul, shall not he know?
and he renders back to man according to his deed.

13 Eat honey, my son, for it is good;
and honey-drippings, sweet to thy palate.
14 So learn wisdom for thy soul;
if thou find it. then there is an end.
and thy expectation shall not be cut off.

an after-time

15 Lie not in wait, wicked man, at the dwelling of the righteous;
despoil not his resting-place.
16 For seven times shall the righteous fall, and arise;
but the wicked stumble into ruin.

17 When thy enemy falls rejoice not;
when he stumbles let not thy heart exult;
18 lest Jehovah see, and it be evil in his eyes,
and he turn away his anger from him.

19 Be not angry against evil-doers;
be not envious at the wicked.
20 For there shall not be an end for the evil;
the light of the wicked shall go out.

an after-time

21 Fear Jehovah, my son, and the king;
meddle not with those given to change.

---

Thirdly, the plea on which the neglect of this duty is justified; *we knew not this*, were not cognizant of the case; in other words, it is not our concern, and we are not bound to know of it.

Fourthly, the falsity of such a plea, in the sight of him who reads the heart, and knows its real motives.

Fifthly, who it is, to whom account shall be given for such wrong; *the keeper of thy soul!*

Sixthly, the retribution; *he renders back to man according to his deed.*

Many such cases will occur to the thoughtful and observant reader; in which life, liberty, and property (for all come under the same rule, and the sacred writer selects the chief one, as an example of the rest) are exposed to imminent peril; and there is no help, for the weak and defenseless, but in the unselfish sympathy of him who "loves his neighbor as himself," and to whom every man in need is a neighbor. For one such, however, there are many who will say, "Am I my brother's keeper?"

VV. 13, 14. *Eat honey*, etc. This is said merely as a ground of the comparison in the following verse, *So learn*, etc. As *honey* is sweet to the palate, so is *wisdom* to the soul (ch. 2 : 10).

*There is an end.* That is, the object or end, the true aim of life, is attained. When *wisdom is found*, then all is secured, and *thy expectation* (founded on the sure promise of God) shall not fail. Margin: compare the remarks on ch. 23 : 18, second paragraph, and below on vv. 19, 20, second paragraph.

VV. 15, 16. Certainty of the final triumph of the righteous, and of the overthrow of the wicked, who plots his destruction.

VV. 17, 18. Against exultation over a fallen enemy; God's just displeasure towards such a spirit.

Every element in such exultation is wrong, and offensive in the sight of God; namely, the spirit of *pride*, triumphing in conscious superiority; of *hatred*, that can not be softened by the humiliation and suffering of its object; of *revenge*, that will not forgive even a fallen adversary; of *self-righteousness*, that discerns not the forbearing goodness of God, which alone has made this difference.

VV. 19, 20. The *anger* here meant (as is evident from the corresponding terms in the second member, *be not envious*) is irritation and dissatisfaction, on account of any apparent advantage which the evil may sometimes have over the good.

*An end* (or, as the margin in the same sense, *an after-time*) must be understood according to the use of the word in similar passages. When trouble comes upon the *evil-doer* and the *wicked*, there is no such *end* (or *after-time*) in reserve for him, as for the righteous. (Ch. 23 : 18). On the contrary, *his light shall go out!*

VV. 21, 22. Against fellowship and intercourse with the discontented and disaffected, who are averse to all authority divine and human, and all settled order in society and government; to whom any change is a welcome relief from irksome restraint.

For their calamity shall rise suddenly; 22
and who knows the ruin of them both?

MARGINAL TRANSLATIONS AND READINGS.

THESE ALSO ARE OF THE WISE. 23

To regard the person in judgment is not good.
He that says to the wicked, Thou art righteous, 24
peoples shall curse him, nations shall abhor him.
But to them that rebuke there shall be delight; 25
and on them shall come the blessing of the good.

He kisses the lips, 26
who answers with right words.

Prepare thy work abroad, 27
and make it ready for thee in the field;
then, afterward, build thy house.

Be not witness without cause against thy neighbor; 28
for wouldst thou deceive with thy lips?

Say not, As he has done to me, so will I do to him; 29
I will render to a man according to his deed.

I passed by the field of the sluggard, 30
and by the vineyard of a man lacking understanding.
And lo, it was all grown up with nettles; 31
its face was covered with brambles;
and its stone wall was torn down.
Then I looked, I considered well; 32
I saw, I received instruction.
A little sleep, a little slumber, 33
a little folding of the hands to rest;

---

*Of them both:* referring to the two characters implied in the double warning, *fear Jehovah—and the king;* namely, those who cast off the restraints of religion, and those who defy the civil magistracy. Both are found among *those given to change.*

PART FOURTH.—Ch. 24 : 23–34.

The fourth division of the book; consisting of a short collection of sayings *of the wise,* as stated in the superscription.

VV. 23–25. *To regard the person, in judgment:* to be influenced, in the decision of a cause, by regard to one or other of the parties to it, and not by the real merits of the case.

The unjust judge is faithless to one of the highest and most sacred trusts that can be committed to man. Hence it is, that even the well-grounded suspicion of such perfidy has consigned many a distinguished name to everlasting and universal infamy. *Peoples curse him; nations abhor him!*

V. 25. *To them that rebuke* (that rebuke the wicked) *there shall be delight:* they shall enjoy the approval of conscience, and *the blessing of the good shall come on them.*

V. 26. *He kisses the lips.* The kiss was a courteous salutation; a token of respect, as well as of friendship and affection. As pleasing, and as acceptable, is an answer expressed in right words. *To kiss the lips* was a special mark of favor.

V. 27. We have here the order of Providence; first, *Bread;* then the *House,* including the *family,* and *household.* Compare (on the word *house*) the remark on v. 3.

V. 28. *Without cause:* that is, without good and substantial reasons. One who appears as a complainant or witness against another, without such grounds, will be strongly tempted to make good his accusation or his testimony, even at the expense of sincerity and truth.

V. 29. Against the *spirit of retaliation;* the indulgence of which is not only highly criminal in itself, and offensive in the sight of God, but is the source of innumerable evils to society. Compare ch. 20 : 22.

VV. 30–34. A striking and justly admired picture of indolence and unthriftiness, with the inevitable consequences.

VV. 33 is not (as understood by some) the language of the sluggard, pleading for a little longer rest. Compare the remarks on ch. 6 : 10.

MARGINAL TRANSLATIONS AND READINGS.

34 and prowling comes thy poverty,
and thy wants as an armed man!

1 THESE ALSO ARE PROVERBS OF SOLOMON, WHICH THE MEN OF HEZEKIAH KING OF JUDAH COPIED OUT.

2 It is the glory of God to conceal a thing;
but the glory of kings is to search a thing out.

3 The heavens for height, and the earth for depth,
and the heart of kings, are unsearchable.

4 Take away the dross from the silver,
and there shall come forth a vessel for the founder.
5 Take away the wicked before a king,
and his throne shall be established in righteousness.

6 Do not bear thyself proudly before the king;
and stand not in the place of the great.
7 For it is better that one say to thee, Come up hither,
than that thou be put lower in presence of the prince,
whom thine eyes have seen.

8 Go not forth hastily to contend at law;
lest thou do aught in the end of it,
when thy neighbor has put thee to shame.

9 Plead thy cause with thy neighbor;
and reveal not another's secret.
10 Lest he that hears reproach thee,
and thine evil report turn not away.

---

V. 34. *Prowling:* compare the remark on ch. 6 : 11. *Poverty* steals on him, like a roving plunderer, prowling round for prey.

*Thy wants:* as of one who has nothing, and is in need of all things. These are the sure result of idleness and neglect, and can no more be resisted than *an armed man.*

PART FIFTH.—Chs. 25—29.

Here commences the fifth division of the book, extending to the end of the twenty-ninth chapter. It consists, as stated in the superscription, of a collection of Solomon's proverbs, made by the men of King Hezekiah.

V. 2. It is not meant that he *studiously conceals;* but that his ways are incommunicable. It necessarily belongs to his infinite nature, that his counsels and ways are beyond finite conception; and this is his glory.

What most distinguishes the sovereign, is his capacity to *search out* and comprehend all that is intricate and obscure in affairs of state.

V. 3. Another trait of kings (not always to be commended, nor so spoken of here) is the *depth of their state-policy.* As the heavens for their height, and the earth for its depth, can not be searched out, so it is with the heart of kings.

VV. 4, 5. *A vessel for the founder.* What will form a vessel, the substance or material for it, is meant. It is now ready for the founder's use, to cast a vessel from it.

*The wicked before a king:* the wicked men who stand before him (see the remark on ch. 22 : 29, second paragraph), as his trusted counselors and executors of his will.

VV. 6, 7. *Do not bear thyself proudly:* such a bearing as becomes only *the great,* the high officers of court.

*Whom thine eyes have seen:* to whose presence thou hast been admitted, and in whose sight thou art justly humbled. Compare Luke 14 : 8-11.

V. 8. *Go not forth:* namely, to the place of trial (compare the remark on ch. 1 : 21).

*Lest thou do aught:* that is (as commonly understood) something rash and injurious to thyself, in the rage and frenzy of disappointment.

More probably, lest thou be required to *do aught in the end,* something not known or anticipated in the beginning, but which the result of the trial will declare.

Be not in haste, therefore, *to contend at law.* The experience of three thousand years has only confirmed the wisdom of this counsel.

VV. 9, 10. *Reveal not another's secret.* a secret known only to

11 Apples of gold in gravings of silver,
is a word spoken in its season.

12 An ear-ring of gold, and a necklace of fine gold,
is a wise reprover, to a listening ear.

13 As the coolness of snow in time of harvest,
is a trusty messenger to them that send him;
for he restores the spirit of his master.

14 Clouds and wind, and no rain,
is a man that boasts of a deceptive gift.

15 By long forbearing a prince is persuaded;
and the soft tongue will break a bone.

16 Hast thou found honey, eat what suffices thee;
lest thou be sated with it, and vomit it up.

17 Restrain thy foot from the house of thy friend;
lest he become weary of thee and hate thee.

18 A war-club, and a sword, and a sharp arrow,
is a man that bears false witness against his neighbor.

19 A broken tooth, and an unsteady foot,
is trust in the faithless in time of trouble.

20 One that puts off a garment in time of cold;
vinegar upon nitre;
so is he that sings songs to a sad heart.

21 If thy enemy hungers, give him bread to eat;
and if he thirsts, give him water to drink.

MARGINAL TRANSLATIONS AND READINGS.

him and thee. Make no third person a party to difficulties, that can be settled between thee and him.

The delicacy of this course commends it to all; and it rarely fails, when pursued in a spirit of honesty and fairness. Compare Matt. 18 : 15.

V. 11. The beauty and fitness of a word seasonably spoken. It is here compared to *golden apples*, inlaid in *graved silver;* the tree, graved in polished silver, with its golden fruit, aptly representing the pertinency and beauty of words suggested by the occasion, and appropriate to it.

V. 12. *An ear-ring of gold* (the most precious of metals) and *a necklace of fine gold*, add beauty and attractiveness to the person of the wearer. Such is the *wise reprover*, as precious, and as decorative, when his counsels fall on *a listening ear*.

V. 13. The snow lies all summer on the summits of Lebanon; and its use in the neighboring vallies, and even in places more remote, to make a cool and refreshing drink *in time of harvest* (April and May), is not impossible nor improbable. To this use of snow and ice many allusions are made in ancient writers.

V. 14. *A deceptive gift* is one that cheats expectation. A man who boasts of what he will give, and disappoints the expectant, is like clouds and wind that bring no rain.

V. 15. By patient forbearance the displeasure of a prince is subdued, or his favor won. It is not hard words that overcome resistance; but *the soft tongue will break a bone*, will make the strongest opposition yield.

V. 16. Against excessive indulgence in pleasure. One instance is given as an illustration of what is true in all others, that excess brings satiety and loathing.

V. 17. *Restrain thy foot:* put restraint on it, make thy visits rare, that they may be the more welcome; lest their frequency should annoy and disgust.

V. 18. The deadliest of weapons is *false testimony;* against which there is often no effectual defense.

V. 19. *A tooth*, that breaks in the moment of need; *a foot*, that fails the weight intrusted to it; such is *confidence in the faithless, in time of trouble.*

V. 20. Three things are here placed in connection and comparison, as being equally incongruous, or out of season; the first two intended to illustrate the third.

Not more unseasonable is *putting off a garment in time of cold*, and not more uncongenial is *vinegar upon nitre*, than is the *singing of songs to a sad heart.*

VV. 21, 22. This is not to be done for the sake of "burning

MARGINAL TRANSLATIONS AND READINGS.

22 For thou heapest burning coals on his head;
and Jehovah will requite thee.

23 The north wind brings forth rain,
and a covert tongue an angry countenance.

24 It is better to dwell in a corner of the house-top,
than with a brawling woman and a house in common.

25 Cold water to the fainting spirit;
so is good news from a far country.

26 A fountain trampled, and a well defiled,
is a righteous man, ready to fall before the wicked.

27 To eat honey in excess is not good;
and their searching after honor is not honor.

28 A city broken down, without a wall,
is a man whose spirit is without restraint.

1 As snow in summer, and rain in harvest,
so honor is not seemly for a fool.

2 As the sparrow in wandering, as the swallow in flying,
so a curse causeless shall not come.

3 A whip for the horse, a bridle for the ass,
and a rod for the back of fools.

4 Answer not a fool according to his folly,
lest thou also be like to him.

his brains out." Such is not the spirit of the command, nor of the obedience required. The reader is incited and encouraged to this kind and generous treatment of an enemy, not by the anticipated pleasure of inflicting pain (which turns it into an act of revenge), but by the assurance that it will be the most effectual rebuke of his wrong, and will be accepted and rewarded by Jehovah. Compare Rom. 12 : 20.

V. 23. *North wind.* Only the four quarters of the heavens are distinguished in Hebrew. The north includes, therefore, all between the north-east and north-west; and a wind from the latter quarter would bring down the vapors of the Mediterranean Sea upon Palestine. There is a reason, in this connection, for saying *north* rather than *west;* the Hebrew word for the northern quarter of the heavens meaning *darkness* and *gloom,* in distinction from the sunny south.

*A covert tongue* is one that uses speech as a cover, or a disguise, for its evil designs; in distinction from one that is open and frank in all its utterances.

Such a tongue brings a storm over the face, as a wind from the north-west does over the sky!

V. 24 is repeated in this collection of Solomon's Proverbs, having already been inserted in a former one, Part second, ch. 21 : 9.

V. 26. When a righteous man falls before the machinations of the wicked, or their lawless violence, it is as when a *fountain is trampled* by the feet, and its pure, wholesome, and refreshing waters *are defiled.* Compare the remarks on ch. 10 : 11.

V. 27. *Honor,* in itself, is good and a thing to be desired. But the eager pursuit of it (*searching after honor*), like excessive indulgence of the appetite for sweets, defeats its own end, and turns enjoyment to disgust.

This eager desire and search after that which should come unbidden, changes the nature of the object sought. It is no longer *honor;* just as the too eager devouring of *honey* makes what was sweet to the palate an object of loathing.

V. 28. *A city broken down, without a wall,* can make no defense, and is an easy prey to every invader.

Such is the man, *whose spirit is without restraint.* He has no self-control, no self-government; and is an easy victim to every outward influence, that may be brought to bear upon him.

Ch. XXVI.—V. 2. As even birds of the air obey a law of nature, in their seemingly irregular wanderings, so the evils that befall men are not fortuitous in their occurrence, but presuppose a reason and a cause.

The meaning may be, that *a curse,* denounced on one without cause, shall not come; the evil so imprecated shall not befall him.

VV. 4, 5. There are two ways of *answering a fool according to his folly;* one in which the answerer comes down to his level, so as to become like him, and equally a fool, which is forbidden;

MARGINAL TRANSLATIONS AND READINGS.

5 Answer a fool according to his folly,
lest he become wise in his own eyes.
6 He cuts off the feet, drinks in damage,
that sends a message by the hand of a fool.
7 The legs hang down from the lame;
so is a proverb in the mouth of fools.
8 As binding a stone in a sling,
so is he that gives honor to a fool.
9 A thorn comes up into the drunkard's hand;
so is a proverb in the mouth of fools.
10 A master-workman forms all things;
but he that hires a fool,
is as he that hires passers-by.
11 As a dog returning to his vomit,
is a fool repeating his folly.
12 Seest thou a man wise in his own eyes?
there is more hope of a fool than of him.
13 The sluggard says, There is a lion in the way,
there is a lion in the streets.
14 The door turns on its hinge,
and the sluggard on his couch.
15 The sluggard hides his hand in the dish;
it wearies him to bring it back to his mouth.
16 The sluggard is wiser in his own eyes,
than seven men that can render a reason.

another, in which the answer so aptly exposes and rebukes his folly, as to take away all his conceit of wisdom, and this is enjoined.

V. 6. *He cuts off the feet.* He deprives himself of all chance of attaining his object; acting as one would, who should send a message by one without legs.

*Drinks in damage:* exposes himself to all the injury which such a representative may bring upon him.

V. 7. A lame leg *hangs down* from the body, ineffective and useless. So it is with a *proverb* (a wise saying) in the mouth of a fool; it loses all its force.

V. 8. He who *gives honor to a fool,* in the hope of serving him thereby, acts as absurdly as he who should *bind a stone in a sling.* The latter, swing it as you may, will never reach the mark; nor can the former, by any effort, be made to reach its object.

V. 9. The drunkard's hand, as he gropes around, blindly grasping at whatever comes in his way, is pierced by a thorn. So fares the fool, when he awkwardly attempts to apply some sharp saying of the wise.

V. 10. *A master-workman:* one who is master of his art. To such one may safely intrust his work. But to hire *a fool* (such as attempt what is beyond their skill) is as if one should hire any that chance *to pass by.*

V. 11. Compare 2 Pet. 2 : 22. He thus proves that there is no cure to his folly. Whatever he may suffer from it, he turns to it again, and thereby shows that he is still the fool he was.

V. 12. *Wise in his own eyes:* filled with the conceit of his own wisdom.

*A fool* is not necessarily 'wise in his own eyes;' but the conceited man is necessarily the worst of fools; one whose folly would not depart from him, though he were 'brayed in the mortar with the pestle' (ch. 27 : 22).

V. 13. Compare the remark on ch. 22 : 13.

V. 14. A lively picture of the sluggard's weary inaction; turning on his couch, with the tedious monotony of a door-hinge, that he may gain relief for one side while he is tiring the other!

The "rack of a too easy chair" is comfort, compared with the miseries of laziness.

V. 15. Compare the remark on ch. 19 : 24.

V. 16. The sluggard's indolent satisfaction with his own ways, and stupid insensibility to all reproof, makes him wiser in his own eyes than seven men that have a reason for their conduct.

MARGINAL TRANSLATIONS AND READINGS.

17 He lays hold of a dog by the ears,
who, passing by, gets angry in a quarrel that is not his.

18 As a madman that hurls fiery darts, arrows, and death,
19 so is a man that deceives his neighbor,
and says, Am not I in sport?

20 Where there is no more wood, the fire goes out;
and where there is no tale-bearer, contention ceases.

21 A coal to burning coals, and wood to fire;
so is a contentious man to the kindling of strife.

22 The words of a tale-bearer are as dainty morsels;
and it is they that go down to the inmost parts of the belly.

23 Dross-silver, spread over pottery,
are ardent lips and an evil heart.

24 He that hates dissembles with his lips;
but in his breast he lays up deceit.
25 When he makes his voice gracious, believe him not;
for seven abominations are in his heart.

26 Hatred covers itself with deception;
his wickedness will be disclosed in the assembly.

V. 17. He who lays hold of a dog by the ears turns his brute rage upon himself; so he is sure to have the worst of it, who gets angry in a quarrel in which he has no personal concern.

V. 18. Many a foolish jest has ended in very serious earnest. Any form of deception, though only in wanton sport, is not less a violation of good breeding than of truth, and in many a sad instance has "scattered fiery darts, arrows, and death." Imposing on another's credulity, setting friends at variance for a time by false surmises for the pleasure of making up, practical jokes of every kind, are dangerous experiments, inconsistent with good manners, often disturbing the harmony of social relations, and proving in the end to be the madman's sport.

VV. 20—22. The three chief promoters of strife. First, the tale-bearer, industriously reporting, where it is most sure to work harm, whatever has been unguardedly or unwisely said or done. Second, the contentious man, needing only the occasion thus or otherwise furnished for the exercise of his peculiar propensities and tastes. Third, the itching ear, to which the tale-bearer's words are "as dainty morsels," eagerly devoured, and made the aliment of much mischief.

Where either of these disturbing elements is wanting, there is little chance for strife.

The tale-bearer is harmless, when his gossip is poured into unwilling and unheeding ears. The contentious man will be harmless, so long as it takes two to make a quarrel, and his peace-loving neighbors are not disposed to be parties to it. A prudent caution, with proper self-denial and forbearance, will make either and all of these pestilent agencies harmless, and will insure the peace of families and communities.

V. 23. *Dross-silver:* silver unrefined, not freed from its impurities; a base but glittring metal, used to gloss over the vilest pottery, and making a fair outside show. So "ardent lips," warm professions, conceal the baseness of an evil heart.

VV. 24, 25. Every proverb is not to be understood as expressing a universal truth. Here is one of the many ways in which hatred manifests itself; dissembling with the lips, while deceit is harbored in the breast.

*When he makes his voice gracious:* speaking so blandly, with such artful adjustment of tones and features to the expression of truest friendship, that no sagacity could of itself detect the counterfeit. The wise man says, "believe him not." And well he may; for there are as many abominations in his heart as went out of Mary Magdalene.

He greets you with both hands; not needing one, in these days of civilization, for Joab's purpose (2 Sam. 3 : 27).

V. 26. As remarked on v. 24, we are not to regard every proverb as expressing a universal truth. Here too is only one of the many phases which hatred assumes. It "covers itself with deception," puts on this disguise, dissembles its enmity, to make more sure of its deadly aim; for openly avowed hatred is comparatively harmless.

But it is seen at length (second member) through all disguises, and "will be disclosed in the assembly,"—that is, before all (Job 31 : 34, revised version). The innocent object of that hatred is sure of ultimate triumph.

Selfish hatred brings its own punishment; and no man acts from personal hatred to another, without injuring himself more than he does the object of his enmity.

27 He that digs a pit shall fall therein ;
and he that rolls a stone, it shall return upon him.

28 A false tongue hates its victims ;
and a smooth mouth will work ruin.

1 Make not thy boast of to-morrow ;
for thou knowest not what a day may bring forth.

2 Let an alien praise thee, and not thine own mouth ;
a stranger, and not thine own lips.

3 A stone is heavy, and the sand is weighty ;
but a fool's anger is heavier than both of them.

4 Wrath is cruel, and anger is impetuous ;
but who can stand before jealousy ?

MARGINAL TRANSLATIONS AND READINGS.

2 Let an enemy praise thee,

V. 27. A graphic expression of a great truth in the Divine economy ; attested by illustrations without number, as striking and convincing as the hanging of Haman on his own gallows.

V. 28. Falsehood and flattery are near akin, and equally are to be distrusted and feared. The false accuser, and the smooth-tongued flatterer, seek the same end. The former " hates its victims " (on the principle, that one " hates most those whom he has most injured ") ; the latter more covertly, but no less surely, " works ruin."

Ch. XXVII.—V. 1. What is it, to " make a boast of to-morrow ?" It is to live to-day, as if to-morrow were certainly our own ; to make arrangements for it, and in reference to it, as if the morrow, and all that shall occur in it, belonged to us, to be disposed and used at our pleasure. This it is to make a boast of to-morrow; and this is the boast we daily make of it.

It was Gibbon (if I rightly remember,—in his autobiography) who put the case : How would it affect the estimate of our hold on life, if we were to decide for each day by lot who of us should be the victims of death on that day ?

So far as concerns ourselves, Gibbon's supposition represents the actual case. To us it is practically the same as if our fate each day were decided by lot ; " for we know not what a day may bring forth." He who leaves his home in the morning, may never return to it. He who lies down at night for rest, to gain strength for the labors of the morrow, may never see it. Such cases are chronicled in every morning and evening journal. Nothing is more certain than the uncertainty of life. So of all other interests and concerns,—health, property, friends, domestic and public relations, honor, power, and influence,—of all these not one is assured to us for a single day. Yet the language of all human life is, " to-morrow shall be as this day, and yet more abundant." This the apostle James (ch. 4 : 16) pertinently calls " boasting ;" adding the just and significant reproof, that men " glory in their boastings."

To hold each day, and its possessions and enjoyments, as God's daily gift, to be used as he wills and resigned at his will, is to make the true estimate of human life, and insure the highest enjoyment of it.

V. 2. The meaning is : Commit your praise to any, even the most remote and unfriendly,—to an alien (margin, an enemy) or a stranger,—rather than take it upon yourself, and employ your own mouth and lips in self-glorification.

V. 3. A wise man's anger, having always reasonable grounds, may be appeased by removing them. But a fool's anger, like the senseless stone and sand, is a dead weight which nothing can lighten.

A *reasonable temper*, happily, is not rare. More rare, but unhappily too common, is a temper that has no reason in it, which is always out of sorts, finding no satisfaction but in being dissatisfied with everything, and no pleasure but in being miserable and making others so ; the curse and dread of the domestic fireside, and a pest in every public relation. These are the two extremes ; and between them are all grades of temperament.

V. 4. *Who can stand before jealousy.* Jealousy of a rival, in whatever relation, is meant. In all relations it is a selfish instinct, unreasoning, as all animal instincts are, and hence is one of the hardest elements in human nature to deal with.

Jealousy is confined to no sphere in life. Wherever there are competing interests, and they are everywhere, there will be rivalry and its attendant jealousies. There are petty jealousies in the family and the neighborhood, in the school, the church, in literature,* commerce, the productive arts, and jealousies on a larger scale in the State and among rival States.

On jealousy in the marital relation, see the striking passage in ch. 6 : 34, 35. In other relations it may be attended with less violent outbreaks, but is not less persevering and unrelenting. Like all selfish instincts, it is essentially mean-spirited. The jealous man sees in a rival's advancement the loss to himself of honor, or of power, or of pecuniary advantage. He can feel no pleasure in another's success, lest it should prove an obstacle to his own.

Yet all observation shows, that he who does well his appointed work, satisfied with serving God and his fellow-men to the extent of his capacity, is the happy and the successful man. His ability to serve, whatever it be, is not likely to remain hidden ; and he that can serve well will be honored with service.

That was noble counsel of Cardinal Ximenes : " Do better if thou canst ; but speak not ill of another's work."

* Pope's character of Addison is but an exaggerated type of it, and in some of its traits is as true a portrait of himself as of his rival

MARGINAL TRANSLATIONS AND READINGS.

5 Better is open rebuke,
than secret love.

6 Faithful are the wounds of a friend;
and plentiful are the kisses of an enemy.

7 A sated spirit tramples the dripping honey;
but a famished spirit—every bitter thing is sweet.

8 As a bird wandering from her nest,
so is a man that wanders from his place.

9 Oil and perfume gladden the heart;
but sweeter is one's friend than fragrant wood.

10 Thy friend and thy father's friend do not forsake;
and do not go to thy brother's house in the day of thy calamity;
better is a neighbor near than a brother afar off.

11 Be wise, my son, and make my heart glad;
that I may answer him that reproaches me.

12 The shrewd saw evil, he hid himself;
the simple passed on,——they were punished.

V. 5. The meaning is (as shown by a comparison of the two members) that the *reproof of a fault* is the surest, as it is the severest test of true love.

*Open rebuke*, (that is, a regard that manifests itself in the rebuke of a fault,) is better than secret love,—a love that ventures no such proof of its fidelity, fearing to hazard the faithful correction of a friend, and thus refrains from manifesting itself in the hour of need. The rough kindness of the former is more to be desired than the barren sentiment with which the latter contents itself.

On the principle, that it is good to be taught though it be by an enemy, the writer may mean, that open rebuke, however administered and from whatever motive, is better than the mere sentiment of love, that seeks no useful expression of itself.

V. 6. That wounds inflicted by true friendship are faithful, is an obvious truth, since (as remarked on v. 5) they are its surest test.

But another truth is implied in the parallelism of the members; namely, that while wounds inflicted by a friend cost him more pain than they do him who receives them, and are therefore sparingly given, the kisses of an enemy cost him nothing, and may be had in any amount.

V. 7. *The dripping honey:* honey as it drips from the comb, clear as crystal, free from the impurities forced out with it by pressure. It is often mentioned as the most delicate of eastern luxuries. Compare Ps. 19 : 10 (revised version), "Sweeter than honey, and the dropping of the combs."

Our homely proverb, "Hunger is the best sauce," finds here a beautiful expression, but does not exhaust the meaning. More than this is intended. They who seek happiness in the indulgence of the appetites have the narrowest range even of earthly enjoyment. Whenever they would go beyond the limits of nature's wants, they find nature in arms against them. Her whole realm has not a delicacy that can tempt a sated appetite,—and yet so soon sated!

V. 8. The attachment of the bird to its nest is proverbial. If driven forth, it wanders away without direction or aim, finding no home and no place of rest.

So it is with the man who wanders from his place, merely from a restless, roving disposition, for want of attachment to home and kindred.

A different case is implied in the now familiar saying,* "Where it is well with me, there is my country."

V. 9. The fondness of the Orientals for "fragrant wood," as an agreeable perfume for their apartments, is indicated in ch. 7 : 17. See the remarks on that passage, in Parts first and second. The point of this proverbial saying is: The sweetness of friendship is more refreshing than fragrant oil and perfume.

V. 10. *Thy friend and thy father's friend* are here the same person, the friend of both father and son; whose long tried friendship may therefore be counted on as unchanging, and more to be relied on, as being voluntary and of inward choice, than the mere outward relationship of birth.

Second member. *Do not go*, etc. This is not to be taken absolutely, as a universal direction, but as qualified by the corresponding member; a "neighbor near" (one ready to help) being better than a "brother afar off," who stands aloof and withholds his aid.

V. 11. *My son* may express the relation of parent or teacher. In either case, the good effect of the instructions given is taken as evidence of the wisdom that dictated them. How many have had occasion to mourn, that no such evidence furnished the answer to undeserved reproach.

V. 12. The instruction is here given by a case in point, a more lively expression of it than in the form of an abstract truth.

The duty of being watchful, and of faithfully using and perfecting

* Ubi bene est, ibi patria.

MARGINAL TRANSLATIONS AND READINGS.

13 Take away his garment, when he is surety for an alien;
and for a strange woman, take a pledge of him.

14 He that blesses his neighbor with loud voice,
rising early in the morning,
it shall be accounted to him as cursing.

15 A continual dripping in a time of heavy rain,
and a contentious woman, are alike.

16 He that confines her confines the wind,
and his right hand encounters oil.

17 Iron is sharpened on iron;
and a man sharpens the face of his fellow.

18 He that keeps a fig-tree shall eat its fruit;
and he who regards his master shall be honored.

19 As face to face in water,
so is the heart of man to man.

20 The underworld and destruction are not satisfied;
and the eyes of man are not satisfied.

---

the faculties given us for self-protection, and for the advancement of our temporal interests, is often inculcated in this book. One of its primary objects is to "give shrewdness to the simple" (ch. 1 : 4); of whom many are sadly in need of it, and often suffer severely for want of it. To such this proverb is (or might be) a useful reminder. (Compare the remarks on chs. 8 : 5, 14 : 15, and 22 : 3.)

V. 13. See the remarks on ch. 20 : 16. The warning, and the precaution, there suggested, apply with additional force to the case here presented in the second member.

V. 14. *Blesses.* Compare the use of this word in formal salutation, Ruth 2 : 4. Ps. 129 : 8. Such ostentatious congratulation shall be accounted *cursing*, as being insincere and designing in proportion as it is ostentatious.

VV. 15, 16. *A heavy rain* soon wets through the mud-covered roof of an Oriental hut, and drips from above. Travelers in Eastern countries often speak of this annoyance. A great domestic discomfort; but not greater than a contentious woman.

V. 16. Where there is the spirit of contention, it will betray itself. As there is no barrier to the wind, and as oil escapes the hand that would confine it, so the spirit of contention is irrepressible.

V. 17. *Sharpens the face:* the *face* as the index of character, where intelligence, thoughtfulness, discernment, and other mental traits are seen. It is the mirror of the mind, where its secrets are read; and as iron is to iron, so is one mind to another, putting a keener edge on all its faculties, and more sharply defining their expression in the face.

V. 18. The first member is only an illustration of the thought expressed in the second. The point of the admonition is: Take care of your employer's interest, and he will take care of yours.

This is the primary law of service. The servant has no right to serve himself, while professing to serve his master or employer. Though there may be occasional exceptions, yet, as a general rule, the faithful servant is as sure of his reward, as he that keeps (takes care of) a tree is of its fruit. He that serves himself, instead of his master, has no such claim to reward, and is sure of nothing.

V. 19. The face is not more truly reflected in water, than is the heart of man in that of his fellow-man. We see ourselves in others, and others in ourselves.

Some understand the proverb to mean, that the feelings we inspire in others correspond to our own,—that what we feel toward them they in turn will feel toward us. But a more profound truth lies in the words than is conveyed in this shallow sentiment.

V. 20 The *underworld*, the common receptacle of all the dead, forever filling and never full, the fittest illustration of insatiableness. *Destruction*,* too, is never satisfied, and however much may be given up to its craving, its demand is ever for more.

So it is with the eye, the chief outlet by which the sensuous spirit holds converse with the world of sense.† The appetites may be appeased, and for the time may become sated and incapable of further indulgence. But "the eye is not satisfied with seeing" (Eccl. 1 : 8); the capacity for its sensuous pleasures is untiring, and the underworld and destruction are not more insatiable.

This may seem to be the most natural turn of the thought in the second member, taken in connection with the first.‡ But "underworld" and "destruction" do not necessarily imply more

* "So that state of existence [of the dead] is called, because in it is swallowed and lost all that was known and cherished on earth." (The writer's note on Job 26 : 6.)

† Compare 1 John 2 : 16, where the Apostle speaks of the "lust of the eyes" as an illustration of his doctrine, that the love of the world cannot co exist with the love of God.

‡ Zöckler (in Lange's Bible-work: "The meaning of clause *b*, as indicated by this parallel in *a*, cannot be doubtful. It relates

MARGINAL TRANSLATIONS AND READINGS.

21 A refining pot for silver, and a furnace for gold;
so is a man to the mouth that praises him.

22 Though thou shouldst bray a fool in the mortar,
among the pounded grain with the pestle,
his folly will not depart from him.

23 Look well to the appearance of thy flock;
give heed to the herds.
24 For wealth is not forever,
nor is a crown to generation and generation. (*Margin:* And is a crown to generation and generation?)
25 The hay is gone, and the tender grass appears,
and the mountain herbs are gathered.
26 There are lambs for thy clothing;
and he-goats, the worth of a field;
27 and goats' milk enough for thy food,
for the food of thy house,
and sustenance for thy maidens.

1 THE wicked flee, when no one pursues;
but the righteous are bold as the young lion.

---

than unsatisfied desire. Hence the words may be understood in a more favorable sense, of the ever active and insatiable observation of man, and his intelligent and inquisitive survey of all things within the range of his vision. It is one distinguishing trait of his nature. Unlike all other creatures of earth, his eye is ever roving, restless, and unsatisfied.

V. 21. What the refining pot is to silver, and the furnace to gold, that a man is to the tongue that praises him. The meaning is,—he himself is to *try* both its sincerity and its truth, and reject what is worthless; not receiving all that that may be favorably said of him as just and deserved, or even as sincerely and truthfully spoken.

Or the thought may be this: The man himself (what he actually is) is to others the true test of the praise bestowed upon him; and by this test true praise may be distinguished from the dross of flattery, or of unmerited commendation.

If the former, as is probable, be the true meaning, the caution is a just and significant one; for few, if any, are wholly free from the weakness here indirectly censured, and from the evils attending it.

V. 22. An example of that grave Oriental humor with which these pointed sayings are occasionally spiced.

What is here meant by a "fool" may be known from his recorded characteristics. Among these are the following: "A fool spurns his father's correction" (ch. 15 : 5); "The fool has no pleasure in understanding" (ch. 18 : 2); "Wisdom and instruction fools despise (ch. 1 : 7); "It is the abomination of fools to depart from evil" (ch. 13 : 19); "The way of a fool is right in his own eyes" (ch. 12 : 15).

It may safely be affirmed, that such folly could not be beaten out of one, though he were brayed in a mortar with the pestle. So ingrained is the folly of the fool that no beating will dislodge it.

The wise man gives no obscure hint of the kind and measure of discipline suited to such a character. Though unavailing for purposes of mercy, it may serve the ends of justice.

VV. 23—27. Admonition, founded on the uncertainty of riches, not to neglect those humbler rural occupations which yield all that is required for nature's wants.

V. 24. Wealth may pass away and be no more (ch. 23 : 4, 5); but the earth, from year to year, supplies all that nature requires.

VV. 25—27. A charming picture of rural life and its occupations, and of nature's provision for the wants of man and beast.

V. 25. The full grown grass, ready for mowing, having been harvested and removed out of the way, the tender grass is now seen springing up in its place, under the kindly influence of showers and sunshine. Compare 2 Sam. 23 : 4.

*The mountain herbs.* Valley, plain, and mountain, all are subservient, and yield their several products for thy use.

VV. 26, 27. The flocks, thus provided for by thy care and foresight, in turn provide clothing and nutritious food for thee and for thy household.

*The worth of a field:* equal in value to a field, and for which a field might be obtained in exchange,—adding to the owner's productive resources.

Ch. XXVIII.—V. 1 is applicable to all the suggestions of a guilty conscience. It pursues the wicked when no other is in pursuit of him, and keeps him in continual alarm.

---

to the really demoniacal insatiableness of human passion, especially 'the lust of the eyes.'" But there is nothing "demoniacal" in the Hebrew conception of the underworld, the receptacle of all the dead, of the good and evil alike.

MARGINAL TRANSLATIONS AND READINGS.

2 When a land revolts, its princes are many;
but, with discerning and knowing men, there may be permanence.

3 A man, poor and oppressing the weak,
is a sweeping rain, when there is no bread.

4 They that forsake the law praise the wicked;
but such as keep the law contend with them.

5 Evil men understand not judgment;
but they that seek Jehovah understand all.

6 Better is the poor that walks in his integrity,
than one of perverse ways, though he be rich.

one perverse in a double way

7 He that keeps the law is a discreet son;
but a companion of the prodigal brings his father to shame.

8 He that adds to his wealth by interest and increase,
shall gather it for him that has pity on the weak.

V. 2. *Its princes are many:* either many rapidly succeeding each other, or many contending simultaneously for the supreme power; in either case inflicting numberless evils on the country.

On the contrary (second member), when there is intelligence in the people, there is stability and permanence in the government.

*There may be permanence:* a prince or ruler (as implied from the first member) may continue long in authority. This, as a rule, is a blessing to a people; revolution, or any violent change of rulers, being ordinarily attended with much suffering.

V. 3. There is already want; and that which should bring hope of supply, lays waste and destroys.

*A sweeping rain:* that instead of refreshing and fertilizing the thirsty ground, only deluges its surface, sweeping away the seed that has been sown.

The poor man may, in many conceivable ways, take advantage of his weaker neighbor and do him wrong, when he might be helpful to him.

V. 4. *Praise the wicked.* The Apostle teaches in like manner (Rom. 1 : 32) that they who do things contrary to the Divine will "have pleasure in those who do them." This is a very significant aggravation of their guilt; and it is an earnest warning to those who are tempted to "forsake the law," and risk the perilous associations and influences of such a course. A man has reached the lowest point of moral degradation, when those who delight in wickedness are his delight, and he approves and commends their ways.

Second member. *To keep the law* is not a man's whole duty. He is bound by his allegiance to it, as the supreme authority, to aid in maintaining it. He does not fully "keep the law,' without asserting its claims to obedience.

V. 5. *Understand not judgment.* They do not understand how to judge rightly in matters of chief concern. Their spiritual perception being perverted and obscured by love for that which is evil, they fail to distinguish between right and wrong. As the Apostle puts the case (Rom. 1 : 21), they become "vain in their reasonings, and their foolish heart is darkened." No wonder that they confound moral distinctions, and impose on themselves even more than on others.

On the contrary, "they that seek Jehovah," who simply desire to do his will, shall know it (John 7 : 17,) and they "understand all" pertaining to it; as the Apostle emphatically asserts (1 John 2 : 20), they "have an anointing from the Holy One, and know all things."

But such are not forward to claim that they *do* know all things. The spirit of self-confidence, the assumption of superior spiritual insight, is not born of the simple desire to know and do the will of God. Of that desire, humility and self-distrust are prime elements.

V. 6. See the remarks on ch. 19 : 1.—(Margin). *In a double way:* not simple and direct in his dealings, always pursuing one and the same course, but sometimes following one sometimes another, in order to deceive and defraud.

V. 7. *That keeps the law.* The law of God is meant. The keeping of it implies "the fear of Jehovah;" and this being the centre of all moral relations (see remarks on ch. 1 : 7–9,) the keeping of the law is wisdom and discretion in all things. A son imbued with this wisdom will not be a companion of the prodigal, and his father's shame.

V. 8. *Interest:* on money loaned. — *Increase:* on produce loaned and to be repaid in kind; as when, for example, three and a half measures of wheat were required in payment of the three loaned.

Both of these terms, and the practices here condemned, will be understood by reference to Lev. 25 : 36, 37. "Take thou no usury [interest*] of him, or increase; thou shalt not give him thy money upon usury [interest], nor lend him thy victuals for increase."

The prohibition of *increase* was justified by the nature of the case. The temporary loan of a commodity, as grain or other articles of living, for the relief of want, did not lessen its value to

* By usury, in the common English version, is meant interest. The modern use of it, in the sense of illegal and exorbitant interest, was unknown to the authors of that version.

MARGINAL TRANSLATIONS AND READINGS.

9 He that turns away his ear from hearing the law,
even his prayer is abomination.

10 He that misleads the upright in an evil way,
shall himself fall into his own pit;
but the blameless shall inherit good.

11 A rich man is wise in his own eyes;
but the poor who has understanding will search him out.

12 When the righteous triumph, great is the glory;
but when the wicked rise, a man hides himself.

13 He that covers his transgression shall not prosper;
but he that confesses and forsakes shall find mercy.

the lender. Hence the demand of *increase* on it was oppressive to the borrower; since, though he was benefited by it, the lender was not a loser. When the full amount loaned was returned, the lender had suffered no loss; for it was the same to him as if the commodity had remained in his own granaries.

The taking of interest on money loaned was also properly prohibited, under the peculiar circumstances of the Hebrews. In the period of their early history, to which these enactments belong, they were an agricultural and pastoral, not a commercial people. Money was not borrowed as a commodity, on commercial speculation as a means of gain, but for the relief of want, and to meet the necessities of life; and to charge interest on it was to take advantage of another's need, and make a gain of charity.

When the lending of money without interest is commended in the later Hebrew writings (as in Ps. 15 : 5; Ezek. 18 : 8, 17), this is to be construed in the spirit of the earlier enactments,* as lending for the relief of the needy,† and not for commercial use, in which it is worth more as a commodity than the price paid for it.

Hence nothing in the early Hebrew enactments, or in later allusions to them, is to be construed as forbidding the taking of interest for the use of money, at its recognized commercial value. It is the same as the merchant's or manufacturer's profit on his goods or wares, and as the farmer's profit on the products of his land.

Second member. It is the general order of Divine Providence that ill-gotten wealth shall not benefit its possessor. He gathers it for others; and the specification, "for him that has pity on the weak," shows for whom Providence designs it, and whom it favors in the enjoyment and use of it.

V. 9. "His prayer is abomination," as being in its essence hypocrisy, and an insult to the Divine Majesty. As he slights him to whom he prays, he may expect to be slighted by him.

* See Ex. 22 : 25, and Lev. 25 : 35–37, where this provision is expressly made on behalf of the poor. That this is the intent of the proverb is clear from comparison with the parallel member, "has pity on the weak."

† See Ezek. 18 : 16, 17, where it is mentioned in connection with relief of the poor.

V. 10. The upright may be misled, by specious devices, into an evil way. But in the end, and in some way, the treacherous seducer will himself be caught in the pitfall prepared for another.

There is a special significance in the words, "misleads the upright." Satan has no truer representative than one who thus follows in his steps, imitating the original seducer and corrupter of the race. He is the Devil's own child, and does the work in which the Devil most delights.

Many a man does wrong himself, who would shrink from enticing another into wrong.

The second member may be understood as intimating, that the character here spoken of is one who misleads the upright, corrupts his principles to his injury and ruin, and misleads him for that very purpose. There are those, happily few in number, who take a fiendish pleasure in overcoming the scruples of the innocent and unwary, and leading them into vice.

Third member. *Shall inherit good:* not simply possess it, have it in possession, which is only a part of the idea; but shall hold it by inheritance, as an heir of the Divine promises.

V. 11. It does not follow, that to be rich is necessarily to be lacking in understanding, or that a rich man is always wise in his own eyes; though wealth, as it always confers power, may sometimes bring with it a conceit of wisdom, and in exact proportion to the lack of understanding.

Second member. *Will search him out:* will find and expose his weak points; that which some men have most reason to dread.

V. 12. *When the righteous triumph:* when they have the ascendency in the State and control its affairs, or exercise the powers of subordinate magistrates, as is evident from the second member; for when the wicked rise, when they come up, and are in power, there is no safety, and men hide themselves.

*Great is the glory:* the prosperity and splendor attained under a wise and beneficent government.

Or, less probably, the pomp and magnificence of parade, with which such triumph is hailed and celebrated; while, on the contrary, men hide themselves when the wicked are raised to power.

V. 13. *Covers his transgression:* indulges in secret sin, continuing to practice it; as is shown by the antithesis in the parallel member, *confesses and forsakes.* The Psalmist says (Ps. 32 : 5, revised version):

MARGINAL TRANSLATIONS AND READINGS.

14 Happy the man that fears always;
but he that hardens his heart shall fall into evil.

15 A growling lion, and a ranging bear,
is a wicked ruler over a feeble people.

16 A prince lacking in understanding and abundant in oppressions;
such as hate plunder shall have length of days.

17 A man oppressed with life-blood,
will flee even to the pit, that they may not lay hold on him.

18 He that walks uprightly shall be saved;
but he whose ways are perverse shall fall at once.

*Or*, he that is perverse in a double way shall fall in one.

19 He that tills his ground shall be satisfied with bread;
but he that follows after vanities shall be sated with poverty.

I will make known to thee my sin, and my iniquity
I have not covered.
I said, I will confess my transgressions to Jehovah;
And thou forgavest the iniquity of my sin.

He who covers his sin from the eye of God,—in other words. does not confess it, will certainly not forsake it; though it may be confessed, and not forsaken.

*Shall not prosper.* The two members point out the two-fold evil of unconfessed and unforsaken sin. No sin can be cherished and persevered in with safety, either to the temporal or spiritual welfare of the transgressor. He knows not whither it will lead him; to what perils it will expose his interests in this life, while it leaves him no hope for the life to come.

V. 14. *That fears always:* that distrusts himself, and hence is ever watchful; that feels his need of Divine help, and hence is ever prayerful; that dreads to do wrong, and hence shuns every temptation to it.

This salutary fear is a moral instinct; as necessary as those natural instincts that warn us of danger from physical evils. Its opposite is hardness of heart; a moral insensibility that discerns no danger, and gives no warning of its approach. The soul, thus unprovided with its needful guard, will surely "fall into evil."

VV. 15, 16. "The Divine right of kings," according to archdeacon Paley, "is the Divine right of constables;" and so the Scriptures seem to treat it. The utterance of this just sentiment is said to have cost him the loss of high preferment in the State Church; and its assertion has cost many others the loss of liberty and life.

While the Scriptures properly require obedience to the civil magistrate, and recognize any government, even the worst, as better than none, it can not be doubted that the sentiments expressed in these verses, and elsewhere, have wrought powerfully in favor of the right of representation by the people in the affairs of State.

*Growling* (in distinction from *roaring*, usually said of the lion) emphasizes the characteristic spirit of such a ruler.

V. 16. The first member only presents the case of such a prince, without expressing a proposition.—The reader will mark the pointed antithesis. In proportion as he *lacks* understanding, he *abounds* in oppressions.

*Such as hate plunder:* such rulers are meant, as is evident from the connection.—*Shall have length of days:* a significant implication, and one that might well have served the purpose of the tribunal that sat in judgment on Charles the First.

V. 17. Of all crimes against Divine and human law, that of the homicide is the least tolerable to the perpetrator. The terrors of a conscience burdened with the guilt of blood, fleeing from the face of man, and seeking refuge even in the grave, have in the rudest ages been felt to be the infliction of Divine justice, and have been portrayed in the most appalling imagery, filling the imagination with horror. Thus has human nature sought to express its dread of this matchless crime. In opposition to this voice of nature, harmonizing with the voice of God in revelation,* the false sentiments of misguided philanthropists of our age, and the mitigation by human law of the penalty demanded by Divine justice, have greatly lessened the horror of the crime, and thus multiplied its victims.

V. 18. Compare the remarks on v. 6, and on ch. 19 : 1.—*Shall fall at once:* that is, suddenly and without warning, and the ruin will be complete, needing no second stroke. This is the law of Providence, and the rule of life. He who heeds it is sure of safety; he who disregards and violates it can not count on being an exception, and risks all upon the experiment.

The reader, who is familiar with the criminal records of the morning and evening journals, will recall numerous examples of this sudden and unlooked for fall into irretrievable ruin.†

V. 19. By *vanities* are meant all objects of pursuit that yield nothing useful or valuable. They may be frivolous as well as worthless, the mere amusement and pastime of idle hours; or they may be the serious aim of earnest but misdirected effort, in which whole lives are often laboriously and fruitlessly spent, effecting nothing.

*That tills his ground* represents all earnest and well-directed effort The significant antithesis, and its apt expression, will not

* See Genesis 9 : 5, 6, and the writer's note on the passage.

† Many translate, as in the margin: *he that is perverse in a double way, will fall in one;* meaning, he who for purposes of deception and fraud, or of dishonest gain, practices double-dealing, pursuing now one course now another, will fall in one of them. The rendering in the text is more probably the true one.

| MARGINAL TRANSLATIONS AND READINGS. | | |
|---|---|---|
| | 20 | A trusty man has many blessings;<br>but he that hastes to be rich shall not be held innocent. |
| | 21 | To regard the person is not good;<br>and for a morsel of bread a man will transgress. |
| | 22 | He that is eager for wealth is a man of evil eye,<br>and knows not when want shall come upon him. |
| | 23 | He that reproves a man shall afterward find favor,<br>more than he that flatters with the tongue. |
| | 24 | He that robs his father and his mother,<br>and says, It is no trespass;<br>the same is a companion for a destroyer. |
| The man of capacious desire | 25 | The proud in spirit stirs up contention;<br>but he that trusts in Jehovah shall be enriched. |

escape the reader's notice. The one will be satisfied with bread; the other, sated with poverty.

V. 20. The "trusty man" is one who can be safely trusted and confided in.—"He that hastes to be rich" is one who makes this the sole and absorbing object of life.

In this proverb, they are placed in contrast; and it is implied, that "haste to be rich" weakens, and may impair and destroy, those elements of character, which are a solid and sure basis of confidence and trust.

The reason is obvious. He who makes the acquisition of wealth his first and chief concern, and is in haste to obtain it, sets before him, as the aim of life, that which has no moral quality in itself, and the pursuit of which has no favorable influence on his own moral development. Whatever regard he may have for commercial honor, and the recognized rules of business, is only a means to an end; and if the end can sooner or more surely be attained by disregarding them, the sacrifice will be made.

The Apostle says (1 Tim. 6 : 9): "They who desire to be rich" (make this their aim) "fall into temptation and a snare, and many foolish and hurtful lusts, which sink men into destruction and perdition." All along the course of human life are seen wrecks of those who have thus fallen "into temptation and a snare," and have sunk "into destruction and perdition." They have not been "held innocent."

On the contrary, he who diligently applies himself to any useful occupation, in accordance with the laws which govern industrial labors and commercial dealings, is sure of that measure of success which Divine Providence sees is best for him; and to desire more is not to seek his own highest good.

He is the "trusted man;" for his aims in life, and his pursuit of them, are a continual discipline of the moral virtues, developing and strengthening those elements of character which all men respect, and honor, and confide in.

He "has many blessings:" either in the testimony of an approving conscience, the Divine favor, and the worldly advantages secured by a life of probity, which is true; or in blessings pronounced upon him by others, to whom his integrity, and his fidelity in every relation, have endeared him,—which is also true.

V. 21. *To regard the person.* By this is meant, to show partiality in judgment; to favor one party, not on the ground of merit and desert, but of some adventitious circumstance, as wealth, power, influence, personal relationship, and the like. Compare the note on ch. 24 : 23, and on Job 13 : 8, 10.

This is often and very pointedly condemned in the Scriptures; and with reason, for it is one of the most common and fruitful sources of wrong. He who is not proof against the temptation thus to wrong his fellow man is not to be trusted; and the proverb only puts the case pointedly when it says, that "for a morsel of bread he will transgress."

V. 22. By an *evil eye* is expressed grudging, distrust, jealousy, envy, malice. For all these there is ample scope in the eager struggle for wealth, and the conflicts, rivalries, stratagems, and disappointments attending it. In the fair competitions of business there is also abundant opportunity for the exercise of the purest and noblest principles. But he whose ruling passion is eagerness for wealth sacrifices to it every higher impulse of his nature.

*Knows not when want will come upon him.* The instability of wealth is often pointedly expressed in these proverbial sayings. See, for example, chs. 13 : 11, 23 : 4, 5.

V. 23. The value of sincere and honest reproof, though it may not always be palatable when administered, will in due time be rewarded with due acknowledgment,—and so will the hollow worthlessness of flattery.

V. 24. The plea, "it is no trespass," is made on the ground of the relationship. But the want of delicate discrimination between right and wrong, in that sacred relation, of necessity lessens it in others, and leads on to the disregard of all moral restraints.

V. 25. Two characters are here sharply defined; the *proud in spirit*, self-confident and arrogant, provoking contention and its uncertain issues, in contrast with him whose trust is in Jehovah, and his sure and rich reward.

*Enriched:* in the consciousness of the Divine favor and protection, the approval of conscience, the esteem and confidence of the good, and the success that rewards his quiet and peaceful industry.

Margin. *The man of capacious desire* (as the words may be rendered): whose boundless cupidity provokes resistance and

MARGINAL TRANSLATIONS AND READINGS.

26 Whoso trusts in his own heart, he is a fool;
but one that walks in wisdom, he shall be delivered.

27 He that gives to the poor is without want;
but he that hides his eyes has many a curse.

28 When the wicked rise, a man hides himself;
but when they perish, the righteous multiply.

1 A MAN often reproved, who hardens his neck,
shall suddenly be destroyed, and without remedy.

2 When the righteous multiply, the people rejoice;
but when the wicked rule, the people mourn.

3 One that loves wisdom rejoices his father;
but a companion of harlots squanders wealth.

contention, in contrast with patient trust in Jehovah, and its peaceful and sure reward.

V. 26. He that *trusts in his own heart*, is one that is sufficient for himself; who has little regard for any opinion but his own; to whom the experience and observation of others are of small account, and for the most part serve only to confirm his own narrow views.

The parallel member intimates, that to "trust in his own heart" is not "to walk in wisdom;" and the latter, as appears by the contrast, is to heed all the lessons, Divine and human, given for the safe and wise direction of our conduct.

The first of these characters is a fool, and will have a fool's reward; the other "shall be delivered" from every evil to which folly is exposed.

Such is evidently the instruction conveyed by the two parallel members, viewed in their connection. But viewing the first member by itself, may there not be exceptional cases, in which a man is bound to consult his own heart alone, following its dictates in accordance with what he believes to be the Divine rule, regardless of the views and convictions of others? Undoubtedly there are. The difficulty is, that the man who most needs this lesson of the Wise, is the one most likely to think himself the exception.—Compare the remark on ch. 18 : 1.

V. 27. *Is without want.* This is the general law of Providence, and is in accord with economic laws. The principles of the Divine government go hand in hand, and are administered in their established relations to each other, and in harmony. It is not meant, that the mere spirit of beneficence, without capacity, without foresight, and without prudent and skillful management, will insure against want. Obedience to one principle will not remedy the neglect of another, or the want of ability for its proper application. But all must concede, that it would not be easy to find a man, who has come to want by giving to the poor.

*He that hides his eyes:* who, with "hard unkindness," turns his eyes away from want and suffering, and refuses relief.

This is the direct meaning and application. But there are other applications includ d in this. There is a spurious sentiment, misnamed benevolence, which can not bear the sight of suffering, and yet is satisfied with escaping the sight of it; mere selfishness, that heeds not the miseries of others, if its own enjoyment is not thereby hindered. There are numbers of the wealthy in every populous city, whose natural sensibilities, given them as a guide and monitor to duty, would be shocked with witnessing the miseries around them, the sight of which would taint every enjoyment. But they "hide their eyes," shut out the sight, and go on reveling in their superfluities, while curses of the destitute and perishing accumulate on their heads.

V. 28. *When the wicked rise:* when they come up, are raised to power in the State. Compare the remarks on v. 12.

Second member. Wicked rulers are a terror to the good, whom they can not use for their evil purposes; and the latter prosper and multiply only when the former are taken out of the way.

Ch. XXIX.—V. 1. *Often reproved:* in whatever manner,—whether by those whose relation, natural or official, confers the right to administer reproof, or by the admonitions of God's Word, or by Divine chastisements in his own person, or in the persons of those dear to him. He who "hardens his neck," who stubbornly resists such repeated reproof, has no moral assurance of safety. He spurns these tender and faithful ministrations of Divine love, seeking his reform, and becomes hardened in sin. Evil, in some form, may at any moment overtake him, and leave him wrecked in character, and in prospects for this life and the life to come.

Such cases may be counted up by scores, in the memory of one who has long observed the course of human life. But whether near or remote in time, the end of all unavailing reproof is sudden destruction, and without remedy.

V. 2. Compare ch. 28 : 12 and 28. *When the righteous multiply:* and by consequence (ch. 28 : 28) the wicked have ceased to be in power.

V. 3, second member. A single instance, and one of too frequent occurrence, of the manner in which the ways of wisdom are forsaken for those of folly.—*Squanders wealth.* Compare Luke 15 : 30. The lavish expenditure in such guilty pleasures is elsewhere referred to in this book (ch. 5 : 10), as is often done in writers of pagan antiquity.

MARGINAL TRANSLATIONS AND READINGS.
a man that takes gifts

4 A king by judgment establishes a land;
but a man that exacts tribute overthrows it.

5 A man that flatters his neighbor,
spreads a net for his steps.

6 In the wicked man's transgression is a snare;
but the righteous shall exult and rejoice.

7 The righteous regards the cause of the weak;
the wicked will not discern knowledge.

8 Scoffers enkindle a city;
but the wise turn away anger.

9 When a wise man goes to law with a foolish man,
whether he be angry or laugh, there is no rest.

V. 4. Oppressive exactions by the government cripple industry, and impoverish the people. The sentiment in each member of this verse is expressed in Ezek. 45 : 9, "execute judgment and justice, take away your exactions from my people."

Second member. Some translate as in the margin. *A man that takes gifts* is one that accepts a bribe, and thereby unfits himself for doing justice between man and man.

V. 5. *Flattery*, in the sense of the text, is the adroit use of praise or censure, or of obsequious attention, to please and gratify its object for some sinister end. Flattery, in this sense, may be addressed to any point in human nature. One may flatter another's prejudices; his enmities and favoritisms; his virtues or vices; his ambition, his love of ease; his pride, his modesty, his humility, his vanity and self-esteem; and easiest of all, his indifference to flattery.

On every side of his character, a man is more or less accessible to flattery; and most accessible on what he regards as his strongest side, because there he feels himself least liable to it, being sure that his merit can not be overstated.

It is well to remember, that he who flatters his neighbor "spreads a net for his steps,"—a net in which many feet are taken.

V. 6. *In the wicked man's transgression is a snare.* The wicked is ensnared in his own crime. His crime is itself a snare, from which there is no escape. The guilt of violated law cleaves to the criminal, and he can not deliver himself. If he evades punishment by man, the guilt remains, and he can not escape the consciousness of it. He can never again be what he was before the offense.

But he is also outwardly ensnared. He has forfeited the immunities of the guiltless, and is no longer master of himself. He is amenable to both Divine and human law. His property and person, his liberty and even life, as the case may be, are in the power of others, and are no longer his own. And what to many is dearer than either or all of these,—character, the esteem and confidence of the good,—are forfeited, and gone forever.

Beyond the immediate purpose of the proverb, perhaps, but within its scope, is the fearful tendency of crime to repeat itself. He who has thus "fallen into the snare of the Devil," has become his prey.

The two members of the proverb express the general sentiment: The righteous escapes the snare into which the wicked falls by transgression, and rejoices in his safety.

V. 7. *Will not discern knowledge.* True knowledge is meant, such as this book aims to impart,—"a true understanding of all our moral relations and duties,"—as already remarked on ch. 18 : 15. These the wicked "will not discern;" implying, in connection with the first member, a disregard of his obligations to the weak, so impressively taught in these sayings of the Wise. See, for example, chs. 17 : 5; 19 : 17; 21 : 13; 22 : 16, 22, 23; 24 : 11, 12.

V. 8. *Scoffers:* men who make a mock of honor and virtue, and of every thing noble; or who, while loudly professing regard for them, practically despise the restraints of social order and of public law. Their rash counsels "enkindle a city," excite popular rage and resentments, which the influence of the wise "turns away."

The direct allusion, in the word "anger," may be to the displeasure of Government, domestic or foreign, provoked by unprincipled leaders of the populace, which wiser counsels would prevent or avert.

All cases are included of popular excitements, raised by reckless and fanatical demagogues.

V. 9. *When a wise man goes to law with a foolish man.* The implication is, that if both parties are wise, they will not go to law; if both are fools, they will be certain to do it.

As a possible case, a wise man may go to law with a foolish one; one party not having wisdom enough for both.

*Whether he be angry or laugh.* One or the other he is sure to do; and which, depends upon his temperament. As to *rest*, that is out of the question.

"Whether he be angry or laugh" is not said as being characteristic of the wise man, but as expressing what there will be abundant occasion for in such a contest. When the wise and the foolish contend, the latter has greatly the advantage, having nothing to lose.

10 Men of blood hate the upright;
but the just will care for his soul.

11 A fool utters all his mind;
but the wise restrains [and keeps] it back.

12 A ruler that gives heed to words of falsehood,—
all his servants are wicked.

13 The poor and the oppressor meet together;
He that gives light to the eyes of them both is Jehovah.

14 A king that truthfully judges the weak,—
his throne shall stand forever firm.

15 The rod and reproof give wisdom;
but a child left to itself shames its mother.

16 When the wicked increase, transgression increases;
but the righteous shall look on their fall.

MARGINAL TRANSLATIONS AND READINGS.

will require his life || *or*, will seek his life [to deliver it]

all his wrath

the wise will afterward appease it

V. 10, first member. For the sentiment, compare v. 27.—Second member. *To care for his soul* means to have a tender and loving regard for him (as in Ps. 142 : 4), in contrast with the bitter hatred of "men of blood," who look upon him as their enemy.

The words may be translated as in the margin,—*will require his life;* as in Gen. 9 : 5, "I will require the life of man." They will hold "men of blood" to a strict account.

The other marginal rendering,—*will seek his life* [to deliver it], is the one commonly adopted. But it is not the sense of the Hebrew phrase as elsewhere used; and the rendering in the text is more strictly antithetic to "hate" in the first member.

V. 11. *Utters all his mind.* Whatever comes into his mind, all his impulses, feelings, and passions, are blurted out, without regard to time, place, or occasion. He exercises no control over the expression of his thoughts and emotions. True wisdom is shown in the self-restraint, which either represses them altogether, or waits the proper opportunity for giving them utterance.

(Margin.) *Afterward:* when he has satisfied himself with the utterance of all his mind, and can listen to reason.

V. 12. When a ruler gives heed to falsehoods, whether it be through perverseness, or through weakness and want of discernment, evil men will take advantage of it, and become his trusted advisers.

V. 13. Compare ch. 22 : 2, and the remarks on it.——Instead of "rich," we have here "the oppressor," one who uses the advantages of wealth to oppress the poor and helpless; instead of "the Maker of them all," the more ornate and comprehensive expression, "he that gives light to the eyes of them both."

*That gives light to the eyes:* that bestows the light of life, or conscious existence (as in Job 3 : 16, and 20 where the parallel member has "life," compare "light of life" in Ps. 56 : 13); that renews life to the fainting spirit (Ps. 13 : 3); that refreshes and cheers the depressed (Ezra 9 : 8).——*Gives light to the eyes of them both:* to both alike the source of life and of every blessing, both being alike dependent on him for all.

There is here a lesson for both. To the self-reliant and self-confident oppressor it is said: What hast thou, that thou didst not receive? And what advantage shalt thou presently have, over him who now receives less?——The poor is taught to remember, that his humbler lot is not the result of chance; and that he shall ere long stand on equal footing with his oppressor, before him who appointed to both their lot in life.

V. 14. *Truthfully:* with "true judgment" (Zech. 7 : 9), according to the actual facts and merits of the case.

*The weak.* Without excluding others, he specifies these, as most of all needing a truthful and impartial administration of justice, and as God's peculiar care.

*Shall stand forever firm.* As already remarked in these notes, the principles of the Divine government go together, and act in harmony; and no one principle, apart from others, can be applied with certainty of success. But there is no principle that implies more of the conditions of a stable government than the one here stated. It may well be asked, what throne, so sustained, was ever shaken down?—Compare ch. 20 : 28, and the remark on it.

V. 15. Nothing is more certain, than that "folly is bound in the heart of a child" (ch. 22 : 15). *Wisdom* is not inborn; it must be taught. *Reproof* is the moral influence by which this end is to be attained, and is generally successful when judiciously applied. It may fail, however, and the aid of the *rod* may be required as an auxiliary to moral influence.

*A child left to itself;* without proper parental care and discipline.—*Shames its mother:* because with her lies the chief responsibility of the early training of the child; and hence her claim to that intellectual and moral culture, to which her nature shows her to be equally entitled with man, and without which she is deprived of the means of fulfilling her mission as a wife and mother.

V. 16. The increase of the wicked and their crimes should not dishearten the lovers of right and of social order. The righteous "shall look on their fall;" shall look on, while they suffer the doom that surely awaits them

| MARGINAL TRANSLATIONS AND READINGS. | | |
|---|---|---|
| | 17 | Correct thy son, and he will give thee rest,<br>and will give delight to thy soul. |
| | 18 | When there is no vision, the people are unrestrained;<br>but he that keeps the law,—happy is he. |
| | 19 | By words a servant is not corrected;<br>for he will understand,—but there is no answer. |
| | 20 | Seest thou a man hasty in his words?<br>there is more hope of a fool than of him. |
| he will be a refractory one in the end | 21 | One brings up his servant tenderly from childhood,<br>and in the end he will be as a son. |
| | 22 | A man given to anger stirs up contention;<br>and a wrathful man abounds in transgression. |
| | 23 | A man's pride will bring him low;<br>but the humble in spirit shall retain honor. |
| | 24 | He that divides with a thief hates his own soul;<br>he hears the curse, but does not inform. |
| | 25 | Fear of man brings a snare;<br>but he that trusts in Jehovah shall be set on high. |
| is a man's right | 26 | Many seek the face of the ruler;<br>but from Jehovah is man's judgment. |

V. 17. The *habit of obedience* should begin with the first opening consciousness of the child. It should never consciously disobey, without such suitable correction as it will soon learn to understand. The habit of obedience may be fully formed while the first elements of language are being acquired, and become the ruling law of childhood. Once established, it is easily obeyed, and not easily overcome.

The parent who desires a son that "will give him rest," and "give delight to his soul," will spare no pains, whatever may be required, to form this early habit in the child, and by its aid correct every later tendency to evil.

V. 18. *No vision:* no Divine communication,—as the word is used in 1 Sam. 3 : 1, compare 1 Chron. 17 : 15,—hence, no Divine teacher. Such were originally called *Seers* (1 Sam. 9 : 9), commissioned to declare the will of God, often communicated in vision, and to watch over the due observance of his law. For such a dearth as is here referred to,—a "famine of the words of Jehovah" (Am. 8 : 11),—compare 1 Sam. 3 : 1, "the Word of the Lord was precious" (properly, rare), and 2 Chron. 15 : 3.

*He that keeps the law:* who, without the influence of the living teacher, observes its precepts.

V. 19. *By words:* that is, by words alone.—*No answer;* namely, in action; there is no responsive obedience.

V. 20. *Hasty in his words:* always in haste to speak, as men ever are who have more words than ideas, whose conceit of wisdom is in proportion to their lack of it, and is always eager for utterance.—*There is more hope of a fool:* there being one chance for him, that of ruminating in silence (ch. 17 : 28), but none for the other.

That this is the sentiment here, is quite evident from comparison with ch. 26 : 12.

V. 21. *His servant:* most probably referring to one born in the house (Gen. 14 : 14), and therefore the more likely to be tenderly reared. As a consequence of such misplaced indulgence, he in the end becomes more a son of the house than a house servant.

V. 22. Anger begets anger, and the passionate man is always stirring up strife, and raising a tempest about him.

The *wrathful man*, in the violence of his passion, loses all self-control, and recklessly commits many an offense, which in calmer moments he deplores, and not seldom expiates with his liberty or his life.

V. 23. See ch. 18 : 12.

V. 24. *He hears the curse:* namely, as pronounced in Lev. 5 : 1 and the following verses, yet does not disclose the offense and its author, and thus brings the curse on his own soul.

V. 25. *Fear of man* is here contrasted with *trust in Jehovah.* He whose trust in Jehovah is overcome by fear of man, is already ensnared, and is the helpless prey of the ensnarer. He is in a bondage that sets no limits to its demands, and the more is yielded the more it requires.

*Shall be set on high:* beyond the reach of harm. Compare Pss. 59 : 1; 69 : 29; 91 : 14; 107 : 41.

V. 26. *Seek the face of the ruler.* They look to him, as though their cause were solely at his disposal, and all rested with him. But, *from Jehovah is man's judgment.* He controls and directs the judgments of man; for "the king's heart is in his hand," and he turns it whithersoever he will" (ch. 21 : 1).

27 An abomination to the righteous is the unjust man;
and an abomination to the wicked is he whose way is right.

1 WORDS OF AGUR, SON OF JAKEH; THE ORACLE.

The saying of the man to Ithiel,
to Ithiel and Ucal.
2 Yea, I am more stupid than any;
and I have not the understanding of a man.
3 I have not learned wisdom,
nor have I knowledge of the Holy.
4 Who has ascended to heaven, and come down?
Who has gathered the wind in his fists?
Who has bound the waters in a mantle?
Who has founded all the ends of the earth?
What is his name, and what his son's name?
For thou knowest!

MARGINAL TRANSLATIONS AND READINGS.

That thou shouldst know

By "man's judgment" some understand the judgment that is a man's due, his right (as in the margin); which is the same in effect, but in form is not so strictly antithetic to the idea of "seeking the face of the ruler," in the first member.

V. 27. The righteous and the wicked are each the abomination of the other; and for the same reason, each being the opposite of the other in principles, as in their aims and acts, one striving for the supremacy of right and the other of wrong. So it has ever been since the Fall, and the conflict still rages with unabated bitterness; the weapons on one side "not carnal but spiritual" when there is liberty to choose; on the other, whatever comes to hand and is most effective.

PART SIXTH.—Ch. XXX.

Here commences the sixth division of the book; containing, as stated in the superscription, words of Agur, son of Jakeh, the oracle.—See Introd. § 5

V. 1. *Agur.* A wise man of the Hebrews, of whom nothing is known beyond what may be gathered from this passage. It contains a small collection of his sayings, remarkable for the pointed expression of profound wisdom, and of practical knowledge, and resting on the same authority as the other collections combined in this book. They consist of what is characterized as the oracle (vv. 1–6); a prayer (vv. 7–9); and brief observations, of various contents (vv. 10–33).

*Jakeh.* Of him also nothing more is known.

*Oracle.* This word, in the sense of *utterance*, something uttered or spoken, occurs twenty-eight times in the Old Testament, always meaning a Divine communication, chiefly prophetic. In the common English version it is translated *burden* (as in Is. 14 : 28; 15 : 1; Hab. 1 : 1). Its import is here admonitory, which is the primary object in many instances where it is prophetic and minatory, foreshowing the consequences of disobedience, as here in v. 6.

*The saying of the man:* namely, of Agur. The form of expression implies that it was used by the one who recorded or collected his sayings.

Of *Ithiel* and *Ucal* nothing more is known than that they were the persons to whom the following admonitions were addressed. By some they are supposed to have been sons, by others pupils, of Agur; and by others still, men of matured views, whose erroneous speculations are here rebuked.

VV. 2, 3. Agur begins with the modest profession of his own want of insight and knowledge, and especially of his inability to comprehend "the Holy;" a suitable preparation for rebuking the arrogant pretensions implied in the following questions. He who feels most his own deficiencies has the best right to challenge the false pretensions of others.

*The Holy:* as in ch. 9 : 10, where it corresponds to *Jehovah*, in the parallel member.

V. 4. In a series of pertinent questions, he unmasks the vain pretense, that we can comprehend the mysteries of the universe, and its Author. They are as pertinent now as when first written. Science, with all its grand achievements, has only brought within our view a wider range of the material universe, and of the substances and organic structures perceptible by the senses. Of the imperceptible forces that are acting in them, it has ascertained nothing, beyond the fact of a certain uniformity in their action and its conditions. What these primary forces are, and how they originated, is still as unknown to science as when these questions were first propounded. No one has yet "ascended to heaven, and come down."

The question, "Who has ascended to heaven, and come down?" is understood by some as of like import with the following questions, and as expressing an activity belonging to God alone. But it more probably means, who of men has ascended where the mechanism of nature and its secret agencies can be traced out, and has brought thence the knowledge thus attained?

*Has gathered the wind in his fists.* Who holds the winds in his control; restraining their violence, and letting loose their wild fury, when he wills.

*Bound the waters in a mantle:* the waters in the clouds, in which they are bound as in a mantle.* Compare Job 26 : 8,

* The mantle was the large outer garment, in shape an oblong

MARGINAL TRANSLATIONS AND READINGS.

5 Every word of God is pure;
a shield is he to them that trust in him.
6 Add not thou to his words;
lest he reprove thee, and thou be found a liar.

7 Two things have I asked of thee;
withhold them not from me before I die.
8 Put far from me vanity and lies;
give me not poverty, nor riches;
feed me with food sufficient for me.

where the waters above are poetically conceived as "bound up" in the enveloping cloud, and the "cloud is not rent under them."

*Has founded all the ends of the earth:* has laid its foundations, in all its length and breadth.

It is implied in these questions, that ONE has wrought these things, of whom this is all that we,—of ourselves,—can know.*

*What is his name* (what is implied in it, what do we know of him),—*and what his son's name?* What know we of him and his?

To know "his name," and "his son's name," implies familiar acquaintance with him and his; consequently, that one knows all about him, and has "found out the deep things of God" (Job 11 : 7). This vain conceit and arrogance are happily rebuked in the ironical concession, *For thou knowest.*—Thou knowest it, of course!

Some translate as in the margin, *That thou shouldst know;* as the same form of expression is properly rendered in Job 38 : 5, but with less grammatical propriety in the connection here (as is clear to the English reader) and with some abatement of the peculiar point that characterizes Agur's words.

In the question, "and what his son's name?" there is supposed by some to be allusion to the Divine Sonship of the Messiah.†

But such an allusion to this great truth, though it is one recognized in the Hebrew Scriptures (Ps. 2 : 7), seems foreign, in manner as well as spirit, to this connection. It is not well to look round for feeble and uncertain supports of great and fundamental truths, which are well established on unquestionable evidence. The cause of truth has often suffered by this course.

VV. 5. 6. Here follows the admonition, to which the preceding questions lead, to cleave to the Divine word, adding nothing to it. In two brief sentences, it contains these weighty suggestions:

1st. Every word of God is pure; is pure truth, without mixture of error, and can not corrupt or mislead.

2nd. He is himself a shield, the sure defense, of all who make him their trust.

3rd. Whoever adds to his words incurs his displeasure, and will be convicted of falsehood.

To "add to his words" is to supplement them with teachings not contained in them, or to substitute others for them.

All that we can know of God, of his nature, of his mode of existence, of his relation to the material universe, of our own moral relation and duties to him, and to ourselves and one another, is revealed in his word. To develope these primary truths, and to apply them in their manifold relations, has been found to be the highest office of human reason; and in doing this, it has achieved its greatest and its only enduring triumphs, in the civilization of the race.

Of the many who have "added to his words," in the ages past, who has been found to be a veritable witness to the truth,—who has not been proved a liar?

Heed, then, the prophetic admonition; and "add not to his words," lest thou too "be found a liar."

VV. 7—9. Here follows the prayer of Agur; and next to the Savior's more complete summary of our daily wants and desires, it is a model prayer.

V. 7. *Before I die.* That is, so long as I live; let them not be withheld from me while I live.

This is sometimes understood to mean, grant them before I die,—let me not die without having enjoyed them. On the contrary, the writer means, let me enjoy them so long as I live,—all the while I live.

V. 8. *Vanity.* Vain and empty seeming, unsubstantial and delusive; hence coupled here with "lies" The two expressions comprehend all that deceives by a mere outward show of unreal good, and cheats and disappoints him that seeks and trusts to it. To this stands opposed real and substantial good, which is the object of his desire, and of which the many fail, in their eager pursuit of the unreal and delusive.

*Not poverty nor riches:* the dictate of true worldly philosophy, as well as of heavenly wisdom. The privations of poverty, and the encumbrances of superfluous wealth, are evils about equally balanced, and equally to be shunned.

"Resolve not to be poor," is a dictate of just prudence; and

square, worn over the shoulders and covering the whole body. At night it served as a covering in sleep; Ex. 22 : 26, 27, Deut. 24 : 12, 13 (properly, mantle, not "raiment").

* So in Job 26 : 7–14, after recounting these and similar exhibitions of power, it is said (the writer's revised version):

Lo, these are the borders of his ways;
and what a whisper of a word is that we hear!

† As by J. Pye Smith (to whose view Dr. Aiken, Lange's Biblework, Am. ed., p. 248, assents): "The concluding clauses of this energetic passage are rationally and easily interpreted, if we admit hat the ancient Jews had some obscure ideas of a plurality in the Divine nature" (Scripture Testimony to the Messiah, I. p. 469).

9 Lest I be full, and deny,
and say, Who is Jehovah;
and lest I be poor, and steal,
and impugn the name of my God.

10 Slander not a servant to his master;
lest he curse thee, and thou be held guilty.

11 A generation,—that curse their father,
and bless not their mother!
12 A generation,—pure in their own eyes,
and not washed from their filthiness!
13 A generation,—how lofty are their eyes,
and their eye-lids are lifted up!
14 A generation,—their teeth are swords,
and their fangs are knives;
to devour the poor from the earth,
and the needy from among men!

15 The leech has two daughters, Give, Give.
Three things there are that are not satisfied;

MARGINAL TRANSLATIONS AND READINGS.

no one can rightfully neglect it, at the risk of becoming a burden to others, and as intimated here, of blaming Divine Providence for his own fault.

On the other hand, the Apostle does not condemn, as offenders, "the rich in this world;"* and none need be overburdened with surplus wealth, while the opportunities are so many for sharing it with the needy.

But many carry the load so long as they have breath, and leave the burden to their heirs, to sweat under it after them.

*Food sufficient for me.* My daily allowance of food, is meant, what is sufficient for my daily wants; agreeing nearly in form, and exactly in sentiment, with the fourth petition in the Lord's Prayer.† We may well apply here (changing a single word) the language of Bishop Hall: "And he that asks for most can use no more."

*And deny:* make the denial implied in the following question,—"Who is Jehovah?"—refusing to own him, and dependence on him. Compare Josh. 24:27, "lest ye deny your God;" Is. 59:13 (properly, "in transgressing, and denying Jehovah"); Jer. 5:12 (properly, "they have denied Jehovah)." What is meant by "denying," is well illustrated in Job 8:18 (the writer's revised version):

"When he shall be destroyed from his place,
it shall deny him, 'I have not seen thee.'"

*Lest I be full* (have more than suffices) *and deny.* He means that fulness of riches, and trust in them, condemned by the Apostle in 1 Tim. 6:17, which loses sight of the Giver in his gifts, and makes them, in place of him, the ground of trust. Compare Hos. 13:6, "They were filled, and their heart was exalted; therefore they forgot me."

*Impugn the name of my God.* As men are prone to do, when suffering either the natural consequences of their own neglect and improvidence,—"his heart is angry against Jehovah" (ch. 19:3),—or the righteous judgment of God,—"when they shall be hungry, they will . . . curse their king and their God" (Is. 8:21).

V. 10. Hasty and groundless accusation of a servant, sometimes too freely indulged in against inferiors in station, is justly and severely resented by the master, from whom protection is due in return for faithful service.

With less probability, the subject of the first clause in the second member (*lest he curse thee*) is by some supposed to be the slandered servant.

VV. 11—14. Four different characters are here held up to view, and briefly sketched in a few well-defined strokes. No comment is made, the statement of their several characteristics being itself condemnatory.

They are distinct types of humanity, that reappear in every passing age, and hang here like pictures in the rogues' gallery, to be abhorred and shunned.

The several traits, so strikingly defined, are:

1st. Filial impiety.

2nd. Self-righteousness, and satisfaction with their own misdeeds.

3rd. Pride and superciliousness, and assumed superiority.

4th. Violence and greed, preying on all the weak and defenceless.

What more is needed, than the prevalence of these traits, to make such a world as perished in the Deluge? How soon would "the earth be filled with violence!" (Gen. 6:11).

V. 11. *A generation:* a progeny, or race, of common parentage, among whom similar traits prevail. The object is, to characterize such, whether races, or classes, or individuals.

VV. 15, 16. Illustration of the insatiable demands of appetite and passion, when not under due regulation and restraint.

V. 15. The *leech*, representing appetite, passion, greed, and

* 1 Tim. 6:17.

† See the writer's note on the passage, in "The Gospel by Matthew, revised version, with critical and philological notes."

MARGINAL TRANSLATIONS AND READINGS.

16 four say not, Enough!
The underworld, and the barren womb;
the earth, that is not satisfied with water,
and fire, that says not, Enough!

17 The eye that mocks at a father,
and scorns obedience to a mother;
the ravens of the valley shall pick it out,
and the young of the vulture shall eat it.

18 Three things there are, too difficult for me;
and four, which I understand not.
19 The way of the eagle in the heavens;
the way of the serpent on a rock;
the way of a ship in the midst of the sea;
and the way of a man with a maid.

every inordinate desire, has *two daughters, Give, Give*, representing their insatiable demands. No matter how much may be given, there is still a twofold cry for more.

V. 16. The thought thus introduced is further illustrated in this verse, by four examples of continually renewed and never satisfied craving.

In referring to the "barren womb" as an example, the sacred writer had in mind the longing for the maternal relation, the natural and proper desire for offspring, of which there are many instances in the Old Testament. See, for example, Gen. 30 : 1; 1 Sam. 1 : 10, 11.*

V. 17. Against filial impiety. This is a violation of one of the purest and strongest instincts of nature. It can exist only where there is no fear of God, and where the noblest elements of human nature are wanting.

"The *eye* that mocks," it is said; the eye being the truest and most significant index of character and feeling. The "mocking eye" is an indication of scornful contempt, such as can find no expression in words.†

Such impiety is here condemned in terms peculiarly characteristic and significant. The point of the statement is, that even the ravens, and the young of the vulture, shall be regarded as more deserving, and as worthy to be instruments of punishment for filial ingratitude.

*Young of the vulture* is set over against an ungrateful and undutiful child.—*Ravens of the valley:* where they congregate. Compare 1 Kings. 17 : 4–6 (*valley* and *brook* being expressed by the same Hebrew word).

VV. 18–20. We have here a peculiar style of oriental teaching, by quaint illustrations, designed to gain attention, and to point the expression of a truth and fix it in the memory.

The object of the sacred writer is somewhat obscure, and has been variously understood. That his object is moral instruction, there can be no doubt; and hence any conception of it as an amusing play of the fancy may be dismissed at once.

V. 19. Of the things difficult to be understood are named, 1st, the way (that is, the flight) of the eagle in the heavens, how his weight is borne up at such vast heights, and moved at pleasure wherever he wills; 2nd, the movement of the serpent on the hard, smooth rock, without any apparent means of locomotion; 3rd, the course of the ship in the sea, borne onward with its huge bulk and immense burdens, in any direction, and to any point intended.*

It matters not that these things can be philosophically explained, and that we now understand how the eagle is sustained in the air by its reacting force, and moves upward or onward by the difference of forces. So can the "balancings of the clouds" (Job 37 : 16) be now understood. The discovery that the air has weight, and is heavier than the pellicles of vapor, has explained the mystery. But there was a time when these were wonders, and to men as wise at least as we are, in matters of greater concern than the truths of physical science. We can all remember when to us too they were wonders; and no illustrations of truth take stronger hold of the imagination and heart, than those drawn from our earliest impressions of nature. The Bible abounds in them; and in this is one secret of its hold on the human heart.

Not less incomprehensible is the mysterious law of reproduction, in the divinely appointed relation of the sexes. In purposed contrast with what follows, we have here the case of the bridegroom and bride, and their chaste intercourse, as a type of the sanctity

* It is well said by Delitzsch (On Genesis 30 : 1), that "The chaste desire for offspring is the highest aim of a virtuous marriage." This chaste desire is what the sacred writer refers to here, and no other thought is to be imputed to him.

† There may be allusion to the habit of the class of birds to which the raven belongs, of first picking out the eyes of its prey.

* Many suppose the sacred writer to mean, that they leave no track behind them, and hence their way is difficult to understand, because it can not be traced. But is it strange that any object, moving through the air, or over a rock, or in the water, should leave no track? It is as true of any other object as it is of the eagle, the serpent, and the ship. This thought is not implied in the expression, it is insignificant in itself, and it is inconsistent with the second example (being no more true of the serpent than of any other animal), and still more inconsistent with the fourth, as interpreted on this view of the case.

| | | MARGINAL TRANSLATIONS AND READINGS. |
|---|---|---|
| So is the way of an adulterous woman ; | 20 | |
| she eats, and wipes her mouth, | | |
| and says, I have done no iniquity. | | |
| Under three things the land is disquieted, | 21 | |
| and under four it can not bear up. | | |
| Under a servant, when he reigns, | 22 | when he becomes king. |
| and a fool when he is sated with food ; | | |
| under a hated woman, when she is married, | 23 | |
| and a maidservant when she is heir to her mistress. | | has dispossessed her mistress |
| Four things there are, the smallest of the earth, | 24 | |
| and they wise, instructed in wisdom. | | |
| The ants, a people not strong ; | 25 | |
| and they prepare their food in summer. | | |

and purity of that relation; for by "maid" is meant a young woman of marriageable age.

V. 20. The moral here culminates in the contrast to which the above fourth example is designed to lead. *So is the way:* just as incomprehensible, in a moral view, is the violation of the sacredness of marital rights by the adulteress, and her hardened indifference to the guilt of the crime. As one who eats and wipes the mouth, she removes all trace of guilt, and fears no reproach, and feels none—*I have done no iniquity!*

VV. 21–23. Four characters, instructive types of humanity in their several spheres, great or small, a kingdom, a neighborhood, or a household.

V. 22. *When he reigns:* when he virtually rules, through the incompetence or negligence of the actual ruler,—compare the remarks on ch. 19 : 10; or (margin, *becomes king*) when he succeeds, by treachery or otherwise (compare 2 Kings 8 : 7–15) to a throne to which he has no rightful title. In both cases, the experience of mankind has generally been as is here stated, though there have been exceptions in both.

Second member. *A fool when he is sated with food.* When his stomach is full, he is independent of everybody, and as insolent as he before was fawning. Hunger and appetite show him his mistake, and teach him better manners.

The *parasite* was once more common than he is now,—at least within the writer's range of observation. But he is sometimes the pest even of modern civilization. In ancient writings he plays a conspicuous part, and elsewhere is characterized much as he is here.

By "sated with food" some understand the writer to mean, when he has come into possession of abundant wealth or power. But this explanation of the words is unnatural and improbable.

V. 23. *A hated woman, when she is married.* There is more than one possible application of these words. They may include such a case as that of Leah (Gen. 29 : 30), the source of the domestic disquiet in the family of Jacob (Gen. 30 : 1) ; for she was not the choice of Jacob (was hated in comparison with Rachel, Gen. 29 : 17, 18) and yet became his wife. But other conditions were in that case the cause of domestic infelicity. The language here indicates a woman not adapted to please, and hence disliked and neglected, who at length becomes the choice of some one, and is taken in marriage. Disappointment, followed by unexpected and delayed good fortune, is apt to engender a a selfish and domineering spirit in one unused to command.

Second member. By a *maid-servant* is meant one in the lowest condition of menial service (Lev. 19 : 20, common version, *a bondmaid not redeemed, nor freedom given her;* Deut. 28 : 68, common version, *sold for bondwomen*), and inferior to that of a *handmaid.* Compare 1 Sam. 25 : 41, properly translated, "Behold thy handmaid for a maid-servant, to wash the feet of the servants of my lord."

*Is heir to her mistress:* that is, by marriage with her master takes the place of her deceased mistress at the head of the household, and over those who were once her equals, or were her superiors. The case is still stronger in another admissible rendering, *has dispossessed her mistress* (margin), in the regard of her master.. In oriental life, the condition of woman was such that this might easily happen. Christian civilization has made it impossible, or has provided an effectual legal remedy.

VV. 24–28. A lesson of wisdom in the direction of worldly affairs, and of God's provident care for the least of his creatures, derived from the instincts of the feeblest of the lower animals.

V. 25. *A people not strong.* As such, they might seem to be barely able to make provision for present wants. But besides doing this, these provident insects lay by a store for winter. Compare ch. 6 : 8.

This opinion, respecting the habits of the ant, was the prevailing one in ancient times, as is shown by numerous allusions to it in ancient writings; and on this prevalent view the moral lesson of the sacred writer is founded.

In modern times this opinion has been controverted, on the ground that the insect is carniverous, needing no vegetable food to be provided "in summer," and is dormant during the cold of winter, having then no need of food. On the contrary, it is an admitted fact that the insect, at least certain species, stores away quantities of vegetable seeds during summer, which it carefully preserves from injury. It is to be considered, moreover, that the ant is not merely carniverous, as every housekeeper knows; that different species, of which there are many, have different habits; that in warm climates they are less subject to torpidity in winter; and that the seeds, which certain species are well known

MARGINAL TRANSLATIONS AND READINGS.

against whom there is no risens up

26 The conies, a people not powerful;
and they make their abode in the cliff.
27 The locusts have no king;
and they go forth all of them in bands.
28 The lizard takes hold with the hands;
and she is in kings' palaces.

29 Three things there are, graceful in step,
and four are graceful in going.
30 A lion, mighty among beasts,
and he turns not back before any.
31 A greyhound, or a he-goat;
and a king, with whom are the people.

32 If thou hast been foolish in exalting thyself,
and if thou hast thought evil,—the hand to the mouth!

to provide in summer, are in some way necessary to their subsistence.—A summary of the views on one side may be found in Smith's Bible Dictionary, art. Ant, and on the other in Wood's Bible Animals, art. Ant, pp. 616–22.

But too much account is made of this and similar matters. The lesson intended by the sacred writer is well grounded, if derived from popular views known to all; and is far more generally useful and instructive than any lessons based on scientific investigations, known only to the favored few. It is not the object of Divine revelation to teach the habits of insects, but to draw moral instruction from what is understood respecting them. Whatever is said on matters of natural science is adapted, in substance and form, to the popular apprehension of these subjects, so as to be intelligible and instructive to the popular mind, which always represents the greater number. Any other course, by which its teachings would be less adapted to their end, might be man's wisdom, but it is not the wisdom of God. Intelligent scoffers can themselves take no other view, and must laugh in their sleeves when they see the believer disturbed by their railings.

V. 26. *Coney* is the Biblical name* for a small, timid, and exceedingly cautious animal, dwelling in the crevices of the rocky cliffs of Palestine. It is described by travelers and naturalists as always on the alert, being never taken off its guard, and hence very difficult to capture or kill.

*Make their abode in the cliff.* Their natural instincts guide them to a secure abode, from which they are not easily dislodged.

V. 27. *The locusts have no king*, etc. By their instinctive sense of order, without the direction of a superior, they move onward in unbroken column, with the regularity of disciplined soldiery. Compare the truthful description in Joel 2 : 7, 8;

They go each one on his ways,
and they change not their courses;
and they thrust not each his fellow,
they go every one on his path.

V. 28. *Lizard:* not "spider," as in the common English version. "The lizard indicated is evidently some species of Gecko" (Smith's Bible Dictionary, art. Spider, 2). One of the species, the Wall-lizard or Fan-foot, is thus described by Wood: "It is exceedingly plentiful, and inhabits the interior of houses, where it can find the flies and other insects on which it lives. On account of the structure of the toes, each of which is flattened into a disk-like form, and furnished on the under surface with a series of plates like those on the back of the sucking-fish, it can walk up a smooth, perpendicular wall with perfect ease, and can even cling to the ceiling like the flies on which it feeds" (Bible Animals, p. 69. Compare Smith's Bible Dictionary, art. Lizard).

*Takes hold with the hands.* This may have reference to the singular provision above described, strange and unintelligible to the ordinary observer, by which one species is able to ascend the smooth surface of a vertical wall, or cling to the ceiling, its hand-shaped toes adhering by atmospheric pressure. This singular power, with the habit of frequenting "kings' palaces," may be the ground of classing it with the other three, endowed with peculiar capacities and instincts.

The relation of the two members may be (without reference to the peculiar structure above referred to), that she takes hold with the hands (a trait common to all the species), and yet she dwells like a queen, in palaces of kings.

This explanation accords well with the sacred writer's meaning in the other three examples.

VV. 29–31. Four examples of graceful and majestic movement. The moral is,—the more impressive beauty and grandeur of rightful authority, as seen in its highest earthly representative.—*With whom are the people:* implying their subordination and devotion.

VV. 32, 33. A lesson of self-restraint and forbearance.—*Hast been foolish in exalting thyself.* Self-esteem, the vain conceit of superiority, and in men too wise for this the assertion of superior merit, and the spirit of dictation, provoke resistance and engender

* "The coney of Scripture is thought to be a pachyderm animal, *Hyrax Syriacus*, called also *daman*. It is small, gregarious, feeble, timid, and easily tamed. It is a native of Syria, Arabia, and Abbyssinia, and lives in the mouths of caves or the clefts of rocks" (Webster's English Dictionary).

MARGINAL TRANSLATIONS AND READINGS.

33 For pressing of milk brings forth cheese ;
and pressing of the nose brings forth blood ;
and pressing of anger brings forth strife.

1 The words of king Lemuel. An oracle, with which his
mother instructed him.
2 What, my son ?
And what, son of my womb ?
And what, son of my vows?
3 Give not thy strength to women,
nor thy ways to that which destroys kings.
4 It is not for kings, O Lemuel,
it is not for kings to drink wine,
nor for princes, or strong drink.
5 Lest he drink, and forget the law,
and pervert the cause of any of the sons of want.
6 Give strong drink to the perishing,
and wine to the sorrowful in spirit.

---

strife.—*If thou hast thought evil.* If in thought, evil has been purposed, whatever may be its aim. In either case,—*the hand to the mouth!* Instant suppression of whatever may thus lead to strife. The wise man's warning is sharp and imperative, and in a form which intimates that there is to be no dallying.

The illustrations are too familiar to need explanation ; and daily observation shows how much is sometimes gained by self-restraint and forbearance, and how much is oftener lost by the want of them.

Part Seventh. Ch. 31 : 1–10. See Introduction. § 5.

In this seventh division, we have the maternal instructions of a wise and virtuous matron to her son, on his duties as a sovereign. If good instruction could impart wisdom, the " most christian " princes of Europe would many of them have been better examples to their subjects, both of justice and morality.

V. 1. *Lemuel.* Of this sovereign nothing further is known. That he, or his mother. stood in any relation to Agur (ch. 30 : 1), as supposed by some, is matter of conjecture, unsupported by any evidence.

*His mother.* Her history is written in the words she was inspired to utter ; words that have come down through the ages, clothed with Divine authority, a warning of power to such as heed them, and a damning record against the many who have dared to despise them.

*What, my son?* The usual form of earnest appeal, when one would arrest attention, and claim consideration for what will spontaneously occur to the thoughtful. Here, as is evident from what follows, she claims heedful attention to what must readily suggest itself, his relations and duties as a son and as a sovereign. What thinkest thou ? What is due from thee ? To me, from the son of my womb,—given in answer to my vows,* to the pledges on which the boon was sought and granted? From thee as a sovereign,—to God who made thee such,—to the people over whom he placed thee, as representing his authority and clothed with his power.

Such, and similar to these, are the thoughts that naturally arise, in answer to her repeated demands for his attention and reflection.

V. 3. *That which destroys kings.* A course of licentious indulgence, and its destructive effects.

V. 4. *It is not for kings,*—for them of all others. They who are highest in station and influence should also be the highest examples of purity in morals ; as they whose responsibilities are greatest, and on whom the general welfare most depends, should most carefully abstain from all that unfits them for their duties.

But it has too commonly been held to be the special prerogative of royalty, to be above all the obligations and restraints of morality. The profligacy of courts has gone far to neutralize the influence of the Bible, the pulpit, and the moral press. It is not easy to teach the young, or even the old, that vice is disreputable, when it is countenanced and commended by the example of those who hold the highest positions in society.

V. 5. *The sons of want.* Another of the many evidences in this book, and in other portions of the Bible, that God has special care for those who specially need it,—the helper of the helpless. The Scriptures abound with these evidences of their Divine spirit and authorship. See, for example, ch. 22 : 22, 23, and ch. 23 : 10, 11, and compare the following sentiment in Ps. 10 : 14 (the writer's revised version) :

> Thou dost look upon trouble and sorrow,
> to set them on thy hand.
> To thee the wretched will commit it ;
> the orphan's helper hast thou been.

VV. 6, 7. The object is to show, by contrast, how unseemly and inappropriate for a king is indulgence in the use of wine. If any require the exhilaration of wine, it is the perishing and the

* Compare the similar case, recorded in 1 Sam. 1 : 11.

MARGINAL TRANSLATIONS AND READINGS.

7 Let him drink, and forget his poverty,
and remember his misery no more.
8 Open thy mouth for the dumb;
for the cause of all orphan children.
9 Open thy mouth, judge righteously;
and judge the poor and needy.

---

10 א A capable woman who shall find?
for far above pearls is her worth.
11 ב The heart of her husband confides in her;
and he shall not lack for gain.

---

sorrowful, in their poverty and misery; how unfit then for the monarch, who has no such plea for its use! The idea of drowning sorrow in intoxication is as much opposed to the spirit and teachings of this book, as it is to sound reason, and the lessons of human experience.

VV. 8. 9. *The dumb.* They who are in no condition to speak for themselves; virtually mute, having no voice that will be heard.—*Open thy mouth.* Be not silent in such a case, when silence is injustice and oppression. Compare the bitter exposure of such criminal negligence, in the taunting sarcasm, Ps. 58 : 1, as correctly rendered in the revised version.

*Judge the poor and needy.* See the writer's note on Gen. 30 : 6. "To judge one, in the scriptural use of the phrase, is to take cognizance of his case as a judge, to see that justice is done him and that he is protected in his rights."

Where else is this truly Godlike prerogative of royalty so justly set forth, and in terms so simple and touching!

PART EIGHTH.—Ch. 31 : 10–31.

The following beautiful description is in the Hebrew an *Acrostic Poem;* the letters of the Hebrew alphabet, in their regular order, being the initial letters of the successive couplets. This was a favorite device of the Hebrew poets; and it sometimes served a useful purpose in aiding the memory, as in the 119th Psalm.* Several examples of it occur in the Book of Psalms. See the writer's Introduction to the revised version of the Psalms, § 8, 1.

V. 10. *A capable woman.* One competent to perform all the duties required of her, as a wife and mother, and as mistress of the household.

I understand the sacred writer as meaning to set forth, in the following description, what woman is capable of under any possible circumstances, and what under some may be expected of her, not what under all circumstances may be required.

The duties of every social relation vary with its exigencies, and with the usages of society in different ages and countries. What may be proper and obligatory under one set of circumstances, may not be required or admissible under others. The duty is here illustrated of activity and diligence in some useful way. It may take the form of care for the husband's estate, and for the comfort and welfare and proper direction of all in the household, where that is necessary; and where it is not, of thoughtful provision for the needy beyond the domestic sphere.

Certainly none are less to be envied than the mere "woman of fashion;" whose only concern is to be admired and pleased, whose existence is of no value to any but herself, and will be missed by no one when it comes to an end.

*Who shall find?* Who so happy! Implying the worth and desirableness of such a treasure (as expressed in the next member), and that it is not always found,—as, indeed, it is not always sought. If the question implies the rarity of what the writer's ideal claims for woman, it must be conceded, that what by parity of rule may be required of her counterpart in man is rarer still. The wife more seldom fails in her duty, than the husband in his; and failure on either side is, happily, the exception.

V. 11. *The heart of her husband confides in her.* What a treasure to the true wife is her husband's confidence; to know that she has the confidence of one who confides in no other, and to whom she is more than all the world beside. How rich a treasure in the possession, and how precious in the remembrance!

And what a trust he confides to her; his home, the sanctuary of his heart, where all his affections and interests centre; his children, whose early training must chiefly be her care, and whose future depends mainly on her instructions and example; his household, which he has made a realm of her own, where her love of order, her prudent management, have supreme sway, and create an abode of peace, a home of intelligence, refinement, and virtue, which royalty might envy.

But how can he confide in her, if compelled to distrust her singleness of devotion to what should be their common interest; if in aught else she finds a higher satisfaction than in her duties as a wife and mother; if she neglects the economy of the household; if she selfishly outruns his income in needless extravagances, thus compromising his good name for honesty and uprightness in his dealings with men; if in any way he is taught to feel, that she does not make his lot her own, and cheerfully share whatever fortune Providence may see fit to grant him.

Happily, such cases are comparatively rare; and their occurrence is more specially noted than are similar or greater faults

---

* This purpose may have been intended here. The acrostic form of the poem, as in some of the Psalms, must be taken into account in considering its peculiar structure, and turns of sentiment and expression.

ג She will render to him good, and not evil, 12
all the days of her life.
ד She seeks for wool and flax ; 13
and works with her willing hands.
ה She is like the merchants' ships ; 14
she brings her food from afar.
ו And she rises while it is yet night, 15
and gives nourishment to her household,
and a task to her maids.
ז She considers a field, and obtains it ; 16
with the fruit of her hands she plants a vineyard.
ח She girds her loins with strength, 17
and strengthens her arms.
ט She perceives that her gains are good ; 18
her lamp goes not out by night.
י She puts forth her hands to the distaff, 19
and her hands lay hold on the spindle.
כ She stretches out her hand to the poor, 20
and reaches forth her hands to the needy.
ל She fears not for her household on account of snow ; 21
for all her household are clothed in crimson.
מ Coverlets she makes for herself ; 22
fine linen and purple are her clothing.
נ Her husband is known in the gates, 23
when he sits with the elders of the land.

MARGINAL TRANSLATIONS AND READINGS.

works cheerfully with her hands

in man, only because more is expected of her truer and more devoted nature.

Second member. *He shall not lack for gain.* Whatever within her sphere may promote the increase of his worldly substance, is made subservient to it.

V. 12. She will render to him good, and not evil,
all the days of her life.

Her domestic history, the secret of her happiness in her husband's confiding love, summed up in two beautiful lines!

V. 14. *Like the merchants' ships.* Like them, in that she neglects no source of needed supplies, far or near.

V. 15. *While it is yet night.* At early dawn.—We have here the three grand requisites of good housekeeping; early rising, timely provision for bodily wants, assignment of the daily task to each of the household. Wherever these three are found, order and efficiency are the certain result.

V. 16. On this, and some other points in the description, compare the remarks on v. 10, second and third paragraphs. Dealings in real estate, though not regarded as one of the "female accomplishments," have been conducted by some women with as good judgment, and as sure success, as is done by men ; showing that want of capacity for business is not a trait of their sex.

V. 17. What is commended here might justly be reckoned among "female accomplishments," and would greatly promote that beauty of person, so justly prized by women, and which all men admire.

V. 18. *Her gains.* What she gets in the exchange of commodities. Like a sensible woman, she takes care that she is not cheated in a bargain.

V. 19. Some readers of these lines, as well as the writer, may remember the time when such labors were performed by women in very good circumstances. But times have changed. It would not now be thought judicious housekeeping, to handle the distaff and the spindle, when machinery does the work at less cost; a good illustration of the statement in the remarks on v. 10 (third paragraph), that social and domestic duties vary in form with time and place, and only the pervading principle remains the same.

V. 20. *She stretches out her hand to the poor.* One of the great rewards of diligence and good management. "Poverty," it has been well said, "makes some duties difficult, and others impossible." Resolve not to be poor, is good counsel for the young, to whom the avenues of successful industry are open. In this country, few can be strictly poor, except by their own fault.

V. 21. *In crimson.* In costly fabrics, showing that there is no lack of means for comfortable clothing.

V. 23. *In the gates.* The open area at each gate of the city, which was naturally the place of public concourse, where men assembled for public business, and for the administration of justice. See the remark on ch. 1 : 21, and the writer's note on Job 5 : 4.

*Known* is somewhat ambiguous; but of course it is to be taken here in a favorable sense. Should the duties of the domestic fireside ever be neglected by women for those of the forum

MARGINAL TRANSLATIONS AND READINGS.

24 ס Fine undergarments she makes and sells,
and delivers girdles to the merchant.
25 ע Dignity and honor are her clothing;
and she laughs at the time to come.
26 פ She opens her mouth with wisdom,
and the law of kindness is on her tongue.
27 צ She watches the ways of her household,
and eats not the bread of idleness.
28 ק Her children rise up and call her happy;
her husband, and he praises her:
29 ר Many daughters have done worthily;
but thou surpassest them all.
30 ש Comeliness is a deception, and beauty is a vain thing;
a woman that fears Jehovah, she shall be praised.
31 ת Give to her of the fruit of her hands;
and let her works praise her in the gates.

and the exchange, their husbands will be known "in the gates," or anywhere else.

*Elders of the land.* Men of age and experience, intrusted with the direction of public affairs.

V. 24. *Girdles.* An essential part of the dress in the East. It was worn by both men and women, and served to confine the loose flowing garments around the waist.

V. 25. *Are her clothing.* With which she is clothed as with a garment. Compare the beautiful use of this figurative expression in Job 29 : 14, in the writer's revised version.

Second member. What the improvident dread, in the dark unknown of the future, is no cause of alarm to her. She is preprepared for every emergency, and laughs at the terrors that appal the unwary.

V. 26. As might be expected of one so practical and judicious, her observation and reflection have taught her wisdom; the knowledge of the true aims of human life and the means of attaining them, and of its relation to the whole life of man. Consequently, when she does open her mouth, she has something to say.

Second member. The power that wins, guides, and controls, is the *law of kindness;* a power that is never resisted as oppressive, and that grows stronger by every victory won.

V. 28. *Call her happy.* Happy in her lot; in the home which her wise direction has made the abode of peace, comfort, and contentment, for all the objects of her love and care; happy in their confidence, affection, and sympathy.*

V. 29 is most probably the language in which the husband expresses his well-merited praise. If in saying, "thou surpassest them all," he did unconscious injustice to the equally deserving, it was sure to be made up to them by a no less admiring judgment in their favor.

*Daughters.* An appropriate designation of the favored sex; expressing their descent from the honored mother of the race, and relation to each other as offspring of a common parentage.†

V. 30. *Comeliness is a deception.* Because men impose upon themselves by taking it above its value, for more than it is worth; bartering for it the more substantial good they might have had, and disappointed in their choice.

*Beauty is a vain thing:* a thing of no account, a vain show, without substantial worth. This is not said absolutely, though in that sense it is too often true, but relatively, and in comparison with more valuable qualities. Personal beauty is of some value to every woman, and as a gift of God that may be wisely used as a just means of influence, should be preserved in all proper ways; the best being the healthful exercise in domestic duties recommended in this chapter.

Second member. *A woman that fears Jehovah, she shall be praised.* An intelligent religious principle is here recognized as the inspiration and the guide of her domestic duties. Throughout this book, the *fear of Jehovah* is regarded as the central law of our moral relations, and the spring of all true moral action.

V. 31. *Give to her of the fruit of her hands.* Many would fare ill, if they could have no more. But what right have any to more than they have in some way earned, or for which they make some equivalent return? The drones of the hive are driven out. But in human communities, they often fare best, who earn nothing.

The sentiment of the verse is: Let her enjoy her well-earned reward, in the fruits of her industry and unselfish devotion, and in the honors due to them.—*In the gates:* as in v. 23.

---

This beautiful sketch of woman, in her domestic and social relations, is an appropriate close to a book of practical wisdom. The proper sphere of her duties, and their healthful influence, were never more truthfully and beautifully set forth; and on the right appreciation of these, more than on any other social element, depends the welfare of society.

* The Hebrew expresses *blessed* and *happy* by two different words, often improperly confounded in the common English version.

† Zöckler (Lange's Biblework), and Hitzig (German Commentary on Proverbs), are surely mistaken. The former supposes that "the husband says 'daughters,' because as an elder he may put himself above his wife;" the latter, because "he who praises places himself above the one praised (Heb. 7 : 7)."

THE END.

Works prepared by T. J. Conant, and referred to in his Notes.

---

The Book of Job; Part First, containing the Hebrew Text, the Common English Version, and a Revised Version, with a Critical Introduction, and Critical and Philological Notes. 1 vol. 4to.

The Book of Job; Part Second, the Revised Version, with an Introduction and Explanatory Notes for English readers. 1 vol. 4to.

The Gospel by Matthew; containing the Greek Text, the Common English Version, and a Revised Version, with an Introduction and Critical and Philological Notes. 1 vol. 4to.

Baptizein; its Meaning and Use, Philologically and Historically Investigated. 1 vol. 8vo.

The Book of Genesis; Revised Version, with an Introduction and Explanatory Notes. 1 vol. 8vo.

The Psalms; Revised Version, with an Introduction and occasional Notes. 1 vol. 8vo.

The Book of Proverbs; Part First, containing the Hebrew Text, the Common English Version, and a Revised Version, with a Critical Introduction and Critical and Philological Notes. 1 vol. 4to. New York, Sheldon & Company, 677 Broadway.

The Book of Proverbs; Part Second, the Revised Version, with an Introduction and Explanatory Notes for English readers. 1 vol. 4to. New York, Sheldon & Company, 677 Broadway.

www.ingramcontent.com/pod-product-compliance
Lightning Source LLC
LaVergne TN
LVHW010229110826
845151LV00004B/1237

* 9 7 8 1 4 2 5 5 2 6 3 8 2 *